FIFTY PLAYS
for
JUNIOR ACTORS

Fifty Plays
for
Junior Actors

A collection of royalty-free,
one-act plays for young people

Edited by

SYLVIA E. KAMERMAN

Publishers   PLAYS, INC.   *Boston*

Library of Congress Catalog Card Number: 66-17944

ISBN: 0-8238-0034-2

MANUFACTURED IN THE UNITED STATES OF AMERICA

Contents

v

CONTENTS

FIFTY PLAYS
for
JUNIOR ACTORS

Treasure in the Smith House

by Grace T. Barnett

Characters

MRS. SMITH
MR. SMITH
DARLENE, *12* ⎫
DIANE, *14* ⎬ *their children*
DENBY, *15* ⎭

SETTING: *The living room of the Smith home.*
AT RISE: DIANE *walks into living room through door at left. Her head is bent over a slip of paper, and she is talking as if unaware that she is speaking aloud.*

DIANE (*Reads*): "If your name begins with D, heed me well, for you shall see a treasure meant for you alone." (DIANE *glances around to make sure that no one is near. Then she continues to read silently, with only her lips moving. At length she stuffs the paper into her pocket and going back to the door, she advances with slow steps, counting as she walks.*) One, two, three, four, five, six, seven, eight. (*She stands in the middle of the floor and looks around in bewildered fashion.*) That doesn't put me near anything. I'll try it again. Maybe I didn't take big enough steps. (*She returns to the door and takes huge strides, counting as before. This time she arrives*

3

near a bookcase filled with books. She speaks again, slowly, as if repeating a lesson.) "Now count ten, and you will find hidden wealth unless you're blind." *(Again she looks about, bewildered. Then her eye falls on the rows of books. She drops on her knees in front of the case, and touching the books as she goes, begins again to count.)* One, two, three, four, five, six, seven, eight, nine, ten. This must be it. I've often heard of people hiding things in books. Wouldn't it be wonderful if I should find a fortune? Then Daddy wouldn't have to worry about—*(As she talks, she pulls out a heavy volume and blows dust off the top.)* Whew! When a house is empty for a few months, the dust takes over in a hurry. *(She starts to turn the pages when a noise outside the door brings her to her feet in a panic. Hastily she tries to stuff the book into place, but the cover catches, and she is struggling with it when* DENBY *enters right.* DENBY *stops abruptly when he sees* DIANE *and stuffs his hand quickly into his pocket.)*

DENBY: What in the world are you doing? Since when did you take an interest in old books? I thought you'd be in the attic exploring those trunks full of old clothes.

DIANE *(Straightening up)*: I thought I ought to start dusting. The house was closed all the time Aunt Agatha was in the hospital and since she died. You could make mud pies on the top of anything in the room.

DENBY: I'm going to like living here. It's the first time we've ever lived in an honest-to-goodness house.

DIANE: I'm going to like it, too. Now with Daddy going into the Smith firm, maybe we can stay in one place long enough to make real friends. I'm tired of moving around. Why don't you go over next door to borrow something? Maybe you could get acquainted with the redheaded boy I saw over there. He looks about your age.

DENBY: Uh, uh. You ought to know your etiquette better than that. He's supposed to come and see me first. Anyway, I'm comfortable right here. (*He flops into a chair with the apparent intention of staying.*)

DIANE (*Glances in irritation at her brother, then obliquely at the books*): Oh, Denby, won't you help Mother with those storage boxes? She said this morning that she wanted to move them out of the basement so that she could check to see what is in them.

DENBY: Why don't you go? Anyhow, Mother is working in the attic this afternoon. I'll bet my hat she needs you.

DIANE (*Sits down, her jaw set stubbornly*): If Mother wanted me she'd tell me. I think a big fellow like you ought to be the one to help up there. I'll get my turn at helping when it comes to sorting the dishes and things. Why don't you at least go and see if you can help?

DENBY: Nope. I moved trunks until my back aches. I'm going to sit right here the rest of the afternoon. I like this old room.

MRS. SMITH (*Calling, offstage*): Diane. Oh, Diane! Please come, dear. I need some help with these cupboards.

DIANE (*Groans*): All right, Mother. I'm coming. (*She gives a hasty look toward the bookcase, glares at DENBY, and runs off at right.*)

DENBY: Whew! I thought I never was going to get rid of her! Now for some sleuthing. (*He thrusts his hand into his pocket, brings out a paper, glances briefly at it and thrusts it back. Then he goes to the door, right, and begins walking, slowly, counting his steps.*) One, two, three, four, five, six, seven, eight. (*He looks around and finds that the only thing near him is the fireplace. He runs his hand through his hair, rumpling it in every direction. He continues as if thinking aloud.*) Well, that fireplace looks mighty solid to me. But you never can tell. In a house as old as this one, you can expect anything. One of the Smiths built it in 1785, Dad says. Probably needed a safe place for his valuables. Couldn't have been many banks in those days. (*While he talks, he begins running his hands over the fireplace.*) Now, let's see. I'll take the top row first. (*Carefully he feels the edges of each brick, counting as he goes.*) One, two, three, four, five, six, seven, eight, nine, ten. This must be the one. (*He pushes and prods with no result.*) Guess I'll have to try another row. It didn't *say* the top row. (*He drops to the floor and begins counting on the lower row.*)

DIANE (*Entering right*): What in the world are you doing, Denby Smith?

DENBY (*Jumping hastily to his feet*): Why, I—I—I was interested in the old bricks in the fireplace. They aren't like the ones they make nowadays.

DIANE: Well, you look kind of silly down on your knees. Besides, I should think you could find something useful to do. With us just moving in and all, there's plenty to do for anyone as husky as you are. (*She wanders toward the bookcase and turns to frown at* DENBY.)

DENBY: You're not such a fragile little blossom yourself. Besides, if Mother needs me, she'll call me. I tell you I like this room. (*He moves over to the table and begins to pick up and lay down the bric-a-brac there.*)

DIANE: *I* like this room, too. And I'd like a chance to enjoy it in peace and quiet for a while without a great creature like you here to disturb me. (*She flings herself into a chair and taps the arm impatiently with her fingers.*)

DENBY: Such sisterly cordiality! I thought— (MRS. SMITH *enters briskly at left. She wears a scarf and carries a broom and dustpan in her hands.*)

MRS. SMITH: I don't know what you two are bickering about. But whatever it is, you can stop right now. There are much more important things to do. Dear Aunt

Agatha was a wonderful housekeeper when she was well. The best way we can show how much we appreciate owning this house is to put it back in apple-pie order and keep it that way. Denby, you go up and take the curtains down in all the bedrooms. Then roll up the rugs in the two back bedrooms and begin on the floors. Diane, you will find rags and cleaner in the kitchen. You may begin on the windows upstairs. Don't try the outside. We'll have a man come to do those. (*She bustles out.*)

DENBY: Now see what you did! We both have to work. (*He follows his mother off.* DIANE *lingers near the bookcase to finger the books in the top row. Then with a backward, regretful glance, she, too, hurries out. They have scarcely gone when* DARLENE *sticks her head around the door at the right. She looks around carefully to make sure that the room is empty. Then she runs in and sits down in the middle of the floor.*)

DARLENE: Jiminy crickets! I thought they never would get out of here! You'd think this was the only room in the house where Diane and Denby could talk! (*She feels in the pocket of her apron, looks startled, draws her hand out empty, then explores the pocket of her blouse. Finding nothing, she jumps to her feet and begins patting her other pockets impatiently.*) Now where did I put that? Diane almost caught me with it in my hand and then Denby barged into the dining room. What did I do with it? (*Suddenly she sits down on the floor again.*) Now I remember. I stuffed it in my shoe. (*She pulls off the shoe and shakes out a bit of paper. She begins to read aloud.*) "If your name begins with D—" D for Darlene—lucky me. With so many of the names in the family starting with D, it could have been meant for Daddy. Or for Diane or Denby, but *I* have it. Now when

I find a great fortune for the family, maybe those other
two will stop treating me like an infant, and one that was
dropped on its head at that! Now let's see. Which way
did I come in? (*She wriggles her foot back into her
shoe and goes over to the door. Then she starts toward
the table.*) One, two, three, four, five, six, seven, eight.
(*She looks over the little figurines and vases.*) The only
thing I can count ten on is this stuff. And who ever
heard of hiding a fortune in a china doll? But here goes.
One, two, three, four, five, six, seven, eight, nine, ten.
(*As she counts, she moves her finger from one to the
other of the things on the table, arriving at a little
carved box.*) I wonder if I cheated a little? I certainly
didn't keep in rows. But this is the only thing that looks
as if it might be *it*. But this room's too popular. I'll take
this where I can look it over without the others poking
their noses in. (*She slips out at left, as* DIANE *comes in
at right.*)

DIANE (*Her hair is tied in a cloth and her dress is covered
by a large apron*): Whew! I didn't know owning a house
was so much work. But it's worth it. It makes a person
feel so—so homey. I'll have to scoot back to my windows in a minute, but I can spare time for one quick
look at that book. (*She goes over and stretches out her
hand for the book, when a noise is heard offstage.*) Oh,
bother! I might as well get back to my job. (*She runs
out.*)

MRS. SMITH (*Entering left. She has removed the cloth from
her hair, but she walks as if she were very tired*): My
gracious! This has been a day! But what fun it has been.
Our own home! A place for the children to grow up
with a feeling of belonging. A good business for David.
A fine community to live in. Dear Aunt Agatha, to give
it to us! Now if we only had a little ready cash to do

some of the things that need doing. (*She looks around the room.*) But I won't sigh about that. I'm too tired to think. I'll just take one of these fascinating old books and go to my room and lie down for a little while. I want to be fresh and rested when David comes home. His first day will have been hard, too. (*She goes over to the bookcase, stoops down and pulls out the big book which* DIANE *has left slightly out of line. She pats and rearranges the others to fill the opening she has made. Then she goes off. In a moment,* DIANE *and* DENBY *enter from opposite sides. Each stops abruptly at the sight of the other one. Both look dismayed.*)

DIANE: Denby Smith! You are the most aggravating person! You tag after me so that I don't have a minute to myself.

DENBY: *I* tag after *you!* That's a laugh. I just can't get you out from under my feet, that's all. (*He walks over to the fireplace and stands looking at it moodily.*) I wish you'd go and play by yourself somewhere. A man wants a little time to himself without a flock of women around trying to boss him all the time. (*He runs his hand over the top row of bricks.*)

DIANE (*Stamping her foot*): You sound as if I were a child! You needn't be so superior even if you are a year and a half older than I am. What are you mooning around that fireplace for? You were down on your knees to it a little while ago, and now you're petting it like—like a dog!

DENBY: I'm not as scatterbrained as you are. I'm interested in serious things. I'd like to know how this old fireplace is made. I might learn something.

DIANE (*Suddenly animated*): Why don't you go over to the library? Aunt Agatha used to say they had a wonderful collection of historical books down there. I'll bet they have books with drawings of old fireplaces in them. Maybe even this one. This is one of the oldest houses in this part of the country.

DENBY (*Excited*): For once, old gal, I think you have a brainstorm! I'll do just that little thing. When my ship comes in, maybe I'll give you a ride! (*He rushes out, upsetting a chair as he goes.*)

DIANE: Well! That was a lucky thought. I had no idea that it would work. I wonder why he's so bothered about that fireplace. It couldn't be that—no. *I* saw the old man first and got the paper. It's just one of those queer streaks boys have, I guess. Anyway, it's a break for me. (*She hurries over to the bookcase, reaches out, then draws back in dismay. She counts aloud, touching the books.*) One, two, three, four, five, six, seven, eight, nine, ten. Why, *that's* not the one. What happened to *my* book? (*She begins pulling out the books, stacking them haphazardly around her on the floor.*)

DARLENE (*Comes running in at left*): Diane, did you— (*She stops to eye the overturned chair and the tumbled books.*) What in the world are you doing?

DIANE (*Jumping up to face* DARLENE *angrily*): Did you take a book out of this cupboard?

DARLENE: What if I did? Is that a crime? And anyway, I didn't. I'm not interested in musty, dusty old books. What *I* want to know is what you did with that little box I left on the table in the upstairs hall. I set it down for just a minute, and when I came back, it was gone.

DIANE: So that means *I* took it, I suppose. Your little old box isn't half so important as my book. I want you to tell me what you did with it. You're the only one who would have taken it, just to tease me.

DARLENE: You and Denby treat me as if I were three years old and a moron at that. Why shouldn't I do something to bother you if I could? When you treat me as if I had some sense, maybe I'll show you some. Anyway, you needn't try to get back at me by taking my box! It's important—so important that you'll be sorry all your life if you've thrown it away just to spite me!

DIANE: You're talking like a nitwit! I tell you I didn't touch your box. It's my book I want. It was here a minute ago and now it's gone, and you're the only one who's been in here. If you think for one minute—(*A dull thud is heard.*)

DARLENE: What is that noise?

DIANE: That's what I'd like to know. It seemed to come from the fireplace.

DARLENE: Where's Denby?

DIANE: He's at the library. There's no one in the house but Mother and us.

DARLENE: And Mother is lying down upstairs. (*The thumping is heard again.*) What can it be? I'm going to find out.

DIANE: We'll go together. (*They rush out at left, as* DENBY *rushes in at right.*)

DENBY (*His face is smudged with dirt*): Boy, oh boy. I think I've hit on it this time. And I didn't need any help from the library, either. Lucky there's no one in this room. (*He rushes over to the fireplace and starts measuring with the yardstick he carries. Then he thrusts his head into the fireplace. He draws back, dragging a trail of ashes onto the hearth. He turns to rush out the door, knocking a china ornament off the table. It smashes on the floor. He pauses.*) Jumping grasshoppers! I didn't mean to do that. Diane will skin me! But I'll see that she doesn't catch up with me for a while. (*He disappears through the door.* DIANE *and* DARLENE *come in by the opposite door.*)

DIANE: Well, we didn't find anything, but the knocking's stopped at any rate. We—

DARLENE (*Interrupting with a wail as she sees the fragments of the figurine*): Who broke this? That was the prettiest one of the whole lot. What's—(*She stops abruptly as the knocking is heard once more, this time louder than ever.*) There it is again. What kind of house is this that we've moved into? First someone steals my little box when I've barely turned my back. Then we hear knocking with no one in the house to do it. While we're looking for the noise, someone or something breaks one of these ornaments. But you and I are the only ones in the house besides Mother, and she's in her room resting. I peeked, to make sure.

DIANE: Don't forget the book that walked off of its own accord. I, for one, don't like it. There's something queer going on and I want to find out what it is.

DARLENE: Well, you aren't going without me. If it's a—a—spook we'll find it together. (*She grabs* DIANE's *arm and looks around as if expecting to see a ghost.*)

DIANE: Don't be childish! Spooks went out of style a long time ago. But I'd just as soon have you along. There's no telling what we *might* find. (DIANE *tries to look nonchalant, but she, too, glances around hurriedly as they leave the room. The thumping continues.* MR. SMITH *enters carrying a newspaper in one hand and a sack of groceries in the other arm. He comes to the center of the room and stares around him.*)

MR. SMITH: Hello! Hello, everybody! Mother! Diane! (*He waits for a minute but gets no answer. Then he, too, notices the pounding.*) What the dickens goes on here? Where is everybody? What is that confounded noise? What's happened to this room? I thought the family was going to spend the day cleaning house. (*He raises his voice.*) Mother! Diane! Darlene! Denby! Where are you? Isn't anybody at home?

MRS. SMITH (*Enters from left*): Why, David, you're home

early. And what is all that stuff? (MRS. SMITH *is carrying
a book under one arm and holds the little carved box
in the other hand.*) I didn't expect you so soon, and
I was resting a little. I thought we'd be all cleaned up
before you got here. (*She suddenly becomes aware of
the confusion of books and the broken ornament and
the littered hearth.*) What in the world has been going
on here?

MR. SMITH: That's just what I'm trying to find out.
Where are the kids? What shall I do with this stuff, as
you call it? I bought some groceries at the corner store
—thought you might not have had time to go out.

MRS. SMITH: That was thoughtful of you, dear. (*She puts
the book and box down on a chair.*) Here, I'll take them
out to the kitchen. (*She goes out, right.*)

MR. SMITH (*As the pounding becomes more vigorous*):
Why doesn't somebody stop that infernal noise! (*He
goes to the door and bellows.*) Denby! Darlene! Diane!
Whatever you're doing, stop it. And come here. (*The
pounding stops abruptly. A confusion of voices is heard
off, and* DENBY *comes in with* DARLENE *and* DIANE.)

DENBY (*Angrily shaking* DARLENE's *hand from his elbow*):
You two leave me alone. I'm tending to my own business. You tend to yours.

DIANE: When someone is trying to tear down the house,
I guess I have a right to find out what he's doing and
make him stop it.

DARLENE: *I* think he's at the bottom of the queer things
that have been going on around here. Denby, did you
take my box? If you've found something interesting or
exciting, I think the least you could do is to let us in
on it. But anyway, I want my box!

DENBY: What box? I don't have any box. If you two don't
leave me alone, I'll—why do girls have to be such pests?
(*Suddenly all three become aware of their father.*)

ALL: Did you call us, Dad?

MR. SMITH: I certainly did. I want some explanation of what's been going on around here. I come home expecting a little peace and quiet, and I find this room looking as if a tornado had been through it and hear noise as if someone were trying to tear the house down. I want to know what it means. (*No one answers for a minute. The three shift uncomfortably, looking around as if each is waiting for the others to speak.* DIANE *and* DARLENE *suddenly rush toward the chair, both speaking at once.*)

DIANE: My book!

DARLENE: My box! How did that get there?

MRS. SMITH (*Entering*): I don't know what all this fuss is about, but I don't want to hear about it now. Diane, you and Darlene straighten up those books. Denby, fix that chair and pick up the pieces of china on the floor. Now, David, just sit down and relax and tell us about the new job. Then we can hear what is on the children's minds. (*She sinks down onto the davenport and pats the place beside her.*)

MR. SMITH: Marilyn, you do have a way of calming things down. (*He sits down beside her, watching the children scurrying about.*) As a matter of fact, I have something mighty interesting to tell, but it's not about the office. It is about this house. (*All stop to listen.*)

DENBY: About the house? What?

MR. SMITH: Well, I ran into the newest, most ingenious racket I've ever come across. The fellow who thought it up had to do some research, and he had to use his brains. I'm almost sorry I couldn't fall for it.

DENBY: What was it, Dad?

MR. SMITH: A little old fellow stopped me on the corner up here this morning and asked me if my name was Smith. When I said *yes*, he asked me what my first name was. Said he had a notion it might be Dan or Donald. I was curious by that time, so I told him. He smiled all over his face and said that David was just as good. He said he had something for me that would make me my fortune. But it seems it wouldn't have been any good unless my first name began with a D. There was only one catch to it. He wanted ten dollars for his secret— something that was supposed to locate a fortune in this house. (MR. SMITH *stops as the three children gasp.*)

DENBY: Did he have kind of a thin face with a scar down one cheek?

MR. SMITH: I believe he did.

DARLENE: Did he have just a fringe of gray hair that curled up around a dirty cap?

MR. SMITH: That's exactly what he did have. This begins to get interesting.

DIANE: Did he have blue eyes that were sort of watery, and made you think he might start to cry the next minute?

MR. SMITH: You have him tagged, all right. Now tell me, where did you run across him?

DIANE: You see, I—I— thought, that is, he said—

DARLENE: Why, the old crook! Did he tell you about it, too? He said I was the only one who could use the secret. That I mustn't tell a soul.

DENBY: Old crook is good. I guess I was the prize sucker. *I* paid him for the secret, and got the paper.

DARLENE *and* DIANE: I did, too!

MR. SMITH: Do you mean you really swallowed that stuff? Does that account for the strange activity around this house?

DIANE (*Looking flustered*): Well, you see, I knew we could use a little ready cash, and he *said* that his great-grandfather had worked for the man that built this house. The secret had been handed down from one generation to another. He said that no one except one whose name began with D—

DARLENE: Why, that old fraud! That's what he told me. That he'd been waiting until the right one came along. He knew his great-grandfather would want me to have it instead of any of the others.

MR. SMITH: And you fell for that? How much did you pay him?

DARLENE: I gave him my allowance for this week.

MR. SMITH: Hm-m-m. Fifty cents. Not much to wait a lifetime to collect, was it? How about you, Diane?

DIANE: I had spent my allowance. I gave him my little gold chain.

MRS. SMITH: Oh, Diane, you didn't!

MR. SMITH: And you, Denby. How much did he nick you for?

DENBY: I offered him my jackknife, but he said that wasn't enough. I gave him the dollar I earned delivering samples.

MR. SMITH: And now the old man has it, and your knife, too. Is that it?

DENBY: Yes, but I'll—I'll—

MR. SMITH: No, you won't. We'll let the old man keep his ill-gotten gains. He's probably a long way from here now, anyway. The point is that I think you've all learned to look carefully before you buy a gold brick to see that it isn't brass. That's a lesson worth learning. What did you think you had found, Denby, in your pounding around?

DENBY: I found that there must be a passage behind the chimney. Perhaps there really is a treasure hidden there. Anyhow, there has to be a room of some kind, from the measurements. I was trying to locate a way into it. (DENBY *hesitates, then blurts out.*) I didn't find anything hidden, but I *did* find something I've been looking for. That's what I want to do for the rest of my life. I want to study to be an architect. I want to study old houses and plan new ones. And I'll bet there *is* a hidden room, and I'm going to find it.

MR. SMITH (*Laughing*): I'll show you the secret door. I played in that room many a time when I was a boy. What did you find, Diane?

DIANE: I didn't find anything, but I don't care. I think this old house is just wonderful. It doesn't need any treasure to make me love it already.

DARLENE: Me, too. But I did find something interesting. I found that my little box has a fake bottom. I was just going to open it when I heard Denby. I put the box down for a minute on the hall table and when I came back it was gone. I'd like to know what happened to it, and how it got here in this room again.

MRS. SMITH: I can solve that mystery. I saw it and picked it up. The book I had taken from the shelf was about antique boxes, so I took that along to study while I read. (DARLENE *goes over and picks up the box. She fusses with a carved bit on the corner and suddenly grabs something from the inside of the box.*)

DARLENE (*Excitedly*): Look! There *is* something here. (*She shakes out a paper.*) Oh! Oh! There *is* treasure in the Smith house, and *I've* found it. Listen to this. (*Reads*) "Dear Curious One: Since you have had the curiosity and the ingenuity to find the secret of this little old box, you are after my own heart, and so to you I shall give my treasures. In the attic under the north dormer, you'll find an old brassbound sea chest. Feel over the window, and you'll find the big key. The chest does not have a treasure of gold, but something which to me is more precious. In it you will find the coat Colonel Jed Smith wore in the Revolutionary War. There's the inkwell that was used on the desk of the first governor of this state. But I'll not spoil your fun by telling you more. Each thing is labeled. And each one tells a bit of the part the Smith family has had in helping to fashion this wonderful America of ours. I hope that my treasures will inspire you to be a true American, with a knowledge of the toil and sacrifice that have gone into the making of a great nation. Agatha Smith." A treasure chest of my very own! I—I feel like crying. Do you suppose I can be the kind of a Smith Aunt Agatha means?

MRS. SMITH: Of course you can, dear.

DARLENE (*Suddenly excited*): Diane! Denby! Come on. I can't wait another minute to open that chest. (*All three run out.*)

MRS. SMITH: Bless the old man, whoever he is. David, I think you should give him something, too. Not really, of course, because he *was* dishonest. He found out how many of us had the initial D, and he made up his scheme. But we *have* found treasure here. Diane has found her joy in the house itself, Denby his decision to become an architect, and Darlene her treasure chest.

MR. SMITH: The old rascal did do the Smith family a good turn in spite of himself. I'm the only D. Smith who didn't fall for his scheme, yet I think I'm mighty lucky. Come on, Mother, let's join the fun in the attic. (*Curtain falls, as the two go out, arm in arm.*)

THE END

On the Fence

by Marcia Moray Beach

Characters

MRS. MILES
TOM MILES
GEORGE
PAUL
JANIE
HORACE
GINNY

TIME: *Saturday morning.*
SETTING: *A backyard with picket fence.*
AT RISE: MRS. MILES *is hanging out some washing while* TOM *paints the fence.*

TOM: Jeepers, Mom! Why did you have to pick today to make me paint this old fence?

MRS. MILES: You've been putting it off for the past week, Tom. As far as I can see, *any* day would be wrong. You might as well settle down and get it over with.

TOM: But there's baseball practice this morning!

MRS. MILES: You had baseball practice all last week, too. You ought to be as good as that Roger Maris (*Pronounces it with long A*) by this time.

TOM (*Correcting her*): Maris, Mom!

19

MRS. MILES: Well, Maris, then. No matter how you pronounce it, I doubt if even he has to spend as much time at practice as you do. Now, get on with that painting, Tom.

TOM (*Muttering*): What a break! Stuck here all day.

MRS. MILES: What's that you're saying, Tom?

TOM: Nothing, Mom. (*He starts painting with exaggerated speed.*)

MRS. MILES (*Coming over to watch him*): Not so fast, there! You've skipped a place. Maybe someone will come along and help you. Remember how it happened in *Tom Sawyer*?

TOM: Who was he?

MRS. MILES: Tom Miles, don't tell me you've never heard of *Tom Sawyer*!

TOM: Is he the guy in "Dick Tracy"?

MRS. MILES: Don't you boys know anyone outside of comic book characters? *Tom Sawyer* is the name of a very famous book written by Mark Twain. (*She sits down on bench.*)

TOM: What has he to do with painting a fence?

MRS. MILES: A great deal. He had a fence to paint on a day just like this one. And he didn't relish the job any more than you do.

TOM (*Hopefully*): Did he get out of doing it?

MRS. MILES: Yes, as a matter of fact, he did. By using his head.

TOM: You can't paint a fence with your head!

MRS. MILES: Don't be facetious, dear. By head, I mean brains. He used his brains.

TOM: I'd use anything to get me out of this job. What did he do, Mom?

MRS. MILES: Briefly, this is the way he managed it. Some of his friends stopped by to watch, prepared to tease him, I suppose. Tom Sawyer paid no attention to them and kept right on at his painting as if he were having the time of his life.

TOM: Some act!

MRS. MILES: It worked, however. His friends began to get interested, and the next thing, they were begging Tom to let them have a try at painting.

TOM: They must have been a bunch of dopes.

MRS. MILES: You may get an opportunity to put his plan to use.

TOM: Go on. What happened?

MRS. MILES: Well, Tom Sawyer held off a while before he pretended very reluctantly to give up the brush. His friends fell all over themselves taking turns painting, and before very long they had the fence all painted while Tom Sawyer sat in the sun watching *them* work.

TOM: Not bad, not bad at all! Thanks for telling me about him.

MRS. MILES: You're welcome, dear. I just hope someone comes along so you can try it out. I have to get at my cake now, so I'll leave you. I don't care who paints the fence just as long as it is done today. (MRS. MILES *exits.*)

TOM (*Calling after her*): Wish me luck, Mom! (*He sits down, leaning against the fence.*) No sense wasting my time on this old fence if I'm going to hook some poor dope into doing it for me. (*A shrill whistle is heard offstage.* TOM *leaps to his feet. He is painting with great zest, as his friend* GEORGE *strolls on stage, tossing a ball into the air and catching it nonchalantly.*)

GEORGE: Hi! Going to ball practice?

TOM: Nope. (*Works with absorption*)

GEORGE: Why not? What's eating you?

TOM: There's something better to do.

GEORGE: Are you kidding? (*Points to fence*) You don't mean *that*? That dumb job?

TOM (*Painting furiously*): That's what *you* think.

GEORGE: What's so special about slapping paint around?

TOM: It's nice work, if you can get it.

GEORGE: All the fellows are coming out for practice today.

TOM: I can play ball any old time. (*Stands off to study his handiwork*)

GEORGE (*Pointing*): You missed one place.

TOM (*Pretending not to see*): Where? Show me.

GEORGE (*Approaching gingerly*): Right in front of your nose. See?

TOM (*Dangling brush in front of him invitingly*): I can do a post in one stroke. Want to bet on it?

GEORGE (*Backing away*): So, what if you can?

TOM: It's fun . . . kind of a game.

GEORGE: Well, I hope you win it! I have a real game waiting. You play it with a bat and ball. So long, Michelangelo! (GEORGE *exits, whistling and tossing ball in air.*)

TOM (*Morosely watching him go*): How do you like that! Some pal. And that Tom Sawyer . . . some actor! (*He returns reluctantly to painting. The sound of a harmonica is heard offstage.*) Oh, well, here comes Paul. Another chance. Here's hoping I don't muff it this time. (*Bends to task with vigor*)

PAUL (*Playing "Yankee Doodle" loudly, as he approaches* TOM): How was that?

TOM: How was what?

PAUL: Are you deaf? I can play it all the way through now.

TOM: Oh, *that?* I'm too busy to listen to kid stuff right now.

PAUL: It isn't kid stuff! This is my new harmonica.

TOM: Anybody can play a tune on those things. I'll bet you can't paint a whole post in one swoosh. Watch this! (*He demonstrates with a flourish.*)

PAUL: Looks simple to me.

TOM: Sounds simple to me . . . playing that thing.

PAUL: I'll bet you can't even play the first bar. Here, try

PAUL (*Starting after her*): I'll help you tomorrow, Tom.

TOM: Tomorrow will be too late, thanks! (*He picks up brush and starts painting.*)

PAUL (*Calling*): Wait for me, Janie! See you later, Tom.

TOM (*Not turning around*): *Much* later.

PAUL: If *that's* the way you feel about it. (PAUL *exits, playing "Yankee Doodle" very loudly.* TOM *continues painting with angry splashes.*)

MRS. MILES (*Entering with a pitcher of lemonade and a plate of cookies*): Poor boy. You look hot. Did you think I was never coming?

TOM: You're too late. They've gone.

MRS. MILES: Who were "they"? And where have they gone?

TOM: Paul . . . and then *she* came horning in.

MRS. MILES: Who is "she"?

TOM: That Janie Fulton. Always chasing after the boys. (*In a falsetto*) Oh, dear. It's *so* hot. I'm thinking about something so cool. (*Disgustedly*) I wish she'd jump in the lake to cool off . . . *deep!* Butting in on a couple of guys who are busy!

MRS. MILES (*Smiling*): Was Paul helping you, by any chance?

TOM: Until *she* . . . I mean Janie, came along.

MRS. MILES: But what did she do?

TOM: Dragged Paul off to swim.

MRS. MILES: I'm sorry, dear. I know it seems harsh, but the fence will never get painted unless I am firm about your finishing it today. (*She pauses while* TOM *drinks his lemonade.*) Tom . . . ?

TOM (*Morosely*): What?

MRS. MILES: I just thought . . . why don't you get the extra brush. Two hands can work faster than one.

TOM (*Wildly*): Gosh, Mom! It's tough enough with one brush in *one* hand!

it. Give me that brush. We'll exchange. (*Holds out harmonica*)

TOM: I don't know if I should take a chance on your messing up this job.

PAUL: Don't be silly. I could do it with my eyes closed. Here, give me the brush, and I'll show you.

TOM (*Pretending great reluctance*): You have to do it just so.

PAUL: Come on! Take this. We'll see which is easier. (*They exchange the brush and harmonica.*)

TOM (*Playing way off key*): There! Hear that?

PAUL (*Covering up his ears*): I wish I hadn't!

TOM: Well, let's see you put some paint on. And you need at least one hand.

PAUL (*Missing part of the post*): You can't do it with just one swish.

TOM: I can. (*Continues playing off key*)

PAUL: Why don't you try something else . . . something easy? (*He attempts to cover post with a single stroke and misses.*)

TOM (*Encouragingly*): You'll catch on to it. Put more paint on next time.

PAUL: You try keeping on key!

TOM: I just need more practice.

PAUL (*Dipping brush deep into paint*): That goes for me and this job, too.

TOM (*Playing*): I think I'm getting it!

PAUL (*Applying paint earnestly*): How am I doing?

TOM (*Inspecting*): Not bad. Not bad at all. You still need a little more paint.

PAUL (*Indignant*): I put too much on last time. Look! It's spilled all over.

TOM: Don't worry about spilling as long as you get the paint on the fence. (*He sits on the bench.*)

PAUL (*Suddenly suspicious*): What do you mean, worry?

Whose worry is this? Not mine, chum! (*Starts to lay down the brush*)

TOM (*Hastily*): I was only kidding. You're going great guns there. Couldn't do as well myself. (PAUL *is drawn into taking another stroke.*)

JANIE (*Wheeling up on her bicycle, surprising both boys*): What's going on?

TOM (*Nervously watching* PAUL): Janie! Where did you come from? Paul and I are doing a job here. We're pretty busy.

JANIE: Looks as if Paul is doing the work part of it.

PAUL: Tom said there was a trick to painting a fence.

TOM: You said there was a trick to playing this old harmonica.

JANIE: From what I heard, and from what I'm seeing, neither of you has mastered the trick. Don't you boys know the team is practicing today?

TOM: Sure. What of it? Paul plays basketball.

JANIE: Why so casual? I thought baseball was your life's work.

TOM: A guy can want a change sometimes, can't he?

JANIE: What are you changing to? The harmonica?

PAUL (*Dropping brush in pail*): He'd better give up on *that* instrument. (*Mops face with a large, red handkerchief*) Whew! It's hot!

TOM: Take it easy a minute. Mom said she'd bring out some lemonade.

JANIE: I'm thinking about something.

PAUL: What?

JANIE: Something very cool.

TOM (*Hopefully*): Like lemonade?

JANIE (*Flatly*): Like water.

TOM: You mean you want a drink? I'll get you one in a jiffy.

JANIE: I don't want to drink it. I want to swim in it.

PAUL: Say, that's not a bad thought, Janie.

TOM: Oh, stick around. There won't be ⟨…⟩ pool now.

JANIE: I know three people who could be t⟨…⟩

PAUL: Who?

JANIE: You, and me, and Tom.

TOM (*Ignoring her to inspect the fence*): ⟨…⟩ your part looks better than mine. (*Sh⟨…⟩* Hey, Mom! How about some lemonade⟨…⟩

MRS. MILES (*Offstage*): You'll have to wa⟨…⟩ Tom. I haven't had time to make it ye⟨…⟩

JANIE: You didn't answer my question a⟨…⟩ ming, Tom.

PAUL: Let's call it quits on this job and ⟨…⟩

TOM: I'm not hot.

JANIE: You don't look like an ad for c⟨…⟩ Your face is as red as Paul's handkerc⟨…⟩

PAUL: What's the matter with my hand⟨…⟩

JANIE: Nothing's the matter with it. I ju⟨…⟩ like it.

TOM: I don't care how I *look*. I'm still ⟨…⟩

PAUL: Well, don't get sore about it. It's ⟨…⟩

JANIE: If it is, then I'm a criminal, bec⟨…⟩ melt. A swim would certainly feel go⟨…⟩

PAUL (*Leaping to his feet*): I've had eno⟨…⟩ around. Come on, Janie.

JANIE: Can't you come with us, Tom?

TOM: I *can*, but I don't want to. On⟨…⟩ finish it. (*Glares at* PAUL)

PAUL: Don't look at *me* as if I'd insu⟨…⟩ it's not *my* job. *I* didn't start it. I was ⟨…⟩ to help you out.

JANIE: I'm not going to hang around li⟨…⟩ argue. I'm off to the pool. So long, ⟨…⟩ *offstage.*)

MRS. MILES: I'm not suggesting that you perform any acrobatic marvel. My thought was that if someone else should come by, two of you could work faster together.

TOM: Oh . . . I get it. The only hitch is, I don't think there's anybody left.

MRS. MILES: Don't give up hope. I'll leave the lemonade here in case you get thirsty. (*She starts off.*) Don't forget the extra brush! (*Exits*)

TOM: O.K. I'll get it now. (*He exits.* HORACE, *all dressed up and wearing glasses, enters and strolls across stage. He pauses in front of the fence and examines it with a critical eye. He picks up brush and dips it extremely cautiously in the paint. Removing his glasses, he peers into the paint mixture.* TOM *re-enters and watches* HORACE *for a moment before speaking.*) Well . . . what's the verdict, Mr. Expert?

HORACE (*Startled, but completely assured*): Mixture's too thin.

TOM: How do *you* know so much about it?

HORACE: I just finished whitewashing our cellar.

TOM (*Flatteringly*): You painted a whole cellar? Wow! Some job, I'll bet.

HORACE: Nothing to it. With the right brush. (*Picks up brush*) This one's too small.

TOM: How about this one? (*Presents extra brush*)

HORACE: Better. (*Holds it*)

TOM: What's wrong with the mixture?

HORACE: I told you. Too thin.

TOM: How do you thicken it?

HORACE: Can't. You've just got to put the paint on heavier.

TOM (*Painting a post*): Like this?

HORACE: That's the general idea. Say, why aren't you out for practice?

TOM: I like doing this. Didn't you like painting your cellar?

HORACE (*With forced enthusiasm*): Sure I did. Good sport . . . painting. (*Urging* TOM *on*) Now, you're getting somewhere!

TOM (*Challengingly*): Ever tried painting a fence?

HORACE: No. It looks simple, though.

TOM: It's not as simple as it looks!

HORACE: You take too long a stroke.

TOM: How would you do it?

HORACE: For one thing, I'd start at the bottom.

TOM: I can't see much difference between these brushes. (*He reverses his stroke.*)

HORACE (*Handing him the other brush*): Here. Take this one. You'll notice the difference, all right.

TOM: Don't *you* want it?

HORACE: Why should *I* want it?

TOM: Well, you seem to know how it's done. Why don't you try out your own theories?

HORACE (*Backing away*): I'm wearing my best suit.

TOM: Oh, go ahead! You won't spill paint on yourself if you're such a great painter.

HORACE: If I did, I'd never hear the end of it. My suit just came back from the cleaners. Hey! Take it easier on the down stroke!

TOM: Yes, *sir,* boss.

HORACE: Well, it's beginning to look like something, now.

TOM (*Sarcastically*): After your expert advice. Don't strain yourself!

HORACE: If I had on working clothes, I could show you!

TOM (*Hopefully*): I can lend you some overalls.

HORACE (*Disregarding the offer and picking up pitcher of lemonade*): Mind if I help myself?

TOM (*Warmly*): Go ahead. Have a swig. I'll go get the overalls.

HORACE: Don't rush. I don't want to bother you.

TOM: It's no trouble. Be back in a jiffy. Have some lemonade. (*He runs out.*)

HORACE (*Fills his glass, and then drains the pitcher. Attempts painting a post, standing well back from it. Shakes his head and drops brush as* TOM *re-enters with the overalls.*): Ah-h!

TOM (*Encouragingly*): Atta boy. Here. Put these on and you can really go to town.

HORACE: No, thanks. I've changed my mind. I can see a fence is more complicated than a cellar. I wouldn't want to mess it up for you. Anyway, it's getting late. I have to be on my way before the library closes. Thanks for the lemonade. Sorry there isn't any left. I guess watching you made me thirsty.

TOM (*Disgusted*): Watching was sure all *you* did!

HORACE (*With injured dignity*): Pardon my intrusion. Goodbye! (HORACE *exits.*)

TOM: Good riddance, Tom Sawyer or no Tom Sawyer! (*Starts painting, whistles as* GINNY *enters.*)

GINNY: Hi, Tom! What are you doing?

TOM (*Not stopping his work*): What's it look like I'm doing? Running for home plate?

GINNY: That's where I thought you would be—at baseball practice.

TOM: That's where I ought to be.

GINNY: I shouldn't think they could spare *you*.

TOM (*Loftily*): They can't. They'll find *that* out.

GINNY: How come you're here, then?

TOM: A guy likes to do a job like this sometimes. It's very complicated work. Nothing a girl could do.

GINNY: I suppose not.

TOM: Of course, with a little practice, and someone to help her get started, she *might* get the hang of it.

GINNY: Maybe having some experience, even on porch furniture, might make a difference.

TOM: It might, at that. Once you get started, you have to keep on going, though.

GINNY: I certainly admire the way you stick at things, Tom.

TOM (*Pleased*): It's the only way you get good at anything.

GINNY: You're the best pitcher we've ever had. Everybody says so.

TOM: Hope this doesn't bother my arm. It goes stiff on me, sometimes.

GINNY (*Worried*): I should think your arm *might* get tired. Going up and down, over and over.

TOM: Oh, I can take it!

GINNY (*Picking up extra brush*): What's this for, Tom?

TOM: Oh . . . that? Just left it there in case somebody turned up who liked painting.

GINNY (*Approaching paint pail*): Would you mind if *I* tried to do a little?

TOM: *Mind?* (*Hiding his eagerness*) Sure, go ahead. Put plenty of paint on the brush.

GINNY (*Dips brush and starts at other end of fence*): Down or up, first?

TOM: Any old way that suits you. (*Watches her*) That's the girl! You're all right, for a beginner.

GINNY (*Anxiously*): Have I too much paint on my brush?

TOM (*Scanning the fence appraisingly*): Looks about right to me. Take your time. Slow and easy does it. (*Returns to his end*)

GINNY: You do it so smoothly, Tom. Mine's sort of blotchy.

TOM (*Joining her*): Take a longer stroke. (*He demonstrates.*) Like this . . . See?

GINNY (*Following his example*): Like so?

TOM: Now you've got it! You're doing fine!

GINNY (*Hard at work*): You have to set a kind of rhythm.

Tom (*Sitting on bench*): You certainly catch on to it quickly . . . for a girl. I'll bet Janie couldn't paint the broad side of a barn.

Ginny: What made you think of *her*? (*She pauses.*)

Tom: Hey! Don't get out of rhythm!

Ginny (*Back at work*): What did?

Tom: What did what?

Ginny: Made you think of Janie?

Tom (*Disparagingly*): Oh, her? She was here a little while ago.

Ginny: She was? Looking for you?

Tom: Looking for trouble. *Making* trouble's more like it. Hey! Easy there. You'd better give that one another lick.

Ginny: What did she want?

Tom: Cooling off.

Ginny: Did you have a fight with her?

Tom: Me? Fight with *her*? She wouldn't get the chance. She's not my type.

Ginny (*Relieved*): She isn't?

Tom: Naw. I like girls who can think of something better to do than go swimming with guys who have something better to do.

Ginny: Guys?

Tom: Yes. Paul was just broken in . . . I mean, interested . . . when she hauled him off.

Ginny (*Smiling*): Oh, I see. Paul was helping you.

Tom: He was crazy to get at this old fence. I *had* to let him mess around. He wasn't even as good as you are!

Ginny (*Demurely*): It's very nice of you to trust me with it, Tom.

Tom (*Grandly*): Think nothing of it.

Ginny: Tom . . .

Tom: Yes?

Ginny: I was just thinking . . . as long as you think I'm

getting along all right, I might as well finish up by myself.

TOM: Is that a hint for me to get back to work?

GINNY (*Innocently*): Why, no, Tom. It's only that there's still time enough for you to sneak in a curve or two. They'll be practicing until lunchtime, won't they?

TOM (*Trying not to appear too eager*): Gosh! You want to paint that much? All by yourself?

GINNY (*Staunchly*): I really like doing this. Honest!

TOM: I sure hate to let the team down. It's not that I need the practice, you understand.

GINNY: Oh, I know that. It's for the team.

TOM (*Edging off gradually*): It has to be done today . . . the fence, I mean.

GINNY (*Calmly*): I gathered that. It will be done. Don't worry.

TOM (*Nearly off by now*): Well . . . as long as you insist. I guess I'd better beat it before Mom . . . before anyone interrupts. 'Bye, now. Keep up the good work.

GINNY: Put one right over the plate for me. (TOM *exits.* GINNY *sets to work with a will, humming to herself.* MRS. MILES *enters with a fresh pitcher of lemonade. She stops in astonishment at the sight of* GINNY.)

MRS. MILES: Why, Ginny Long! What are you doing here all alone? And working so hard. Where's Tom? Don't tell me he talked *you* into taking over!

GINNY (*Serenely*): He just *thinks* he did, Mrs. Miles. I've read *Tom Sawyer,* too!

MRS. MILES: Well, Tom Sawyer or no, it's very good of you to take over for Tom, Ginny.

GINNY (*Embarrassed*): I'm not doing this just for Tom. I'm really doing it for the team. Tom *is* our star pitcher, you know.

MRS. MILES: I just hope Tom wasn't trying to back out.

GINNY: He wasn't thinking of himself. The team just comes first with Tom. That's all.

MRS. MILES (*Sits down*): Well, Ginny, let's you and I enjoy this lemonade. (*Pours two glasses*)

GINNY: Thanks, Mrs. Miles. I guess I am a little thirsty. (*Drinks lemonade*)

TOM (*Suddenly re-entering, tossing ball in air and then catching it as he approaches*): Hi, Mom. Hi, Ginny.

GINNY: For heaven's sakes! Ball game over?

TOM: Nope. It's still going strong.

GINNY: Why did you come back, then?

TOM: I got to worrying.

GINNY: Worrying? About what? Me?

TOM: Not you. The fence.

GINNY: Well! I like that! I was doing all right by your darned old fence.

TOM: It doesn't look right.

GINNY (*Enraged*): Doesn't *look* right!

TOM (*Hopelessly mixed up*): I don't mean the fence doesn't look right. I mean you!

GINNY (*Raises hands to her hair*): And what's wrong with the way I look, may I ask?

TOM (*In agony*): You look swell, Ginny. You aren't getting the point.

GINNY (*Somewhat placated*): What *is* the point?

MRS. MILES: Yes, what is the point, Tom?

TOM: It doesn't look right for a girl to be working on a job like this all alone. That's the point.

MRS. MILES (*Rising from bench*): And a very good one, Tom. I'm glad you came back in time. If you two will excuse me . . . (*She exits quickly.*)

TOM: There's not much left to do, anyway. (*He grabs brush.*)

GINNY (*Taking the other brush*): Would it look all right for me to work *with* you?

Tom: You aren't mad at me?

Ginny (*As they both start in painting*): I haven't made up my mind about that yet. (*They paint in silence a moment.*)

Tom: Ginny . . . could you make up your mind at the movies this afternoon?

Ginny: Maybe. It depends.

Tom (*Anxiously*): On what?

Ginny (*Teasingly*): On whether we finish the fence! (*Curtain*)

THE END

The Key to Understanding

by Louise Biggs

Characters

BOB
TOM
INNKEEPER
INNKEEPER'S WIFE
MR. JONES
MR. MORRIS
SALLY
CAROL
HENRY
JOE
GREECE
NETHERLANDS
RUSSIA
ITALY
ENGLAND
JAPAN
SPAIN } *children of the nations*
INDIA
UNITED STATES
CANADA
MEXICO
NIGERIA

GENERAL ASSEMBLY
SECURITY COUNCIL
INTERNATIONAL COURT
  OF JUSTICE
THE SECRETARIAT
TRUSTEESHIP COUNCIL
ECONOMIC AND SOCIAL
  COUNCIL

} *children representing the United Nations*

SCENE 1

SETTING: *An inn. Upstage is a counter with food, glasses, etc., on it. In front of the counter are several small tables with chairs around them.*

AT RISE: *The* INNKEEPER *and the* INNKEEPER'S WIFE *are standing behind the counter.* MR. JONES *and* MR. MORRIS *sit at one table, talking quietly to each other.* HENRY *and* JOE, *sitting at another table, are also talking quietly.* BOB *and* TOM *enter and sit at one of the tables. The* INNKEEPER *goes over to their table.*

INNKEEPER: Good day. May I help you?

TOM: We would like a bite to eat before we go on our way.

INNKEEPER: My wife will feed you well.

INNKEEPER'S WIFE: We have some tasty, tender roast beef today.

BOB: I'll have a Coke and a roast beef sandwich, then.

TOM: The same for me. (INNKEEPER *goes behind counter.* MR. MORRIS *and* MR. JONES *rise to pay their check. As they go to counter, they talk to each other.*)

MR. MORRIS (*Angrily*): You can't mean you'd vote for Mr. Wright!

MR. JONES: Why, he's the best man.

MR. MORRIS: Howard Finch is a much better candidate than Wright. (*He pays* INNKEEPER.)

MR. JONES: You're wrong there. I'd never vote for Finch. (*They start toward door.*)

MR. MORRIS: You're crazy. Wright would be no good at all in that office. (*They exit, as* SALLY *and* CAROL *enter left.*)

SALLY: Let's play checkers.

CAROL (*Arguing*): No, I'd rather play rummy.

SALLY: Oh, you always choose what you want. I won't play at all.

CAROL: Don't, then. (*They exit right.*)

HENRY (*Loudly, to* JOE): He was out!

JOE (*Angrily*): He was not! He touched you first before you put your foot on base.

HENRY: You need glasses. He was out!

JOE: He was not.

HENRY: Oh, come on, let's go. You'll never have any sense. (*He gets up and pays* INNKEEPER.)

JOE (*Getting up*): You're the one who could use some sense. (*They exit.*)

BOB: What a lot of trouble is going on in the world.

TOM: Yes. People argue so much with their friends, it's no wonder that nations can't get along with each other.

BOB: I wish there were something we could do to bring about peace in the world.

INNKEEPER'S WIFE (*Bringing food to* BOB *and* TOM): Here is your lunch.

BOB (*As they start to eat*): What an interesting old inn you have here.

INNKEEPER'S WIFE: We try to make it so for our guests.

INNKEEPER: If you haven't been here before, perhaps you haven't seen our interesting collection of keys.

TOM: No, we haven't. We'd like to see them.

INNKEEPER (*Taking a board with keys from the counter and going to table*): Here are a few of the keys we have collected over the years.

TOM: Please tell us about them.

INNKEEPER: When people first came to our inn, we gave each person a key as a souvenir.

INNKEEPER'S WIFE: This plan seemed to please many of our customers. However, it became a little too expensive for us to continue.

INNKEEPER: Now, all of our customers leave us a key as a souvenir of their visit.

INNKEEPER'S WIFE: As you see, we have a very large collection.

BOB: How many keys do you have in your collection?

INNKEEPER'S WIFE: We have over ten thousand keys. This is the key to Buckingham Palace. (*Holds up a key*)

INNKEEPER: Show them the ignition key to the first mail plane to fly over the Rocky Mountains.

BOB: How interesting!

TOM: What is that odd-looking key with a tag attached?

INNKEEPER'S WIFE: This is a key left by two soldiers who visited our inn following the war.

BOB: What is it a key to?

INNKEEPER: Read the tag the soldiers attached to the key.

BOB (*Reads*): "The World Needs A Key to Understanding."

TOM: That certainly would be wonderful.

INNKEEPER'S WIFE: Perhaps such a key could be found, if only someone would search for it.

TOM: Bob, shall we try to find the key to understanding?

BOB: I'm all for it.

INNKEEPER: How wonderful it would be if you could return to our inn and give us a key to unlock a door of understanding among nations.

BOB: Let us begin our search for this key at once. (*He rises and takes a key from his pocket.*) Here is a key we would like to give you for your collection, but we hope we can return soon with the key to understanding.

TOM: Here's hoping our search will not be too long.

INNKEEPER: Farewell and good luck!

INNKEEPER'S WIFE: May you meet with success. (BOB *and* TOM *exit as the curtain closes.*)

*   *   *

SCENE 2

TIME: *Many months later.*

SETTING: *The area before the curtain represents a meeting place, and the curtain represents a great door.*

BEFORE RISE: BOB *and* TOM *enter with* INNKEEPER *and* INNKEEPER'S WIFE. BOB *carries a large cauldron, which he places on the floor.* TOM *pins on curtain large sign reading "Door of Understanding."*

BOB: We've searched far and wide to find the key to understanding.

INNKEEPER: Have you found it?

TOM: You will soon see. Many other people have helped us search for the key. Children from all parts of the world have gathered keys which they hope will open this great door.

INNKEEPER'S WIFE: Perhaps one of them will have the key.

BOB (*As* CHILDREN OF THE NATIONS *enter on both sides*): Here are the children of many nations. They have come to unlock this great door of understanding.

TOM: Tell us who you are, and what kind of key you have brought to unlock this door.

GREECE: I come from Greece. My key is the key of kindness. There should be kindness in the world, without prejudice as to race, color or creed. (*He takes a key and attempts to unlock the "door."*)

BOB: It doesn't work. (GREECE *drops key in cauldron.*) [Note: *After each child tries unsuccessfully to open "door", he throws his key into the cauldron.*]

NETHERLANDS: My country is the Netherlands. My key is the key of unselfishness. We all should share with those who need any kind of help. (*Tries key*)

TOM: That one doesn't fit either.

SPAIN: My home is Spain. Faith in others is needed in the world. My key is faith. (*Tries key*)

INNKEEPER: Still no luck.

ITALY: Italy is my homeland. Good deeds, not just words, are needed in the world. Perhaps this is the key that will open the door. (*Tries key*)

BOB: No, again. I hope *one* of the keys does the trick!

ENGLAND: I live in England. What we need in this world is knowledge. We need to learn many things about other nations. (*Tries key*)

INNKEEPER'S WIFE: The door's still locked.

JAPAN: Japan is my homeland. There is so much wrong in the world that we need most the key of judgment between right and wrong. This is the key I have brought with me. (*Tries key*)

BOB: No success yet.

RUSSIA: My country is Russia. We need hard work to achieve better living conditions. Perhaps my key is the one most needed. (*Tries key*)

TOM: We aren't getting anywhere.

INDIA: My land is India. Food for the hungry is greatly needed. My key supplies this great need. (*Tries key*)

INNKEEPER: We don't have the right key yet.

INNKEEPER'S WIFE: It's so important for us to find it soon!

UNITED STATES: I am from the United States. In my country we work for freedom from fear and for the protection of all. Maybe my key will open this door. (*Tries key*)

Bob: That's not the right key either.

Canada: I represent Canada. Medical help is important in the world. This is the key I have brought with me. (*Tries key*)

Innkeeper: But we still have to try others.

Mexico: From Mexico I come with the key of responsibility. All of us need to be responsible in carrying out our duties. Perhaps I can open this door. (*Tries key. Shaking his head he walks away from door and throws key into cauldron, as all of the others have.*)

Innkeeper's Wife: I'm still hopeful that the next key will open the door.

Nigeria: My land is Nigeria. We need truth to bring about respect in the world. Here I have the key to truth. Maybe it will open this great door. (*Tries key*)

Bob: All these wonderful keys have not been able to open this great door by themselves.

Tom: Maybe by uniting them all together we can produce the key for which we've been searching. (*He stirs the keys together in the cauldron, then pulls out an enormous key.*)

Innkeeper: What an enormous key!

Innkeeper's Wife: Do you think that this will be the key to understanding?

Tom: I hope that it will be. (*He walks to curtain and tries to unlock it. As he does so, the curtains open.*)

* * *

Scene 3

Time: *Immediately following previous scene.*

Setting: *The United Nations. The counter of the inn has been removed, and the tables have been put end to end to make one long table, like a conference table. Six*

CHILDREN *representing the United Nations sit behind the table.*

TOM: We have opened the door of understanding!

BOB: But where are we?

GENERAL ASSEMBLY: This is the United Nations.

INNKEEPER: Then the United Nations is the way to understanding!

INNKEEPER'S WIFE: Will you tell us who you are and what you do? (TOM, BOB, INNKEEPER, INNKEEPER'S WIFE, *and* CHILDREN OF THE NATIONS *stand to one side.*)

SECURITY COUNCIL: We are a group of one hundred seventeen nations.

TOM: What are your purposes?

INTERNATIONAL COURT OF JUSTICE: Our purposes are to keep peace, to develop friendly relations between nations, to help improve living conditions and promote human rights and freedom for all, and to provide a place where nations may meet together to solve mutual problems.

BOB: I count only six of you here, but you say you have one hundred seventeen members in the United Nations.

SECRETARIAT: We represent the six main divisions of the United Nations.

TOM: Tell us about these divisions.

GENERAL ASSEMBLY (*Showing a sign marked "General Assembly"*): I represent the General Assembly. It is the town meeting of the organization. We meet once a year, talk about problems, and try to come to agreements about them. Each nation has one vote and five delegates.

SECURITY COUNCIL (*Showing sign*): The Security Council has eleven members. We are like forest rangers and policemen. We spot trouble. Our permanent members are the United States, Great Britain, China, France and

Russia. There are six members who are not permanent. They are elected by the Assembly for two-year terms.

INTERNATIONAL COURT OF JUSTICE (*Showing sign*): I represent the International Court of Justice. There are fifteen nations on this court, elected by the General Assembly for nine-year terms. We handle disputes. For example, a dispute may arise over boundaries of a country. This court also interprets treaties or agreements between countries.

SECRETARIAT (*Showing sign*): The Secretariat does the day-to-day work of the organization. All business is carried on by the Secretariat. It serves all nations impartially.

TRUSTEESHIP COUNCIL (*Showing sign*): The Trusteeship Council safeguards the rights of people in territories that are not self-governing. The object of this council is to give these people a chance to be on their own as soon as possible. In this way it helps to bring about peace.

ECONOMIC AND SOCIAL COUNCIL (*Showing sign*): The Economic and Social Council helps to promote better living standards. There are committees in this group which work on unemployment, care of children, and freedom of the press. The Economic and Social Council helps all specialized agencies to work together.

Many kinds of help are needed. Struggling countries need loans. People need to know how to raise more food. It is this branch of the United Nations which helps solve all these problems.

BOB (*Coming forward*): Certainly the United Nations is *our* Key to Understanding.

TOM (*Bringing* INNKEEPER *and* INNKEEPER'S WIFE *forward*): We have found the key to understanding, and now you can add this wonderful key to your collection. (*He gives them key.*)

INNKEEPER: Thank you. We will never forget what we have seen here.

INNKEEPER'S WIFE: We will keep this key and take good care of it. It will remind our guests that the United Nations is the key which opens the door of understanding, and that every nation and individual has an important part to play in helping to bring about understanding in the world. (*Curtain*)

THE END

The Rosy-Cheeked Ghost

by Betty Gray Blaine

Characters

SCARY LARRY, *the rosy-cheeked ghost*
MOANA
MAD MABEL } *witches*
WEIRD WILLIE
EERIE EDDIE } *ghosts*
PROFESSOR GRUESOME, *a monster*
TONY
DICK
KATHY
PETER } *children in Halloween costumes*
BETSY
LINDA
OTHER GHOSTS
OTHER WITCHES

TIME: *Halloween.*
SETTING: *A deserted barn, the classroom of Spookane Ghoul School. Straw, cornstalks, and old boxes and crates are strewn around the room.*
AT RISE: SCARY LARRY *is sitting on an old crate, looking dejected.* MOANA, WEIRD WILLIE, *and* EERIE EDDIE *are standing around him, trying to comfort him.*

45

MOANA: Don't worry, Scary Larry, I know you'll graduate.

SCARY LARRY (*Sadly*): I just don't look like a successful ghost, and I can't moan and shake like you can, Moana.

EERIE EDDIE: We'll help you, Scary Larry, and show you how to be a real ghost. Then you'll pass the Spookane Ghoul School final exam with flying colors.

SCARY LARRY: Tonight is my last chance. I *must* be mysterious tonight. But I'm afraid it's no use. I guess I just don't have what it takes for haunting.

WEIRD WILLIE: Oh, don't be so modest, Larry. All it takes for haunting is no body and a hollow head, and you have that.

EERIE EDDIE: I think your main difficulty is that you look too healthy. Can't you do something about those rosy cheeks?

SCARY LARRY: I've tried rubbing them, but they just get redder and rosier.

MOANA (*Patting* LARRY *on the back*): Well, don't you worry, Larry. You are the healthiest and handsomest ghost we have had around here in a long, long time. (EDDIE *and* WILLIE *make frightening gestures at* MOANA.)

SCARY LARRY: Thanks, Moana! I think you are a very bewitching witch.

EERIE EDDIE: Hey, stop the soft talk. We came here to help Larry be scary. Remember?

WEIRD WILLIE: You're right, Eddie. You show him how to shake and quake. That is your specialty! (EDDIE *flaps arms under sheet and shakes and quakes*)

EERIE EDDIE: Now you do it, Scary Larry. (LARRY *tries unsuccessfully*.) Oh, that's terrible. You'll never frighten anyone with that smile and those rosy cheeks.

WEIRD WILLIE: Eddie's right, Scary Larry. You act positively human, and that's the worst thing that can happen to a ghost.

EERIE EDDIE: I give up. Moana, take over and see what you can do to help him.

MOANA: Well, first of all, you must stop looking so happy all of the time, Larry. To be a successful ghost, you must learn to suffer, like this. Oh-h-h! (MOANA *moans mournfully.*)

SCARY LARRY: Oh-ha ha ha! There, you see I really tried and I can't moan. I can only chuckle. (MAD MABEL *enters.*) Hello, Mad Mabel.

MAD MABEL (*Cackling*): There's nothing wrong with chuckling. I do it all the time and everyone knows I am a wicked witch. Why, just the other day some young scamp gave me a compliment. He pointed to his head and said, "Sick. Sick. Sick. The poor thing's sick." I guess that is about the nicest thing anyone ever said about me. (*Sits down away from the rest of the group and cackles from time to time.*)

WEIRD WILLIE: Poor Mabel. She really is mad. Well, Larry, now it's my turn to try to help you. I'll teach you the greatest trick of all. It will get you out of many a difficult situation.

SCARY LARRY: What is that, Weird Willie?

WEIRD WILLIE: I will teach you how to vanish into thin air. Every good ghost must be able to vanish when he wants to. Now follow my instructions carefully. Close your eyes. Press the pulse in your left wrist and say *presto,* and whisk—you will be gone.

SCARY LARRY (*Follows directions*): *Presto* . . . Where am I? Where am I?

EERIE EDDIE (*Moans*): You're at Spookane Ghoul School—just where you were before.

SCARY LARRY: Oh, no. (*Opens eyes*) Oh, yes. I am. It's no use, my friends. You have done all you can do. I'm a ghastly ghost. Besides, it's too late. Here comes Professor Gruesome.

MOANA: Please do your best on the examination tonight, Scary Larry. We want you to graduate with us. (PROFESSOR GRUESOME *enters with other ghosts and witches.*)

SCARY LARRY: It's a miserable evening, sir.

PROFESSOR GRUESOME: Fine, fine! I'm glad to hear it. Arise, Spirits. (*Everyone stands*) We will repeat our pledge.

ALL:

We pledge to all the spirits past
That over us a spell is cast.
We will haunt each Halloween night
And do our best with all our might.

(*All sit*)

PROFESSOR GRUESOME: Do you all know what night this is?

SCARY LARRY: It is our graduation night, Professor Gruesome. We will be graduate ghosts when we complete our examination.

PROFESSOR GRUESOME: True. True. I hope you will be so fortunate, Scary Larry, but your healthy appearance is certainly a handicap. However, I shall try to overlook that and judge you only on your performance tonight. And now are you all ready for your final test?

SCARY LARRY: I guess so, Professor. I'm as ready as I'll ever be.

PROFESSOR GRUESOME: Tonight is Halloween and every eligible ghost and witch who has completed this education gets a jittery feeling. Your final test will be to show me what you have learned in this school.

MOANA: But Professor, how can we practice haunting if there is no one to frighten?

PROFESSOR GRUESOME: I have made all of the arrangements. Our little visitors will arrive very shortly and it is your job to frighten them. It's all in fun, of course. Do you understand?

ALL: We understand.

PROFESSOR GRUESOME: Then come with me into the back corner of the barn where we cannot be seen. When I run my finger down your spine it is your turn to frighten our visitors away. (*All go to the back of the stage and wait in the shadows.* TONY, DICK *and* KATHY, *in costume, tiptoe into barn.*)

TONY: Sh-h-h. Do you see anything in this old barn?

DICK: No, it's too dark and scary.

KATHY: I don't like it in here. Let's get out!

TONY: Girls are 'fraidy cats. I'm taking care of you so don't worry.

MOANA (*Begins to moan softly and then louder*): Oh-h-h! Oh-h-h!

KATHY: Did you hear something?

DICK: I—I think so, but I'm not sure.

TONY: Oh, don't be silly. There's no one here but us.

MAD MABEL (*Begins to cackle*): Sick. Sick. The poor thing's sick.

KATHY: There it is again. Oh, I don't care if I am a 'fraidy cat. I'm getting out of here.

TONY: Go ahead if you want to, but it's just the wind. I don't see anything.

EERIE EDDIE (*Appears waving arms and moaning*): Oh-h-h! Oh-h-h!

TONY: Now I see something. Come on. Let's get out of here. (*All exit squealing.*)

PROFESSOR GRUESOME (*Laughing*): Moana, Mabel and Eddie, you passed the test. You were very convincing ghosts. (MOANA, MABEL *and* EDDIE *dance around*) Quiet! I hear our next victims. Scary Larry, are you ready?

SCARY LARRY: I hope so. (PETER, BETTY, *and* LINDA *in costume tiptoe in.*)

PETER: Boy, it's really dark in here. It kind of makes chills run up and down your spine, doesn't it?

BETSY: Yes, it's mysterious, spooky, and kind of scary, too. That is, if you scare easily, but I don't. Where's Linda?

LINDA: I'm right here. I think this is silly. We came out for trick or treat and we won't get anything from this old barn but a bad cold. It's drafty here!

PETER: It's funny you mentioned that just then because I think I feel a cold chill. Do you, Betsy?

BETSY: I feel it, too.

LINDA: And it's coming from behind us. (*All turn and see* LARRY.)

SCARY LARRY: Boo!

PETER: Hey, is that you, Larry?

SCARY LARRY: Yes, but how did you know?

BETSY: Why, Larry Jones, we ought to know you. You live next door to us.

SCARY LARRY: Oh, no, you've made a mistake. I'm Scary Larry. (*Children laugh.*)

PETER: Ha, ha! That's a good one. Your ghost costume is wonderful.

LINDA: Yes, he almost looks like a real ghost except for his rosy cheeks.

BETSY: Come on, let's get out of this silly barn and fill our treat bags. Here's one for you, Larry. (*Hands trick-or-treat bag to* LARRY)

SCARY LARRY: But I'm a ghost! I'm not Larry Jones! Please, I'm a ghost! A ghost! (*Children exit pulling* LARRY *after them.*)

MOANA: Oh, poor Larry. Now he'll never pass the final test.

WEIRD WILLIE: He's the goofiest ghost I have ever seen.

PROFESSOR GRUESOME: It appears that we have lost one of our ghosts to the children. That's certainly a switch!

EERIE EDDIE: I feel sorry for Scary Larry. He wanted so much to be a ghost, but those rosy cheeks just didn't look right.

PROFESSOR GRUESOME: Well, we haven't time to worry about one failing ghost. Let's go on with the test. Sh-h! I hear someone! Weird Willie, it's your turn. (*Curtain is lowered or lights dimmed for a few moments to indicate passage of time. When curtain rises or lights come on again,* PROFESSOR GRUESOME *is seated on a large box, holding several diplomas. The pupils of Spookane Ghoul School are seated on the floor in front of him.* SCARY LARRY *is not on stage.*)

MOANA: I wonder where Scary Larry is. He hasn't been back since the children dragged him away.

WEIRD WILLIE: Maybe he's ashamed to come back, since he didn't pass the test.

MOANA: I'm worried about him.

PROFESSOR GRUESOME: Quiet, ghosts, quiet! (*He stands.*) The time for our ghostly graduation has come. I have taught you all I know about haunting and you have learned your lessons well. Spookane Ghoul School is proud of you. (*Mysteriously*) Now the time has come for you to go out in the wide, wide world and do your ghostly duty. I know you will be successful. As I call your names you may come up for your diplomas. Moana. (*She comes forward*) Goodbye, Moana, and good luck. (*A low mysterious moan is heard from offstage.*) Please be quiet until I finish handing out the diplomas. Eerie Eddie. (*As he comes forward, there is a louder moan offstage.*) Goodbye, Eddie, and good luck. (EDDIE *sits down and moaning gets louder.*) Weird Willie. (WEIRD WILLIE *stands up. Suddenly* SCARY LARRY, *carrying a treat bag, enters and darts around the room. His cheeks are no longer rosy.*)

ALL (*Frightened*): Who is it? Who is it?

WEIRD WILLIE (*Sitting down again*): Is it Scary Larry?

EERIE EDDIE: No, it can't be. Larry has rosy cheeks.

MOANA: Besides, this one's very mysterious and he moans as well as I do, and Larry could never do that.

PROFESSOR GRUESOME: He is certainly a convincing ghost. He must be one of my students who graduated last year and he has returned to show you how well he is doing. Who are you, Mr. Ghost? Who are you?

SCARY LARRY (*Stops darting and moaning*): I am Scary Larry. (*Begins to moan again*)

ALL: Larry?

OTHER GHOSTS (*Ad lib*) : Oh, no, I can't believe it. It's impossible! Where are your rosy cheeks? (*Etc.*)

PROFESSOR GRUESOME: Larry, stop shaking and moaning and tell us what you saw to inspire you to be such a good ghost.

SCARY LARRY: Not what I saw, what I *ate*! (*Begins to moan again and drops his treat bag.*) I have a terrible pain.

MAD MABEL: Sick. Sick. The poor boy's sick.

MOANA (*Picks up* LARRY's *treat bag*): Mabel's right. Larry really is sick. Look, he has eaten the whole bag of treats.

PROFESSOR GRUESOME: Is this true, Scary Larry?

SCARY LARRY (*Rubbing stomach*): Yes, sir. I feel awful.

WEIRD WILLIE: You will have to give Larry his diploma, Professor Gruesome, because he is the best ghost of all now.

ALL: Yes. Yes. Give Scary Larry his diploma.

PROFESSOR GRUESOME: Wait a minute. I can't give a diploma for just one good act. How do I know Larry will always be a good ghost just because he is sick tonight?

SCARY LARRY: Oh, Professor, I will never think of Halloween (*Groans*) again without remembering how terrible I feel (*Groans*), and it will be easy to moan and shake like a ghost. Once a ghost, always a ghost. I will never forget this miserable feeling in my stomach.

PROFESSOR GRUESOME: All right, Scary Larry. I guess you have earned your diploma the hard way. I'm sure you will be a successful ghost. Here is your diploma and good luck to you. (*Class claps for* SCARY LARRY.)

SCARY LARRY (*Comes to front of stage and says to audience*):

On Halloween when the lights are low,
If you should hear a mournful "Oh-h-h,"
I warn you, friend, do not tarry
Or you'll meet up with Scary Larry.
(*Curtain*)

THE END

Cinder-Riley

by Claire Boiko

Characters

LEPRECHAUN
THE STEPMOTHER
AGGIE ⎱ *stepsisters*
MAGGIE ⎰
CINDER-RILEY

FAIRY GODMOTHER
JACK O'CLOCK
DANCERS
PROP BOYS

BEFORE RISE: *The piano sets the scene with a lively Irish jig. While the music is playing, the* LEPRECHAUN *pokes his head through the curtain opening. He turns his head first to one side, then to the other. Then he leaps out and seats himself on the apron of the stage, cross-legged. The music stops.*

LEPRECHAUN: Whist now, it's a fine audience ye are! We have a grand play for you to watch this day. 'Tis the old Hibernian legend, "Princess Cinder-Riley, or The Lost Brogan." Our actors are guaranteed to make you split your sides with laughter one minute, and cry your way through three handkerchiefs the next! But first, we'll need your cooperation. In order to make the play begin, we'll need some loud clapping. This clears the air for the actors. Now, would you mind applauding, please? (*He taps his stick, and all applaud. The curtains open.*)

SETTING: *The stage is bare. The backdrop is hung with drawing of large knives, forks, spoons and skillets.*

AT RISE: *Two* PROP BOYS *carry in a large screen which they set at center. The* BOYS *walk behind the screen, so that they are not seen, and remain behind the screen. A table covered with a cloth reaching to the floor is "walked" onstage by* FAIRY GODMOTHER *and* PROP BOY, *who are hidden beneath it, giving the magical effect of a walking table. On the table are a pile of papers, a quill pen and an inkstand.*

LEPRECHAUN (*Stops the applause*): Sure, that was fine! Now, just applaud a bit more and our actors will come out and begin the play. Ready? Let's clap for the Princess Cinder-Riley, her wicked stepmother, and her two disgustin' stepsisters. (*He taps his stick again. All applaud. The* STEPMOTHER, AGGIE, *and* MAGGIE *enter, noses in the air. They are followed by* CINDER-RILEY, *who wears a long gown, a crown, and silver slippers.* CINDER-RILEY *is crying and wringing her hands.*)

STEPMOTHER: Now, Princess Cinder-Riley, it's no good cryin' at all, at all! You must keep to the schedule. Riding lesson at two o'clock. Music lesson at three. Etiquette lesson at four. Dancing lesson at five. And at six, the royal state banquet with the Duke of Downderrydown, the Earl of Earlyrise and your betrothed, the King of West Muffinland!

CINDER-RILEY: Must I? Oh, please don't make me marry the King of West Muffinland! He has turned-up toes and a wart on his nose, and he's as fat as a tub of butter!

AGGIE *and* MAGGIE (*Linking arms and dancing around mockingly*): Ha! Ha! Cinder-Riley's going to marry the King of West Muffinland!

AGGIE: With turned-up toes!

MAGGIE: And a wart on his nose!

AGGIE *and* MAGGIE (*Together*): Fat as a tub of butter! (*They pantomime big stomachs and puffed out cheeks.*)

STEPMOTHER: Now don't carry on so, Cinder-Riley. After all, you are a princess, and I am your regent. Princesses must marry kings. I shall see to it that you do! While we're at it, you must send out a proclamation that your sister Aggie shall marry the Duke of Downderrydown.

AGGIE: The Duke of Downderrydown—ah! He's so handsome!

STEPMOTHER: And your sister Maggie shall marry the Earl of Earlyrise.

MAGGIE: The Earl of Earlyrise—ah! He's so rich!

STEPMOTHER: And speaking of proclamations, here are thirty-three dozen more matters of proclamation to be signed before sundown. (*She points to a large stack of papers on the table.*) Come, girls, we must go rest ourselves for the royal banquet this evening. Princess Cinder-Riley, I'd advise you to hustle your bustle if you wish to be finished before the sun goes down! (*They exit.* STEPMOTHER *leads and* AGGIE *and* MAGGIE *follow, noses in the air.* LEPRECHAUN *bounces to the side and shouts "Boo," encouraging audience to do likewise. As* CINDER-RILEY *comes downstage, he puts finger to lips, shushing audience.*)

CINDER-RILEY: Alas! Alack! Well-a-day! Sure, and woe is me! (*She sobs.* LEPRECHAUN *takes out large red hanky and pantomimes woe.*) I do not love the King of West Muffinland. Nay! Nay! A thousand times nay! I love handsome Jack O'Clock. But oh, bitter fortune, Jack O'Clock is only a kitchen boy. Oh, would I were a simple scullery maid. I would give all my satins, all my jewels, yes, my very crown itself, just to be a kitchen maid. For this is the night of the Pantry Frolic . . . all the lads and colleens who work in the kitchen will be dancing and singing. And Jack O'Clock, my own true love, will be crowned Prince of the Potatoes! I cannot be there. Oh, my heart is breaking!

FAIRY GODMOTHER (*Pokes head out from under the table-cloth*): Pssst! Cinder-Riley! (CINDER-RILEY *looks around, startled.*)

CINDER-RILEY: My goodness! Who might you be?

GODMOTHER (*Steps out dressed in kitchen outfit*): Sure, I'm your fairy godmother, I am, I am. I've come to help you out of your miserable plight. Dry your tears, me pretty. We must be quick. Now, let me see.

CINDER-RILEY: But, fairy godmother, I have thirty-three dozen matters of proclamation to sign before the sun goes down!

GODMOTHER: Pish posh, macushla! That's a simple thing for a fairy to fix. Here now—just write your name in the air, whilst I wave me wand. (CINDER-RILEY *writes her name in the air.* FAIRY GODMOTHER *waves broom as she chants.*)

Dimple-dee, dample-dee, dumple-dee dined
Proclamations—Be ye signed!

(CINDER-RILEY *claps hands in amazement as she looks at papers.*)

CINDER-RILEY: Oh, how *marvelous!* 'Tis a miracle to be sure!

GODMOTHER: Tonight you shall be a simple kitchen maid. First, you need a raggedy dress . . . aha! Me magic shears. (*Takes huge pair of shears from reticule, snips at* CINDER-RILEY'S *dress, turning it into a short gown with a ragged hem.*) Now, a mop cap. (*She takes off her cap. Underneath it, she wears another cap, so that she always stays perfectly dressed.*) And a sweet little apron. (*Takes off her own apron. There is another apron beneath it.*) Now you are all ready to go to the Frolic!

CINDER-RILEY (*Takes off crown, puts it on table. Puts on*

cap and apron, looks down at feet): Ah—but my shoes!

GODMOTHER: Sure, I almost forgot. You need some nice comfortable brogans. You could never dance the night in those slippers. *(She takes off her own shoes. Underneath she has another pair.* CINDER-RILEY *takes off her slippers, puts them on table, and puts on the brogans.)* There is only one more thing, Cinder-Riley. You must be home at twelve o'clock to the minute. Are you ready now?

CINDER-RILEY: Indeed I am, fairy godmother.

GODMOTHER *(Waving broom):*
Rimple-dee, rample-dee, rumple-dee row
Bring us the Pantry Frolic now!
(The PROP BOYS *behind the large screen move it off so that it looks as though it is moving by itself.* PROP BOY *under table moves that off. The music of an Irish jig is heard, and the* DANCERS *enter, clapping hands to music. They may dance a reel. When music stops,* JACK O'CLOCK *enters, dressed in tatters with a crown of potatoes.* CINDER-RILEY *and* GODMOTHER *stand to one side, watching.)*

DANCERS:
Here's Jack O'Clock, let's give him a cheer,
He's the Potato Prince without a peer!
Hip hip, Potato! Hip hip, Potato! Hip hip, Potato Prince!
*(*LEPRECHAUN *cheers and leads audience in cheers and applause for* JACK O'CLOCK.)*

DANCER: Lead us in a jig, Jack!

JACK: That I will! *(Piano begins jig.* DANCERS *freeze in pose.* JACK *spots* CINDER-RILEY, *holds up hand. Piano changes to "When Irish Eyes Are Smiling" which is played sentimentally throughout remainder of scene between* JACK *and* CINDER-RILEY.)* Wait! Here's a colleen the like of whom I've never seen. She's as lovely as a

May morning. 'Tis herself I shall dance with and none other. Come, me little flower. (GODMOTHER *exits, as* JACK O'CLOCK *and* CINDER-RILEY *dance together. At end of dance* JACK *goes downstage and speaks in an aside to the audience.*) Me heart! Me heart is not in its rightful place! Sure, it's been stolen! Stolen by the maid with the raggedy dress. Dare I speak me deepest thoughts to her? (LEPRECHAUN *nods eagerly.*)

CINDER-RILEY (*Goes downstage other side, speaks in an aside to the audience as she holds her hand on her heart*): My heart! My heart is beating like the drums in a marching band! Ah! He's so manly! Ah! Dare I speak my mind to him? (LEPRECHAUN *nods and takes each one by hand, joining their hands center stage. He holds his finger to his lips to warn audience not to make noise.*)

JACK: Oh, lovely kitchen maid!

CINDER-RILEY: Oh, Jack! (*They strike a pose.* LEPRE-CHAUN *beams and claps hands, motioning audience to applaud, also. Chime sounds twelve times.*) Oh, dear! 'Tis midnight. I must go! (*On the stroke of twelve the screen and table come back.* GODMOTHER *has hidden herself beneath table again.* DANCERS *go behind screen.* CINDER-RILEY *leaves one shoe on stage as she runs back near screen.* JACK *picks up shoe, scratches head, goes behind screen with shoe.* STEPMOTHER, AGGIE *and* MAGGIE *enter, noses in air.*)

STEPMOTHER (*Horrified*): Princess Cinder-Riley, where in the great rollin' world were you this evening?

AGGIE: We looked hither and yon for you!

MAGGIE: And the King of West Muffinland was so angry, he popped three gold buttons off his coat!

STEPMOTHER: Cinder-Riley! What are you doing in that dreadful rag? Take off that apron! (*She snatches the apron off* CINDER-RILEY.)

AGGIE: Put on your crown! (*Takes cap off* CINDER-RILEY'S *head and thrusts crown on*)

MAGGIE: Put on your slippers! (*Tosses the slippers to* CINDER-RILEY, *who puts them on*)

STEPMOTHER: And throw my cloak over that tattered dress! (*Puts cloak around* CINDER-RILEY'S *shoulders*) Foolish girl! You must prepare to marry the King of West Muffinland immediately!

CINDER-RILEY: Oh, no! Please! Wait! The marriage cannot be official unless there is a proclamation.

STEPMOTHER: I took care of the proclamation. It was in this great pile. You signed it yourself.

AGGIE *and* MAGGIE (*Together*): So there!

CINDER-RILEY: Oh, woe! Alas! 'Tis true. Oh, I shall fade away and die. I'll be in my grave with the sorrow of it all!

STEPMOTHER: Come, Cinder-Riley. (*Starts to lead her off.* JACK *comes around the screen, puts his hand up and shouts.*)

JACK: Wait! (*They turn and stare.* STEPMOTHER *eyes him icily.* CINDER-RILEY *sighs longingly.* LEPRECHAUN *signals for cheers, and piano plays a fanfare.* JACK *bows.*) I beg your pardon, me ladies and Your Royal Highness, but I have a boon to ask ye.

CINDER-RILEY (*Aside*): Handsome Jack O'Clock. My own true love! (*To* JACK) Speak, young man, I command you.

JACK: I have in me hand a darlin' little brogan which a fair lass, the pride of me life, wore to the Pantry Frolic. And I swore to meself that I would not rest until I tried it on the foot of every maid in the kingdom.

AGGIE (*Giggles*): Oh, isn't he a fine broth of a lad! Let him try it on my foot!

JACK: I must try every maid until I find her. (*He puts the brogan on her foot. The toe of the shoe is slit so that her stocking, stuffed with cotton, protrudes visibly.*)

MAGGIE: You silly colleen! Your foot is the size of an elephant's! Here, young man—try my dainty foot! (JACK *puts shoe on her. The same thing happens.*)

JACK (*Sadly*): Well, I suppose that is that! Your ladyship is the last girl in the kingdom—except of course you, Your Highness. I suppose I shall never find my lost kitchen maid. (*He turns to go.*)

CINDER-RILEY: Wait! Try the shoe on my foot.

JACK: But, Your Highness!

CINDER-RILEY: Please.

JACK: Very well, but I hardly think the shoe could belong to Your Royal Highness. (*He slips the shoe on* CINDER-RILEY. *The piano plays a fanfare.* DANCERS *come from behind screen and cheer, "Hip, hip Potato Prince!"* LEPRECHAUN *leaps up and down and leads cheers. All show astonishment as* GODMOTHER *comes out from under table, slips cloak off* CINDER-RILEY, *and replaces the cap and apron.*) Princess Cinder-Riley! You are me lost love!

STEPMOTHER: Lost love? The likes of you, Jack O'Clock, speakin' about the Princess Cinder-Riley as your lost love. What impudent nonsense! The Princess is promised to the King of West Muffinland. It is officially proclaimed! (GODMOTHER *waves broom over the papers.*)

GODMOTHER (*Steps up and curtsies*): Begging your pardon, madam, but if you will examine this proclamation (*Picks up paper and waves it*), you will find that she is promised to someone quite different.

STEPMOTHER (*Snatches paper angrily*): Indeed! Let me read it! Why I wrote the proclamation myself. I certainly should know what I have written! (*Righteously*) Ahem! (*Reads*) "Hear ye! Hear ye! The Princess Cinder-Riley is hereby promised in marriage to the Prince of Potatoes, Jack O'Clock." (*She stares at paper, astonished.*) Bejabbers! All is lost!

GODMOTHER: And 'tis signed by the Princess' own hand. That makes it official. (LEPRECHAUN *cheers in pantomime.*)

STEPMOTHER: But what shall I tell the King of West Muffinland?

GODMOTHER: Dear me, the good King still needs a wife, does he not? (*Snaps fingers*) Ah! The very thing. Another proclamation. (*Hands one airily to* STEPMOTHER)

STEPMOTHER: Ahem! "To Whom It May Concern" (AGGIE *and* MAGGIE *poke their noses over the paper to see better as she reads*) "The King of West Muffinland shall be married this morn to her ladyship, the former regent of the realm, stepmother of Princess Cinder-Riley." (*She screams.*) Oh, no!

AGGIE: And 'tis signed by her own hand!

MAGGIE: That makes it official!

STEPMOTHER (*Throws up hands*): Oh, no! Oh, woe! He has turned-up toes and a wart on his nose.

AGGIE *and* MAGGIE (*Together*): And he's fat as a tub of butter!

STEPMOTHER: Help me, daughters, I am about to faint! (*She faints in their arms. They drag her offstage.* LEPRECHAUN *boos and invites all to boo.*)

JACK: Come, Cinder-Riley, let us prepare for our joyous weddin'. Oh, happy day! (*Piano may play "Wedding March" as they strike a pose.*)

CINDER-RILEY: Yes, dear Jack. And you shall be my prince regent and the king of my heart, forever!

GODMOTHER: Faith now, I've done a full day's work. I've banished the wicked stepmother and the disgustin' sisters; I've joined the lovers, and I've even found a wife for the King of West Muffinland. (*She strikes a pose as*

LEPRECHAUN *steps up and shakes her hand. All make tableau as* LEPRECHAUN *motions for applause, then runs to help close curtain. Piano concludes with fast jig. Curtains close.* LEPRECHAUN *turns his head from right to left, then waves goodbye and disappears.*)

THE END

The Dreadful Dragon

by Margaret Wylie Brydon and Esther Ziegler

Characters

NARRATOR
PROPERTY MAN
MOTHER
CHANG, *elder son*
LI WAN, *second son*
WILLOW, *elder daughter*
POPPY, *second daughter*
TAO, *Chang's friend*
EMPRESS SU H'SAI, *a little girl*
MOONGLOW, *Goddess of Night*
PRECIOUS JADE, *Goddess of Earth*
SILVER CLOUD, *Goddess of Sky*
RADIANT PEARL, *Goddess of Sea*
DRAGON (PRINCE LIN)
STEWARD
SERVANTS OF EMPRESS
VILLAGERS

SETTING: *The stage is bare except for a red paper-covered screen up center upon which has been painted the figure of a household god.*
AT RISE: *The NARRATOR enters, goes to center stage, and bows to audience.*

NARRATOR: Most honorable ones, this lowly person appears before you to welcome you to our humble play. With your gracious permission, I introduce to you a Chinese fairy tale of long ago. Be so kind as to follow our Chinese custom and imagine before you the miserable home of Chang, the elder son of a widowed mother, while our esteemed property man sets up our stage. (PROPERTY MAN *enters from right, carrying two stools and a small black box representing a charcoal stove. Ignoring the audience, he places one stool down right of center, the other down left of center, and the box directly up center stage in front of the screen. Then he nonchalantly strolls off in the direction from which he came.*) Since our property man is completely invisible to your celestial sight, I hasten to assure you that he bumps his head in the dust ten thousand times in your august presence. (PROPERTY MAN *re-enters during the preceding line, carrying a kettle and a basket. He glances at the* NARRATOR *indifferently and then places the kettle on the stove and the basket on the floor, left of the stove, after which he walks off right again, scratching his back as he goes.*) Our hero, Chang, his mother, his two sisters, and his little brother are all very unhappy for reasons you will soon learn. Ah me! They come! Forgive me if I withdraw my feet with unseemly haste from your honored presence, but it would be most improper for this worthless servant to intrude upon such depths of misery as I see approaching. (NARRATOR *bows and hurries out right.* MOTHER, CHANG, LI WAN, WILLOW, *and* POPPY *enter in single file, each carrying sewing. They bow in turn as they reach center stage, and then take their places. All look unhappy.*)

LI WAN (*Tilting empty kettle to look for rice, and turning away disgusted*): Venerable Mother, I'm hungry. Isn't there anything in this house to eat?

MOTHER (*Dropping sewing in despair*): No, not even a bit of rice. Oh, my children, how am I to feed you?

CHANG (*Turning to* MOTHER): Never mind, my mother, I am the man of the house. I will find a way.

WILLOW (*Pausing in her sewing*): If only our honorable father had not been taken to his ancestors!

MOTHER (*Resuming her work*): Aye, he would take care of the family he loved so much. How it must grieve him to see us unhappy.

POPPY: If only I could eat, I would not be so unhappy.

MOTHER (*Reprovingly*): We should not despair. Think of our little Empress, searching the world for her playmate Prince who disappeared in the year of the Kia-Yin. (*Courageously*) Come, let us hurry with this coat for the merchant Wong. He will give us a few coins.

LI WAN (*Disgustedly*): We will starve to death before that time. (*Going left to* MOTHER, *and gesturing toward coat*) Why, the padding is not yet in.

POPPY: Why can't I go out and get work—real work—not all this sewing?

CHANG (*Rising determinedly*): You are only a girl child. I will go out in the village and see if I can get work.

LI WAN (*Going to* CHANG. *Eagerly*): I can work, too.

MOTHER: No, Second Son, you are too young.

LI WAN (*Turning to her*): I'm not too young, Honorable Mother. I'm almost seven years old!

MOTHER: Aye, a great age!

WILLOW (*Teasingly*): You're just a baby.

LI WAN: I am not! I could fight the Dreadful Dragon himself! (*Drawing an imaginary sword*)

MOTHER (*In alarm*): Hush, Li Wan, you mustn't mention the dragon. It is bad luck.

LI WAN: It would be bad luck for him if I should meet him.

CHANG (*Bowing to* MOTHER): Farewell, Honorable Mother. (*Exits left*)

MOTHER: Goodbye, Elder Son.

CHILDREN (*Calling after him*): Farewell. Bring back something to eat.

LI WAN (*Following him to door, and calling after him*): Or bring back that old dragon, and we'll eat him!

MOTHER: Hush! If he should hear you! (*In Chinese fashion, all actors exit right.* PROPERTY MAN *enters, removes furniture of Scene 1, reverses screen to show sign, "Street of the Locusts," and exits right.* TAO *enters left with* CHANG.)

TAO (*Walking along beside* CHANG *toward center stage*): Where are you off to so early in the morning, friend Chang?

CHANG: To get food for my family. We are starving. But no one will give me work.

TAO (*Nodding his head wisely*): Everyone in the village is poor. They say it is bad luck, caused by the hungry dragon who guards our hills. They say our crops will fail until he is given his just due from our village.

CHANG: His just due?

TAO: You know the story.

CHANG: True, I once knew it, for my honorable father told me, but it has been many moons since he went to join his ancestors, and I have forgotten much of what he said.

TAO: Hear it then. It is said that we must send one of our prettiest young maidens to him each year, if our village is to prosper. He is angry, for the girls have not been sent, and often you can hear him roaring in the hills.

CHANG: That is thunder that you hear, my friend.

TAO: You do not believe this story?

CHANG: No. And even if it were true, I think it would be

dreadful to send anyone up there to be eaten by a dragon, even a useless girl.

TAO: Yes, they are useless, and there are too many in our house. I could spare him a sister easily.

CHANG: Not so in our house. There are too few hands now to earn the rice. (*Squatting on his haunches*) Sometimes, if I were not a man, I would cry. (*Turning his head to hide his tears*)

TAO (*Squatting beside him, and sniffling in sympathy*): And I. (*Quickly*) Of course we wouldn't think of it.

CHANG: Oh, no. (*Blowing nose vigorously*)

TAO: This water on my cheeks is caused by a speck of something in my eye.

CHANG: I know. It is the same with me. It is a dusty road. (*Getting up, and looking around*) Tao, where does this dragon live?

TAO (*Springing up in alarm*): Chang, you wouldn't go there? He would eat you at once, and wonder who you were later.

CHANG: This dragon, if there be one, surely guards a treasure, and if I can kill him, the treasure will be mine.

TAO (*Impressed*): Oh, Chang, you wouldn't dare!

CHANG (*Stoutly*): I would do anything to fill an empty stomach.

TAO (*Dreamily*): Yes. Think of rice flavored with just a small piece of fish.

CHANG (*Rubbing his stomach*): And the little cakes my mother used to make. Ah, I can taste them now. (*Licking his lips*)

TAO: I wish I could.

CHANG: I taste them only with my mind.

TAO: That does not fill your stomach. Chang, I will show you where the Dreadful Dragon lives. I will even go with you to the low hills. (*Starts forward eagerly, then halts*) But you must go to his cave alone. Even for food I cannot go.

CHANG: All right. Show me the way. (*They start off right.*)

TAO (*Hesitating*): Aren't you going to tell your honorable mother?

CHANG: Of course not. She would weep, and I must spare her tears.

TAO (*Thinking it over*): That is so. I will spare my mother also. Come, it is this way, toward the eastern sky. (*The little boys exit right. The* PROPERTY MAN *comes in left, and removes screen.*)

NARRATOR (*Entering*): The little boys set off with eagerness and also with fear, for this is truly a Dreadful Dragon whom they go to find. He is as large as the palace of the mighty Empress herself, and his wings are the color of the clouds at sunset, amber and turquoise and rose. It is said his eyes shoot flame, and he speaks with the voice of thunder. (*Thunder rolls.*) The children walk for a long time, then prepare to rest beside a small stream. (PROPERTY MAN *enters, puts down stream.* NARRATOR *gestures down left.*) Here is our stream; there, the mountains toward which the boys are journeying. (PROPERTY MAN *re-enters with mountains which he places up right.*) This is the cave of the Dreadful Dragon. (PROPERTY MAN *places cave behind mountains up right.* NARRATOR *and* PROPERTY MAN *exit right.* CHANG *and* TAO *now enter left.*)

TAO (*Sits by stream*): When I am rested, I must leave you. My mother will worry.

CHANG: You mean you are afraid of the Dreadful Dragon.

TAO: I must spare my mother trouble, and if her only son were lost, she would weep many tears.

CHANG: It is not your mother's tears that bother you; it is your own skin. (*Impatiently*) Get up and show me that cave! What makes you such a coward?

TAO (*Indignantly*): I am not a coward! It is just that my departed father would wish me to guard myself for the sake of my ancestors.

CHANG: You are a mouse!

TAO (*Sniffling*): Do you mean that, O Chang-who-was-once-my-friend?

CHANG (*Checking his anger*): No, it is the hunger that speaks in me. Come, let us find the dragon. (*Jumps stream at left*)

TAO (*Reluctantly*): I will go. My bones will be found in the cave, and my mother will weep, all my ancestors will weep, and my sisters, too, but I will go. (*Leaping stream at left*) Ai-ya, ai-ya, ai-ya!

CHANG: Hush, and lead me to the cave. (*Pushes* TAO *ahead of him*) Night approaches.

TAO (*Turning back eagerly*): That is true. Let us wait until morning for this task. (*Edging behind* CHANG) In the morning I will gladly go with you.

CHANG (*Striding ahead*): We are going now. (TAO *hesitates, afraid to stay, or to go back alone.*)

TAO: Ai-ya, ai-ya, ai-ya! My poor mother, my poor ancestors, my miserable sisters! (*Grumbling to himself, he joins* CHANG *center. The boys wind in and out around the stage, as if following a winding mountain path. As they reach the foothills, upper right, a loud roar is heard.* CHANG *falters, while* TAO *skitters down the path, and hides behind the mountain.*) Let us return to our village. Oh, please, friend Chang, please!

CHANG (*Sturdily*): I am not afraid of that dragon.

TAO: Then why are your knees shaking?

CHANG: A slight chill. Hurry, before it is too dark to see him, if he is there. (*Starting on*) My ancestors were mighty men, and I am not afraid—much. (*The boys walk on toward stage right, more slowly now. Suddenly, a voice speaks.*)

DRAGON (*Appearing in entrance to cave*): Who is there? Who comes to the cave of the Dreadful Dragon?

TAO: I go. (*Races back along winding path, hops over stream, and exits left*)

CHANG: Wait, wait! Oh, he is gone into the darkness, and I am left alone with this terrible dragon. What shall I do? (*Appealing helplessly to audience*)

DRAGON: What should you do but sit down and have a cup of jasmine tea with me? You've no idea how lonely I get way off here in the mountains with no one to keep me company!

CHANG: But I thought—that is—

DRAGON: You thought I would eat you. Is that it?

CHANG (*Embarrassed*): Well, you see—

DRAGON: Yes, I see. Those silly people down in the village think I am a terrible creature of fire and wrath, when really I am a most gracious and charming animal. Won't you come in?

CHANG (*Faltering*): A thousand thanks for your gracious invitation, Honorable Monster, but—

DRAGON: You don't seem pleased by my humble hospitality. Aren't you hungry?

CHANG: Oh, yes. But I am afraid you are, too.

DRAGON: Now, then, why do we delay our feasting, esteemed guest? I have bird's-nest soup, bamboo shoots, tea fit for the Empress herself, and many little cakes. (*CHANG goes toward cave, hesitates briefly, then bravely plunges into darkness. DRAGON withdraws into cave, followed by peals of thunder. PROPERTY MAN removes mountains, cave, and stream, and sets up house scene again.*)

NARRATOR (*Entering*): I beg you to excuse this most unseemly intrusion, but I have been sent by the Dreadful Dragon to convey his most humble apologies. Because of the limited space within his wretched cave, he is not able to give himself the sublime pleasure of being your host, as well as Chang's. Lest I do you the discourtesy of leaving you too long in the dark, permit me to place the sun once more in the sky, and we shall go on with the play. It is the next morning, and Tao has reached the village. (*Exits right*)

MOTHER (*Enters with family and sits on stool*): Oh, my son, my son! What shall I do without my elder son?

POPPY: Honorable Mother, perhaps he is all right.

WILLOW (*Who has been standing center with hands over eyes. Aside to* POPPY): All right? Have your miserable wits deserted you? The dragon will eat him, of course.

LI WAN: I, Li Wan, the Tiger, will go to rescue him. (*Starts off left*) Farewell, my mother.

MOTHER (*Springing up and crossing left of center*): No, no, my Small One, you shall not go. You are now my only son, the honorable head of this house.

POPPY (*Steps toward down right*): Li Wan, stop boasting.

WILLOW (*Coming down right center*): I won't take orders from a child, even if he is the only son.

LI WAN: Silence, women! (*Crossing center past* MOTHER) Your master speaks. (*Turns back to* MOTHER) Mother, I am still hungry. Though my eyes weep for my brother, my stomach remembers it has not been fed. (*Gong sounds, and* TAO *rushes in.*)

TAO: The Empress comes. The Daughter of Heaven comes to our lowly village.

MOTHER: Li Wan, wash your face. Willow, and Poppy, your best clothes.

WILLOW: I have nothing to wear. (*Hurries off right, followed by* POPPY)

MOTHER: Hurry! They say the Empress is good and beautiful. They say she possesses the power to control the very winds themselves. Surely she could subdue even the Dreadful Dragon, if only she will take pity on us.

LI WAN (*With great interest*): Will she give me food?

POPPY (*Rushing in right, followed by* WILLOW, *both dressed in best robes*): Hush, Small One, the Empress comes to our lowly home. (*Rushing to doorway and peering out*) Is she not glowing as the sun at mid-day?

LI WAN (*Pushing in beside her*): She is only a little girl, like Poppy.

WILLOW (*Looking over her shoulder*): But beautiful and stately. And see her jewels, and her servants. Oh, to be an empress!

MOTHER: Quiet, children. (*She motions them back behind her, up right, where they go and stand.* EMPRESS *enters left, followed by* STEWARD *and her* RETINUE, *and several curious* VILLAGERS. *All bow.*)

EMPRESS: Rise, my friends. The people tell me you have a great trouble here.

LI WAN: Honorable Empress, we have nothing to eat.

MOTHER: Hush, Li Wan. O Most Gracious Queen, our unworthy abode is exalted by your most august presence.

EMPRESS: Tell me what sorrow burdens this worthy mother's heart.

MOTHER: Ah, Exalted One, a thousand pardons for intruding the sorrows of this lowly person upon your flower-like presence. Since all the kingdom knows your own sorrow at the loss of the noble Prince, your beloved, it is in my mind that you can understand my deep despair.

EMPRESS: Alas, yes. (*Pause*)

MOTHER: O Most Honored Queen, my elder son went to find the dragon of the hills, and he has not returned.

EMPRESS (*Wistfully*): Dragons, dragons, Chinese dragons!

MOTHER: Did you speak, Exalted One?

EMPRESS: 'Tis nothing. (*Pause*) When did your son disappear?

MOTHER: This morning. He went to seek work in the village, but his friend Tao has told me there was no work to be found, and now we are starving, his brother, his lowly sisters, and I.

POPPY (*Unexpectedly*): I am not lowly. (*Moving forward*)

EMPRESS (*In astonishment*): What did you say, my child? (MOTHER *gasps in consternation, and steps back left, as* EMPRESS *crosses center to meet* POPPY.)

POPPY (*Courageously*): Why are all boys worthy, and all girls lowly? Is not Your Highness a girl?

EMPRESS: I know. Often even I have found it difficult to be a girl.

MOTHER (*Crossing to left of* EMPRESS): She is a thoughtless, ignorant child, Gracious Empress, but she means no harm. I implore you, do not have her beheaded.

EMPRESS (*Impatiently*): Of course not. She is a girl of spirit. I like her.

POPPY (*Happily*): And I like you.

LI WAN (*Eyeing* VILLAGER *who has wandered in with food in his hand*): I like bean sprouts.

MOTHER (*Fearfully*): Forgive their unpardonable boldness, Exalted One.

EMPRESS (*Looking from one to the other in amusement. To* POPPY): Do *you* think your brother is dead, child?

POPPY: Of course not. Chang will kill that nasty dragon.

EMPRESS: How nice, if he can. I have always wanted to see a dragon myself. Perhaps I will rescue the boy.

MOTHER (*Falling at the* EMPRESS' *feet, touching head to floor*): Illustrious One! May you live forever!

POPPY: If only I could go!

LI WAN: I am still hungry.

EMPRESS (*Clapping for* SERVANTS): Feed these people. Remain in the village, and give them whatever else they require. (SERVANTS *bow, and depart left.*)

MOTHER: How good you are.

WILLOW: And how beautiful! (SERVANTS *enter with food on trays.*)

EMPRESS: Here is food. Eat then. I will go to find your elder brother. (*Starts out left*)

STEWARD: Permit me to accompany you, Celestial Queen.

EMPRESS: I go alone.

STEWARD: No, no! You will be killed.

EMPRESS (*Haughtily*): Not the Empress of China. Not even that terrible monster would dare to harm the Royal One who sits upon the Dragon Throne. (*Exits left*)

LI WAN (*Receiving his share of the food*): I shall eat until I cannot move. (*Exits right, followed by others.* PROP-ERTY MAN *removes house, and sets up mountains and stream as before.*)

NARRATOR (*Entering*): While the happy villagers are feasting, if it is the pleasure of our augustly noble audience, we shall follow in the fragrant footsteps of our Honorable Empress. She goes alone, small and beautiful and wise, to meet the dragon. On her way in the dark night she encounters three goddesses—Precious Jade, Silver Cloud, and Radiant Pearl. (*He bows and exits right, as the goddesses enter and dance about. As* SILVER CLOUD *catches sight of the approaching* EMPRESS, *she stops dancing and jumps lightly over the stream to look offstage at the* EMPRESS.)

PRECIOUS JADE: What is it? Why did you interrupt our dance?

SILVER CLOUD: Sh-sh. A mortal makes her way toward our mountains.

RADIANT PEARL: What is she like?

SILVER CLOUD: She is beautiful.

PRECIOUS JADE: Do you suppose she is on her way to the Dreadful Dragon?

SILVER CLOUD: I don't know.

RADIANT PEARL: If not, perhaps I can persuade her to travel that way. (*Giggles, as she goes right, to meet the* EMPRESS. *Then her expression changes as the* EMPRESS *comes onto the stage.* RADIANT PEARL *bows sadly, covering her face with her hands.*)

EMPRESS: Oh, oh, a real goddess! Now I am glad I came to seek the dragon. Why do you weep, Celestial One?

RADIANT PEARL: The Dreadful Dragon of the hills has taken our moon from the sky, and we cannot see.

EMPRESS: How truly dreadful of him!

RADIANT PEARL: He was lonely. He said no mortals came to see him, so he must have the moon for company. If only one mortal had the courage to visit him, perhaps he would give back our lovely moon.

EMPRESS: He is truly a terrible monster. Stealing the moon indeed! (*Crossing center*) Who are these other beautiful creatures?

RADIANT PEARL: They are Precious Jade, Goddess of Earth, and Silver Cloud, Goddess of the Sky. (GODDESSES *bow, as they are introduced.*)

PRECIOUS JADE: We, too, are sad because our sister, Moonglow, is a prisoner of the dragon.

SILVER CLOUD: We need our sweet Goddess to make the nights beautiful with her shining light.

RADIANT PEARL: Without her, the waves no longer stretch a silver path to the shore.

PRECIOUS JADE: Even the dolphins are sad, and the seahorses no longer ride in the misty moonlight.

SILVER CLOUD: We are lonely without our sister.

EMPRESS: I have often been lonely.

RADIANT PEARL: We know you lost your playmate prince.

PRECIOUS JADE: We of Earth wept with you for many crescent moons.

EMPRESS: You are very kind. I shall return the moon to you. It will be a simple task for a Manchu.

PRECIOUS JADE: You are going to see the dragon! (*Pretending to be impressed*)

RADIANT PEARL: You are not afraid? (*Giggles a little*)

EMPRESS: Of course not. I am the Empress of China. I am not afraid of anything.

SILVER CLOUD: That is splendid, but (*More laughter*) be very careful of the Dreadful Dragon.

RADIANT PEARL: He is a terrible creature, breathing fire, and flashing his hundred horrible claws in the air. (GODDESSES *exit, still laughing, down right, as the* EMPRESS *goes on alone, up imaginary path. As she reaches the summit, there is a mighty roar.*)

EMPRESS (*Stopping*): This feeling I have is new to me. It must be fear. (*Starts on*) But I will not stop. (*Loud roar.* EMPRESS *braces herself, and walks on, talking to keep up her courage.*) It is a good thing that the blood of a thousand fighting ancestors runs in my veins! (*A third roar announces the appearance of the* DRAGON's *head at the cave entrance.*)

DRAGON: Who comes to my cave in the deep, deep hills?

EMPRESS (*Standing her ground bravely*): The Empress of China. Make way!

DRAGON: Su! Not the beautiful Su H'sai? Oh, my little friend, you have come at last!

EMPRESS: Do not try to flatter Su H'sai! She would not acknowledge as a friend a dragon who would devour a helpless little boy, and who makes the evening hideous with his dreadful roars!

DRAGON: If I had known *you* were coming, I would have produced a much more terrifying roar. Listen to *this*. (DRAGON *jerks his head back into cave, and produces*

*loud roar, making the cave tremble. Suddenly his head
darts out again, and he shouts at her.*) What do you
think of that one? (EMPRESS *lifts chin bravely.*) And
what if I have eaten this boy, and will eat you as well?

EMPRESS: I am not afraid.

DRAGON: Spoken like a true Manchu. I am proud of you.

EMPRESS: Proud of me?

DRAGON: Don't you remember the fete they gave to honor
the throne, and the little doll-faced children with their
lanterns full of moon-flowers, glowing like a pale flame?

EMPRESS (*Slowly*): Who are you?

DRAGON: Don't you remember the ancient celestial spirit
who cared for our lives in the long ago?

EMPRESS: You are—you cannot be, Prince Lin, my betrothed?

DRAGON: I am he. (*Steps out of dragon skin into sunlight
to the sound of thunder and the flash of lightning, as*
EMPRESS *retreats downstage in terror.*) See, I am no
longer a raging dragon, but your own Prince. (*He follows her downstage.*) You have saved me by your courage.

EMPRESS (*Sinking to her knees in thanksgiving*): Lin! My
playmate, my gentle Prince.

LIN (*Raising her tenderly*): Yes, my beautiful Empress,
it is I. When the bandits stole me, I was only a child. I
cried for help to the God of the Dragons, and the only
way he could help me was to make me a dragon like
himself. I made short work of those bandits then, I can
tell you!

EMPRESS (*Admiringly*): How brave you were!

LIN: Then, because people no longer believe in dragons,
no one would build a pagoda for me, as was once the
custom, especially since being a very inexperienced
dragon, I was shy, and didn't know how to assert myself.

EMPRESS (*Sympathetically*): How sad.

LIN: Yes. So I had to live in this cave that no one else wanted—a dark and drafty old place it is, too.

EMPRESS (*Steps toward him*): Poor Lin.

LIN: I roared to attract attention, but it only frightened the people. (*Sighing*) So I just sat down in my cave to wait.

EMPRESS: Alas, then! Did no one take pity on my Prince?

LIN: Only the Goddess of the Moon. She heard my roars, and brought to me her beautiful light. But after all, she is only a spirit. She could not free me from my enchantment. So there I sat in my cave, waiting.

EMPRESS (*Surprised*): Waiting for what?

LIN: The God of the Dragons wove a spell to help me. If I were to regain my human form, two mortals, for unselfish reasons, must seek me out. At last it has happened. I am a boy again, for which I am deeply grateful to you, O Most Exalted Empress. (*Bowing to her with grave dignity*)

EMPRESS (*Returning bow automatically*): And the second person?

LIN: The little boy, Chang. He was afraid, but he came to the cave anyway, that he might save his family from starvation. I am afraid the poor boy was disappointed; I have a treasure chest, but it is filled with toys, and for little girls at that.

EMPRESS (*Withdrawing*): Indeed?

LIN: You see, by magic I caused the legend to grow up that the crops would fail, and the people starve, unless beautiful maidens were sent to keep me company.

EMPRESS (*Coldly*): Beautiful maidens! Why not boys?

LIN (*In confusion*): Well—we—you see I had grown used to having you for a playmate, and I longed for another little girl to take your place.

EMPRESS (*Stiffly*): Where is this child from the village?

LIN: In the cave, still stuffing himself with sweetmeats.

EMPRESS: I would see him. But first bring forth the Spirit of the Night who lights your cave.

LIN: The Goddess Moonglow? Why, of course. (*Calling within cave, upstage*) Moonglow, here is someone to see you.

MOONGLOW (*Appearing at cave mouth*): Yes, friend Dragon. (*Coming downstage, and passing him without recognition. Stops and looks about*) But where is my friend, the Dreadful Dragon?

LIN (*Coming down between the two*): Here I am, Goddess. There was a spell upon me, but now it has been broken.

EMPRESS: At least now there will be no other playmates for you.

LIN: I am sorry it displeased Your Highness.

EMPRESS: And don't call me Highness. You are royalty yourself.

LIN: Yes, Small One.

EMPRESS (*Crossly*): And I am not your "Small One" either. Stop trying to act grown-up. You are only a little boy.

LIN (*Turning away from her, and looking wistfully at his lost refuge*): Ah me, perhaps I should have stayed a dragon. At least then, everybody was afraid of me.

EMPRESS: So this is the Spirit of Night that you have kept prisoner! Humph!

MOONGLOW: I was not a prisoner here. I stayed only to light up that black cave. He was so lonely there in the dark. And frightened. I found him weeping.

LIN: Now, Goddess, dragons aren't afraid of anything. And they *don't* weep.

MOONGLOW: You did. And he cried mostly for you, Highness.

EMPRESS: He did? Really? Oh, Lin!

MOONGLOW: My silly sisters were jealous because he valued my light above all their treasures.

EMPRESS: So that is why they laughed.

LIN (*Turning away, pouting*): A fine dragon I was, a constant source of amusement to everyone!

MOONGLOW (*Consolingly*): You couldn't help it. And your roars were getting better all the time. (*Babble of voices is heard off left.*)

LIN (*Peering down imaginary mountainside*): What's that?

EMPRESS: People from the village. (LIN *climbs back to top of mountain.* EMPRESS *follows him, and stands beside him in front of entrance to cave.* LIN *peers down at the people, shading his eyes, as* TAO, MOTHER, POPPY, WILLOW, LI WAN, STEWARD, VILLAGERS, *and the retinue wind their way slowly up the path.*)

TAO (*In the lead*): This is the place. I'm sure of it. Look, there is the Empress!

STEWARD: Exalted Empress, praise to the Celestial Guardians, you are safe!

EMPRESS: Naturally I am safe! Why are all these people here, when I bade everyone stay in the village?

STEWARD: We heard the horrible thunder, and saw the red flash of lightning, Your Highness. We feared for your life, and with the boy Tao to lead us, we rushed to the mountain-top to aid you if there were yet time. Forgive your miserable servants if we did wrong.

MOTHER (*Coming forward*): I beg you, blame no other. It is I who urged your servants to disobey, for love of you, gracious Empress, and in anxiety for the life of my son.

EMPRESS (*Graciously*): As you can see, there is no danger here.

MOTHER: The boy, Chang. Highness, I do not see him. (*Thunder rolls and all but the* EMPRESS *and* LIN *start back in terror.*) Alas, alas, too late! The Dreadful Dragon has devoured my boy. Ai-ya, ai-ya! My darling son!

CHANG (*Appearing at entrance to cave with thunder sheet*

and drumstick. His stomach is noticeably bulging. He speaks to MOONGLOW): Where's the dragon? (*Sees* PRINCE *and* EMPRESS) Oh, I beg your pardon, Excellencies! (*Making a deep obeisance*) I seek the dragon. He left his sound effect in there, and he can't be fearsome at all without it. (*He bangs on the metal sheet again, and then stops in amazement as he catches sight of the crowd beyond the royal couple.*)

MOTHER (*Shrieking, and clutching her daughters*): The Spirit of my departed Chang! Ai-ya, ai-ya, the dragon has truly devoured my son, and sent his shade to haunt us!

POPPY (*Doubtfully*): He looks extremely fat for a spirit.

CHANG (*Dropping the sheet and hammer and running to* MOTHER): Mother! Mother! I am no spirit, but your son Chang.

MOTHER (*Backing away in disbelief*): Do not try to deceive me, ghost. You spoke with the voice of the Dragon.

LI WAN (*His eyes wide*): Surely it is a dragon's stomach he wears, and not Chang's.

CHANG: But I tell you, the dragon is a friendly fellow. As for devouring (*Glancing sheepishly at his protruding stomach*), I'm afraid I was the one who did that. All the good things he gave me! Eggs a hundred years old! Duck flesh roasted brown and dipped in the jellied sauce of wild berries. There is plenty for all! (*Children, quite convinced, surround him, and eagerly receive sweetmeats which* CHANG *gets for them.*)

MOTHER: For shame, Unfilial Son, to frighten your mother with such hideous noises! Such rudeness in the presence of the Exalted Empress of China is unforgivable!

CHANG (*Starting*): The Empress! (*Falling to his knees*) A thousand pardons, Celestial One!

EMPRESS: Rise, Worthy Chang. All China owes you a debt of gratitude, for your courage has helped to free from enchantment the noble Prince who stands beside me.

LIN: Yes. He is very brave. No doubt he would have made a wonderful dragon, if he had had the chance. (*Wistfully*) A better dragon than I could ever hope to be.

MOONGLOW (*Comfortingly*): But everyone who knew you loved you, and love is better than fear.

EMPRESS: Humph!

LIN (*Aside to* EMPRESS): I wish you would get over your habit of saying, "Humph!", Su H'sai. It isn't becoming.

EMPRESS: When I want your advice, my Prince, I shall ask for it, graciously.

CHANG (*Bewildered by the praise heaped upon him*): Where is my friend, the Dreadful Dragon? I don't understand.

MOONGLOW: He was enchanted, and he is now the little boy you see here, quarreling with the Empress of all China.

EMPRESS (*Turning to* MOONGLOW *and speaking sweetly but firmly*): Hadn't you better join your sisters now? They are lonely for you.

MOONGLOW: I doubt it, but I will go. Farewell. I will keep a light for you in the sky. (*Exits right*)

LIN: Thank you, beautiful Moonglow. Farewell.

EMPRESS: Goodbye. (*Turning to* CHANG) Now, worthy son of a noble mother, you shall be rewarded for your bravery with a place in my court. (CHANG *kneels again. Turning to* POPPY) And Poppy here, who thinks girls are important, too. She will have a chance to prove that she is a worthy sister of the noble Chang, as a handmaiden in the Royal Court. (*To* SERVANTS *and* VILLAGERS) Hurry back to the village, and prepare a feast to celebrate the victorious homecoming of Chang, Liberator of Princes, Honored Retainer in the Celestial Court of the Empress of China, First Lord of the Sacred Inner Court of the Golden Dragon Throne!

LI WAN: Whew!

EMPRESS: Prepare a feast at the teahouse of Wang.

VILLAGERS: The best place!

EMPRESS: At the Hour of the Dragon.

VILLAGERS: The best time! (*At a wave of dismissal from the* EMPRESS, VILLAGERS *and* SERVANTS *start gaily down the mountainside and disappear off left. Then* EMPRESS *turns again to the astounded* CHANG *who has prostrated himself at her feet, and now arises as if to hurry after the others.*)

EMPRESS: Noble Chang, the Prince and I would have you go before us and lead the way to the village.

CHANG: Your humble servant is honored in obeying your command, O Gracious Empress! Deign to follow in my unworthy footsteps. (*He starts down the path, followed by the* EMPRESS, *with* PRINCE LIN *lagging behind.*)

EMPRESS (*Over her shoulder to* LIN *who is looking back at the deserted cave*): Come, Prince Lin, away from your lonely cave, for you are no longer the Dreadful Dragon. (*Laughing merrily*) You, the Dreadful Dragon. It's amusing!

LIN (*Irked*): I was really a very good dragon, wasn't I, Chang?

CHANG (*Continuing his walk down the path and speaking back to the others who are coming in single file behind him*): Well—er—certainly, Your Highness—a—a most unusual dragon.

LIN (*Pressing him for reassurance*): A magnificent dragon?

CHANG: Well—er—your nostrils did smoke a little, I think, but (*In a sudden burst of honesty*)—but you didn't breathe fire as I thought you would.

LIN (*Annoyed*): A pity, but I could never get the hang of it.

EMPRESS: Your wings certainly weren't as bright as some

I've seen, and those roars were simply silly! Thunder indeed!

LIN (*Striding past the* EMPRESS): Have done, woman. Your chatter intrudes upon the lofty thoughts of the mighty Prince Lin, descendant of the Mandarins, and Ex-Dragon of the Western Hills. I go.

EMPRESS (*Demurely*): Yes, my lord. I follow. (*To audience, with a twinkle*) Moonglow was right. His roars are getting better all the time. (*They descend the mountain and disappear in the direction of the village to the sound of distant music, and merrymaking. Curtain*)

THE END

The Mystery of the Gumdrop Dragon

by Gerry Lynn Burtle

Characters

TWO GUARDS
PRINCESS
LADY CANDY FLOSS ⎫
LADY LEMON DROP ⎬ *ladies-in-waiting*
LADY DIVINITY ⎭
PAGE
COURT WRITER
TOWN CRIER
THREE CLOWNS
WIZARD
BUTTERSCOTCH ⎫ *storytellers*
BUTTERCRUNCH ⎭
GATEKEEPER
PRINCE PEPPERMINT-STICK
SIR LICORICE
GUMDROP DRAGON

SCENE 1

SETTING: *The throne room in the Kingdom of Candyland.*
AT RISE: TWO GUARDS *stand at either side of the stage,*
at attention. The PRINCESS *enters weeping, followed by*

the LADIES-IN-WAITING, *who are wringing their hands and whispering to one another. The* PRINCESS *takes her seat on the throne, surrounded by the* LADIES-IN-WAITING.

PRINCESS: Alas, what woe has fallen on our Candyland Kingdom today!

LADY CANDY FLOSS: Yes, my Princess. Your favorite pet, the Gumdrop Dragon, has been stolen.

PRINCESS: He has disappeared. Who could have taken him?

LADY LEMON DROP: If you ask me, my Princess, I'd say it was the Keeper of the Town Museum. He always did think the Gumdrop Dragon would look lovely stuffed and mounted. (PRINCESS *begins to wail.*)

LADY DIVINITY: Now, now, little Princess, I'm sure the Museum Keeper would never take your pet. He knows how much you love the Gumdrop Dragon. He would never think of such a thing.

PRINCESS: That is a relief, but it doesn't help much. We still don't know who *did* steal the Gumdrop Dragon.

LADY CANDY FLOSS: Princess, I have an idea!

LADY LEMON DROP: I hope it's better than most of your ideas are. If it isn't, you're wasting our time.

PRINCESS: Don't be unkind, Lady Lemon Drop. I should like to hear Lady Candy Floss's idea.

LADY CANDY FLOSS: Thank you, Princess. I thought you might send the Town Crier throughout Candyland, with a proclamation.

PRINCESS: What sort of proclamation?

LADY CANDY FLOSS: You could offer a reward to the person who finds the Gumdrop Dragon for you.

PRINCESS: Why, that's a wonderful idea, Lady Candy Floss.

LADY CANDY FLOSS: Thank you, Princess.

LADY LEMON DROP: If it's such a good idea, answer me one question.

PRINCESS: Certainly, Lady Lemon Drop. What is it?

LADY LEMON DROP: Just what are you planning to offer for a reward?

PRINCESS: Why, I hadn't thought about that. I don't know.

LADY LEMON DROP: I thought not. Then I'd say it isn't a very good idea.

PRINCESS: Perhaps you're right. (LADY CANDY FLOSS *begins to cry softly.*)

LADY DIVINITY: There, there, Lady Candy Floss. Your idea is a very good one, and it will still work.

LADY LEMON DROP: And just how, may I ask?

PRINCESS: Yes, how, Lady Divinity?

LADY DIVINITY: Don't worry your head about the reward, Princess. Simply put in your proclamation that whoever finds the Gumdrop Dragon may choose his own reward.

PRINCESS: Of course. That's the very thing. Oh, thank you, Lady Divinity. (*Pause*) But how does one go about sending a proclamation? I've never done it before.

LADY DIVINITY: Call in the Court Writer, Princess. He will write down the proclamation on a scroll, and the Town Crier will read it throughout the land. (PRINCESS *claps her hands together once, and the* PAGE *enters and bows.*)

PRINCESS: Send the Court Writer to me at once, please.

PAGE: Yes, Your Majesty. At once! (*Exits*)

PRINCESS: I do so hope this will work. I should be lost without my Gumdrop Dragon.

LADY DIVINITY: Don't fret, Princess. I'm sure the Dragon will be found.

PAGE (*Enters and bows*): The Court Writer! (WRITER *enters and bows as* PAGE *exits.*)

WRITER: Court Writer at your service, Your Majesty. What will it be—a poem, a story of magic?

PRINCESS: I want none of those, my friend. Today the task I place before you is not a happy one.

WRITER: In that case, if you'll excuse me, Your Majesty,

I'll get my handkerchief ready. I always cry when I write sad things. (*He pulls handkerchief from sleeve, and holds it ready at his nose.*) Now then, Princess, if you will, proceed.

PRINCESS: Just today, my pet Gumdrop Dragon was stolen from his cage in the courtyard. No trace of him can be found. (WRITER *begins to sniffle sadly*) I would like you to write me a proclamation to send throughout the kingdom, offering a reward for his return.

WRITER (*Sobbing into handkerchief*): Your every word is my command, Princess. (*He removes his cap, takes paper from the lining, and pulls the long feather from the cap.* LADY DIVINITY *brings him an ink well, he dips his pen, then goes toward one of the* GUARDS, *holding the pen and paper. The* GUARD *bends over, and the* WRITER *places paper on his back.*) Begin, Princess.

PRINCESS: First of all, I should like to address this proclamation to all the people of the kingdom.

WRITER: Uh-h-h, how about something like this: Hear ye! Hear ye! All ye good people of the kingdom!

PRINCESS: The very thing. It's perfect. I couldn't have said it better.

WRITER (*Writing*): Always willing to help, Your Majesty. What's next?

PRINCESS: I suppose I'd better tell them who's sending the proclamation.

WRITER: That's simple. This is a proclamation from the Princess of Candyland.

PRINCESS: Yes, that's it exactly. Now say something about the reward for bringing back my Gumdrop Dragon.

WRITER: What is the reward, Princess?

PRINCESS: They may choose anything they want.

WRITER: Anything?

PRINCESS: Anything!

WRITER: Very handsome of you, Princess. It will go this

way then: The Princess of Candyland offers a reward to anyone who finds her missing pet, the Gumdrop Dragon, and the villain who stole him away. The person returning both to her may choose anything he desires for a reward.

PRINCESS (*Clapping her hands*): It's very well worded. And it says exactly what I want it to. Now it must have an ending.

WRITER: We will end with: Hear ye! Hear ye! (*He writes busily.*) There. Is that all, Princess?

PRINCESS: Yes, that's all. Roll it up, please, and hand it to me. (*He does so.*) I am very grateful to you. When the dragon is found, you also will be rewarded for your help.

WRITER: Thank you, Princess. Don't hesitate to call whenever I can be of service. (*Bows and exits.* PRINCESS *claps her hands once and* PAGE *enters.*)

PAGE: Yes, Your Majesty.

PRINCESS: Bring the Town Crier to the throne room, please. Immediately.

PAGE: Yes, Your Majesty! Immediately! (*Exits*)

PRINCESS (*Holding up the paper*): And now to send my proclamation throughout the kingdom for all to hear.

PAGE (*Enters and bows*): The Town Crier, Your Majesty! (TOWN CRIER *enters, bows, draws himself up to his full height, takes a deep breath, clears his throat importantly and speaks.*)

TOWN CRIER: I hope you can make this brief, Your Majesty. I'm about to begin my morning rounds with the news, and I can't be late. A Town Crier can never be late, you know.

PRINCESS: I shall take only a minute of your time, Town Crier. I want you to take this proclamation throughout the kingdom for me, and read it to all my people. (*Hands proclamation to him.*)

TOWN CRIER: Glad to do it, Princess. (*He unfolds procla-mation and reads.*) Um—certainly, I see.

PRINCESS: Is it all right?

TOWN CRIER: Fine, just fine. Would you like to hear me read it now? I've a very good voice, you know.

PRINCESS: I should like that very much, thank you. But won't you be late with the news if you take the time?

TOWN CRIER: Well, just a little late. After all, business be-fore pleasure, you know.

PRINCESS: Yes, of course.

TOWN CRIER: Now that that's settled—(*He again draws himself up, takes a deep breath, clears his throat, and continues in a loud voice.*) Hear ye! Hear ye! All good people of the kingdom! This is a proclamation from the Princess of Candyland . . .

LADY CANDY FLOSS: My, such a nice strong voice!

TOWN CRIER: Thank you, madam, but please, no inter-ruptions. I cannot work with interruptions.

LADY LEMON DROP: Oh, fiddlesticks! That's a lot of non-sense!

TOWN CRIER: Madam, please! It is not a lot of nonsense! It is one of the rules!

PRINCESS: Please continue, Town Crier. No one will inter-rupt again, we promise.

TOWN CRIER: Thank you, Princess. Now let me see, where was I?

LADY CANDY FLOSS: You were just at the part that says, "This is a proclamation from the Princess of Candy-land."

TOWN CRIER: You promised me no more interruptions. I am afraid I shall be unable to continue with the read-ing, under the circumstances.

PRINCESS: Oh, please, please continue. Lady Candy Floss just forgot, didn't you, Lady Candy Floss?

LADY CANDY FLOSS: Oh, yes. I was only trying to help. You

couldn't find your place, and I remembered where it was, so I thought I could help by telling you. That's all.

TOWN CRIER: Madam, when I have lost my place, I am perfectly capable of finding it myself. That's one of the rules.

LADY CANDY FLOSS: I'm sorry. I didn't know that.

TOWN CRIER: Well, you know it now, and if I am to continue with the reading, I must ask all of you to abide by the rules.

PRINCESS: We will, Town Crier. You have our undivided attention.

TOWN CRIER: Thank you. To continue—"The Princess of Candyland offers a reward to anyone who finds her missing pet, the Gumdrop Dragon, and the villain who stole him away. The person returning both to her may choose anything he desires for a reward. Hear ye! Hear ye!" (*Looks around for approval. The others sit looking at him, without saying a word.*) Well, have you nothing to say? Didn't you like the reading? Why don't you say so?

LADY DIVINITY: We're afraid of interrupting.

TOWN CRIER: But I'm finished now. The rule says no interruptions while the reading is going on, and it's not going on now.

LADY DIVINITY: Well, we just wanted to be sure.

TOWN CRIER: Since you're sure now, what about the reading?

PRINCESS: The reading was beautifully done. Thank you, Town Crier. I shall depend on you to read it throughout the kingdom, and to see that every one of my subjects hears it. Perform your duty well, and you also shall be richly rewarded.

TOWN CRIER: You can depend on me, Your Majesty. I will not fail you. (*Clicks heels together, bows low and exits.*)

PRINCESS: And now I must hope with all my heart that the

Dragon will be found. Perhaps because I believe it will be so, my Gumdrop Dragon will be returned to me.

CURTAIN

*   *   *

SCENE 2

TIME: *One week later.*
SETTING: *Same as Scene 1.*
AT RISE: *The* PRINCESS *is seated on her throne, surrounded by the* LADIES-IN-WAITING, *who appear dejected.*

LADY CANDY FLOSS: Princess . . . Princess, please lift your head. The sun is shining this morning, and the birds are singing. Won't you try to smile?

PRINCESS (*With a deep sigh*): I will never smile again now, for a week has passed, and no one has found my beloved Gumdrop Dragon. Now, at last I must give up hope. I am sure he will never be found.

LADY DIVINITY: You must learn to live without him, Princess. I fear you are right, and the Gumdrop Dragon is gone for good.

LADY LEMON DROP: If you'd asked me, I could have told you that a week ago. Never did think we'd find that Dragon. (PRINCESS *sobs softly.*)

LADY DIVINITY: Princess, you must be cheerful again. When you are sad, the whole Kingdom of Candyland is sad.

PRINCESS: How can I be happy again, when my heart is broken?

LADY CANDY FLOSS: Perhaps we can mend it again.

PRINCESS: Oh, if you only could. But how?

LADY DIVINITY: Will you let us try, Princess?

PRINCESS: Yes, you may try, but I am sure nothing will ever make me smile again, unless my Gumdrop Dragon is found.

LADY DIVINITY: Nevertheless, we will try. May I have your permission, Princess, to call the clowns?

PRINCESS: You may call them. (LADY DIVINITY *claps her hands once, and the* PAGE *enters.*)

LADY DIVINITY: Send the Clowns to the throne room, please.

PAGE: Yes, my lady. At once. (*Exits*)

PRINCESS: I do not think the clowns will seem funny to me today.

LADY DIVINITY: But, on the other hand, perhaps they will. We shall see.

PAGE (*Entering*): The Clowns! (CLOWNS *enter tumbling over each other. All but the* PRINCESS *laugh.* CLOWNS *tumble to their feet and bow.*)

FIRST CLOWN: Good evening. We're here as you can see . . . somewhere. (*He looks around to see where, and all but the* PRINCESS *laugh again.*)

LADY CANDY FLOSS: It's not evening. It's morning.

FIRST CLOWN: Oh, is it? I hadn't noticed. Well, morning or evening, we're here and at your service. What would you like? A song, perhaps? Come, Clowns.

CLOWNS (*Singing*):
Hurray, hurray, today's the day,
Today's the day, we've chosen to play.
Of course today could be any day,
'Cause any day is the day that we play.
(*They proceed to tumble and jump and play hide-and-seek behind the throne, but the* PRINCESS *remains glum.*)

LADY DIVINITY: Enough, enough. You have done your best, but it does not make the Princess happy. We must try something else. You may go now, and thank you for trying. (CLOWNS *exit dejectedly*.)

LADY LEMON DROP: Well, let's not give up. Try the Wizard. He's a master of magic. Might be he could cheer the Princess. (LADY DIVINITY *claps her hands again.* PAGE *enters*.)

PAGE: You called, my lady?

LADY DIVINITY: Bring the Chocolate Wizard to me at once. At once, do you hear?

PAGE: I hear, my lady. At once. (*Exits*)

LADY CANDY FLOSS: Oh, my Princess, if you will observe the Wizard carefully, his tricks will fascinate you, I know, and you will soon forget all about the Gumdrop Dragon.

PRINCESS: I will never forget the Gumdrop Dragon.

PAGE (*Entering*): The Chocolate Wizard! (*Exits as* WIZARD *enters, removes his hat and bows*)

WIZARD: Good day. And what would the good people of the court like to see this morning? Perhaps a white rabbit would suffice. (*Pulls one from his hat*) Or if not, a wave of my wand brings moonlight. (*He waves wand, and lights change.*) But come, this is a mere sample of my art. Perhaps you would care for something else.

PRINCESS: You are a wizard, and wizards are supposed to be very wise. Can you read the future?

WIZARD: Alas, my Princess, you have touched upon my one failing. I cannot read the future. You see, once when I was a very young wizard, I turned a man into a stone, and when I tried to turn him back into a man again, I failed. An older, wiser wizard had to do it for me. Since I failed so badly in this, the Wizard's Union decided to make me a second-class wizard. Actually, though I hate to admit it, Princess, (*He begins to sob into his hat*) I am nothing but an over-glorified magician.

PRINCESS: Oh, I am so sorry for you. I know how you must feel. I too am unhappy.

LADY LEMON DROP: Here, here, that will do, you so-called Wizard. You've done enough damage. Begone!

WIZARD (*Recovering himself*): I beg your pardon. I forgot myself for a moment. Don't send me away. My tricks are still the best in these parts. Name something else, and I will do it gladly.

LADY LEMON DROP: You've already had your chance, and all you've done is harm.

WIZARD: Alas, I have failed again.

PRINCESS: That's not so. It's not the Wizard's fault that he failed to cheer me. He tried very hard. It just can't be done, that's all. I am too unhappy.

WIZARD: May I ever come back again?

PRINCESS: Of course, Chocolate Wizard. I want you to come often.

WIZARD: Thank you for your kindness, Princess. I hope you find your Gumdrop Dragon and your happiness again. (*Bows and exits*)

PRINCESS: Ah, if only I *could* find my Gumdrop Dragon. How wonderful it would be!

LADY DIVINITY: Let us talk no longer of this. We will call the Storytellers. Perhaps a gay story will cheer you, Princess.

PRINCESS: Perhaps. (LADY DIVINITY *claps her hands and the* PAGE *enters*)

PAGE: Here I am, my lady. What may I do for you now?

LADY DIVINITY: Fetch me the Storytellers. And tell them to bring their gayest tale with them.

PAGE: I will do so, my lady. (*Exits*)

LADY DIVINITY: Now then, Princess. You will soon be happy again, when you hear the gay tale the storytellers weave.

PRINCESS: Is it fair to be gay, when my poor Gumdrop

Dragon may be lonely somewhere, and a prisoner of the terrible villain who took him from me? Oh, what a dreadful thought—my Gumdrop Dragon may be a prisoner!

LADY CANDY FLOSS: Princess, you must try not to think of that.

PAGE (*Entering*): The two storytellers, Buttercrunch and Butterscotch. (*They enter, cackling to themselves.*)

BUTTERCRUNCH: Understand someone here wants a gay story.

LADY DIVINITY: That's correct. The very gayest you have to offer.

BUTTERSCOTCH: Fine, then we'll tell you about the silly butterfly.

BUTTERCRUNCH: Once upon a time, there was a lovely butterfly.

BUTTERSCOTCH: This butterfly had beautiful lacy wings, and every day she flew from flower to flower. (*Imitates butterfly*)

BUTTERCRUNCH: But, the butterfly decided one day that it was silly to fly from flower to flower. She wanted to do something useful. So what do you think she did?

LADY CANDY FLOSS: What did she do?

LADY LEMON DROP: Sh-h-h.

BUTTERSCOTCH: One day she flew off to a nearby town to find something useful to do, and the first shop window she came to, she peeked in. Lo and behold, there sat an old man trimming hats. (*Acts it out*)

BUTTERCRUNCH: So the lovely butterfly flew in the door of the shop and asked the old man if he had something useful for her to do.

BUTTERSCOTCH: The old man was delighted to see the butterfly, and said yes, indeed he did have something useful for the butterfly to do.

BUTTERCRUNCH: He held up a beautiful yellow bonnet,

that was badly in need of an ornament, and told the butterfly that if she liked, she could become the decoration for that hat.

BUTTERSCOTCH: And that's exactly what the butterfly did. She became a hat decoration. It was such a pretty hat that the loveliest lady in town bought it.

BUTTERCRUNCH: At last the silly butterfly was doing something useful. She was making a pretty lady even prettier.

BUTTERSCOTCH: And the butterfly led a very gay, happy life, for she went to many parties and balls and nice dinners, perched on the lady's bonnet.

BUTTERCRUNCH: And that's the story of the silly butterfly, who wasn't so silly after all. Wasn't it gay?

LADY DIVINITY: It was indeed. Did you like it, Princess?

PRINCESS: Yes, I did, but I couldn't help thinking how gay and happy I might be if only I had my dear Gumdrop Dragon here with me.

LADY LEMON DROP: What did I tell you? It's hopeless to try to cheer the Princess.

LADY CANDY FLOSS: We've tried everything, and nothing has worked.

BUTTERCRUNCH: Wasn't the story gay enough?

LADY DIVINITY: It was a lovely story. And you've both done your very best, storytellers. For that, we thank you. You may go. (*They exit, dejected, shaking their heads.*) Princess, is there anything more we can do to help?

PRINCESS: Only find my Dragon. Other than that, there is nothing.

LADY DIVINITY: There is no hope left of finding him now, I fear.

LADY CANDY FLOSS: No one has seen a trace of him.

LADY LEMON DROP: The Gumdrop Dragon is gone forever. I think, Princess, you had better make up your mind to that.

PRINCESS: My hope is gone. I have nothing left to cling to. My Gumdrop Dragon is gone forever, and my heart is broken. (*She sobs.*)

CURTAIN

*   *   *

SCENE 3

TIME: *That afternoon.*
SETTING: *Same as before.*
AT RISE: *The Court is assembled as in Scene 2. The PAGE is standing before the throne.*

PAGE: Your Majesty, I came as fast as I could. The Gate-keeper begs an audience with you. He says he has important news.

PRINCESS: About my Gumdrop Dragon? A week and a day have passed since he disappeared.

PAGE: He wouldn't say, Your Majesty. He will talk only to you. Will you see him, Princess?

PRINCESS: Oh, yes indeed. At once! Please send him in.

PAGE: Yes, Your Majesty. At once. (*He exits. The LADIES-IN-WAITING break into a buzz of excitement.*)

PRINCESS: Perhaps my Gumdrop Dragon has been found at last!

LADY CANDY FLOSS: Perhaps he has, Princess. Why else would the Gatekeeper want to see you?

LADY LEMON DROP: We shall soon know. He is coming now.

PAGE (*Entering*): The Keeper of the Gates! (*Exits as the GATEKEEPER enters, bows and approaches the PRINCESS.*)

GATEKEEPER: Your Majesty—Your Majesty—a strange thing! Yes, indeed, a very strange thing. It's happening now, happening right now!

LADY LEMON DROP: Speak up, old man, and stop sputtering. The Princess is waiting.

GATEKEEPER: Yes, my lady. Yes, yes indeed. Right away.

PRINCESS: What have you to tell me, old man? No, don't hurry. Take your time. We will be patient.

GATEKEEPER: I'm sorry, Princess, but I am out of breath. I ran all the way from the gate to tell you what I've seen.

PRINCESS: Yes. And what have you seen?

GATEKEEPER: This morning from my tower in the gate-house, I saw a strange procession winding its way toward the Town.

PRINCESS: Yes, and—?

GATEKEEPER: I could not see at first what it was, but as it came nearer, I began to make out certain figures. First came a young man, a very handsome young man. And next—

PRINCESS: Next?

GATEKEEPER: Next, Your Majesty, came the Gumdrop Dragon!

PRINCESS: The Gumdrop Dragon! Are you sure?

GATEKEEPER: Yes, Your Majesty. They have already passed through my gates, and are even now winding their way to the castle.

PRINCESS: At last! My Gumdrop Dragon is found. Prepare a feast. Let there be laughing and rejoicing! We must celebrate the return of my Gumdrop Dragon!

GATEKEEPER: Your Majesty, there were others in the procession.

PRINCESS: Let them come, old man. They shall be made welcome, every one of them.

GATEKEEPER: Even the villain who stole the Dragon?

PRINCESS (*Slowly*): Does the villain also come with the procession?

GATEKEEPER: Yes, my Princess. He comes, slowly, at the end of the line. He is in chains.

PRINCESS: Ah, then he too will know what it is like to be a prisoner, as my Gumdrop Dragon was. Thank you, old man, for your joyful news. Such loyalty will be rewarded, I promise. And now you may go.

GATEKEEPER: Thank you, Princess. Yes, indeed. Thank you very much. (*Bows and exits, as* PAGE *enters.*)

PAGE: Your Majesty, they come: the victor with your dragon and his prisoner.

PRINCESS: And the victor, my Page, is a man, is he not?

PAGE: Yes, Your Majesty.

PRINCESS: And is he a handsome man?

PAGE: Oh, yes, Your Majesty. He is wonderfully handsome, and a prince.

LADY CANDY FLOSS: A prince! Oh, my!

PRINCESS: A prince! Bring him to me at once. I must welcome him royally.

PAGE: With pleasure, Your Majesty. (*Exits*)

LADY CANDY FLOSS: A prince. A handsome prince. Do I look all right?

LADY LEMON DROP: What does it matter how you look? He wouldn't be bothered with you.

LADY DIVINITY: He must be a very brave prince to have found the Gumdrop Dragon, and captured the thief who took him.

PRINCESS: Oh, I am sure he is brave and good.

PAGE (*Entering*): Prince Peppermint-Stick! (PRINCE PEPPERMINT-STICK *enters alone, removes his hat and bows sweepingly to the* PRINCESS.)

PRINCE: Princess of Candyland—at last we meet. For many years, I have heard tell of your wondrous beauty. Now I see for myself that you are far more beautiful than could ever be told.

PRINCESS: You are very kind, noble sir, and I thank you, for the compliment and the service you have done me today. Is it true you have found my beloved Gumdrop Dragon?

PRINCE: Yes, Princess, it is true. I have found the Gumdrop Dragon and the thief who took him. Both I return to you.

PRINCESS: Again my thanks to you, sir. May I ask you from whence you come?

PRINCE: I come from the neighboring kingdom of Peppermint Green, Princess. I was traveling through your Kingdom when I heard the proclamation. I immediately joined the search, hoping that luck would be with me, and that I might find the Dragon, and at last behold you, face to face.

PRINCESS: And luck was with you.

PRINCE: Indeed, luck has been very kind to me, for I was fortunate enough to stumble upon the entrance of a tiny cave hidden away in the Marshmallow Mountains. I stopped to investigate, and found your Gumdrop Dragon tied up inside.

PRINCESS: How cruel! But what of the villain?

PRINCE: Ah, yes, the villain. I was coming to that. I loosed the cord that bound the Gumdrop Dragon, and since the villain was not to be seen, I settled myself at the mouth of the cave to await his return.

LADY CANDY FLOSS: Please, please tell us what happened then.

PRINCE: At once, fair maid.

LADY CANDY FLOSS: Oh-h-h. Did you hear that? He called me a fair maid.

LADY LEMON DROP: Hush. Let us listen to the prince.

PRINCE: I had not long to wait. Just as night was falling, the villain sneaked back to the cave, with food for the Gumdrop Dragon.

PRINCESS: Oh!

PRINCE: I challenged him with my sword, but he was a coward, and surrendered immediately without a fight. This done, I had only to make the long journey to you, with the Gumdrop Dragon and my wretched prisoner.

PRINCESS: You are very brave, my Prince, and you shall have your reward. But first I must see to the villain. (*She claps her hands together.*)

PAGE (*Entering*): Yes, Your Majesty.

PRINCESS: Bring the villain who stole my Gumdrop Dragon to me at once.

PAGE: Y-yes, Your Majesty. (*Exits*)

LADY CANDY FLOSS: The villain! I don't think I want to see him. He might harm someone.

PRINCESS: Never fear. He will harm no one, for he is in chains, and even if he were not, we are well protected, for here stands the brave prince, and there, the soldiers who guard the Throne Room.

LADY CANDY FLOSS: I had forgotten that. Thank you, Princess.

PAGE (*Enters*): The—the villain! (*He runs out.* SIR LICORICE *enters in chains. He stands before* PRINCESS, *without bowing.*)

PRINCESS: You are now in the presence of a princess, villain. You will please bow, as you are required to do. (SIR LICORICE *bows.*)

SIR LICORICE: 'Scuse me, Your Majesty, but I've never been in the presence of a princess before. I didn't know I had to bow.

PRINCESS: Now, villain, what is your name?

SIR LICORICE: My name is Sir Licorice.

PRINCESS: You are Sir Licorice, and you stole my dragon. That was a very wrong thing to do, you know.

SIR LICORICE (*Sadly*): I know.

PRINCESS: Then why did you do it?

SIR LICORICE: It's this way, Princess. The people of Candyland are all gay and bright and happy, except me. I'm terribly unhappy. And of course, I don't like being unhappy. So one day, I decided to do something about it. First of all, since the people of Candyland were all so happy, I looked around to see what was making them happy. And I discovered what was making them happy was you, Princess.

PRINCESS: Me!

SIR LICORICE: Yes, you, Princess. The people of Candyland were all happy because you were happy, so next, I looked around to find out what was making *you* happy. And I discovered that you were happy because you had the Gumdrop Dragon. So I decided to take the Gumdrop Dragon. I thought since he made you so happy, he'd make me happy, too. Only it didn't work. I was still unhappy, even with the Gumdrop Dragon, and not only that, but when I took him, I made you unhappy, and all the people of Candyland, too. Everybody was unhappy, but I was the most unhappy of all.

PRINCESS: Oh, poor Sir Licorice. You aren't a wicked villain at all. You're just an unhappy one.

SIR LICORICE: You can say that again. (*Sobbing*) I wish I'd never taken the Gumdrop Dragon. It only made things worse than ever.

PRINCESS: Listen to me, Sir Licorice. You didn't have to take the Gumdrop Dragon to be happy. What you need are friends.

SIR LICORICE: I do?

PRINCESS: You do. Then you can be very happy.

SIR LICORICE: I can?

PRINCESS: You can.

SIR LICORICE: But where am I going to find any friends?

PRINCESS: That's easy. We're all your friends here. Aren't we, Court of Candyland?

ALL: Yes!

SIR LICORICE: They are! Oh, I'm so happy. I'm so happy.

PRINCESS: See, what did I tell you? You aren't unhappy any more.

SIR LICORICE: You're right! I'm not. Oh, joyful day! I'm not unhappy any more. I'm just me. Everybody loves me, and I'm happy, happy, happy!

PRINCESS: Now you can help us to celebrate the return of my Gumdrop Dragon. Guards! Remove Sir Licorice's chains. He is no longer a villain. (*While* GUARDS *remove chains,* PRINCESS *claps her hands.* PAGE *enters.*) Page, bring in the Clowns, the Wizard, the Storytellers, the Court Writer, the Town Crier, the Gatekeeper— everyone who tried to cheer me up and help me find the Gumdrop Dragon.

PAGE: Yes indeed, Your Majesty! (*Exits*)

SIR LICORICE: Oh dear, oh dear. How can I be happy when I caused so much trouble for so many people, and made them all unhappy?

PRINCESS: Well, you did cause some trouble, and you did make us unhappy.

SIR LICORICE: I'm so sorry. I'm so sorry for what I did.

PRINCESS: We forgive you. You're sorry you took the Gumdrop Dragon, and that's all that matters.

SIR LICORICE: Then I will stay for the celebration. Thank you, Princess. You are kind and merciful. (PAGE *enters, followed by* CLOWNS, WIZARD, STORYTELLERS, WRITER, TOWN CRIER, *and* GATEKEEPER.)

PRINCESS: Welcome! And now, Sir Licorice, before all these people, you must promise that you will never be bad again.

SIR LICORICE: Oh, I wouldn't even think of it again. From now on, I'll always be good Sir Licorice.

ALL (*Ad lib*): Hurray for good Sir Licorice! Hurray! Hurray! (*Etc.*)

PRINCESS: Let us begin the celebration, and welcome the Gumdrop Dragon home.

ALL: Hurray! (*The* GUMDROP DRAGON *runs in, and trots to the* PRINCESS, *who throws her arms around his neck.*)

PRINCESS: Oh! Oh, my darling Gumdrop Dragon! You're home! You're home, thanks to Prince Peppermint-Stick!

PRINCE: I was only too happy to be of service, Princess.

PRINCESS: And now, Prince Peppermint-Stick, you must choose your reward. For as you know, my proclamation said that the person who found my Gumdrop Dragon could choose anything he might desire for a reward.

PRINCE: And if I want no reward?

PRINCESS: Ah, but you must choose a reward. I have promised it. You must, to please me.

PRINCE: To please you, Princess, I would do anything. And there is one thing I do want more than anything else in the world. I choose that.

PRINCESS: And that is?

PRINCE: I choose you, my Princess. (LADIES-IN-WAITING "oh" and "ah.")

PRINCESS: What?

PRINCE: I choose your hand in marriage, Princess. Will you do me the honor of being my wife?

PRINCESS: Why, I never dared hope for this.

LADY CANDY FLOSS: Imagine, a handsome prince choosing the princess for his reward!

LADY LEMON DROP: He couldn't have made a better choice, if you ask me.

LADY DIVINITY: And neither could she, for the prince is good and wise.

PRINCE: Will you grant me my reward, Princess? Will you be my wife? (*Everyone leans forward waiting for the answer.*)

PRINCESS (*Softly*): Yes, my Prince. (PRINCE *takes her hand*

and they stand together with the GUMDROP DRAGON, *as all cheer.*)

ALL:

Hurray for the Gumdrop Dragon!
Hurray for our Princess fair!
Hurray for the Prince who claims her!
And the Villain who gave us a scare!
(*Curtain*)

THE END

The Bookworm

by Gwen Chaloner

Characters

LIBRARIAN	HANSEL
BETTY	GRETEL
BOOKWORM	CAPTAIN HOOK
SEVEN REFERENCE BOOKS	TOM SAWYER
ALICE	GINGERBREAD MAN

TIME: *Late afternoon on a rainy day.*

SETTING: *A public library.*

AT RISE: LIBRARIAN *is seated at her desk, working on library cards. She looks at her watch, then stands up and straightens the books on her desk.* BETTY *tiptoes in. She reaches center stage before* LIBRARIAN *sees her.*

LIBRARIAN: Where are you going, little girl?

BETTY (*Startled, swings around to face* LIBRARIAN): Oh! I—I—

LIBRARIAN (*Coming around desk and facing* BETTY): Where did you come from?

BETTY: I was just walking home from school and then the thunderstorm came. It rained buckets. I had no coat or umbrella, so I ran in here.

LIBRARIAN: But we are closed until six o'clock. Wasn't the front door locked?

BETTY (*Shaking her head*): No.

LIBRARIAN: That's strange. It should have been. I'll lock the door, then I must go upstairs for a while to check some magazines. You may stay here until I come back. Perhaps the storm will be over by then. You'll find plenty to read.

BETTY: Thank you.

LIBRARIAN (*As she turns to exit*): What is your name?

BETTY: Betty.

LIBRARIAN: Well, Betty, you must promise to be very quiet.

BETTY: I promise.

LIBRARIAN: You may look at those books on the side of my desk, if you'd like to. I won't be very long. (LIBRARIAN *exits.* BETTY *starts leafing through books on desk.* BOOK-WORM *enters quietly and climbs onto a high stool which stands near center stage. He carries several books. He opens one of the books, then turns toward* BETTY, *who has not yet seen him.*)

BOOKWORM (*Suddenly and loudly*): Good after-hours to you!

BETTY (*Jumping and turning around*): Oh! I beg your pardon!

BOOKWORM: I said, "Good after-hours."

BETTY: Good—good afternoon.

BOOKWORM (*Loudly and distinctly, but with dignity*): *After-hours.* Don't you know the library is closed? This is after-hours.

BETTY: Oh, yes. This is the library, isn't it?

BOOKWORM: Why, bless my books and eyeglasses! Don't you know a library when you see one?

BETTY: Well, it was raining and—

BOOKWORM (*Severely*): No excuse at all. I suppose you do know what a library is?

BETTY (*Brightening*): Oh, yes, sir. A library is where books

are kept, and where you may borrow books. Are you a
librarian?

BOOKWORM: Bless my books and eyeglasses again! Of
course not. Librarians aren't here after-hours. After-
hours is *my* time.

BETTY: Then who are you, sir?

BOOKWORM: I? I am the bookworm.

BETTY: Oh!

BOOKWORM: You must have heard of me.

BETTY: Yes, I think I have. What do you do?

BOOKWORM (*Indignantly*): Do? Why, I work my way
through all these books during after-hours. I do believe
I am the best-fed and best-read bookworm in any library.

BETTY: There are so many books in a library.

BOOKWORM: Never enough. Always glad to welcome new
friends. How many have you read? Ten thousand?

BETTY: Oh, no, sir.

BOOKWORM: Five thousand? (BETTY *shakes her head and
steps back a little.*) One thousand?

BETTY: No.

BOOKWORM: Five hundred?

BETTY: No.

BOOKWORM: One hundred?

BETTY (*Slightly worried*): I don't think so, sir. But I read
a book during the vacation.

BOOKWORM: I see. (*He seems satisfied and begins to open
one of his own books, then turns inquiringly to* BETTY
again.) One book a day, of course?

BETTY: No, sir. One book.

BOOKWORM (*Excitedly*): Why, bless my books and eyeglasses, child! You are missing the greatest treasures of
the world. You are losing the finest friends of your life.
What are books for? Books! Books! (*Glaring at* BETTY.)
Can you spell the word "book"?

BETTY (*Smiling*): Oh, of course, sir. B-o-o-k.

BOOKWORM: Can you spell "library"?

BETTY (*Hesitatingly*): L-i-b—L-i-b-e—

BOOKWORM: No!

BETTY (*Nervously*): L-i-b-a-

BOOKWORM: No, no, no! We'll have to do something about this right away. (BOOKWORM *sits thinking.* BETTY *stands by, looking very unhappy.* BOOKWORM *sits up straight.*) The Reference Books! That's the idea! (*He claps his hands.*) Reference Books, come to our rescue. (SEVEN REFERENCE BOOKS *enter. They stand in a straight row across the back of the stage. Each* REFERENCE BOOK *carries or wears a poster resembling a large book on which a letter is painted in bright colors. Together the letters spell* LIBRARY) Let's see if you can learn your lesson, now. Tell me how to spell the word "library."

BETTY: Li-b-r-a-r-y. (REFERENCE BOOKS *nod their heads in encouragement as* BETTY *spells.*)

BOOKWORM: There! That's more like it. Library! Books! Wonderful books! (*Turning to the row of* REFERENCE BOOKS) Books, tell this child some of the wonderful things you can offer her.

1ST REFERENCE BOOK:

We have a book on every sort of science,
We can give you any special information,
With facts that can be quoted with reliance,
Should you wish to build a bridge or rule a nation.

2ND REFERENCE BOOK:

If you prefer excitement or adventure,
There are books to make your hair stand straight on
    end,
You can travel round the world or to a planet,
Yet never leave your home or lose a friend.

3RD REFERENCE BOOK:

Perhaps you'd rather read of jungle lions,

Or dogs or pussy cats or kangaroos.
You'll find a story of a horse or camel,
Or any animal you find in zoos.

4TH REFERENCE BOOK:

Old fairy tales of little elves and witches,
And fables that are wonderful to know;
Strange mysteries and myths of ancient wisdom—
Such curious treasure-troves our pages show.

5TH REFERENCE BOOK:

All kinds of people packed inside the covers,
Great Presidents, a scientist, a queen,
A dancer, builder, fireman, explorer,
The old, the young and every age between.

6TH REFERENCE BOOK:

Fine craftsmanship and paintings worth a ransom,
Sweet music which to all men may belong;
Oh, what a world of beauty to discover,
In poetry and literature and song!

7TH REFERENCE BOOK:

A library is like a mighty harbor,
Where you may board a boat for distant seas;
Then when your ship's in port you choose another,
And journey out again where'er you please.

BOOKWORM: What more could one ask? I have journeyed to every port in the world—and other places besides. Wonderful, wonderful books! (*To* BETTY) Don't you agree?

BETTY: Oh, yes! Yes, I do, indeed.

BOOKWORM: Of course you do. Thank you, Reference Books.

1ST REFERENCE BOOK: You're welcome, Mr. Bookworm.

ALL REFERENCE BOOKS (*Ad lib*): Goodbye, Mr. Bookworm. Goodbye, Betty. (*Etc.*)

BETTY: Goodbye, and thank you! (REFERENCE BOOKS *exit.*)

BOOKWORM (*Sitting up very straight*): Now it must be about time for my book party.

BETTY: Did you say book party or tea party, Mr. Bookworm?

BOOKWORM (*Emphatically*): I said book party. I entertain a few dear friends every after-hours. Just three or four at a time. Perhaps you will know some of them. That is, if you've read any books. Ah, here they come. (ALICE *enters*.) Good after-hours, dear Alice.

ALICE (*Curtsying*): Good after-hours, Mr. Bookworm. I am sorry the White Rabbit isn't here yet. He is always late.

BETTY (*Excitedly*): I know you. You are Alice in Wonderland!

ALICE: I remember you, too. We became acquainted when you had the measles.

BETTY: Why, yes. My cousin gave me your book. I still have it.

ALICE: Sometimes I think you have forgotten me. You never take me out or even look at me any more.

BETTY: Oh, but I will. Truly I will, Alice.

ALICE: The White Rabbit and the Mad Hatter and the Sleepy Old Dormouse get very lonesome when their friends forget them. And I do, too.

BETTY: I'm going to read about you all over again as soon as I get home. (HANSEL *and* GRETEL *enter, hand in hand*.)

HANSEL: Hello, everybody.

GRETEL: I hope we're not late, dear Mr. Bookworm.

BOOKWORM: Good after-hours, Hansel and Gretel. You'll notice that I didn't invite the old witch today. She has her points, but there are times when I can't stand having her around.

GRETEL: We feel the same way, Mr. Bookworm.

BETTY (*Clasping her hands together with pleasure*): More friends of mine!

HANSEL: Hello, Betty. You found us under your Christmas tree, didn't you?

BETTY: I did. All my friends know about you, Hansel and Gretel.

GRETEL: And the Witch?

HANSEL: And the Gingerbread House?

BETTY: Of course, of course! (BETTY, ALICE, HANSEL, *and* GRETEL *stand together as if chatting.* CAPTAIN HOOK *and* TOM SAWYER *enter.*)

BOOKWORM: Well, bless my books and eyeglasses, if it isn't that old rascal, Captain Hook! Hasn't the Crocodile caught up with you yet, Captain? Tick-tock! Tick-tock!

CAPTAIN HOOK (*Looking nervously around, alarmed*): Is the Crocodile here?

BOOKWORM: Never fear, Hook. You're safe with me. (*He chuckles.*) Here's another rascal, but a young one, this time—Tom Sawyer. Or should I say "Thomas"?

TOM SAWYER: No, no. Not Thomas! You know very well that's the name they lick me by. I'm Tom when I'm good. Just call me Tom.

BOOKWORM (*Teasingly*): How's Becky Thatcher?

TOM SAWYER: Just fine, I reckon, thank you.

BOOKWORM: And that trouble-making friend of yours?

TOM SAWYER: You mean Huckleberry Finn?

BOOKWORM: That's the one.

TOM SAWYER: Old Huck's just as adventurous and troublesome as ever.

BOOKWORM: Tell him to come around to see me some day soon, after-hours.

TOM SAWYER: I'll do that. Well, look who's here! (TOM *points to entrance as* GINGERBREAD MAN *runs in and across the stage.*)

BOOKWORM:
Run, run, as fast as you can—
GINGERBREAD MAN:
You can't catch me, I'm the Gingerbread Man!
BETTY: I met you when I was in first grade, Mr. Gingerbread Man. You were one of my favorites. Don't you get tired of running away and being chased?
GINGERBREAD MAN: Not me. As long as I keep running, the story keeps on going. You can't catch me—I'm the Gingerbread Man. (*He runs behind* BOOKWORM *and exits. A bell rings. It rings again and everyone becomes quiet. When the bell rings for the third time,* BOOKWORM *looks around at all his guests.*)
BOOKWORM: It's time for the library to open again. We'd better go.
ALICE: Good after-hours, Mr. Bookworm. Thank you for a lovely book party. I'll come again soon, if I may. (ALICE *curtsies to* BOOKWORM.) Good after-hours, Betty. Don't forget to look me up! (*She starts toward exit.*)
HANSEL: Remember us, too, Betty. Good after-hours, everyone.
GRETEL: Good after-hours, and thank you, dear Mr. Bookworm. Wait for us, Alice. (*They follow* ALICE *out right.* BETTY *waves goodbye.*)
CAPTAIN HOOK: Good after-hours, old Bookworm! And make sure you don't invite Peter Pan here at the same time you ask me. I don't know what the children see in him, I'm sure.
BOOKWORM: Tick-tock, tick-tock. Watch out for the crocodile, Captain Hook! (CAPTAIN HOOK, *frightened, holds* TOM SAWYER'S *arm.*)
TOM SAWYER: Never you fear, Cap'n Hook. I'll watch out for you. Old Mr. Bookworm is just having a little fun, I reckon.

CAPTAIN HOOK: All the same, I think we'd better go. (*He looks all around and holds on tighter to* TOM's *arm.*) Come along, Tom. Let's go! (*They exit.*)

BOOKWORM (*Gathering up his books and getting down from his stool. He stands looking at* BETTY *for a moment.*): Books, child. Wonderful books! Wonderful, wonderful books! (BOOKWORM *exits. As* BETTY *stands looking after him, the* LIBRARIAN *enters.*)

LIBRARIAN: Why, Betty, I'd forgotten you were here. (*She goes over to her desk.*)

BETTY: That's all right, ma'am.

LIBRARIAN: I'm sorry I left you here alone for so long, Betty.

BETTY: Oh, but I wasn't alone. There were Alice in Wonderland, and Hansel and Gretel, and Captain Hook and Tom Sawyer and the Gingerbread Man. (BETTY *counts them on her fingers.*)

LIBRARIAN: I see you've been busy reading some of our children's books. But I think you had better run home now. It has stopped raining and your mother will be wondering where you are.

BETTY: Yes, ma'am. May I borrow some books? I have Alice in Wonderland and Hansel and Gretel at home, but I'd love to borrow Tom Sawyer and Peter Pan. Peter Pan has Captain Hook in it.

LIBRARIAN: Of course you may. Here they are. (*She takes a couple of books from the shelf.*) I'll give you a library card.

BETTY: Thank you very much. (LIBRARIAN *checks books out for her.*) Miss Librarian—

LIBRARIAN: Yes, Betty?

BETTY: Miss Librarian, have you ever heard of a Bookworm?

LIBRARIAN: A Bookworm? (*Smiling*) Why, yes. Many times.

BETTY: Have you ever *seen* a Bookworm sitting on that

stool? (BETTY *points to the stool.*) All dressed in stripes, who keeps saying, "Bless my books and eyeglasses"? Have you?

LIBRARIAN: Why, Betty, I do believe you have been dreaming. You must have fallen asleep.

BETTY (*Looking around the room*): I don't think so, but I'm not sure.

LIBRARIAN: Well, Betty, run along now. Be sure to come in again soon.

BETTY: Thank you. As soon as I finish these books, I'll be back to check out some more. Good after-hours! (BETTY *exits.*)

LIBRARIAN (*Looking after* BETTY): Good—after-hours! What a funny thing to say! (*She busies herself at the desk.* BOOKWORM *appears again silently, climbs on his stool, and sits reading intently.* LIBRARIAN *looks up, then jumps with a startled gasp as she sees* BOOKWORM. *She blinks her eyes, shakes her head unbelievingly, then turns her back on him. She takes off her eyeglasses and cleans them thoroughly. She breathes on them and rubs them. Then facing the audience, she holds her eyeglasses up to the light and inspects them carefully. She speaks slowly.*) How strange! How very, very strange! I think I need new eyeglasses. (*She polishes them once more.*)

BOOKWORM: Well, bless *my* books and *your* eyeglasses! (*He slides off stool and exits.* LIBRARIAN *puts her eyeglasses on, then looks cautiously over her shoulder at the stool. It is empty. She smiles with relief and turns to audience again.*)

LIBRARIAN: Do you know, I *almost* thought I saw that Bookworm myself. (*Quick curtain*)

THE END

The Court of King Arithmetic

by Gwen Chaloner

Characters

ROMAN NUMERALS, *two guards*
KING ARITHMETIC
PRINCESS ADDITION ⎫
PRINCESS DIVISION ⎬ *his four daughters*
PRINCESS SUBTRACTION ⎪
PRINCESS MULTIPLICATION ⎭
SIR PROBLEM, *the Court Ambassador*
TIMOTHY SCHOOLBOY
LORD CALCULATION, *the Court Magician*
TEN NUMBERS (ZERO *through* NINE), *Lords and Ladies of the Court*
DOLLARS *and* CENTS, *two more guards*

SETTING: *The throne room of King Arithmetic's palace.*
AT RISE: KING *is seated on his throne, and his four daughters—*PRINCESS ADDITION, PRINCESS DIVISION, PRINCESS SUBTRACTION, *and* PRINCESS MULTIPLICATION—*are seated around him.* TEN NUMBERS—ZERO *through* NINE—*the Lords and Ladies of the Court, stand behind the throne, five on each side.* ROMAN NUMERALS *stand guard at the door, left;* DOLLARS *and* CENTS *stand guard at door, right.*

1ST ROMAN NUMERAL (*Taking a few steps toward* KING *and standing at attention*): Your Majesty, Sir Problem has arrived.

KING: Tell my ambassador to come in. He may have some interesting news to give us.

1ST ROMAN NUMERAL: Yes, Your Majesty. (*Exits left*)

PRINCESS ADDITION: I like Sir Problem.

PRINCESS DIVISION: I find him hard to understand, sometimes.

KING: So do I, but he's a very useful fellow, for all that.

PRINCESS SUBTRACTION: And very important!

PRINCESS MULTIPLICATION: And . . . and handsome, too, don't you think?

KING: Tut, tut, daughters. Stop the chatter. Here comes Sir Problem, himself. (1ST ROMAN NUMERAL *enters*.)

1ST ROMAN NUMERAL (*Proclaiming loudly*): Sir Problem, Ambassador of the Court of King Arithmetic! (*Takes stand at left door*)

SIR PROBLEM (*Enters from left side and bows with a flourish before* KING): Your Majesty, King Arithmetic! (SIR PROBLEM *bows graciously to each* PRINCESS, *naming them in turn*.) Princess Addition. Princess Subtraction. Princess Multiplication. Princess Division. (*The four* PRINCESSES *smile and curtsy to* SIR PROBLEM.)

KING: Welcome home again, Sir Problem. What news do you bring us this time?

SIR PROBLEM (*Dramatically*): Bad news, Your Majesty, sad news, Your Majesty.

KING (*Sternly*): Out with it, then.

SIR PROBLEM: Timothy Schoolboy has renounced—oh, I find it difficult to say it, Your Majesty. . . .

KING: Go on! Go on!

PRINCESSES (*Ad lib*): Yes, do! Please do! (*Etc.*)

SIR PROBLEM: Timothy Schoolboy has renounced arithmetic! He has given it up.

KING (*Shouting*): What!

PRINCESSES (*Ad lib*): Oh, no! How dreadful! How could he! Impossible! (*Etc.*)

SIR PROBLEM: I know how you must feel. But that is the case.

KING (*Sternly*): The facts, Sir Problem. Give us the facts.

SIR PROBLEM: Well, Your Majesty, Timothy threw his arithmetic book into the river. (PRINCESSES *scream and put their hands over their faces.*) And he put his arithmetic homework assignment into—into the trash can! (PRINCESSES *scream again.*)

DOLLARS (*Shouting*): Scalp him!

ROMAN NUMERALS (*Together*): Put him in chains!

CENTS: Boil him in oil!

KING: Silence! Silence, all of you! (*To* SIR PROBLEM) Where is this—this schoolboy?

SIR PROBLEM: In the guardhouse, Your Majesty.

KING: Send for him at once.

SIR PROBLEM: Yes, Your Majesty. (*Turning to* 2ND ROMAN NUMERAL) Guard, bring in Timothy Schoolboy. (2ND ROMAN NUMERAL *exits left and returns with* TIMOTHY SCHOOLBOY, *holding him by the collar and pushing him before him.* SIR PROBLEM *points to* TIMOTHY) This is Timothy Schoolboy.

KING (*Glaring at* TIMOTHY): So! I understand you have been making trouble.

PRINCESS MULTIPLICATION: He doesn't *look* bad.

PRINCESS ADDITION: He doesn't look stupid!

PRINCESS DIVISION: Nor even dull!

PRINCESS SUBTRACTION: I think he's cute!

KING: Silence, daughters, silence! (*To* TIMOTHY) Well, Timothy, what have you to say for yourself?

TIMOTHY: Nothing.

SIR PROBLEM (*Indignantly*): Bow, and say, "Your Majesty."

TIMOTHY (*Bowing*): Your Majesty.

KING: What did you do with your arithmetic book?

TIMOTHY: I threw it into the river.

SIR PROBLEM: Bow, and say "Your Majesty."

TIMOTHY (*Bowing*): Your Majesty.

KING: Why did you do that, Timothy?

TIMOTHY: I hate arithmetic. I don't like numbers. I'm no good at addition. I can't do subtraction. I don't understand multiplication. And division scares me.

PRINCESSES: Oh-h-h! Oh-h-h!

SIR PROBLEM: That is no way to speak of the King's daughters!

TIMOTHY: But it's true. I don't want to learn any arithmetic. Ever!

DOLLARS: Let me take care of him, Your Majesty.

KING: No. This case must be solved according to the rules. Send for Lord Calculation, the Court Magician.

SIR PROBLEM (*To* 1ST ROMAN NUMERAL): Bring in Lord Calculation. (1ST ROMAN NUMERAL *exits left and returns with* LORD CALCULATION.)

LORD CALCULATION (*Bowing with dignity*): At your service, Your Majesty.

KING: Lord Calculation, Sir Problem has a problem.

SIR PROBLEM: A very serious problem.

LORD CALCULATION: What are the facts, Your Majesty? I will give them my most profound attention.

KING: Of course, of course. Proceed, Sir Problem.

SIR PROBLEM: Here is the culprit—Timothy Schoolboy.

LORD CALCULATION (*After looking* TIMOTHY *over*): He looks harmless.

PRINCESS SUBTRACTION: He threw away his arithmetic book.

LORD CALCULATION: Oh, dear!

PRINCESS ADDITION: Into the river.

LORD CALCULATION: Oh, no!

PRINCESS MULTIPLICATION: And threw his homework papers—

PRINCESS DIVISION: Into the trash can!

LORD CALCULATION: What a monstrous boy, to be sure!

TIMOTHY: But I don't *like* arithmetic.

SIR PROBLEM: You see what I mean?

KING: Lord Calculation, what is your advice?

LORD CALCULATION (*After a moment of deep thought*): Bring me volume seven of my latest book, *Multadd-subtravision for the Billions.* (CENTS *exits and returns with a huge book.* DOLLARS *helps him hold it up.*) Look up chapter 93, page 827, section 34, paragraph 6, line 2, first answer.

ZERO (*Comes forward and looks through book as* DOLLARS *and* CENTS *continue to hold it*): Here it is, Your Lordship.

KING (*Eagerly*): What does it say?

PRINCESSES: What is it? Tell us.

LORD CALCULATION (*Puts on very big eyeglasses, which hang on a cord around his neck*): Just as I thought. Hm-m-m-m.

KING: Well, what does it say?

LORD CALCULATION: It says, "Subtract the product of the evidence from the sum of the facts, and divide by the difference of opinion." (DOLLARS *and* CENTS *close book and set it down.*)

SIR PROBLEM (*Stroking his chin*): How extraordinary! Exactly what I thought myself. Exactly!

LORD CALCULATION (*Snubbing* SIR PROBLEM): But *I* prefer my *short version.* (*He takes a very tiny book from his pocket and looks at it through a huge magnifying glass.*)

KING (*Watching as* LORD CALCULATION *peers into his little book*): What does *that* one say?

LORD CALCULATION: It says, "Check results before going on."

KING: That sounds reasonable. How do we do it?

LORD CALCULATION: With Your Majesty's permission, we will give this boy his greatest wish. We will take arithmetic out of his life. He will not be able to use numbers in any way.

TIMOTHY: Oh, good! I like that!

KING: Must the punishment be so severe?

LORD CALCULATION: We will give Timothy just *one* chance to change his mind.

TIMOTHY: I don't need any chances. This is too good to be true. No multiplication tables. No addition. No subtraction. No division ever again. Oh, boy! What fun!

LORD CALCULATION: Wait, boy! We will proceed in an orderly manner. The book says, "Check results before going on." (*To the Court*) Your Royal Highnesses, Lords and Ladies of the Court, let us show Timothy Schoolboy what this punishment would mean. (*To* KING) With your permission, Your Majesty?

KING (*Impatiently*): Proceed, proceed.

LORD CALCULATION (*Turning his attention to* TIMOTHY): When is your birthday, Timothy?

TIMOTHY: January 12th.

ONE: No more birthdays, Timothy. You may not use days or months, for they are counted by numbers. They are dates.

PRINCESS ADDITION: And they add up, too.

TWO: No birthday cakes, no cookies, no pies any more. You need numbers and tables and fractions to measure what goes into them.

TIMOTHY: I'll buy them at the store.

THREE: You cannot buy anything, Timothy. To buy, you must figure—add and subtract.

DOLLARS: And use dollars—

CENTS: And cents.

TIMOTHY: I don't care about the cakes. I'm going to have a bicycle. I'll ride my bike.

FOUR: Bikes cost money. Money means numbers, too. And bicycles have many parts—two wheels, two handles, many spokes. It is the same with toy trains and planes and cars.

TIMOTHY: We-e-ell, I just like playing games.

FIVE: No. You cannot keep score without numbers. You cannot choose teams without dividing.

TIMOTHY: I—I—could read a book.

SIX: A book has pages and chapters, all numbered. You won't be able to use numbers at all.

TIMOTHY: I would travel.

DOLLARS: But you'd need to know how to count to pay fares on buses, trains, and boats.

CENTS: Yes, indeed.

SEVEN: And you'd have to use numbers to read timetables and schedules and the distances between places.

EIGHT: Without numbers, there would be no minutes or hours.

1ST ROMAN NUMERAL: And no numbers on clocks to tell the time.

TIMOTHY: I'd get a job and work all day.

NINE: There'd be no dollars or cents to pay you with.

DOLLARS *and* CENTS: Certainly not!

ZERO: And so, Timothy, you would be nothing, a little round nothing.

TIMOTHY: *You* are nothing. It is written right on you.

ZERO (*Smiling*): Oh, no, Timothy. I am *Zero*. I am nothing when I am alone, as you would be, Timothy; but when I belong to the group, I am very important. See, like this. (ZERO *puts his arm around shoulders of* NINE.)

I can change *Nine* into *Ninety*. *You* can't make numbers. *(Pats* NINE *on shoulder)* See?

TIMOTHY: I—I—I want to go home!

ONE: Mustn't ask directions.

TWO: Mustn't count streets.

THREE: Mustn't have numbers on the door.

TIMOTHY: I'll phone.

FOUR *(Warningly)*: Phone numbers!

TIMOTHY: Oh, I wish—I wish—

KING: What do you wish, Timothy Schoolboy?

TIMOTHY: I wish I'd never said those horrid, mean things about arithmetic.

FOUR: Nor thrown us all away in the river?

TIMOTHY: Yes.

FIVE: Nor thrown us in the trash can?

TIMOTHY: Yes, yes—I mean, *No!* No, I wish I hadn't.

KING: Timothy, perhaps we could solve this problem. We'll erase the errors and begin all over again. We'll be friends instead of enemies.

TIMOTHY: Oh, could we, Your Majesty? Could we?

KING: What do you say, Sir Problem?

SIR PROBLEM: I'd say that was a sensible answer to the problem, Your Majesty.

KING: And you, Lord Calculation?

LORD CALCULATION: Check, and double check, Your Majesty.

TIMOTHY: Oh, thank you, sir. Thank you.

KING: And now, Timothy, let my four daughters give you some good advice.

TIMOTHY: Yes, Your Majesty.

KING: Princess Addition.

PRINCESS ADDITION *(Stands)*: Make your figures carefully. Add from the top down; check from the bottom up. Always keep your columns straight, Timothy. Then the *addends* will give you the right sum.

TIMOTHY: I will, I will, Princess Addition. (PRINCESS ADDITION *returns to her seat. Each* PRINCESS *follows the same procedure.*)

KING: Princess Subtraction.

PRINCESS SUBTRACTION: The minus sign tells you to take away. Copy carefully. Keep your work neat, Timothy. And remember, you subtract the *subtrahend* from the *minuend* to find the *difference.*

TIMOTHY: Yes, yes. I will remember.

KING: Princess Multiplication.

PRINCESS MULTIPLICATION: When you have learned to add and know all your times tables, you will like to multiply. You will see numbers grow and grow. Remember to keep your figures in straight lines, then the *multiplier* times the *multiplicand* will give you the *product.*

TIMOTHY: Yes, Princess Multiplication.

KING: And now Princess Division.

PRINCESS DIVISION: You probably know more about division than you think, Timothy. You see—you divide whenever you share things—candy or cookies or toys. You must learn to subtract and multiply and study your times tables thoroughly, then you will be ready to divide larger numbers. You will divide the *dividend* by the *divisor,* and the answer will be called the *quotient.* Promise you will try hard, Timothy.

TIMOTHY: I promise, I promise. I didn't know arithmetic was so important. I'm not going to fight it ever again. I'm going to make arithmetic one of my best friends.

PRINCESS ADDITION: I *knew* he was a nice boy.

PRINCESS MULTIPLICATION: Yes, so did I.

KING: You will find that arithmetic will work for you every day of your life, Timothy.

TIMOTHY: Thank you, Your Majesty. Thank you, everyone. But now I must hurry. I don't want to be late for school.

KING: One moment, boy. (*Turning to* LORD CALCULA-TION) Lord Calculation, you are the Court Magician. Can you bring his books and papers back?

LORD CALCULATION: Certainly. Certainly. (*To* ROMAN NUMERALS) Stand at the gates while I work my magic. (*Guards exit.* LORD CALCULATION *makes elaborate magic signs with wand while he chants.*)

Three plus four makes seven,
Nine take away five leaves four.
Book, rise out of the river,
And come to the castle door!

(1ST ROMAN NUMERAL *re-enters with book.*)

1ST ROMAN NUMERAL (*Handing book to* TIMOTHY): Here it is, Timothy. A trifle damp, but almost as good as new.

TIMOTHY (*Taking book*): Oh, thank you.

LORD CALCULATION (*Making more magic signs*):

Four times two makes eight,
Six divided by two makes three.
Papers rise out of the trash can,
And return to Timothy!

(2ND ROMAN NUMERAL *re-enters with papers.*)

2ND ROMAN NUMERAL (*Handing papers to* TIMOTHY): The papers, Timothy.

TIMOTHY: Thank you. Thank you very much.

KING: Our problem has been solved. (*He extends his sceptre toward* TIMOTHY.) Timothy is a real schoolboy once more. (KING *stands ceremoniously, holding his sceptre aloft.*) Case dismissed. (*Curtain*)

THE END

A Prince Is Where You Find Him

by James R. Chisholm

Characters

TWO GUARDS	PRINCESS
KING	LADY ASTER
PRIME MINISTER	THREE LADIES-IN-WAITING
QUEEN	PRINCE SQUARE
BEGGAR	COOK

SCENE 1

TIME: *Long, long ago.*

SETTING: *The throne room of the King and Queen of Pneumonia. There is a sundial to the left of the two thrones.*

AT RISE: *The* KING *and* QUEEN *sit on their thrones. The* TWO GUARDS *stand at the doorway.*

1ST GUARD: Your Majesty! Announcing the Prime Minister, Count Shuvoff! (PRIME MINISTER *enters, strides toward throne, and bows.*)

KING: What have you learned, Shuvoff? Have your spies reported to you?

PRIME MINISTER: They have, Your Majesty, and I have learned much. As you know, your uncle, the Emperor Mendacious, has to find a ruler for his kingdom of

Petunia. He wants your daughter, the Princess Emma, to become Queen of Petunia, but he insists that she must be married to a prince by tonight, or she cannot rule Petunia.

QUEEN: Come, come, Shuvoff! We know all this already. What else have you learned?

KING: Yes, Shuvoff. What?

PRIME MINISTER: Your Majesty, as you know, the only prince in the country is Prince Square. Yesterday you told Princess Emma and Prince Square that they were to be married this evening. (BEGGAR *wanders in while* PRIME MINISTER *speaks.*)

BEGGAR: Alms! Alms! Any old money you don't need, for a starving man? (GUARDS *grab him.*)

2ND GUARD: All right, fellow! Out you go! This is no place to beg. (*They push* BEGGAR *offstage.*)

PRIME MINISTER: As I was saying, Your Majesty, the people want the Princess to marry a common man. There may be a revolution if she marries a prince. Of course, she cannot marry *both* a prince *and* a commoner, so you have decided that she must marry a prince, since you must not offend the Emperor.

QUEEN: Worries! Always worries!

PRIME MINISTER: My spies tell me that the Princess does not want to marry Prince Square, and that she is coming at any moment to tell you so.

KING: Worries! Always worries! Is there anything else, Shuvoff?

PRIME MINISTER: One little thing, Your Majesty. (*Eagerly*) Do you have any executions that need to be done? As you know, I am also the Royal Executioner, and it has been such a long time since I've beheaded anyone. You know how it helps my golf swing. (*Stands to the rear of the throne.*)

1ST GUARD: Your Majesty! Announcing the Princess

Emma! (*The* PRINCESS *enters, followed by* LADY ASTER *and* THREE LADIES-IN-WAITING.)

KING: Hello, Emma. What do you want?

PRINCESS: You know what I want, Father. That horrid little man, Pushoff—or Jumpoff or Kickoff or whatever his name is—tells you everything. Even one of my own attendants, Lady Aster, spies on me for him. (*Turns to* LADY ASTER.) Don't you, Lady Aster?

LADY ASTER: Princess, you know how poorly paid a lady-in-waiting's job is!

PRINCESS: See, Father? Well, I refuse to marry that horrid tennis-playing Prince Square, and that's that!

BEGGAR (*Emerging from behind throne*): Alms! Alms! Any old dollars you want to dispose of? Alms!

2ND GUARD (*As* GUARDS *hustle him off left*): You'd better get away from here—fast. Didn't you see that look in the Royal Executioner's eyes?

QUEEN: Worries! What did I tell you?

KING (*Pleading*): Now Emma, you know you have to marry a prince by tonight. Prince Square is the only prince around, so unless you can come up with another prince by nine o'clock tonight, palace sundial time, you'll just have to marry Prince Square!

QUEEN: That reminds me, Henry. The palace sundial is running fast and will have to be repaired by tonight.

KING: I've been looking for a good sundial repairman. (*Turns to* EMMA) The trouble with you, young lady, is that you're too romantic. You've been reading too many Prince Charming stories.

QUEEN: I think Prince Square is rather nice.

KING: Square has a good head on his shoulders.

PRINCESS: A square head. All he ever thinks of day and night is playing tennis. Tennis, tennis, tennis!

KING: Hush, child! He should be coming here any minute now. (GUARDS *re-enter and stand at either side of door.*)

1st Guard: Your Majesty! Announcing Prince Square!

Queen: I wonder what he'll say when he learns you won't marry him.

Prince Square (*Bounding in, waving tennis racket*): Tennis, anyone? Hello, Your Majesty, everybody, Emma. Care for a fast set or two? (Guards *exit and quickly reenter, dragging in the* Beggar, *wrapped in a tennis net.*)

2nd Guard: Sire, the guards at the gate caught this beggar trying to sneak in behind Prince Square, disguised as a tennis net. What shall we do with him?

Beggar: Give him some alms and let him go.

1st Guard: Silence, knave!

Prime Minister (*Eagerly*): Let me behead him, Your Majesty, I'm so out of practice.

King: You might as well, Shuvoff. I can't have beggars running around my kingdom.

Beggar: No, Your Majesty! Wait! I'm not just a beggar. I'm a common citizen. You must listen to me!

King: Common citizen? Oh, that's different. I always listen to the common citizens.

Prince Square: I surely thought he was a tennis net.

King: What are you, if you're not a beggar? Do you have a trade?

Beggar: Indeed, sire. I am a sundial repairman—but very few people seem to want their sundials repaired these days.

Queen: Henry! He can repair the palace sundial for the wedding.

King: You're right! (*To* Beggar) You'd better have that sundial working at nine o'clock tonight!

Prime Minister: If you don't, I'll get a little practice on my golf swing. (*He swings his arms.*)

CURTAIN

*   *   *

SCENE 2

TIME: *A few minutes later.*
SETTING: *The same.*
AT RISE: *The* PRIME MINISTER *and the* BEGGAR *examine sundial.* BEGGAR *holds satchel.*

PRIME MINISTER: Now that everybody's gone to prepare for the wedding, you'll be able to work on the palace sundial. There it is! (*Gestures*)

BEGGAR: Thank you, sir.

PRIME MINISTER: Don't thank me! Just be sure you have it ready by tonight. Farewell, I must leave now. I have some axes to grind. (*Exits.* BEGGAR *puts down satchel and starts looking over the sundial.*)

BEGGAR (*To himself*): If I don't have any interruptions, I should be just about able to do it in time.

2ND LADY-IN-WAITING (*Enters left and calls back offstage*): Princess! Girls! Here's that beggar fixing the sundial! I must say he's a handsome beggar. Let's watch him work. (PRINCESS, LADY ASTER, *and other* LADIES-IN-WAITING *enter and gather around.*)

3RD LADY-IN-WAITING: Oh, yes, let's!

PRINCESS: My, he *is* handsome! I hadn't noticed before.

1ST LADY-IN-WAITING: I love to watch people work.

LADY ASTER: I'll bet he'd love to have us watch him. Wouldn't you, fellow?

BEGGAR: Look, lady, I just came here to beg.

3RD LADY-IN-WAITING: But you're not just a beggar! You're a sundial repairman.

1ST LADY-IN-WAITING: I'll bet you're not even that! You don't seem to be repairing that one very fast.

BEGGAR: Lady, you'd be surprised at how little help you are.

PRINCESS: *I* think he's a Prince Charming in disguise!

BEGGAR: Honestly, Princess, I'm only a tennis net in disguise.

2ND LADY-IN-WAITING: Princess, you read too many romantic stories.

LADY ASTER (*Pointing off right*): Look! Here comes the new cook that the King hired this morning!

PRINCESS (*To herself*): I still think he's a prince. At least I wish he were a prince.

COOK (*Entering, loudly*): Prince! Charlie Prince! How are you, Charlie? Still fixing sundials? (*Starts to watch BEGGAR working*)

PRINCESS: Prince?

BEGGAR: Hello, Sam. What's cooking?

PRINCESS: *Charlie* Prince?

BEGGAR: How's your wife, Sam?

COOK: Putting on weight, Charlie. Must be my cooking, I guess. Look, Charlie, I'd like to talk with you, but the King's having some kind of party tonight and I have to bake a cake. Take care of yourself, Charlie! (*Exits left*)

BEGGAR: I'm trying! (*Turns back to work*) Look at that sun! With all of these interruptions I'll never have this fixed on time.

PRINCESS: Is your name Charlie *Prince?*

BEGGAR: That's right.

PRINCESS: You're not really a *prince,* are you? I mean— royalty?

BEGGAR: Well, yes and no. I am a Prince. So was my father. All of my people have been Princes, but we're not *royalty.* Prince is just our name. We're common people.

PRINCESS (*Aside*): The Emperor wants me to marry a prince. The people want me to marry a commoner. (*Looks at BEGGAR*) Charlie *Prince,* a common man. (*Looks at LADIES-IN-WAITING, then at BEGGAR again*) Oh, girls, it's getting late. You'd better go and get ready for the wedding—*now!* (LADIES-IN-WAITING *start to exit left, except* LADY ASTER. BEGGAR *looks at his work, shrugs his shoulders, and stops working. He takes an apple from his pocket.*)

LADY ASTER: Aren't *you* coming, Princess? *You* have to get ready, too.

PRINCESS: Lady Aster, some day I'll be queen. You will want to be my friend then, won't you?

LADY ASTER: Yes. Goodbye, Princess. (*Exits*)

PRINCESS: Are you all finished with the sundial, Charlie?

BEGGAR (*Eating apple*): No, it's too late now. These interruptions will be the death of me.

PRINCESS: Do you like me, Charlie?

BEGGAR: I don't know. When you kept me from finishing my work on time, I didn't like you. But now that it's too late, I'll probably be losing my head over you.

PRINCESS: If I saved you from being beheaded, would you like me, Charlie Prince?

BEGGAR: I'd love you.

PRIME MINISTER (*Off left*): This way, Your Majesty. Oh, I hope he's not finished!

KING: Beggar, are you finished? And you, Emma, have you found another Prince yet?

BEGGAR: No.

PRINCESS: Yes. (*Pause*) Father, this beggar is really a prince, and he can *prove* it, too. He's Charlie Prince, and he's also a commoner. If I marry him, both your uncle and the people will be pleased!

PRIME MINISTER: Oh, dear! I won't get to execute him!

KING: What! Why, this is marvelous! There will be no war with the Emperor and no revolution by the people! Wonderful! Quickly, my children—go get ready for the wedding. We'll have to get along without a sundial.

BEGGAR: No, we won't, Sire! I have my portable sundial

that I invented to wear on my wrist. Whenever I want to know what time it is, I watch my wrist.

PRIME MINISTER: What do you call it?

BEGGAR: A watch-wrist.

PRINCESS: Come along with me, my Prince. (*They start to go off left.*)

BEGGAR (*About to take a bite of the apple*): Call me Charlie. (*They exit.*)

PRIME MINISTER: Your Majesty, what about Prince Square? He may feel insulted when he hears what has happened.

KING: Worries! Always worries!

PRIME MINISTER: Oh, dear. What *will* Prince Square say?

PRINCE SQUARE (*Enters right, bounding in with tennis racket*): Anyone for tennis? I say, Your Majesty, I just saw the Princess with a tennis net. She says she's going to marry it.

KING: That's true, Prince Square.

PRINCE SQUARE: I say, that is jolly. That will leave me much more time for my tennis. Always did prefer a good game of tennis to these beautiful princesses.

KING: Marvelous, my boy! That's worthy of your ancestors —spoken like a real Square! (*Quick curtain*)

THE END

The Magic Bookshelf

by Patricia Clapp

Characters

SALLY
TIM
FAIRY GODFATHER ⎫
PETER PAN   ⎪
CINDERELLA   ⎪
ALICE IN WONDERLAND   ⎬ *storybook people*
JACK THE GIANT KILLER   ⎪
DOROTHY OF OZ   ⎪
CHRISTOPHER ROBIN ⎪
RED RIDING HOOD ⎭

SETTING: *A living room.*

AT RISE: SALLY *is sitting in a chair reading to* TIM, *who sits in a second chair with a blanket over his knees.*

SALLY (*Reading from a book open on her lap*): "—and when the Prince tried the glass slipper on Cinderella's dainty foot, it fitted perfectly! Taking her hand he helped her to her feet and said—"

TIM: I'm tired of being read to! (*He rises from chair and goes to the window.*) I wish I could go out.

SALLY (*Putting down the book*): You know you can't go out when you're just getting over measles.

TIM: I wish I had somebody to play with.

SALLY: You're not supposed to play; you're supposed to be quiet. And listen.

TIM: I wish I didn't have to be quiet. Or listen.

SALLY: Come back here and sit down. You have to keep warm and quiet. Mother said so.

TIM (*Returning reluctantly to the chair*): I'm tired of keeping warm and quiet, and I'm tired of having measles, and I'm tired of hearing about silly Cinderella! I wish I had real, live, honest-to-goodness people to play with.

SALLY (*Rising and tucking the blanket firmly around TIM*): What would you play?

TIM: Boy things. Pirates and wild animals and giants and things like that. Anyhow, Cinderella's a dopey story!

SALLY (*Indignantly*): It is not!

TIM: The only good part is the Fairy Godmother. I wish *I* had one.

SALLY: Good gracious, stop wishing! All you've done all afternoon is wish for things!

TIM: If I wished hard enough, do you think I'd get a Fairy Godmother?

SALLY: You'd have to be *really* miserable, just like Cinderella.

TIM (*Dropping his head against the back of the chair and groaning*): Oh-oh! I'm *really* miserable! My measles hurt!

SALLY: Measles can't hurt! You're just pretending!

TIM: I am not! I'm *very* miserable and I'm suffering like anything! Please, Fairy Godmother, please come and help me! (FAIRY GODFATHER *suddenly appears in the doorway. He carries a baseball bat.*)

FAIRY GODFATHER: Since you put it like that—

TIM (*Sitting up straight and opening his eyes wide*): Who are you?

SALLY (*Reaching out quickly and taking* TIM's *hand*): Where did you come from?

FAIRY GODFATHER: What a reception! (*Mimics their voices*) "Who are you? Where did you come from?" I'm Tim's Fairy Godfather, of course, and I came from— well, never mind where I came from. I'm here.

TIM: I don't have a Fairy Godfather!

FAIRY GODFATHER: Now there's a ridiculous statement if ever I heard one! I'm standing right here in front of him, and he says he doesn't have a Fairy Godfather!

SALLY: I thought there were only Fairy God*mothers*.

FAIRY GODFATHER: That just shows how much *you* know about it! Girls have godmothers, boys have godfathers!

SALLY (*In a small voice*): Oh. Well, won't you sit down please?

FAIRY GODFATHER: Thank you. I always sit on floors.

SALLY (*With her best manners*): You'll find our floor very comfortable.

FAIRY GODFATHER (*Sitting cross-legged on the floor and bouncing a little*): Thank you. Yes, it is delightfully soft. Now, Tim, just why did you call me?

TIM: I didn't know I was calling you.

FAIRY GODFATHER (*Sternly*): Young man! If I am going to be your Fairy Godfather, the very least you can do is make sense when you talk to me. I distinctly heard you calling for a Fairy Godmother. Well, that can be forgiven, I suppose. You didn't know about *boys* having god*fathers*. So—there you were, saying you were miserable, and calling for me.

SALLY: But Tim wasn't really miserable; that was just pretend.

FAIRY GODFATHER: I'm just pretend, too, so that takes care of that.

SALLY: But I can see you!

FAIRY GODFATHER (*Impatiently*): Of course you can see me! I'm right here!

TIM: Then why did you say you were just pretend?

FAIRY GODFATHER (*Shaking his head*): Oh, me! Such children! Don't you know there is *real* pretend as well as *pretend* pretend?

TIM: No, I guess we didn't. What's the difference, please?

FAIRY GODFATHER: It's perfectly plain. *Real* pretend things are fairies, and wishing wells, and magic and flying around the room. *Pretend* pretend things are toy guns and the horses on merry-go-rounds and marshmallow bananas, and things like *that!* Do you understand?

TIM (*Doubtfully*): I *think* so. (*Pauses*) Why do you carry a baseball bat?

FAIRY GODFATHER: Who ever heard of a fairy without a wand?

SALLY: But I thought wands were very slim and had shiny stars on top.

FAIRY GODFATHER: Now wouldn't I look just fine waving around a skinny wand with a shiny star on top? Fairy God*fathers* don't go in for that dainty stuff. Besides, you never know when you might just happen on a good baseball game. It pays to be ready.

TIM: Oh, I see.

FAIRY GODFATHER: Now, let's get down to business. What did you call me for, child? I haven't all day, you know.

TIM: I don't think I remember.

SALLY: I do. He was tired of listening to me read out loud and he wanted someone to play with. He's a very ungrateful boy sometimes. *I* like to listen to me read. I read very well.

TIM (*Scornfully*): Cinderella! All that dopey stuff about Prince Charming and pumpkin coaches. Everyone knows you can't ride in a pumpkin.

FAIRY GODFATHER: I suppose everyone knows there aren't Fairy Godfathers, too!

TIM: I'm sorry.

FAIRY GODFATHER: That's better. Learn a little respect for your elders, my boy, and don't go around doubting everything. You'll get along much better. So—you wanted someone to play with, did you? What's wrong with storybook people?

TIM: I wanted a real person to play boys' games with.

FAIRY GODFATHER: There you go again! Real—pretend— you still don't know the difference! I can see I'm going to have to do something about this. (*He rises and scans the titles of books on the shelf.*) Let's see. How about Peter Pan to start with?

TIM: To start what with?

FAIRY GODFATHER: To start playing with, of course! You *did* want someone to play with, didn't you?

SALLY: I think Tim means he wants some real, live children, to play boys' games with—like pirates.

FAIRY GODFATHER: You can't beat Peter Pan when it comes to playing pirates. You do remember about him and Captain Hook, don't you?

TIM: No, I don't think I do.

FAIRY GODFATHER: You mean you never read about Peter Pan?

SALLY: Tim doesn't like books much.

FAIRY GODFATHER: Well! Where do you think *I* came from, for goodness' sake? You read about Cinderella's having a Fairy Godmother, and you wanted one, didn't you?

TIM: Yes.

FAIRY GODFATHER: So you called me. And I came. Here I am. Now! Wasn't that out of a book?

TIM: Yes, I guess it was.

FAIRY GODFATHER: All right, then! Let's have no more

nonsense about book people not being real! (*He takes the book "Peter Pan" from the shelf, and holding it in one hand, lightly taps the cover with his baseball bat.*) Peter, Peter, in the book,
Come out and give our Tim a look!
(*As* FAIRY GODFATHER *turns to replace the book on the shelf,* PETER PAN *bounds through the door.*)

PETER PAN: Somebody call me?

SALLY: Peter Pan!

PETER PAN (*Sweeping off his cap and making a deep bow*): At your service!

TIM: It can't be!

FAIRY GODFATHER: And why can't it be?

TIM: Because Peter Pan is just somebody in a book!

PETER PAN (*To* FAIRY GODFATHER): What's he talking about?

FAIRY GODFATHER: It's a very sad case! This boy, Tim— my own godson—doesn't believe in book people!

PETER PAN (*Shocked*): No!

FAIRY GODFATHER: That's right. He thinks that just because he *reads* about us, we're not real people!

PETER PAN (*Jumping suddenly to stand beside* TIM'S *chair*): Pinch me!

TIM (*Hesitantly*): I beg your pardon?

PETER PAN: I said—pinch me! (TIM *pinches him.*) Ouch! There! Am I real or not?

TIM: You *feel* real.

PETER PAN (*Politely to* SALLY): Would you care to try? (*He extends his arm to her, and she gently pinches it.*) Thank you. Very ladylike. Well?

SALLY: You *do* feel real.

PETER PAN: I should hope so! Look! *I'm* real, (*Points to* FAIRY GODFATHER) he's real, (*Points to* TIM *and* SALLY) *you're*—well, I'm not so sure about you. *We're* real pretend, and that's the realest kind of real there is!

SALLY: Are there more of you?

PETER PAN: Are there more—? (*To* FAIRY GODFATHER) Listen to her! Are there more of us, she wants to know! Come on, old-timer, show her!

FAIRY GODFATHER (*Turning to bookshelf again*): Well, how about—

SALLY (*Holding out the book she was reading*): I want to see Cinderella!

PETER PAN (*Taking the book from* SALLY *and handing it to the* FAIRY GODFATHER): She wants to see Cinderella.

FAIRY GODFATHER (*Taking the book and tapping on the cover with the bat*):
Cinderella in the book,
Come, let Sally take a look.
(CINDERELLA *comes through the door.*)

SALLY (*Joyfully*): Cinderella!

CINDERELLA: Hello, Sally.

FAIRY GODFATHER: You know one another?

CINDERELLA: We've never really met before, but Sally and I are old friends. She's always reading about me.

SALLY: I read about you to Tim today, but I don't think he really—well—believed in you.

CINDERELLA: It's understandable, I suppose. He probably prefers Peter Pan, and Jack the Giant Killer, and Aladdin, and people like that. Boys usually do.

FAIRY GODFATHER: He doesn't believe in them, either!

CINDERELLA: This is terrible! Imagine not having people believe in you! What can we do to prove we're really us?

PETER PAN: I know. Let's have a meeting! Old-timer, you stand there by the bookshelf and call some of the others in. Who's there?

FAIRY GODFATHER (*At bookcase, scanning the titles*): There's Alice in Wonderland.

CINDERELLA: Oh, she's lots of fun! Ask her—I haven't seen her in ages!

FAIRY GODFATHER (*Starting to take book from the shelf*):
Alice, Alice in the book—

PETER PAN (*Impatiently*): Do it the short way, old-timer!
You know—

FAIRY GODFATHER: Very well, then. (*He runs his bat
lightly over the backs of as many books as he can reach.*)
Everyone within a book,
Give Tim and Sally both a look!
(*Through the door come as many storybook people as
desired.* PETER PAN *stations himself on one side of the
door and* CINDERELLA *stands on the other, where they
take turns announcing the guests.*)

CINDERELLA: Miss Alice, from Wonderland!

ALICE (*Entering*): Cinderella! How nice to see you!

PETER PAN: Master Jack, Killer of Giants!

JACK (*Entering*): Hi, Pete—how's Wendy?

CINDERELLA: Miss Dorothy, from the Kingdom of Oz!

DOROTHY (*Entering*): Why, hello! For a minute I thought
I was back in the cyclone, being whooshed into Oz! Is
this a party?

CINDERELLA: No, a meeting. We'll explain in a minute.

PETER PAN: Christopher Robin, and Pooh Bear! (CHRIS-
TOPHER ROBIN *enters, carrying a teddy bear.*)

CHRISTOPHER ROBIN: Are we in time for tea? Pooh is rather
hungry.

CINDERELLA: Maybe later, Christopher Robin; not just
now. (RED RIDING HOOD *runs in.*) Ah, here's Red Riding Hood. Don't *rush* so, dear!

RED RIDING HOOD: I can't help it! It's that dreadful Wolf!
He keeps following me!

CINDERELLA: Peter Pan will protect you. He scares wolves
by making faces at them.

PETER PAN (*Bending down and peering horribly through
his legs*): Like this!

RED RIDING HOOD (*With a little scream*): Oh! That should work—it even scared me!

ALICE: Will somebody please tell me what we're doing here? I can't stay very long. The Queen is having another of her tea parties.

CHRISTOPHER ROBIN: Could Pooh Bear and I go? Pooh's a little hungry.

RED RIDING HOOD: Here, Christopher dear, I have some lovely things in my basket. (*She hands him a cookie from the basket on her arm.*)

CHRISTOPHER ROBIN (*Politely*): Pooh Bear says thank you.

PETER PAN (*Clapping his hands*): Now, the reason we're all here is that these two—(*Pointing at* SALLY *and* TIM) —don't believe in book people!

JACK: They *don't?*

PETER PAN (*Shaking his head*): No, they don't!

SALLY: I believe—a little.

PETER PAN: A little's not enough!

CINDERELLA: Oh, Peter—a little is better than nothing. I think Sally sort of believed in *me*. At least, I'm sure she was very fond of me.

SALLY (*Eagerly*): I believe now!

FAIRY GODFATHER: Anyone can believe in what he sees! It's believing in what you can't see that counts. (*To the storybook people*) You see, it started when Tim wished I would appear and bring him someone to play with. Naturally, I did. After all, that's what I'm around for— to appear when he calls me.

TIM: Why didn't you ever appear before, Fairy Godfather?

FAIRY GODFATHER: You never asked me.

TIM: Oh.

FAIRY GODFATHER: So—as I was saying—he wanted playmates, and I invited you to come and play with him.

JACK: Here we are—what shall we play?

PETER PAN: That comes later. First we have to have a meeting. Old-timer, you be the chairman.

FAIRY GODFATHER: Very well. (*Raps with his bat for attention.*) Will this meeting please come to order? (*Everyone is quiet*) Ladies and gentlemen—and Pooh Bear—please be seated. (*Everyone sits on the floor in a semicircle.*) Now. The first item on the agenda—

CHRISTOPHER ROBIN: Pooh Bear wants to know what an agenda is.

DOROTHY: It's a thing you have at meetings. Sh-sh!

CHRISTOPHER ROBIN: Pooh says, "Is it like honey?"

FAIRY GODFATHER (*Sternly*): This meeting cannot proceed until there is silence! (*He waits a moment, glaring at* CHRISTOPHER ROBIN.) As I was saying, the first item on the agenda—is how to prove to Tim that we're real pretenders. Has anyone a suggestion?

ALICE: May I ask Tim a question, sir?

FAIRY GODFATHER: You may.

ALICE (*Standing and addressing* TIM): What makes you think we're not real?

TIM (*Starting to get to his feet*): Well—

FAIRY GODFATHER: Get back into that chair! (*To the others*) He's getting over measles. Continue, Tim.

TIM (*Slipping back into his chair*): When Sally and I were little—that is, littler—before Sally could read (*Glances sidelong at* SALLY) so beautifully—Mother and Daddy used to read to us.

FAIRY GODFATHER: Yes?

TIM: They used to read about Jack and Jill and Peter Rabbit and Sleeping Beauty and all those things—er—people.

PETER PAN: Peter Rabbit is *not* a person!

FAIRY GODFATHER: Quiet, Peter. Give the boy a chance.

TIM: Thank you, sir. Our Mother and Daddy said that they were just made-up stories about made-up things—

er, people and animals—and that they didn't really happen. That they were fairy stories!

FAIRY GODFATHER: Well! *That* explains it.

SALLY: It does?

FAIRY GODFATHER: Of course. You see, there are some things that grownups don't know.

SALLY: There are?

FAIRY GODFATHER: Yes, and it's too bad, really, because they're very important things.

TIM: Like what?

FAIRY GODFATHER: Like what kind of noise the grass makes when it's growing, and whether there really is a pot of gold at the end of the rainbow.

TIM: There is, isn't there?

FAIRY GODFATHER: Of course! And what the outdoors feels like when it's dark—and things like that. But the most important thing they don't know is about real pretenders.

SALLY: I thought grownups knew everything.

FAIRY GODFATHER: They know a great many very useful things about making cookies, and what to do for a scraped knee, and how to build a model airplane—but some of the most important things they ever knew, they've forgotten!

TIM: You mean the pretend things?

FAIRY GODFATHER: That's right. They *used* to know, because all children are part fairy themselves, and fairies know all about pretend. But somehow, as grownups get older, they forget. It's very sad, and yet it almost always happens.

SALLY: Oh, Mr. Godfather, I don't want to grow up and forget!

FAIRY GODFATHER: That's the way Peter Pan felt. That's why he decided always to remain a little boy.

SALLY: I don't think I could manage that.

FAIRY GODFATHER: There *is* another way—a way to keep the magic that children and fairies know about.

SALLY: Oh, how? Please tell.

FAIRY GODFATHER: *Read!*

TIM: Read?

FAIRY GODFATHER: Read! Read and read and read until you've stored up so much magic and pretend and make-believe that you can never lose it all. Read fairy stories and nursery rhymes and children's books. Read about animals that talk—

ALICE: Like the White Rabbit.

FAIRY GODFATHER: Read about toys that are alive.

CHRISTOPHER ROBIN: Like Pooh Bear.

FAIRY GODFATHER: Read about Fairy Godmothers.

CINDERELLA: Like mine.

FAIRY GODFATHER: And magic places.

DOROTHY: Like Oz.

FAIRY GODFATHER: Read about giants.

JACK: That's my story!

FAIRY GODFATHER: And pirates and Indians.

PETER PAN: That's mine!

FAIRY GODFATHER: Read about them all until they're a part of you that you won't ever lose. Read about them until they are your friends and your companions and your playmates. Read about them until you can never be lonely, and never be bored and never forget!

SALLY: Will it work?

FAIRY GODFATHER: I said it would, didn't I? (*Turning to the storybook people*) Am I right?

ALL: Yes! Yes!

PETER PAN: You can read about anything you like. Whatever sort of friend you want, you'll find in a book. We're always there—we never go away.

ALICE: It doesn't matter whether it's raining out, or

whether you're sick in bed—you can still have us to keep you company.

TIM: Then—if I wanted to have a big adventure, for instance—

JACK: Try *Robin Hood* or *Treasure Island*.

TIM: Or if I just wanted to sit and laugh at something funny—

RED RIDING HOOD: Read about Babar, or Mary Poppins.

TIM: Then I wouldn't ever be alone, would I? Even if Sally was at school, and Daddy was at work, and Mother was busy, I'd always have somebody with me!

FAIRY GODFATHER: That's right.

TIM: And when we grew up, the magic wouldn't ever rub off?

FAIRY GODFATHER: Not if there was enough of it. And if it did, you could always shine it up a little.

SALLY (*Triumphantly*): By reading another book!

FAIRY GODFATHER: Or an old one over again. Now that you know the secret, there's only one thing more. (*Very sternly*) Tim!

TIM: Yes, sir?

FAIRY GODFATHER: Do you believe in us?

TIM: Oh, *yes,* sir!

FAIRY GODFATHER: And you won't forget?

TIM: Oh, *no,* sir!

FAIRY GODFATHER: Now it's time for us to go. We're all very busy, and we must get back to our chores. (*To the storybook people*) Will someone make a motion that the meeting be adjourned?

CHRISTOPHER ROBIN (*Waving Pooh around wildly*): Pooh makes a motion. He's hungry. (*All start to rise.*)

RED RIDING HOOD: Walk home with me, Christopher Robin, and you can have the rest of my cookies.

CHRISTOPHER ROBIN (*Warily*): What about the Wolf? Pooh doesn't like wolves.

PETER PAN: I'll walk with you and scare him. Don't worry! (*Runs to bookshelf and takes a book.*) Here, Tim— here's my story. You'd better start with me, because I'm so clever! Oh, the cleverness of me! (*Puts book in* TIM's *lap.*)

JACK (*Taking his book from shelf*): And don't forget my story—it's a real thriller! Wait till you get to the Fee Fi Fo Fum part! (JACK *piles his book in* TIM's *lap, and the others follow suit, taking books from the shelf and piling them in* TIM's *chair until he is nearly hidden.*)

ALICE (*With her book*): I think the bit about the Cater-pillar is best.

RED RIDING HOOD (*With her book*): And don't worry about the Wolf—I always get away.

FAIRY GODFATHER: Come along, everybody. (*The story-book people shout "goodbye" and leave.* TIM's *hand waves to them above the pile of books. Suddenly he moves enough so his face is visible.*)

TIM: Fairy Godfather!

FAIRY GODFATHER: Yes, Tim?

TIM: Will you ever come back?

FAIRY GODFATHER: If you ever really need me, Tim, I'll be here! But I think you're going to be *very* busy! (*He exits.*)

SALLY: Tim, were they really here?

TIM (*Opening book and giving her only half his atten-tion*): Who?

SALLY: The book people. Did you see them, too?

TIM (*Starting to read*): Uh huh.

SALLY: Tim, do you believe they were real?

TIM (*Looking at her*): Oh, Sally—they were real pretend, of course, just as they said! And that's the realest kind of real there is. Now don't bother me. I'm reading! (*He returns to his book.* SALLY *stares at the doorway for a minute, and then, taking a book from* TIM's *pile, curls her feet under her in the chair and settles down to read, as the curtain falls slowly.)*

THE END

A Message from Robin Hood

by J. G. Colson

Characters

ROBIN HOOD
WILL STUKELEY
TOM THACKER
LITTLE HUBBERD
MUCH
JACK PEDLAR
DUFFY

LITTLE JOHN
FRIAR TUCK
WILL SCARLET
SHERIFF OF NOTTINGHAM
SOLDIERS
OUTLAWS

TIME: *Early on a summer evening in the days of Robin Hood.*

SETTING: *The grove of the Trysting Oak in Sherwood Forest.*

AT RISE: DUFFY *is sitting on a log with his bow beside him, putting goose feathers on an arrow with the aid of his knife. On his left sit* WILL STUKELEY *and, further downstage,* TOM THACKER. *On his right, downstage, are* MUCH, *who is practicing with his quarterstaff, and* JACK PEDLAR, *who is mending a bow.*

DUFFY: Ow! (*He drops his knife and sucks his finger. The outlaws stop their activities to look at him.*)

STUKELEY: What have you done now, Duffy?

DUFFY: Ow! My finger! I've cut it!

STUKELEY: Let me see. (*He crosses to* DUFFY.)

DUFFY: It hurts, friend Stukeley.

PEDLAR: Don't bother with him, Will, he's soft.

MUCH: Ay, soft! That's what he be—soft! (WILL STUKELEY *examines* DUFFY'S *finger.*)

STUKELEY: Can't see anything.

DUFFY (*Points*): There!

STUKELEY (*In disgust*): That! Pah! A scratch! What do you want to make such a fuss for?

THACKER: 'Cause he's daft, Will.

DUFFY: Don't you call me daft, Tom Thacker. I was just putting this goose feather on this arrow when the knife slipped—

PEDLAR: And we thought we cut our hand off, didn't we, Much?

MUCH: Ay, Jack, that we did. I thought it were his head he'd lost.

STUKELEY: Pah! (*He moves back to his former position.*) What you'd be like in a fight, Duffy, I don't know.

PEDLAR: You wait till you meet the Sheriff's men, Duffy.

THACKER: Soldiers, with swords and lances.

MUCH: That'll be the day, Duffy. That's when the blood will flow thick and fast. You'll see.

DUFFY (*In dismay*): Blood!

MUCH: Ay, blood, Duffy, blood. Many's the time we've sent the soldiers from Nottingham home with their skulls cracked.

DUFFY: Don't say any more, friend Much. I don't like it.

PEDLAR: You wait till Little John comes back. He always tries out new members of Robin's band with his quarter-staff.

THACKER: New members like you, Duffy.

DUFFY: Oh, he does, does he? Where's he gone?

MUCH: Where's he gone! Didn't you hear what Robin said? Be you deaf as well as daft?

STUKELEY: Little John's gone with the rest of the band to look for the Sheriff.

DUFFY: Which sheriff, friend Stukeley?

STUKELEY: The Sheriff of Nottingham.

DUFFY: Where is he?

PEDLAR: He's in Sherwood somewhere looking for us. He wants to hang Robin Hood.

THACKER: And us with him.

DUFFY: He can't do that.

STUKELEY: Oh, yes, he can.

MUCH: But he won't! Don't ye worry, Duffy. Little John'll see to that.

STUKELEY: It's Robin he wants most.

PEDLAR: But Robin's always too clever for him.

DUFFY: Clever! Is Robin Hood clever?

STUKELEY: You'll see how clever, Duffy. The Sheriff's looking for us, but Little John with Will Scarlet and the rest of the band are out looking for the Sheriff.

MUCH: And he doesn't know about it. There be a surprise in store for that Sheriff.

PEDLAR: They're going to meet him four or five miles from here.

MUCH: I wish Robin had let me go with them. (*He flourishes his quarterstaff.*) I be fair aching to use this.

THACKER: Ay, it's too quiet here, Much.

DUFFY: I like it. I like sitting here in the sun making arrows. (*He takes up his knife and resumes whittling arrows.*)

STUKELEY: There's no fun in just idling about. I hate it. But somebody has to wait here, I suppose.

MUCH: It be too dull, Will.

STUKELEY: It won't be so dull when they bring back the Sheriff.

PEDLAR: It won't take Little John long to do that.

DUFFY: Bring back the Sheriff! You can't do that, friend Pedlar.

THACKER: Little John can, and will, Duffy. We shall have him a prisoner here before nightfall.

MUCH: And his soldiers with him.

DUFFY (*Cutting himself again*): Ow!

STUKELEY: Here, give me that. (*He takes the knife and the arrow.*) You'll never make a bowman. I'll finish it for you.

MUCH: A disgrace to the Lincoln green, that's what he be.

THACKER: Why Robin let you join us, I don't know.

MUCH: That be Robin all over. Always looking after some poor fellow that can't look after himself.

DUFFY: What do you mean, friend Much? I can look after myself. I can read and write. That's more than you fellows can do.

MUCH: Ay, you be a proper clerk, Duffy, but you don't be a fighting sort of clerk.

DUFFY: Perhaps I'll learn.

PEDLAR: You'll have to learn a lot more yet, Duffy, before you're as good a fighting man as the Clerk of Copmanhurst.

DUFFY: Ay, Jack Pedlar, those be true words. Friar Tuck, the Clerk of Copmanhurst, be a rare fighter.

STUKELEY: And doesn't he love it! He knows how to use a quarterstaff.

MUCH: That he does, Will, but I haven't set eyes on him all day.

STUKELEY: I have.

MUCH: Where be he, then?

STUKELEY: He was talking to Robin about an hour since. After that I saw him walking through the forest.

DUFFY: Won't he get lost?

MUCH: Lost! Friar Tuck lost! He knows the paths through Sherwood as well as Robin himself.

DUFFY: Oh! I didn't know.

STUKELEY: You'll learn, Duffy. (*He gets up and moves to* DUFFY.) Here's your arrow. Now be careful.

DUFFY: Thank you, friend Stukeley. (*He begins to fit the arrow to the bow.*)

STUKELEY: Some time I'll show you how to flight an arrow properly.

MUCH: He be too daft to learn, Will. (DUFFY *turns towards* MUCH, *pulling the arrow back on the bowstring.*) Hi! You put that bow down, Duffy. I don't want an arrow in me.

DUFFY (*Putting down his bow*): Sorry, Much. Didn't think you were scared. (*The outlaws laugh.*)

MUCH: Scared! Me! I'm not scared. But you be dangerous with that bow and arrow. (LITTLE HUBBERD *enters from between the trees at left.*)

HUBBERD: Where's Robin? They're coming! Where's Robin?

STUKELEY: Steady, Little Hubberd. Who's coming?

HUBBERD: The Sheriff's men. Sherwood's full of them. They're all around us. They're sure to find us here. Where's Robin?

THACKER: He's over there. (*He points right.*) He's resting in his usual place. You know it, Little Hubberd.

HUBBERD: I'll find him. (*He crosses to the left.*)

STUKELEY: Just a moment, Little Hubberd.

HUBBERD (*Turning*): What is it, Will?

STUKELEY: How far away are they?

HUBBERD: About half a mile.

PEDLAR: How many of them?

HUBBERD: About fifty soldiers with the Sheriff. I'll tell Robin. (*He goes out upstage left, between the trees.*)

MUCH (*Rising*): Now for a fight. (*He brandishes his quarterstaff.*)

STUKELEY: Don't be a fool, Much. There are only six or seven of us here. We're no match for them.

MUCH: Oh, yes, we be. Now you'll see the blood flow, Duffy.

DUFFY: Six can't fight fifty, friend Much.

MUCH: Oh, yes, they can. You'll see.

PEDLAR: What's happened to Little John?

STUKELEY: Mayhap he's been beaten.

THACKER: Or captured.

PEDLAR: That Sheriff couldn't beat Little John.

STUKELEY: But Little Hubberd said there were fifty or more soldiers with the Sheriff.

MUCH: Little Hubberd be a big talker at times.

PEDLAR: He's reliable enough.

STUKELEY: We're no match for them, Much.

MUCH: We'll break a few heads afore they catch us.

PEDLAR: They won't catch us. Leave things to Robin; he'll think of something.

STUKELEY: Ay, leave it to Robin.

MUCH (*Looking right*): And here he be. (ROBIN HOOD *enters from the right, followed by* LITTLE HUBBERD. *The outlaws rise to their feet.*)

ROBIN: Ha, my friends, you wear anxious looks.

STUKELEY: The grove is surrounded, Robin.

ROBIN: That I know. Thanks to Little Hubberd's vigilance, we have been warned in time.

MUCH: Let me send a few arrows into them, Robin.

ROBIN: No, Much, we are too few to match them in combat. We will abide here in this Grove of the Trysting Oak. 'Tis well hidden and the Sheriff will pass us by.

MUCH: But we have sworn to capture him.

ROBIN: And keep our oath, we shall. But, good Much, we cannot keep our oath if we are prisoners. Little Hubberd has told me that we are encircled. Little John and the band are several miles to the north.

STUKELEY: Ay, the Sheriff must have outwitted them.

ROBIN: Yes, Will, I'm afraid he did. Little John and Will Scarlet must be still waiting in ambush for the Sheriff.

PEDLAR: And the Sheriff is almost here. What shall we do, Robin?

ROBIN: Send for Little John.

THACKER: That's it. Send for Little John.

ROBIN: Now that we know where the Sheriff and his men are, Little John and his men can attack them from behind.

MUCH: That be sense.

ROBIN (*Producing a scroll from his tunic*): I have written a message to Little John, telling him to return.

DUFFY: May I take it, Robin? I know the forest. I learnt the paths when I was a tinker.

STUKELEY: Better let me go, Robin.

MUCH: I be the man to take it.

ROBIN: Not you, Will, nor you, Much. Duffy shall take it.

DUFFY: Thank you, Robin.

ROBIN: Little John is about four miles to the north, between here and Nottingham. Fetch him and tell him to attack and capture the Sheriff from behind. Take the path by the brook—you know it?

DUFFY: Ay, Robin, over the Stepping Stone Ford.

ROBIN: Follow it and you'll come to him. Give him this message. (ROBIN *hands the scroll to* DUFFY.)

DUFFY: Thank you, Robin.

ROBIN: Read it, Duffy.

DUFFY (*Reading the scroll*): Come at once to the Grove of the Trysting Oak. Robin, his sign.

ROBIN: When he sees that sign, he will act at once. Tell him how we are placed.

DUFFY: I will. Trust me, Robin.

MUCH: I don't think Duffy ought to go, Robin. His wits be that slow.

ROBIN: Don't you trust my judgment?

MUCH: Ay, Robin, we trust you.

ROBIN: Very well, you shall go, Duffy. You have a chance to prove your worth. And Little Hubberd—

HUBBERD: Robin?

ROBIN: Go and keep careful watch. Inform us immediately of any danger.

HUBBERD (*Moving to the left*): I go, good Robin. (*He goes out down left.*)

ROBIN: Come, Duffy, I will set you on your way.

DUFFY: Many thanks, friend Robin. (ROBIN *and* DUFFY *move upstage and go off left. The outlaws seat themselves on the ground.* MUCH *sits on the log.*)

PEDLAR: I don't like this.

THACKER: Can't think what made Robin do it.

MUCH: Now if I'd gone—

STUKELEY: If you had gone, you'd have broken your staff on the first Sheriff's officer you met.

MUCH: That I would, Will. I'd have cracked the skulls of a few of 'em.

STUKELEY: Robin knew that. That's why he didn't send you.

MUCH: What be you getting at, Will Stukeley?

STUKELEY: Robin didn't want his messenger to fight, Much. He needed someone who would hide if necessary, and get his message to Little John.

PEDLAR: Didn't want Much, the fighting miller, for that sort of work.

MUCH: And ye don't want a witless wight like Duffy, either. Now you mark my words—no good be coming out of this. (ROBIN HOOD *re-enters.*)

ROBIN: No good will come out of what, Much?

MUCH: Sending that soft Duffy to fetch Little John and the others.

ROBIN: Poor old Much. You're too anxious.

STUKELEY: We're all anxious, Robin. We don't feel sure that Duffy has the brains to reach the band.

ROBIN: Brains or no brains, Will, Duffy is a good workman. I watched him creep away. Not one of us could have done better.

MUCH: But he be no fighter.

ROBIN: I don't want him to fight.

THACKER: There'll be no help coming for us if he gets caught, Robin.

PEDLAR: They'll hang us all.

ROBIN: They won't. Little John will come.

MUCH: If Duffy gets to him.

STUKELEY: But Little John's miles away, Robin. He can't get here for an hour or more.

ROBIN: Well, we'll just lie low and wait, Will. (LITTLE HUBBERD *enters excitedly*.)

HUBBERD: The Sheriff's men are all over the forest. There's a soldier behind every tree. They're all round us and coming closer.

ROBIN: Don't be alarmed, Little Hubberd. This grove is well hidden.

THACKER: They'll not find us.

HUBBERD: I tell you they will, Tom. They're heading this way.

MUCH (*Handling his staff*): At last I be going to use this.

ROBIN: Go, Little Hubberd, and keep watch.

HUBBERD (*Moving towards left*): I'll climb into a tall tree—

MUCH: And don't ye go to sleep. (LITTLE HUBBERD *goes out down left*.)

PEDLAR: He won't.

STUKELEY: What next, Robin?

ROBIN: All we can do is wait. I believe the Sheriff's men know more about us than you think.

STUKELEY: Do you mean they have spies, Robin?

ROBIN: I can't say, Will, for certain. You know there's a heavy price on our heads.

STUKELEY: Perhaps some wayfaring tinker or roaming charcoal-burner may have let slip a careless word.

THACKER: Maybe so, Will.

ROBIN: Maybe not. The forest wanderers are loyal. Now we'll be quiet and lay low till Little John comes.

MUCH: Do ye think he will, Robin?

ROBIN: I'm sure of it, Much. Little John will get the Sheriff of Nottingham. (*The* SHERIFF OF NOTTINGHAM *enters silently from upstage right.* SOLDIERS, *with their bows drawn, take up positions covering the outlaws from all sides.*)

SHERIFF: Little John won't. Aha! The Sheriff of Notting-ham has got you. (*He moves downstage.*)

MUCH: Trapped!

SHERIFF: Don't move, any of you—unless you want an arrow in your heart. I've caught you this time, Robin Hood.

ROBIN: My old friend, the Sheriff. So we meet again.

SHERIFF: For the last time. There's no escape for you, Robin Hood. Try to get away and my soldiers will shoot you down like the dog you are.

ROBIN: Well, you've brought enough men. (*He notices* MUCH *moving.*) No. Keep still, Much, and you others. I order it. (LITTLE HUBBERD *is brought in struggling between two soldiers.*)

HUBBERD: Let me go, knaves. Keep your hands off me.

SHERIFF: Another of them! Knock him on the head. That'll quieten him.

ROBIN: Stop, Little Hubberd. Don't struggle. (*Turns to* SHERIFF.) There's no need to injure a prisoner, Sheriff.

HUBBERD: I didn't see the soldiers, Robin. Jumped on me from behind a tree, they did.

SHERIFF: That's the last one. Now we have all who were left here.

ROBIN: How do you know that?

SHERIFF: You'd be surprised if I told you, Master Robin Hood. You're not so clever as you think. I know all that goes on in this grove.

MUCH: He be a proper cleversides, be the Sheriff.

SHERIFF: Silence, knave! (*The* SOLDIERS *have advanced on* ROBIN HOOD.)

ROBIN: You have enough men, Sheriff.

SHERIFF: Too many for you this time. I made sure of that. You've sneaked out of my hands before, but you won't this time. No, by thunder, you won't. Take him and disarm him, you men. See to his followers, too. (SOLDIERS *move towards the outlaws, two to each, one covering with a bow and arrow, the other with a sword.*)

1ST SOLDIER: Yes, my lord.

SHERIFF: And don't let them get away.

2ND SOLDIER: We won't, my lord.

MUCH (*As a* SOLDIER *touches him*): Keep your hands off.

ROBIN: Stop, Much. Fighting is of no avail.

SHERIFF: So you have come to your senses at last, Robin Hood. I'm pleased you've brains enough to realize there's no escape.

ROBIN: You've caught me for once, Sheriff. I thought our grove was securely hidden. Tell me, Sheriff, how did you manage to find it?

SHERIFF: That's a secret, Robin Hood, but—yes—(*He looks off right*) you shall learn in a moment. (DUFFY *enters from down right.*)

PEDLAR: Watch out, Duffy! Go back! (*One of the* SOLDIERS *moves towards* DUFFY *with pointed sword.*)

SHERIFF: Stop, you fool! You touch him with that sword and you'll rot in the deepest dungeon in Nottingham! (*The* SOLDIER *lowers his sword.*)

STUKELEY: So you didn't get through, Duffy.

SHERIFF: Get through! Ho! Ho! Get through! What fools these outlaws are. (*He approaches* DUFFY *and slaps him heartily on the back.*) Well done, Robert, my boy. I'm proud of you.

MUCH: Robert? His boy? This smells of treachery.

SHERIFF (*Turning to* MUCH): Treachery! Loyalty, you mean, fellow. This is my son, Robert.

DUFFY (*Gloating*): Ay, Daft Duffy is the Sheriff's son. You fools! You poor fools! Robin Hood and his Merry Men! Pah! Haven't the brains of a gnat. I just took your message to my father and showed him the way to the grove.

SHERIFF: And here we are. Thanks to you, Robert, the clever Robin Hood is captured at last.

DUFFY: The not-so-clever Robin Hood you mean, Father.

MUCH: The scoundrel. Let's make a fight of it, Robin.

ROBIN: No, Much. We are outnumbered.

MUCH: I told ye not to send that Duffy.

SHERIFF: Come, Robert, we'd better get these outlaws to Nottingham.

DUFFY: And the reward, Father? Don't forget the reward.

SHERIFF: You shall have it. One thousand crowns for Robin Hood and two hundred for each of the outlaws.

MUCH: Two hundred crowns for me! Wouldn't my old mother be pleased if she knew I was worth that.

SHERIFF: Robert, my boy, you will be rich. Er—perhaps we can share the reward—just you and I.

DUFFY: We'll see about that later, Father. It wouldn't look well for you to take any part of it really, would it?

SHERIFF: Why not, Robert?

DUFFY: Well, it's *your* duty to suppress outlaws, not mine. You couldn't have done your duty without my help.

PEDLAR: The help of a traitor.

THACKER: A treacherous spy.

DUFFY: That's enough from you. You robbers! You common outlaws! I'll teach you to respect your betters before I've done with you. I'll have you all thrown into the dungeons. That'll make you change your tune. Come, Father, let's get these twisty knaves out of Sherwood.

MUCH: Twisty knaves! You wait, Duffy!

DUFFY: Silence!

MUCH: This is what comes of sending the wrong man for Little John.

ROBIN: The wrong man, Much? (LITTLE JOHN, SCARLET *and numerous* OUTLAWS *come silently in from upstage right and left. Some have their bows drawn while others carry quarterstaffs. They are as yet unseen by* SHERIFF *and his followers.*)

SHERIFF: The wrong man with a vengeance! (*He roars with laughter.*) This will amuse the people of Nottingham. The great Robin Hood sends Robert, the Sheriff's son, to capture his own father.

SOLDIERS: Ha! Ha! Ha! (*The* OUTLAWS *close in.* ROBIN HOOD *has seen them.*)

ROBIN: Very funny, Sheriff. But I sent the right man. I sent Duffy for his father. I knew he was a spy, Sheriff. I knew he would bring you to me.

SHERIFF: I don't believe it.

DUFFY (*To* ROBIN): Why?

ROBIN: Well, Duffy, I wanted a thousand crowns or so.

SHERIFF: Bravado! Mere bravado! Well, we've come, Robin Hood. Now what are you going to do?

ROBIN: Just hold you for ransom.

SHERIFF: Hold us for ransom! Ha! Ha! You're coming with us to Nottingham, and we shall claim the reward for putting you in jail.

ROBIN: I'm staying here. Look behind you, Sheriff. (*The* SHERIFF, DUFFY *and the* SOLDIERS *see the* OUTLAWS.)

SHERIFF: Betrayed! Someone will suffer for this, by thunder.

ROBIN: Welcome, Little John. You're just in time.

LITTLE JOHN: Don't move, any of you. Take their weapons, Scarlet.

SCARLET (*To the* SOLDIERS): Give me your swords. No nonsense! (SCARLET *and the other* OUTLAWS *proceed to disarm the* SOLDIERS.)

MUCH: This be better. (*He turns to the* SOLDIER *who was guarding him.*) My turn now. (*He picks up his quarterstaff and flourishes it.*)

LITTLE JOHN: Friar Tuck brought your message, Robin. I came straight away.

ROBIN: You have done well, Little John.

LITTLE JOHN: I've brought two hundred men. (*Blows his horn*) That will bring them. We took the soldiers by surprise. They're not fighting men. They soon gave in or fled. (*There is an answering hail from offstage.*) That means that all is well. (FRIAR TUCK *enters from down right.*)

STUKELEY: The worthy Friar.

TUCK: Hail, Robin Hood!

ROBIN: Greetings, Friar Tuck. So you have accomplished your mission. Good work, Friar.

TUCK: An easy task, Robin. We made prisoners of some of the soldiers; the rest fled back to Nottingham. (*A* SOLDIER *rushes in from down right, near* MUCH.)

SOLDIER: The wood's filled with outlaws. They've taken most of us.

MUCH (*Tapping him on the head with his quarterstaff*): We've captured you, too. (*He shakes him.*)

SOLDIER: Ow!

MUCH: Give me that sword. (*He takes the* SOLDIER'S *sword.*) Just what I be wanting. (DUFFY *moves towards the trees near* LITTLE HUBBERD.)

HUBBERD: Oh no you don't. (*He taps him on the head with his quarterstaff.*)

MUCH: Give him another, Little Hubberd. Give him one for me!

ROBIN: Enough! Do not ill-treat him. He's worth a thousand crowns to us.

PEDLAR: And the Sheriff, Robin?

ROBIN: The Sheriff, Jack, is worth two thousand.

SHERIFF: You can't hold us for ransom, Robin Hood.

ROBIN: Now, Sheriff, I can. I shall keep you and your rascally son here as our guests until three thousand crowns are paid for your release. I guessed your son was a spy and knew he would deliver to you the message destined for Little John.

STUKELEY: And we thought you had made a mistake, Robin.

TUCK: There was no mistake. Robin knew there was a spy in the camp.

ROBIN: So my old friend, Friar Tuck, took the proper message an hour before I sent Duffy.

LITTLE JOHN: And I came here as quick as an arrow from a bow.

STUKELEY: Just in time, Little John.

SHERIFF: I'll get even with you for this, Robin Hood.

MUCH: Three thousand crowns first, Sheriff—then we'll let ye start again.

THACKER: But think of something better next time, Sheriff.

PEDLAR: Don't send Daft Duffy again.

ROBIN: Do you intend to pay, Sheriff?

SHERIFF: The ransom shall be paid. My son can fetch the money.

ROBIN: Your son would fetch more of your soldiers, Sheriff. He stays here, too. Friar Tuck will take a message for you to Nottingham.

SHERIFF: Very well.

ROBIN: Now, Scarlet, and you, Much, go kill a fat buck. Kindle a fire, Will Stukeley. The Sheriff and his son shall sit down to the merriest feast ever held in Sherwood Forest. (*Curtain*)

THE END

A Turtle, a Flute
and the General's Birthday
by Lavinia R. Davis

Characters

LUDWIG VON BRAM, *aged 12, cook's boy in the Continental Army*

MASTER BRIDGEMAN, *chief cook*

PRIVATE LANKY ⎱ *cook's helpers*
PRIVATE SCOPES ⎰

DESERTER

MR. WOODSTOCK ⎱ *members of the Fourth Artillery Band*
BANDMASTER ⎰

GENERAL WASHINGTON

BARON STEUBEN

COLONEL JOHN LAURENS

MARTHA WASHINGTON

MAJOR NATHANAEL GREENE

"MAD ANTHONY" WAYNE

OTHER OFFICERS

THREE FLUTISTS

DRUMMERS, FIFE PLAYERS, PIPERS, FLUTISTS *and* OTHER BAND MEMBERS

168 A TURTLE, A FLUTE AND THE GENERAL'S BIRTHDAY

Scene 1

Time: *February 22nd. Early in the morning.*
Setting: *Valley Forge. The kitchen and dining room of General Washington's headquarters. The kitchen end of the room is divided from the dining end by a screen. The kitchen has an open fireplace, cranes with black pots, a plain table and stools, cooking utensils, and a sideboard with china and pewter on it. The dining room has a large table with plain chairs.*
At Rise: Master Bridgeman *and* Private Scopes *are in the kitchen.* Bridgeman *is sharpening a knife and* Scopes *is cleaning up at the hearth.* Private Lanky *comes in, carrying two buckets of water.*

Bridgeman: Where is that lazy lout of a cook's boy? Where is Ludwig? He is late!
Lanky (*Putting down water*): Right here behind me. I saw him when I went to fetch the water. It seems he slept through reveille.
Ludwig (*Hurrying in with his flute tied to string around his waist*): I am sorry, Master Bridgeman. I truly am. But I had the most amazing dream. It was that I, Ludwig von Bram, was playing the flute for General Washington! Then Private Lanky told me that tonight there was to be a banquet to celebrate the General's birthday, and that the Fourth Artillery Band was to play. It seems almost a miracle!
Bridgeman: I'll miracle you for being late on such a day! Here I am, chief cook of the whole Continental Army, asked to prepare a banquet for General Washington and his lady, and I have nothing fit for a pig to cook with. I have half a mind to put you into the stew pot, young Ludwig von Bram.
Ludwig (*Dodging a cuff on the ears*): But Master Bridge-

man, I did not know it was the General's birthday. I did not hear until just now that Martha Washington had come from Virginia.

BRIDGEMAN (*Searching for coat and moving with* LANKY *and* SCOPES *towards door*): Oh, you did not know. Bah! If you paid less attention to that precious flute of yours and more to what your elders and betters were saying, you would have heard as soon as I did myself. But now, boy, set to work. Sweep and clean the dining room. Rake out the ashes, polish the spit and tend the kitchen fire. Lanky, Scopes and I are off to the quartermaster's for supplies. So step lively, boy! 'Twill go hard with you if all is not shipshape at our return.

LUDWIG (*Reaching for broom*): Yes, sir. Yes, Master Bridgeman. I will do as you say. (BRIDGEMAN, LANKY, *and* SCOPES *exit.* LUDWIG *goes into the dining room to sweep. The flute gets in his way and he puts it gently, almost reverently, on the dining table.*) Oh, how I wish I could play the flute for General Washington. (*He works as he talks, but his work gradually slows down.*) They say he is very fond of flute music, and this is such a fine flute. Why, Grandfather Van Zarn says that when he was in the Hussars Band in Bavaria, there was not a finer flute in the whole country. (*He keeps looking at the flute as he talks about it. Finally, he can't resist it, and he picks it up and sits down before the kitchen fireplace. He strokes it lovingly, then begins to play. He plays a simple tune, then breaks into "Yankee Doodle."*) Ah, that's a brave tune. 'Tis no wonder that every man in camp, from the General down, feels new heart in him when he hears it. (*He puts the flute to his lips again as* BRIDGEMAN, SCOPES, *and* LANKY *enter.*)

BRIDGEMAN: So! Look, Scopes! Look, Lanky! This is what happens when my back is turned. This lazy rascal has let my fire go out. (BRIDGEMAN *cuffs* LUDWIG *about the head and shoulders, while* LANKY *stoops to fan fire and* SCOPES *puts down bundles of grain, etc., which they have brought from the quartermaster's stores.*)

SCOPES: Perhaps it is not so grave a matter after all. We can soon set it going again. If we only had enough good kindling!

BRIDGEMAN: If, if, if! If we had enough of anything— wood, flour, spices, meat, cream, or butter! But no, we have next to nothing and yet I, a master chef, am expected to prepare a banquet. And to make matters worse, I am cursed with a good-for-nothing flute player to work in my kitchen. Give me that flute, you lazy young rascal. I have half a mind to use that for kindling.

LUDWIG: No. No, sir! Please! The flute belongs to my grandfather Van Zarn. He said it is the finest flute—

BRIDGEMAN: Oh, he did, did he? Well, 'twould serve you right if I were to beat you black and blue with your grandfather's flute and *then* use it for kindling! This is *too much.*

LANKY (*Straightens up from fire and gives* LUDWIG *a push toward door*): Send the lad off, Master Bridgeman. Let him find other kindling, or perhaps a bit of food.

SCOPES (*Giving* LUDWIG *another push*): Ay, that's a sound notion. After all, he might snare a bird, or at the least find some pine boughs to keep out the chill. (*He whispers in* LUDWIG's *ear.*) Run, lad. Run for your life.

BRIDGEMAN: And come back with food or fuel, if you value your skin! If you come back empty-handed, I shall beat you until your own mother would not recognize you. I'll teach you a lesson you'll never forget. I'll boil you in oil! (*Curtain falls.*)

*　　　*　　　*

SCENE 2

TIME: *A few minutes later.*

SETTING: *A country path. (If desired, this scene may be played in front of the curtain.)*

AT RISE: LUDWIG *enters left and* DESERTER *enters right.*

DESERTER: Well, lad, where are you going? Had your fill of this mockery at last?

LUDWIG: Yes. No. I do not dare go back to Master Bridgeman empty-handed, and I have not found as much as a sparrow to bring to him.

DESERTER: Better do as I am doing, then. Take French leave of the Continental Army. 'Tis a hopeless cause.

LUDWIG: You mean run away for good? Desert?

DESERTER (*Sneering and looking cautiously around him*): That is one way of looking at it. Older and wiser heads think the time has come to go back to His Majesty's forces. At least the English feed and clothe their soldiers.

LUDWIG (*Looking down at his flute*): I cannot go. You see, when my grandfather lent me this, he said it was because he could trust me to use it as—as a soldier and musician. I cannot desert.

DESERTER (*Going offstage left*): More fool you! I doubt if a cook's boy has much time to play a flute. You spend your days cleaning up the swill which in this wretched army passes for food. Well, I am off.

LUDWIG: Goodbye. (*He looks down at his flute and begins talking to himself.*) I can play now. And then—and then—I shall not be so frightened of Master Bridgeman. (*He plays "Yankee Doodle." MR. WOODSTOCK, holding a large turtle, comes on stage right as LUDWIG finishes.*)

MR. WOODSTOCK: Ah, good day there. Look at what I have caught! And 'twas your music brought me luck. I have spent the whole morning searching that pond over

yonder, and slap me if I saw as much as the claw
of a turtle till you began to play.

LUDWIG (*Fingering his flute and looking hungrily at the
turtle*): 'Tis a mighty fine creature. If only I could
catch one for soup!

MR. WOODSTOCK: Not a hope, lad. Not a hope in the
world. There is not another turtle left in the whole of
creation. Or at least not in this corner of it, or my
name is not Jonathan Woodstock.

LUDWIG: But I must find another. I must. Master Bridgeman could make a soup out of it for the banquet tonight.

MR. WOODSTOCK (*Reaching out for* LUDWIG'S *flute*): That
is an uncommon fine flute that you have there. Mind
if I try it?

LUDWIG: Yes. No. I must go catch another turtle.

MR. WOODSTOCK: There is not a chance, boy. Not the
least bit of use even looking. I tell you I searched every
inch of the pond, and there is not another. (*He plays
a few bars on the flute.*)

LUDWIG: Sir. Sir! I want—I need—I'd give anything I
own for another turtle.

MR. WOODSTOCK (*Flipping the flute casually as he speaks*):
Oh, I don't doubt you'd like one. There is not any
one of us in the whole of Valley Forge who would
not enjoy a good bowl of soup.

LUDWIG: No! No! I would not taste it myself. I want the
turtle for General Washington.

MR. WOODSTOCK (*Holding flute out of reach over* LUDWIG'S
head): Enough to pay for it with your flute?

LUDWIG: Oh, no! I can't! It—it isn't really mine!

MR. WOODSTOCK: So the flute is not yours! I might have
known it was stolen.

LUDWIG: But it isn't. Grandfather Van Zarn gave me the
flute to play in the band. He did not know they would

set me to work in the kitchen as a scullery boy. Grandfather Van Zarn played the flute himself in the Hussars Band in Bavaria.

MR. WOODSTOCK: So that is how the land lies, is it? Well, I shall let you prove your story. You may take the turtle, and after I know that the General has supped on it, I shall return your flute. Meanwhile, a friend of mine will know if it really did come from Bavaria.

LUDWIG: It did. I swear it.

MR. WOODSTOCK: What is your name, lad?

LUDWIG: Ludwig von Bram, sir. My grandfather brought the flute with him when he came to America.

MR. WOODSTOCK (*Putting down turtle and pocketing flute*): Capital. Excellent. And if this story is true, you shall soon have the flute back. But now, my lad, don't forget the turtle. (*He walks quickly off right.*)

LUDWIG: My flute! My beautiful flute! Shall I ever see it again? (*He picks up turtle and exits left, wiping away tears on his ragged sleeve.*)

*   *   *

SCENE 3

TIME: *That evening.*

SETTING: *Same as Scene 1.*

AT RISE: GENERAL WASHINGTON, MARTHA WASHINGTON, BARON STEUBEN, MAJOR NATHANAEL GREENE, "MAD ANTHONY" WAYNE, COLONEL JOHN LAURENS, *and* OTHER OFFICERS *are at the table in the dining room being served by* LANKY *and* SCOPES. *The table is set for a banquet, with white tablecloth and silver candlesticks.* LANKY *carries a pudding from the kitchen to the dining room as* SCOPES *goes from dining room to kitchen. The people at the table pantomime conversation.* LUDWIG, *heartsick over the loss of his flute, sits dejectedly in the kitchen, not even looking towards the dining room. BRIDGEMAN is busy at fireplace.*

SCOPES: Come, Ludwig, look in at the party. 'Tis a brave sight to see the General celebrate.

LUDWIG (*Shaking his head*): No. No, thank you.

BRIDGEMAN: Cheer up, lad. Never be downhearted; that is my motto. Why, only this morning I was fearful about this banquet, and then the turtle appeared as though by magic.

LUDWIG: But my flute! I gave it to Mr. Woodstock. (*He is interrupted by the sound of band music outside. The clear note of a flute is heard above the snare drum, pipes, tabors, oboe, etc.*)

SCOPES: Hark! There is the sound of a flute this moment. They say the General plays one himself, back at home in Virginia.

GENERAL WASHINGTON: Major Greene, be so kind as to bid the bandmaster and the flutists come in. Their music is capital.

MAJOR GREENE: Yes, General. At once, sir. (*He goes out, then returns with* BANDMASTER, MR. WOODSTOCK, *and* THREE FLUTISTS. *Other* BAND MEMBERS *may also enter, if desired.* MARTHA WASHINGTON *and* OFFICERS *applaud.*)

MARTHA WASHINGTON: Delightful! Excellent!

COLONEL LAURENS: Indeed it is, ma'am. A worthy finish for a great occasion. (LUDWIG *knocks into* BRIDGEMAN *on his way into dining room.* LANKY *and* SCOPES *try to keep him back but he reaches* MR. WOODSTOCK, *who is beside* GENERAL WASHINGTON.)

LUDWIG: Mr. Woodstock. My flute. My grandfather's flute. The General has supped on turtle soup, so remember your promise. You said you would—

MR. WOODSTOCK: Sh. Later. Not now.

GENERAL WASHINGTON: Bandmaster, what is the meaning of this? I should like an explanation of this—er—unusual interruption.

BANDMASTER (*Clicking heels and saluting*): Yes, sir. Woodstock, tell the General the story you told me.

WOODSTOCK: General Washington, sir, this is Ludwig von Bram's flute. His grandfather brought it from Bavaria. I was not sure it was Bavarian myself until I showed it to the bandmaster. You see, sir, young Ludwig seemed too ragged and hungry to have come by such a beautiful Bavarian instrument honestly. When I met him this morning, he wanted a turtle which I had just caught. He said that he did not want it for himself, but for Your Excellency's table. So I thought it wise to bargain with him and keep the flute until I was sure the turtle actually reached the headquarters kitchen.

GENERAL WASHINGTON: Indeed it did reach the kitchen. And Bridgeman made a fine soup out of it.

MARTHA WASHINGTON: Delicious. I do not know when I have tasted better.

OFFICERS (*Ad lib*): Capital. Excellent. Splendid! (*Etc.*)

GENERAL WASHINGTON (*Turning back to* WOODSTOCK): This sounds like a fair bargain faithfully kept. So now give the lad his flute. I should like to hear him play. (LUDWIG *grasps flute, puts his fingers around it, starts to play, becomes desperately shy and trys to scuttle out of the room.* MARTHA WASHINGTON *stops him.*)

MARTHA WASHINGTON: The General has asked you to play for him, Ludwig. You must play a tune for his birthday.

LUDWIG (*Trembling with shyness*): But what can I play, ma'am, for so great an occasion?

MARTHA WASHINGTON: Do you know "Who Is the Man," Ludwig? The one that begins, "Do good and evil quite eschew; seek peace and after it pursue?" (LUDWIG *nods and begins to play, tentatively at first, then with growing confidence. As he finishes, all applaud.*)

GENERAL WASHINGTON: Well played, lad. Excellent.

MARTHA WASHINGTON: Beautiful, Ludwig, beautiful!

ANTHONY WAYNE (*Bowing to* GENERAL *and* MARTHA WASHINGTON): And a splendid choice of song. Not one of us here can listen to that noble song without thinking of Your Excellency.

OFFICERS (*Ad lib*): Hear! Hear! Encore! (*Etc.*)

COLONEL LAURENS: Play us another tune, lad. (LUDWIG, *once more confident, plays "Yankee Doodle." As he finishes, there is a roar of applause.*)

GENERAL WASHINGTON: A good tune, that one. A tune to be proud of. The British first played it to make fun of the Colonists in Boston. Then the good Bostonians took it up and played it back to the British. Since then it has swept the country, so that now it belongs to each and every one of us.

MAJOR GREENE: And 'twas played like a master.

BARON STEUBEN (*In German accent*): A master musician! General Washington! In this country why do you keep such a one cleaning the pots? (*Laughter and applause*)

GENERAL WASHINGTON: Why indeed, Baron? Major Greene, Bandmaster! This boy is to be transferred to the Fourth Artillery Band.

MAJOR GREENE *and* BANDMASTER: Yes, sir!

LUDWIG (*As though to himself*): It is like my dream, only better. I would rather play my flute with the Fourth Artillery Band than with the Royal Hussars in Bavaria.

BRIDGEMAN: But, General, I cannot lose my scullery boy. He has just begun to be useful, Your Excellency, due to the most careful and kindly training on my part.

GENERAL WASHINGTON (*Dismisses* BRIDGEMAN *with a nod*): Major Greene! The order of Ludwig von Bram's transfer is to take effect at once. Now, play "Yankee Doodle" again, lad. 'Tis a good air with which to end the celebration.

LUDWIG (*Draws himself up very straight and salutes*): Yes, sir! (*He plays as the curtain falls.*)

THE END

Valentine's Day

by Lucille M. Duvall

Characters

TWO FAIRIES
TEAMSTER'S VOICE
LITTLE VALENTINE, *an orphan*
TEARDROP DAN
JACK THE KNAVE, *leader of Elves*
TOMPKINS

PETERKINS
A BAND OF ELVES
QUEEN OF THE FAIRIES
KING
KING'S FOLLOWERS
OFFSTAGE VOICES

TIME: *Nightfall.*

SETTING: *A forest glen.*

AT RISE: *There is a quiet hush over the forest. An owl hoots in the distance. Two figures creep in from right stage. They are* FAIRIES, *and they move stealthily toward a fallen tree at the center of the stage. The* 1ST FAIRY *carries a covered tray.*

1ST FAIRY: Oh-h, I dropped one.

2ND FAIRY: Sh-h! Someone will hear you. (*As the* 1ST FAIRY *stops to search for the missing article*) Never mind the one you dropped. We'll have enough without that one, and no one can find it in the dark. Come now, we must hide them quickly before the elves miss us and come looking for us.

1ST FAIRY: Are you sure they're safe here?

2ND FAIRY: As safe as anywhere I know with Jack the Knave and his wicked men abroad.

1ST FAIRY (*Sniffing the contents of the tray*): M-m-m-m. They smell so delicious. I hate to part with them. Why do we have to leave them here?

2ND FAIRY: It's part of the magic charm, don't you remember? The recipe said—
"Bake well, until done.
Then leave a while
Twixt moon and morning sun
In the dell."

1ST FAIRY: And then, they're really magic?

2ND FAIRY: Of course. Why else would the queen want them for the king's birthday?
"He who eats the magic tart
Becomes one of us
Forever young, pure in heart—
A true fairy."

1ST FAIRY: The king has tried so hard to be a good ruler. It's a shame Jack the Knave and his thieving band have caused him so much trouble.

2ND FAIRY: That's because both the King and Jack are part mortal, and the fairy prophecy says no mortal can live in fairyland without causing trouble.

1ST FAIRY: And that's why the queen is coming to us?

2ND FAIRY: Yes, I told her about the magic tarts. They can be baked only once in a hundred years. This is the night—the last full moon of winter before the spring begins. (*The sound of children's gay voices can be heard offstage.*)

1ST FAIRY: Hark! What's that?

TEAMSTER'S VOICE (*Offstage*): Load up! We're off. Is everyone here? Count noses, please.

2ND FAIRY: Mortals! Can't you tell by their voices? We passed them over on the hill, remember? They had sleds and a big bonfire. Every year they have a sleighing party.

1st FAIRY: Of course, I remember. They're the children from the monastery orphanage, aren't they? Listen, I hear someone coming.

2nd FAIRY: Quick, hide the magic tarts in this tree. We must not be found here! It may be the elves and they'll guess our secret. (1st FAIRY *hides the tray in the tree trunk, and they slip quietly out left stage.*)

TEAMSTER'S VOICE (*Offstage*): Here we go. Giddap, Dobbin! (*Great jingle of sleigh bells as children's voices die off in the distance.* LITTLE VALENTINE *comes running in from left.*)

LITTLE VALENTINE: Wait! Wait! Don't leave. I'm coming. Wait! (*As voices recede in distance,* LITTLE VALENTINE *drops down on the log, tired out and frightened.*) Oh, how could they go without me? I didn't mean to get separated from them. But it was such a lovely hill. The moon made a beautiful path right down here into the heart of the forest. And now they've gone without me and I'm afraid they won't even miss me until morning. Everyone will be so tired that no one will check the rooms tonight. Oh dear, oh dear, what shall I do? (*Cries softly. As he sobs,* TEARDROP DAN *appears at his shoulder.*) Who are you?

DAN: I'm Teardrop Dan, good humor man. I come whenever you're in trouble to try and cheer you up.

LITTLE VALENTINE: But I've never seen you before.

DAN: I can only come to fairy places.

LITTLE VALENTINE: Fairy places?

DAN: Yes, you're in the dell—the fairies' meeting place. Didn't you know?

LITTLE VALENTINE: No. (*Looks around*) It *is* different, isn't it? It doesn't seem to be cold and there's no snow here.

DAN (*Pointing in a circle*): See, you're safe in the magic circle. Storms and human troubles cannot bother you here.

LITTLE VALENTINE (*Entranced*): A magic circle with no troubles. How wonderful!

DAN: No human troubles. But alas, there's fairy trouble to spare. Believe me, I've been working overtime. (*Looks at his rotund figure anxiously*) If this keeps up, my store of good humor will disappear.

LITTLE VALENTINE: But fairies have no troubles. Valentine told me.

DAN: Who's Valentine?

LITTLE VALENTINE: One of the monks at the orphanage. He's my favorite. He found me in the hills one night. No one knows where I came from or who I really am.

DAN: Don't you know who you are?

LITTLE VALENTINE: Oh, yes, I'm Little Valentine. Everyone calls me that because, you see, I belong to Valentine.

DAN: Fair enough. But if he says fairies are always gay, he just hasn't seen any of them since it happened.

LITTLE VALENTINE: What happened?

DAN: The war. You see, fairies never used to fight. But when our queen chose a part mortal to be king, human troubles came into the kingdom.

LITTLE VALENTINE: You mean the king is bad?

DAN: Oh, no, he's very good. But he has a cousin, Jack the Knave, who has gathered up a band of cutthroat elves and is trying to take over the kingdom. You see, there is a fairy prophecy that says no mortal can rule in fairyland without causing trouble. These elves have caused us so much trouble that the king has promised the fairies he will leave us and turn the kingdom back to the queen at midnight tonight. It is his birthday, and it will be a very sad one for all of us.

LITTLE VALENTINE: Is there nothing that you can do?

DAN: One of the fairies is baking some magic tarts. If they are successful, they can change the king into a full-fledged fairy, and then the black elves will have no power against him.

LITTLE VALENTINE: Then there's nothing to worry about.

DAN: But of course there is. It's a very, very magic recipe and can be used only once in a hundred years. If anything should go wrong, all would be lost. Oh, my, I hear tears falling, don't you? (*Both listen intently.*) I'll bet it's the queen again. Poor thing! I must go to her right away. Are you all right now?

LITTLE VALENTINE: Yes, somehow I'm not frightened any more.

DAN: Good! I'll tell you what. Curl up here and go to sleep. Morning will be here before you know it, and then you'll be able to find your way home. That is, if they haven't come to find you before that.

LITTLE VALENTINE: Maybe I will. I am tired. (*Settles himself comfortably, as* DAN *hurries off left. There is silence for several moments, as* LITTLE VALENTINE *drops off to sleep. There is the scamper of footsteps offstage, and* JACK THE KNAVE, *disguised in a cloak, tiptoes in.*)

JACK THE KNAVE: Pssst, are you there, men? To the conquest. Heigh ho! (TOMPKINS, PETERKINS, *and* ELVES, *armed, rush in and run all over the stage, dancing madly here and there until the leader calls*) Attention! (*As* ELVES *await his command, he skips lightly to center of stage but stops short at the sight of* LITTLE VALENTINE *asleep.*) What's this? Investigate, Tompkins.

TOMPKINS: I-I-I think it-it's a mortal.

JACK: A mortal? In the glen? Impossible! Take another look. (*Several of the* ELVES *hurry to look at* LITTLE VALENTINE *asleep.*)

TOMPKINS: A-a-a dead one, sir.

JACK (*Bending over to investigate the sleeping figure*): It's not dead. It's asleep. Leave it there. We've no time to lose. Peterkins!

PETERKINS (*Speaking briskly*): Yes, sir.

JACK: You're sure this is the spot?

PETERKINS: Yes, sir. I was hiding behind the kitchen stove when they made their plans. I heard them say the glen.

JACK: Why they'd go to all the trouble of hiding tarts in the glen I'll never know. To the search, men! We must find them. (*The* ELVES *scatter around looking here and there.*)

TOMPKINS (*Picking up the lost cookie*): L-l-look, I've found something. It looks like a tart. (ELVES *stop search.*)

JACK: Don't pay any attention to him. It's probably a stone. We're not looking for a single tart. We're looking for a tray of them. Now where would I hide a tray of tarts? (*Looks around the glen*) Why in that tree trunk, of course. (*Darts over to tree*) Stop the search! Here they are. (*Pulls out tray*)

PETERKINS: That's the very one, sir, the very one.

JACK: Magic, huh? They look like regular tarts to me.

ELVES (*Ad lib*): And oh-h, they smell like tarts. Can we eat them? (*Etc.*)

TOMPKINS: Oh, no, they're for the king. Peterkins promised me you'd do the king no harm if I let him hide in the kitchen. H-he said you were going to help the queen catch Jack the Knave.

JACK (*Taking off cloak and pointing to large heart on front of costume*): I'm Jack the Knave, stupid.

TOMPKINS: Y-Y-You're Jack the Knave? Oh, oh, oh, what have I done! I was trying to help the queen. I'm a good elf.

JACK: Oh, my, how tiresome. Tie him up, fellows, and see if you can keep him quiet. (ELVES *tie the protesting* TOMPKINS *to a tree, gagging him with a handkerchief.*)

Now then, let's see. You say the queen is coming here?

PETERKINS: The fairies are bringing her. The king is to meet her here at twelve for the surprise.

JACK: At twelve, you say? We don't have much time to lose. You're sure you don't know what the magic is?

PETERKINS: No, sir, they mumbled a lot, but the only thing they said aloud was,
"The king alone must eat
These tarts
And then he can defeat
Those elves."

JACK: Oh, ho, is that it? Then, if we eat them, we'll be twice as strong, no doubt. Fall to! Let's clean up. (*As they eat the last of the tarts, there is the sound of a bugle.*)

ELVES: The queen!

JACK: Hide quickly. Let's watch the fun. We'll see now who's the leader. (ELVES *crouch behind trees and stones, as* TWO FAIRIES *guide the* QUEEN *to the fallen log.*)

QUEEN: Quick, the king will soon be here. Let's spread our cloth and prepare for our surprise. Where are the tarts?

1ST FAIRY (*Hastening to the hiding place*): They're gone!

QUEEN: Gone!

2ND FAIRY: Oh, no, they *can't* be gone! No one knew where we hid them. Look again. Here. I'll help. (*Stumbles over sleeping child*) A mortal! He must have taken them. (*Shakes* LITTLE VALENTINE *furiously*) Give them back, I say!

LITTLE VALENTINE (*Waking in alarm*): What is it? Please. Who are you? What are you doing to me?

2ND FAIRY: What did you do with the tarts?

LITTLE VALENTINE: Tarts? Oh, I didn't see them. Honestly, I didn't.

1ST FAIRY: He probably ate them all up.

2ND FAIRY (*Slowly*): No, he couldn't have. He'd be a fairy if he had.

1ST FAIRY: That's right. Oh me, oh my!

QUEEN (*Beginning to sob*): Now I shall lose the King.

DAN (*Running in all out of breath*): Dear, dear Queen, I'll be but a shadow of myself if you keep calling me with your tears. *Now* what's wrong?

QUEEN: The tarts are gone! (*Cries afresh*) The king will soon be here and I don't even have a farewell present for him. (*At a rustle in the bushes*) There he is now. (*Jumps up in fright as* JACK *and his men appear silently before her*) Run for your lives! Warn the King!

JACK: No, stay. We are your loyal subjects now. (*They drop on their knees before her*) We ate the tarts but now we are sorry.

1ST FAIRY: It's a trick. Don't trust them.

LITTLE VALENTINE: No, I don't think so. They ate your magic tarts. Teardrop Dan said whoever ate them would turn into full-fledged fairies.

2ND FAIRY: That's right! They'll never bother you again and the king can stay!

QUEEN: I wish I could believe that. But the king is still mortal and his mind is made up. He leaves us tonight after the fairy presentation. Presentation! (*Cries again*) We have nothing to give him. (*The assembled company look at each other in panic.*)

JACK: It's all our fault. I'd undo the damage if I could, but we ate the tarts—every one.

LITTLE VALENTINE: Valentine says—(*They all look inquiringly at him.*) Valentine is the monk who found me—he says there's magic in any gift, if it's given from the heart.

JACK: The heart, why didn't I think of that? My decoration from the war, the thing I treasure most. Here, take it. It's the least I can do. (*Hands her heart*)

LITTLE VALENTINE: I have this handkerchief of lace. I think it was my mother's. It was found with me. I have always kept it with me. But now I want you to have it for the king. Perhaps it will bring good luck to him. (*Gives it to the* QUEEN)

PETERKINS: If I hadn't spied and led the Elves here, the tarts would still be safe. This morning I found a miracle, a perfect rose blooming in a sheltered spot in the sun. Let me see if I can find it again. (*Goes to rear of stage*) Yes, here it is, a perfect one—a deep red rose in February's wintry sun. The only one, I'll wager, in the land. (*Brings rose to* QUEEN)

QUEEN: How perfect! See, I'll take Jack's precious heart and lay the child's snow white lace upon it. And here in the center we'll place the single rose and fasten it all with my pin.

1ST FAIRY: Not your pin!

QUEEN (*Taking arrow pin from her dress and fastening the flower and lace upon the heart with it*): It is my prize possession. My loyal subjects gave it to me upon my coronation. It's supposed to be one of Cupid's diamond darts. (*A fanfare offstage announces the* KING's *arrival. As* KING *appears with his followers, the* QUEEN *falls on her knees before him.*) My lord, I wish you the happiest of birthdays. I would that my gift were the magic one we had planned for you, but alas, things went wrong, and there is no magic. (*In a sweeping gesture*) But each of us has wrapped up his heart's desire in this farewell gift to you. (*Presents the gift to the* KING)

KING (*Raising* QUEEN *to her feet*): Arise, dear one, your gift of love means more to me than life itself. I arrived early, and as I stood outside the dell, I could not help but hear your plans.

QUEEN: Then you know all about the missing tarts. (*At*

the mention of the tarts, ELVES *throw themselves at the* KING's *feet as if to beg for mercy.*)

KING: Yes, but see how well they've served their purpose. (*Turns to kneeling* ELVES) Arise, Sir Elves, I make you knights and welcome you to Fairyland. Protect your queen when I am gone.

QUEEN: But surely you can stay now that the black elves are our friends.

KING: How I wish I could! No, although it breaks my heart, I must leave you now. (*As the* KING *turns sadly away, he is attracted by the frantic struggles of* TOMPKINS.) Who is that tied to the tree?

JACK: Oh, that's Tompkins, one of your most loyal subjects. We lured him here by telling him he could help the queen if he found the tarts. We had to tie him up when he found out who we really were. Unloose him, men.

TOMPKINS (*Throws himself at the* KING's *feet as* ELVES *release him*): P-P-Please don't go away.

KING: I'm afraid I must.

TOMPKINS: They all gave you a gift. I want to give you something, too. (*Feels frantically in his pockets and discovers the tart he had put there earlier.*) I guess I have only this old stone I found over there. (*Points to spot where he found tart*)

2ND FAIRY: Stone! That's not a stone. That's one of the magic tarts. Where did you get it?

1ST FAIRY: The one I dropped, remember?

ALL (*Ad lib, excitedly*): The tart, the tart! The magic tart! The King is saved! Long live the King! (*Etc.*) (*The bells toll out the hour of twelve, as they all count out the strokes*)

QUEEN: It is tomorrow and the magic has not failed us. Eat the tart, my lord. (*As the* KING *complies*) You're safe now. You'll never have to leave us. (*Turning to*

LITTLE VALENTINE) Thank you, little one. If you had not suggested our giving the king a gift from our hearts, Tompkins would never have thought to give him the magic tart.

KING (*Holding up* QUEEN's *offering*): Not only Tompkins, but each of you gave from your heart. (*Holds up their offering*) Surely there has never been a more fitting gift to mark a more joyous day. Such a precious gift deserves a special honor. What is your name, lad?

LITTLE VALENTINE: Valentine, sir.

KING: Then we'll call this gift a valentine. And because you've helped to make my birthday such a perfect day, I shall name this day, February 14th, Valentine's Day in honor of you. That day shall be set aside each year to send our heart's regards to those we love.

OFFSTAGE VOICES (*From the distance*): Valentine, Valentine! Where are you?

KING: Your friends have come for you. (*To the group*) Come, we must be gone before they arrive. Goodbye, little one, Happy Valentine's Day! (*Exits, followed by everyone but* LITTLE VALENTINE.)

LITTLE VALENTINE: Happy, happy day! (*As voices offstage call again*) I'm coming! Wait for me. (*Starts offstage as curtain falls*) I have so much to tell you!

THE END

Saving the Old Homestead

by Maxine Fay

Characters

MASTER OF CEREMONIES
CAROLINE, *a sweet young girl*
WILLIAM, *a good young man*
MURDOCK, *the villain*
MARTHA JONES, *the sweet mother*
CLARENCE JONES, *the stern but just father*
SAM, *the hired man*
PANSY, *the hired girl*
I. M. TRUE, *the lawyer*
JIMMY, *the errand boy*

BEFORE RISE: *The* MASTER OF CEREMONIES *gives a welcoming speech. This can include various credits, etc. It should also contain the following:*

MASTER OF CEREMONIES: This old-time melodrama which you are about to see is the sort of show people all over America enjoyed about fifty years ago. The actors this evening will act as actors did in the period known as the "gay '90's." You will make the villain happy if you hiss and boo him when he appears. The hero and heroine you will cheer by applauding. I tell you these things because you are a part of the show, and since "old time" audiences were not dignified, please do not be dignified now. On with the show! And remember—tonight is just for fun.

Scene 1

SETTING: *The living room of the Jones farmhouse.*

AT RISE: CLARENCE *is sitting at the table working over bills.* CAROLINE *is embroidering.* MARTHA *is moving about straightening the furniture.* PANSY *enters from left.*

PANSY: How many's goin' to be here for dinner, ma'am? I want to know so I won't peel any more spuds than we'll need.

MARTHA: Nobody but the family, Pansy. Why do you ask?

PANSY (*Hesitating*): Oh—I just wanted to know, that's all. (*Exits left*)

CLARENCE: Gad, Martha, even the hired help knows we are in dire circumstances!

MARTHA (*Dramatically*): Oh, Pa, though the whole world would condemn you as a failure, Caroline and I know you have done only what you thought was right.

CAROLINE (*Rushes to* CLARENCE, *kneels at his side*): Oh, Father, dear Father, I have faith in you. Mother has faith in you—haven't we, Mother dear?

MARTHA: Yes, Caroline, we have indeed. Clarence, we will always stand by your side no matter what happens.

CLARENCE (*Arising and placing his hand on* MARTHA's *shoulder*): Martha, good wife, I knew you would say that. And you too, my sweet Caroline. I never dreamed I would bring you to this sad end.

CAROLINE (*Cheerfully*): Father, it is not the end!

CLARENCE: If I had not invested all our money from the

last harvest in that oil well, we would be able to pay off the mortgage. Now we have only forty-eight hours left in this home we came to when we were young.

MARTHA: Clarence, there is still hope. Lawyer I. M. True said he would take good care of our money. Perhaps he may bring us good news yet. I still have those stocks hidden in my dresser drawer.

CLARENCE: I wish I had never seen those stocks. (*Despairingly*) Oh, a pity that man is forever taken in by get-rich-quick schemes. And I am caught in the net with all the other poor fish.

CAROLINE: Father dear, soon William, my dearest love, will be here. He will help us. He will think of some way out of our trouble.

MARTHA: Dear, kind William. (*A knock is heard.* CAROLINE *runs to door and admits* WILLIAM)

CAROLINE: Here is dear William, Mother and Father.

CLARENCE (*Extending hand to* WILLIAM): Welcome, William. You find us a troubled family indeed.

WILLIAM: I came as soon as Sam brought me your note, Caroline. (*Dramatically*) Oh, to help you I would give my all; but alas, I can think of nothing. (SAM *enters, accompanied by* MURDOCK. *Audience should hiss, as* MURDOCK *twirls mustache.*)

SAM: Here is Mr. Murdock, folks. I told him the mortgage wasn't due yet, but he said he wanted to see you anyhow.

CLARENCE: Murdock, could you not let us have our last hours in our old home in peace? (*Strikes pose*) I am a man of honor. You shall have the money to pay off the mortgage or the farm is yours.

MURDOCK (*With a slick voice and manner*): You wrong me, Mr. Jones. I cannot throw your little family out into the cold. I am gentle, tender-hearted. No, Mr. Jones, you may keep your home.

WILLIAM (*Aside to audience*): I like not the looks of this Murdock.

CAROLINE: Oh, Mr. Murdock, you are so good, so kind. I knew people had wronged you.

CLARENCE: How can we ever repay you for your kindness?

MURDOCK: There can be no talk of repayment among friends. But since you insist, there is a small thing; just a token—they are not worth the paper they are printed on, but I'll take that worthless oil stock off your hands for you, and we'll call it square.

CLARENCE: You are welcome to it, and may it bring you better luck than it has me. Martha, get the stock for Mr. Murdock.

WILLIAM: Wait! The time is not up for forty-eight hours. Keep the stock in your home until the time is up!

MARTHA: William is right, Pa. We still have forty-eight hours.

CLARENCE: All right, Mother, if you think it best. In forty-eight hours, Murdock, you may have the stock, and we will keep our home.

MURDOCK: I have urgent business elsewhere. I would like to have the stock now and be on my way.

WILLIAM (*Suspiciously*): Since the stock is worthless, why are you in such a hurry? I smell a *rat* somewhere.

MURDOCK (*Strikes pose*): Sir, you insult the honor of a gentleman!

CLARENCE (*A little angrily*): William, this man has done us a great kindness. You must not insult him in my house. You were not able to help us, but he, out of the goodness of a noble heart, has shown us how to keep a roof over our heads in our old age. (WILLIAM *looks properly subdued while* MURDOCK *smirks at the audience*) As Murdock says, what do a few hours matter? Get the stock, Martha.

MARTHA: No, Pa! I have faith in William. The stock must have my signature, and I say *wait*.

MURDOCK (*Hissing at audience*): Foiled! !

CURTAIN

* * *

SCENE 2

TIME: *Later that evening.*

SETTING: *Same as Scene 1.*

AT RISE: PANSY *is dusting furniture with exaggerated movements. She is singing to herself.*

WILLIAM (*Enters stealthily, whispers loudly*): Pansy, are you alone? Is there anyone else about?

PANSY (*Startled*): Oh, Mr. William, you sure surprised me! I am alone; just straightening up the parlor.

WILLIAM (*Urgently*): For all of Murdock's slick manners, I don't trust him. I think he has trickery up his sleeve!

PANSY: I don't like him either. He's a handsome devil— but that is just what he is—a devil.

WILLIAM: He's too anxious to trade the oil stocks for the mortgage. If the stocks are worthless, why does he want them? Murdock has never been known to give something for nothing. I cannot believe that a heart of stone can turn to a heart of gold so easily!

PANSY: Mr. William, I think you are right! But what can we do?

WILLIAM: Pansy, do you know where those stocks are hidden?

PANSY: Well, I did see Mrs. Jones put them in her dresser drawer. But what are you thinking of, Mr. William?

WILLIAM: Pansy, I am going to take those stocks and hide them myself, until the forty-eight hours are up! (*He exits.* PANSY *looks worried, paces up and down twisting apron. As* WILLIAM *re-enters left,* SAM *enters from right.*)

SAM: Why, Mr. William, I thought you had gone home long ago. What are you doing coming out of Mr. Jones' bedroom?

PANSY: Mr. William, you can trust Sam. You can tell him anything. Maybe he can help us.

WILLIAM: Well, I didn't trust that Murdock so I have taken the stocks until forty-eight hours have passed, because I fear foul play.

SAM: You can be sure I won't tell. I don't like the looks of that city slicker, either.

WILLIAM: The stocks are safe here. (*Thumps his chest*) I substituted blank papers for these.

PANSY: We better clear out of here before anyone finds us. (*Turns down lamp, and all exit.* MURDOCK *enters stealthily, starts searching, turns toward audience*)

MURDOCK: They would not be so foolish as to hide them in here. I will search the next room. The old lady said her signature was needed—Ha, ha, ha! I have signed many names to many other things. (*He leaves and returns soon with envelope, a look of triumph on his face.*) The fools! Right in the top drawer! The envelope is marked "Greasy Oil Stocks." (*Opens envelope, takes out blank paper*) Foiled again!

CURTAIN

*   *   *

SCENE 3

TIME: *The next day.*

SETTING: *The same.*

AT RISE: CLARENCE, MARTHA *and* CAROLINE *are on stage.* CAROLINE *is arranging flowers in a vase.*

CAROLINE: What beautiful posies. And they came out of our own garden, too. Aren't they lovely, Mother dear?

MARTHA: Yes, Caroline, and to think these may be the last flowers we shall pick from our own little garden! (*She begins to weep*)

CLARENCE (*Walks over to* MARTHA, *puts a hand on her shoulder*): Now, now, Mother, all will be well. That kind and unselfish gentleman, Mr. Murdock, will let us keep our home. All we have to do is turn that worthless stock over to him. Oh, he is a fine man who has been greatly wronged!

CAROLINE: I have always had such faith in William, but how he has misjudged Mr. Murdock. (*A knock is heard, and* MARTHA *admits the smirking* MURDOCK.)

MURDOCK: Good day, good day, and how is the happy little family this afternoon? (*Does not wait for an answer*) I came today because I find I must leave town. Business, you know. I have the mortgage with me, and if you will give me the stocks, it is yours.

MARTHA: But there are twenty-four hours left. William said we must wait!

MURDOCK: Bah! That callow youth, what does he know of business? The deal must be made here and now! Or I shall withdraw my generous offer. What say you, Jones? Is it give up the stock and a cozy home today, or keep the stock and a bed in the street tomorrow?

CLARENCE: Martha, there is nothing else to do. Get the stock for Mr. Murdock.

MARTHA: Yes, Pa, I can see waiting would gain us nothing. I'll get it at once. (*As she leaves,* MURDOCK *looks anxiously after her*)

CAROLINE: Mr. Murdock, why do you want this worthless stock? You will gain nothing from it.

MURDOCK: My dear, beautiful child, I want it for sentimental reasons. Some day, when I am old, I shall be able to take it out and look at it and remember that once I was able to save a home for some old people. Yes, and keep a roof over the head of their lovely daughter! I will then know that I have not lived in vain! (*Strikes a sentimental pose*)

CAROLINE: Oh, what a beautiful sentiment!

MARTHA (*Rushing in and crying*): The envelope is gone! Someone has taken it!

CLARENCE (*Dazed*): Taken it! Oh, no, Martha, there must be some mistake!

MARTHA: No, Pa, I looked everywhere. (*Dramatically*) The stocks are gone, gone!

CAROLINE: But, Mother dear, who would do such a dreadful thing?

MURDOCK: The servants, perhaps? I thought that Sam had a shifty eye!

CLARENCE: Sir, our hired man and our hired girl have been with us for years. I trust them completely. However, we will see what they have to say. (*Calls off*) Pansy! Pansy!

PANSY (*Offstage at first and then entering*): Coming, Mr. Clarence, coming as fast as I can. (SAM *enters with her.*) Sam and I have just been having some coffee in the kitchen. (*Looks around at the group*) Is—is something wrong?

CLARENCE: A most terrible thing has happened, Pansy. The stocks are gone!

PANSY: The stocks, sir? What stocks, Mr. Clarence?

CLARENCE: The only stocks we have—the oil stocks.

PANSY: Oh, the oil stocks. They'll probably show up. I must be getting back to the kitchen. (*Tries to edge out*)

MURDOCK: Stay, my crafty one; methinks you know more about this than meets the eye! And you, (*Turns to* SAM) what do you know, my man?

SAM: Me—? I don't know anything. I don't know a thing about those stocks. I wasn't here when those stocks were taken last night, was I, Pansy?

PANSY: Sam, you fool!

MURDOCK: Ah, ha! so you have a viper in your home, Jones. (*Advances toward* SAM) What did you do with those stocks, Sam? Where are they now?

CLARENCE: Sam, if you know where they are, speak up now, before it is forever too late.

SAM: I—I, please, Mr. Jones, don't ask me.

PANSY: Sam didn't do it. Sam never took anything.

MARTHA: Pansy, do you know who took the stocks? Are you shielding someone? Answer with the truth, Pansy. If those stocks are not recovered, all will be lost.

PANSY (*Crying*): I promised not to tell. I gave my word.

CAROLINE: Pansy, dear, (*Puts arm around* PANSY's *shoulder*) your loyalty belongs to this family before all others. If you know, you must tell.

PANSY: But I promised, Miss Caroline, I promised him I wouldn't tell, and I can't go back on a promise to Mr. William.

ALL THREE JONESES: William! (*At this moment* WILLIAM, *who has been listening conspicuously at the door, enters.*)

WILLIAM: Yes, William! Thanks for trying, Pansy, and you too, Sam. (*Turns to* CAROLINE) Caroline, you understand why I did it, don't you? (CAROLINE *just stares.*)

CLARENCE: Do I understand that you are the thief? You whom we have trusted and taken into the bosom of the family? (*Strikes dramatic pose*)

WILLIAM: I did it, Mr. Jones, for the good of all. I don't trust this Murdock. (*Turns again to* CAROLINE) Oh, Caroline, my sweet, tell me you believe me!

CAROLINE (*Strikes pose*): Oh, William, how can you speak of trust when you have just betrayed us? How can you speak sweet words when you have just done such a foul deed?

MURDOCK: And where are the stocks now? What have you done with them? (*Strikes a sentimental pose*) Ah, it makes my heart bleed, to see such a trusting little family betrayed. (*Turns again to* WILLIAM) Where are they, I say?

WILLIAM: I shall not tell until tomorrow. They are in a safe place.

CAROLINE: Here is your ring, William. You have broken a maiden's tender heart. Go, and never darken this doorway again!

WILLIAM: I go, but some day you will understand; some day you will want me back. As for you, Murdock—you shall not have the stocks. (*Exits*)

MURDOCK: Foiled again!

CURTAIN

*   *   *

SCENE 4

TIME: *Later, the same day.*

SETTING: *The woods.*

AT RISE: WILLIAM *is pacing back and forth.* JIMMY *runs in, followed by* I. M. TRUE.

JIMMY: I brought him, Mr. William, just like you said to do.

WILLIAM: Thank heaven, Lawyer True, you have come at last! You find me in great trouble indeed.

TRUE: I left everything to come to you when Jimmy said I should keep this rendezvous with you here in the woods. William, my boy, what is this all about?

WILLIAM: Do you remember the oil stocks which you bought for Clarence Jones?

TRUE: Yes, I know the ones you mean. In fact this very morning, just as Jimmy delivered your note to me, my stockbroker was starting to tell me something about those "Greasy Oil Stocks." I told him to talk to me later, and I dashed out of my office to meet you here. What about the stock, William?

JIMMY: We live on a ranch . . . my father has lots of stock . . . horses, cows, bulls, pigs. . . .

WILLIAM (*Impatiently*): We don't want to hear about your cows and pigs.

JIMMY: Yes, yes, I like animals.

WILLIAM (*To* TRUE): Now, about those stocks. Murdock, the leech, wants to trade the mortgage on the Jones home for the stock, which *he* says is worthless.

JIMMY: My mother says my father's worthless.

TRUE: Did they give the stocks to Murdock?

WILLIAM: No—I stole them from the house; I have them here. (*Pats chest*)

TRUE: My boy, you could find yourself in grave trouble for doing that. However, I see it was the only thing to do. But what did you want of me?

WILLIAM: Here. (*Hands stock to* TRUE) Take them. Find out for me if they have any value. There are only four hours left to save the Jones farm! Now hurry—go!

TRUE: I go. (*Exits*)

WILLIAM: Jimmy, run and find Miss Caroline. Tell her

to come quickly to this spot in the woods. Tell her that it has something to do with her dear parents' future. (JIMMY *runs out.* WILLIAM *paces back and forth.* MURDOCK *enters.*)

MURDOCK: So! This is where you have been hiding! I am asking you, for the last time—what have you done with those stocks? Answer me!

WILLIAM: I no longer have them. They are in a safe place, where you will never find them.

MURDOCK: You lie, William. I will get that stock if I have to take it off your dead body! (*Pulls out gun, as* CAROLINE *enters running.* WILLIAM *turns toward her with back turned toward* MURDOCK.)

CAROLINE: William, William!

WILLIAM: Go back, Caroline! Go back! (MURDOCK *raises pistol and strikes* WILLIAM *on head.* WILLIAM *falls to ground.*)

CAROLINE (*Rushes to* WILLIAM's *side and kneels beside him*): Oh, William, my dearest love! What has he done to you? (*Turns to* MURDOCK) What have you done to him, Murdock?

MURDOCK (*Searches* WILLIAM *and finds nothing*): Foiled again!

CURTAIN

*   *   *

SCENE 5

TIME: *An hour later.*

SETTING: *The sawmill.*

AT RISE: WILLIAM *is gagged and tied to a chair.* CAROLINE *is tied to the sawmill.* MURDOCK *surveys them triumphantly.*

CAROLINE: Help! Help! Someone save me!

MURDOCK: Your cries will avail you nothing, my proud beauty. Soon I will find out from your William the location of those stocks. Only he can save you now. (*Goes over and removes gag from* WILLIAM'S *mouth*)

WILLIAM: Release her, you villain!

MURDOCK (*Laughs*): Not until I know where those stocks are.

CAROLINE (*In panic*): Tell him, William, please tell him!

WILLIAM: You win, Murdock. I gave the stocks to Lawyer True.

MURDOCK: You lie! You didn't have time to take the stocks to him.

WILLIAM: Nevertheless, Lawyer True has the stocks. Now release Caroline from the saw!

MURDOCK: Bah! I still do not believe you, William!

CAROLINE: William always tells the truth—release us— you villain—Help! Help!

MURDOCK (*Ties handkerchief over* CAROLINE'S *mouth. He puts gag back in* WILLIAM'S *mouth. Turns to audience*): I am not called Murdock, the Villain, for nothing! (*Starts sawmill and pushes* CAROLINE *toward it.* LAWYER TRUE, *and* JIMMY *enter, followed by* CLARENCE *and* MARTHA)

TRUE: What is the meaning of this? (*Catches* MURDOCK *off guard, holds him tightly.* MURDOCK *tries to get loose.*)

MURDOCK: Unhand me! Unhand me! (JIMMY *cuts* WILLIAM *loose.* WILLIAM *runs to turn off sawmill and untie* CAROLINE. CLARENCE *comes to* TRUE'S *aid and knocks* MURDOCK *on head with pipe which is lying on floor.* MURDOCK *falls to floor.*)

MARTHA (*Rushing to* CAROLINE): Caroline, my sweet baby, are you hurt? Oh, what you have suffered! Tell me what has happened!

CAROLINE: Oh, it has been terrible!—just terrible!—too terrible to talk about!

MARTHA: My poor, poor child. Time will erase this from your memory!

WILLIAM: Lawyer True, you are indeed a true friend. If you had not come when you did, we would not be living this minute. Your timely arrival indeed saved us! But what news do you have for the Jones family?

TRUE: Good news indeed! Those "Greasy Oil Stocks" are very valuable. I can sell them for you at a tremendous profit. You will not have to worry about money for the rest of your lives!

CAROLINE: William, oh, William! You are so clever! You knew better than all of us. Will you once again let me wear your ring upon my finger? (WILLIAM *pulls ring out of pocket and kneels as he puts it on her finger.*)

CLARENCE: Forgive me, William, for having doubted you. You are indeed a true-blue friend. (*Turns to* TRUE) And you, too, True, are a true friend. A friend in need is a friend indeed.

MARTHA (*To audience*): They saved our home!

CAROLINE: And now we will be rich—oh, William, you are so very clever!

WILLIAM: I, too, own some of those "Greasy Oil Stocks." When I sell them, I will have a tidy sum. We can be rich together, my dear, sweet Caroline.

CAROLINE: Oh, William! (*All step forward and sing "Home Sweet Home" as curtain falls.*)

THE END

The Emperor's New Robes

by Marie Agnes Foley

Characters

EMPEROR OF JAPAN
EMPRESS
KIYOMORI, *Prime Minister*
LADY OF THE COFFERS
LADY OF THE WARDROBE
FAN BEARER
COURT FOOL
DANZO
TARO } *impostors from China*
SAKURA, *little girl*
COURTIERS
TWO STORYTELLERS

SCENE 1

TIME: *Evening.*

SETTING: *The throne room of the palace of the Emperor of Japan, and the Flower Path before the palace.*

AT RISE: EMPEROR *is seated on the divan examining his face in a mirror, while* FAN BEARER *slowly fans him. The* LADY OF THE COFFERS, LADY OF THE WARDROBE *and* COURTIERS *stand nearby.* STORYTELLERS *stand right and left.*

1ST STORYTELLER (*Speaking directly to audience*): His Worshipful Highness, the noble Emperor of Japan, is thinking of tomorrow, the Feast of Lanterns, as he looks at himself in the mirror. Because he has grown stouter than he was at the Feast of the Cherry Blossoms, he thinks he will look very handsome in the new robes he is having made in China.

2ND STORYTELLER: His long mustache will glisten, black and shiny in the golden sunshine of his kingdom. He is happy in his heart. But see—Kiyomori, the Prime Minister, is hastening hither. (KIYOMORI *enters.*) In his heart is great anxiety. So worried is he that for a moment he cannot speak, while his feet patter a nervous tattoo upon the floor.

KIYOMORI: Your Worshipful Highness . . . Your Worshipful Highness . . . I have bad news for you!

EMPEROR (*Picking up his fan*): What bad news have you for me? (*Thundering*) Speak!

1ST STORYTELLER: Kiyomori fears the anger of his Worshipful Highness, and his fear chokes him.

EMPEROR (*Snapping his fan in his hand*): Speak!

KIYOMORI: The—the—ship that was bringing your robes from—(*Stammering*) from China for the Feast of Lanterns sank off the coast of Shantung!

LADY OF WARDROBE: Sank!

LADY OF COFFERS: Sank!

FAN BEARER: Sank? (LADIES *nod "yes" to* FAN BEARER.)

EMPEROR (*Rising in great anger*): What? Sank! Say that again!

KIYOMORI: The ship that was bringing your robes from China sank off the coast of Shantung.

EMPEROR: You shall be killed with the seven knives for this! Out of my sight!

LADY OF COFFERS: He shall be killed with the seven knives for this!

LADY OF WARDROBE: He shall be killed with the seven knives for this!

FAN BEARER: What? What? (LADIES *nod "yes."*)

KIYOMORI (*Runs forward with tiny steps to* EMPEROR. *At first he only opens and closes his mouth. Finally he speaks.*): But Your Worshipful Highness—*I* was not to blame for it. It was the storm. Your Worshipful Highness, I was not to blame—Your Worshipful Highness, I was not to blame . . . (*His voice trails off, then can be heard repeating the phrase over and over, as he hurries backwards and exits.*)

EMPEROR (*Running frantically about with tiny steps, fanning himself furiously*): What shall I do? What shall I *do?* What *shall* I do? Oh, what *shall I do?* Now I have nothing to wear, *nothing to wear*—and tomorrow is the Feast of Lanterns! *What shall I do?*

LADY OF WARDROBE: What shall he do?

LADY OF COFFERS: What shall he do?

2ND STORYTELLER: No one can answer his Worshipful Highness for no one has an idea in his head. (EMPRESS *enters, preceded by* COURT FOOL, *who sits down and listens.*)

EMPRESS (*Watching* EMPEROR, *and running up and down with him*): My Maple Tree, whatever is the matter?

LADY OF COFFERS: She asks her Maple Tree: Whatever is the matter?

LADY OF WARDROBE: She asks her Maple Tree: Whatever is the matter?

EMPEROR (*Running about excitedly*): Disturb me not in my sorrow, my dear. Tomorrow is the Feast of Lanterns, and I have nothing to wear in the procession.

LADY OF WARDROBE: He has nothing to wear in the procession!

LADY OF COFFERS: He has nothing to wear in the procession!

EMPRESS: Why don't you wear the robes they have been making for you for the last six months in China, my Maple Tree?

1ST STORYTELLER: The Emperor's most loved one asks futile questions, for in her head is little knowledge.

EMPEROR: I've just received news that the ship bringing the robes from China has (*Drops on divan*) sunk! What shall I do?

LADY OF COFFERS: What shall he do?

EMPRESS: Why does not my darling Lantern-Face wear the black satin robe embroidered with chrysanthemums?

LADY OF WARDROBE: She asks her darling Lantern-Face. . . .

EMPEROR (*Impatiently dropping his head first on one hand and then on the other*): I wore that for the visit of the King of England. I can't wear that *again!*

LADY OF WARDROBE: He can't wear that again.

EMPRESS: How about the crimson, silk-lined robe with the dazzling jewels upon it?

LADY OF COFFERS: Yes, with the dazzling. . . .

EMPEROR (*Interrupting*): The crimson, silk-lined robe with the dazzling jewels upon it? I wore it at the Feast of the Cherry Blossoms. I cannot wear *that* again!

LADY OF COFFERS: *That* again!

EMPRESS: Why not wear the heliotrope robe with the green-eyed dragon painted upon it?

LADY OF WARDROBE: Yes, with the green-eyed dragon painted upon it!

EMPEROR (*Glaring at each* LADY): Don't you remember, I wore the heliotrope robe with the green-eyed dragon painted upon it at the Feast of the Sacred Gong? I cannot wear that either. Oh, what shall I do?

LADY OF COFFERS (*Quickly*): What shall he do? What *shall* he do? What shall he *do?*

EMPRESS: We *must* think of something!

LADY OF WARDROBE (*Quickly*): Think of something. Think of something.

LADY OF COFFERS: We can't—we can't—we can't! (*Both* LADIES *hit their heads.*)

EMPEROR: We *must!* (*They all strike first their foreheads, then, with right hands, the right sides of their heads, and with their left hands the left sides of their heads, and last, with right hands, the tops of their heads.*)

2ND STORYTELLER: Hollow and empty—hollow and empty —nothing within!

FOOL (*Jumping up and down toward the entrance*): Hollow and empty—hollow and empty—nothing within! *Something* without. (*Exits, as* KIYOMORI *enters.*)

KIYOMORI: Your Worshipful Highness, there is a great commotion in the outer court.

EMPEROR (*Rising and thundering*): Who dares disturb my unhappiness?

KIYOMORI (*Mildly*): I do—and—(*Pointing*) others! Two strangers desire to bring their loathsome selves before your celestial eyes, Most Worshipful Highness! (FOOL *enters.*)

EMPEROR: At this momentous moment?

FOOL (*Dancing about*): They say they are Chinamen, and that they are expert *weavers.*

EMPRESS: Weavers!

BOTH LADIES: Weavers!

2ND STORYTELLER: A silver stream of blood rushes to the brain of his Most Worshipful Highness. An *idea* is born!

EMPEROR: Weavers! Show them in at once! (KIYOMORI *goes to the door.*)

1ST STORYTELLER: Celestial atoms of joy are bubbling in the sacred soul of his Most Worshipful Highness! (EMPEROR *smiles at everyone and dances about with* FOOL.)

KIYOMORI (*Joyously announcing the weavers*): Here are the weavers, Taro and Danzo, Your Worshipful Highness! (TARO *and* DANZO *enter and bow.*)

1ST STORYTELLER: Here is trickery. Much is steaming in these lowly minds but that which brews is tainted. The eye windows of their souls show forth that which is not good.

EMPEROR: You say you are expert weavers?

DANZO: Yes, Your Most Worshipful Highness, we have been weaving since we were *one* year of age! (*They continue to bow with hypocritical humbleness, enjoying their own shrewdness.*)

LADY OF COFFERS: One year of age?

EMPEROR: Why, when were you born?

TARO: On the day that the first Sacred Cherry Tree was planted.

EMPEROR: A thousand years ago!

DANZO: Yes, Your Most Worshipful Highness, and we have been weaving ever since.

EMPEROR: Then you *must* be expert weavers. How *quickly* can you weave?

TARO: So fast we work, that no mortal eye can see our needles. (*All put fingers to eyes.*)

2ND STORYTELLER: Much is here that honest eyes see not!

EMPEROR: If I wanted a robe woven and made by tomorrow morning, could it be done?

DANZO: Yes, if Your Worshipful Highness will provide materials and candlelight, and we work all night.

EMPEROR: Good! And what is the price?

TARO: We work for *love,* Your Most Worshipful Highness, and merely for our food until the task is done. Bring forth the materials, and we shall set ourselves to work.

EMPRESS: They work for love?

LADY OF WARDROBE: They work for love? (*Soulfully*) Ah-h-h-h!

1ST STORYTELLER: These souls are not planted in the golden dust of sacrifice. They do not blossom with love. Their thoughts are buried in the mire of deception.

EMPEROR: I know of no one in my household who works for love. But we shall see. Lady of the Coffers, what do my coffers contain?

LADY OF COFFERS (*Coming forward*): There are enough yards of satins, silks and golden threads that were they stretched out in a double line, they would reach from here to Shantung. Jewels and precious stones there are to supply the Emperor's needs until the cherry blossoms are no more, and in the treasury we have a hundred thousand yen.

EMPEROR: Excellent. See that everything is at their disposal. (*Turning to the secretly grinning impostors*) Weavers, you will work here in the throne room until the robe is finished. And if you do not make the most beautiful robe I have ever worn, so that I shall shine at the Feast of Lanterns tomorrow, (*Suddenly*) you shall be *buried alive!*

COURTIERS: Buried alive! Oh-h-h-h! (*They lie down with hands on chests and* FAN BEARER *turns face to back wall, as* FOOL *pretends to dig hole like a dog.*)

2ND STORYTELLER: The wicked hearts of these impostors, Taro and Danzo, are thumping in fear now, but the men dare not show their feelings.

DANZO (*Swallowing hard*): Gladly do we accept your royal commission. And the robe that we make will not only be the most beautiful one ever made, but it will contain magic.

COURTIERS (*Jumping up and facing forward*): Magic!

FAN BEARER (*Facing front*): What?

TARO: Yes, Your Worshipful Highness, you will find this robe we shall weave can be seen *only* by the eyes of the *good* and *noble!*

EMPRESS: The robe can be seen only by the eyes of the good and noble?

DANZO (*Winking slyly at* TARO): Yes. To all other eyes the robe will be invisible.

1ST STORYTELLER: Many hearts are thumping now in the court.

LADY OF WARDROBE (*Repeating in amazement*): The robe can be seen only by the eyes of the good and noble? To all other eyes it will be invisible?

TARO: It is true, most noble courtiers.

FOOL: To see or not to see. Where does that leave me? (*Jumps up and down*)

2ND STORYTELLER: Each soul now smiles and says to itself: "*I* shall certainly be able to see it, but I wonder, who of my neighbors will?"

EMPEROR: Auspicious time! (*Walks about rubbing his hands together happily*) I shall be able to find out who of my people is worthy of his high office.

EMPRESS: My Bubbling One, life may be happier if it flows not over into too much enlightenment!

DANZO: Will it please Your Worshipful Highness to be measured?

EMPEROR (*Clapping three times*): Bring tape measure, ink, brush, and pad. (*The* LADIES *exit and return immediately with articles mentioned and a low table.*)

DANZO (*Measuring* EMPEROR): From shoulder to shoulder, four hundred royal inches!

TARO (*Writes as he repeats and enlarges on* DANZO's *directions while an attendant holds the ink jar.* NOTE: TARO *must begin his brush writing at the bottom of the page and write upwards instead of down the page*): From shoulder to shoulder four *thousand* royal inches.

DANZO: From shoulder to wrist seventy and one-eighth noble inches.

TARO: From shoulder to wrist seventy and one-quarter noble inches.

DANZO (*Correcting him*): One-eighth, Taro!

TARO: One-quarter!

DANZO: From shoulder to feet six hundred seventy-eight and seven-eighths celestial inches.

TARO: From shoulder to feet six *million* and seventy-eight and seven-eighths celestial inches!

DANZO: His sacred chest measures three hundred fifty-seven and six-eighths voluminous inches.

TARO: His sacred chest measures three *billion* fifty-seven and six-eighths voluminous inches!

DANZO: The measuring is done, Most Worshipful Highness. We are ready to begin. (*During above scene each COURTIER tries to figure measurements, but gives up in despair.*)

EMPEROR: Bring the loom at once. (*Two COURTIERS exit and return with loom, as EMPEROR offers his arm to EMPRESS.*)

EMPRESS: The robe indeed will be marvelous if by it you will be able to know whether or not your courtiers are worthy of their high offices. But if they are not worthy, my pet, what then?

COURTIERS: What then? What then? (*All exit, except DANZO, TARO, STORYTELLERS and FAN BEARER.*)

DANZO (*Jumping about and laughing*): They are all taken in! Now when they bring the jewels, we must hide them until we can get away.

TARO: Sh-h-h! Here they come. (*A few of the COURTIERS enter with boxes of jewels and beautiful silks.*)

DANZO (*While COURTIERS are within hearing*): Hurry now, Taro, thread twenty needles with golden thread for me. Let us begin. In this corner— (*Pointing to empty loom*) we will weave a green and gold dragon's head.

TARO: Yes, just above a yellow chrysanthemum. Weave quickly. (*All* COURTIERS *exit.*)

DANZO: Quick, they are gone. Hide those silks. Empty those jewels here in my hidden pockets!

TARO (*Dancing around with the empty loom over his head*): Ha, ha, ha! We shall be buried alive, the Emperor said. Ha, ha, ha!

DANZO: Ha, ha, ha! Even the Emperor himself won't be noble or wise enough to see the robes we weave upon this loom!

1ST STORYTELLER: The wickedness in these men is coming forth in their deeds.

TARO (*Hurriedly placing loom before him and pretending to work upon it*): Here they come again! To work! (*They both work frantically.* COURTIERS *and* LADIES *enter and place more boxes of materials upon the floor, food and candles on table. They peer, much worried, at the empty loom, as* TARO *and* DANZO *pretend to weave imaginary threads back and forth through the empty frame.*)

LADY OF WARDROBE: We bring you boxes of the finest of jewels, rarest silks, and food for the quick-passing hours of the night.

LADY OF COFFERS: And candles that we pray will last you the hours through, until the sunrise of the day on which our noble Emperor must wear the robe you fashion. We bid you speed the night through till we see you in the morning!

FAN BEARER (*Looking into mirror*): I see myself. I see my robe. (*Looking at empty loom*) Am I blind if I see no other robe?

DANZO (*Quickly*): Give me those scissors, Taro. (*To* FAN BEARER) Will you give me a drink of the wine, kind sir?

We have not time even to raise the goblet to our lips. (FAN BEARER *gives* DANZO *drink.*) There, I feel better. Also please place food in the mouth of my assistant. My brow is dripping with perspiration, (*He wipes his forehead*) but it must be so if we are to have this robe woven by daylight.

TARO (*Holding up a jewel*): Here is a jewel with a flaw in it, Danzo.

DANZO: A flaw! Return the jewel to the coffers! Only flawless jewels must go into the making of his Worshipful Highness's robe. Hand me that large emerald, Taro, for the dragon's eye. Exquisite! The Emperor's robe will be true perfection! (*All except* DANZO, TARO, *and* STORYTELLERS *exit.*)

TARO: They've gone. Let us eat and sleep while we may. Hide the candles. In the morning only a low burnt one will remain as if we had worked all night.

DANZO: Fill your secret pockets with more jewels first. This large emerald goes into my pocket. (*They stuff their pockets with jewels and their mouths with food, arrange candle, then throw themselves idly upon the divan.*)

TARO (*Laughing*): Won't the Emperor look ridiculous walking in the grand procession without any clothes on? He wouldn't dare say he cannot *see* the robe!

DANZO (*Also laughing*): And all the courtiers who say they see no clothes will lose their high positions, or their heads! Ha, ha!

TARO (*Still laughing*): We may not know who is noble, but we shall soon find out who is *wise!* (*Curtain*)

*   *   *

SCENE 2

TIME: *The next morning.*

SETTING: *Same as Scene 1.*

AT RISE: STORYTELLERS *are onstage.* DANZO *and* TARO *are asleep on divan.* TARO *wakes up and stretches.*

TARO: Wake up, Danzo! Sh-sh! Here they come! (*They put low burnt candle between them, dash to their places and pretend to work again, now near the bottom of the loom.* KIYOMORI *enters. Taken unawares, he stares in amazement at empty loom.*)

2ND STORYTELLER: These rogues have planned well. Never were minds to be so tested for nobleness and wisdom!

DANZO: We need the last candle no longer. (*Blows it out*) Ah! We have almost finished with our work. (*Continuing to work, but looking slyly up at* KIYOMORI) Is not the robe beautiful? Do you not admire the exquisite blending of colors in this flower? (*Turns loom toward* KIYOMORI)

1ST STORYTELLER: See, Kiyomori grows pale. He is thinking: (KIYOMORI *pantomimes deep thought.*) Am I not fit to hold my great office of Prime Minister? Am I lacking in nobleness? For to my eyes this loom is empty and these weavers are weaving nothing!

DANZO (*Slyly*): I see you are speechless with admiration!

KIYOMORI (*Suddenly pulling himself together*): Oh, yes, the coloring is exquisite! The Emperor will be greatly pleased. *Greatly* pleased!

2ND STORYTELLER: In his heart, Kiyomori is worried about losing his high position, so he quickly makes believe he sees the robe.

TARO: And the train is over there! It is finished. Twenty-two and a half yards long. Is it not beautiful? (*Pretends to unroll train*)

KIYOMORI (*To himself*): Alas! I see no train! (*Aloud*) Oh, yes, the train is the most beautiful piece of weaving I have ever seen. (FAN BEARER, LADY OF COFFERS, LADY OF WARDROBE *enter. They, too, stare in amazement at the empty loom, but do not dare to look at each other.*)

FAN BEARER: The Emperor wishes to see his robe while it is still in place on the loom.

DANZO: It will be ready for his celestial eyes in two minutes. (FAN BEARER *exits.* DANZO *turns to* LADIES) You, also, seem lost in wonder over our marvelous work, just as the Prime Minister was when he saw it for the first time.

KIYOMORI (*Quickly*): Yes. Do you not greatly admire it, Lady of the Coffers and Lady of the Wardrobe? And look at the train over there. See, have you ever seen anything so finely wrought?

1ST STORYTELLER: Woe to the hearts of *these* two people. They are amazed in their hearts that they can see nothing of the Emperor's new clothes. They also decide to pretend to see, for the sake of their positions. Neither wisdom nor nobility are coupled here!

LADY OF COFFERS: Beautiful! Exquisite! How heavenly the design! Marvelous! Gorgeous!

LADY OF WARDROBE: How stunning the pattern! The Emperor will be pleased. How could he help being pleased! (FAN BEARER *appears at door.*)

FAN BEARER: His Worshipful Highness! (EMPEROR *enters and all step back to let him gaze at loom.*)

EMPEROR: I wish to see the robe while it is still on the loom. (*He looks, blinks, looks again and is puzzled.*)

2ND STORYTELLER: All hearts beat with the same puzzled throbbing! Highest of the high and lowest of lesser men!

DANZO: Ah, I see Your Worshipful Highness speaks not for sheer amazement and delight at beholding such beauty in a gown! Forgive us for praising our own work.

TARO (*Smirking*): We were inspired by your worshipful self to make so exquisite a piece.

1ST STORYTELLER: Alas! Deliver us from temptation! In so great a person as his Worshipful Highness a thorn has sprung among blossoms!

EMPEROR (*Coming down front, to himself*): Am I not worthy to be Emperor of this great Empire?

DANZO: You murmur words of approval, Worshipful Highness?

TARO: Do not these golden threads and dazzling jewels in your new robe cast a radiance upon all the faces in the room?

EMPEROR: Yes, yes! All the faces shine alike!

DANZO: I see you are pleased with your new robe. The train is there on the cushion. (EMPEROR *crosses to see train.*) And, Taro, show his Worshipful Highness the obi.

TARO (*Taking imaginary obi from other side of room*): Here is the obi, Your Worshipful Highness. We have lined it with the rich purple of the wisteria.

EMPEROR (*With forced emphasis*): Beautiful indeed! No one in all the world has ever woven clothes like unto these. I will be robed in them at once.

DANZO: We are ready. Take the gown from the loom, Taro. Now, if Your Worshipful Highness will disrobe, we will at once see that our handicraft fits you as your smile becomes your benign countenance. (LADIES *turn their faces to the wall while* KIYOMORI *disrobes the* EMPEROR *until he stands in a one-piece suit of long underwear.*)

TARO (*Pantomiming business of dressing* EMPEROR): Now, Your Worshipful Highness, just slip your arm in this sleeve. Now the other one. There! It fits you perfectly! Let us straighten out these folds. Ah, it becomes you admirably. (LADIES *all turn about to admire and gasp with shock.* TARO *and* DANZO *continue with elaborate gestures to dress the* EMPEROR *in the imaginary clothes, smoothing and brushing imaginary folds and unrolling imaginary train to stretch the width of stage.*)

DANZO: Now the obi, Taro. Ah, Your Worshipful Highness, you have a delightful surprise awaiting you when you look into the mirror. Around your waist—there, how the jewels dazzle! Now last, but not least, the train, Taro. Unwrap its two hundred and a half yards and lay it carefully on the floor. Now we fasten it to the shoulders, so! (*Again they smooth and straighten out the imaginary folds of the robe with the attached train.*)

KIYOMORI: Is not our Emperor's train the most beautiful you have ever seen, noble Lady of the Wardrobe?

LADY OF WARDROBE: Yes—yes—I have never seen anything like it!

LADY OF COFFERS: Nor I. It is most stunning to the senses!

EMPEROR (*Crosses to stand before the mirror. He suddenly starts when he sees himself without the robe. He quickly recovers, however, and turns from side to side as though admiring his robe.*): Yes. It is stunning to the senses! Nothing like it has ever been made for me. I am *quite* pleased, quite *pleased* . . .

LADY OF WARDROBE: *Quite* pleased! Quite *pleased!*

LADY OF COFFERS: Quite pleased!

KIYOMORI: Is Your Worshipful Highness now ready for the grand procession of the lanterns?

EMPEROR (*Nods his head*): Yes. (EMPRESS *enters*)

EMPRESS: Oh, here you are, my butterfly. I have been looking for you everywhere. (*Starts to cross room from behind the* EMPEROR)

DANZO (*Dashing to her*): Look out—the train! The train! Don't walk on the royal train!

LADY OF COFFERS: The train—the train—the royal train!

EMPRESS (*Looking about*): What train?

EMPEROR: Of my new robe, my spouse. Look, is it not beautiful?

EMPRESS (*Puzzled*): Why, you haven't. . . .

EMPEROR (*Hastily breaking in*): See—do you not admire the green and gold dragon with crimson fire spouting from its mouth?

2ND STORYTELLER: The poor Empress stands speechless with horror as she realizes that she cannot see the robe the Emperor and all the court apparently see. To her, the Emperor is without clothes.

EMPRESS (*Crosses to front stage and talks to herself*): Am I a simpleton? Am I not worthy to be the wife of my noble Emperor? Alas! Alas!

EMPEROR: And the obi. Do you not admire the obi?

EMPRESS (*Swallowing hard and pulling herself together*): Obis are beautiful!

EMPEROR: See how splendidly the robe fits across the shoulders. Now we are ready for the grand procession! (COURTIERS *enter carrying canopy and lanterns.*)

EMPRESS: You are going out in the streets like—like—

EMPEROR (*With emphasis, looking hard at* EMPRESS): We march at once about the palace and down the Flower Path. Who will carry my train?

KIYOMORI: I myself will carry it, Your Worshipful Highness. (*He proceeds to pick up imaginary train and, with empty hands raised, walks behind the* EMPEROR.)

EMPEROR (*Taking the arm of the* EMPRESS, *starts the procession*): Now I can surely find out who is worthy of his office, my dear!

COURTIERS (*Preceding* EMPEROR *with grand lantern and many smaller ones*): Make way for the grand procession. Make way for the Procession of the Lanterns! (*All fall into procession, one attendant carrying a canopy-parasol* over the head of the EMPEROR. *The* FAN BEARER *gently fans him as they progress. The* EMPEROR *shivers a little as they reach the open air upon the Flower Path where the populace (the audience) are waiting to see the procession and the new clothes.*)

SAKURA (*Entering and pulling at* DANZO's *sleeve*): Where is the Emperor? (*Pauses*) Where is the Emperor?

DANZO: There he is under the canopy-parasol in the procession being fanned by the fan bearer.

SAKURA: Now I see him, but I don't see his new clothes!

TARO: Sh-sh! Look! His clothes are beautiful, never more beautiful.

SAKURA: But I don't see *any* clothes on him.

FOOL (*Running in*): Oh, I'm late, I shall miss the procession.

SAKURA: There's the Emperor, but you mustn't look at him. He has no clothes on. Shame on him!

FOOL (*Suddenly sees* EMPEROR): Oh-oh-oh! (*Jumps up and down*) The Emperor has no clothes on! The Emperor has no clothes on! (*Laughs*)

SAKURA (*Laughing gleefully*): Of course, he has no clothes on.

FOOL (*Jumping again*): The Emperor has no clothes on!

SAKURA: The Emperor has no clothes on! (SAKURA *and* FOOL *dance about stage, then follow procession, repeating their words with great glee.*)

EMPRESS: My dear, listen to what that child and the fool are saying. They are saying that you have no clothes on.

EMPEROR (*Unabashed*): But, my dear, what can you expect from a fool and a child? (*Twirls his mustache. The procession proceeds down the Flower Path. As soon as it is out of hearing,* TARO *and* DANZO *gather up their spoils, not forgetting to steal the* EMPEROR's *robe which he had taken off.*)

DANZO: Now is our chance to get out of the kingdom with

our spoils. Quick, Taro, bundle up the robe the Emperor took off. We might as well take it, too.

TARO: Have you all the jewels, golden threads, and silks?

DANZO: I surely have. Ha, ha, ha! What fools these people are. Now we're off for parts unknown. We shall wipe the dust of Japan from our shoes forever! (*They start to sneak out of the palace.*)

1ST STORYTELLER: And so, with evil thoughts in their minds, these two wicked impostors will taint another nation of people. But hold! Listen to the cries of the people! Many there are who speak the truth with their eyes and their voices.

PEOPLE IN AUDIENCE (*Ad lib*): The Emperor—the Emperor. He has no clothes on. Get him a blanket—a blanket! (*A* COURTIER *brings a blanket, which is wrapped about the* EMPEROR.) Where are the impostors who perpetrated this hoax? The impostors! Where are they? (*Etc.*)

FOOL (*Rushing back up aisle with* SAKURA): There they are, there they are, stealing all the Emperor's money and jewels. Run, child, run! Catch that one by the pigtail. Quick, I'll catch this one. (*Grabs* TARO's *pigtail*)

SAKURA: I will, I'll pull his hair *hard!* (*Grabs hold of* DANZO's *pigtail.* TARO *and* DANZO *cry out in pain.* EMPEROR *re-enters, shamefaced.* LADY OF THE WARDROBE *puts his robe on him.* COURTIERS *re-enter.*)

EMPEROR: We thank you, honest child, and my noble fool, for what you have done for us by telling the truth this day.

FOOL: What is to be done with these wicked creatures, Worshipful Highness?

EMPEROR: Tie their pigtails together until punishment is meted out to them. (*The* FOOL *and* SAKURA *tie the two pigtails together and usher the impostors offstage.*)

COURTIERS: And what of us, O Emperor? Our eyes should be blinded in shame for our duplicity!

EMPEROR: And your Emperor also, my people! (FOOL *and* SAKURA *return to stage.* EMPEROR *draws them to his side, and places his hands upon their shoulders.*) A fool and a child have indeed led us now!

2ND STORYTELLER (*Rises and comes toward center stage*): And so in each and every mind is a new resolve for truthful thoughts and better deeds forever after! (*Curtain*)

THE END

Father Hits the Jackpot

by Juliet Garver

Characters

PAUL EVANS, *father*
LORRAINE EVANS, *mother*
SHEILA, *16* ⎫
TOMMY, *15* ⎪
CINDY, *14* ⎬ *their children*
PATRICE, *13* ⎭
AUNT MARION
COOK
TV ANNOUNCER
REPORTER

SCENE 1

TIME: *A Saturday afternoon.*
SETTING: *The Evans living room.*
AT RISE: PAUL EVANS *is sitting at his desk, working on a pile of bills.* MRS. EVANS *sits in armchair, sewing.* SHEILA *is doing her nails.* CINDY *is sprawled on the floor, absorbed in a movie magazine, while* PATRICE *is writing on a magazine in her lap.*

MR. EVANS: Bills, bills, and more bills—that's all I ever get in the mail these days. Tomorrow morning, I'm going to dump all the mail in the wastebasket, without even looking at it.

PATRICE (*Looks up, alarmed*): Oh no, you can't do that!

SHEILA: Patrice is afraid you'll throw away one of her precious samples—face powder, salve for aching muscles, baby cereal—what are you sending away for this time, Patrice?

PATRICE: Never you mind. (*Continues to fill out coupon, biting her pencil*)

MRS. EVANS: There's nothing wrong with Patrice's sending away for free samples.

MR. EVANS: How about sending away to Fort Knox? Maybe they'll send you a few nice samples. We sure could use them.

PATRICE: But it's fun sending away for samples! I like to collect things, all kinds of funny things.

SHEILA: She's getting almost as peculiar as Aunt Marion.

MR. EVANS (*Looking up*): Huh . . . your Aunt Marion. I wish she'd part with some of that money she stuffs her mattress with!

CINDY: Aunt Marion's a female Scrooge, if you ask me.

SHEILA: Imagine carrying an umbrella twelve months a year, rain or shine, and a purse with a lock and key—

PATRICE: And she wears the key on a chain around her neck!

MRS. EVANS (*Reprovingly*): Now, girls . . .

MR. EVANS: Well, I do think Aunt Marion ought to use her money for a good cause.

SHEILA: Us, for instance. We're her only relatives, after all.

MR. EVANS (*Sighs*): I'd almost agree . . . there's our wedding anniversary coming up next week. And I don't think I'll be able to afford anything more than going out for dinner.

MRS. EVANS: I don't mind, dear . . . really I don't.

MR. EVANS: There's so much I want for you, Lorraine, and
for the children. But there just never seems to be any
money left for anything extra.

SHEILA: Well, I've been baby sitting for years and buy lots
of my own clothes.

PATRICE: Being a sitter isn't so rough.

SHEILA: No? One evening with little Butch McWilliams
and you'd quit. Butch is a Space Man these days and
every Saturday night he kills me with his magic ray gun.
I have to lie down on the floor and pretend to be dead.

PATRICE: That should be a snap . . . for you.

MRS. EVANS (*Scolding*): Girls!

SHEILA: I wish we didn't always have to worry about
money.

CINDY (*In her best movie star manner*): So vulgar . . .

PATRICE: If we were rich, I'd buy twenty-nine cashmere
sweaters, one in every color of the rainbow. When they
got dirty, I'd just throw them away.

CINDY: If we had loads of money, I'd have a bedroom like
a movie star's, with white satin, quilted walls, shim-
mering satin sheets, and a white and gold telephone.

SHEILA: I'd have a car of my own—a purple convertible
with a pink top. (TOMMY *enters left with a letter in his
hand.*)

TOMMY: What's everybody so happy about? Dad get a
raise?

MR. EVANS: This is the most mercenary family.

TOMMY: Here's a letter from Aunt Marion. Just found it
in the mailbox when I came in.

MRS. EVANS: She never wrote us a letter before.

TOMMY: She has now. Her name's on the envelope. Here.
(*Hands it to* MRS. EVANS)

MRS. EVANS (*Reads envelope*): "Do not open till your
anniversary."

SHEILA: That's funny . . . it must be a present.

PATRICE: Probably an old family recipe for apple dumplings.

CINDY: Or a page from her mother's diary.

MRS. EVANS: Whatever it is, I won't open it till our anniversary. It wouldn't be right. (*Puts envelope down on desk*) There.

PATRICE: Tommy, what would *you* want, if we were rich, and you could have anything at all?

TOMMY: Food and more food—and then dessert. I'm starving! I had only three measly hamburgers for lunch.

PATRICE: I don't know how you had the strength to get home.

TOMMY: You be quiet. (*Heads for doorway upstage center.*) Think I'll have a little snack.

MRS. EVANS: Don't touch the fried chicken! We're having that for dinner—cold, with potato salad.

TOMMY (*Turns and faces them*): I know what *I'd* want if we were rich. Yeah . . . I'd sit on a banquet couch like Caesar and those guys and eat all day long . . . have servants bring steaming food . . . hot roast beef . . . golden brown turkey . . . mountains of French fries . . . mmm . . . that would be the life. Pardon me while I go console my aching stomach with a cheese sandwich or two. (*He exits.*)

CINDY: All he ever thinks about is his stomach.

SHEILA: Say, Mom, what would *you* want if you could have anything in the world?

MRS. EVANS (*Smiling*): Lots of things . . . a dishwasher, a freezer, a trip around the world . . .

MR. EVANS (*Grumbling good-naturedly*): Stop spending all the money I don't have! (*Gets up for his newspaper and settles himself on the couch*) My aching head. Why don't you women go dream somewhere else so I can work my trick crossword puzzle in peace? (*Concentrates on his newspaper*)

SHEILA: You still doing those puzzles for the *Daily Tribune* Contest?

MR. EVANS (*Without looking up*): Mm-hm . . . there's $25,000 in prizes. Maybe I'll win. There's a winner every week. They haven't announced last week's winner yet. They will any day now.

MRS. EVANS: I'd better see what Tommy's eating. He can make food disappear so fast. (*She goes.*)

SHEILA: Cindy, let's go upstairs and work on our secret project . . . you know . . . (*Hums "The Anniversary Waltz"*)

MR. EVANS (*Smiling*): I don't hear a thing . . . (*They exit.*) Oh, Patrice, how about mailing your new coupon?

PATRICE: All right. (*Takes her coupon and pen with her*) I can take a hint. (*She exits.*)

MR. EVANS (*Aloud, to himself*): Children . . . hm . . . I don't know what the world is coming to these days— talk, talk, talk. A man ought to wear ear muffs when he lives with so many women . . . (*Yawns*) I'm getting sleepy . . . (*Closes his eyes*) Maybe I'll close my eyes for a minute . . . feels good . . . (*Opens his eyes as* TV ANNOUNCER *comes onstage, wearing top hat.*)

TV ANNOUNCER: Mr. Paul Evans?

MR. EVANS: Yes?

TV ANNOUNCER: Congratulations! You've just won $25,- 000 on the TV Gold Mine Show. (*Hands him check*)

MR. EVANS: $25,000? *Me?*

TV ANNOUNCER: Yes, sir. Yours was the winning entry: the best 25 words on why you wanted to find a gold mine in your own backyard. Congratulations again! (*He exits.*)

MR. EVANS: $25,000? I can't believe it. (*Looks at check*) Yes, it's made out to me all right. . . . (REPORTER *enters, wearing felt hat way back on his head.*)

REPORTER: Mr. Paul Evans?

MR. EVANS: Yes?

REPORTER: I'm Carsons from the *Daily Tribune*. You're a mighty lucky man—yes, sir!

MR. EVANS: I am?

REPORTER: Yes sir. You've won the *Daily Tribune* trick crossword puzzle contest. First prize, $50,000. (*Hands him stack of play money*)

MR. EVANS: But—but I never won anything before in my life . . . (*Looks at money as* REPORTER *exits*) $50,000! We're rich! (*Starts throwing money into air*) Whee . . . we're rich! I'm going to buy a new car, a foreign one with air conditioning. And I'll buy Lorraine a fur coat! (MRS. EVANS *enters.*) Here, Lorraine, buy yourself a mink coat, buy two, one for everyday and one for Sunday. (*Throws money into air*) Whee! We're rich! (MRS. EVANS *looks astonished, as the curtain slowly closes.*)

*   *   *

SCENE 2

TIME: *The dream continues.*

SETTING: *The Evans living room.*

AT RISE: TOMMY *is reclining on the couch, Nero style, eating a giant bunch of grapes.* COOK *enters and looks at him anxiously.*

COOK: Will there be anything else, sir?

TOMMY (*Tearing off another grape and eating it*): Of course. What did I have? Just three small steaks, some French fries, two banana splits with hot fudge and now a measly bunch of grapes.

COOK: Three pounds of grapes.

TOMMY: A mere drop in the bucket.

COOK: You must have an awfully big bucket.

TOMMY: I beg your pardon?

COOK: Oh, I'm sorry. I didn't mean anything.

TOMMY: Well, I want some food—not right this minute, but in a little while. But don't keep me waiting. If my stomach growls, I'll growl at you!

COOK: Yes, sir, anything you say.

TOMMY: How about a pizza?

COOK: Begging your pardon, sir, are you sure all this won't kill you?

TOMMY (*Smiling*): My dear woman, can you think of a better way to die?

COOK (*Looks at him strangely*): N-no . . . I'll go to work on the pizza. Sausage or anchovy?

TOMMY: Both. And don't forget the onions and garlic.

COOK: I won't. Maybe I'd better call a doctor, too—just to stand by, in case . . . (*She exits.*)

TOMMY (*Dangling the grapes*): Ah, this is the life! (SHEILA *enters.*)

SHEILA: Tommy, I'm worried. You know, ever since I got my convertible, I've been so popular . . .

TOMMY: So what's so horrible?

SHEILA: Is it me the boys like or is it the convertible? (MRS. EVANS *enters.*)

MRS. EVANS: I don't know where we should go, Hawaii or Bermuda . . .

TOMMY: This family really has problems. . . . (PATRICE *enters, wearing four or five sweaters.*) What are you supposed to be, a mummy?

PATRICE: If you weren't so befuddled by food, you'd see I'm wearing my cashmere sweaters.

TOMMY: Why so many? Going to the North Pole to welcome Santa Claus?

PATRICE: Very funny.

MRS. EVANS: Aren't you too warm, dear?

PATRICE: I'll get used to it. (CINDY *enters, dressed theatri-*

cally, a feather in her hair, tottering on high heels, carrying a fan, etc.)

MRS. EVANS: Cindy . . . for goodness' sakes!

CINDY: How do I look? (*Turns around*)

TOMMY: Awful.

MRS. EVANS: Is this a costume for a play at school? You didn't tell me.

CINDY: Oh Mother, how can you be a mother and still be so naïve? I copied this from *Movie Moments* magazine —it's what Teresa DuLaine wore for the premiere of her latest picture!

MRS. EVANS: You're not going to school in that, are you?

CINDY: No. I went outside like this and some of the kids from school . . . well . . . they just don't understand. They don't even know what sophistication means. (MR. EVANS *enters.*)

MR. EVANS: And how's my happy family today?

PATRICE: A little warm . . .

MR. EVANS (*Not hearing her*): Wait till our anniversary next week! I'll have more surprises for everyone . . . especially for you, Lorraine.

MRS. EVANS: Paul, it's so wonderful to have money.

MR. EVANS: You bet it is. You know, I've been thinking. I'd like to paper one room in the house with dollar bills . . . the den upstairs . . . or should I make it five-dollar bills?

PATRICE: But that's showing off . . .

TOMMY: Look what's talking—Miss Eskimo of the Year.

PATRICE (*Tugging at the sweaters around her neck*): Whew! I can't stand all these sweaters. I guess I need only one sweater at a time. I'm going upstairs to change. (*She exits.*)

CINDY: I'll bet even Teresa DuLaine doesn't have a room papered with dollar bills . . . (*Looks down at her clothes*) Maybe I'll take off these clothes and put on a skirt and blouse . . . kinda lonely just parading around in here . . . (*She exits.*)

TOMMY (*Gets up*): If you'll excuse me, I'm going up to lie down. (*Puts his hand on his stomach*) I'm going to have the worst stomach-ache in history. (*Smiles wanly*) And I'm not even sure it was worth it. (*He exits.*)

MRS. EVANS: Paul, you didn't mean that about papering a room with dollar bills?

MR. EVANS: Mmm . . . I don't know. I've worried about money all my life. This is more fun . . . (*Takes money out of his pocket*) See, I can just throw it around . . . (*Throws money into the air. Curtain slowly closes.*)

*   *   *

SCENE 3

TIME: *A short time later.*

SETTING: *The Evans living room.*

AT RISE: MR. EVANS *is alone onstage, asleep on couch. He opens his eyes and looks around him slowly.*

MR. EVANS (*Stretches, yawns*): I thought it was a dream . . . too good to be true . . . and I don't think I could ever throw money around like that. (*Throws his hand up into the air as if he had money in it*) Whee . . . wasn't that something? (*Gets up and scans* AUNT MAR-ION's *envelope*) Wonder what's in this? For our last anniversary, Aunt Marion gave us a set of pot holders she made herself. (*Holds envelope up to light*) I can't believe it, but it looks like a check. I wonder if I should open it. (*Phone rings. He puts envelope down and goes to phone*) Hello? Paul Evans speaking. . . . What? . . . *Daily Tribune* Puzzle Contest? I did? Well! Thank you . . . yes . . . thank you very much! (*Hangs up*) What do you know? (*Weakly*) I won a prize in last week's contest. $2500. (*Looks around room a moment*) I *think* I'm awake now. (*Pinches himself*) Ow . . . yes . . . I must be awake—where is everybody? Lorraine! (*Shouts*) Tommy! Cindy! Patrice! (Mrs. EVANS *and* TOMMY *rush onstage, followed by* CINDY, PATRICE, *and* SHEILA)

MRS. EVANS: Paul, why are you shouting so?

MR. EVANS (*Smugly*): I'm a smart man, Lorraine, a smart man.

MRS. EVANS (*Impatiently*): Yes, yes, I know, but why all the shouting?

MR. EVANS: I just won a prize in the *Daily Tribune* Puzzle Contest. They called me on the phone.

PATRICE: I ought to try that instead of sending away for free samples.

MRS. EVANS: Paul, that's wonderful. How much did you win?

MR. EVANS (*Tries to be nonchalant*): Oh, a mere $2500.

TOMMY: Wow!

PATRICE: Double wow!

MR. EVANS: I'm going to buy you a nice present for our anniversary, Lorraine . . .

CINDY: Mother's going to be smothered in mink!

MR. EVANS (*Shakes his head*): No, nothing like that. I think we should be wise about this money. Maybe put it in the bank and save it to help put our children through college.

CINDY: What a horrible, sensible idea.

MR. EVANS (*Smiling*): Raising children can be horrible and sensible, too, at times.

PATRICE: Nothing exciting is ever going to happen to this family.

MRS. EVANS: Why, it just did. Your father won $2500, just like that! You never can tell what tomorrow will bring. (*Doorbell rings.*) I wasn't expecting anyone . . .

SHEILA: I'll get it. (*She goes to door and in a moment re-enters with* AUNT MARION.)

MR. EVANS: Why, Aunt Marion . . .

AUNT MARION: The weatherman said "Rain," but I thought I'd take a chance and come here anyway.

MRS. EVANS: That was very nice of you, Aunt Marion. Come on in.

AUNT MARION (*Walks towards others*): Of course, I brought my umbrella, just in case.

MRS. EVANS: We've just had some wonderful news.

PATRICE (*Not happily*): Yeah . . . Father won $2500 in the *Daily Tribune* Puzzle Contest.

AUNT MARION: My, think of that! $2500 . . .

MR. EVANS (*Pleased with himself*): Mm-m . . . think of that!

AUNT MARION: I suppose you have all sorts of plans for the money.

MR. EVANS: At first, I was kind of excited and thought maybe we'd all take a trip, to Hawaii or some place like that. But then, all of a sudden, I changed my mind. Most of that money's going right in the bank towards my children's college education.

CINDY: I'm not even sure I want to go to college. I don't know if an actress has to go to college.

AUNT MARION: Be quiet a minute, Cindy. Paul, you mean to tell me you're not going to spend that money foolishly?

MR. EVANS: No, I'm not. Oh, I might send a check to the Greenview Orphan Home, too. I always send them a check for Christmas, and I'd like to send them something extra, now that I've won this money.

AUNT MARION: I'd better sit down. (*She sits.*) This is all rather surprising to me.

MR. EVANS: I'm a little surprised myself. Oh, we've talked

about what we'd do if we had some extra money . . .

SHEILA: We sure have!

MR. EVANS: But when you actually have some, well . . .

MRS. EVANS: It's not the same thing at all.

AUNT MARION: I had no idea you felt like this about money. Hm . . . By the way, did you get my letter?

MR. EVANS: Yes, we did, but we didn't open it. You said not to, till our anniversary. (*Doorbell rings.*)

PATRICE: Maybe Father won some more money!

TOMMY: I hope it's the groceries—I'm starving! (*He goes to the door. REPORTER enters.*) No, it's not the grocery order.

REPORTER: Is this the Evans house?

TOMMY: Yes, but if you're selling encyclopedias, we have two sets already, and Mom's vacuum cleaner's in good shape.

REPORTER (*Laughing*): Now wait a minute, young fellow. I'm Jim Harrison from the *Daily Tribune.* You've probably read my column.

MR. EVANS (*Goes over to greet REPORTER*): Come in, Mr. Harrison. I'm Paul Evans, this is my wife, my aunt, Miss Selby, my children—Tommy, Sheila, Cindy, Patrice— (*The children nod as he says their names.*)

REPORTER: A fine family, Mr. Evans . . .

MR. EVANS: Thank you.

CINDY: Aren't you going to take our picture?

REPORTER (*Smiles*): No, afraid not, young lady. I'm here to interview Mr. Evans. The *Daily Tribune* likes to get a statement from each contest winner. (*Takes out pad and pencil*)

MR. EVANS: I'm the happiest man in the world since I won that $2500, and you can quote me.

REPORTER: Wait a minute—did you say $2500?

MR. EVANS: Why, yes . . . that's what I . . . you mean, I didn't win anything?

AUNT MARION: Well, speak up—speak up, young man.

REPORTER: Oh, yes, sir, you won a prize, but not $2500. I'm sorry, but you must have misunderstood my editor on the phone. He always talks with a cigar in his mouth.

MR. EVANS (*Weakly*): How—how much did I win?

REPORTER: Twenty-five dollars.

TOMMY: Oh, brother . . .

MR. EVANS: I see . . . (*Shrugs*) Well . . .

REPORTER: This would make a good story, but my paper wouldn't print it. My editor would hit the ceiling. Now, in a few words, just give me your reaction when you heard you were a contest winner.

MR. EVANS (*Still dazed*): I don't know what to say.

MRS. EVANS (*Helping out*): It's a—a surprise.

MR. EVANS: Yes . . . yes . . . that will do . . .

REPORTER: I'm sorry you didn't hear my editor right, Mr. Evans. We'll . . . uh . . . mail your check this afternoon. (*Starts to leave*)

MR. EVANS: Thank you. (REPORTER *leaves.*)

PATRICE: Don't feel bad, Father. We'll work our way through college, all of us.

CINDY: Tommy can work in a restaurant—maybe he'd get his meals free.

SHEILA: And I've had years of experience baby sitting. I could baby sit like mad for all the professors' wives.

MR. EVANS (*Tries to smile*): Things aren't that bad, really. We still have some money in the bank. Of course, I'm disappointed—and I did want to buy you something special for our anniversary, Lorraine.

MRS. EVANS: It doesn't matter, dear. Really it doesn't.

AUNT MARION (*Gets up*): I've changed my mind.

MRS. EVANS: You don't have to go home yet, Aunt Marion. I don't think it's going to rain.

AUNT MARION (*Goes to desk and gets her letter*): I'm going to open this letter.

CINDY: But Aunt Marion . . .

MRS. EVANS: You said we should wait.

AUNT MARION (*Opens letter and pulls out check*): I wrote you a check, but I'm going to tear it up. (*Tears up check as they all watch*)

SHEILA: I guess we're just not destined to be rich.

AUNT MARION: I wrote you a check for twenty-five dollars, but that was before I found out how sensible you could be about money, Paul. Now I'm going to write you another check for your anniversary. (*She goes to desk, unlocks handbag, pulls out checkbook and writes check.*) This check is for $2500.

MRS. EVANS: I'm speechless.

MR. EVANS: I'd better sit down . . . too much excitement for one day.

AUNT MARION: I'll admit I've been selfish, but I'm going to be different from now on.

TOMMY: I'm so surprised I've practically lost my appetite!

AUNT MARION (*Gets up and hands check to MRS. EVANS*): Here you are, Lorraine.

MRS. EVANS: I—I don't know how to thank you . . .

AUNT MARION: You don't have to. (*Gets her umbrella*) You see, Santa Claus doesn't always wear a beard. (*She winks.*) This time, he's carrying an umbrella. (*Waves her umbrella in the air*) Happy Anniversary!

MRS. EVANS (*Still amazed*): This is an anniversary we'll never forget . . . but never! (*Curtain.*)

THE END

The Mystery Ring

by Nathalie F. Gross

Characters

NANCY FOSTER, *twelve*   MRS. SIMPSON, *a neighbor*
JANE FOSTER, *eleven*   TIMID LADY
SALLY FOSTER, *nine*   MEAN LADY
MRS. FOSTER, *their mother*   FRIENDLY LADY

SCENE 1

TIME: *Saturday morning.*
SETTING: *The front lawn of the Foster home.*
AT RISE: NANCY *and* JANE *are sitting at a table at center.*

NANCY: I wish Sally would hurry up out here.
JANE: Why did we ever promise to play Treasure Hunt with her?
NANCY: Oh—we're just obliging to our little sister. (*Lightly*) Or maybe we have nothing better to do, and Mom worked out all the clues.
JANE: Boy, wouldn't I like to be seated on a horse right now—trotting through open country—sniffing cows and cactus—
NANCY: I'd settle for a pony ride in the park. Your horse fever is catching.

JANE: I don't think I've ever wanted anything as much as I want a horse.

SALLY (*Calling from off*): Here I come, Nancy and Jane. (*Enters, waving paper*) The Treasure Hunt can start! Mom gave me the first clue. It says: "Jump twice, starting from the table. Reach as far as you are able." I'll go first.

NANCY: Oh, no. We're all playing. Come on, Jane. Let's jump.

JANE: I'm going thataway. (*Takes two jumps upstage from table and hunts around. SALLY and NANCY jump and hunt in other directions.*)

NANCY (*Finding scrap of paper*): I found it! (*Reads*) "Second clue: Hop, hop, hop. You'll know when you must stop."

JANE: Hmm. What does Mom mean?

SALLY: I'll get this one. (*Starts hopping. NANCY and JANE hop, too. SALLY finds a small package.*) Say, look at this!

JANE: What is it?

NANCY: Why, it's a package! Maybe Mom put the next clue inside!

JANE: Open it up. (*SALLY unwraps package.*)

SALLY: Wowee—there's a ring! What a big red stone!

NANCY: That doesn't look like one of our clues.

SALLY: I don't see any note.

JANE: We'd better show Mother. (*Calling*) Mother. Mom!

MRS. FOSTER (*Entering*): How's the Treasure Hunt, girls?

SALLY: Look, Mommy. I just found this!

MRS. FOSTER: Well, my goodness! Where did that come from? It looks valuable. I wonder whose ring it is.

NANCY: It was right over there.

MRS. SIMPSON (*Entering*): Good morning, everybody.

ALL: Good morning, Mrs. Simpson.

MRS. SIMPSON: I couldn't tell from my yard what all the

jumping around was about, so I thought I'd better come over.

MRS. FOSTER: Glad to have you. I planned a Treasure Hunt for the girls, but see what they just found. (*Shows ring*)

MRS. SIMPSON: Ginger and jam! That's some ring. Let me look at it. (*Examines it*) That's a real ruby or I'm a homing pigeon. There's writing in here. 18 K—that's 18-karat gold! And here's something. D—A—I—Why, it says "Daisy H."

SALLY: Can we keep it, Mom?

NANCY: We could all take turns wearing it, even Mom.

MRS. FOSTER: No. We can't keep it, girls. I think we'd better put an ad in the paper.

JANE: I know. "Found. Gold ring. Ruby stone. Inscribed 'Daisy H.' Call at 1399 Middle Avenue."

NANCY: No, Jane. Let's not tell about the stone or the name. We'll just say "gold ring." Then we can be sure that the right owner comes for it.

MRS. FOSTER: Very good idea!

MRS. SIMPSON: Well! You've found quite a treasure while you were hunting, haven't you, girls?

SALLY: I'm going to look for more clues and more rings. Gangway, everybody!

CURTAIN

*　　*　　*

SCENE 2

TIME: *Next morning.*

SETTING: *The same.*

AT RISE: MRS. FOSTER *is showing a newspaper to* NANCY, JANE *and* SALLY.

MRS. FOSTER: There's our ad, at the top of the column, under "Lost and Found."

SALLY: Let me see.

JANE: It looks important.

NANCY: What if no one comes to claim the ring?

MRS. FOSTER: I guess we'll turn it over to the police. Maybe we should have done that right away.

NANCY: Oh, no! It's much more exciting to meet the person who lost it. (*Telephone rings offstage.*) There's the telephone.

JANE: I'll answer. (*Races off*)

SALLY: If it's for me, I'm not playing with anybody. I don't want to miss anything right here.

NANCY: That's how I feel.

JANE (*Re-entering*): Mother, it's the Red Cross office. They need you to drive a patient to the Veterans' Hospital.

MRS. FOSTER: Oh, dear. I can't leave you girls this morning.

NANCY: Sure you can. Probably no one at all will come for the ring. And you don't want to spoil your record with the Red Cross.

JANE: What should I say?

MRS. FOSTER (*Hesitates*): Well—say I'll do it. And get the patient's address. (JANE *exits. Thoughtfully*) I'm not at all sure I ought to leave.

SALLY: I'll call for help if we need it. Mrs. Simpson can always hear me.

NANCY: Don't worry about us, Mom. (JANE *re-enters.*)

JANE: The Red Cross lady sounded very pleased. I left the address near your purse.

MRS. FOSTER: Thanks, dear. Now look, girls. I'm putting the ring right here. (*Takes ring box from pocket and places it on table*) Keep your eye on it.

SALLY: With the three of us, it's safe.

Mrs. Foster: And I'll hurry back. (*Exiting*) Please be careful!

Sally: 'Bye, Mommy.

Nancy: I hate just waiting. What can we do?

Jane: Wish we lived on a ranch. I'd gallop round and round on my horse!

Sally: We could *play* horse.

Nancy: We're kind of big for that, Sallykins.

Sally: Want to play croquet?

Jane: That's not a bad idea.

Nancy: Get the croquet set, Sally. (Timid Lady *enters, carrying newspaper.*)

Sally (*Alerting her sisters*): Psst! Psst!

Timid Lady (*Reading*): 1399 Middle. 1399 Middle. (*To girls*) Is this 1399 Middle Avenue?

Jane: Yes. It is.

Timid Lady: May I speak to your mother, girls?

Nancy: Mother isn't home. May we help you?

Timid Lady: Well, I'm here about a ring. A ruby ring I lost.

Sally (*Squealing*): Oh!

Nancy: Can you describe it for us?

Timid Lady: It's a very precious ring. It has been in my family for three generations. It's always worn by the oldest daughter on her right hand.

Jane: What does it look like, please?

Timid Lady: Why—the band is a wide piece of silver— very wide.

Nancy: Did you say silver?

Timid Lady: Yes. And there are little flowers stamped near the stone.

Nancy: Oh. I'm very sorry. That isn't like the ring we found. Ours is gold.

Sally: We said so in the paper.

Timid Lady: Oh, dear. Are you *sure* yours is gold?

SALLY: Yes.

TIMID LADY: I'm so sorry I bothered you. So sorry indeed.

JANE (*Kindly*): It's too bad we don't have your ring. We hope you find it soon.

TIMID LADY: Thank you, girls. Thank you. (*Exits*)

NANCY: Poor dear.

JANE: Sally, you sounded rude about our ad in the paper.

SALLY: Well, she should read more carefully and not waste our time.

NANCY: Don't be so impolite, or we'll send you inside.

SALLY: Huh. Think you're the boss! (MEAN LADY *enters.*) Just 'cause Mom isn't home!

JANE (*Grimly*): Just wait till Mom gets back!

MEAN LADY: Girls! Can you stop quarreling long enough to listen to me?

NANCY: Why—what can we do for you?

MEAN LADY: I've come for my ring. It's advertised at this address. I'll reward you, all three of you. Now give it to me, please.

JANE: You'll have to identify it first. What does it look like?

MEAN LADY (*Huffily*): Now you don't think I'm telling a story, do you? (SALLY *sits down on the table in front of ring box.*) It is a gold ring. All gold.

JANE: We mentioned that in our ad.

NANCY: Does it have a stone?

MEAN LADY: A stone?

SALLY: Yes. What does the stone look like?

MEAN LADY: Oh—the stone. Let me see. It's—a beautiful diamond.

SALLY: Well, you're wrong! (*Jumps off table*) It isn't!

JANE: I'm sorry. (*Firmly*) We don't have your ring.

MEAN LADY (*Angrily*): Well, I'm not so sure of that. Where's your mother?

242 THE MYSTERY RING

NANCY: Mother stepped out—for a moment. But we don't have your ring.

MEAN LADY: I've a good mind— (*Spying ring box on table*) I'll just look for myself. (*Grabs for box*)

JANE: Don't you dare—

NANCY: Leave that box alone!

MEAN LADY (*Seizing box and opening it*): This box is empty! There's no ring in it! You never found a ring. You're fakers! Why—I ought to have you three arrested! Making me come all the way across town—I'll report you to the police, that's what I'll do! (*Exits*)

NANCY: Phew! What an old crow! Glad she's gone!

JANE: But where's the ring?

NANCY: That's right! What happened to it?

JANE: Do you think the first lady took it?

SALLY: Uh-uh. She didn't.

NANCY: How do you know so much, little one?

SALLY: See? (*Holds up right hand, with ruby ring on it*)

JANE: Why, you blessed idiot.

SALLY: That lady scared me. So I thought the ring was safest on me.

NANCY: You're fresh—but not so dumb!

SALLY: Thank you, sis.

NANCY: Let's put the ring in the house. Maybe we shouldn't talk to anybody else till Mom gets home.

JANE: That old witch looked mean enough to grab the ring and run.

SALLY: Bet she didn't even lose one! (*Exits with ring box*)

NANCY: This is more complicated than I expected.

JANE: I guess we really shouldn't trust anyone who claims the ring. (FRIENDLY LADY *enters.*)

FRIENDLY LADY: Pardon me, young ladies.

NANCY: How do you do.

FRIENDLY LADY: I'm sorry to trouble you, but there was an ad in the paper about a ring—

JANE: Yes, I believe Mom put one in.

FRIENDLY LADY: May I speak to your mother?

NANCY: She's out now.

FRIENDLY LADY: Oh, dear. I'll just have to come back again. Oh, dear. Thank you, girls. (*Starts to leave*)

NANCY: Maybe we can help you.

FRIENDLY LADY: It's such a valuable ring. My husband tells me the ruby is most unusual.

JANE: The ruby?

FRIENDLY LADY: Yes. You see, my husband is a jeweler. He knows all about precious gems. He asked me to deliver this ring the other evening. I was carrying some toys for my grandchildren, and I was sure I had the little package safe in my pocket, but somehow—(SALLY *appears and stands listening.*)

NANCY: Can you describe the ring for us?

FRIENDLY LADY (*Slowly*): I've only seen it once. Let me think. There was a narrow gold band—and an oval-shaped ruby.

JANE: Was there any inscription in the ring?

FRIENDLY LADY: Hmm. I think not.

NANCY (*Uncertainly*): Well, I don't believe we—

JANE: We'll have to wait till Mother gets here. She'll— (SALLY *starts to hum loudly the song "Daisy, Daisy, give me your answer, do."*)

FRIENDLY LADY: Why, it's just come to me. There *was* an inscription. My husband mentioned it. It was— "Daisy H."

SALLY: That's right! Let's show the lady the ring! (*Dashes off to get ring*)

JANE (*Excitedly*): I think we have your ring!

FRIENDLY LADY: Oh, I hope so. It will mean so much to my husband and me to get it back.

NANCY (*Calling*): Hurry up, Sally.

SALLY (*Dashing in with ring*): This is yours, isn't it?

FRIENDLY LADY: Yes, it is! It is! Well, my goodness me!

SALLY: I knew it! I could tell. That's why I gave you a hint.

FRIENDLY LADY: Why, bless you all! What good, honest children you are! Now, I shall have to see about a fine reward for you.

NANCY: Oh—that won't be necessary.

SALLY: But maybe the lady wants to give *me* something. After all, I found it—

JANE (*Scolding*): Sally!

FRIENDLY LADY: My husband will probably want to give each of you some jewelry.

NANCY: Thank you very much. I don't know whether Mother will let us accept.

FRIENDLY LADY: Well—do you girls like to ride horses?

JANE: Do we!

FRIENDLY LADY: I thought so! Now, we own a little farm outside town and you girls are welcome to come out and ride our horses any time you like.

NANCY: Thank you! Mother won't object to that!

SALLY: What a break! Is there a horse for each of us?

FRIENDLY LADY: Yes, there is.

SALLY: Hooray! (*Gallops around happily as though riding a horse*)

NANCY: Maybe Mother will let us go today!

JANE: This is the nicest thing that ever happened! Ever, ever, ever! (*Curtain*)

THE END

The Gypsy Look

by *Anna Lenington Heath*

Characters

PAUL MORTON
NORA MORTON, *his older sister*
SUE CONWAY, *his cousin*
BUTCH DAVIS
RHODA LESTER
VIC ADAMS

SETTING: *The living room of the Morton home.*
AT RISE: PAUL *is pacing the room impatiently. He looks at his watch, shakes his head, and mutters to himself as* NORA *enters carrying* PAUL's *suit, several books and a purse.* NORA *thrusts the suit into* PAUL's *hands, crosses to a big chair and drops into it, keeping the books and purse on her lap.*

PAUL: Where on earth have you been, Nora? I've been waiting an hour.
NORA (*Smiling*): My, my. You're even better than the Marines, brother.
PAUL: And what does that crack mean?
NORA: They specialize in the difficult—you do the impossible.
PAUL: Yeah?

NORA: You've waited an hour in the twenty minutes it took me to get your suit from the cleaner's and stop at the library. There must be a lot of lead sinkers sewed into your coat, from the weight of it. (*Rubs her arm*)

PAUL (*Contritely*): Thanks, sis. I'm sorry I snapped. It seemed an hour to me. I'm sort of upset.

NORA: Skip it. What's the trouble? (PAUL *goes to table, takes an apple from basket, and bites into it.*) You'll get indigestion, gobbling an apple that way.

PAUL (*Diffidently*): You—you remember Rhoda Lester, don't you?

NORA: Of course. The California girl who visited the Hendersons last year. You wrote a poem to her beginning:
"Sweet Rhoda of the redwoods,
The West's most fairest flower—"

PAUL (*In annoyance*): No need to bring that up.

NORA: You're right. Rhoda's a good kid. What about her?

PAUL: She's at the Hendersons' again this week. I've asked Mother to have her here to dinner tonight.

NORA: Good. It will be nice to see her again. What's upsetting about it?

PAUL: Well—well—Butch is having his meals here while his folks are away, and—well—you know Butch—he'll give Rhoda a rush, and I want to talk to her myself.

NORA: You'll just have to be more entertaining than he is.

PAUL: Oh, sis, have some sense! I don't have the line of chatter he has. You'll have to help.

NORA: How?

PAUL (*Gulping desperately*): Make yourself attractive to Butch.

NORA (*Indignantly*): *Make* myself attractive to Butch. I *am* attractive to Butch Davis. He likes me fine.

PAUL: Oh, I know he likes you. He likes Mother and Sue and all of us. I want you to interest him—well—sort of —romantically.

NORA (*Letting books and purse fall to floor*): Romantically? Butch? I'd have more chance with the man in the moon.

PAUL: Now don't be like that, Nora. You're pretty. You're smart, and you can be mighty come-hitherish when you want to be.

NORA (*With conviction*): Not with Butch. He's in and out of this house like the family. He's seen me at my worst; before breakfast, after baby-sitting; after I'd fallen into the river, and once, asleep with my mouth open.

PAUL: He knew you had a cold and couldn't breathe any other way.

NORA: True, but the revolting picture remains. It's no use, brother.

PAUL: But, Nora! You must have something! The Blake boys are forever here, and I'm always stumbling over Vic Adams. They sure don't come to see me.

NORA: Oh, they're different—guests. They see me at my best. Charming, all prettied up and maybe, a bit mysterious. Butch practically lives here.

PAUL (*Pleading*): This means a lot to me, Nora. You could charm and mystify Butch, too, if you'd try.

NORA: Butch would laugh his head off. And besides, Paul, I have no time to waste on him. I baby-sit with the Neven twins through the dinner hour.

PAUL (*Looking at watch*): You'll have time enough before that. Butch will be here any minute now. I have to do an errand for Mother and then pick up Rhoda. Do this for me, sis. "I'm asking," as we used to say when we were little.

NORA: Paul, it wouldn't be any use.

PAUL (*Turning back after moving toward door upstage right*): "I'm asking," Nora.

NORA (*Throwing up her hands*): Oh, I'll give it a try, but it'll flop. Butch is sure going to be surprised.

PAUL: It'll wake him up to what he's been missing.

NORA (*Coldly*): Don't be silly. And don't expect— (SUE *enters at right.*) Hi, Sue.

SUE: Hi, Nora—hello, Paul.

PAUL: Don't you have anything to do at home to keep you out of our hair?

SUE: I do. I haven't been over here before today.

PAUL: And why are you here now?

SUE: I've been studying a book on acting, and I've come to practice what I've learned.

PAUL: Practice on Nora then. I've something more important to do. And don't stay long. Nora has a job, too. (*Exits at left*)

SUE (*Reflectively, after watching* PAUL *go*): My cousin Paul has a vexed, distraught look. What's on his mind? And what's the job you have to do?

NORA: Plenty, on both counts. Rhoda Lester's in town, and she is coming to dinner tonight. Butch Davis is eating here while his folks are away at a convention. Paul has set me the job of distracting Butch's attention from Rhoda.

SUE: So-o-o. With all due credit to you, coz, that's quite an assignment.

NORA: Are you telling me?

SUE: I could invite him over to our house.

NORA: He wouldn't go. Mother's having chicken pie, and he knows it.

SUE: Maybe we could induce him to go off on some wild goose chase where he'd get lost.

NORA: You could lose a homing pigeon easier. Sleeping potions and blunt instruments are out, too. We're stuck with Butch, and I'm elected to charm him.

SUE: Then talk to him about himself, the things he likes and can do. That's supposed to win any man. Butch plays good baseball.

NORA: He has told me all he knows and thinks he knows about baseball a hundred times. That goes for football, track, hot rods, and wrestling, too. We've worn them all out. (NORA *walks about, troubled.*)

SUE: Skating?

NORA: A thousand times, *No.* I can skate rings around Butch.

SUE: Parlor games? Anagrams?

NORA: Don't be foolish. Butch isn't the intellectual type. I'd do better trying to draw him out about something he doesn't like.

SUE: It's all over but the shouting, then. Just bring up the subject of gypsies and stand clear.

NORA: Gypsies? What gypsies?

SUE: Oh, I forgot. You've been away for two weeks. Has no one told you of the ruckus Butch had with the gypsies over his cousin, Maisie Fenner?

NORA: Not a word. What gypsies and what about? Talk fast. My time is short.

SUE: A big outfit, rigged up like a gypsy caravan, is camped at the Trailer Park advertising sporting goods: guns, fishing poles, skis, camp equipment, and the like.

NORA: I saw it as I came in on the bus, but I didn't know what it was.

SUE: There's an old chief, a fat woman who tells fortunes, and six or eight others, all in gypsy costumes. *And* a devastating young man named Tonio. He's really something. Maisie met him first.

NORA: She would.

SUE: She dropped some bundles when she was passing, and Tonio picked them up for her.

NORA: Things like that happen to Maisie. Then, what?

SUE: Tonio met her several times, just happened to, you know, then took her on a tour of the camp and the old woman told her fortune.

NORA: Promised riches, travel, romance and a lot of sporting goods, I suppose.

SUE: And charged her a dollar for the fortune. Maisie told about it and took to wearing big hoops in her ears and a scarlet head scarf like Tonio's.

NORA: Which Butch objected to.

SUE: Girl, that's the understatement of the year. He tore up an acre of grass! Then he went out to the camp and bawled out the fortuneteller for robbing a simpleton of a kid. He threatened to lick the socks off Tonio, who wasn't there at the moment.

NORA: Butch has a pretty low boiling point. Maisie's only his second cousin. Is that all?

SUE: No. The old gypsy chief told him to get off the lot and stay off, or he'd have him arrested.

NORA: And Butch took off. I suppose he's still boiling and waiting to catch this Tonio off base.

SUE: Yes, and to make him still sorer, a lot of the other girls have taken to wearing ear hoops and gay head scarves. "The Gypsy Look" they call it. (*Takes pair of hoop earrings from her pocket*) I have a pair but haven't dared to wear them yet.

NORA (*Examining the earrings*): There's a box of hoops like these and several sashes and head scarves among the costumes Mother brought here after the guild play. (*Returns the rings*) Sue, what does this Tonio look like?

SUE: He's a slender, dark boy about my height, has a little

black mustache—handsome, really. Just mention him, and Butch'll forget everything else, Rhoda included.

NORA (*Thoughtfully*): I think I have a better idea. You say you have been studying how to be an actress. Here's where you get a workout. Come with me. (NORA *leads* SUE *out right. A moment later* BUTCH *enters left, very much at home. He tosses cap to couch, helps himself to candy after careful examination, finds funny paper on table, sits sprawled in big chair, reading and eating. A few seconds later, he rises, gets more candy, returns to chair and starts reading. Voices off right.* NORA *and* SUE *re-enter.* SUE *has small suitcase.*)

BUTCH (*Half rising*): Hi, girls. (*Slumps back into chair.*)

NORA *and* SUE: Hi, Butch.

BUTCH (*Noticing suitcase*): Are you leaving us, Susan? Going away?

SUE: Only a short way—be back before you miss me.

BUTCH: Good. Want me to walk you home?

SUE: No, thank you. It's exactly sixty-two steps from this door (*Indicating door at left*) to mine. I can get there before you can swallow that candy, untangle yourself and find your cap.

BUTCH: I don't doubt it. Have a good time on your little trip. Go slow and hurry back. 'Bye.

SUE: 'Bye. 'Bye, Nora. (*Exits left*)

BUTCH: Where's everybody?

NORA: Mother's at a meeting, and Paul's on some errand for her. I'm going to get ready to baby-sit.

BUTCH: The Wilson terror?

NORA: No, the Neven twins. (*Walks to door.* BUTCH *stands at table looking over candy left in dish.*)

BUTCH: Is this candy for the boy friend?

NORA (*Turning*): No, I told Vic I was baby-sitting. But don't eat it all. Paul might like a piece, and it'll spoil your appetite, anyway. (*Exits*)

BUTCH: Not my appetite. (*Selects candy, then sits and reads. A moment later* NORA *re-enters wearing gay head scarf and big hoop earrings.* BUTCH *speaks without looking up.*) I left the hard pieces Paul likes. I wish sometime you'd make—(*Looks up, stares an instant, speechless, bounds up, yells*) Suffering seacats! You, too, Nora? I thought you had more sense!

NORA (*Undisturbed*): It's becoming, isn't it?

BUTCH: If you like that gaudy sort of thing, but that isn't the idea.

NORA: What is the idea, if any?

BUTCH: The idiocy of the thing. Regular girls like you putting bandannas on your heads and curtain rings in your ears because a kooky cousin of mine went ga-ga over a mail-order gypsy.

NORA: I haven't seen Tonio, but I hear he is very handsome.

BUTCH: Like a drugstore cowboy. This whole thing's unfitten—

NORA: The word is "unfitting." Have some candy?

BUTCH: I've had candy. I begin to think you're no brighter than Maisie. Of all the cock-eyed—(*Voices off left.* PAUL *ushers in* RHODA. BUTCH *becomes badly flustered.*)

NORA (*Welcoming* RHODA *warmly*): Rhoda, it's good to see you again. How have you been?

RHODA: Fine, thank you, Nora, and I am so glad to be here again. I had such a wonderful time last year. (*Stands back from* NORA *admiringly*) You have the new Gypsy Look. It's really cool. I'm going to get a scarf and hoops tomorrow. (PAUL *beams and* BUTCH *glowers.*)

PAUL (*To* RHODA): You remember Butch, don't you?

RHODA (*Turning to* BUTCH): Of course I do. How are you, Butch? Nice to see you again.

BUTCH (*In confusion*): Yes, it is nice. Nice for you, I mean.

No, I don't—it isn't—Oh, gosh, how do you do. (PAUL
and NORA *smile at each other.*)

RHODA (*Puzzled, but kind*): You must take me shopping,
Butch, as you did when I was here last year. I must have
some hoop earrings. I'm crazy about the Gypsy Look.
(NORA *nervously watches door at left.*)

BUTCH (*Without thinking*): You sure must! Oh, I didn't
mean—I'm going to be busy tomorrow. Maybe you'd
better. I mean—(*A knock is heard at door left.* PAUL
opens door, and VIC *breezes in.*)

VIC: Hi, everybody. How's every little thing? (NORA *is
plainly dismayed. She was not expecting* VIC. BUTCH
mumbles reply to VIC.)

PAUL (*Trying to save situation*): Rhoda, this is Vic Adams.
Vic, Rhoda Lester.

RHODA: How do you do, Vic.

VIC: Glad to meet you, Rhoda. You're the girl from the
Golden West, aren't you. Paul's been lyric in your praise,
and I hear even the other girls love you.

RHODA (*Bowing mockingly to* VIC): Silver-tongued flat-
terer, isn't he, Paul?

PAUL (*Not too pleased with* VIC): He has quite a line.
Come, sit down. (*Leads* RHODA *to couch, sits beside her.*
BUTCH *takes big chair.* NORA *and* VIC *stand by table.*
PAUL *and* RHODA *talk pleasantly in low tones.* BUTCH
sulks.)

NORA (*Covertly watching left door*): I'm due to baby-sit
in a little while, Vic. I'm sure I told you.

VIC: Sure. I'll walk you down.

NORA: No need to bother. It's just a few blocks.

VIC: No bother. A pleasure.

NORA (*In desperation*): But I don't want—

VIC (*Oblivious of her agitation*): Aw, I'm glad to do it.
The streets are pretty dark. You don't have to tear off

right now. Let's talk to Rhoda. (VIC *goes to couch.*
NORA *remains at table, watching door*) Did you have a
good trip, Rhoda?

RHODA: Not too good. I was delayed by washouts, some in
—(*Knock is heard at door left.* NORA *opens door,
and* SUE *stands revealed in doorway dressed in slacks,
gay shirt, sash, head scarf, hoop earrings and a small
black mustache. All stare in silence a moment.* BUTCH
yelps "Tonio!" and plunges belligerently toward SUE.
VIC, PAUL *and* RHODA *step forward into space between*
BUTCH *and door.* NORA *pushes* SUE *out and slams door.
She stands in front of it facing* BUTCH.)

BUTCH: Let me out there!

NORA: You'll make no scenes here, Butch Davis.

BUTCH: I'll make one outside all right. There are two
doors to this room. (*Turns and plunges toward door at
right rear. Collides with* RHODA, *who is saved from falling by* PAUL. BUTCH *finds* VIC *in his way, jumps right to
avoid him.* VIC *makes simultaneous move and they face
each other again. They repeat this movement twice.*)
Stand still, you lug, and I'll go around you! (VIC *complies.* BUTCH *rushes out, right.*)

VIC: Impetuous guy, friend Butch, isn't he?

PAUL: Are you all right, Rhoda?

RHODA (*Clinging to* PAUL): Yes, thanks to you, Paul. I'd
have been on the floor if it hadn't been for you. You
are so strong and gentle. (PAUL *is very pleased*) Whatever ails Butch? (*As* PAUL *and* RHODA *talk,* NORA *again
opens door at left, pulls* SUE *inside and closes door. All
gape at* SUE *in astonishment.* RHODA *squeals delightedly,
runs to* SUE. *They embrace, and* SUE *shows exaggerated
gallantry and affection toward* RHODA. PAUL *wraps his
arms about his head and groans in anguish.* VIC *is astonished,* NORA *poker-faced.*)

VIC: For Pete's sake, Nora. Do something. This is getting all out of control.

RHODA (*Seeing reaction of* PAUL *and* VIC): Oh, you precious sillies. It's Sue Conway. (SUE *bows deeply, hand on heart.* PAUL *stares dumbly.* VIC *steps close to* SUE, *gives her a long look.*)

VIC: As I live and breathe, it is cousin Sue. Gals, you are beyond me. Marvelous and wholly unexpected. Is this some sort of a run-around you are giving Butch?

NORA: He made fun of our Gypsy Look—thinks we're a lot of silly sheep.

VIC: So you're making a monkey out of him. Fair enough. (*Sound of steps off left*) If I'm not mistaken, here he comes back for more. (NORA *clutches* SUE's *arm, points to big chair.* SUE *scuttles behind it and crouches out of sight. Others face door at left, as* BUTCH *enters.*)

PAUL (*Relaxed and happy again*): Well, did you catch him?

BUTCH: No. Didn't even see him. Think I heard him splitting the breeze over toward B Street. That mail-order gypsy won't bother you again, Nora.

NORA (*Much too sweetly*): Thank you so much. You've saved me from a terrible fate.

RHODA: His looks are simply ravishing, Butch. (*Clasps her hands in mock ecstasy*) And that mustache!

VIC: You shouldn't have run the guy off, Butch. He's so romantic!

PAUL: You might like him fine if you got to know him, kid. (SUE *has bobbed in and out of sight from behind chair several times.*)

NORA (*Reluctantly, after glance at watch*): Much as I hate to leave this party, I must get along to my baby-sitting.

BUTCH: I'll walk you down, Nora.

VIC (*In protest*): Just a moment, laddie, just a moment.

I came here for the express purpose of escorting Nora to her job.

BUTCH: She wasn't expecting you. She told me so herself.

VIC: That makes no difference. Expected or not, I'm here, and I walk Nora to wherever she's going. (PAUL *and* NORA *exchange worried glances.*)

BUTCH: That's what you think.

VIC: It is, and I'm going—(*Sees* SUE *shaking her head wildly at him*) to let you do it. (*Helps himself to candy*) You win, and I hope the gypsy sticks out a foot and trips you flat on your face. Goodbye, Nora. I shall cherish you in my heart. (BUTCH *ignores* VIC, *leads* NORA *left.* NORA *throws kiss to* PAUL *who raises hands in "O.K." sign.* NORA *exits.*)

BUTCH (*To* VIC): In case you have any ideas about the return trip, I'm waiting on the curb till the baby-sitting's over, no matter how late it is, and will see Nora safely home. (*Exits, slamming door*)

VIC (*Calls after* BUTCH): On your way! (*Walks to big chair.* SUE *comes out. He pulls mustache from her lip*) Now tell the folks good night, Susan, and I'll walk *you* home, the long way, around four blocks, and you'll tell me all about this goofy business. There's more in the dish than floats on the surface, I well know. (SUE *nods good night to* PAUL *and* RHODA *with mock meekness, and exits left with* VIC.)

RHODA: I do have the greatest times when I come here, Paul, even if I don't know what's going on.

PAUL: You don't know the half of it, lady, but Mother's home now. Come on out and see her. (*They exit at right rear, as curtain falls.*)

THE END

Poet's Nightmare

by Elbert M. Hoppenstedt

Characters

Maryann Martin	Jim
Alfred Martin, *her brother*	Andy
Mrs. Martin	Steve
Jane	Carol

Setting: *The living room of the Martin home.*

At Rise: Maryann *is dialing a number on the telephone. She glances furtively around and then speaks in a subdued voice.*

Maryann: Hello, Jane? Maryann. Listen. I need your help . . . about Alfred. He's up to one of his old tricks again. He's acting the poet . . . yeah, since he published that poem . . . what's wrong with *that?* Ye gods, you should live with him now. He's impossible. The doors aren't high enough to get his nose under. You've got to help, Jane. The Christmas vacation will be ruined if we don't do something to get him straightened out. (*Hears noise offstage.*) Somebody's coming. Can you come over? I'll tell you all about it. Yes. Yes. All right. Goodbye. (*Hangs up, as* Mrs. Martin *enters*) Oh! It's you, Mother.

Mrs. Martin: Of course it is, dear. Who else would it

be? Your father's at work. You're here, and Alfred—well, who knows where *he* is! (*Sitting on couch and picking up knitting*) Your brother is a famous poet now, I suppose you know. He told me so himself.

MARYANN: Poet! Just because he got one sticky, slushy love poem published in the *Youth Journal of Poetry*! It's all Carol's fault, and I told her so. Ever since he wrote her that love letter from prep school, and she was dope enough to answer it, he's been so lovesick you can't talk to him. That's what started all this poetry writing, I know! He's putting on an act to impress Carol.

MRS. MARTIN: You're not being fair to your brother, Maryann.

MARYANN: I'm not, huh! This is just another one of his acts. Mother, we simply *must* do something to get him over this. He'll be the laughingstock of the town before he's finished. You know, I think people look at me now and smile to themselves. I can almost hear them whisper: "That's the sister of that screwy, half-baked poet—"

MRS. MARTIN: Maryann, watch your language.

MARYANN: Well, those are the only words I can think of to express what I think. Mother, something *has* to be done.

MRS. MARTIN: Let the boy alone. He'll get over it by himself—the way he did all those other times.

MARYANN: Yes—like the time he thought he was a great detective, and went around looking for things with a magnifying glass. Only now he's a poet, and *that's* worse! Why he hasn't seen any of his old pals since he's come back from prep school. Jim Tilkens called and wanted to go ice skating. I just had to let him know the truth.

MRS. MARTIN: The truth?

MARYANN (*Sadly*): Yes. That—that my brother is—out of this world.

MRS. MARTIN: Maryann! You didn't!

MARYANN: But it's the truth, Mother. What else could I tell him?

MRS. MARTIN (*Setting down knitting*): Well, I'll speak to your father about it. (*Starts to exit*) He went to prep school, too, so maybe he'll know what can be done.

MARYANN: Don't tell me Father ever acted like this!

MRS. MARTIN (*Smiling faintly*): Well, he did write poetry to me from school. (*Exits*)

MARYANN: Poetry. . . . phooey! I hope I never hear another line of it. (*Doorbell rings.* MARYANN *exits, returning after a minute with* JANE.) Gosh, I'm glad you've come.

JANE: Now, really, Maryann, it can't be as bad as all *that!*

MARYANN: No? Here, sit down. Now listen. This is the poem Alfred had published, the one he wrote to Carol. You listen to it and tell me if anyone in his right mind could write something like this: (*Reads*)
"Sweet Carol, lovely as a summer breeze,
Hair as soft as zephyrs through the trees,
Lips as fragile as a rare wine glass;
See! The very flowers bow to let you pass.
Sweet Carol, lovely as an orchid's bloom . . .

JANE (*Interrupting*): "And skinny as an old used broom . . ."

MARYANN (*Laughing with* JANE): That *would* be a better line. (*Reads again*)
"Sweet Carol, lovely as an orchid's bloom,
Sunlight in my heart to chase away the gloom.
I see your loveliness whene'er I close my eyes,
Like summer beauty, your beauty never dies."

JANE: I see what you mean. Has Carol seen this?

MARYANN: I don't think so. Certainly *Alfred* wouldn't have the nerve to show it to her.

JANE: No, I guess he wouldn't. (*Doorbell rings.* MARYANN

puts down poem and exits. JANE *picks it up and begins to read to herself, shaking her head as she reads.*)

JIM (*Offstage*): Where's that half-baked brother of yours? (JIM, ANDY *and* STEVE *enter with* MARYANN.)

ANDY: Yeah, what's he doing—going into hiding?

STEVE: We hear he's joined the Muses.

MARYANN: Come on in, boys, and be prepared for the worst.

STEVE (*Looking about*): Well, where is he? Hi, Jane.

JANE: Hi!

ANDY: Where's this ethereal paradise he's hidden himself in?

JIM: No kidding, Maryann, where is he? We're all set for an ice skating party, and you know we can't possibly have any fun without Alfred.

MARYANN: Here, read this and find out.

JIM (*Scanning*): Holy smokes! Great guns! What's happened to the kid—writing drivel like this. "Sweet Carol, lovely as a summer breeze. Hair as soft as zephyrs through the trees. . . ." How could he?

STEVE (*Snatching paper*): Let's see that! (*Reading, half aloud*) Wow! This is sen-sa-tion-al. "Dear, sweet Carol, with hair as soft as a tornado" . . . er . . . I mean zephyr. And have you seen the dame! Wow!

JANE: Now wait a minute. You're exaggerating.

STEVE (*Paying no attention to her*): "The very flowers bow to let you pass . . ." (ALFRED *appears at left. His head is held high and there is a dreamy, far-away quality to his voice. He carries a pad in his left hand, and lifts a pencil slowly to his lips, and makes an occasional notation.*)

ALFRED: Like the soft touch of spring on a sleeping bough. Say! That's *good!* (*Goes over to geranium on table and touches flower gently*) Petals as soft as moss—no, soft as a sunset's glow on a quiet lake. Say! That's *good!*

(Pretends to see others for first time. Says nothing, but comes over and gently removes paper from STEVE'S *hand)* Please. Let us not defile that which is good and sacred. That is meant only for the eyes that have been opened; the gifted, the lover of art and nature, the transcendentalist . . .

STEVE: Huh?

ALFRED: And sorry as I am to say this, dear Steve, you are a plebeian, one of those whose eyes are closed to the wonders and greatness of beauty. Do not defile the sacredness of that page by touching it.

STEVE *(Looking at his hands in shame)*: Huh?

ALFRED: And now, gentlemen, if you will excuse me, I shall return to the solitude of my room, where the passion of my new-found talent may pour forth from the pen unmolested, unrestrained by vulgar presences.

ANDY *(Stepping over toward* ALFRED*)*: I say, old bean, would you mind translating that for me? I'm a little slow, don't you know, on that incoherent jibber-jabber you just expounded.

ALFRED *(In dead seriousness)*: Quite understandable, Andrew. I don't hold it against you. The flowers look forth boldly with their beauty; the weed must turn its head in shame. *(Writing on pad)* Say! That's *good!* Good day, gentlemen. *(Exits)*

JIM *(Starting after him)*: But the ice skating party. That is, we want you. . . .

ANDY *(Collapsing onto couch)*: No! *(Slapping head with palm)* I'm dreaming. This can't be true.

MARYANN: But it is, most horribly true—*Andrew.*

ANDY: Oh, don't. Please. It's *Andy.*

JANE *(Mockingly)*: Like a yellow moon amid the pines— say, *that's good!*

JIM: Please, Maryann. I can't stand any more. This is the limit. We have to *do* something.

JANE: Yes, but *what?*

MARYANN (*To* ANDY): You're the one who can think up the practical jokes, Andy. Now's your chance to shine.

STEVE: Andy, come on—give. He'll ruin our whole vacation going on like this.

MARYANN: You see, Andy, we have to get Alfred to forget this gag.

STEVE: If it is a gag.

ANDY (*Pacing floor*): You're right, all of you. We have to bring him down to earth again. (*Talking to himself*) But how—that's the question. We'll have to use psychology, that's it. (*Stopping suddenly and facing others*) How about getting Carol to read it; you know, burlesque it, so he sees how lousy it really is?

JIM: I—I'm afraid that wouldn't work, Andy.

ANDY (*Slumping into chair*): I can't think of a thing. (*Wailing*) And all the times I've had such a fertile brain—when it got me into nothing but trouble. And now when I need it, what happens?

JANE (*Coming to him; others cluster about*): There, there, Andy. It'll come to you. You need to relax, that's what's the matter. Let your head rest against the back of the chair. Now close your eyes, and think, *think,* Andy, while I stroke your head. Blood in the head makes the brain work faster, you know.

STEVE: Brain? Who said he had a brain?

JANE: Concentrate . . . concentrate. (*To others*) You know, I actually think I feel something percolating.

STEVE: Feels like pins and needles, doesn't it?

JANE: No, more like cogwheels grinding. Concentrate. . . .

ANDY (*Jumping up*): I have it! I have it!

MARYANN: Great! Out with it!

ANDY: It's colossal, stupendous. Quick, Maryann, call up Carol and tell her to come over right away.

MARYANN: O. K. I'll take your word that it's good. (*At telephone*) Oakland 6-9101, please.

ANDY (*To others*): All right. Now, you, Jim. See how many books of poetry you can find in the bookcase.

JIM: Poetry? What for? We've got too much now around here.

ANDY: Don't ask questions. Jane, get all the paper and pencils you can find from the desk. (*Stands surveying the scene with satisfaction*)

MARYANN (*At telephone*): Hello, that you, Carol? . . . Maryann. Say, can you come over? The gang's all here and we have a plan to cure Alfred. . . . Yes, that's what I said, cure Alfred. . . . You didn't know he was sick? Well, this is *mental* illness. . . . You understand? . . . That's right. His poetry. . . . You feel morally responsible? . . . O. K., we'll see you. (*Hangs up. To others*) She'll be right over. Says she feels responsible for Alfred's condition.

JIM (*Coming over with several volumes*): Here you are. Three volumes. Gosh, they're heavy. Probably just as heavy reading.

JANE (*With pencils and paper*): There's just enough to go around, if that's what you want.

ANDY: Great! Put them on the table. The books, too. Now gather around, and I'll give you the low-down. (*They move up close.*) All right. Here's what we do. We'll show Alfred we can play his little game, too. We'll act like poets, too. We'll give him so much of it he'll have to give up. We'll give it to him until it comes out of his ears. So go to it, folks! Start writing. The sillier the better. We'll see who's the real poet around here!

CURTAIN

* * *

Scene 2

Time: *An hour later.*

Setting: *Same as Scene 1.*

At Rise: Maryann, Jane *and* Andy *are seated on the couch, pencils poised, deep in thought.* Jim *is pacing the floor, and carries pad melodramatically in his hand.* Steve *is seated on the armchair and stares dreamily into space.*

Jim: Your eyes are like great big blue marbles. Say! *That's good!*

Maryann: Lips as soft as down . . . no, *goose* down, that's softer. Let's see. Down . . . frown, brown, clown. (*To others*) You know, I'm beginning to enjoy this. You make me somersault like a clown. *That's good!* (*Doorbell rings; she goes to answer it, still talking dreamily.*) And your eyes are the deepest brown . . . darling, you're simply the talk of the town . . . (*Exits, still talking*)

Jane: What rhymes with Constantinople?

Steve (*Biting pencil thoughtfully*): The stars are never as deep as that faraway look in your eyes. (*To others*) Has Alfred passed by yet?

Maryann (*Entering with* Carol): Please, dear, take away that withering frown. (*Stops to write it down; seats herself*)

Carol (*Dumfounded*): Say, what's going on here, anyway?

Jim (*Without looking up*): There are pencil and paper over there on the table. . . . Little Robin, fairest creature of spring, are you thinking about anything, as you soar on motionless wing? That's *good.*

Jane: I just can't think of a thing to rhyme with Constantinople.

CAROL: Will somebody *please* tell me what's going on?

JANE: Hurry, Carol. Alfred might see you. Get into the poetic mood, quick. It's our plan—we're giving him a dose of his own medicine.

MARYANN: And you're the center of attraction. If Alfred sees *you* acting like this, too, he'll really be convinced.

CAROL: All right. I'll string along. What do I do?

JANE: Write poetry, of course! What else? Sit down here. Move over, Andy.

ANDY: Huh? Oh, move over. All right. Little yellow flower, fairest of spring, what secret message of summer do you bring? That's *good*. (CAROL *settles down to work.* ALFRED *appears at door, still carrying pad and staring off into space.*)

ALFRED: Little elfin mischief dancing in your eyes. Say! That's *good!* (*Looks toward others*) What's going on here? I thought you were. . . . (*Remembering role he is playing*) Starlight, sifting through a moon-gold sky, listens quietly to the bobcat's cry. I say, *that's good!* (*Looks around to find no one paying attention to him*) Starlight (*Louder*) sifting through a moon-gold sky, listens to the bobcat's cry . . . I say, that's *good*, isn't it? (*Stares off into space*)

STEVE: A whisp of smoke, like a tiny finger spreads, curls, rises, and into the air is fed. Say, *that's good.*

ALFRED (*Approaching* STEVE, *taps him cautiously on shoulder*): I say, would you mind telling me what you're doing?

STEVE (*Shrugging shoulder*): And the night closes in, and there is blackness everywhere; the trees, the camp, the very thickness of the air.

ALFRED (*Moving away from* STEVE, *catches sight of* CAROL): Carol! What on earth are *you* doing here?

CAROL (*Indifferently*): Hello.

ALFRED: "Hello"? Is that all you can say to me?

CAROL: Please, Alfred, don't bother me now.

ALFRED: B-bother you?

CAROL: Soft silver, tropical silver, the moon glows . . .

ALFRED: Say, just what's coming off here?

ANDY (*Rising slowly*): It means, Alfred, that you've convinced us, old man. We were fools, going merrily on our plebeian way, unknowing . . . unfeeling. . . .

ALFRED: But—

ANDY: Never mind, old man. (*Puts hand on his shoulder*) We owe *you* the apology. We just never understood, that's all—until *now*.

JANE (*Looking up momentarily*): Andy's right, Alfred. We never realized what joy creative expression could bring a person. We owe it all to you, Alfred.

JIM (*Looking up*): I say, Alfred. Now that we're one of your kind, why don't you honor us by sitting down and doing your writing here?

ANDY: That's a beastly good suggestion, James, old man. I say, Alfred, do join us.

ALFRED: Well—er—I was going to join you at—yes, at writing! Of course! (*Settles himself uneasily on edge of chair, looking about furtively*)

JANE: Mocking bird, mocking bird, where art thou gone?

STEVE: "Never!" quoth the villain, and slithered through the dark. . . .

ALFRED: Say, fellows, shall we. . . .

JANE: S-h-h-h!

ANDY: Stop talking. How can I concentrate?

MRS. MARTIN (*Running into room suddenly holding paper*): It's wonderful! Oh, I tell you it's simply the most exciting, wonderful thing that has ever happened to me.

MARYANN (*Coming to her*): We understand, Mother. We've had the same glorious experience. Come, read us what you've written. What have you named it?

MRS. MARTIN: "Fireflies."

ALFRED: Mother, you don't mean to tell me . . . !

MRS. MARTIN (*Coming over and kissing him*): I do, Alfred. And I owe it all to you.

ALFRED: Oh, no!

JANE: Read it to us, Mrs. Martin.

MRS. MARTIN: How could I refuse? I can't hold it within me any longer. It must out. (*Reads*) "Fireflies."
"At night I see your tiny, golden lamps aglow,
Fairy lanterns, dancing to an elfin's bow,
Reflecting glory of the stars above,
A song enchantment; a song of ethereal love."
Isn't it wonderful? I tell you, it just f-l-o-w-s from me. (*Confidingly*) It isn't finished yet. But I simply had to share it with you. Now I won't disturb you any longer, children.

JANE: Please, Mrs. Martin, promise us you'll come back and read the rest when it's finished.

MRS. MARTIN: Oh, I will, I *will*. I promise. (*Exits*)

ALFRED (*Watching others settle back to work*): Say, fellows and gals, what say we go out for a. . . .

JIM: Sh-h-h!

STEVE (*Looking up for a moment*): Really, Alfred, you should know better than to interrupt so often.

ALFRED: Oh. . . . bother! (*Everyone settles down to work. ALFRED paces the room several times. Suddenly he stops and faces the others boldly.*) All right, so I was wrong. So I am no poet. For heaven's sake, stop this nonsense, and let's go out for a sleigh ride or ice skating or—or anything. (*Stops, waiting*) All right! All right! You've had your fun. I'm cured. You know as well as I that you're no more poets than—than I was. I'm cured. (*No one answers or looks up.*) Ye gods! Of all the stupid, imbecile, idiotic tricks. I told you I'm punished, strictly and severely punished. Now let's get out of here and have some fun. (*Still no one answers.*) All right then, stay here. But *I'm* going! (*Quick exit*)

CAROL (*Rising quickly, laughing. Others continue to write*): Wasn't he *funny!* I could hardly keep a straight face. Well, anyway, he's cured. Your plan worked like a charm, Andy. He's completely cured. In fact, he's so cured, he'll probably never even want to *look* at another line of poetry. Well, what about it? Do we go ice skating or sleigh riding? Maryann, which'll it be?

MARYANN (*Glancing up*): If you don't mind, Carol, I think I'd like to finish this. Really, it's *good,* and I mean that.

CAROL: Oh, *no!* How about you, Steve? They say the ice is as smooth as glass. (*Mockingly*) Say, that's *good.*

STEVE: Not right now, Carol. I'd like to, but, well, to tell you the truth, I've become kind of interested in this poem.

CAROL: Well, I'll be . . . ! All right, Jane, I guess it's up to us. You've finished your poem, haven't you?

JANE: Yes, my *first* one. But really, Carol, it would be sinful to stop now. That first poem was—well—call it a warm-up period. I just have to see what I can do with my next one.

CAROL: Ye gods, what's happened here anyway? We cured Alfred. Now *who's* going to cure you? Come on, Jim, you've got more sense than the rest. Up and at the ice skating.

JIM (*Momentarily aroused*): What?

CAROL: Oh, no, not you, too!

MARYANN: Would you all mind talking a little less? There's more paper in the desk if that's what you want.

CAROL: I don't *want* any more paper. I don't *want* to write any more poems. I never *did* want to write any. I never *will* want to write any more either. Now is that clear? All I want to do is to get out of here and get in some ice skating. Now do you all understand?

ANDY: What rhymes with "sadder" except "gladder" and "madder"? There's no such word as "madder" is there? (*No answer*) I didn't think so.

MARYANN (*Dramatically*): "Lithely leaping, like a lily's lilting leaves." Isn't that wonderful alliteration?

CAROL: This has gone far enough. Now, for the last time, is anyone coming with me or not? (*No answer*) Very well, then, *I* am going. And do you know where I'm going? I'm going to find Alfred and go ice skating. I'm going to find someone who's *sane*. Goodbye. (*Quick exit*)

JANE (*Shaking her head sadly*): Poor girl. She just doesn't have the stuff that poets are made of.

MARYANN: No depth to her character.

STEVE: All she was interested in was getting Alfred out of here.

JIM: Alfred's genius was short-lived, too.

MRS. MARTIN (*Bursting in*): It's finished! Finished at last.

JANE: Read it to us, Mrs. Martin. Please.

MRS. MARTIN: Thank you, Jane, I will. (*Reading*)
"And now the first faint flush of dawn shows in the east,
And from the purple mountains, like a beast,
The angry, swollen sun comes roaring up,
To make a streak of gold—out of a yellow buttercup."

JANE: Splendid!

JIM: Bravo!

ANDY: It's the best thing any of us has written. Stay here with us, Mrs. Martin. We need you—for inspiration.

MRS. MARTIN: Really, I couldn't. It was nothing . . . well, all right. (*Sits down*)

ANDY: And—now shall we all return to work, with no more interruptions? (*All nod solemnly.*)

JANE: Chirping, chirping little robin . . .

MARYANN: Slithered and slip, the slimy serpent stole softly, swiftly southward . . . it's marvelous what one can do with alliteration.

JIM: Morning . . . warning . . . adorning . . . corning . . . torning . . . nothing rhymes with morning. (ALFRED *enters steathily, holding* CAROL *by the hand. They cross stage and exit.* ALFRED *reappears carrying ice skates, followed by* CAROL. *As they get near to right exit,* ALFRED *stops and looks over the group. No one notices him. He shakes his head sadly, and making a circling motion near his head, he starts to exit.*)

ALFRED: Come on, Carol. Let 'em be. The poet's nightmare settles o'er the Martin dwelling. Say! *That's good!* (*Pretends to go back to join the others, but* CAROL *pulls him laughingly offstage, as curtain falls.*)

THE END

The Feast of the Thousand Lanterns

by Betty Tracy Huff

Characters

EMPEROR OF CHINA
SENG, *his chief minister*
O BAN YING, *a little girl*
CHANG, *her brother*
OLD WOMAN
BEGGAR
LEE ⎱
WING ⎰ *children*

SELLER OF LANTERNS
SELLER OF SINGING BIRDS
SELLER OF PARASOLS
SELLER OF REFRESHMENTS
IMPERIAL GUARDS
CROWD

TIME: *Long ago in ancient China.*
SETTING: *An open space.*
AT RISE: EMPEROR *hurries onstage, followed by* SENG.

SENG (*Breathlessly*): Your Majesty! Your Majesty!
EMPEROR (*Stopping and turning*): Ah, so the honorable chief minister has changed his mind about coming with me today!
SENG (*Bowing with his hands in his sleeves*): It is not seemly for the Emperor of all China to walk about alone like an ordinary man, O Celestial One!
EMPEROR: How else can I find out how my people live,

271

Seng? How else can I know whether or not they are happy?

SENG: But today of all days, Celestial One, you should remain at the Palace. Has Honorable Emperor forgotten that today at the Hour of the Tiger the Feast of the Thousand Lanterns will begin?

EMPEROR: Then what better day could there be, Seng, for me to meet everyone? At any moment now the people will be coming from all the cities to compete for the prize for the finest lantern.

SENG: But, Emperor—!

EMPEROR: Enough, lowly one! And remember, from now on I am no longer to be addressed as befits the Emperor of all China. I am only Mr. Wu, a poor scholar. You understand, Seng?

SENG: I live only to obey your wishes, O Celestial Majesty!

EMPEROR: Seng!

SENG: I . . . I mean yes, Mr. Wu, Your Majesty . . . or do I mean, yes, Your Majesty, Mr. Wu. (*Gong sounds three times offstage.*)

EMPEROR: The Hour of the Tiger! The Feast of the Thousand Lanterns has begun! (*A crowd of people come running on. They carry lanterns in their hands, or hung on poles.*) Seng, let us step aside and watch as my people enjoy the celestial delights of this day when happy moments are as numerous as golden butterflies in the Garden of Willows. (O BAN YING *and* CHANG *enter, left. They have no lantern, but they carry a drawstring bag. They both look around admiringly at the lanterns the others carry.*)

O BAN YING: The lanterns are more beautiful than the blossom of the almond tree that stands in the garden of the Mandarin!

CHANG: The lantern we will buy will be even more lovely. And we will win the prize.

O Ban Ying: Then we will never be hungry again! (*Enter* Lee *and* Wing)

Lee: A cordial greeting to you both from this unworthy one. (*They bow to one another.*) But do you not have your lantern yet?

Chang (*Waving his purse*): We are going to buy it as soon as the seller of lanterns arrives.

O Ban Ying: We have twenty yen!

Wing: Twenty yen! But it is said in the city that you and your brother Chang are among the poor who wait at the gate of the Mandarin for bread.

Chang: It is true we are among the unworthy ones. But all the year long, from the time of peach blossom to the moon of the chill time, we have worked and saved.

O Ban Ying: So now at last we have a chance to buy a beautiful lantern that may win the purse of gold for our honorable mother. Then no longer will she have to work so hard to buy us food. (Seller of Lanterns *enters. He is practically hidden by his load of merchandise.*)

Seller of Lanterns: Come buy, come buy! (Chang *and* O Ban Ying *run over to him.*)

Chang: Honorable sir, how much is your finest lantern?

Seller of Lanterns: Twenty yen, boy. Take your choice.

O Ban Ying: They are beautiful. Which one shall we choose, brother? (*They examine the stock.* Seller of Singing Birds *enters.*)

Seller of Singing Birds: Come buy a pretty singing bird! Come buy! (*He holds up a covered cage.*) Come buy a caged wild bird.

Chang: Poor little prisoners!

O Ban Ying: Can't we do something, Chang? Please, please, Chang. (Chang *strides over to* Seller of Singing Birds.)

Chang: How much for the wild birds, sir?

SELLER OF SINGING BIRDS: Ten yen and the whole cageful of sweet singers is yours, young sir.

O BAN YING: Buy them, Chang, so that we may set them free!

CHANG: We can still buy a very nice lantern with the ten yen we will have left. We may yet win the prize. (*He counts out the coins into* SELLER'S *palm, taking the cage in exchange.* SELLER OF BIRDS *exits.*) CHANG *and* O BAN YING *run to the side of the stage.* CHANG *holds the cage up high, just out of sight behind the curtain in the wings. Everyone on stage looks up. Some point upward. Some cry "There they go!"*)

O BAN YING: Go home to the forest, little ones! (EMPEROR *steps forward with* SENG *running behind him.*)

EMPEROR (*Bowing with his hands in his sleeves*): I am Mr. Wu, an unworthy scholar from the province of Wan How. (*Stooping and picking up some feathers from the stage*) May I keep these feathers from the wings of the wild birds you set free?

O BAN YING (*Bowing*): You are welcome, Mr. Wu, if you think you have a use for them.

EMPEROR: Confucius says, "Everything in its time is useful." (*He gives the feathers to* SENG, *who puts them ceremoniously away inside his voluminous sleeves.* SELLER OF PARASOLS *enters with several paper umbrellas under his arms, and one open in his hands. This one he spins and twirls about.*)

SELLER OF PARASOLS: Come buy, come buy! (*Several people run up and buy parasols which they open and twirl about. As* SELLER OF LANTERNS *handles a brisk trade,* CHANG *and* O BAN YING *cross over to him again.*)

O BAN YING: Pray sir, show us the finest lantern you have for sale for ten yen.

SELLER OF LANTERNS: There are many, lovely as lotus blossoms.

O BAN YING: Oh, Chang, they are beautiful! We still have a chance at the prize. Which one shall we buy? (OLD WOMAN *enters, wailing mournfully and holding up four golden tassels.*)

CHANG: Honorable aged one! What can be the cause of your distress?

OLD WOMAN: My parasol . . . oh, my parasol! It is gone! Alas, a great wind came and blew it away. I held onto the tassels which decorated the handle, and they are all that is left to me.

O BAN YING: Your sorrow is ours.

OLD WOMAN: All year long I had been saving to buy it. From the time of the rice harvest I had been looking forward to the Feast of the Thousand Lanterns, and now I shall not be able to go to witness the judging of the prize. A woman as old as I am may not appear at the Imperial Palace without a parasol.

O BAN YING: Do not distress yourself, honorable one. My brother and I will buy you a new parasol! Come along with us. (*They take her over to* SELLER OF PARASOLS *and buy her a parasol. She turns and spins it about with delight.*)

OLD WOMAN: May your honorable ancestors bless you both! (*The* EMPEROR *steps forward with* SENG.)

EMPEROR: Aged one, since you have no further use for the tassels from your lost parasol, may I have them?

OLD WOMAN: Certainly, if they are of use to you.

EMPEROR: Who can say when a thing may become useful. (*He hands the tassels to* SENG, *who puts them into his sleeves.*)

O BAN YING: How much money do we have left now, brother?

CHANG: We still have five yen, little sister. We will see if we can buy a lantern with that. (*They go over to* SELLER OF LANTERNS. CHANG *holds out the coins on his palm.*)

SELLER OF LANTERNS: Only five yen? There are few lanterns left as you can see. It is the wish of this unworthy one that you had bought from me while you had twenty yen. But I will give you good value for what you have left. See, there is this good red lantern still on my pole.

SELLER OF REFRESHMENTS (*Entering with a tray of colorfully wrapped packages of food*): Come and eat! Sesame candy—rice cakes. Come and eat! (*People go to him to buy.* BEGGAR *enters and goes up to* CHANG.)

BEGGAR: Food, food . . . I cannot walk for hunger.

O BAN YING: Over here honorable Seller of Refreshments! Quickly! (SELLER OF REFRESHMENTS *comes over.* O BAN YING *takes several packages, in exchange for four of the coins. She gives the packages to the* BEGGAR, *who unwraps them and eats hungrily.*)

BEGGAR: May the blessings of your honorable ancestors descend upon you both. (EMPEROR *comes forward and picks up the pieces of wrapping paper*)

EMPEROR: Of your charity, sir, I beg these papers.

BEGGAR: Honorable scholar, you are welcome, if they are of use to you.

EMPEROR: In its time everything and everyone are of use in this world. Take this to the Imperial Overseer of Rice Fields. He will give you work that you may never hunger again. (*He gives* BEGGAR *a token.* SENG *takes the wrapping papers and puts them in his sleeves.*)

BEGGAR: Blessings be upon you. (*He exits, bowing.*)

O BAN YING: Still there is one yen left, brother.

CHANG: I wonder if it is any use trying to buy a lantern with that.

O BAN YING: We can try, Chang. (*They cross over to* SELLER OF LANTERNS. *He now has only one lantern left. It is larger than the average, but it is undecorated, and it is broken.*) How much for your last lantern, sir?

SELLER OF LANTERNS: You may have it for one yen. If only you had bought when you had twenty yen, or ten, or even five! I would like you to win the prize. (*He shrugs, handing over the broken lantern in exchange for the last remaining coin.* EMPEROR *comes forward.*)

EMPEROR: Alas, I have no lantern. None are left! Now I shall not be able to go to the feast and see the competition, for no one is allowed to enter the Imperial Palace on this day of the year without a lantern.

CHANG: Take our lantern, honorable scholar, and welcome. Poor as it is, it will at least gain you admittance.

EMPEROR: May your ancestors reward you for your kindness to this unworthy one. (*He takes the lantern and gives it to* SENG *who tries in vain to cram it up his sleeve. He is still trying when he exits with* EMPEROR.)

O BAN YING (*Looking about her*): I wonder which lantern will win.

CHANG: Oh, little sister, if only . . . if only we could have done as we planned! Think how much the prize money would have meant to our honorable mother.

O BAN YING: Chang, say you are not sorry for the way we spent our savings. Please say you are not!

CHANG: I would not have had things happen otherwise for all the tea in China, little sister. (IMPERIAL GUARDS *enter, followed by* SENG)

1ST GUARD: Pray silence for the honorable Seng, chief minister of all China!

SENG: Know good people, that this year his Celestial Greatness, the Emperor, has decreed that the competition for the finest lantern is to be held here in the Square, instead of at the Palace, so that even those unfortunate ones who have no lanterns will have the opportunity of witnessing the ceremonies.

CHANG: Ah, how fortunate for us, O Ban Ying. At least

now we shall see what goes on. (*Crash of gong.* GUARDS *enter ceremoniously carrying a table. On it, covered with a dark cloth, is a lantern. They set the table at center. The gong sounds again.*)

SENG: His Imperial Greatness, the Emperor of all China! (*Enter the* EMPEROR *in his royal robes. Everyone bows.*)

EMPEROR: Arise, my people! (*He hands a parchment to* SENG.)

SENG (*Bowing and reading from parchment*): To O Ban Ying and her brother Chang, the prize for the best lantern.

CHANG: But Your Majesty, there has been some mistake. We have no lantern. (EMPEROR *signals to* GUARDS. *They pull away the cloth, disclosing a magnificent lantern*)

EMPEROR: The prize is yours, children. (CHANG *and* O BAN YING *step forward to stand on either side of the table.*)

CHANG: But, Celestial One, that lantern is not ours!

EMPEROR: Ah, but it is. Let me show you. (*Pointing out design on large central lantern as he speaks*) Here are the feathers from the little wild singing birds you set free. (O BAN YING *and* CHANG *kneel down on either side of the table.*) Here are the golden tassels from the old lady's parasol. Here are flowers cut from the colored wrapping papers that were around the food you gave to the starving beggar man. The lantern is the one you gave to the poor scholar, and he straightened it out and repaired it, and now he gives it back to you.

O BAN YING (*Rising, and bowing*): Your Majesty, you were the poor scholar, and we did not recognize you!

EMPEROR (*Handing them the purse of gold*): Here is your prize. Nowhere in the world could there be a more beautiful lantern than the one you have earned today. Now, to the Palace, everyone! On with the Feast of the Thousand Lanterns! (*People line up in couples and march out.* SENG *and* GUARDS *exit, bowing ceremoni-*

ously. EMPEROR *stands behind the table, bending low over the central lantern. The children kneel on either side of him. Slow curtain as the gong sounds.*)

THE END

The Courage Piece

by Eleanore Leuser

Characters

JOHNNY	LEPRECHAUN
WIDOW O'CONNOR, *his mother*	MIKE
KATHY, *his small sister*	DAN
NOREEN, *his invalid sister*	JIM
NEIGHBOR DUNN	

SETTING: *The old-fashioned kitchen of an Irish cottage.*

AT RISE: WIDOW O'CONNOR *is busy with her pots and pans.* KATHY *is playing on the floor.* NOREEN *sits looking out of the window. She has a rug over her feet and a pillow at her back.*

NOREEN: I can't see Johnny on the road, Mother.

WIDOW: I wish he'd hurry with the milk now. It's nearly time for our supper.

KATHY (*Looking up from her play*): Something might have happened to him. Johnny's always getting into trouble.

NOREEN: That's because he's afraid of the likes of his own shadow.

WIDOW: Whisht, now, Noreen! I won't have you speaking of your brother in that fashion. It's a good boy Johnny is.

NOREEN: Oh, he's good all right. It's just that . . . (*Breaking off short*) Here's Johnny coming now. Sure, something's happened to him!

KATHY (*Running to the window*): Let me see! Oh, poor Johnny! (WIDOW *also goes over to look. In a moment the door opens and in comes* JOHNNY, *muddy and bedraggled, carrying a broken pitcher. He is almost in tears.*)

WIDOW: What's happened to the lad?

KATHY: Johnny, did you fall in a big mud puddle?

NOREEN: It's little milk that you'll be bringing in a broken pitcher.

JOHNNY (*Breathing hard and stumbling in his story*): I . . . well . . . the boys in the village chased me . . .

NOREEN: Again?

JOHNNY: Well, the truth of it is . . . I was coming home with the milk when three of them jumped out at me.

KATHY: Oh, Johnny, what did you do?

JOHNNY: I stopped and then they dared me to fight any one of them and they'd let me by. But I ran back the other way and round about. They came after me. First thing I knew, they'd pushed me flat in the ditch and my milk pitcher was in pieces beside me.

NOREEN: And where were the boys?

JOHNNY (*Slowly*): They just stood and laughed. I got up and came home.

WIDOW: The miserable spalpeens! (*Putting her hand on* JOHNNY'S *shoulder*) But, Johnny, lad, when will you be learning to take care of yourself? Since your father's gone, you're the man of the house. If you can't take care of yourself, how will you be taking care of your sisters and me?

JOHNNY (*Miserably*): I don't know, Mother. There's something inside of me that makes me afraid. I'm sorry, that I am. But that's the way of it every time.

WIDOW: Some day, lad, you'll grow up inside you and then you won't be frightened any more. Till then we'll just stand by together. . . . Now, go along and get cleaned up, lad. Kathy, you help set the table. Noreen, you can be spreading the bread with this good dripping. We'll just go without milk, the night. Get busy, all of you. (JOHNNY *goes into the other room to clean up.* KATHY *starts putting things on the table.* WIDOW *puts some bread, a knife and a bowl of dripping on a small stand close to* NOREEN. NOREEN *is just starting to spread the bread when there is a knock at the door.*) Come in. (NEIGHBOR DUNN *enters.*)

NEIGHBOR DUNN: Good even to you, Widow O'Connor!

WIDOW: Good even to you, Neighbor Dunn. How are your folks?

NEIGHBOR DUNN: That's what brought me here, Widow O'Connor. The wife is in bed . . . took ill all of a sudden. We've done all we know how. Would you come over? There's no one like yourself for getting a person well in a hurry.

WIDOW: Indeed and I'll be with you right away, Neighbor Dunn. Kathy, get my cloak. (JOHNNY *re-enters with some of the mud cleaned off*) Johnny, you get my basket. There's sickness at Neighbor Dunn's. (*The children scurry round getting her things. She packs her basket with a few homemade remedies, then stops by the door before she leaves*) Now, Johnny, lad, I'm leaving your sisters and the house in your care. It's not likely I'll be back tonight. I'd best stay as long as they have need of me, so you carry on.

NOREEN: I wish you didn't have to go, Mother. Johnny will be small comfort.

KATHY (*Hanging onto her mother*): Take me, too.

WIDOW: Now . . . now, children, that's no way to be talking when a neighbor's in trouble. Johnny, just keep the fire going and look after your sisters. After all, there's little can happen.

JOHNNY: Sure and I can do that much, Mother. (NEIGHBOR DUNN *and* WIDOW *go out, closing the door behind them.*)

NOREEN (*Spreading the bread and handing one slice to* KATHY *and another to* JOHNNY): We'd best eat. But we'll have to be drinking water instead of milk.

JOHNNY (*Getting her some water from a jug on the table*): I'm that sorry, Noreen!

NOREEN: If it wasn't the milk you spilled it would be something else that happened because you were frightened. I wish I could be up and about.

KATHY (*Going over to* JOHNNY *to comfort him*): Don't talk to Johnny like that. He's our brother.

JOHNNY: It's all right, Kathy. Noreen's right. It's not good when a lad gets into trouble over being frightened all the time. I don't blame her for being ashamed of me.

NOREEN: I wouldn't be ashamed if you'd do something about it. But do you think I like having my brother the laughingstock of the village?

JOHNNY: I'd give anything to be different. You know that, Noreen.

NOREEN: All you have to do is to start, then.

JOHNNY: I've started a hundred times but it always ends up the same way.

NOREEN (*Looking out of the window*): You'd best be getting in some turf for the fire. There's a storm coming up . . . a big one.

KATHY: Oh, I don't like storms and Johnny doesn't either.

JOHNNY: Hush, Kathy! Don't be talking about it. I'd best

go and get the turf and be quick about it. (*Opening the door and looking out*) The storm's coming up fast. Look how dark it's getting!

KATHY: I'll help you, Johnny, so we can get it in fast before the storm comes. (*She trudges back and forth a couple of times with* JOHNNY, *carrying turf. Then* JOHNNY *puts down his armful and shuts the door.*)

JOHNNY: I think I won't be getting any more till the storm's over. I don't like the look of it. It's a black one. Noreen, if you'd be closing the window and pulling the curtain, we wouldn't see the lightning.

NOREEN: But I like to watch the storm. It's a grand sight. Hark! Hear the thunder. (*The room has grown dark.* JOHNNY *closes the window but doesn't pull the curtain. Flashes of lightning are seen through it. Distant thunder is heard.* JOHNNY *is lighting the lamp when a knock is heard at the door. The three children start and look at each other.* JOHNNY *backs slowly away.*)

KATHY (*Almost whispering*): Who's that?

JOHNNY (*Frightened*): I should have bolted the door.

NOREEN: Don't be silly now. Is there reason to fear? (*Calling*) Come in, then. (*Door opens and the* LEPRECHAUN *enters, with some turf in his arms.*)

LEPRECHAUN: Don't be frightened now, Johnny. I just brought in some turf you dropped in your hurry to get in from the storm. I thought likely you'd need it. (*He puts it down on the hearth and advances smiling.*)

JOHNNY (*Keeping his distance*): You're strange hereabouts?

LEPRECHAUN: That I am but I get around. How about a bite of that nice bread and dripping, little girl?

NOREEN: Of course, sir, excuse me for not offering it before. I'm sorry we have no milk to go with it. (*She hands him the bread which she has spread.*)

LEPRECHAUN: Now that you don't need to be telling me. I know that Johnny dropped the pitcher.

JOHNNY (*In surprise*): Were you there, sir? I didn't see you.

LEPRECHAUN: As I said before, I get about . . . here, there and a little bit of everywhere, I'm a-thinking.

KATHY (*Staring at him*): You're a funny little man. Who are you?

NOREEN: Kathy . . . that's rude!

LEPRECHAUN: Faith, and I admire people who aren't afraid to ask questions. (*Bowing to* KATHY) Little maid, you see before you—a leprechaun!

ALL: A leprechaun!

LEPRECHAUN: Yes . . . that's myself! 'Tisn't often a human being sees a real one and knows it.

KATHY (*Delighted*): I've always wanted to meet a real Leprechaun. What do you do, sir?

LEPRECHAUN: Well, I can't deny I've an eye for mischief now and then. You might say, though, I get people who deserve it *into* trouble and those that need it, I help.

JOHNNY (*Eagerly*): Would you help me, Mr. Leprechaun? Sure, and I'm needing it.

LEPRECHAUN (*Scratching his head*): Well, now, I saw that for myself when you ran away from those boys. You shouldn't do that, you know. But if you're really wanting to be helped, maybe I could do something for you.

JOHNNY (*Eagerly*): Indeed I do want to be helped, sir. I want to have courage. Could you do anything about that? I've heard leprechauns were magic.

LEPRECHAUN (*Taking something out of his pocket and looking at it*): Now, this might be just the thing.

KATHY (*Coming close to look at it*): O-oh! What is it? It's bright, like a new coin.

LEPRECHAUN (*Holding up so all can see*): That, my little maid, is a Courage Piece.

NOREEN: A Courage Piece!

JOHNNY (*Excitedly*): A Courage Piece for sure?

LEPRECHAUN: That's what I said. It's quite a remarkable piece, too. Just to be knowing you have it will fill you with all the courage you need. It's belonged to all the brave Irish heroes you've ever heard about.

KATHY: St. Patrick himself?

LEPRECHAUN: St. Patrick and probably every other body who has ever forgotten himself and done something brave—to say nothing of Brian Boru or Robert Emmet. Here, Johnny lad, it's for you. Carry it in your wallet wherever you go. Remember that you have it, and I'll promise it will give you the courage you need.

JOHNNY (*Taking it gratefully*): I can't be thanking you enough, sir. (*He holds it and looks at it carefully*) I believe I feel better already.

LEPRECHAUN: That's the stuff, my lad. Now, I'll be on my way. I've another little errand I'll take pleasure in doing.

KATHY (*Going to the door with him*): Goodbye, nice leprechaun. Thank you for Johnny's Courage Piece.

NOREEN: Yes, we ought all to be thanking you.

LEPRECHAUN: You're welcome entirely. As I said before, I like to do a bit of good, now and then, to people who deserve it. Now, Johnny, believe in your Courage Piece, and it will work for you as well as for St. Patrick himself. Good night to you all. (LEPRECHAUN *goes out as the thunder rolls and the lightning flashes.* JOHNNY *closes the door and goes over to the fire, looking at the Courage Piece in his hand.*)

JOHNNY (*Slowly and thoughtfully*): I'm thinking of all the brave men who have held this. You know . . . it's a funny feeling I'm beginning to have. It's almost as if I could stand anything that could happen to me. (*He puts the coin in his wallet carefully and puts the wallet in his pocket.*)

NOREEN (*Softly*): I'm glad that you feel that way, Johnny, very glad.

KATHY (*Dancing up and down*): The Courage Piece! The Courage Piece! I like the Courage Piece!

JOHNNY (*With new vigor*): I'll just get a few more bits of turf and maybe a little wood from the shed to keep the fire burning. I can put it under my coat to keep it dry. (*He marches straight out the door into the storm, holding his coat over his head for protection.*)

NOREEN: He never would have gone out in a storm before.

KATHY: It's the Courage Piece! (*She dances with glee. JOHNNY comes in with some turf under his coat and stirs up the fire. The storm continues; the door blows open unexpectedly.*)

KATHY (*Alarmed*): What's that?

JOHNNY (*Goes over to the door quite calmly and looks out, then calls*): Anyone there? (*He turns to his sisters.*) It's so black out, I can't see. (*Calls again*) Anyone there? (*Closing the door and bolting it*) It must have been the wind. I'll just bolt the door and keep the wind out. (*A loud crash of thunder is heard.* KATHY *puts her fingers in her ears and runs to put her head in* NOREEN's *lap.*) Don't you be frightened now, Kathy, girl. That's only the thunder talking.

NOREEN (*Quietly*): Johnny, the lamp's going out.

JOHNNY (*Going over to it*): That's queer! I filled it this morn. (*Going over to the supply can*) There's no oil in this, either. I could have sworn there was plenty to last the week out. Well, we'll just have to put up with the dark and maybe make the fire burn a bit brighter. (*He makes the fire burn brighter.*)

KATHY (*Whimpering*): I don't like storms. I don't like the dark. Johnny didn't either. Now he doesn't seem to mind a bit. I want my mother.

JOHNNY (*Comforting her*): Whisht, now, Kathy! Be a brave girl. I'll have to be lending you my Courage Piece. It works fine, I'm noticing.

KATHY (*Sobbing*): I want my mother!

JOHNNY: Noreen, sing her one of your songs and she'll feel better and not notice the dark. (NOREEN *sings an Irish lullaby in the firelight, as* KATHY *sits on the floor by her side. The thunder sounds only in the distance. As she finishes, there is a moment's silence. Then the lightning flashes—the thunder sounds closer—there is a hammering at the door. They all look toward door.*)

NOREEN: Now who would that be, out in such a stormy night?

KATHY (*Half-crying*): I-I'm scared. Johnny, don't let them in.

JOHNNY: You couldn't be leaving a dog out in a storm like this.

NOREEN: I wish we had more light.

KATHY (*Trying to hold him back*): Johnny, don't open it. (*More rapping at the door.*)

VOICES (*Outside*): Johnny, let us in. There's someone after us. Open the door, quick.

JOHNNY (*Stopping short*): It's the boys from the village.

KATHY: The same ones that were after you?

NOREEN: Do you think you'd better let them in, Johnny?

VOICES: Hurry, Johnny! Open up this door!

JOHNNY (*Takes out wallet and looks at it as there is a louder crash of thunder than before*): Listen to that storm. I'm going to let them in.

NOREEN: Be careful, Johnny. (*He unbolts the door, and three badly bedraggled boys come in, breathing hard as if they had been running. They hurry to bolt the door.*)

MIKE (*Out of breath*): We're not after you right now, Johnny. We just want shelter from the storm . . . and *things!*

JOHNNY: Well, that's all right, fellows. You can come over to the fire and get dried out.

DAN (*As he goes over to the fire*): We think there's someone following us.

JIM: Someone or *something!* First it was a strange pig. We followed it, thinking to have a bit of fun.

MIKE: But I'll swear that pig went wild. He led us up hill and down dale and through thistles and thorns. Once we thought we had our hands on him and there we were standing up to our necks in a pool of water that hadn't been there five minutes before.

DAN: And instead of a pig it was a little man we were following and he was chuckling and laughing fit to kill.

JIM: So we turned and ran, and the last we saw, he was coming after us still chuckling, and the storm was growing worse.

MIKE: The whole thing took little time at all but faith, it seemed hours while we were running.

JOHNNY: Well, you can stay here till the storm's over. But I'll have you know, you're not to bother my sisters or me. I'll be ready to fight any one of you outside, first thing tomorrow when it's daylight. You can come right here and I'll be waiting for you. (*The boys look at each other in surprise.*)

DAN: What's happened to Johnny?

JIM: Faith and he's different!

MIKE: He's not frightened at all.

KATHY: It's the Courage Piece.

BOYS: The *what?*

JOHNNY: Yep . . . my Courage Piece. You can't be frightened when you have a Courage Piece.

DAN: What's a Courage Piece?

JOHNNY: Oh, it's something I was given. It's belonged to some of the bravest men of Ireland. I keep it in my wallet here. (*Taking out wallet.*)

BOYS (*Crowding about; ad lib*): Let's see it. Show it to us. Let me look. (*Etc.*)

JOHNNY: Just a bit. Don't push me. I'll be showing it to you when I get ready. (*A knock sounds on the door. The three boys start and move back, afraid.* JOHNNY *stands calmly.*)

DAN: The Saints preserve us . . . that's him!

JIM: Don't let him in. He's after us.

MIKE: There's no telling what he'd do to us . . . to you, too.

JOHNNY: You boys can hide if you want to. I'm not going to be keeping anyone out in a storm like this. I let you in, didn't I? Well, I'm going to let this person in. (*He moves over to the door.*)

BOYS (*Ad lib*): Are you crazy? Don't open the door! If it's that man, he's up to no good. (*Etc.*)

NOREEN: I think Johnny's braver than the lot of you. Go ahead, Johnny, open the door. (*There is continuous sound of thunder. The boys all stand stock-still as* JOHNNY *puts his hand on the bolt. Then at a louder knocking they move in mad haste.* DAN *gets back of the table.* MIKE *hides behind a chair, and* JIM *seizes a broom as a weapon.* KATHY *holds tight to* NOREEN, *as* JOHNNY *unbolts and opens the door.* LEPRECHAUN *is standing there, smiling.*)

MIKE (*Terrified*): That's him! That's the little man! He's after us. Keep him out. (*But* JOHNNY *is ushering in the* LEPRECHAUN, *as the boys watch amazed.*)

JOHNNY: Don't mind the boys, sir. They don't know who you are and they're a bit afraid.

LEPRECHAUN: Serves them right—serves them right.

They're fond enough of playing tricks on other people. Well, I've just had a little fun with them myself. Thought I'd teach them a little lesson. Come out, boys, come out. No hard feelings, I hope. That's right. (*As the boys come out shamefacedly*) Just remember, never play tricks on a Leprechaun or if you must, never run away. You only get more frightened.

KATHY: What did you come back for, Mr. Leprechaun?

LEPRECHAUN: Well, I wasn't quite finished with Johnny here. I thought I'd better see how much he'd minded the storm, the dark and these boys here. I headed them to your house, Johnny, just to try you out a bit. How about it?

JOHNNY: I wasn't afraid. I had my Courage Piece.

LEPRECHAUN: Now, are you sure you have it, son?

JOHNNY: I have it right here in my wallet. I was just going to show it to the boys.

LEPRECHAUN: Come over to the light, and let's see it for sure. By the way (*Turning up the lamp*), the oil's back in your lamp now. I thought the dark would be another little test for you. You didn't use to like it, you know.

JOHNNY: I know, sir, but my Courage Piece is wonderful.

LEPRECHAUN: Show it to the boys, then. (*The boys have come up to see what is going on. They watch intently, as* JOHNNY *opens his wallet.*)

JOHNNY (*In great dismay*): It isn't there!

LEPRECHAUN: That's what I thought. But be sure, now. Look again.

JOHNNY (*Turning wallet upside down*): There's nothing inside! Wait, how did that bit of shamrock get in there? I didn't have that before.

LEPRECHAUN: That's it, Johnny. That's all you've really been carrying all this time.

JOHNNY: You mean I've had no Courage Piece at all that belonged to St. Patrick and all the other brave men?

LEPRECHAUN: That's right, my lad. And why would you really be needing the Piece itself? The secret is . . . you *thought* you had it and that did just as well.

JOHNNY: I didn't have the Courage Piece, and still I wasn't afraid!

LEPRECHAUN: That's why I came back . . . to make sure you'd find out what all the brave ones know . . . that when you realize your courage is within you . . . you can never lose it.

JOHNNY (*Gratefully*): I think I understand what you mean, sir, and faith, I'm glad to find out. I'll never forget.

NOREEN: It's a fine boy Johnny is, now that he's found his courage.

KATHY (*Dancing up and down*): I like the Courage Piece!

LEPRECHAUN (*Smiling mischievously*): Now, if anyone else here should ever want a Courage Piece, I might just happen to have the very same Piece I gave Johnny, right here in my pocket. (*He puts his hand in his pocket and draws it out closed. The boys crowd around to see.*)

BOYS (*Ad lib*): Let's see it, sir. Let's see it. Couldn't we try having one? (*Etc.*)

LEPRECHAUN (*Opening his hand and holding up the Courage Piece so everyone can see it*): Well, now, what do you think of that? It seems as if almost everyone could do with a bit of courage, doesn't it? (*Curtain*)

THE END

The Honored One

by Eleanore Leuser

Characters

KING	NURSE
PRIME MINISTER	DOCTOR
COURT JESTER	SINGER
PAGE	ARTIST
FARMER	SCIENTIST
BALLERINA	OLD WOMAN
RICH MAN	

SETTING: *A room in the palace.*

AT RISE: *The* KING *is on his throne talking to the* PRIME MINISTER. *The* COURT JESTER *sits nearby, twirling a baton. A* PAGE *stands at one side.*

KING: I am much pleased with this plan of yours, Prime Minister, and the way you are carrying it out.

PRIME MINISTER: It is really your idea, Sire. You wanted to find the most worthy of all your subjects and honor him or her.

KING: But it was your suggestion to have the most outstanding of my people come to the court and let us judge them. You even sought them out. I am waiting eagerly to see them.

PRIME MINISTER: I have been searching diligently throughout your kingdom, Sire, and I feel that I have selected only the most noteworthy. Any one of them would be deserving of your consideration.

KING: Ah, I did not realize I had so many worthy subjects. I foresee that it may be difficult to choose the best.

JESTER: Not difficult at all, Your Majesty. I have seen them all and they are good, but I am submitting a candidate of my own.

PRIME MINISTER: You!

KING (*Smiling*): A Court Fool always knows more than the wisest King and his Prime Minister. Come, save us trouble, and whisper in my ear whom you have brought. It might even guide my decision.

PRIME MINISTER (*Alarmed*): Nay, King, give no heed to a Fool. See the people I have brought, then make your decision.

JESTER (*Gaily*): The Prime Minister is right. You must see them all. Then, I venture to say that Your Majesty will agree with me that my candidate is the best of all.

KING: You mean your choice and mine will be the same?

JESTER: Nay, that I did not say. But I will wager my cap and bells against the Prime Minister's job that the person I have selected will be the most worthy.

KING: Done! I have great confidence in my judgment and that of the Prime Minister.

PRIME MINISTER: The Court Jester would never dare to disagree with the King.

JESTER: You mean, the King would never disagree with the Court Jester. Bring on your most worthy subjects, Prime Minister. The King would see them.

PRIME MINISTER: I shall. They are so good, that I cannot, for the life of me, see how you will choose who is best, Your Majesty.

JESTER: Choose mine.

KING: Be quiet, Fool! Send them in one at a time, Prime Minister. Remember, if by any unlikely chance I should agree with the choice of the Court Jester, you will exchange your office for his bells.

PRIME MINISTER: Heaven forbid! I cannot see how such a thing would be possible.

KING: Come, let us delay no longer. Page, bring in the first worthy subject. (PAGE *bows, leaves and returns with* FARMER, *who is carrying a basket or tray of fruits and vegetables.*)

PRIME MINISTER: Your Majesty, this is the Farmer. He has rich lands and good crops. Without him you could not eat.

FARMER (*Bowing*): O King, I bring you products of the soil. The sun has shone upon them. The rain has watered them and the slow days of summer have ripened them. Your Majesty's storehouses are filled with grain from my fields. Here is some more of the fruit of my labor. (*He gives the basket to the* KING.)

KING (*Thoughtfully*): My thanks! Prime Minister, you are right. This is a most worthy man. Without him, all of us in the land would starve. What think you, Jester?

JESTER: A good man indeed, my King. But ask him to wait until you have seen all the others, including mine.

KING: Good advice! I will see all before I choose. Wait over there, good Farmer. Send in your next choice, Prime Minister. (FARMER *goes over to one side.* PRIME MINISTER *motions to* PAGE *who brings out* BALLERINA.)

PRIME MINISTER: This is the Ballerina. She represents both beauty and grace. She gives delight to all who see her. Will you watch her dance, O King?

KING: Gladly! (BALLERINA *bows and dances to offstage music. She curtsies as the music ends and then goes to one side.*) Her dancing is indeed a thing of beauty. You did well to select her, Prime Minister. These two have been so good, I am anxious to see the rest.

PRIME MINISTER (*Pleased*): I had many worthy subjects to choose from, Your Majesty. I think you will be pleased with all of them.

KING: Hm! It will be difficult indeed to choose the one who is best. They are so different.

JESTER (*Striking an attitude*): Not at all! Not at all!

PRIME MINISTER (*Sternly*): You speak foolishly, Jester, and are too sure of yourself. (*He claps his hands and* PAGE *brings in* RICH MAN *who carries a large money box.*) Your Majesty, this is the richest man in your kingdom.

KING (*Curiously*): You are the richest of my subjects! How do you measure your wealth?

RICH MAN (*Bows and clinks his box*): Sire, I measure it by money in the bank and by stocks and bonds and by businesses that I own or have an interest in.

KING: It is people like you who pay my taxes and keep the nation wealthy.

PRIME MINISTER (*Quickly*): He not only makes money, Sire, but he gives part of it away to help others.

KING: This is indeed a worthy man. To whom do you give your money?

RICH MAN: I feel that part of all that I have earned should go to hospitals for the sick, to schools so that others may learn, and to charity, for the poor and needy.

KING: That is indeed praiseworthy. The Prime Minister has done well in choosing you. Will you wait with the others? (RICH MAN *goes over to one side.*) I vow, I will have a most difficult time in choosing the most worthy of all these. I wish we had not decided to choose the best. To my mind, they all seem to be amazingly good.

JESTER: But there is one above the others, Sire.

PRIME MINISTER (*Ruffled*): I cannot imagine whom you are talking about, Jester. I know of no such person. My choices are equally good, and I foresee that the King may have to honor them all.

KING: Stop arguing and bring in the next.

PRIME MINISTER: The next two will come together, Your Majesty. I could not separate them. They work together and are equally worthy. (*He claps his hands, and* PAGE *brings out* DOCTOR *and* NURSE.) Your Majesty, these are the Doctor and Nurse. I need not remind you of all they do for those who suffer.

KING: Indeed I know, and I welcome you both. Where is your work?

DOCTOR: I am head of a large hospital in your city, Sire. I also lecture to young students who are just beginning to learn about medicine. But my first love is research, so that I may find ways to prevent disease.

KING: A most worthy ambition. And you, Nurse, what do you do?

NURSE: I work in a hospital for babies and children, Your Majesty. I try to see that children have a chance to grow up strong and healthy. We try to help little ones who are sick.

KING: Nurse, we could not do without you and all the other nurses like you in our kingdom. You, like the Doctor, are invaluable. (DOCTOR *and* NURSE *bow and move to side.*)

PRIME MINISTER: And now, O King, let me call someone very different, one who will add joy to your life as you listen.

KING (*Thoughtfully*): I had not thought there were so many different kinds of people who make a kingdom worthwhile. Yes, call the next one on your list.

PRIME MINISTER (*Claps his hands.* PAGE *brings in* SINGER): O King, here is one who will sing for you and fill your moments of relaxation with the happiness of music.

KING: Welcome, Singer of songs. Sing for us now. It would

give me great pleasure. (*The* SINGER *sings a light classical selection. She bows as she finishes.*) Lovely indeed, O Singer! Do you do this for others?

SINGER: It is my profession. I learned to sing as a child. I enjoyed it so much that I went on with the study of music so that I could sing for others.

KING: You must give much pleasure to all who hear you. (*She bows and goes to stand with the others.*) The choice of who is the best of all grows more perplexing by the moment. Is that not true, Jester?

JESTER: I grant you that all of the choices made by the Prime Minister have been excellent. I grant you that you have a long list of worthy subjects, skilled in many ways. But I still say that the one I have selected is best of all. These people would be the first to say so.

KING (*Perplexed*): I do not understand. How are you so sure?

PRIME MINISTER (*Alarmed*): Sire, pay no attention to this Fool. He is just babbling like a brook. Will you not see the others?

KING: Ah, yes indeed! (PRIME MINISTER *claps his hands and the* PAGE *brings in* ARTIST, *who carries a large painting.*)

PRIME MINISTER: This is the Artist. His portraits of your wise men will live through the ages. He paints scenes of your countryside which are shown in all the museums of the land.

ARTIST (*Bowing*): I try to make both truth and beauty come to life here on canvas. I paint what I see both of the old and of the new. (*He gives the picture to the* KING.)

KING (*Looking at it*): Ah, you have caught the beauty and simplicity of living. You have captured the loveliness of our land. I thank you. (*To others*) This man is a master.

(ARTIST *bows and moves away.*) What say you now, Jester? Have you any better than he?

JESTER: I ask Your Majesty to wait and see.

PRIME MINISTER: I have but one more, O King, one more out of many others that I might have chosen.

KING: Call him. I am indeed humble at the thought of so many worthy ones in my kingdom.

PRIME MINISTER (*Claps hands.* PAGE *brings in* SCIENTIST, *who brings his equipment on a rolling cart. It should have a microscope, test tubes and any scientific instruments possible*): Your Majesty, the Scientist. Through his research he has brought all Nature to our doorstep and has started to harness it. Nothing is too big or too small for his investigation.

SCIENTIST (*Bowing*): My findings are at your disposal, Sire. I can look deep into the earth. My search leads to the farthest planet. I can make new substances or discover new ways to use the old. My microscope and my test tubes examine everything. I ask questions of the universe.

KING (*Awed*): New discoveries—new methods—new things waiting to be discovered. This man, I think, must be the most worthy of them all.

JESTER: Yet who is to say which is the best of all these who are so good? Do we not need them all: Food for the hungry, riches wisely used, grace and beauty, music and art, healers of the sick, and science which finds out about the world? Let me offer my candidate and you will see why she would be the most worthy of them all.

PRIME MINISTER: Impossible! I say he does not know what he is talking about.

KING: Bring in this unknown person. But I warn you, Jester, that you will be banished from the kingdom forever if I find that you are playing tricks.

JESTER: It is no trick. Moreover, I warrant you will both agree with me. I will go to bring her. (*Exits*)

PRIME MINISTER: The Fool is carrying his jests too far.

KING: But his choice deserves a hearing like the rest.

JESTER (*Returns with a dignified* OLD WOMAN): This is my choice, O King.

KING (*Sternly*): Who is this woman? What has she done to earn her entry into a company such as this?

JESTER: O King, you have seen and heard all the others. This is the one who was their teacher when they were young.

KING (*Rising*): You say, the *teacher* of all these others? Then, Jester, I commend your choice. It would be mine also.

OLD WOMAN: Nay, O King, all these had seeds of greatness within themselves. I helped only to bring them out.

KING: Speak on, O Teacher of so many.

OLD WOMAN: The little ones who love all growing things; the young who find joy in the sound and feel of music; the children who use colors to paint life as they see it; the boys and girls who bind the wing of a bird or heal the hurt of a small child; the young students who find keen satisfaction in performing experiments or doing higher mathematics—all these and many more are in every class throughout the land.

KING: The seeds of greatness may be in all, but it takes a wise and skillful teacher to bring them forth. You have made possible the greatness of all these others. I crown you most worthy of them all. (*He places wreath of honor on her head. Others clap hands.*)

PRIME MINISTER (*To* JESTER): Jester, your choice is right. But I confess I have no wish to wear your cap and bells.

JESTER: And I would sooner keep them than have your

job—for a Prime Minister and a King have agreed with a Jester this day.

KING: That is because a Fool is sometimes nearer the truth than the wisest of men. (*Curtain*)

THE END

Angel of Mercy

by *Esther Lipnick*

Characters

FLORENCE NIGHTINGALE
PARTHENOPE, *her sister*
AGNES, *a friend*
MARY MORSE
DR. HALL
DR. GOODALE
SIR HARRY VERNEY, *Parthenope's husband*
LORD ASHWORTH, *Agnes's husband*
BUTLER
BOY'S VOICE

SCENE 1

TIME: *1837.*

SETTING: *The living room of the Embley Park home of the Nightingales.*

AT RISE: FLORENCE NIGHTINGALE, *a gangly girl of seventeen, is standing beside a globe of the world. There is an unfinished sampler on a footstool beside her.* PARTHENOPE, *her older sister, is seated on an elaborate divan, embroidering;* AGNES, *seated across from* PARTHENOPE, *is also embroidering intently.* FLORENCE *seems upset as she twirls the globe around almost angrily.*

PARTHENOPE (*Looking up from her work*): Flo, have you finished the sampler you were doing for Aunt Mai?

FLORENCE (*Shakes her head without looking up*): No.

AGNES (*Looking up at* FLORENCE): I can't make you out, Florence. Nothing seems to please you any more, not even the prospect of being presented at court.

FLORENCE: Court. Humph! (*The two girls look at* FLORENCE, *shocked.*) I don't mean to be disrespectful. It's just—oh, it's just that I'm not made for this sort of life. Summer at Lea Hurst near the quaint village of Lea in Derbyshire, winter at fashionable Embley Park near Romsey. Surrounded by flowers and birds and servants. Ladies! Humph! Music and grammar, composition and modern languages. A lady must know Greek and Latin and mathematics and the antics of Caesar and Hannibal! It's—it's like lying on one's back and having liquid poured down one's throat. (*Pauses for a moment to get her breath; picks up her sampler, looks at it scornfully as she speaks.*) Embroidery! Like a bird in a gilded cage —like a fool I sit here sewing verses I don't mean. (*Reading from sampler.*)

"When I was young and in my prime
You see how well I spent my time.
And by my sampler you may see
What care my parents took of me."

(FLORENCE *begins to laugh, almost hysterically.*)

PARTHENOPE (*Stands up, very angry*): Stop that, Florence. You're forgetting your position. (FLORENCE *drops sampler onto floor; then sits down dejectedly on the footstool, her hands covering her face.*)

FLORENCE (*Barely audible*): Yes, my position.

AGNES (*After a brief silence*): But, Florence, what else can an English lady do?

PARTHENOPE: That's just it. Sometimes I feel that my sister isn't English at all. You know she was born in Florence, Italy, and seems to have inherited some of that Italian temperament. (*She smiles at* FLORENCE, *as if trying to cajole her.*)

AGNES: Your parents were traveling there at the time— (*There is a sudden sound of crying outside the window as* AGNES *speaks.* FLORENCE *jumps up as though electrified and runs to window.*)

FLORENCE: What has happened out there?

BOY'S VOICE (*Off, from outside window*): Cousin Jerry fell out of the tree and skinned his leg.

FLORENCE: Don't move him or touch him in any way. I'll be right out. (*She looks almost radiant as she turns to go, talking as if to herself.*) I must heat some water and get some clean bandages. (*Exits, left*)

AGNES (*Suddenly, to* PARTHENOPE): I have it, Parthenope. Your sister wants to be a—

PARTHENOPE: Nurse.

AGNES: How dreadful! Such a lowly profession, worse than being a kitchen-maid! (FLORENCE *re-enters with basin and bandages, crosses stage almost running, and exits. The girls look after her.*)

PARTHENOPE: Yes, and she'll have her way. Mark my words, it won't be long before she'll be traveling on the continent to start her training. I know my headstrong sister and (*Lowers her voice*) I've seen her devour in the privacy of her room reports of medical commissions, pamphlets of sanitary authorities, and histories of hospitals and homes!

AGNES: But your parents, what will they say?

PARTHENOPE (*Resignedly*): Oh, they'll be most unhappy, but they'll give in after a struggle. (*Looks up*) I can hear my mother saying, "We are ducks and have hatched a swan."

CURTAIN

*   *   *

SCENE 2

TIME: *1855, during the Crimean War*

SETTING: *"Sister's Tower," Florence Nightingale's head-quarters in the Barrack Hospital at Scutari.*

AT RISE: FLORENCE NIGHTINGALE *is sitting bent over a rough, unpainted table, writing letters.*

FLORENCE (*Aloud, as she writes*): My dear Mrs. Conrad, your boy, Jim, has asked me to say "hello" to you. He is doing very well and has shown much progress since he's been brought here. Do not worry. His eye, which we were afraid he would lose, has improved greatly. (*There is a knock at the door.* MARY MORSE, *a nurse, enters, carrying scrub brush and pail.*) Come in, Mary.

MARY: Oh, Miss Nightingale, I thought I'd drop in to say good night. The wards have all been scrubbed clean.

FLORENCE: Good girl, Mary. You're on the way to becoming a fine nurse. You're learning the importance of cleanliness—I'll never be able to stress that too strongly.

MARY (*Smiling*): Thank you, Miss Nightingale. You know I was thinking while I was scrubbing the floors, wouldn't they be surprised back home if they saw me doing such work. They'd think I'd gone plumb mad.

FLORENCE (*Smiling*): Yes, they called me mad, too, when I came here, because the first thing I asked for was a supply of sacking and two hundred hard scrub brushes for washing floors.

MARY: You mean you didn't even find that here?

FLORENCE: No, not a basin, not a towel, nor a bit of soap, nor a broom—

MARY: Heavens, Miss Nightingale, then all those stories are true, about the laundry, and the cooking, and the storekeeping.

FLORENCE: I don't know what you've heard, Mary, but it's the same thing all over again. Cleanliness, cleanliness is the thing I've had to fight for time and again. It can be such a simple thing, too. Why shouldn't a soldier wear a clean shirt on the front as well as at home. And isn't it more important that a sick man should eat food that is appetizing, like broths and jellies, rather than hunks of bread and raw meat?

MARY (*Nodding*): It's just common sense, Miss Nightingale. Then why is it so hard to make them understand? Why did Dr. Hall oppose you so?

FLORENCE: My dear girl—that's an age-old question. Man versus woman. Man still believes that a woman's place is in the home.

MARY: In the home. (*Musingly*) I wonder what they're doing at home now?

FLORENCE (*Rather dryly*): Drinking their afternoon tea.

MARY (*Straightens her shoulders and looks squarely at her superior*): I'm glad I'm here with you, Miss Nightingale. Good night.

FLORENCE: I'm glad you're here, too, Nurse Mary Morse. We need more women like you. Good night. (MARY *exits.* FLORENCE *looks after her, then resumes her writing. Aloud, as she writes*) Your son will soon be writing to you himself, God willing. Yours truly. (*There are footsteps outside the door, and men's voices can be heard. A knock follows.*) Come in, come in, gentlemen. (*Two medical officers enter, one dressed in white, the other in military uniform.*)

DR. GOODALE: Good evening, Miss Nightingale.

DR. HALL: Good evening, Miss Nightingale.

FLORENCE: Good evening, Dr. Goodale, Dr. Hall. Be seated, gentlemen. (*They sit down on the bench.*)

DR. GOODALE: We'll be but a moment, Miss Nightingale. I see you are busy as usual.

DR. HALL: I have news for you, Miss Nightingale. I am leaving for England tonight on official business.

FLORENCE: For England! I am sorry to see you leave, Doctor. We shall miss you.

DR. HALL (*Waves her last remark aside*): No, you won't, Miss Nightingale. I am leaving the hospital in good hands—in yours and Dr. Goodale's. But I haven't merely come to say goodbye; as a matter of fact the reason for my visit is twofold.

FLORENCE (*Interrupting him*): Yes, Dr. Hall. You're going to ask me if I have a message to send them back home. Well, I have. (*Stands, facing him and becomes very businesslike and brisk*) Tell them that the supplies I stocked up on at Marseilles are running out. Tell them for heavens' sake to stop this red tape which entwines all the official stores sent from England. Tell them dying men can't wait for a Purveyor who in turn has to wait for a Board of Survey to examine goods sorely needed. Delay is maddening. We're fighting a war and we're dealing with human lives. Human lives, Dr. Hall!

DR. HALL: Yes, Miss Nightingale, I shall see what I can do.

DR. GOODALE: And while you're at it, Dr. Hall, you might tell them how Miss Nightingale put to work the women who followed their husbands to the front. Tell them how these women work in the laundry, washing clothes. Tell them that before Miss Nightingale came only six shirts a month were washed. Tell them of the diet kitchen she set up. And tell them what fools we doctors were and how we opposed her every move.

FLORENCE: Come, come, Dr. Goodale, let's forget that.

DR. HALL: That indeed is the second motive for my call. I've come to apologize for being a stubborn mule and to salute a woman who is my superior. I salute you, Miss Nightingale, and wish you luck and health that you may continue your work of mercy here.

FLORENCE (*Shakes hands with* DR. HALL *as he rises, ready to leave*): Thank you, Doctor, and Godspeed.

DR. GOODALE (*Shakes hands with* FLORENCE *too*): Good night, Miss Nightingale.

FLORENCE: Good night, Doctor. (*They exit, center.* FLORENCE *returns to her work, sits for a moment with her head in her hands, then rises. She goes to shelf and gets a kerchief which she ties around her head, throws a shawl over her shoulders, lights her lamp, puts some paper and a pencil in her pocket, picks up her lamp.*) And now I must visit my dear children. (*Starts off, as curtain falls.*)

*   *   *

SCENE 3

TIME: *August 7, 1856.*

SETTING: *Living room at Lea Hurst, summer home of the Nightingales.*

AT RISE: *The lamps are lighted. There is much laughing and gay conversation.* LADY AGNES *and her husband,* LORD ASHWORTH, *are seated on a divan. Directly opposite* PARTHENOPE *is reclining comfortably on a chaise longue, while her husband,* SIR HARRY VERNEY, *sits on an elaborate footstool beside her. A serving table is laden with fruit and sweets, and the ladies are eating almost continuously.*

LADY AGNES (*Between bites of candy*): And when was the last time you heard of your sister?

PARTHENOPE: Oh, just the other day.

LORD ASHWORTH: I say she ought to be in any day now. The man-of-war on which she is expected is due to arrive very shortly.

SIR HARRY: Oh, yes. Preparations are all complete for the

homecoming of my illustrious sister-in-law. Three military bands have been rehearsing ceaselessly for weeks on end.

LADY AGNES (*Taking another candy*): Somehow I can't picture Florence accepting all this fanfare. She never had any use for the conventional things.

PARTHENOPE (*Reaches out for candy*): No, not our wild swan. Sometimes, I almost lose patience with her. I was quite angered when she refused to come home after contracting Crimean fever. Stubborn as ever.

SIR HARRY: What is it she wrote you? "I am ready to stand out the war with any man," and by Jove she has!

LORD ASHWORTH: I say, I almost forgot. One of my tenants showed me a letter his son sent him from the Crimean front, and I've always intended to read it to you. (*Searches in his pocket and brings out a much wrinkled piece of paper; adjusts his glasses and reads*) "What a comfort it was to see her pass, even. She would speak to one and nod and smile to many more, but she could not do it all, you know. We lay there by hundreds, but we could kiss her shadow as it fell, and lay our heads on the pillow again content."

SIR HARRY: I say, that's a fine tribute.

PARTHENOPE (*Wiping her eyes*): May I see it? (LORD ASHWORTH *hands it to her.* SIR HARRY *gets up as if to break this sentimental moment.*)

SIR HARRY: I think we could all do with a spot of tea.

LORD ASHWORTH: Splendid idea. (SIR HARRY *rings for* BUTLER *who rushes in, obviously upset.*)

BUTLER (*Excitedly*): Master, what am I to do?

SIR HARRY: Control yourself, Albert. We'd like some tea.

BUTLER: But, sir, what am I to do about the woman all in black?

PARTHENOPE: What are you talking about, Albert?

BUTLER: There's a woman all in black who insists on

coming in the front entrance, and I swear she looks like cook's younger sister. I just can't make her come in the servants' entrance.

PARTHENOPE: Why, Albert, let her in. (FLORENCE, *dressed in black, face veiled, enters.*)

FLORENCE: She is in. (*They all stare in astonishment as* FLORENCE *lifts her veil.*)

PARTHENOPE (*Running over to* FLORENCE *and embracing her warmly*): Flo, darling.

BUTLER: Oh, Miss Florence, begging your pardon a thousand times, I didn't know—

FLORENCE: That's all right, Albert— (*Everyone shakes hands with* FLORENCE; PARTHENOPE *helps her remove her hat and veil, which* BUTLER *takes away. All sit down.*)

PARTHENOPE: But, Flo, why didn't you let us know so we could meet you?

LADY AGNES: They said you were coming on the man-of-war.

FLORENCE: I couldn't take all the excitement. (*Looking around*). It's good to be back—to see you all.

LORD ASHWORTH: And you—all England has been awaiting your return.

LADY AGNES: You must be dreadfully tired, dear. We ought to leave and let you rest.

FLORENCE: No, I'm not really tired.

LORD ASHWORTH: I do think we ought to leave you to your family. (AGNES *and* LORD ASHWORTH *rise and hold out hands to* FLORENCE.)

LADY AGNES: My dear, I hope we'll see you soon. Dinner, perhaps.

FLORENCE: Thank you. I am sure we shall see you soon.

LORD ASHWORTH: Good night, Florence Nightingale. (*They shake hands.*)

LADY AGNES: Good night; good night, everyone. (*She*

waves her hand, kisses FLORENCE *on cheek, and she and*
LORD ASHWORTH *move to door.*)

OTHERS: Good night. (SIR HARRY *goes out with guests,
while* FLORENCE *and* PARTHENOPE *move to divan and
sit side by side.*)

SIR HARRY (*Re-appearing in doorway*): Shall I have Albert take care of your bag, Florence?

FLORENCE: Thank you, I wish you would. It's in the vesti-
bule.

PARTHENOPE (*Looking at her sister*): It's been a long time.

FLORENCE: Yes, and yet everything here is just the same.
Peaceful and restful.

PARTHENOPE: You need rest badly. You must stay now and
forget your nursing for a while.

FLORENCE: Forget nursing! I could no longer live without nursing than you without air.

PARTHENOPE (*Sighing*): I see that I won't be able to stop
you. With the war over, now what?

FLORENCE: There are wars to be fought here at home and
in the army—wars for sanitation. Too many deaths result from neglect, sister. There's so much of it. You
might just as well take a million men every year and
shoot them upon Salisbury Plain!

PARTHENOPE: Your task won't be easy. You forget that
you're a woman.

FLORENCE: Yes, I am a woman. I must fight for a more useful life for women. Women must be at the forefront of
reform. It will not be easy, but it must be done—

PARTHENOPE: At the expense of your own health!

FLORENCE: My health? I shall guard my health, but I cannot stop. I cannot rest; there is too much to do.

PARTHENOPE (*Standing*): Be that as it may. You win. If
you'll excuse me now, I'll see that your room is made
ready for you so that you'll rest at least tonight. (*Exits*)

FLORENCE (*Closing her eyes*): So much to do. I cannot

forget those heroic dead. (*She rises, extinguishes one lamp and dims another. Then, with determination*) They shall not have died in vain! (*Offstage voices are heard singing "Angel of Mercy", as the curtain slowly falls.*)

THE END

Fiesta the First

by Jean A. McArthur

Characters

PEDRO	DOLLMAKER'S WIFE
MARIA	COOK
CARLOS	COOK'S WIFE
JANE	MAYOR
MANUEL	JANE'S FATHER
CONCHITA	FIESTA ANNOUNCER
TWO WOMEN	CROWD
DOLLMAKER	

TIME: *The morning of Pan American Day.*

SETTING: *The marketplace. There are several stalls set up.*

AT RISE: *The marketplace is almost deserted. A few people are outside the stalls and the* COOK *and the* COOK'S WIFE *are inside their stall.* CARLOS *and* PEDRO *enter, carrying their baskets wearily.* MARIA *enters, wipes her forehead. As they approach their stall,* JANE *peers out from behind it, then ducks behind the stall once more.*

MARIA (*Looking around*): Did you hear something?

CARLOS: Girls, they are always hearing things. We have work to do, Maria. (*They set down their baskets and begin to put vegetables into their stall.*) I hate these old baskets. If only we had a donkey, a little burro!

313

PEDRO (*Kicking angrily at one basket*): A donkey! If only we had some money!

MARIA (*Excitedly*): Maybe we will. You know there's going to be a big celebration here today.

PEDRO: So? We are workers, not watchers, Maria. We will have to stay here. (PEDRO *continues to pile vegetables*.)

MARIA: Wait, Pedro. There's going to be a contest for the children. Some will represent Mexico and some Latin America, and some will even sing songs of our good friends in North America.

CARLOS (*Hopefully*): It might be fun, Pedro.

MARIA (*Coaxingly*): There is a prize, Pedro. Money.

PEDRO (*Busy with the vegetables*): A few pennies.

MARIA: No, no. Enough to buy many sweets and clothes—a burro, even.

PEDRO (*Turning*): A burro? (MARIA *nods*) That settles it! Carlos, Maria, we are going to win the contest!

MARIA (*Clapping her hands*): Oh, Pedro!

CARLOS: But how, Pedro? We can't sing, and we can't dance.

MARIA: At least, not well.

PEDRO: Why, we'll—act out the meaning of Pan American Day. We can represent the countries.

CARLOS (*Looking around doubtfully*): All twenty-one of them?

MARIA: Of course not, silly! (*Making up her mind*) I shall be Colombia, the land of emeralds and coffee. (JANE *peeps around the corner of another stall as they talk*.)

CARLOS: How? Will you paint yourself green and wear a coffee plant in your hair?

MARIA: You *are* foolish! I will mention the coffee plantations and act out how the emeralds are found. My green beads (*Touches beads*) will be the emeralds.

PEDRO (*Nodding*): Good! Then I shall be Brazil, the land of rubber. I can show how men get rubber.

CARLOS: I'll give you my ball to show. It's my favorite, but you can have it. And I shall be—I shall be—Bolivia, land of tin and silver. I can tell about the great mines, but (*Sadly*) I have no silver.

PEDRO (*Trying to be casual*): I—I have a few coins you may use.

MARIA (*Surprised*): Pedro!

PEDRO (*Hastily*): A few, not many.

MARIA: Then we shall surely win the contest, and we'll buy a burro and— (JANE *sneezes loudly.*) What was that?

PEDRO (*Turning around*): See there, behind the stall! Catch her! (*Children quickly surround* JANE, *who stands still.*) Who are you, and what are you doing here?

JANE: I'm Jane, and I'm lost.

PEDRO (*Sternly*): So you spy on us.

MARIA (*Looking at* JANE *closely*): Look at her dress. How odd it is!

JANE (*Proudly*): I am an American.

CARLOS: Huh, so are we!

JANE: I mean a United States American.

MARIA (*Surprised*): A Yankee. Oh!

JANE: We're strangers here, my father and I. He stopped to talk to someone, and I wandered off, and—I'm lost.

MARIA (*Putting her arm around* JANE): Why don't you stay with us? Everyone will come to the marketplace today. It's Pan American Day, the day when the twenty-one American countries celebrate their friendship. There's going to be a contest for children. Everyone comes—perhaps your father will, too. (MANUEL *and* CONCHITA *enter from right.*)

MANUEL (*Watching* CONCHITA): Don't cry, Conchita. We're going to a fiesta.

CONCHITA (*Weeping*): But I lost my present.

MANUEL: Do you want those children to see you crying? Mother will understand.

CONCHITA: But we worked so hard making the baskets. And you got up so early to sell them. And now I have lost the present we bought for Mother with the money.

MANUEL (*Gruffly*): Stop crying! They were only beads.

MARIA (*Touches her own beads*): Oh!

MANUEL: We will go home and explain what happened. Perhaps Mother is too old for beads.

CONCHITA: Oh, no, Manuel! Why was I so careless? (*Weeps*)

MARIA (*Slowly*): I have some beads, little one. See, I will give them to you.

CONCHITA (*Reaching out for them*): Manuel, look. Oh, how pretty they are!

MARIA (*Quickly*): I have others. These are nothing. Do not let her cry.

CONCHITA (*Curtsying*): Thank you, senorita. Oh, thank you! (MANUEL *and* CONCHITA *exit.*)

JANE: You are very kind.

PEDRO: But now you can not be Colombia.

MARIA (*Quickly*): I can help you, instead. (*She turns as* TWO WOMEN *enter from left.*)

1ST WOMAN (*Putting her hand up to her head*): I have forgotten it!

2ND WOMAN: What have you forgotten? You have your basket.

1ST WOMAN: The present for little Juan.

2ND WOMAN: Oh, that. Take him some flowers. Or give him some pennies.

1ST WOMAN (*Sadly*): I have no money. If I had, I would take him something from the fiesta. He has never been to one. We live so far from town, and he could never come here on his little lame legs.

2ND WOMAN: He will not mind.

1ST WOMAN: You do not know how he waits for me with his eyes always watching the road. I had promised him a rubber ball so that he might play with it like other boys. And now I can give him nothing. (CARLOS *turns away from her and looks at his rubber ball.*)

2ND WOMAN: Come, I will make little Juan some candy, and next time—

CARLOS (*Quickly*): Here, give my ball to the lame one. I am too big for childish toys, anyway.

2ND WOMAN (*Taking the ball*): Thank you, thank you, senor.

PEDRO (*Stepping forward*): And take my money. It will buy something for the little lame one. I have two strong legs myself. I can earn more any time.

1ST WOMAN: Thank you, thank you both. Juan will be very happy! (WOMEN *exit.*)

CARLOS: Now we are really finished! We have no way to represent Pan American Day. Goodbye to our burro!

MARIA: There is so much trouble in the world.

PEDRO: But why must we always be the ones to right it? Another year of lugging these vegetables! (*Kicks at basket*) I hate them!

JANE: Such sour faces!

PEDRO (*Sitting down*): No sermons, please.

CARLOS: Our hearts are good, but our backs (*Rubs his back*) will be sorry.

JANE: Isn't there anything you could do for the contest?

CARLOS (*Sitting beside* PEDRO): Nothing.

JANE: There's always a way. That's what my father says and—I think I have an idea. (*Bends down and whispers to children*)

MARIA (*Excitedly*): That's it! That's it! Jane, you're wonderful!

PEDRO (*Slowly*): It might work. (*As* DOLLMAKER *and* DOLLMAKER'S WIFE *enter.*) But when will the contest begin?

DOLLMAKER (*Cheerfully*): Any moment now. The people are parading through the streets.

DOLLMAKER'S WIFE: Stop your silly chatter, man! There are dolls to be finished.

COOK: How ugly she is! Well, Carlos, how about a pancake?

CARLOS (*Sadly*): We have no money.

COOK'S WIFE: You need none. It's a holiday. This once we will treat you.

CHILDREN (*Taking pancakes*): Thank you, senora, senor. (*As they eat,* MAYOR *and* FIESTA ANNOUNCER *enter right, followed by crowd.* JANE'S FATHER *enters with crowd, unnoticed by others.*)

MAYOR (*At front of crowd*): Welcome to our marketplace. We are met here on this great occasion—

DOLLMAKER'S WIFE: Enough of speeches! Where are the performers?

MAYOR: To pay tribute to Pan American Day, the day when all the American nations celebrate their unity.

COOK'S WIFE: How beautifully he speaks.

MAYOR: It is a day of great rejoicing, a day on which we remember all we have done together, but, above all, it is a day of fiesta. So, now let the entertainment begin. Musicians, announce your songs.

ANNOUNCER: Thank you. First, a Mexican folk song, a tribute to our beloved country.

MAYOR: You may begin. (*A group from crowd sings an appropriate Mexican folk song.*)

COOK (*As song ends*): Beautiful voices, beautiful voices!

MAYOR: A fine start, indeed, for our fiesta. Who is next?

ANNOUNCER: We are indeed fortunate to have with us to-day a group of children from the American school. Their first number will be a folk song from the United

States. (*A group from crowd sings any appropriate American folk song.*)

COOK'S WIFE: How well they do! Such intelligent children!

MAYOR: Well done, well done. It will be hard to pick the winner today.

ANNOUNCER: Next, we will hear a South American song. Begin, singers. (*A group from crowd sings any appropriate South American folk song.*)

DOLLMAKER (*Loudly*): They are the best. Give them the prize!

ANNOUNCER: Wait! The children from the American school will now sing their second number. (*Second group sings another American folk song.*)

COOK'S WIFE: Oh, they are good!

DOLLMAKER'S WIFE: No, the others are better! Give them the prize.

COOK'S WIFE (*Coming out of stall, angrily*): Who are you to give the prizes? You know nothing of singing.

DOLLMAKER'S WIFE: How dare you speak like that to me! Husband! (*Turns to him*)

COOK'S WIFE (*Angrily*): Husband, indeed! Husband, my husband. (COOK *and* DOLLMAKER *come from behind the counters and stand glaring at each other.*)

MAYOR: Stop that! The judges will decide the winner. But, first, is there anyone else who wishes to compete for the prize?

PEDRO (*Stepping forward with* CARLOS *and* MARIA): Please, sir—

MAYOR: Speak up, speak up. Are you children singers?

PEDRO: Well, no, sir.

COOK: Do you dance?

MARIA: Oh, no, sir!

DOLLMAKER: They give plays, no doubt.

CARLOS (*Slowly*): Not exactly.

DOLLMAKER'S WIFE (*Scornfully*): They neither sing, dance

nor act. Are we to listen to them talk all day? (*Crowd laughs.*) Tell us the winner. Let these little ones return to their mother.

MAYOR (*To* PEDRO): I am sorry, but, since you have nothing to offer, we must continue. (*To crowd*) We have with us today a famous North American who has come to advise us on our farming. While the judges are making their decision, he will speak to us on the meaning of Pan American Day.

JANE's FATHER (*Stepping forward*): My good friends—

JANE (*Running to him*): Father, Father, it's me!

FATHER: Jane, I looked everywhere for you.

MARIA: But she did not tell us her father was to speak.

JANE (*To* FATHER): My friends took care of me. See, here they are.

FATHER: The three who entertain without entertaining.

JANE: Oh, they would entertain if they only had a chance. Please help them, Father.

FATHER (*Turning to* MAYOR): Mr. Mayor—

MAYOR: Perhaps we have been too hasty. (*Turning to* PEDRO) If you wish, you may begin.

PEDRO: Then, back, all of you, back. (*Waves the others to the rear of stage*) And now an American game, a real North American game, by name, Farmer in the Dell. Form a circle. I shall be the Farmer. (CARLOS, MARIA, JANE *and some of the crowd form a circle and begin to play, as the children from the American School sing.*)

DOLLMAKER's WIFE: Oh, what fun! Choose me, choose me! (DOLLMAKER's WIFE *is chosen and, in turn, chooses the* COOK's WIFE.)

CROWD (*As game ends*): Do it again, do it again!

MAYOR: Wait. First we must award the prize.

CROWD: Give it to them. Give it to the children.

FATHER: I think they deserve it. From what my daughter has told me, they are as kind as they are clever. By all means, give them the money. They have shown that in sport there is friendship for all.

MAYOR (*Happily*): I shall! I shall!

PEDRO (*Almost shouting*): A burro, a burro at last! Maria, Carlos, we've won!

CARLOS (*Frowning*): But what shall we call our burro?

MARIA: Call it? Why, Fiesta, of course. Fiesta Maria Carlos Pedro the First. Our wonderful, beautiful burro! (*Crowd cheers as the curtain falls.*)

THE END

The Cross Princess

by Esther MacLellan and Catherine V. Schroll

Characters

EDWARD ⎫
CATHERINE ⎭ *two children*
KING
QUEEN
PRINCESS ANNABELLE
NURSE
PAGE
MASTER KNOW-IT-ALL ⎫
MRS. WORDSWORDS ⎬ *royal teachers*
MISS SPELL ⎭

SETTING: *Bedroom of the* PRINCESS ANNABELLE.
AT RISE: *The stage is empty.* EDWARD *and* CATHERINE
enter from the left.

EDWARD (*Motioning toward games and toys*): There,
Catherine, what did I tell you? Did you ever see such
a room? It has more toys than a toy shop.
CATHERINE: Yes, yes, it really does. (*Examining dolls*)
Look at the dolls! Big ones and little ones. Dozens and
dozens of dolls.
EDWARD: And every kind of game. Puzzles and paints and
skates and sleds.

CATHERINE (*Darting to bookcase*): And best of all—books. Oh, Edward, just see how many books the Princess Annabelle has.

EDWARD (*Picking up a book and leafing through it*): Here's a good one. It's full of pirates and fights and buried treasure.

CATHERINE (*Wistfully*): So many books. If I borrowed one till tomorrow, do you think the Princess would mind?

EDWARD: How would we get it back? We're supposed to be in the kitchen delivering vegetables, not wandering around the palace. If the cook found out where we were, she'd . . . she'd skin us. We'd better get out of here. (*Noise is heard offstage*)

CATHERINE: It's too late. Somebody's coming now.

EDWARD: Well, don't just stand there. Do something. If we're caught, we may be thrown into the dungeon.

CATHERINE: Into the dungeon!

EDWARD: Why not? That's what dungeons are for. Quick! Crawl under the bed. No one will see us there. (*They hide under bed.* PRINCESS ANNABELLE *enters with* NURSE, *who carries a tray.*)

ANNABELLE: I tell you I don't want it. I won't eat and you can't make me!

NURSE: Princess Annabelle! What's the matter with you? You never used to talk so to your poor old nurse. A sweet baby you were, always polite and good.

ANNABELLE: I'm sorry, Nurse.

NURSE: You've hardly tasted your nice luncheon.

ANNABELLE: I'm not hungry.

NURSE: I'll leave the tray on the table. Maybe you'll want something later. Let me brush your hair. It's almost time for your arithmetic lesson.

ANNABELLE: I don't want to do arithmetic. I'm tired.

NURSE: Now, now, don't be silly. You always have your

arithmetic lesson after lunch. A fine princess you'd turn out to be if you didn't learn how to add and subtract. (PAGE *enters.*)

PAGE: Master Know-It-All. (*He bows and exits.* MASTER KNOW-IT-ALL *enters.*)

NURSE: Here's your teacher, Princess Annabelle. Where's your silver pencil and your notebook with the golden cover?

ANNABELLE: Out the window, I suppose. That's where I threw them yesterday.

NURSE: Just for that you can use a plain pencil and a paper tablet. (*Hands her paper and pencil*)

ANNABELLE (*Folding her arms*): I don't want to write. I don't feel like doing numbers.

NURSE: None of that. Do what your teacher says. (*Exits*)

MASTER KNOW-IT-ALL: Good afternoon, Princess Annabelle. Open your book to page two.

ANNABELLE: Page two! Haven't we finished with page two yet?

KNOW-IT-ALL: How can we finish with it? You don't know it. Begin with the first problem. If Prince Henry has one diamond ring, and his mother gives him another diamond ring, how many rings does he have?

ANNABELLE: Who's Prince Henry?

KNOW-IT-ALL: What does it matter who he is? It's the arithmetic part that's important. If Prince Henry has one diamond ring, and his mother gives him another, how many rings would Prince Henry have?

ANNABELLE: How do I know? I've never heard of him.

KNOW-IT-ALL (*Tapping book with pencil*): Answer the question, please. Answer the question.

ANNABELLE: Very well. Twenty.

KNOW-IT-ALL: Twenty!

ANNABELLE: *I* have twenty diamond rings. Why shouldn't Prince Henry have twenty diamond rings?

KNOW-IT-ALL: The book doesn't ask how many he *should* have. What's one and one?

ANNABELLE (*Yawning*): Three.

KNOW-IT-ALL: Three!

ANNABELLE: Yes, three.

KNOW-IT-ALL: One and one are two.

ANNABELLE: I say one and one are three, and I'm the princess. I command one and one to be three! (KING *and* QUEEN *enter.*)

KING: What's this? What's this? You can't command one and one to be three.

QUEEN: One and one are two, Annabelle dear. They've always been two.

KING: Master Know-It-All, I thought you were the best teacher in the country.

KNOW-IT-ALL: I am, Your Majesty.

KING: Then why does the Princess say that one and one are three? Everyone knows it isn't true.

KNOW-IT-ALL: Everyone but the Princess. She knows nothing.

QUEEN: Nothing!

KNOW-IT-ALL: Nothing. (*Opening small black book*) On Monday, her mark was zero. Tuesday, zero. Wednesday, zero. Thursday . . .

QUEEN: Stop! Stop!

KING: Master Know-It-All, we will speak to our daughter. You may return tomorrow.

KNOW-IT-ALL: Yes, Your Majesty. (*Exits*)

KING: Annabelle! This is dreadful. A princess who doesn't know arithmetic.

ANNABELLE (*Stamping her foot*): I don't care.

QUEEN: That's not true, Annabelle. Of course you care. (PAGE *enters.*)

PAGE: The riding master is ready to give the Princess her riding lesson, may it please Your Majesties.

KING: Very well. Run along, Annabelle. (PAGE *exits.*)

ANNABELLE: Yes, Father. (*Exits right*)

QUEEN: If Annabelle is so poor in arithmetic, can she be learning her other lessons?

KING: We'll soon find out. Ho, Page! (PAGE *enters.*)

PAGE: Yes, Your Majesty?

KING: Call the royal teachers.

PAGE: Yes, Your Majesty. (*Calling*) Ho, the royal teachers! (*Enter* MISS SPELL *and* MRS. WORDSWORDS)

KING: Miss Spell, you teach the Princess Annabelle her spelling, do you not?

MISS SPELL: I try, Your Majesty.

KING: What are her marks?

MISS SPELL (*Opening small black book*): Monday, zero. Tuesday, zero. Wednesday, zero. Thursday . . .

QUEEN: Stop! Stop! Let the reading teacher speak.

MRS. WORDSWORDS: I have had no lessons with Princess Annabelle this week, Your Majesty.

KING: No lessons? And how is that?

MRS. WORDSWORDS: Monday, the Princess threw a teacup at me. Tuesday, the Princess threw a pincushion and a bedroom slipper. Wednesday . . .

QUEEN: Stop! Stop! I can bear no more.

KING: Page, you may show the royal teachers to their rooms. Tell the royal treasurer to give each one an extra piece of gold. They've earned it.

PAGE: Yes, Your Majesty. (*Teachers exit, followed by* PAGE)

QUEEN (*Weeping*): What are we to do? What can be the matter with dear Annabelle?

KING (*Pacing the floor*): Zero, zero, zero. Such a report! The child knows nothing.

QUEEN: And why is she so cross and bad-tempered? Whoever heard of a rude princess?

KING: It's a disgrace. A terrible disgrace. I tell you, my

dear, I would give a bag of gold—yes, a bag of gold—
to know what's wrong with our daughter. (PAGE *enters.*)

PAGE: May it please Your Majesties, it is time for the
royal bridge game. Queen Hildegarde and King Archi-
bald are waiting in the throne room.

KING: Very well. (*Exits left with* QUEEN. EDWARD *and*
CATHERINE *crawl out from under the bed.*)

CATHERINE: Goodness! Isn't Princess Annabelle cross! I
wonder if all princesses act that way.

EDWARD (*Grandly*): "I command one and one to be
three!" I wish *I* could do that.

CATHERINE: It would make school easy, wouldn't it?
Though it doesn't seem to work so well for the Princess. Zero, zero, zero. Our mother wouldn't like those
marks.

EDWARD: Neither did hers.

CATHERINE: The King is willing to give a bag of gold to
the one who finds out what's wrong with the Princess.
(*Slowly*) A bag of gold. Edward, if we could win the
bag of gold, think what we could do for Mother. She
works so hard.

EDWARD: How can we tell what's wrong with the Princess? I don't know anything about princesses.

CATHERINE: She's just a girl. Mother says that when children are cross, there's always a reason. Maybe Princess
Annabelle needs more exercise. Babies fret and cry when
they don't get enough fresh air.

EDWARD: She's no baby. Besides, look at the balls and
sleds and other games. And she just went for a riding
lesson.

CATHERINE: That's true. (*Walks toward table*) Here's her
lunch. Vegetable soup, whole wheat bread, salad, milk,
fresh fruit. There's certainly nothing wrong with her
food.

EDWARD: She didn't eat it.

CATHERINE: I wonder why she didn't? Everything looks so good.

EDWARD (*Eating slice of bread*): It tastes good, too. (PRINCESS ANNABELLE *enters right.*)

ANNABELLE: How dare you eat my lunch! Who are you, you . . . nibblers!

CATHERINE: I'm Catherine.

EDWARD: I'm Edward.

CATHERINE: We sell vegetables to the cook, and we just happened to be passing, and . . . Oh, Princess Annabelle, you have so many lovely things.

ANNABELLE (*Proudly*): Of course.

CATHERINE: I like the books best. Please read us one.

ANNABELLE: No. I don't want to.

EDWARD: I didn't think you could read.

ANNABELLE: I'm an excellent reader. No one can read better than I.

EDWARD: Then let's hear this pirate story. (*Hands book to* ANNABELLE) I like something exciting.

ANNABELLE: Very well. (*Opening book*) It's called "The Pirate's T . . . Tree . . . The Pirate's Tree Stump."

EDWARD: "The Pirate's Tree Stump"! What a funny name.

CATHERINE (*Peering over* ANNABELLE'S *shoulder*): No, no. It's "The Pirate's Treasure."

ANNABELLE (*Closing book*): I don't feel like reading.

EDWARD: Humph!

CATHERINE: How about a game?

EDWARD: All right. (*Getting ball and bat*) Catherine, you pitch and I'll catch. As long as you own the ball, Princess, you can be first batter.

ANNABELLE: Of course.

CATHERINE: Ready? (*She throws ball to* ANNABELLE, *who misses it.*)

EDWARD: Strike one.

ANNABELLE: It wasn't a strike. Catherine didn't throw properly.

EDWARD: You mean you didn't hit properly.

ANNABELLE: I always hit properly. I'm a good hitter.

EDWARD: With your fists, maybe, but not with a bat.

ANNABELLE: How dare you say I can't bat!

EDWARD: Because you can't. You can't read either. The Pirate's Tree Stump!

ANNABELLE: You rude, disagreeable boy. I'll have my daddy throw you into the dungeon.

CATHERINE: Indeed you will not!

ANNABELLE: And who will stop me? (KING *and* QUEEN *enter left*)

KING: What's all this fuss and shouting?

ANNABELLE (*Pointing to* EDWARD): Have this boy thrown into the dungeon!

KING: Have you forgotten, Annabelle? You know that's where the cook keeps the potatoes and turnips. There's no room for anything more.

QUEEN: My dear boy, why do you want to go to the dungeon? It's damp and quite uncomfortable.

ANNABELLE: It's good enough for him. Daddy, he said that I can't bat. (*Stamping her foot*) He's a perfectly horrid boy, and I don't like him.

QUEEN: Annabelle! How can you be so rude?

KING: What's the matter with you, Annabelle?

CATHERINE: I think I know, Your Majesty.

QUEEN: You do? Can you tell us why the Princess is so cross?

KING: And why she doesn't learn her lessons?

CATHERINE: Yes, I think I can. My cousin, Oliver Donald, used to behave just like the Princess.

EDWARD: Oliver Donald! You're right, Catherine. I remember. He was always shouting and stamping his foot and getting bad marks in school until we found out.

QUEEN: Found out what? Was he ill?

EDWARD: Not Oliver Donald.

CATHERINE: He didn't get enough sleep.

QUEEN: What?

KING: The Princess is sent to bed early every night.

EDWARD: Oliver Donald was sent *and* put.

CATHERINE: He only pretended to sleep, Your Majesty. As soon as Mother went out of the room, Oliver Donald hopped out of the bed.

KING: Aha! Page, ho! (PAGE *enters*.) Call the royal nurse!

PAGE: Ho, the royal nurse! (NURSE *enters*.)

KING: At what hour did the Princess go to bed last night?

NURSE (*Curtsying*): Oh, Your Majesty! Very late. I stopped in at ten o'clock to see if all was well with my darling, and she was wide awake.

QUEEN: Never!

NURSE: Playing with her paper dolls, Your Majesty.

KING: And the night before?

NURSE: Coloring a picture, may it please Your Majesty.

QUEEN: And the night before?

PAGE: I remember that night, Your Majesty. I was out late taking care of a sick pony. When I returned, the palace was dark—completely dark—except for a light in the Princess's room. And there I saw the gleam of a candle!

QUEEN (*Sadly*): Is this true, Annabelle?

ANNABELLE: I did not feel like going to bed.

QUEEN: No wonder you have been so cross. No wonder you have had so many zeros.

KING: You've broken a rule of the kingdom. A rule I wrote with my royal hand. Page, bring hither the Rules of the Kingdom. (PAGE *brings in large book.* KING *points to place on page*.) Look, Annabelle, look. "Every grown-up must have eight hours of sleep each night. Every child must have at least ten." *At least ten.*

ANNABELLE: I'm sorry, Daddy.

QUEEN: You've broken a law, Annabelle, and you must be punished.

KING: Not one candy, not a single piece for thirteen days.

QUEEN: And your promise, Annabelle, never to stay up late again.

ANNABELLE: I promise.

EDWARD: See why you couldn't bat? Everyone that's good in sports must get enough sleep. That's one of the first training rules.

CATHERINE: Sleep will chase away zeros, too. When you're tired, you can't learn anything.

KING: True. Very true.

QUEEN: How fortunate that you knew what was wrong with Annabelle!

CATHERINE: I just remembered when Oliver Donald wasn't getting enough sleep, either.

KING: Goodness! I just remembered something, too. (*Exits hurriedly*)

ANNABELLE: Mama, if I go to bed early tonight, may I play tomorrow with Catherine and Edward?

QUEEN: Certainly, dear.

ANNABELLE: We'll have our game on the lawn. And I won't be striking out. I'll prove that I can hit. (KING *enters, carrying two bags*)

KING: I promised a bag of gold to the one who found out what was wrong with Annabelle. And a king never breaks his royal word. As both knew the answer, both shall have a reward. (*To* CATHERINE) Here, my child, a small bag of gold for you. (*To* EDWARD) And another small bag of gold for you, my boy.

CATHERINE: Thank you, Your Majesty.

EDWARD: Long live the King!

CATHERINE: And the Queen, too, Edward. Remember your manners.

EDWARD: Long live the King! Long live the Queen!

CATHERINE (*Nudging him*): Don't forget the Princess. You'll hurt her feelings.

EDWARD: Long live the King! Long live the Queen! Long live the Princess Annabelle! (*Curtain falls.*)

THE END

The Secret of the Windmill

by Esther MacLellan and Catherine V. Schroll

Characters

MR. CARTER   MR. VAN DYKE
MRS. CARTER   JULIANA VAN DYKE
PAULA CARTER   JAN VAN DYKE
JIMMY CARTER   GRANDMOTHER VAN DYKE
MRS. VAN DYKE

TIME: *Late morning one day in spring.*
SETTING: *The Van Dyke living room in Amsterdam.*
AT RISE: MRS. CARTER *sits front right reading.* PAULA *and* JULIANA *enter.*

PAULA: Mother, Aunt Susan is making us a delicious lunch. We're having the best cheese sandwiches. (*Holds up Edam cheese*) I brought the cheese to show you. Doesn't it look like an apple? Did you know the Dutch were famous for cheeses? Can we buy Edam cheese in America?

MRS. CARTER: Yes, to every question.

PAULA: Why don't we? Buy it, that is. Why haven't we had Edam cheese at home?

MRS. CARTER: I don't know. Maybe it's because Americans make good cheeses, too.

PAULA: But now that I'm in the Netherlands, I love every-

thing Dutch. I'm crazy about the tulips, and the wind-
mills, and the canals, and the—

JIMMY (*Enters as she speaks*): You're just crazy, that's all.

PAULA: I don't care. (*She opens her arms wide.*) I love
everything. (*She hugs* JULIANA.) I love my Dutch cousin,
Juliana, who's named for the Queen. And I love my
Dutch Aunt Susan—

MRS. CARTER: Susan is my sister. She's about as Dutch as a
hot dog. Your Uncle Hans and Susan met at an American university.

PAULA: And wasn't it lucky? That's why everybody in this
house speaks English, even our Dutch grandmother.

JIMMY: She isn't our grandmother. She's Juliana's and
Jan's.

PAULA: Juliana said she could be our grandmother, too,
didn't you, Juliana?

JULIANA: Yes.

PAULA (*Whirling around the room*): Dear Holland! Wonderful country! If this house only had a mystery, it
would be perfect. Wouldn't it add just the right touch
to discover a secret treasure right here!

MRS. CARTER: Paula, stop your nonsense! Secret treasures,
indeed! Next you'll be breaking something. You just
missed the lamp.

MRS. VAN DYKE (*Entering*): Where's my Edam cheese?
What became of my two helpers?

PAULA: We started talking about mysteries, Auntie.

JIMMY: Old houses should have mysteries. How long has
the Van Dyke family lived here, Aunt Susan?

MRS. VAN DYKE: Forever, I think.

JULIANA: As a matter of fact, we do have a little mystery,
a tiny one. Tell them, Mother.

PAULA (*Whirling around the room again*): A mystery! A
real-life mystery! I'll solve it! I know I can!

JIMMY (*Shaking his head*): There she goes again, Mom. She'll ruin something for sure this time.

MRS. CARTER: Paula, stop this minute! You almost knocked over the vase.

JIMMY: Come on, Aunt Susan, tell us your tale. I hope it's a horror story.

MRS. VAN DYKE (*Laughing*): Well, it isn't. It's just an old story that may or may not be true.

PAULA (*Leading her aunt to a chair*): Tell us! Right now!

MRS. VAN DYKE (*Sitting*): Long ago, your grandmother had a young and beautiful aunt named Katrinka, who became a famous opera singer.

JULIANA (*Sitting at her mother's feet*): Aunt Katrinka was supposed to have had a collection of marvelous diamonds—all given her by an ardent admirer—a ring, earrings, a diamond necklace . . .

PAULA: Wonderful! Go on, go on!

MRS. VAN DYKE: Aunt Katrinka died young. She was vacationing on a yacht, when a sudden storm came up. Everyone aboard was drowned.

PAULA: How sad!

JULIANA: And after her death nobody ever found *one* of her famous diamonds.

JIMMY: That's no mystery. The diamonds went down with the yacht.

JULIANA: No, Aunt Katrinka never wore jewelry in the summer. She didn't have them with her.

JIMMY: Wasn't there any clue to where the diamonds were hidden?

PAULA: There must be a clue! Otherwise how would we begin to solve the mystery?

MRS. VAN DYKE: Yes, there was one. Before she left on the yacht trip, her father asked Katrinka about the jewels. But she just said they were hidden in a secret place.

PAULA: Didn't she tell her own father where the jewels were?

MRS. VAN DYKE: She started to, but her friends rushed in and she had no time to talk. As she kissed him goodbye, she whispered something to her father. But he didn't hear very well and all he was sure of were the words "secret" and "windmill."

PAULA: The secret of the windmill! Why that's not hard at all.

JIMMY: Just find the nearest windmill and dig.

MRS. VAN DYKE: It isn't that simple. The Van Dykes did have a windmill on their property and they did dig.

JIMMY: But nothing was found?

MRS. VAN DYKE: Nothing.

JIMMY: Where's the windmill? I'll go over it myself this afternoon, applying scientific methods of research.

MRS. VAN DYKE: You do that, Jimmy. Come, girls, I'm going to make the dessert now if you want to learn.

PAULA: Oh, yes, learn and taste. (*To* MRS. CARTER) Mother, Aunt Susan is making the dessert with delicious Dutch chocolate.

MRS. CARTER: And she'll cover it with delicious Dutch whipped cream, and I'll gain another pound or two. Run along, girls, and I'll join you in a minute. (PAULA, JULIANA *and* MRS. VAN DYKE *exit*.) Now, Jimmy, have you written your English paper?

JIMMY: Not yet, Mom. I was . . .

MRS. CARTER: Did you do yesterday's geography paper?

JIMMY: I don't think I quite remember. Let's see now— (*Picks up paper from desk and reads*) was that the one where I said the Netherlands was a small country, only a little larger than Maryland? That the name "the Netherlands" comes from the word "Nederlanders," which means lowlanders?

MRS. CARTER: No, that's not the one.

JIMMY (*Selecting another paper*): Was it the paper where I told that the climate is often damp and chilly but seldom very hot or very cold? Where I told about the chief products? In agriculture: wheat, barley, oats, potatoes, fruits, flowers, and flower bulbs? Dairy: cheese, condensed milk, butter . . .

MRS. CARTER: No. You're just reading from a travel booklet and you know it, and more important, I know it. And still more important, your teacher will know it.

JIMMY (*Pacing up and down*): Maybe that was the time I wrote about the large cities of the Netherlands—Amsterdam first, of course, the biggest diamond-cutting center in the world. The Hague. Rotterdam, greatest seaport in Holland . . .

MRS. CARTER: No. No to everything. You haven't done any of your school work for three days and you're to get busy right now.

JIMMY: Now?

MRS. CARTER (*Firmly*): Now.

JIMMY: But, Mother, I've the day planned—all the educational things I really must do. And then there's the mystery to solve. Jan and I . . .

JAN (*Enters right, staggering in with a huge packing case*): Did you call, dear cousin? Here I am. (*He sets the box down near center.*)

JIMMY (*Inspecting box*): What's all this stuff?

JAN: Old clothes. Ancient dishes. Mother cleaned out the storeroom yesterday when you were taking that long canal ride through the city.

MRS. CARTER (*Picking up lamp shade from box*): What an old lamp shade! It's positively black with age. But isn't it early for spring housecleaning?

JAN: Mother has been trying to get our storeroom cleaned for years, but Grandmother wouldn't let her throw anything away. The room was so full you could hardly get the door open. Yesterday, Granny finally gave in and told Mother to throw out anything she didn't want. So Mother started before Granny changed her mind.

JIMMY: I'll help you get the box out of here. We have to go down to the windmill quickly. We've work to do.

JAN: I can't. I've about twenty loads of junk to move out of the storeroom—old chairs, broken-down tables . . .

JIMMY: But we have to look for Aunt Katrinka's diamonds. It's terribly urgent. We must find them before we leave for America.

PAULA (*Dashing in and running to box*): What's this? (*Puts old lamp shade on her head and does a few dance steps*)

MRS. CARTER (*Mechanically*): Paula!

JIMMY: Hurry up! Let's go, Jan.

MRS. CARTER: You're not going anywhere, Jimmy. We're leaving for home soon, and your school work must be done, and done well.

JIMMY: Why doesn't Paula do something?

MRS. CARTER: She does.

PAULA: I finished writing today's paper early this morning. Want to hear it? It's very good.

JIMMY: No.

PAULA: I'll get it. It's right here on the table. (*She takes paper from book with a flourish.*) Ahem.

MRS. VAN DYKE (*Offstage*): Jan!

JAN (*Without moving*): Yes, Mother?

MRS. VAN DYKE (*Appearing at left*): Come to me when I call, please. I want you to go to the store. (*She and* JAN *exit left.*)

PAULA (*Walking downstage*): Though the Netherlands is a small kingdom, the patience, intelligence, and hard work of its people have made it one of the most prosperous countries in the world. Other nations have added to their size by waging war, but the Dutch have actually created more land by pumping salt water out of marshes and swamps. Slowly and patiently over the years they have saved up layers of soil washed up by the tides. Even the great Zuider Zee, once the largest bay in the country, is being drained to make more farm land.

JIMMY: Mother! Is she going to read all day?

MRS. CARTER: I think Paula has done very well. Now you sit right down here (*Points to chair right*) and start your work.

JIMMY: But, Mother, hadn't I better wait till we've had lunch? I'm weak with hunger. I can't think.

MRS. CARTER (*Handing him paper and pencil from table upstage*): Begin.

JIMMY: Shouldn't I go to my room where it's quiet?

MRS. CARTER: It will be quiet here. Paula, don't talk to your brother.

PAULA: I won't. I'll just set the table for lunch. (*She removes books and papers from table.*)

MRS. CARTER: I'll help Aunt Susan. (*She exits left, followed by* PAULA.)

JIMMY (*Striding back and forth*): What shall I write? That the Netherlands is a great place for bicycles because it's so flat? There's not a mountain in the whole country. (*Looks at paper*) It says here that the highest elevation is about 1,000 feet. How about natural resources? Teachers always like natural resources. (*Consults paper*) Most important natural resources: clay, salt, coal, and oil. Hm. Oh, I'd much rather be hunting for diamonds than writing reports. If we don't find them before we leave, our family will lose its great chance. Well, I'd better finish this. Clay. Salt. Huge beds of salt are located in the east near Hengelo. There's enough salt in this area to supply the entire world for about 100 years. What do you know about that? Everything else may be shaky, but the salt situation is O.K. Very interesting.

(He sits right, chewing on pencil. PAULA *enters with tray. She puts knives and forks on table. She looks at* JIMMY *but he pays no attention.)*

PAULA: *Ahem!* (JIMMY *starts to write.*) Watch me do the Dance of the Tea Tray. *(She dances around and thrusts the tea tray under his nose.* JIMMY *jumps up. She laughs, waves the tray, and bumps against the lamp which falls to the floor.)*

JIMMY: Grab the lamp!

PAULA *(Hands over eyes)*: Did I break it?

JIMMY *(Kneeling)*: I don't know. Nothing seems to be wrong with the lamp, but there's a piece of glass on the floor.

MRS. CARTER *(Enters left, followed by* JULIANA*)*: Oh, dear! Paula, you see what your wildness has done!

JULIANA: But the lamp can't be broken. The base is made of wood. Besides, what if it is? It's terribly old. Nothing lasts forever.

JIMMY *(Still kneeling)*: If the lamp's wooden, then where did these chips of glass come from?

MRS. CARTER: Paula, get a broom to sweep up the glass. Then you'd all better get back to your work and stop breaking things.

PAULA *(Beside him)*: Wait a moment, Mother. Look! There's a little hole here in the lamp. Oh, Jimmy! *(Examining stones)* This isn't glass!

JIMMY: What is it?

PAULA *(Holding up ring)*: They're diamonds!

JULIANA: A ring!

MRS. CARTER: Let me see. *(Takes ring)* Why, Paula, you're right. It is a diamond ring. And look what else is here! (MRS. VAN DYKE *and* JAN *enter.*)

JAN: What's going on? What's the excitement?

PAULA: Earrings! *(Holds them up)*

JULIANA: It's the lamp, Jan. Paula found a diamond ring in it, and now earrings.

MRS. VAN DYKE: Aunt Katrinka's jewels! After all these years.

JULIANA: What about the necklace?

JIMMY (*Standing up*): That's all. One ring, one pair of earrings, and three stones.

PAULA: And the mystery is solved. But what about the windmill?

JULIANA: And where's the necklace?

MRS. VAN DYKE: I think I know the answer to that. (*Points to stones*) Your Aunt Katrinka was gay and extravagant. She probably sold the diamonds in the necklace one by one until only these three were left.

MRS. CARTER (*Kneeling*): Isn't it strange? The lamp must have fallen right on the catch that opened a hidden door in the hollow base.

JAN: It's a good thing we had Paula jumping around, or we'd never have found the diamonds. Won't Father be surprised?

MRS. VAN DYKE (*Looking at her watch*): Your father! He'll be home any minute. I must finish lunch. You boys guard the treasure! (*She exits left, followed by* PAULA, JULIANA *and* MRS. CARTER.)

JIMMY (*Inspecting diamonds*): Pretty good work, finding these jewels so easily. I'd planned to tear that old windmill apart this afternoon. (*Crosses left, puts ring on finger and holds it up*) How do I look with a diamond ring?

JAN: Ravishing.

GRANDMOTHER (*Entering*): Hello, boys. Lunch ready?

JAN: Not yet, Grandmother, but soon. Wait till I tell you the . . .

GRANDMOTHER (*Going toward box*): What's this? What's in the box?

JAN: Old stuff to be thrown out.

GRANDMOTHER: *Stuff!* (*She picks lamp shade from box and goes to lamp.*) This shade was hand painted by a fine artist. Your Aunt Katrinka bought it specially for this old oil lamp. (PAULA *and* JULIANA *enter with trays holding glasses and dishes and go to table at rear.*)

JIMMY: Hand painted? (*Holding shade to light*) I can't see a thing on it.

GRANDMOTHER: Can't you? (*Points*) Here's the picture. A lovely little windmill.

PAULA (*Rushing from table*): Windmill?

GRANDMOTHER: What's so strange about a windmill in Holland?

JIMMY: Nothing really—but it does explain what Aunt Katrinka meant.

PAULA: The secret of the windmill wasn't in the real windmill, but in the windmill lamp. (MR. VAN DYKE *and* MR. CARTER *enter.*)

MR. CARTER: Hi, family! What's new?

PAULA (*Running to him*): Plenty! We found Aunt Katrinka's jewels. They were in the base of the old lamp.

GRANDMOTHER: You found them! But why didn't you tell me? I've wondered about them for years.

JAN: But you didn't give us a chance. Here they are. (*Shows her the jewels*)

JULIANA (*Carrying lamps over to* MR. VAN DYKE): And look, Father, here's the secret hiding place, right in the lamp.

MR. CARTER: Clever work, isn't it?

MR. VAN DYKE (*Turning lamp*): You'd never know it had a hollow space. Let's see the jewels.

GRANDMOTHER: Earrings, ring, three diamonds. (*She hands them to* MR. VAN DYKE *one by one.*)

MR. CARTER: What will you do with your treasure, Granny?

GRANDMOTHER: I'll wear the jewels for a few years, until my granddaughters are ready for them. Then (*Taking earrings and handing them to* JULIANA) these shall be yours, and (*Turning to* PAULA) the ring will be for Paula.

PAULA: How beautiful! (*She tries ring on her finger.*)

GRANDMOTHER: As for the loose diamonds, I'll sell them, and when the boys are ready for college, they'll get a nice present. (MRS. CARTER *and* MRS. VAN DYKE *enter, carrying soup bowls on trays.*)

MRS. VAN DYKE: Come everybody, lunch is served. (*She sets bowls on table.*)

MR. VAN DYKE (*Walking to table*): Now, I want to hear the whole story.

MR. CARTER: Yes, let's hear the tale from the very beginning. It isn't every day that a treasure is found.

PAULA (*Going to table*): Well, it was this way . . .

JULIANA: It was all because of Paula, really. (*The curtain slowly begins to fall as they sit down.*) Paula was so excited about being in Amsterdam, that she—well—walked a little fast, and over went the old lamp and . . . (*Curtain*)

THE END

A Doctor for Lucinda

by Margaret Mantle

Characters

JEREMY, *the doctor*
SQUIRE GERONDE
LUCINDA, *his daughter*
ROBIN, *a youth*
LUKE, *a servant*
JACQUELINE, *Lucinda's maid*

SETTING: *A room in Squire Geronde's home.*
AT RISE: LUCINDA *and* JACQUELINE *enter.*

JACQUELINE (*Indicating chair*): Do you wish to sit here, Lucinda? (LUCINDA *nods.*) Would you like a footstool? (LUCINDA *shakes her head.*) A pillow? (LUCINDA *nods.* JACQUELINE *gets pillow and is adjusting it, when* SQUIRE GERONDE *enters.*)

GERONDE: Ah, I see you have brought my daughter downstairs. We will have the doctor shown in here. I wish to be present when he makes the diagnosis. Of course we may have a long wait.

JACQUELINE: Luke said he would try to return soon.

GERONDE: I hope he finds a doctor who can cure Lucinda. (*Sighs*) Poor child. Will she ever speak again? Such a strange malady.

JACQUELINE: It is that, sir, and it happened so suddenly.

GERONDE: Just the day before her wedding . . . and now Anthony, her betrothed, says the marriage must be postponed until she is cured. We have tried the best doctors, but not one seems to know what is wrong. What are we to do?

JACQUELINE: Perhaps today Luke will find a doctor who can cure her.

GERONDE: No ordinary practitioner will do. Luke will have to find a really clever physician. (*Sound of voices offstage*) Jacqueline, do I hear voices?

JACQUELINE: Yes, sir. Perhaps it is Luke

GERONDE: So soon? Then he has failed.

JACQUELINE: I do hope not. (LUKE *enters.*)

GERONDE: Alone, I see. (*Angrily*) Death and furies, Luke, my orders were to find a doctor or never return.

LUKE: I have found one, sir, the most skilled doctor in the world. He has performed cures which can only be described as miracles. He—why he brings folks to life that were dead as stones. There was a twelve-year-old boy that fell off a steeple . . .

GERONDE: Bother the boy and the steeple. What can he do for Lucinda? And (*Suspiciously*) more to the point, where is he?

LUKE: I left him in your room, sir.

GERONDE: Why didn't you say so? I'll consult him in private. (GERONDE *exits.*)

JACQUELINE: Luke, are you up to one of your tricks?

LUKE: Why, no. What made you say that?

JACQUELINE: Why didn't you show the doctor right in here?

LUKE: Because he is changing into clothes more fitting a doctor.

JACQUELINE: There is something odd in all this. Why isn't a doctor dressed as befits a doctor?

LUKE: He was chopping wood when I found him.

JACQUELINE: Chopping wood? You mean you've brought a woodcutter? What will the Squire say?

LUKE: A woman I met told me he is a doctor, but he likes to pretend he is not one, so as to keep his knowledge to himself.

JACQUELINE: A great mind, with a grain of lunacy, just as a lofty roof may have a loose tile.

LUKE: He's a whimsical fellow, all right. You'd never take him for a real doctor. (GERONDE *re-enters.*)

GERONDE: For a doctor, he is the strangest person. Hurry him along, Luke, and bring him here.

LUKE: Yes, sir. (LUKE *exits.*)

GERONDE: I warrant you he'll turn out no better than the rest.

JACQUELINE: The best treatment for your daughter, sir, would be a good husband. (LUCINDA *nods her head, indicating that though she is speechless, she can hear and understand everything which is said.*)

GERONDE: Zounds, woman, didn't I find one for her?

JACQUELINE: Yes, you found that ancient Anthony Houndsdell, but he's not the one Lucinda wants. Lucinda loves Robin and if you would consent to that marriage . . . (LUKE *enters, followed by* JEREMY)

LUKE: Dr. Jeremy Owles. (JEREMY *skips forward. He is the caricature of a doctor, but a real one, never.*)

GERONDE: Ah, my dear Dr. Owles. Your services are badly needed here. My poor daughter has been afflicted with a most grievous disorder.

JEREMY: I'm delighted to hear it. I wish from the bottom of my heart you and all your family were afflicted with grievous disorders.

GERONDE (*Amazed*): You do?

JEREMY: So that I might have the pleasure of curing you.

GERONDE (*Still not sure how to take these remarks*): I'm obliged, of course, but only my daughter is ill.

JEREMY (*Going to* JACQUELINE, *and putting his arm around her*): You're a fine, healthy girl. What is your name?

JACQUELINE: Jacqueline.

JEREMY: Give me your hand, and let me feel your pulse.

JACQUELINE: Here is my hand, and let it feel your ear. (*She hits him.*)

GERONDE: This is my daughter, sir.

JEREMY: Yes, of course. (*Going to* LUCINDA) So. Hm-m. For an invalid, I find nothing repulsive in her general appearance. (*He studies her.*) Aha. Hm-m-m. Ah. (*Everyone waits impatiently for the doctor's next words.*) I find your daughter marriageable, very much so.

GERONDE: Lucinda is my only daughter, and you can understand that if I were to lose her . . .

JEREMY: Don't be alarmed. She's too much of a lady to think of dying without doctor's orders. Let me feel her pulse. (*He takes her hand, fondles it, then tickles her under the chin.* LUCINDA *laughs.*)

GERONDE (*Pleased*): Why, you've actually set her laughing.

JEREMY: Part of my treatment. (*To* LUCINDA) Well, young lady, where do you feel ill?

LUCINDA (*Touching forehead, lips, throat*): Eh, uh, ah.

JEREMY: Very few languages I don't understand. That's one of them.

GERONDE: That is what is wrong with her. For no reason that we can discover, she has suddenly become dumb. Her future husband will not marry her until she is cured.

JEREMY: He's a fool. I wish my dear wife had the same complaint. (*To* LUCINDA) Now open your mouth. (*He studies her tongue.*) From the condition of the patient's tongue, I diagnose speechlessness. I always put my finger on the complaint at once, and I have the honor to inform you that, in my professional opinion, your daughter is dumb.

GERONDE: I know that. In fact, I told you. What I should like you to tell me is why she is dumb.

JEREMY: That's a perfectly fair question, and I'll give you a fair answer. The reason your daughter is dumb is that she has lost the power of speech.

GERONDE (*Impatiently*): But what caused her to lose it?

JEREMY: Best authorities—I mean authorities like me— hold it is due to an obstruction of the tongue.

GERONDE: What causes the obstruction?

JEREMY: The vapors formed by the exhalations in the region of the malady produce—by the way, do you know Latin?

GERONDE: No, I'm no scholar.

JEREMY: That's fine—I mean what a pity. You're sure you don't know one Latin word?

GERONDE: All I learned, I have forgotten.

JEREMY: All the better—I mean so much the worse. As I was about to say, Cambricus, arci, catalampus, hic, haec, hoc.

GERONDE: I don't understand a word. How I wish I'd heeded my books when I was a boy.

JEREMY (*Sternly*): No interruptions. Moreover, oratio Latinas? Etiam. Quere? You follow me?

GERONDE: Well—er—not entirely.

JEREMY: Then I'll translate. These vapors pass from the left side where the liver is situated to the right side in which lies the heart . . .

GERONDE: Just a moment, doctor. You said the liver was on the left and the heart was on the right. I thought it was the other way 'round.

JEREMY: It used to be, but I changed all that. My latest discovery.

GERONDE: Now that you know what is wrong with Lucinda, what do you advise?

JEREMY: I advise you to put her to bed, and give her a quantity of bread soaked in wine.

GERONDE: Seems a strange remedy. Why do you recommend that?

JEREMY: Because there is a sympathetic virtue in wine that stimulates speech. (*To* JACQUELINE) Go, follow my directions. (LUCINDA *and* JACQUELINE *exit.*) Good. Now I must think out the next part of the treatment. If you will leave me alone to meditate . . .

GERONDE: By all means. Come, Luke. (GERONDE *and* LUKE *exit.*)

JEREMY: Let me think: how do you cure a dumb girl? If the bread and wine won't work, and I don't know why they should, what do I do next? Make a hasty departure —that's what I prescribe. (ROBIN *enters through window.*)

ROBIN: Are you the famous doctor?

JEREMY: None other.

ROBIN: I heard you were here. I've been watching for a chance to see you alone.

JEREMY: Sit down and show me your tongue, though I'm sure it will look no different from other tongues I've seen.

ROBIN: I want your help.

JEREMY: Most people do.

ROBIN: I'm not a patient. I'm not ill. My name is Robin Luckcraft. I'm in love with Miss Lucinda. Her father objects to me so strongly that he has forbidden me to see her. Will you help me?

JEREMY (*Indignantly*): Young man, young man, have you

the audacity to ask a famous family physician to be-
tray his trust?

ROBIN: Believe me, sir, I would not think of insulting
you with such a suggestion, but—(*Holding up purse
full of money*)

JEREMY (*Taking purse*): Think nothing of it. You are
too much of a gentleman to insult me, and I am too
much of a gentleman to refuse. What is it you wish me
to do?

ROBIN: Introduce me here as your apothecary.

JEREMY: Have you had any experience in curing cases of
dumbness?

ROBIN: You mean Lucinda's dumbness? I assure you she
is pretending to be dumb to postpone her marriage to
Anthony Houndsdell.

JEREMY: Pretending, did you say? (*Greatly relieved*) I'm
glad you mentioned that, but of course, I knew it. Now,
if I do say you are my apothecary, won't Lucinda's father recognize you?

ROBIN: I will disguise myself.

JEREMY: Come back as soon as possible, and I will see
what I can do for you.

ROBIN (*Starting out, then returning, as a thought occurs
to him*): Oh, there's one thing. You must do all the
talking. I know nothing about medicine. (ROBIN *exits.*)

JEREMY: Neither do I! But (*Happily*) I see a perfect way
to cure Lucinda now. (JEREMY *starts to count the
money given him by* ROBIN, *but puts it into his pocket
quickly, as* GERONDE *enters.*) Ah, Squire, has the patient
begun to benefit by my treatment?

GERONDE: She is much worse.

JEREMY: Excellent, excellent.

GERONDE: It is?

JEREMY: Indeed, yes. That tells me what to try next. I
have sent for my apothecary. He will carry out the rest

of the treatment under my instructions. (LUCINDA *en-ters*.) Ah, my patient. Come, my dear, I predict a cure in a few minutes. (ROBIN *enters, disguised*) This is my apothecary. (*To* ROBIN) Now, sir, you will take the patient to the side of the room, and proceed according to the usual methods, formula 99, amo, amas, amat. You comprehend? (ROBIN *leads* LUCINDA *down right, while* JEREMY *takes* GERONDE's *arm, and leads him down left. Whenever* GERONDE *tries to return center,* JEREMY *turns him away from* ROBIN *and* LUCINDA.) Now, Squire, the incongruous opacities of the feminine temperament induce a preponderance of . . . you understand?

GERONDE: Completely. (JEREMY *continues speaking in a low voice, ad lib.*)

LUCINDA (*In a voice that carries above* JEREMY's): I promise you, Robin, I promise you that nothing, nothing will make me change my mind.

GERONDE (*Turning toward his daughter*): Did you hear that? My daughter has spoken, spoken at last!

JEREMY: My formula never fails.

GERONDE (*Shaking* JEREMY's *hand*): How can I ever repay you?

JEREMY: The usual way will be quite satisfactory.

GERONDE (*To* LUCINDA): So, my child, you have recovered your speech, thanks to the good doctor here.

LUCINDA: No, Father, thanks to the good apothecary, here. But I have recovered it only to tell you that I shall never marry anyone but Robin, and that it is quite useless for you to insist on Anthony. He's old, he's . . .

GERONDE: Your wedding will take place tomorrow.

LUCINDA: I won't marry a man I dislike. I would sooner die. I won't marry Anthony. (LUCINDA's *voice becomes louder and louder.*) I won't. I won't.

GERONDE: She has recovered her speech. Doctor, I'll trouble you to make her dumb again.

JEREMY: Sorry I can't do that, but my apothecary will apply the treatment I prescribe in these cases.

GERONDE: You mean he can bring the girl to reason?

JEREMY: When you see her next, I assure you she will be a different person. Apothecary! Lead the patient into the garden. As soon as she is composed, exhibit a pinch of amo, amas, amat, then proposium matrimonium, and be off in secretum ad parsonio. You comprehend?

ROBIN: Perfectly. (*To* LUCINDA) Permit me. (*He escorts her out.*)

JEREMY: Well, Squire, as there's nothing more I can do for you, I will take my—er (*Holding his hand out for money*)—leave.

GERONDE (*Giving him a purse*): Here is your fee.

JEREMY (*Putting purse into his pocket*): Oh, I couldn't think of taking it. I labor, not for money, but for love. (LUKE *enters, running*)

LUKE: Master, Squire, sir, sir! Here's nice doings. Miss Lucinda . . .

GERONDE: Calm yourself, Luke. Miss Lucinda is in the garden being treated by the apothecary.

LUKE: That's who I mean, sir, the apothecary. He's kissing Miss Lucinda. (JEREMY *hurries to the door.*)

GERONDE (*Running after* JEREMY, *and holding him by the collar*): Doctor, what kind of a cure is this?

JEREMY: Kissing exercises the lips, and since the lips are essential to good articulation . . .

GERONDE (*Shaking* JEREMY): You scoundrel, you villain!

LUKE: Squire, I saw him take off that cap and cloak, and do you know who the apothecary is?

GERONDE (*Still holding* JEREMY): Quickly, Luke, there is no time to lose. Go to the garden. Bring my daughter back. Use force, if necessary.

LUKE: Yes, sir. (*Exit* LUKE)

GERONDE (*Shaking* JEREMY): You renegade. You scoundrel.

JEREMY: Squire, desist. You will unravel my vertebrae. (LUCINDA, ROBIN, *and* LUKE *enter.* ROBIN *is again disguised.*)

GERONDE: You—you apothecary, how dare you kiss my daughter? Lucinda, what does this mean?

LUCINDA: It means I will never marry Anthony. (*Takes* ROBIN's *hand*) I'm going to marry him.

GERONDE: First Robin, now an apothecary. I will not have my daughter marry a penniless apothecary.

ROBIN: I'm not penniless.

LUKE: He's not an apothecary. Make him take off that cap. (LUKE *removes it.*) See, it's Robin that's the apothecary.

LUCINDA: Yes, Father, it's Robin, and I love him.

GERONDE: What has love to do with it? Anthony is rich; Robin is poor.

LUCINDA: Robin will be rich.

JEREMY: The learned Hippocrates says you must agree to this marriage.

GERONDE: Hippocrates said that 2300 years ago! I'll never consent!

JEREMY (*To* LUCINDA *and* ROBIN): Well, then, you'd better elope.

ROBIN: We don't want to elope. We want the Squire's consent. I haven't even told Lucinda this, but my uncle has just made me his only heir.

GERONDE: Your uncle has made you his heir? Why didn't you tell me?

ROBIN: Every time I tried, you had me thrown out.

GERONDE: There must have been some misunderstanding, my boy.

JEREMY: Then, Squire, you will consent to this marriage?

GERONDE: Of course.

JEREMY (*Standing between* LUCINDA *and* ROBIN):
A mere medic would be content to restore his patient's
   voice,
But I give Lucinda, Robin, the husband of her choice.
(*Curtain*)

THE END

Thirteen

by Anne Coulter Martens

Characters

SUSAN
ROBERTA
CAROL
PATTY
JOAN
EMMY · *the Twelve Teens Club*
DIANE
MARGIE
LYNN
FRANNY
GINNY
BONNIE
GRACE, *a visitor*

TIME: *A Friday evening.*

SETTING: *Susan's living room.*

AT RISE: SUSAN *is sitting at the desk taking notes from several open books. Pages of her notes are scattered on the desk. She crumples a piece of paper and tosses it toward the wastebasket which is already overflowing with papers. There is a rap on the door at left, and* CAROL *comes in.*

355

CAROL (*At the door*): Hi! Am I the first one here? (*Enters room*)

SUSAN: That's right.

CAROL (*Eagerly*): Have you heard from Bonnie? She's coming, isn't she? Do you think she suspects a surprise party? And tell me, did Roberta bring the birthday cake? (SUSAN *laughs and cover her ears.*) Well, say something!

SUSAN: Give me a chance, will you? Roberta should be here with the cake any minute.

CAROL: Oh, good!

SUSAN: And, yes, Bonnie's coming—I hope.

CAROL: What do you mean—you *hope?* Aren't you positive?

SUSAN: She promised to come. I tried to get her on the phone just now, but the line was busy.

CAROL: Oh, wouldn't it be awful if she changed her mind?

SUSAN: Relax, Carol, relax. Bonnie thinks this is just an ordinary meeting of the Twelve Teens Club. We can't make too much of a fuss, or she'll suspect something.

CAROL: I guess you're right. (*Opens her handbag*) I brought the money we collected for her gift. (*Takes out an envelope*) Dad took our change and gave me a crisp five-dollar bill. (*Puts envelope on edge of desk*)

SUSAN: That's fine. I saw some darling shoulder bags downtown. Bonnie can pick out just the kind she wants. (*Moves some papers on the desk, crumples one and throws it toward the basket*)

CAROL: What are you so busy about—homework?

SUSAN: A special report for English. All about superstitions.

CAROL: Never walk under a ladder. (*Scoffing*) It might fall on you!

SUSAN (*Indicating a large book*): Make a wish when you

see a load of hay pulled by a white horse. (*Laughs*) How
often do I see a load of hay?

CAROL: Nobody believes those things any more.

SUSAN: You'd be surprised what some people still believe.

CAROL: I'll be surprised if we can pull off this party without Bonnie's finding out.

SUSAN: It's not easy for eleven girls to keep a secret.
(*Glances at some notes, crumples them and tosses paper
toward basket*)

CAROL: You ought to empty that basket before it overflows.

SUSAN: Pretty soon. (*Gathers her scattered papers together
and puts them inside the large book, not looking at
them. Then she gets up, stretching*) I think I've worked
long enough. (*There is a knock on the door at left.*)

CAROL (*Excitedly*): I hope it's not Bonnie—before the
cake is here!

SUSAN: If it is, act natural. (CAROL *sits down quickly, picking up a magazine.* SUSAN *opens the door.*) Hello! (*To*
CAROL) Stop worrying. The cake has arrived! (ROBERTA
comes in, carrying a pretty cake plate with a cover.)

CAROL (*Getting up*): Oh, Roberta, let me see it!

SUSAN: I can't wait to have a peek.

ROBERTA: Don't swarm all over me or I'll drop it! (*Walks
to center and sets cake on coffee table. As* SUSAN *and*
CAROL *watch,* ROBERTA *lifts the cover*) There!

CAROL: Beautiful!

SUSAN: Yum-my! (CAROL *puts out a tentative finger toward
the icing.*)

ROBERTA: Oh, no, you don't! (*Slaps* CAROL's *finger and
puts cover back on cake*) You sample that icing when
all twelve of us are here, and not before.

CAROL: I can dream, can't I?

ROBERTA: Your dream had better not have sticky fingers.
(*There is the sound of a car horn from offstage.*) I have
to dash. Mother's out front waiting for me in the car.

SUSAN: You're leaving?

ROBERTA: Because I promised to do a little errand with Mother. If I'm a few minutes late, try to stall things till I get here, will you?

SUSAN: Sure, we'll do that.

ROBERTA (*At door*): Oh, I almost forgot. My cousin Grace is here for the weekend. Do you mind if I bring her along?

SUSAN: Of course not.

CAROL: We all like Grace. The more the merrier.

ROBERTA: O.K., then. (*There is a knock on the door and she opens it.*) Hi, Patty. (PATTY *comes in.*) Be seeing you. (*Goes out*)

PATTY: Where's Roberta going?

SUSAN: She'll be back.

CAROL: Look, Patty—the cake! (*Displays it*)

PATTY (*Impressed*): Out of this world! (*Sits in chair at right.*) Oh, won't it be simply terrible if Bonnie doesn't come?

SUSAN: What makes you say that? Of course she's coming.

PATTY: I was talking to her on the phone just now.

SUSAN: No wonder her line was busy.

CAROL: Yakety-yakety-yak!

SUSAN: What did she say?

PATTY: That the woman next door wants her to baby-sit.

CAROL: Oh, no—she can't do that tonight.

SUSAN: I'll go over to her house and talk her out of it. Come on, let's all go. (*There is a knock on the door.*) Come in! (BONNIE *comes into the room.*)

ALL (*In pleased surprise*): Bonnie! (*They start toward her.*)

PATTY (*Remembering the cake*): Oh-oh. (*Dashes back and stands in front of it.*)

BONNIE: Why is everybody looking at me?

CAROL: What do you mean?

SUSAN: We're just glad to see you, that's all.

PATTY: And glad that you're not going to baby-sit.

BONNIE: Oh, but I am. (*Comes center and* PATTY *moves, hiding the cake from* BONNIE) I just stopped in to ask if Mother may borrow your pinking shears. She's making a dress.

SUSAN: Of course. (*Goes right and* BONNIE *follows her.* PATTY *shifts again to hide the cake.*) Bonnie, please don't baby-sit tonight. We want you at our meeting.

BONNIE: Honestly, I hate to miss it, but I need the money. I'm saving for a new shoulder bag. (*The girls exchange glances.*)

SUSAN (*At the door up right*): Carol and Patty, you talk to her. (*Goes out*)

CAROL: Everybody will be so disappointed if you don't come.

PATTY: Please, Bonnie.

BONNIE: Anything special going on?

CAROL *and* PATTY: Oh, no!

BONNIE: Then I'd better baby-sit. Anyway, this woman is counting on me now.

CAROL: Can't you get some other girl?

PATTY: Your sister. Ask your sister if she'll do it.

CAROL: Oh, do you think she would? Ask her, Bonnie. Please ask her.

BONNIE (*Weakening*): Well, all right. (SUSAN *comes in with a pair of pinking shears.*)

CAROL (*Happily, to* SUSAN): She'll come!

BONNIE: If my sister will take over the baby-sitting job.

SUSAN: Oh, I'm so glad. (*Holds out the shears*) Here you are. Take them home and then come right back.

BONNIE: Just a minute. (*Takes a penny from her purse*) A penny for you.

SUSAN (*Surprised*): A penny? (*Takes it*)

BONNIE: Because you're giving me something with a sharp

edge. (*Gets up, putting her purse on chair as she takes shears*) Keeps away bad luck. (*Knocks on wood*)

SUSAN: Listen to her, knocking on wood! I didn't know you were superstitious.

BONNIE: Maybe I'm just careful. (*Laughs*) Thanks for the shears. (*As she starts left,* PATTY *shifts to hide the cake and* BONNIE *pauses beside her.*) You've been standing there ever since I came in, giving me the oddest looks.

PATTY (*Uneasily*): Not really!

BONNIE: Is there something going on that I don't know about?

PATTY *and* CAROL: Oh, no!

SUSAN (*Quickly*): Of course not, Bonnie. (*Anxiously*) You *will* ask your sister to do the baby-sitting, and you'll surely come back?

BONNIE: I guess so. (*Goes to door left*)

SUSAN (*Following her*): Promise you will. Promise.

BONNIE: O.K., I will. (*Goes out, forgetting her purse on chair*)

CAROL: Gol-ly! Am I glad we straightened that out!

SUSAN: She really had me worried.

PATTY: And I thought sure she'd see the cake. (*Picks up cake*) I'd better get it out of here fast. (*There is a quick knock on the door, and* BONNIE'S *voice is heard.*)

BONNIE (*Offstage*): Me, again! (CAROL *and* SUSAN *step quickly in front of* PATTY *as* BONNIE *hurries in.*) I forgot my purse.

CAROL: There it is. (*Indicates chair. As* BONNIE *crosses to right,* CAROL *and* SUSAN *turn, but stay in front of* PATTY. BONNIE *pauses beside the chair, then begins to turn around slowly.*)

BONNIE (*As she turns*): One. (*Turns again*) Two. (*Again*) Three.

SUSAN: What in the world—?

BONNIE: If you forget something and have to go back for it, you turn around three times and then sit down. (*Sits in chair*) Bad luck if you don't. (*Knocks on wood*)

CAROL: Oh, Bonnie—really!

BONNIE: I *always* do it. (*Gets up with purse and goes to door left.*) See you later. (*Goes out*)

SUSAN: How can she possibly believe such nonsense?

PATTY: Just habit, I guess. (*To the cake*) Come on, cake, let's go! (*Goes out right.*)

SUSAN: I'll burn these papers in the incinerator. (*Picks up wastebasket, pauses near door at right.*) Carol, I'm still worried. Suppose Bonnie changes her mind about coming back?

CAROL (*Worried*): Or suppose her sister won't take the baby-sitting job?

SUSAN: Why do things always go wrong at the last minute? (*There is a knock on the door at left.*) You go. (*Goes out right.* CAROL *goes to the door, opening it.* EMMY *and* DIANE *come in.*)

EMMY: Hi.

DIANE: How's everything?

CAROL: Under control—we hope. Sit down, girls.

EMMY (*Sitting on the couch*): When do you expect Bonnie?

CAROL: Pretty soon.

DIANE (*Sitting on the couch*): I do hope she doesn't suspect anything.

CAROL: I'm pretty sure she doesn't.

EMMY: After all, her birthday's not till tomorrow.

CAROL: That part doesn't worry me. (*Sighs*)

DIANE: But something else does?

CAROL: Well, a little. (*Brightly*) But I guess it will work out all right. (*There is a knock on the door.*) Come in! (MARGIE, LYNN *and* FRANNY *come in, happy and excited.*)

MARGIE: Here we are! (SUSAN *comes in right with the empty basket.* PATTY *follows her.*)

SUSAN: Find yourself a chair or a cushion.

LYNN: I'm glad we got here before Bonnie.

FRANNY: This is going to be fun. (*They take cushions from couch and sit on floor.* SUSAN *puts basket beside the desk.*)

MARGIE: Is everybody coming?

CAROL: They all said so.

EMMY: How many more to come now?

SUSAN: Let's count how many are here. (*Counts*) Eight of us. Joan and Ginny still to come. That makes ten.

DIANE: Bonnie—eleven.

LYNN: And Roberta—twelve. All accounted for.

CAROL: Roberta's bringing her cousin Grace.

FRANNY: Oh, good! I'm glad Grace is coming. (*There is a knock on the door, and* JOAN *and* GINNY *come in, looking around.*)

JOAN: Bonnie isn't here yet?

SUSAN: Any minute now.

JOAN: We practically ran all the way. (*They sit down.*)

SUSAN: I hope you girls have kept the secret.

GIRLS (*Ad lib*): I have! Of course we have! Sure thing! (*Etc.*)

SUSAN: Remember, we won't say a word about her birthday till Roberta and Grace get here. Then Patty can bring in the cake, and we'll all yell, "Surprise!"

CAROL: When you give the signal. (*There is a knock on the door.*)

SUSAN (*Warningly*): Sh! (*Calls*) Come in! (BONNIE *comes in. This time she has a sweater over her arm and carries an umbrella.*)

BONNIE (*To* SUSAN): My sister put up a stiff fight—but I won! (*To the others*) Hi! (*They greet her.*) Susan, I brought back the sweater I borrowed last week.

SUSAN: Thanks, Bonnie. No hurry.

PATTY: Hey, why the umbrella? Not a cloud in the sky.

BONNIE (*Laughing*): That's why I carried it.

CAROL: Say that again?

BONNIE: I set my hair, and you know how if you don't carry an umbrella, it always rains—and if you do carry one, it never does. (*Knocks on desk, then leans umbrella there and looks around*) Where do I sit?

SUSAN: Anywhere you can find room.

BONNIE: I'll take your sweater upstairs first. (*Goes right, then turns*) Is everybody here?

SUSAN: All but Roberta. (*Follows* BONNIE) I'll go up with you.

CAROL: And her cousin Grace.

BONNIE: Grace is coming? Good. (*About to go out, she turns, suddenly upset*) Oh, no!

SUSAN: What's the matter?

BONNIE: You're sure Grace is coming?

SUSAN: Positive.

PATTY: I thought you liked her.

BONNIE: Oh, I do.

CAROL: Then why all the fuss?

BONNIE: There'll be thirteen of us!

SUSAN: That's right.

BONNIE: Thirteen! And on a Friday, too.

CAROL: So?

BONNIE: I'm sorry, but I won't stay.

SUSAN (*Surprised*): Oh, Bonnie, don't be silly. As if thirteen means anything. (BONNIE *knocks on wood.*)

PATTY: There she goes, knocking on wood.

CAROL (*Impatiently*): Don't start that again.

BONNIE (*Upset*): I shouldn't even have come. As I was crossing the street, a black cat ran across my path.

CAROL: I like black cats.

BONNIE: *I* don't. (*Shivers*) My grandmother knew a

woman who fell and broke her arm after seeing a black cat.

CAROL: Because she tripped over the poor animal?

BONNIE: No! (*Annoyed*) You don't believe me.

CAROL: I certainly don't think the black cat had anything to do with it. Or that thirteen is an unlucky number.

BONNIE: Oh, it is!

PATTY (*Cheerfully*): I'm not worried.

BONNIE: *I* am.

SUSAN: Not really?

BONNIE (*After a pause*): I'll take your sweater up, and then I'll go home and baby-sit after all.

PATTY: Oh, Bonnie—no!

JOAN: Honestly, nothing will happen.

DIANE: Nothing bad, anyway.

EMMY: Maybe even something good.

BONNIE: My grandmother knew a woman who had a dinner party for thirteen. They all seemed well and happy, but that night—

SUSAN: Stop it! Bonnie, you're staying here, and we don't want to hear any more nonsense.

BONNIE: Sorry, but I'm *not* staying. (*Goes out right.*)

SUSAN (*Quickly, to the girls*): What are we going to do?

CAROL: Talk some sense into her.

SUSAN: I tried. (*Upset*) *You* think of something—and quick! (*Goes out right. All the girls are worried now.*)

JOAN: If she leaves—there goes our party!

LYNN: We have to stop her from going.

FRANNY: But how?

GINNY: Even if we tell her about the surprise, she might not stay.

MARGIE (*Slowly*): I suppose we could call Roberta and ask her not to bring Grace.

EMMY: And hurt Grace's feelings, when we all like her?

DIANE: Hurt Roberta, too.

LYNN: It wouldn't be *fair*.

MARGIE: You're right. We can't call Roberta.

CAROL: It would be giving in to superstition.

PATTY: We all know thirteen isn't unlucky, but how can we convince Bonnie?

EMMY: Instead of bad luck, *good* things are going to happen if she stays.

CAROL (*Thoughtfully*): Maybe we *can* prove that to her.

DIANE (*Eagerly*): How?

CAROL: Are any of you girls the least bit superstitious?

GIRLS (*Ad lib*): No! Not me! Of course not! (*Etc.*)

CAROL: Then we can do it! We'll deliberately invite bad luck.

PATTY: How?

CAROL: Quick. Tell me some easy superstitions.

PATTY: Breaking a mirror.

CAROL: You have one in your purse. When Bonnie comes in, drop it. And if it doesn't break—step on it!

PATTY: On purpose?

JOAN: Bonnie will have a fit.

CAROL: Let her, for a few minutes.

JOAN: I've heard it's bad luck to put a pair of new shoes on a table.

CAROL: Susan has new flats. You get them and put them on this table! (JOAN *goes out right.*)

PATTY: What else?

CAROL (*Noticing* BONNIE's *umbrella*): This umbrella!

PATTY: Poor Bonnie! I know just what you're going to do.

MARGIE: Now I catch on. Bonnie will see that in spite of everything, she has *good* luck.

CAROL: And that should cure her of all these silly superstitions.

PATTY: Carol, you're a genius.

CAROL (*Laughing*): Maybe I am, at that. (SUSAN *enters, right.*)

SUSAN (*Anxiously*): Do you have any ideas?

CAROL: Plenty! (BONNIE *enters, right.*)

BONNIE: Well, I'm on my way. Sorry I'll miss the meeting.

CAROL: You don't have to leave this minute. Only eleven of us are here.

BONNIE: Please don't be angry with me. I know you think I'm foolish—but—well,—I won't stay with thirteen. (JOAN *comes in right, carrying a pair of new shoes in her hand.*)

JOAN (*To* SUSAN): The girls wanted to see your new shoes. (*Walks center, pausing beside the coffee table*) Aren't they snappy? (*Reaches out as if to set the shoes on the table*)

BONNIE (*Quickly*): Don't do that! (*Walks center.*)

JOAN (*Innocently*): Do what?

BONNIE: Never put new shoes on a table. It's bad luck. (*But as she speaks,* JOAN *sets the shoes on the table.*) Oh, you've done it! (*Knocks on wood*)

JOAN: So I have.

BONNIE: Something will happen. Just you wait.

JOAN: Oh, I guess not.

EMMY: Aren't there any *good* luck signs?

BONNIE: Oh, sure. The horseshoe—

CAROL: If it doesn't clonk you on the head.

BONNIE: And the four-leaf clover. A rabbit's foot brings good luck, too.

CAROL: But not for the poor rabbit. (*Signals to* PATTY, *who gets her purse and moves down left, opening it.*) Looking for something, Patty?

PATTY: My mirror. (*Drops it, giving a little cry*) Oh, I dropped it! (*Takes a step back, presumably stepping on the mirror*) And now I've stepped on it!

BONNIE (*Sharply*): Is it broken?

PATTY: Right in half! (*Picks up the pieces, putting them on the desk*) Too bad.

BONNIE (*Upset*): Oh, dear! (*Knocks on wood*)

CAROL: You really think Patty's going to have seven years of bad luck because she broke a mirror?

BONNIE: I hope not. (*Unhappily*) But that's what they say.

PATTY: Do I look worried?

BONNIE: Let's not talk about it. I'm leaving.

CAROL (*Picking up the umbrella*): Don't forget your umbrella. A very pretty one. (*Raises it as if to open it*)

BONNIE: Never open an umbrella in the house!

CAROL: I want to see how it looks. (*Opens umbrella*)

BONNIE: Then don't hold it over your head!

CAROL: Bad luck? (*Holds umbrella over her head and saunters about*) When does the sky begin to fall on me?

BONNIE: Oh, stop it! (*Suddenly*) I think you're all doing these things on purpose!

CAROL: Do you? (*Closes umbrella*)

BONNIE: Now I know you are.

CAROL: I wondered how soon you'd catch on.

PATTY: We want to prove that they don't really bring bad luck.

JOAN: Something *good* is going to happen.

BONNIE: Sorry, but I've stayed long enough.

DIANE: Don't go yet.

BONNIE (*Going to door left*): I really must.

CAROL: Stay just a few minutes longer.

PATTY: Oh, why doesn't Roberta come?

BONNIE: 'Bye, now.

LYNN: We can't let her go!

CAROL: Wait! (BONNIE *pauses.* CAROL *turns to the other girls.*) Shall we tell her *why* we want her to stay?

GIRLS (*Ad lib*): Yes! Tell her! Hurry up! (*Etc.*)

CAROL: First, the envelope. Where did I put it?

SUSAN: On the desk. (*Looks on desk*) I don't see it.

CAROL (*Looking*): And neither do I. (*Grabs her handbag and looks in it*) It's not in my bag. Where *is* it?

MARGIE: Look on the floor. Maybe it fell down. (SUSAN and CAROL *look on the floor, getting more and more excited.*)

SUSAN: I can't find it!

CAROL: But it simply must be here!

BONNIE: Why is the envelope so important?

CAROL (*Alarmed*): If it fell—oh, Susan—maybe it fell into the wastebasket!

SUSAN: Oh, my glory! I burned the papers without looking at them!

CAROL (*Near tears*): All our money—burned! (*There are murmurs of concern from the girls.*)

BONNIE: What is it? Tell me!

CAROL: I—can't. Oh, this is awful!

BONNIE (*Slowly*): Don't you see—this happened after Patty broke that mirror.

EMMY: That's right, it did.

DIANE: I wonder—?

CAROL: No! There simply couldn't be any connection.

PATTY (*Unhappily*): I'm beginning to be sorry I did it.

CAROL: Patty, don't you go back on me! You know very well that Susan burned the papers quite a while ago. (*The telephone rings, and* SUSAN *picks it up.*)

SUSAN (*On the phone*): Hello . . . (*To* JOAN) For you.

JOAN: Me? (*On the phone*) Hello . . . What is it, Johnny? (*To the others*) My little brother. (*On the phone*) You want me right away? . . . (*Excitedly*) What happened? Tell me! (*Hangs up, very worried.*)

CAROL: What's the matter?

JOAN: He says something's happened, and I have to go home right away. (*Hurries to left.*) Oh, dear! He wouldn't say *what* it is! (*Hurries out*)

BONNIE: Maybe it's an accident.

CAROL: Don't say that!

BONNIE: I warned Joan not to put those shoes on the table.

LYNN (*Shivering*): This gives me a very funny feeling.

FRANNY: I'm getting scared, too.

GINNY: Oh, Carol, I wish you hadn't opened that umbrella in the house!

CAROL: I just won't believe in such stuff!

SUSAN: We'll have to call Roberta and tell her the bad news. Carol?

CAROL (*Unhappily*): You do it.

SUSAN (*Dials a number*): Hello . . . Mr. Patton, may I speak to Roberta, please? This is Susan. . . . (*Startled*) Oh! . . . Oh! When did she go? (*She drops the receiver on the desk, turning to the others.*) Mr. Patton says her mother just took Roberta to the hospital!

PATTY: Oh, good heavens!

GINNY (*Excitedly*): Why?

LYNN: For an operation?

EMMY: Is it very serious?

DIANE: Poor Roberta!

CAROL: What's the matter with her? Ask him.

SUSAN (*On the phone*): Hello . . . Mr. Patton . . . Hello! (*To the others*) He hung up.

MARGIE: That does it. I'm going home, too. (*Rises*)

FRANNY: I guess I won't stay either. (*Rises*)

BONNIE (*To* CAROL): Oh, why did you put that umbrella over your head?

GINNY: All our plans are ruined.

LYNN: The money gone—

EMMY: Roberta in the hospital—

DIANE: And goodness knows what's happened at Joan's house! (*They all get up and look at* CAROL.)

CAROL: Why are you all looking at me like that? Do you think it's *my* fault?

SUSAN: I hardly know *what* to think. (*Picks up her large book, looking at it in a puzzled way.*)

PATTY (*Reproachfully*): Breaking those superstitions was your idea.

CAROL: Have you *all* deserted me? (*They look at her in silence.*) But I only wanted to prove—

MARGIE: You proved it, all right. The wrong way.

CAROL: No! (*Upset*) Oh, I don't know. I'm all mixed up.

BONNIE: And I'm going home. (*There is a knock on the door at left.*)

SUSAN: What now? (*Calls*) Come in! (*The knock is repeated. SUSAN opens the door and steps back in surprise, throwing up her hands and dropping her book. Papers scatter on the floor.*)

GIRLS (*Ad lib*): Roberta! She's here! Look! (*Etc.*) (ROBERTA *and her cousin* GRACE *enter.*)

PATTY: We thought you went to the hospital!

ROBERTA: I did. Why all the excitement? I told you I had an errand to do with Mother. She left some things there for a bake sale. (*Sighs and murmurs of relief come from the others.*)

SUSAN: I could hardly believe my eyes when I opened the door. (*Starts to pick up papers, then cries out happily*) Oh, my glory! (*Drops everything else and picks up the missing envelope, holding it high.*)

CAROL: Our money!

SUSAN: In the book with my papers!

PATTY: Yea! (*Goes out right.* JOAN *hurries in left*)

JOAN: Girls, what do you think? Our Persian cat just had three kittens!

DIANE: Is *that* why your little brother called?

JOAN: Can you imagine? We're tickled pink. (PATTY *comes in with the birthday cake.* SUSAN *gives the signal.*)

ALL: Surprise! Happy birthday, Bonnie!

BONNIE (*Excitedly*): For *me*? Oh! Oh, how nice of you!

(*As* PATTY *puts the cake on the coffee table*) It's simply beautiful!

SUSAN (*Handing her the envelope*): And here's some money to buy yourself a shoulder bag.

BONNIE (*Overwhelmed*): I—I don't know what to say. No wonder you tried so hard to make me stay. Thank you all so much.

CAROL: Now what about your silly superstitions? They don't mean a single thing!

BONNIE: I'm sorry I was so foolish.

CAROL: And you'll never be superstitious again?

BONNIE: Oh, never, never! Who cares about thirteen? Nothing can spoil our party now. (*Without thinking, she knocks on wood.*) Oh-oh. I did it again!

CAROL (*Laughing*): I give up. You're a hopeless case! (*They all laugh, then sing "Happy Birthday," as the curtain falls.*)

THE END

Visit to the Planets

by Hathaway Kale Melchior

Characters

MARK	MARS
LEIF	JUPITER
JANET	SATURN
NADINE	NEPTUNE
KIT	URANUS
DIANE	PLUTO
SUN	METEOR
MERCURY	HEAD OF THE COMET
VENUS	TAIL OF THE COMET
EARTH	

SCENE 1

TIME: *The present.*

SETTING: *The corner of the school playground. At right center is a rocket ship, in launching position.*

AT RISE: MARK *and* LEIF, *in space suits, are putting final touches on the rocket ship.* LEIF *uses a monkey wrench, and* MARK *is hammering.*

MARK (*Standing back to observe the rocket*): There, that's that. Leif, it's finished!

LEIF: I can't wait to blast off.

JANET (*Running on*): Say, what's *that* you're making?

LEIF (*The boys exchange disgusted looks*): Ugh! Girls! It's a spaceship, can't you see?

JANET (*Calling*): Hey, kids, come look at what Leif and Mark are making. (KIT, DIANE *and* NADINE *enter.*)

NADINE: What is it?

KIT: What are you going to do with that thing?

LEIF (*Rather sarcastically*): My dear, it isn't a *thing*, it's a spaceship.

MARK: And we're going to take a trip to visit the planets, that's all.

KIT: That's *all?* You're crazy!

JANET: Why do you want to visit the other planets? Earth is the only one you can live on.

KIT: Sure, Earth is the best.

MARK: How do you know? Have you seen all the others?

NADINE: If you two are so smart, how are you going to blast off?

MARK (*Mysteriously*): Oh, we have a way. I'll show you. (*He gets a small gadget from the ship. The girls follow, inquisitively*) See this little gadget.

DIANE: What is it? (MARK *and* LEIF *exchange glances.*)

MARK: Come closer and see. (*Girls reluctantly draw closer. The boys tease the girls by holding out the gadget, and springing at the girls with a "Ps-s-st." Girls jump back.*)

NADINE: Now stop kidding. What is it really?

LEIF: This gadget is *imagination.* If you have some imagination, you can do anything—even visit the planets if you want to. (MARK *returns gadget to ship and gets into ship.*)

NADINE: Do you suppose they're right?

LEIF: It's time for the final check-up (*To* MARK, *who is in ship*) Check the gyros.

MARK: Check!

LEIF: Radar.

MARK: Check!

LEIF: Oxygen.

MARK: Check!

LEIF: Cooling pumps.

MARK: Check!

LEIF: Check the jet propeller! (MARK *takes a "Make-It-Snow" gadget and sprays it from back of ship*) That checks! Now, we'd better take a look at our helmets. (MARK *gets out of ship, bringing bowl-shaped helmets.*)

KIT: Look at those fish bowls.

DIANE: Are you going to take goldfish with you on the trip? (*Girls laugh.*)

LEIF: Oh, brother! (*Looks at watch*) Ten seconds to blast-off time. Let's go. (*Boys hurry into ship.*)

MARK (*Calling*): Stand back for blast off.

NADINE: They really think they can do it.

KIT: Aren't they silly?

LEIF (*Calling from inside ship*): 5—4—3—2—1—0. *Blast off!* (*Lights flash, a fire extinguisher behind the spaceship is set off, and the ship starts vibrating and slowly ascends.*)

GIRLS (*Ad lib*): They did it! They're off! Imagine that. Good luck. (*Etc.*)

CURTAIN

* * *

SCENE 2

SETTING: *In space. Dim light reveals glowing constellations.*

AT RISE: *Music of "The Planets," by Holst, is heard in the background. After a short pause,* SUN *enters, lighted by a bright spotlight.*

SUN: I am the Sun. For thousands of years people on Earth have looked up at me and wondered what I am. Because they did not know, they made up stories to explain me . . . But I am not the Egyptian sun God, Ra; nor am I the golden wheels of Apollo's chariot; nor am I carried in a canoe across the sky each day as the American Indian thought. No. . . .

I am a mass of atomic explosions. I lose four million tons of myself every second. As my atoms fuse, I give off terrific energy. This is the heat and light you know on Earth.

You may think of me as a Mother with a family of nine children, nine planets which constantly travel around me in circles as though they were tied to my apron strings. . . . You are on *one* of my planets. (*Looking at dial*) Oh, now my sundial tells me it's time for roll call. I will call my children in order and have them stop rotating in their orbits just long enough for you to meet them. I'll call my smallest child first, the one who keeps closest to me. (*She calls*) Mercury, oh, Mercury!

MERCURY (*Offstage*): Coming, Mother. (*He makes two small revolutions around the* SUN, *then stops, hot and panting.*) Oh, dear, Mother, I get very hot and tired running around you so fast.

SUN: Yes, dear, but I've explained to you why you must travel so quickly.

MERCURY: I know, if I didn't twirl around you once every eighty-eight days, your magnetic force would pull me out of my orbit. I'd collide with you and *Puff!*, that would be the end of poor little me.

SUN: Now stop feeling sorry for yourself, and tell the people how you got your name. That always cheers you.

MERCURY: May I? (*He comes down and talks to the audience*) I was named after a Roman God, Mercury. He could run more swiftly than anyone. He had wings on his heels and wings on his head, so they made him the messenger of the gods. And because I travel the fastest of all the planets, they named me after him. I can tell you some stories about this god, Mercury. One day . . .

SUN (*Interrupting*): All right, dear, no time for stories now. I must get on with the roll call. (*Calling*) Venus! Oh, where is that girl? . . . Venus, get into your orbit this minute.

VENUS (*Entering with mirror, and fussing with her veils*): Here I am, Mother. I was arranging my beautiful, cloudy veils.

MERCURY: Always trying to make herself beautiful!

VENUS: I heard what you said, Mercury, but I don't have to try to make myself beautiful . . . I *am* beautiful. The Earth people think I'm one of the most beautiful sights in the sky. One of their poets wrote a poem about me that begins, "Oh, brightly shining morning star."

MERCURY: Ugh!

VENUS: They didn't name me after the goddess of beauty for nothing.

SUN: Yes, dear, you are beautiful, and your veils make you very mysterious looking, but try not to be so vain about it. Now let me get on. (*Calling*) Earth, Earth.

EARTH (*Entering excitedly*): The most exciting thing has happened. You should just hear the news I have.

MERCURY: Stop, and tell us about it.

EARTH: Two of my little boys are at this very moment wandering around in space. They're going to visit all of you. Isn't it exciting. . . . But I do hope after seeing you, they'll like me best. Just imagine, two of my little Earth boys.

MERCURY (*Rather bored*): From which continent?

EARTH: From North America.

VENUS: Sister, you're always talking about *your* people.

EARTH: My Earth people are very nice people—at least

most of them are. Oh, you should see some of the things they've learned to do. The children can read and write and do arithmetic. They build skyscrapers a hundred stories high, and even little boys know about rocket ships—

SUN (*Interrupting*): Yes, I'm sure your people are very special.

EARTH: Yes, they are special, and I'm special too, in a way. All of my brothers and sisters have Latin names. Of course, I have a Latin name too, Terra, but not many people call me that. But Earth, my special name, comes from an old Nordic goddess called Erde, so you see that makes me different.

SUN: Each one in my family is different, Earth; that's what makes it such an interesting family. (*Calling*) Mars, Mars!

MARS (*Entering with broad strides. In gruff voice*): Yes, Mother, what do you want?

SUN: Mars, just because you were named after the god of war, you don't have to be so pugnacious—always ready for a fight.

MARS: Then why did they name me "Mars"? Just because I'm the red planet? I can't help it if a lot of my surface has oxidized and looks like rust. I try to be a good boy, I keep in my orbit, but since my name is "Mars", everybody's always expecting trouble from me. (*He brandishes his sword*)

SUN: Mars, relax before you melt your polar cap. Since you're in this mood, I think I'd better call in Jupiter. (*Calling*) Jupiter, Jupiter!

JUPITER (*Calling from offstage*): Yes, Mother Sun, did you call me?

SUN: That's Jupiter. He's the biggest in the family and sometimes likes to show off. (*Calling*) You may come in now, Jupiter. (JUPITER *struts in.*)

EARTH: What a show-off! My little Earth boys would never act like that.

JUPITER: I was named after the king of the gods, and I'm the biggest one in the family. I'm not afraid of anyone, not even Mars. (*He glowers at* MARS, *who frowns back*)

SUN: Tut-tut-tut-tut—Just sit down there, Jupiter, and behave yourself.

JUPITER (*Obeying*): Yes, Mother.

SUN: Now for my next child. (*Calling*) Saturn, Saturn! (*Pause*) Saturn, what are you doing?

SATURN (*Entering*): I'm polishing my rings. I'm the only one in this family with rings.

JUPITER: Rings . . . they're only a lot of exploded moons.

SATURN: I still have nine moons. You're just bragging, Jupiter, because you have twelve moons. But you don't have any rings. The Earth people think my rings look very beautiful in the sky. I'm glad I look pretty, because I'm not so sure I like my name, Saturn. That's a man's name. Saturn was god of the harvest and agriculture, and was Jupiter's father. The old Romans thought of me as having a dark, unpleasant face, but I don't think I have an unpleasant face at all.

SUN: No, dear, your face is very bright and shiny. Now let me call Uranus. (*Calling*) Uranus, Uranus! Oh, he's probably getting dressed up, pretending he's grandfather. Perhaps I should explain. In Roman mythology Uranus was the grandfather of Jupiter, and so this child likes to pretend—

URANUS (*Enters, bent and leaning on stick*): Oh-h-h, my moonitism, oh-h-h, my moonitism. I have five moons you know. Oh, oh, oh.

SUN: See what I mean?

JUPITER (*Getting up*): Shall I help you, grandfather?

URANUS: Thank you, grandson, thank you. I guess I feel creaky because there's not enough heat way out here so far from the sun. Over a billion and a half miles from the sun. And I'm so far away from you, Earth, that your people don't know too much about me; even though they did name uranium, the radioactive, metallic element, after me.

SUN: My children are so talkative this solar day, I hope I can finish this roll call. There are just two more. Neptune is next. (*Calling*) Neptune!

SATURN: He's probably swimming around somewhere. Neptune is always swimming.

NEPTUNE (*Swimming in*): Here I am, Mother Sun. How do you like this breast stroke?

SUN: It's very good.

NEPTUNE: I get a lot of practice way out here in space. I was named Neptune after the god of the sea, so I guess that's why I like swimming so much. There's only one thing wrong with the swimming here. It's so far away from Mother Sun, it's mighty cold in my orbit.

PLUTO (*Entering*): You're cold, what about me? Br-r-r-r.

SUN: Oh, this is my last child, little Pluto. He was named after the god of the dark underworld. Wrap yourself up now, Pluto.

PLUTO: I'm tired of the winter out here; it's always cold and dark.

MERCURY: Well, isn't that better than roasting the way I do?

PLUTO: I don't know, I'd like to get warm just once. And, Mercury, I have another problem you don't have. I'm on the outer rim of our solar system and closer to all the stars in the other galaxies, so I'm afraid of getting "starlit fever."

EARTH: Stop worrying, Pluto, and tell me something. Since you can see farther out into space than I can, is there by any chance another planet beyond you? Some of my people think there might be.

PLUTO: I'm too cold to look. If your Earth people want to know, tell them to build a bigger telescope and find out for themselves.

EARTH: All right, I'll tell the astronomers on Mount Palomar, and at the Hayden Planetarium what you said. My people will find out in time; they're getting more intelligent every day.

SUN (*Looking off, very excited*): Children, children, I see two figures approaching. Earth, it's probably your little boys. Now get into your orbits, children, and remember we're having guests. So, for goodness' sake, *please behave yourselves.*

PLANETS (*Rise, bow or curtsy*): Yes, Mother.

CURTAIN

* * *

SCENE 3

SETTING: *Same as Scene 2.*

AT RISE: *"The Planets" music is heard.* MARK *and* LEIF *enter, jet propelled, in a spaceship. They wear space suits.*

LEIF: This is a good, dependable jet propeller.

MARK: Yes, who would have thought that it would bring us way out here in space?

LEIF: Look, Mark, the stars seem bigger out here.

MARK: Let's see if we can pick out some constellations. There's Orion, the hunter, and the brightest star, Sirius.

LEIF: And I found the twins, Castor and Pollux. Over here is the Big Dipper.

MARK: This is fun being able to recognize them, but we'd better move on. (*As they move slowly across the stage, the* SUN *appears, lighted by a spot.*)

SUN: Stay back, stay back. Don't come too close. My heat would turn you into a vapor. Do you know who I am?

LEIF: Of course, you're the Sun, and you're really a star.

SUN: Hm-m-m-m. Earth said her children were very intelligent. Do you know the difference between a star and a planet?

LEIF: Yes, we do.

SUN: Well, what is the difference?

MARK: A planet is a body which revolves around the Sun and has no light of its own.

LEIF: And a star is a celestial body which *has* heat and light of its own.

SUN: Very good, very good!

MARK: We came to visit with your children. Is that all right?

SUN: Of course, I'll go out and send them in . . . except Earth. You know her. But don't expect them to talk too much. As a family our motto is "Find Out for Yourselves." Besides, the children must get right back into their orbits. (*She exits, calling, "Mercury, Mercury."*)

MERCURY (*Running in*): Hello, I'm in a hurry.

LEIF: Mercury, could we visit you for a while?

MERCURY (*Stopping*): Oh, I don't think you'd like it here with me. On my hot side, I'm 770 degrees, and on my cold side I'm close to absolute zero, which would freeze anything. No, you couldn't live here. Now, if you'll excuse me, I'm in a hurry. (*Exits*)

VENUS (*Entering*): Hello, little boys.

MARK: Venus, would you tell us something about yourself? On Earth you're called the "mystery planet" because of those clouds which cover your face. What are those clouds?

VENUS: If I told you that, I wouldn't be a mystery any more, and I like being a mystery. (*She starts to exit when suddenly there is a flash of light. Planets offstage shout, "Watch out—watch out", as a comet streaks on, just missing the boys)* There's that sky wanderer again.

HEAD OF THE COMET: Sky wanderer, indeed! We happen to be a comet—Halley's Comet, to be exact. I'm the head.

TAIL: And I'm the tail.

HEAD: We're sorry we almost hit you, but you were in our orbit.

LEIF: You have orbits, too?

HEAD: Of course we do. The planets call us "wanderers" just because our paths around the Sun aren't the same as theirs. But we know where we're going. Let's see now, Tail, when do we visit Earth again?

TAIL: Well. . . . *(Figuring this out loud)* every seventy-six Earth years . . . we'll be by there next in 1986. So remember the date; look for us in 1986.

HEAD: You understand you won't see anything too fantastic, just millions of pieces of stone and iron and frozen gases, that's all we are. But we look interesting in the sky. *I* lead when we're going toward the sun, but tail leads us away. Now we must be on our way. Lead on, Tail. *(They turn)*

TAIL *(Leading off and waving)*: Don't forget 1986.

MARK: Whee-ee. That was a close shave! *(Enter SUN, with MARS and JUPITER.)*

SUN: I thought I'd bring in Mars and Jupiter myself. They're a little difficult!

MARS: I know the question they want to ask me, "Are there any Martians living on the planet, Mars?" The Earth people will just have to find out for themselves. But if you do visit us, be sure to bring plenty of water and oxygen. Mine are just about used up.

JUPITER: And you won't like my atmosphere either. It's made up of two poisonous gases, ammonia and methane.

LEIF: Jupiter, would you tell us what your famous red spot is that we see from Earth? Is it a volcano?

JUPITER: I refuse to answer that!

SUN (*Leading them out*): They weren't very helpful, I'm afraid. I'll send in the rest of my children. Maybe they'll be more cooperative.

MARK: Leif, I'm beginning to think that Earth is the best planet, after all. (*Enter* SATURN, URANUS, NEPTUNE *and* PLUTO)

LEIF: Saturn, would the Earth people ever be able to visit you?

SATURN: I'm surrounded by poisonous gases too, you know. (*At this point* METEOR *streaks across the sky. All shout, "Look out, look out . . . It's a Meteor" The* METEOR *bumps into the boys.*)

LEIF: Mark, watch out!

MARK: Ouch, I'm hit!

PLUTO: Why don't you watch where you're going?

NEPTUNE: Really, you're the clumsiest thing in the universe.

METEOR: Well, I couldn't help it. I'm just a piece of space junk on my way down to Earth. I'll end up as a meteorite in the Hayden Planetarium, you'll see. Come visit me there one of these days. (*Exits*)

LEIF: Are you hurt, Mark?

MARK: My oxygen tank was hit. I'm losing oxygen fast—hard to breathe.

EARTH (*Entering*): Oh, my Earth boys, my poor little Earth boys.

LEIF: Take it easy, Mark. Hold on. We've got to land on some planet fast. I'll try these. (*They approach* URANUS.)

URANUS (*Sadly shaking head*): Too cold here.

PLUTO (*As boys approach him*): *Very* much too cold here,

and no *atmosphere*. (LEIF *puts his arm around* MARK *and tries to share his oxygen.*)

EARTH (*Holding out her hands*): Little boys, listen to me. Come back to Earth. I'm the only planet you can live on. Please, *please come back to earth.*

CURTAIN

* * *

SCENE 4

BEFORE RISE: JANET, NADINE, DIANE, *and* KIT *enter in front of curtain, running.*

JANET: I hear a rocket!

NADINE: It must be the boys coming back! (*At the other side of the stage, the girls stop, looking up*)

DIANE (*Pointing*): Look, there they are.

KIT: The rocket's headed this way.

JANET: It's right over the school. (*There is the sound of a terrific crash offstage. Curtains rise.*)

SETTING: *Same as Scene 1, except that instead of the rocket ship there is a pile of rocket ship debris.*

AT RISE: LEIF *and* MARK *are sitting on a pile of rocket debris. From time to time, bits of debris fall from above.*

GIRLS (*Ad lib*): They've landed! They've landed! Look, they've landed! (*Etc.*)

LEIF (*Raising his head and removing helmet*): Landed, and how! (*Boys rise slowly, dazed, and brush each other off*)

MARK: Are you all right, Leif?

LEIF: I—I guess so. How are you?

MARK: I'm all here. (*Looking about*) Say, where are we?

LEIF (*As he looks all around*): Why, this looks like the school. It *is!* (*Pointing*) There are the girls. Mark, we made it! We're home! (*Looking up*) Oh-h-h! I hope Mr. Moore can fix that hole in the roof.

DIANE (*With something like admiration for the boys*): Boys, we're certainly glad to see you again. Did you really get out into space?

MARK: Did we? Wait 'til you hear!

NADINE: Did you see any planets? And what was it like on the Moon?

MARK: The *Moon?* (LEIF *and* MARK *look at each other incredulously.*)

LEIF: Oh, *no!* Mark, how did we ever forget to stop on the Moon? (*He shrugs his shoulders, looks around at the smashed ship and picks up a part of it.*) Well, let's try to put this rocket ship together again. We're going to make another trip. Want to help us, girls?

GIRLS (*Ad lib*): Sure! O.K.! I'll help—if you'll let us go with you next time. (*Etc.*)

LEIF: All right, we'll take you. Now, let's get to work on this. (*Looking skyward, and with a kind of salute*) See you soon, Moon! (*Curtain*)

THE END

The Invisible Dragon of Winn Sinn Tu

by Rosemary G. Musil

Characters

THE DRAGON
WUN SUN TU, *a student magician*
PEASANT
PEACH BLOSSOM
BARON

SETTING: *A Chinese village.*

AT RISE: *The stage is empty. Chinese music is heard in background; it stops as* WUN SUN TU *enters, whistling. He pauses at center, notices the pit or space in front of stage, and looks down into it.*

WUN SUN TU: Aha, water! And where there is water, sometimes there is a fish for a hungry man's dinner! (*Looks about*) If only I had a fishing pole and a worm, I would —(*Stops and purses lips*) There I go, forgetting that I have just completed a course in magic! The students there were taught to produce a fishing pole by magic. Let's see now. How did it go? Oh, yes! You clap your hands three times and bow to the left (*Does so*), bow to the right (*Does so*), then bow to your audience (*Bows*).

Then you snap your fingers (*Does so*), and a fishing line will drop out of your (*Starts to shake sleeve*) . . . sleeve . . . into . . . your . . . (*Shakes head sadly, drops to the floor cross-legged, his head in hands*). I knew it wouldn't work. Magic works for every magician in the school except me! The Master Magician said that it is because I have no faith in myself, and he is right. I am a coward! Every time I go to perform my magic in front of somebody, I get butterflies inside my stomach, start shaking up and down and, in general, make a clown of myself. (*Jumps up suddenly*) I know! Suppose you don't look at me—that's it. If you don't look, maybe I'll get more confidence in myself and be able to perform the magic trick. Now close your eyes, everybody. Put your hands over your eyes; that's right. Thank you so very much. Now stay that way, please do, till I perform the trick. Now, I bow to the right. (*Acts out previous routine again, then puts hand inside coat sleeve, and looks chagrined.*) It didn't work. There is no fishing pole. One of you peeked. Yes you did, I know you must have. Because I really know how to perform magic—it's just that I am shy with people! (*Folds hands inside coat, then suddenly draws them slowly out of sleeve*) Wait a moment. What's this? (*Draws out long string*) A fishing rod? It is! I did perform the magic trick. (*Jerks at string*) No, I didn't. It's just a string hanging down from my coat sleeve. Oh well, I might as well use it. (*Jerks it off and pulls it out*) Now if I had a bent pin. (*Searches in his clothing*) Aha, here is one. (*Attaches it to string*) Now if I could only find a worm. (*Searches on ground*) Worm, worm, where are you, little worm? Come, come, I need you on the end of my line. Oh, well. Maybe some hungry fish will bite without a worm. (*Sits, takes off sandals and ties the end of the string to his big toe. He lies back, crosses leg and dangles string over pit*.) There's more than one way to catch a fish, and I might as well be comfortable. I'll sing to the fish. Maybe he will get angry when he hears my sandpaper voice and bite on my hook to stop me. (*Sings*)

Oh there once was a dragon from Winn Sinn Tu,
An invisible dragon was he,
He came to the aid of one who was brave
When a magic word spoken would be.

(*He sits up, alert*.) Here now. Where did I ever hear those words before? Oh, now I remember. My Master Magician taught them to me. He said that if I couldn't perform magic, I should try to find the invisible dragon of Winn Sinn Tu, and the dragon would help me. You see, the dragon is invisible, so I would pretend to do magic, but the dragon would do what I ordered instead. People would think it was I who did it, because they couldn't see the dragon, of course. Now let's see. There was a magic word he taught me to say that would call the dragon to me at once. What was that word? (*Shakes head despairingly, and begins to pace, beating head with fists*.) What was the word that would produce the magic dragon! (*To audience*) Perhaps you can help me. Try saying a magic word. Come on, please help me. (*If audience responds, he can say the words they suggest and look each time for dragon. If he gets no help, he can shake his head and continue*.) It was a queer word, something like Rickey-tin-tin. (DRAGON *comes bounding on immediately and stands in front of* WUN SUN TU, *paws up like a dog begging.* WUN SUN TU *can't see him and keeps pacing*.) No, that wasn't the word, but it is close though. What *was* the word? (DRAGON *attempts to show* WUN SUN TU *that he is there by pulling at his shirt, tripping him, pointing to himself, etc.* WUN SUN TU *is unaware of him. If the audience calls attention to the* DRAGON, WUN SUN TU *shakes his head and asks them not to tease him.* WUN SUN TU *suddenly pauses.*) I must remember not to say the word twice if I think of it. You see, when I say the word once, the dragon appears, but no one can see him. If I say it twice, the dragon becomes visible and everybody can see him, and that would do me no good, of course. And if I say the word three times he disappears for good, so I must not repeat any of the words I have said. But, oh, dear. If I did say the word once, I couldn't see the dragon anyhow! For all I know, I have said the word and he is here. And if I say it twice —(*Shakes head and sits dejectedly*) Oh, dear. I am sunk, no matter what I do. (DRAGON *sits beside him, imitating his every action.* WUN SUN TU *suddenly jumps up.*) I have a thought! To do my magic, I need confidence. I wonder if I could get confidence by *pretending* I had an invisible dragon. By pretending, I might fool myself into believing I had help to perform my magic, and then I could do it. I'll try, and you help me. Cross your fingers. Thank you. Now. (*Shuts eyes and repeats slowly three times*) "I have an invisible dragon to help me." (*Opens eyes*) Now, I'll do my magic with my invisible dragon's help. First I bow to the right. (*Repeats routine*) Then I put my hand inside my sleeve and I will pull out a worm. (*Does so. As he draws hand out, the* DRAGON *reaches down and picks up a worm and drops it into his hand.*) It worked! It worked! The worm came to me. See, it is a worm! (*Holding it up*) I pretended to have an invisible dragon, and it gave me the courage to make my magic work! Oh happy day! Oh wonderful world! Now I can practice my magic and it will work, work, work! (*Jumps about ecstatically and bumps up against a* PEASANT *who comes out on the stage with a peach tree which he carefully sets on a mat.*)

PEASANT: Stupid dolt!

WUN SUN TU: Oh! I beg your pardon!

PEASANT: You almost made me drop my peach tree! Leave! (*Pushes him*) Get off my land! Go!

WUN SUN TU: Now see here! You stop pushing me about like this or I'll . . .

PEASANT (*Flexing his muscles*): You'll what?

WUN SUN TU: I'll send my invisible dragon after you and you'll be sorry!

PEASANT (*Astonished*): You'll what?

WUN SUN TU: I'm a magician, and I can do things to you, so you'd better stop pushing me about.

PEASANT: What things will you do to me?

WUN SUN TU: I'll . . . I'll make your peach tree disappear into the sea!

PEASANT: Bah! You are stupid. Go! (*Pushes again*)

WUN SUN TU (*Desperately*): Invisible dragon, make the peach tree go! (*The* DRAGON *bows, then goes behind the mat and pulls the peach tree out. The* PEASANT *stands in amazement.*)

PEASANT: Make it stop! Make it come back before it slides into the sea!

WUN SUN TU: Very well. (*Claps hands*) Invisible dragon, bring the peach tree back! (DRAGON *bows and slides tree back.*)

PEASANT (*Grabbing tree*): My tree! My peach tree! (*Looks fearfully at* WUN SUN TU *and runs out.* WUN SUN TU *swaggers to the right and dusts his hands.*)

WUN SUN TU: And let that be a lesson to you, my good man, not to tamper with magic! (*Struts about boastfully*) Now what do you think of my magic! I told you! I told you all along that I was a great magician. It was just that I didn't have confidence. Now, by pretending to have a dragon to help me, I can do any trick on earth! Oh, happy day! (*Cavorts about*) I'll go down to the village of Winn Sinn Tu and perform magic tricks in the square, and the people will give me money! I'll be rich!

(*Stops cavorting about and looks around*) Let's see now. Which road do I take to the village? (DRAGON *gets in front of him and motions to the left.*) Something seems to tell me that I should try this direction. Yes, I shall try it. Oh, it is wonderful to have confidence in what you can do. I should have pretended to have an invisible dragon long ago. (*Exits. From the left, a plank with a door frame and door and a small tea table and two small stools are slid out to the center of the stage. From behind the center screen,* PEACH BLOSSOM, *with a potted plant and trowel, comes onto the plank, opens the door and steps outside. She sets the plant down and begins to dig about the roots.*)

WUN SUN TU (*Coming from left, followed by* DRAGON): Whew! I'm tired. I've walked for miles, and haven't come to the village yet. (*Looks about*) Oh, here is someone who can perhaps tell me in what direction Winn Sinn Tu lies. (*Approaches* PEACH BLOSSOM *and bows*) I beg your pardon!

PEACH BLOSSOM (*Rises in alarm*): Oh, you—you are a stranger!

WUN SUN TU: Permit me to introduce myself. I am . . .

PEACH BLOSSOM: Go! Go at once! Hurry! (*Greatly agitated, she tries to push him*)

WUN SUN TU: Now, see here. I'll be very glad to go, if you will only tell me the way to the village of Winn Sinn Tu.

PEACH BLOSSOM (*Shaking her head violently*): No, no! You must not go there either. (*Starts pushing again*) Go back where you came from!

WUN SUN TU: Wait a moment. I'm tired of being pushed around. If you will just tell me the way to the village, I will—

PEACH BLOSSOM (*Buries face in hands and cries softly*): Oh, foolish man!

WUN SUN TU: All right, all right. Please don't cry. I'll go. (*Turns to go, but* DRAGON *holds him by the coattails.* WUN SUN TU, *thinking that* PEACH BLOSSOM *has changed her mind and is holding him, folds his arms and stands grinning.*)

PEACH BLOSSOM (*Noting his hesitation*): Hurry! Go before the Baron returns.

WUN SUN TU: How can I go when you hold on to me!

PEACH BLOSSOM: Forgive me, I do not mean to be rude to one as kind as you seem, but if the Baron catches a stranger near his castle, he will be angry and make the earth quake again!

WUN SUN TU: Come now. A man can't cause the earth to quake.

PEACH BLOSSOM (*Beginning to cry again*): He will toss you over the mountain and break your bones like matchsticks!

WUN SUN TU: In that case then, perhaps it would be better if I . . . (*Turns to go but* DRAGON *holds his coattails again.*) Well, make up your mind. Do you want me to stay or go?

PEACH BLOSSOM: I would want you to stay, very much, but we dare not risk making the Baron angry.

WUN SUN TU: And why not? Who is this Baron?

PEACH BLOSSOM: He is a man who possesses a magic gong. When he is angry, he strikes it and the earthquake comes. Whoever else strikes it is killed instantly.

WUN SUN TU: Poppycock!

PEACH BLOSSOM: No, it is true. Look about you. Once this castle, these lands, even the village of Winn Sinn Tu belonged to my father, the rightful Baron. He was good and kind and the people loved him and he served them well. One day the big earthquake came and killed my father and many people. Then the Baron appeared with the gong and said that he had caused the quake, and that now the people must obey him and make him Baron. I, Peach Blossom, who was a Princess, am now his servant. He will not tolerate strangers!

WUN SUN TU: Well, I'm not going away! I would have gone once, but not now. You see, now I have discovered a great secret about myself, and I am no longer afraid.

PEACH BLOSSOM: A great secret?

WUN SUN TU: Yes. I've discovered that I am a coward.

PEACH BLOSSOM (*Wringing hands*): You joke. You joke when any moment—

WUN SUN TU (*Holding up hand to stop her*): But a coward who can become a brave and wonderfully talented magician. Watch me. (*Repeats words to give himself confidence*) I have an invisible dragon. I have an invisible dragon. (DRAGON *bows and nods each time he says it.*) Now, observe. Banish the castle! Make it disappear! (DRAGON *bows, steps behind the flat and pulls castle by string, and it slides behind the screen.*)

PEACH BLOSSOM (*Frightened*): You're making the castle disappear. Make it come back!

WUN SUN TU: Gladly. (*Claps hands*) Invisible dragon, make the castle reappear! (DRAGON *slides the flat back.*)

PEACH BLOSSOM: You are a wonderful magician indeed, but why do you speak of an invisible dragon?

WUN SUN TU: As I told you, I was a coward, and had no confidence in myself. Then I thought of the old story of an invisible dragon who could help a poor magician with magic, and I pretended I had one. It gave me the confidence I needed to perform my magic. (*Bows*)

PEACH BLOSSOM: You are a great and wonderful magician indeed. Perhaps you could help us!

WUN SUN TU: I could make the Baron disappear.

PEACH BLOSSOM: But he must disappear of his own free will.

WUN SUN TU: How's that?

PEACH BLOSSOM: The Baron must *want* to go when he leaves us, or he will make the earthquake come and kill us all.

WUN SUN TU: Come, take me inside and show me this terrible gong that causes the earthquakes.

PEACH BLOSSOM: Hurry then, before the Baron wakes from his afternoon nap and sees a stranger in his castle.

WUN SUN TU: After you and the flowerpot. (*Bowing, he claps his hands and motions.* DRAGON *understands, bows and wafts the flowerpot through the doorway.*)

PEACH BLOSSOM: My rose tree is flying through the air!

WUN SUN TU: My magic, fair lady . . . and now you! (*Claps hands*) Invisible dragon, transport the lady inside her castle! (DRAGON *bows, picks her up.*)

PEACH BLOSSOM: Oh, I'm being carried through the air! (DRAGON *carries her inside and sets her down.*)

WUN SUN TU: And now, where is this terrible gong that causes earths to quake?

PEACH BLOSSOM: Here, but be careful. Be very, very careful. With my own eyes, I once saw a brave man like you just touch the gong, and be instantly killed.

WUN SUN TU: Wait—I will manufacture some courage. (*Repeats three times, "I have an invisible dragon who will keep me from harm."*) Now, let me examine this silly gong. (*Walks around gong. A loud yawn sounds from inside left screen.*)

PEACH BLOSSOM (*Nervously*): Oh, the Baron is waking! Go, go quickly! He will have us hanged from the highest tree—

WUN SUN TU (*Allowing himself to be pushed to door*): Yes, yes indeed. I certainly don't want to be hanged from the—(*Stops*) What's the matter with me? I forgot I have an invisible dragon to make me brave!

PEACH BLOSSOM: Invisible dragon or no, the Baron does not permit strangers.

WUN SUN TU: Then I won't be a stranger. Quickly! Doesn't some servant help you serve the Baron sometimes?

PEACH BLOSSOM: Yes, my cousin Wang. But you look nothing like him!

WUN SUN TU: What does he look like?

PEACH BLOSSOM: He has long hair that goes across his lips and hangs down each side of his face.

WUN SUN TU: Watch! (*Repeats "The invisible dragon will help me," as he reaches inside his sleeve and draws out two long mustaches. He puts them on his lip and bows.*)

PEACH BLOSSOM: You grew Wang's mustaches!

WUN SUN TU: I'm glad you think so. Now do I resemble Wang?

PEACH BLOSSOM: Perhaps, but you have a deep voice, and he speaks with a high, thin one.

WUN SUN TU (*Falsetto*): Like this?

PEACH BLOSSOM: No, no! Oh, you'd better go! Your voice would give you away!

WUN SUN TU: I have it. I'll wrap my scarf about my neck. You tell him that I have been ill and have lost my voice. Then you can speak for me!

PEACH BLOSSOM: Oh yes, then I can say the proper things.

WUN SUN TU (*Wrapping scarf around throat and chin*): Good. Now what shall I do?

PEACH BLOSSOM: Help me serve the Baron. When I get the trays, remove the dishes of food, set them before the Baron, then remove them when he has finished. But, oh dear! How are you going to make the Baron want to disappear?

WUN SUN TU: One thing at a time. The dragon and I will find a way!

BARON (*Roaring as he enters*): My supper! Serve my supper! (*Enters quickly and sinks onto stool*) My supper!

Where is my food? (*Pounds on table, head down, not looking at anything*)

PEACH BLOSSOM (*Bowing*): It is prepared, my lord. It is served! (*Goes behind screen, gets small tray with four red plastic bowls and hands them one at a time to* WUN SUN TU, *who hands them to* BARON, *who does not look up. Propping his head with one hand, elbow on table,* BARON *wolfs the food, setting each bowl in turn on the table.*)

BARON: Food, more food. Perhaps it will help me overcome my sleeplessness! Quickly, more food!

PEACH BLOSSOM: Indeed, my lord! (*Bows and brings out a heavier tray with larger plastic dishes.* WUN SUN TU *claps his hands, and* DRAGON *bows, lifts the tray, and deposits it in front of* BARON.)

BARON (*Bellowing in fear*): The tray! It came through the air by itself!

PEACH BLOSSOM (*Quaking in fear*): No, no, my lord. It only seemed to!

BARON (*Rising, sees* WUN SUN TU): Strangers! There are strangers here!

PEACH BLOSSOM (*Puts herself between* BARON *and* WUN SUN TU): No, no, my lord. It is Wang, my cousin! He is here to help me serve you!

BARON (*Shaking head and backing down onto stool again*): Wang? You are sure?

PEACH BLOSSOM: Of course, my lord. Remember, you asked for him!

BARON: Yes, yes, of course I did. (*Mumbles*) Sleep, can't sleep. Makes me imagine things. Take food away. I go to the garden . . . night air may make me sleep. (*Goes out the door and sits on the stoop.* PEACH BLOSSOM *turns on* WUN SUN TU *angrily.*)

PEACH BLOSSOM: Would you ruin everything with your foolish magic? If the Baron had not been so ill from lack of sleep, he would have known that you were not Wang.

WUN SUN TU: But I have the way to make the Baron disappear! We give him this sleeping potion. (*Takes bottle from pocket*) Then while he sleeps, I hypnotize him and make him want to go.

PEACH BLOSSOM (*Shaking head*): He will never take it. He is suspicious of everyone. That is why he can't sleep. He is afraid someone will do away with him at an unguarded moment.

WUN SUN TU: When he comes back inside, I shall be asleep at the table. Tell him that I have tested a wonderful sleeping potion, to see if it is harmless for him to take. (BARON *yawns, gets up mumbling and starts back inside.*)

PEACH BLOSSOM: Oh, dear, I don't know if it will work or not. But give the bottle to me and we can try.

WUN SUN TU: Don't worry. My invisible dragon will help us!

PEACH BLOSSOM: There is no such thing, and you know it!

WUN SUN TU: Sh-h-h-h. Don't say it so loudly. I might believe it, and then I'd get cowardly and run away. He returns—take the bottle. (*Hands her the bottle and spoon and sits at the table, head on folded arms.* PEACH BLOSSOM *stands uncertainly with the bottle in her hands, watching as* BARON *enters dazedly.*)

BARON (*Suddenly awake and angry*): Wang—your cousin! (*Pointing*) The oaf sleeps at my place!

PEACH BLOSSOM (*Bows*): Most illustrious lord, he sleeps but to show *you* how to sleep!

BARON: I *know* how to sleep.

PEACH BLOSSOM: But you are ill from lack of it, my lord. Wang is testing this medicine that promises a deep refreshing sleep to all who swallow it.

BARON: Medicine? Medicine that makes one sleep?

PEACH BLOSSOM: Yes, yes. He is doing it to help you.

BARON (*Approaches* WUN SUN TU *suspiciously*): Bah! I do not think he is sleeping at all.

PEACH BLOSSOM: My lord, observe him! How can you doubt it? (WUN SUN TU *starts to snore a little.*)

BARON: We shall soon see if he sleeps. I'll tickle him with this feather. (*Takes feather from floor and starts to tickle the back of* WUN SUN TU's *neck.* DRAGON *puts his paw over* WUN SUN TU's *neck to keep it from being tickled.*) Hm-m-m. He must really sleep if the feather doesn't bother him. I'll tickle his foot. If that doesn't waken him, I will know he truly sleeps. (*Removes* WUN SUN TU's *slipper and tickles his foot. Again* DRAGON *intervenes.* BARON *puts slipper back.*) He really is sleeping!

PEACH BLOSSOM: Of course, dear Baron. And if the Baron will but take a sip—(*Holds bottle out to him*)

BARON: It is most tempting. If I slept, would I be safe here?

PEACH BLOSSOM: Wang would waken and guard you.

BARON: You are sure of this?

PEACH BLOSSOM: Of course, dear Baron. It is why he came tonight.

BARON: Give me the medicine. (PEACH BLOSSOM *hands it to him. He sniffs it carefully.*) It doesn't smell bad. How does it taste?

PEACH BLOSSOM: It has the taste of lotus blossoms, dear lord.

BARON: How do you know? You haven't tasted it! You drink it! (*Holds it out to her. Behind* BARON's *back,* WUN SUN TU *rises worriedly.*)

PEACH BLOSSOM: I—I (*Begins to back away.* WUN SUN TU *motions to her to drink. She takes the bottle.*) Very well. (*Pretends to drink, and sinks to floor.* BARON *grabs the bottle and watches her pillow her head on her hands and sleep, with a blissful smile on her face.* BARON *goes to the other side of the table as* WUN SUN TU *quickly goes back to pretended sleep.* BARON *sits and contemplates bottle.*)

BARON: I'll take it! (*Gulps down medicine, then sighs and sinks down at the table. Snores gently.* WUN SUN TU *rises and tests him with the feather.* BARON *does not move.*)

WUN SUN TU (*Going to* PEACH BLOSSOM): Poor Peach Blossom. What a pity she had to take the potion also. How sweetly she sleeps! How lovely she is! (*Gently caresses her hair*) If only I can get rid of the Baron, and become courageous enough for her! (PEACH BLOSSOM *jumps to her feet and stands smiling before him.*) Peach Blossom! You were not asleep!

PEACH BLOSSOM: Of course not. I only pretended to swallow the medicine! But what were you saying, dear cousin Wang?

WUN SUN TU: There are other things to do at once. I shall test the Baron and see if I can make him do my will. Invisible dragon, help me! Baron—Baron—(BARON *stirs.*) Get up, and go to your nice soft bed.

BARON (*Mumbles, stirs, lifts head*): Sleep in nice soft bed.

WUN SUN TU: That's right. Rise and go to bed.

BARON (*Starting out*): Nice soft bed.

PEACH BLOSSOM: He is doing as you suggest. Quickly, tell him to leave!

WUN SUN TU: Baron, go away. Go over the mountain and never come back.

BARON (*Pauses in his sleep-walking*): Baron go over mountain. (*Starts to turn toward door*)

PEACH BLOSSOM: He is doing it!

BARON (*Gets to door, stops, goes back to table*): Baron sleeps.

PEACH BLOSSOM: He isn't going to do it. He's gone back to sleep.

WUN SUN TU: Yes, I know. I had forgotten what the Master Magician said never to forget—that the subject you hypnotize will do only that thing he wishes to do in the first place!

PEACH BLOSSOM (*In despair*): And he would never wish to leave. Oh, dear. We are right back where we started from. Dear Wun Sun Tu, you must go. You cannot help us! If he wakens, he will know you are not Wang and will hurt both of us! Go! (*Starts to push him to door. He stops to consider.*)

WUN SUN TU: But that gong! I wonder why people are hurt when they use it. (*Goes to gong, and* PEACH BLOSSOM *wrings her hands.*)

PEACH BLOSSOM: Don't start that all over again! If you touch the gong, you and many with you will die in the earthquake!

WUN SUN TU: Hm-m-m-m. . . . (*Suddenly he dashes outside, behind the screen and back in again.*) It is as I thought. The sly Baron has balanced a great rock behind the gong on the mountainside. When the gong is sounded, the vibration topples the rock and starts an enormous landslide toward the village, hurling rocks and dirt down upon it! So you see, Peach Blossom, he has no magic! He is just a man. He cannot hurt you. Quickly, go get the villagers and show them the rock. Have them remove it. Then I shall strike the gong and waken the Baron. The villagers will come and we shall toss him over the mountainside.

PEACH BLOSSOM: No, no, do not strike the gong, or you shall die. I have seen it again and again with my own eyes. He who strikes the gong, dies!

WUN SUN TU (*Pacing up and down*): I have it! All we really want to do is get rid of the Baron, right? (PEACH BLOSSOM *nods.*) Then suppose I use my invisible dragon to make him so frightened that he will leave!

PEACH BLOSSOM: But you have no invisible dragon! (DRAGON *tries to make them see him.*)

WUN SUN TU: True. But if the *idea* of such a thing can make me brave, why couldn't the same idea make him frightened? I'll waken the Baron, then pretend there is an invisible dragon who hates evil men. (DRAGON *nods.*) Then I shall perform magic to make it seem as if a dragon were getting in his way, putting stools in front of his feet (*Picking up stool*), grabbing his food away from him (*Picking up dish*), tripping him (*Sticking out foot*).

PEACH BLOSSOM: Yes, he might become frightened by that.

WUN SUN TU: It is our last chance to rid ourselves of him. Get fresh food. I shall waken him and make him hungry again. (PEACH BLOSSOM *goes to get fresh tray of dishes.* WUN SUN TU *repeats, "I have an invisible dragon," three times, and each time, the* DRAGON *bows before him. He snaps his fingers.*) Baron, wake up!

BARON (*Wakes, rises, looks about*): I slept! . . . I had a good sleep!

PEACH BLOSSOM (*Entering*): Indeed you did, and now you must be hungry. Come sit down.

BARON: Yes, yes, I am famished. (*Starts across in front of the table.* WUN SUN TU *claps hands and* DRAGON *places the stool in his path. He flops over it and lies flat on the floor at* WUN SUN TU's *feet. Then he sits up.*) You put the stool in my path. You made me fall!

WUN SUN TU: No, no, honorable Baron. It was the dragon —the invisible dragon!

BARON (*Rising*): The what?

WUN SUN TU: There is an invisible dragon about. I know because he always changes my voice for me when he comes, and he is mean and cruel to people who have done evil things.

BARON (*Angrily advancing*): You are not Wang! (*Advances towards* WUN SUN TU, *who claps his hands.* DRAGON *nods, bows, and places other stool in* BARON's *path. He falls over it.*) You tripped me!

WUN SUN TU: No, no, dear Baron. The invisible dragon tripped you. Although why he should hate one as kind, as considerate as you, I cannot think!

PEACH BLOSSOM (*As* WUN SUN TU *helps* BARON *up*): Come eat. Perhaps you will feel better. (WUN SUN TU *places stool for* BARON. *The* BARON *starts to sit down carefully, and just as he is about to sit,* DRAGON *jerks the stool out, and* BARON *falls down.*)

BARON (*To* WUN SUN TU): It was you! I know it was you!

WUN SUN TU: Baron! Baron! It was I who tested the sleep medicine and helped you sleep. Would I do a thing like this to you?

BARON: You are not Wang. Your voice is deep; his is high!

WUN SUN TU: As I explained, that is why I know the dragon is about.

BARON: He—he changes your voice?

WUN SUN TU (*Nods solemnly, then holds the stool for* BARON): I shall help you my lord. This time the dragon will not take the stool from you. (*Holds the stool firmly.* BARON *approaches stool timidly, starting to sit several times and jumping up to make sure of the stool. At last he sits.* WUN SUN TU *goes to opposite side of the table, and* PEACH BLOSSOM *hands* BARON *a dish of food. As he starts to take it,* DRAGON *grabs it and sets it down.*)

BARON (*Jumping up*): He did it! It wasn't you! I've stayed too long! I'm going! (*Walks to the door.* WUN SUN TU *opens it with a flourish, and as he does, his long mustaches catch on the door and pull off.*) You are not Wang! You are playing a joke on me! (*Advances on* WUN SUN TU *menacingly.* PEACH BLOSSOM *gets between them.*)

PEACH BLOSSOM: Let him go, my lord. He is only a poor traveling magician who is trying to help me.

BARON: Out of my way! (*Pushes her down.* WUN SUN TU *places hand on gong.*)

WUN SUN TU: Leave her alone, or I shall ring the gong and expose you to the villagers.

BARON (*Surprised*): Expose me? How?

WUN SUN TU: You have a rock balanced to cause a land-slide when the gong is hit. I know it. You pretend it to be an earthquake.

BARON: It kills as effectively as an earthquake. And may I suggest to you that if you strike the gong, you shall also die?

PEACH BLOSSOM: Yes, yes, do not hit the gong, dear Wun Sun Tu!

WUN SUN TU: I shall not hit it if the Baron will promise to go away!

BARON: With you killed, I shall have no need to go away. Hit the gong!

PEACH BLOSSOM (*Holding* WUN SUN TU's *hand*): No! No! (DRAGON *nods and holds* WUN SUN TU's *hand also.*)

BARON: You'd better follow the lady's advice, young man!

WUN SUN TU (*Reaches for clapper to hit gong, and shouts out suddenly*): Rickey-tin-tin! (*A large rock, attached to clapper by a string, is pulled from top of screen when* WUN SUN TU *grabs the clapper.* DRAGON, *now visible due to the repetition of the magic word, catches the rock, thus saving* WUN SUN TU *from being hit.* WUN SUN TU, BARON, *and* PEACH BLOSSOM *now see* DRAGON *for the first time.*)

PEACH BLOSSOM: The dragon! There *was* a dragon! (WUN SUN TU *stares in astonishment at* DRAGON, *who returns the look lovingly. The* BARON *utters a frightened squeal, turns, and runs out the door and disappears behind the far screen in a manner indicating that he will never stop running.* WUN SUN TU *drops the clapper and turns to the door.*) Where are you going?

WUN SUN TU (*Sadly*): Away. You don't need me any longer —you have the dragon!

PEACH BLOSSOM: But I do need you! I need you to rule with me and be the Baron of the village!

WUN SUN TU (*Sadly*): You would not want a coward for a husband!

PEACH BLOSSOM (*Angrily*): A coward? You are not a coward. You are brave; very, very brave. (DRAGON *nods.*)

WUN SUN TU: It is the dragon who was brave. (*Bitterly*) I thought myself such a great magician. I wasn't a magician at all. The dragon was doing those things for me while he was invisible! I am not only a coward, but a failure at the one thing I was born to do—magic! I must go. (*Starts off again.* DRAGON *grabs his coattails.* WUN SUN TU *turns, and* DRAGON *points to the rock.*)

PEACH BLOSSOM: I understand! I know what he is trying to tell you! The gong! You hit the gong when you thought it would kill you! You hit the gong not knowing that the dragon would catch the rock and keep you from death!

WUN SUN TU (*Taking heart*): Yes—yes I did do that, didn't I?

PEACH BLOSSOM: You are brave! Very, very brave. And even if you were not—

WUN SUN TU: Yes?

PEACH BLOSSOM (*Softly*): I would still want you for my Baron. (WUN SUN TU *starts to take her in his arms, then suddenly turns away.*)

WUN SUN TU: The dragon would be here always doing things we wanted done. I would not keep on being brave. I would grow soft and lazy and you would come to hate me. No, I cannot stay, while a dragon does my

work for me. (*Walks sorrowfully to door.* PEACH BLOS-
SOM *gets in front of him and shuts the door bravely.*)

PEACH BLOSSOM: Then we shall send the dragon away!
(DRAGON *nods.*)

WUN SUN TU: No, no, the dragon saved my life. He deserves a better fate. (DRAGON *shakes head.*)

PEACH BLOSSOM: No. See, he is shaking his head. He wants
to go. He wants you to stay. Isn't that right, dragon?
(DRAGON *tries to answer both questions at once, shaking
his head one way, then the other. He shrugs helplessly.*)

WUN SUN TU: Of course he doesn't want to go. He deserves this good home. He was working hard for it,
while all the time I was only fooling myself. I must go.

PEACH BLOSSOM: Stay! Stay, or I shall banish the dragon
forever!

WUN SUN TU (*Astonished*): Banish the dragon? How?

PEACH BLOSSOM: By saying the secret word. Remember,
you said it once, and the dragon came to help you, but
no one could see him. I, too, know this legend of the
invisible dragon—my father taught it to me. You say
the magic word once and the dragon comes to help you,
but remains invisible. You say it twice and the dragon
stays on, but everyone can see him!

WUN SUN TU: Yes, yes, that is right. I must have said the
word twice. But I didn't know I said it. I must have
known the word all along, but could only say it when
I didn't think about it.

PEACH BLOSSOM: When you were under great pressure!

WUN SUN TU: Yes, of course. The first time I said it, I
was worried about my magic and hoping to get the
dragon.

PEACH BLOSSOM: The second time you said it, you were
risking your life and longing for such a dragon to help
you.

WUN SUN TU (*Turning affectionately to* DRAGON *and placing a hand on his shoulder*): And he did help me, didn't you, old friend? You deserve a good home. I shall never rob you of it. Thank you, and—goodbye. (*Goes to* PEACH BLOSSOM, *who turns to weep, head in hands*) I don't want to leave. I—I love you Peach Blossom, but I could never rob the dragon of his right to happiness. (*He starts out.*)

PEACH BLOSSOM (*Shouts defiantly*): Rickey-tin-tin! (DRAGON *puts down his rock, nods happily and starts out the door.*)

WUN SUN TU (*Searching about*): Invisible dragon, come back! She didn't mean it! Invisible dragon! (*Angrily*) Now what have you done?

PEACH BLOSSOM: I have released him from you so that he can serve another. You do not need him, but someone else might.

WUN SUN TU: You need him. You need him to protect you! (PEACH BLOSSOM *smiles and shakes her head, looking fondly at* WUN SUN TU. DRAGON *waits in doorway, smiling at them.*) You need me? You want me instead? (*She nods vigorously.*) But I am not even a good magician. I am only a poor traveling peasant.

PEACH BLOSSOM: You are a brave man, and my Baron!

WUN SUN TU (*Runs to door as* DRAGON *starts slowly away toward screen at right. Calls*): Dragon, dragon, if you can hear my voice—we will put a cup of milk each night for you on our doorstep! (*He waits a moment, then* PEACH BLOSSOM *holds out her hand. He takes it, still looking off toward right. They go behind screen at left. Curtain*)

THE END

The Rebellious Robots

by Deborah Newman

Characters

AGATHA FOLLANSBEE	DAN
HENRY FOLLANSBEE	ELLEN
SIX ROBOTS	JOE
ANN	LISA
SUSIE	MAYOR PORTLY
TOMMY	

TIME: *The present.*

SETTING: *A gift shop. At one side there is a display of flowers, at the other, a display of jewelry, candy, and other gifts. Various signs are placed around the store, giving gift suggestions, price information, etc.*

AT RISE: AGATHA *enters, carrying a large box marked "candy". She puts the box down in the center of the stage.*

AGATHA (*Calling*): Henry! Henry, I need you. The candy is here. Henry! Oh, where is that husband of mine? A fine help he is—always in that workshop of his, inventing something when there's work to be done. Well, I guess I'll just have to open this myself. (*She takes a scissors from her apron pocket and begins cutting the strings.*) This candy should have come days ago. I suppose Henry forgot to mail the order again. That man! All he thinks about are his inventions. (1st Robot *enters slowly, knocking down a chair as he comes forward.* Agatha *does not see him; her back is to him, and she does not look up as she tugs at the strings.* 1st Robot *stops near her.*) Well, Henry, it's about time you got here. Now, you just listen to me. I want you to stop all this foolish inventing and get to work. This candy must be put on the shelves, and then I want you to oil the door, and—Henry, are you listening to me? (*She turns around, sees* 1st Robot, *screams, and falls to floor, covering her eyes. Then she slowly looks up, and gets up angrily.*) Henry Follansbee! You can't fool me. (*She goes over and pokes at* 1st Robot.) I know it's you. So *this* is your new invention—a suit of metal to make you look like a robot. Well, you can just take the suit off right now, and get to work. Our customers will start coming in any minute. (*She pushes* 1st Robot.) Go ahead, Henry! You heard me. (Henry *enters briskly. He carries some coiled tubing and some boxes with colored buttons on them.*)

Henry: Good morning, Agatha, my dear. It *is* a good morning, isn't it? (Agatha *stares at him, putting her hand over her mouth.*) The sun is shining, the sky is blue—and I'm really excited about my latest invention.

Agatha (*Pointing to* 1st Robot, *then to* Henry): Henry —I thought—Henry—who—who—

Henry: Now, now, my dear, stop saying "who, who" like an owl. As you always say, we have no time to play games when our customers will be coming any minute.

Agatha: Henry—who is that creature?

Henry: Why, that's my new invention, of course. I told you I was working on something wonderful. (*Pats* 1st Robot) Oh, you are a marvel, you wonderful creature!

Agatha: Henry, get it out of here.

HENRY: Oh, my dear, I can't do that. We're going to sell these in the shop. As a matter of fact, I have a little surprise for you. Yesterday while you were gone, I sold two of them. And I'm sure I'm going to sell the rest today. We'll make a fortune. I'll bring in the rest of them now, my dear. (*He presses buttons on his boxes, and* 2ND, 3RD, *and* 4TH ROBOTS *march in and stand beside the* 1ST ROBOT. AGATHA *tries to get them to go out.*)

AGATHA: Go away! Shoo! Get out of here! Henry, make them go away. I won't have them in the shop. (*She takes candy out of big box and puts it on counter.*)

HENRY (*Fussing over* ROBOTS): Agatha, my dear, you don't understand. These robots are marvels of science. Customers love them.

AGATHA: Last year you invented an electric back-scratcher. How many of those did you sell?

HENRY (*Hopefully*): One?

AGATHA: You didn't sell any! The year before that, it was the automatic fire maker.

HENRY: Well, you must admit the automatic fire maker was a good idea. How was I to know I had invented matches?

AGATHA: Henry, I am going out to do the marketing. I want you to stay in the shop while I'm gone—and I want you to get those—those creatures out of here. Now! (AGATHA *goes out the door of the shop.* HENRY *dusts off* ROBOTS *as the door opens, and* ANN, SUSIE *and* TOMMY *enter.* HENRY *greets the children happily, rubbing his hands.*) Aha! Our first customers today. Good morning, children.

ANN: Good morning. We've come to buy a birthday present for our mother.

SUSIE: We have three dollars. Each of us saved a whole dollar.

TOMMY: We'd like to buy the same candy we bought last year. It was delicious.

ANN: Tommy, we're not going to buy candy this year. Last year you ate almost the whole box, all by yourself.

SUSIE: He got sick, too.

TOMMY (*Indignantly*): I did not!

ANN: This year let's buy something just for Mother. I think she'd like some jewelry.

HENRY: Ah, my young friends, candy and jewelry are all very nice, but this week the gift shop has something very special. (*He gestures to* ROBOTS.) This week, the gift shop is offering, for the very first time anywhere, the Mother's Mechanical Helper.

TOMMY (*Examining* ROBOTS): Mother's Mechanical Helper? What's that?

SUSIE: What can it do?

ANN: Does it do the dishes? Will it scrub the floor?

HENRY: Well, no. These Mother's Mechanical Helpers are the very first models, and they can do only one job. They pick things up off the floor.

TOMMY: Wow! Do you mean that if I left my pajamas on the floor, one of these robots would pick them up?

ANN: If I dropped my schoolbooks on the floor, would a Mother's Mechanical Helper pick them up?

HENRY: Yes, yes, of course! What bright children you are.

SUSIE: I'm not sure I understand how they do it.

HENRY: Let me give you a demonstration. Now, we'll need lots of things on the floor for the robots to pick up. (*He looks around, sees some large wastebaskets loaded with paper at one side of the stage.*) Aha! The wastebaskets! Now children, each of you take a wastebasket and throw the papers in it all over the floor. (*The children take the wastebaskets and scatter papers all over the stage.*)

TOMMY: Whee! This is fun.

ANN: I hope the robots really do pick this up. I'd certainly hate to do it.

SUSIE: The floor looks like my room when I've been making something.

TOMMY (*Looking around*): It sure is a mess.

HENRY (*Rubbing hands*): It's just fine. The messier the better, for my robots. Now, I wind up the robots. (*He turns a crank in back of each* ROBOT.) One—two—three. Then I press the button marked "Walk" and then the button marked "Pick Up." (*He presses buttons on the back of each* ROBOT. *As he does so, the* ROBOTS *set to work. They walk around the stage stiffly, picking up the papers and putting them back in the wastebaskets.*)

TOMMY: Wow! Look at them work!

ANN: They really do pick things up.

SUSIE: Mother would never have to scold us again when we leave things on the floor. (2ND ROBOT *picks up* HENRY'S *coiled tubing and puts it in a wastebasket.* HENRY *gets it back.*)

HENRY: Now, now, now, I need this. (*When the* ROBOTS *have finished, they march back to their places and stand stiffly.* HENRY *smiles proudly.*) Well, what do you think of my robots?

TOMMY: They're great.

ANN: We certainly need one in our house.

SUSIE: But how much do they cost? We have only three dollars.

HENRY: Well, they would be rather expensive—but I'm anxious to have mothers try them out, so I'm offering them at a special price. They cost just three dollars. But if you buy one now, you must promise me that you'll let your mother try it out right away.

SUSIE: But we shouldn't give Mother her present before her birthday.

ANN: Just this once, we could. Besides, we could never hide the robot in a closet. It's too big.

TOMMY: Come on, girls. Let's buy one. (*He gives* HENRY *the money.*)

HENRY: Thank you. Now, which color belt would you like? All the robots are the same, but I've given them different belts.

SUSIE: I want the red belt. (*She points to* 3RD ROBOT.)

HENRY: Fine, fine. Now, just press the button marked "Walk," and the robot will come with you. (TOMMY *presses the button, and* 3RD ROBOT *begins to walk.*)

TOMMY: Come on, girls. We'd better go.

ANN: Goodbye.

HENRY: Goodbye—and let me know how your mother likes the Mother's Mechanical Helper. (ANN, SUSIE, *and* TOMMY *go out with* 3RD ROBOT. HENRY *rubs his hands happily.*) Well! Another sale already. My robots are a success. (*The door opens, and* DAN *and* ELLEN *enter with* 5TH ROBOT.)

ELLEN: Hello.

HENRY: What's this? Aren't you the children who bought the Mother's Mechanical Helper yesterday?

DAN: We certainly are.

ELLEN: We want to return it and get our money back.

HENRY: What's wrong? Did the robot break down? (*He turns the dials at the back of* 5TH ROBOT.)

DAN: It works all right, but our mother doesn't like it.

HENRY (*Astonished*): What? Your mother doesn't like the Mother's Mechanical Helper? I can't believe it!

ELLEN: My mother says we can't go through life expecting a robot to be around to pick things up.

DAN: She says we have to learn to pick up our own things.

ELLEN: So she told us to return the robot and get her something else for her birthday instead.

HENRY (*Insulted*): Very well. If that is the way your mother feels, I will certainly return your money.

DAN: Thank you. We'll buy Mom a box of candy, instead. (DAN *and* ELLEN *go to candy counter with* HENRY *and pick out a box of candy. He puts it in a bag, and* DAN *and* ELLEN *exit.* HENRY *goes to the* 5TH ROBOT *and brushes it off.* JOE *and* LISA *enter with* 6TH ROBOT.)

LISA: Good morning. We've come to ask you if we could return our Mother's Mechanical Helper and get our money back.

JOE: Our mother doesn't want the Mechanical Helper.

HENRY (*Annoyed*): Indeed! And *why* doesn't your mother want a Mechanical Helper?

LISA: Well—we've had the Mechanical Helper for two days. Every time something was dropped on the floor, we pressed the buttons and the robot picked it up.

HENRY: But that is exactly what the Mechanical Helper is supposed to do! What, may I ask, is wrong with that?

LISA: We have seven children in our family—and our mother is used to having things all over the place.

JOE: She says she can't stand a neat house. She likes to have stuff around.

LISA: Mother says she feels sorry for the people who have no children. Their houses are always neat.

JOE: She says children just naturally make things messy— but she *likes* it that way.

HENRY (*Shaking his head and pulling at his beard*): I just can't believe it! I just don't understand it!

LISA: So please, sir, could we have our money back?

HENRY: Very well. I certainly don't want any dissatisfied customers.

JOE: Thank you very much, sir.

LISA: Let's get Mom some flowers. She always likes lots of flowers. (*They go to flower display.*)

JOE: These are very pretty. (*He points to some flowers.*)

LISA: O. K. May we have a nice big bunch, please?

HENRY (*Taking flowers and wrapping them*): Yes. I hope your mother likes these.

LISA: I'm sure she will. (JOE *and* LISA *take flowers and exit.* HENRY *straightens counter as* TOMMY, ANN, *and* SUSIE *enter with* 3RD ROBOT.)

HENRY (*Brightly*): Ah, children! What fine children you are! You promised to let me know how you liked the Mother's Mechanical Helper, and here you are back, good as your word. Well, how are things going? I'm sure you're delighted, simply delighted!

TOMMY: Well, no—we're not exactly delighted.

ANN: In fact, we don't like the Mechanical Helper.

SUSIE: I don't like it at all.

HENRY (*Bewildered*): You—you don't like it? (*The three children shake their heads "No."*) Why—why don't you like it?

TOMMY: Well, you see, when we pick things up, we put them where they belong.

ANN: But the robot can't think. It just throws everything into the wastebasket.

SUSIE: I had a paper doll on the floor with all the scraps of paper from my cutting—and the robot threw the doll away with everything else. When my mother picks up, she always saves the important things.

TOMMY: The robot threw out my pajamas, my new baseball mitt, and my sneakers.

HENRY (*Stroking his beard*): Hm-m. I never considered this. I shall have to give it some thought.

TOMMY: While you're thinking, could we have our money back?

HENRY: Very well. (*He gives* TOMMY *the money.*)

ANN: I guess we should buy candy after all.

TOMMY: O. K. Let's get a big box of chocolates. (TOMMY,

ANN *and* SUSIE *go to candy counter.* HENRY *sits sadly at center.*)

HENRY (*Gesturing to* ROBOTS): All of them—returned. All my wonderful, marvelous robots. My whole life's work—and no one wants them. (*He takes out a large handkerchief and dabs sadly at his eyes.* AGATHA *enters carrying a shopping bag, which she places on the counter.*)

AGATHA: Henry! I thought I told you to get those robots out of here.

HENRY (*Rising*): Yes, my dear. I'll take them back to my workshop now. You were right. No one wants to buy them.

AGATHA: Of course I was right. You and your inventions.

HENRY: I just can't understand it. I was sure I had invented something wonderful. (MAYOR PORTLY *enters.*)

MAYOR: Good morning, good morning. I've come to buy an anniversary present for my wife.

AGATHA: Good morning, Mayor Portly. I'm sure we can help you.

MAYOR: I've made out a list of what my wife needs. Let me see—where did I put that list? (*The* MAYOR *begins to pull papers out of his pockets. He reads from each paper, then shakes his head and pulls out another paper.*) "Bacon, lettuce, cheese . . ." No, that isn't it. "New lights for the City Hall . . ." No, that isn't it. "Dog licenses . . ." No, that isn't it, either. Oh, dear, where is my list of presents? (*The* MAYOR *drops his papers all over the floor.*) Good gracious, now look what I've done! (TOMMY *runs up to* 4TH ROBOT *and presses the buttons. The* 4TH ROBOT *picks up the papers and starts for a wastebasket with them.* TOMMY *gets the papers from* 4TH ROBOT *and gives them back to the astonished* MAYOR. *The* 4TH ROBOT *returns to place.*)

TOMMY: Here are your papers, Mr. Mayor.

MAYOR (*Pointing to* 4TH ROBOT): What did that creature do? What *did* that creature do?

TOMMY: It picked up your papers. That's Mr. Follansbee's Mechanical Helper. It picks up anything on the floor and puts it in a wastebasket.

MAYOR: A Mechanical Helper? A Mechanical Helper? (*He smiles, jumps up in the air, and drops the papers again. This time* HENRY *pushes the buttons,* 4TH ROBOT *picks up the papers,* HENRY *gets them and hands them to the delighted* MAYOR, *who hugs* HENRY.) My dear Mr. Follansbee! My dear, dear, dear Mr. Follansbee! How wonderful! How perfectly wonderful!

HENRY (*Sadly*): Your wife won't like a Mechanical Helper, Mr. Mayor.

MAYOR: Wife? Wife? Who said anything about a wife? These robots are just what I've always dreamed about.

HENRY: Your secretary won't like one, either.

MAYOR: My dear Mr. Follansbee, will you let me speak? Ahem! As you know, this town has a litter-bug problem. Every town has a litter-bug problem, but in this town, the litter-bug problem is my problem because I am the mayor. Now, for years, I have tried to think of some way to keep the streets of our fair town clean. People do forget, you know. They drop papers, gum wrappers—oh, all sorts of things—on the streets of our town.

HENRY (*Becoming excited*): My Mechanical Helpers wouldn't stand for that. They'd pick up all the litter and put it in the wastebaskets on the street corners.

MAYOR: Exactly. We'll use your robots to keep our town clean. They'll be wonderful.

HENRY (*Excited*): They'll be perfect!

MAYOR: We'll buy all you have! We'll send them all over town!

HENRY: My Mechanical Helpers will keep the town clean!

(HENRY *and the* MAYOR *shake hands and dance around happily. The children and* AGATHA *cheer.*) I'll re-name the robots. Instead of the Mother's Mechanical Helpers, I'll call them the Mayor's Mechanical Helpers.

MAYOR (*Pleased*): Wonderful, wonderful! (*He stops and thinks.*) Now, let me think. Why did I come in here?

AGATHA: You came in to buy a present for your wife. (*She picks up various items from counters.*) Now, Mayor, your wife might like flowers, or jewelry, or—

HENRY: Agatha, my dear, I'm afraid that will have to wait. The Mayor and I have business to talk over. I know you will excuse us while we go to my workshop to make plans. (*He takes the* MAYOR's *arm.*)

MAYOR: Yes, yes, of course. We must make plans. (*They start off slowly, arm in arm.*)

AGATHA: Henry! Come back here at once.

HENRY: I can't do that, my dear. I must get back to work on my inventions. After all, *I* am the inventor of the Mayor's Mechanical Helpers. (*He bows to her, then leads the* MAYOR *off as she stares after him.*)

AGATHA: Well, I never! (*She drops the flowers and jewelry on the floor.*)

SUSIE (*Coming over*): I'll help you pick them up.

TOMMY: No, let the robots do it. (ANN, TOMMY, *and* SUSIE *quickly press buttons. The* ROBOTS *start over.* AGATHA *is already kneeling on the floor, picking up flowers. The* ROBOTS *pick up* AGATHA *and go toward the wastebasket with her, while she screams for help and the curtains close.*)

THE END

The Mysterious Stranger

by Jessie Nicholson

Characters

PETER LISTER
NATALIE, *his sister*
MRS. LISTER
MR. LISTER
BERNICE, *the maid*
TWO POLICE OFFICERS

TIME: *Late afternoon.*

SETTING: *The living room of the Lister home.*

AT RISE: PETER *is crawling around the living room floor, a large magnifying glass in his hand, examining every square inch carefully. Several times he picks up something between thumb and finger and puts it carefully between the folds of a sheet of paper.*

NATALIE (*Entering from hall*): For goodness' sake, Peter Lister, what are you doing? Still looking for that nickel you lost last week?

PETER (*Growling*): No, silly, I'm looking for clues—ah! (*Holding up something triumphantly between thumb and finger*)

NATALIE: Clues? What on earth are you talking about?

And what do you have in your hand? I don't see anything.

PETER (*Excitedly*): Look closely, my girl. It's a hair—a
red hair! If that isn't a clue, I don't know what is.
Nobody in our family has red hair.

NATALIE: Nobody in our family has a screw loose, either,
except you, Peter Lister!

PETER: Just wait till I build up my case. Then we'll see
who has a screw loose.

NATALIE: Case—what case? I never heard anything so
ridiculous.

PETER: Perhaps you hadn't noticed it but things have
been disappearing around here (*Lowering his voice*)
mysteriously! Tuesday, Bernice couldn't find the clean
dust cloths she'd cut up the day before; Wednesday,
one of Pop's best blue socks was gone from the drawer
and Thursday (*Looking all about cautiously*), Mom's
toothbrush was missing!

NATALIE (*Sarcastically*): And so today you went out and
bought a book on "How to Become a Detective" in
six easy lessons.

PETER: Yes—and that wasn't all. (*Whipping a Sherlock
Holmes plaid cap and a false beard out of his pocket
and putting them on hastily and rather crookedly*) How
do I look?

NATALIE: Like something that belongs in a zoo. Of all
the kid stuff!

PETER: All right, you just wait and see, Miss Smarty. Once
I really get my teeth into this detecting job—

NATALIE (*Interrupting*): We'll all be able to sleep safely
in our beds, I suppose—ha, ha!

PETER (*Coldly*): Some day you will thank the brother who
was willing to take his life in his hands to solve a crime.

NATALIE: Oh, you make me hysterical—really hysterical.
(*Laughing shrilly*)

PETER (*Bitingly*): Just like a hyena. You even look something like one.

NATALIE: Very funny. Well, I'm going to go and do something *constructive*.

PETER: Like tying up the telephone on the upstairs extension for an hour or two talking to Jack Mills, I suppose?

NATALIE (*Tossing her head*): I'll be too busy getting my clothes ready for the high school dance tomorrow night to bother with telephone calls. You may have the rest of the afternoon to talk to your little friends! Before I go, I just have to find my gold shoes. (*She begins to look under chairs, sofa, table, etc.*)

PETER (*Looking up with interest*): Another mysterious disappearance, eh?

NATALIE (*Disgustedly*): Don't be silly! (*Calling offstage*) Mother—oh, *Mother!*

MRS. LISTER (*Coming to door*): Yes, dear. What is it?

NATALIE: Have you seen my gold evening shoes? They aren't in my shoe bag and they aren't in the closet.

MRS. LISTER: Why, no, I haven't seen them. Better have another look.

NATALIE (*Wailing*): But I have looked—just everywhere.

MRS. LISTER: They must be somewhere. Come and I'll help you look. (NATALIE *and* MRS. LISTER *exit.*)

PETER: We really need a detective in this house. (*Telephone rings. With a groan of disgust,* PETER *gets up and answers phone.*) Hello. . . . Natalie? Sorry, old man, she's too busy to bother with telephone calls today. . . . Yes, too busy—that's what she said. . . . Well, you don't have to believe me.

NATALIE (*In doorway*): Peter, who's that on the phone?

PETER (*Nonchalantly, holding hand over mouthpiece*): Nobody particular. Just Jack Mills. You don't have to worry—I told him you were too busy to bother with telephone calls this afternoon.

NATALIE (*Rushing to phone furiously*): You didn't! Give me that phone!

PETER (*In disgust*): Oh, all right—here. I might have known I couldn't have any privacy to carry on my important investigations.

NATALIE: Hello—hello—are you there, Jack—hello— HELLO. (*Slams down receiver, and turns on brother*) You beast!

PETER: Don't tell me good old Jack fell for that line. Of all the absolutely killing situations! (*Laughs noisily*)

NATALIE (*Approaching her brother threateningly*): Killing situations is right. Oh, what I'd like to do to you!

MRS. LISTER (*Entering from back of house*): What are you two quarreling about now?

NATALIE: He told Jack I wouldn't speak to him on the phone and— (*Sniffling unhappily*) and Jack hung up.

MRS. LISTER: What did you do that for, Peter?

PETER (*Defensively*): She said she didn't want to be bothered with any telephone calls this afternoon. What was I supposed to do?

MRS. LISTER: Did you tell him that, Natalie?

NATALIE (*Desperately*): Well, yes—in a way. That is, not exactly.

MRS. LISTER: Either you did or you didn't, dear.

NATALIE (*Bitterly*): Well, yes, then, but—but (*Miserably*) I wasn't really expecting any calls. Jack was supposed to be working this afternoon after school. Now, my whole life is probably ruined. He'll probably never speak to me again.

MRS. LISTER (*Hiding a smile*): Oh, dear, I don't think it will go as far as that. I'm sure Peter will be willing to call up Jack and explain.

NATALIE (*Tearfully*): Explain? How can anyone explain a thing like that?

PETER: Easy as pie. I'll just tell Jack you wanted to make sure you didn't talk to any old Tom, Dick or Harry.

NATALIE: Tom, Dick or Harry—oh! You just keep your hands off that phone from now on. You know Jack is jealous. (MR. LISTER *enters, carrying a briefcase and looking decidedly annoyed.*)

MRS. LISTER: Why, Frank, you're home early. Is there anything wrong?

MR. LISTER (*Explosively*): Is there anything wrong? I'll say there is! That paper I worked over last evening and had ready for my client to sign today disappeared right out of my briefcase. I was never so embarrassed in my life!

MRS. LISTER: You mean you forgot to take it with you, don't you? You could have phoned, dear, and I would have sent Peter right down with it.

MR. LISTER: No, Cora, I did *not* forget it. That paper was the last thing I put in my briefcase before going to bed.

MRS. LISTER (*Persisting*): But it must be here, dear. (*Going through papers on desk hurriedly*)

PETER (*Cheerfully*): You won't find it, Mother. Something tells me it's completely disappeared.

MR. LISTER (*Sharply*): See here, Peter, what do you know about it?

PETER (*Hastily*): Oh, nothing, nothing.

MR. LISTER (*Suspiciously*): If you've done anything with that paper, young man—

PETER: Oh, not me. It's the mysterious stranger who's responsible for this mysterious disappearance. That's where your paper went, Dad, along with everything else.

MR. LISTER: Everything else? What gibberish are you talking?

PETER (*Checking items off on fingers*): Well, first, it was

Bernice's dustcloths that were missing, then your blue
sock, then Mom's toothbrush; this afternoon, Natalie's
gold slippers, and now— (*Shrugging, with hands out-
stretched*)

MR. LISTER: Nonsense. You aren't implying we're harbor-
ing a thief in our midst, are you?

PETER: What else? I call him the mysterious stranger. But
never fear, Dad, you have me working on the case. I'll
soon have it solved.

MR. LISTER (*Dryly*): I'm sure you will. In the meantime,
I'll ask for complete quiet in the living room for the
remainder of the afternoon while I rewrite the paper
which so *mysteriously* disappeared.

PETER (*Protesting*): But, Father, I'm working in here. I've
already dug up some very leading clues. I assure you I
won't make a sound.

MR. LISTER: You'll look for your clues elsewhere, young
man.

MRS. LISTER: Now, Frank, just because you mislaid your
papers, there's no reason for taking it out on Peter.

MR. LISTER: Mislaid! How many times do I have to tell
you—(BERNICE *enters, looking panicky*)

MRS. LISTER: Why, Bernice, what's the matter?

BERNICE: I tell you, the strangest thing happened. I was
cleaning celery at the sink and I went to stir something
on the stove and—and—

MR. LISTER (*Roaring*): And what, Bernice? I asked for
peace and quiet, but I can't seem to get it around here.

MRS. LISTER: Sh-h-h, Frank. Go on, Bernice, what happened?

BERNICE (*Twisting her apron around her finger nervously*):
Well, you won't believe it but that celery disappeared
right out from under my nose!

PETER: Aha!

MR. LISTER (*Irritably*): Keep still, Peter, for heaven's sake!

MRS. LISTER: What do you mean, Bernice?

BERNICE: Well, ma'am, when I turned around from the stove, that celery was gone—clean gone! (PETER *hastily puts on cap and beard and slips out of room unnoticed.*)

MR. LISTER: Nonsense. You'll probably find it in the bottom of the soup kettle. If you'd get that boy friend off your mind once in a while, we'd all be better off. (BERNICE *bursts into sobs, throws her apron over her head and runs out.*)

MRS. LISTER: Frank, now you've hurt her feelings. Bernice broke up with her boy friend two weeks ago.

MR. LISTER: Broke up with her boy friend, eh? Probably spends all her time trying to figure out how to get him back. We'll very likely get a dish of stewed celery for dessert. There's nothing like a woman scorned! (*At these words* NATALIE *also bursts into tears and runs out.*)

MRS. LISTER: See what you've done now, Frank Lister? You ought to be ashamed of yourself. Besides you needn't worry about what you're getting for dessert tonight. We're dining with the Merediths.

MR. LISTER (*Protestingly*): Oh, no—not tonight! What about my paper?

MRS. LISTER (*Looking at her watch*): You'll have at least twenty minutes to work on it. It won't take you any longer than that, will it?

MR. LISTER (*Groaning*): I spent four hours on that paper last evening. And now you want to know if I can rewrite it in twenty minutes!

MRS. LISTER (*Calmly*): You'll just have to do the best you can, Frank. It's your own fault, you know. If you hadn't been so careless with your first copy—

MR. LISTER (*Ominously*): Now, Cora! (*Then throwing up his hands*) Oh, what's the use? I'm going upstairs and lock myself in the den and I don't want to be disturbed.

Is that clearly understood? (*Without waiting for an answer, he snatches up his briefcase and exits.*)

MRS. LISTER (*Going about and putting on lights*): I'll give Bernice the evening off. It may cheer her up. (*She exits. PETER, wearing cap and beard, tiptoes in carrying something before him in folded sheet of paper. He looks all around cautiously and then removes large stalk of half-eaten celery from paper.*)

PETER (*Holding up his find*): My most important clue to date. The missing celery. (*Looking straight out at audience*) Now who would want to eat celery in the bathroom, I ask you?

NATALIE (*Entering from hall*): So, it was you who took Bernice's celery? You ought to be ashamed of yourself, scaring her like that. Of all the kid tricks!

PETER (*Indignantly*): I did not! I found this in the bathroom. You know I never eat celery.

NATALIE: You'd do anything for laughs.

PETER: Not eat celery. I loathe the stuff. (*BERNICE enters, still sniffing and carrying tray with napkin over it. PETER hastily hides celery behind him.*)

BERNICE (*Looking neither to right nor left*): Here's your supper. (*Sniff, sniff*) Your ma told me to leave it here on the table for you. (*Sniff, sniff*) I hope you enjoy it. (*Glancing up, she sees PETER in cap and beard and screams in fright, and stands rooted to the spot.*)

NATALIE: Don't be scared, Bernice. It's just Peter. He thinks he's Sherlock Holmes, stalking criminals.

PETER (*Leering at BERNICE*): Oh, no, I'm just stalking, Bernice. First celery stalks, then Peter stalks! (*Grinning horribly*)

NATALIE (*As BERNICE throws her apron over her head and runs from room*): Of all the mean, contemptible things to do! As if taking the celery right out from under her nose wasn't enough, without taunting her about it.

PETER: Oh, what's the use? I might as well go and lock myself in my room like Dad, where I can give this case my undivided attention. (*Just then* MR. *and* MRS. LISTER *enter, wearing coats,* MR. LISTER *looking martyred.* PETER *conceals cap and beard hastily.*)

MRS. LISTER (*To* PETER *and* NATALIE): Eat your supper, and go to bed as soon as you get your homework done.

MR. LISTER (*Groaning*): Homework! When I think of all the homework I still have to do—

MRS. LISTER: Please, Frank.

PETER (*Aside, to his father, man to man*): I know how you feel, Dad. Women just don't understand.

MR. LISTER: You're so right, son. And what can we do about it? (*Sighs and starts to go. At door*) Goodbye, Peter—Natalie. (*Exits*)

MRS. LISTER: Goodbye, children. (MRS. LISTER *exits.* PETER *goes over to table and lifts napkin from tray.*)

PETER: Ye gods! Cold bean sandwiches and stewed prunes!

NATALIE (*Coldly*): It's your own fault. If you hadn't upset Bernice, it would probably have been chicken and chocolate cake.

PETER: *Me* upset Bernice? (*Groans*) Here we go again. (*A loud bang is heard from offstage.*)

NATALIE: What do you suppose that was?

PETER (*Hastily putting on cap and beard*): Don't be frightened, my girl. I'll handle this.

NATALIE: Who's frightened? It was probably just that window upstairs with the broken cord falling. You were supposed to fix that days ago.

PETER (*In disgust*): You just aren't taking this thing seriously enough. If you'd let me work this case out in my own way—

NATALIE: For heaven's sakes, go work it out upstairs and leave me alone. I've some important reading to catch

up on and besides I may get a telephone call any minute
now—which I want to take in complete privacy.

PETER: If Jack Mills is as smart as I think he is, he'll know
when he's well off and keep his ugly mug away from
the telephone. (*Starts out door.*)

NATALIE: Get out of here! (*Flings a magazine at his hastily
departing figure. She then retrieves it and holds it open
in front of her so that it can be seen by audience. It is
a copy of "Romances." She takes box of chocolates from
under sofa cushion and tossing herself down on her
stomach, begins reading and munching a piece of candy.
Suddenly, the door leading to back of house opens just
a trifle and then closes again. She sits up abruptly.*) Is
that you, Peter? (*She gets up and moves cautiously toward the door. The door handle turns squeakily, and
NATALIE gives a loud shriek. As she turns to rush out
into the hall, she collides with PETER, rushing in.*)

PETER: What's the matter? What happened? (*NATALIE
points speechlessly to the other door. PETER tiptoes toward it and presses his ear to the crack. Then he reaches
for paper knife on desk and with finger raised to lips for
silence, he drops on knees and runs paper knife hastily
beneath door. When nothing happens, he looks decidedly chagrined.*) My detective book says that a trick
like that ought to make anyone lurking on the other
side of the door give himself away.

NATALIE (*Furiously*): You and your detective book! I probably just imagined this whole thing. The way you've
been talking about clues and mysterious strangers is
enough to give *anyone* the creeps. You can go right back
upstairs and stay there. I'm going on with my reading
and improve my mind.

PETER (*Jeeringly*): With this? (*Picking up magazine. Then
he spies open box of chocolates beside it. Pounces on it*)
So, you've been holding out on me?

NATALIE: Well, it was a present to *me*. Besides, I just opened it. I didn't have a chance to give you any.

PETER: Just opened it? Whew? You're a fast worker. Half of the top layer is gone already!

NATALIE (*Staring at open box in amazement*) But *I* ate only one piece!

PETER (*Shaking his head*): You really ought to start checking up on yourself, my girl. Your mind is slipping. Here, I'll just relieve you of the rest of the layer so you won't be tempted to eat too many. (*He helps himself generously, setting box back on sofa and leaving his sister staring in bewilderment at candy as he leaves.*)

NATALIE: I can't understand it. I'm sure I didn't eat more than one. (*Staring straight out at audience with hand over mouth in gesture of dismay*) Or did I? Like that girl in the picture the other night who got all mixed up and had to be put away in an asylum? (*Suddenly the phone rings and* NATALIE *jumps nervously, then answers it.*) H-Hello—oh, hello, J-Jack. . . . No, I'm all r-right. (*Hopefully*) Are you coming over? . . . You're what? You're helping the police look for an escaped—hello—Jack—hello! (*Frantically jiggling receiver*) Hello—hello—oh, dear, we've been cut off. Oh, Peter! (PETER *enters on the run*)

PETER (*Breathlessly*): What's happened now?

NATALIE: I was talking to Jack and we were cut off!

PETER: Shucks, is that all?

NATALIE: He was just telling me he was helping the police look for someone who'd escaped, when the line went dead.

PETER: Whew, that sounds bad. I hope the poor chap hasn't been taken for a ride.

NATALIE (*In horror*): Peter!

PETER (*Cheerfully*): Well, it can happen to the best of us, you know. We who are in charge of law and order walk a dangerous path. Say, wait a minute. If there's some criminal loose in the community, he might—(*Swallowing hard and running a finger inside his collar*) he might be right here in this house now! (*Looking fearfully towards door leading into kitchen*)

NATALIE: Oh, Peter, do you really think so?

PETER: There've been a lot of strange things happening around here lately. Look at all the stuff that's disappeared.

NATALIE: But what would any thief want with Mom's toothbrush or—or one of Dad's socks?

PETER: Maybe he's a klepto—klepto—

NATALIE: Kleptomaniac. They do take strange things, don't they?

PETER: Here, give me that phone. A good detective always knows when it's time to call in the police. (NATALIE *hands him the phone.* PETER *lifts the receiver and listens. Frowns.*) The line's as dead as a dodo bird. (*In sudden dismay*) It was at our end you were cut off—not Jack's! (*He gets down on hands and knees and follows the telephone cord out into the hall. From there he emits a low groan.*)

NATALIE (*Fearfully*): What is it, Peter?

PETER (*In doorway*): The line's been cut with Mom's shears! They're here on the floor.

NATALIE (*Wailing*): Oh, Peter, we have to call Mother and Dad right away.

PETER (*Returning to living room*): How can we do that, silly, with the wire cut? (*Panicky now*) We have to get away from here—pronto! (*Starts to dash out, then turns back somewhat sheepishly for his sister*) What are you just standing there for? Come on!

NATALIE (*Weakly*): My l-legs feel sort of funny, Peter, as if they didn't want to move!

PETER: Shucks! (*Goes back and pushes her ahead of him,*

without noticing that he has dropped his false beard he was carrying in his hand) Girls get so scared! If it weren't for you, I'd stick this thing out and capture the criminal myself. *(They exit, the front door closing noisily after them. Presently, MR. and MRS. LISTER enter.)*

MRS. LISTER *(Removing her wraps)*: Well, I hope you're satisfied, Frank Lister—coming home this early. I don't know what Fred and Alice must have thought of you, I'm sure. All through dinner you kept looking at your watch. I'm sure they were glad to have us go home.

MR. LISTER *(Chuckling)*: That was just the way I wanted it.

MRS. LISTER: Oh, you were clever all right. But just remember Alice Meredith is—was *(Falteringly)* my best friend.

MR. LISTER *(Soothingly)*: And still is, my dear. She won't blame you for my shortcomings, only pity you for being married to such a big boor.

MRS. LISTER: Don't think you can soften me up because it won't work. *(Suddenly a loud thud is heard offstage.)* What was that?

MR. LISTER: Probably Peter, throwing his book on the floor before he puts out the light. I'll just run up and say good night and bring my papers downstairs to finish. *(He exits.)*

MRS. LISTER *(Going about straightening up living room; she picks up box of candy)*: My, my, Natalie shouldn't eat so many sweets. She knows it's bad for her complexion. *(Replaces lid and puts box back on table. Picks up PETER's false beard.)* Goodness gracious, what's this? It looks like a man's beard! *(Looking about a little fearfully)*

MR. LISTER *(From offstage, excitedly)*: Cora, my papers are gone again, *(Rushing in breathlessly)* and the children aren't in their rooms!

Mrs. Lister: Oh, Frank! And I found this—this thing on the floor!

Mr. Lister: Good heavens—a false beard! I'll call the police right away. (*Rushing to phone*) Hello—hello! (*Jiggles receiver up and down. Nervously*) The phone is dead!

Mrs. Lister (*Falteringly*): That noise that—that we heard upstairs—there must be a burglar in the house.

Mr. Lister: I never suspected that paper I was preparing had criminal implications.

Mrs. Lister: What are we going to do—oh, Frank, the children!

Mr. Lister: Now, Cora, be calm. (*His voice rising*) We must think this thing out sensibly. (*Paces back and forth nervously running fingers through his hair*)

Mrs. Lister (*Regaining her self-control*): We'll think it out more sensibly with the help of the police. Come along, Frank, we'll go next door and telephone them. (*Leads him determinedly through hall door. A moment or two later, PETER enters from outside, looking very crestfallen. He flings Sherlock Holmes cap into wastebasket in evident disgust, then going to table, picks up bean sandwich which he consumes mournfully. Finally, gathering up schoolbooks on desk, he slouches out of room. MR. and MRS. LISTER enter, followed by a POLICE OFFICER.*)

Mr. Lister: I'm certainly glad you were in the neighborhood, officer.

Officer: Sure now, they've had the boys out all day combing this area. Nothing but complaints it is we've been having.

Mr. Lister: You mean there've been other robberies, officer?

Officer: That I do. Not a house on this street has been missed. Why even the flag was removed from the precinct station flagpole, in the broad light of day, too, mind you.

MR. LISTER: Some important papers of mine have been stolen. The thief must be very crafty and intelligent, officer. Why, he knew enough to attach more importance to those papers than I did myself. He stole them twice!

MRS. LISTER (*In great distress*): How can you talk about papers, Frank, when our children have been kidnapped?

OFFICER (*His jaw dropping in amazement*): Saints alive, that's a new angle. You wouldn't be trying to kid me now, would you?

MRS. LISTER (*Indignantly*): Certainly not!

OFFICER: I'm sorry, ma'am. No offense meant, I can assure you. But I thought you folks knew—(*Just then the doorbell rings loudly.* MR. LISTER *rushes to answer it, while* MRS. LISTER *leans against the sofa for support, looking frightened.* 2ND OFFICER *enters with* MR. LISTER. *The* OFFICER *is carrying small valise.*)

2ND OFFICER: Well, it's all over, folks. They finally have him in custody down at headquarters. He was caught red-handed right outside your own house. Had his cache stowed away in the shrubbery. We've had quite a time getting the stuff straightened out, I can tell you. Hope I have all your belongings here. (*Dumping contents of bag out on table, he holds up each item for inspection*) One pair of gold shoes—guess he had a girl friend. (*Chuckling*) One blue sock—choosy, wasn't he? One toothbrush with blue handle—blue must have been his favorite color—an assortment of rags—(*Looking blank*) this one has me stumped—and last but not least (*Inspecting the missing papers critically*), somebody's after-dinner speech—he must *really* have been hard up!

MR. LISTER (*Stiffly*): Those are some important law papers of mine, officer.

2ND OFFICER: My apologies, Mr. Lister. I guess we're all

feeling a bit silly after the merry-go-round we've been on. If it hadn't been for your son, we'd still be going round and round.

MRS. LISTER: Our son—Peter—where is he? (PETER, *who has come downstairs stealthily to listen, hastily conceals himself beyond hall doorway.*)

2ND OFFICER: Why, he was the one responsible for the capture, ma'am. A real hero. Saved us a lot of trouble.

MR. LISTER (*With pride*): My son! Capturing a criminal. (*Modestly*) It was I who taught him the art of fisticuffs, officer.

2ND OFFICER (*Scratching his head*): Well, now—I think this turned out to be more of a wrestling match than a fist fight. You might even call it a tooth-and-nail sort of affair, so to speak. (*At that moment* PETER *tries to slip back upstairs unnoticed, but* MR. LISTER *sees him.*)

MR. LISTER: Peter, come here. (MRS. LISTER *rushes and throws her arms around* PETER.)

MRS. LISTER: Oh, my poor boy, are you hurt?

PETER (*Disgustedly*): Shucks, no—you just don't understand, Mom.

MR. LISTER: We understand you are a hero, son. This officer said so. Now come and tell us all about it. How many blows did it take to knock the bruiser out?

PETER: I didn't knock him out. (*Desperately*) I—I sat on him!

MR. LISTER (*Boastfully*): Well, it must have taken a powerful lot of sitting, anyway.

PETER (*Miserably*): Not to sit on a—a monkey!

MR. LISTER (*Explosively*): A *what?* (*The* OFFICERS *exchange looks and exit hurriedly on tiptoe.*)

PETER: Yes—a trained monkey from the traveling circus over in North Dover. He escaped last Tuesday. (*In despair*) Oh, I'll never live this down!

NATALIE (*Entering from hall*): I should say you won't. Not

if I have anything to say about it—Mr. Sherlock Holmes!

PETER (*Sinking down on sofa dejectedly*): Life just isn't worth living! (MR. LISTER *is looking very exasperated, while* MRS. LISTER *is trying to restrain her smile.*)

2ND OFFICER (*Sticking his head back around door again, a broad grin on his face*): Forgot to tell you, Sherlock—there's a ten-dollar reward offered by his master for the capture of Roy, the Ringside Rocket. You're in the chips, young fellow. May make life worth living for you again.

PETER (*More cheerfully*): Ten dollars—whew! Now, that's just the price of the Astro-Kit I saw in McLean's window. I always did want to build a spaceship! (*Curtain*)

THE END

Teapot Trouble

by Jessie Nicholson

Characters

PETER TODD	MRS. THORPE
JILL TODD	MRS. BOUNCE
SALLY TODD	MR. HIGGINS
MRS. SLADE	MR. SNIFTER

SETTING: *The interior of an antique shop. Bells hanging on shop door ring as customers enter.*

AT RISE: SALLY *is sweeping the floor,* JILL *is dusting the shelves and antiques, and* PETER *strolls about supervising the job.*

PETER: Don't leave any dust in the corners, Sally. Jill, you're getting finger marks on that copper bowl! We have to keep everything looking just right while Mother's away, and prove to her that she didn't need to worry about leaving us alone while she went to take care of Grandmother.

JILL (*Grumbling*): That's all very well, but I still don't see why you shouldn't help with the cleaning up.

PETER: Mother left *me* in charge. You and Sally have to do what I tell you to.

SALLY: Well, I'm sick of all this dusting. It seems to me the dirtier things are, the older they look, so there!

435

(Gives duster an angry flip, knocks a cup on the floor and breaks it)

JILL: Now look what you've done. A fine way to show Mother how careful we're being!

SALLY: It's just a silly old cup without a handle. Who'd want a cup without a handle?

PETER *(Scornfully)*: Our ancestors did. You just don't know anything. The ladies used to pour their tea into little cup plates from cups without handles and sip it politely. It was considered very elegant.

SALLY *(Giggling)*: You don't think I'm going to believe that, do you? You're just trying to be funny. Imagine anybody drinking tea out of a plate!

JILL: And you're just showing your ignorance, Sally. Mother told us all about cup plates a long time ago. I can see you're going to be no help around here. Suppose somebody came in and wanted to buy a cup plate. You wouldn't even know what to sell them.

SALLY: But Mother said we weren't supposed to sell anything. Just show people around and tell them she'd be back again in a couple of days.

JILL: Wouldn't it be wonderful, though, if we could surprise her and make some good sales?

PETER: Or maybe make a real buy at the auction. A priceless heirloom for a mere—a mere pittance. *(Snapping his fingers)*

SALLY: How can you tell a priceless heirloom when you see it?

PETER: Oh, lots of ways. But my secret method *(Lowering his voice and looking around)* is by the smell. There's nothing like a good, old, musty smell. Yes, sir, a good, old, musty smell!

SALLY *(Aside)*: A good, old, musty smell. Now, I must remember that. A good, old, musty smell.

PETER: I thought maybe I'd go to the auction in the village

for a while. Who knows but what I might pick up something for a mere—

JILL: Yes, we know. A mere pittance. But where were you expecting to get the mere pittance to buy this choice piece with?

PETER: Out of the cash box, of course. (*Mysteriously*) That is, if the money *were* still in the cash box, which it isn't.

JILL: What do you mean?

PETER: Just that I hid the money someplace else. Where's a thief going to look first for money? In the cash box, of course. A stupid place to keep cash, I say.

SALLY (*Giggling*): I suppose you'd keep it in your sock.

PETER: No, I wouldn't, Miss Smarty.

JILL: Don't you know he gets too many holes in his socks to keep anything in them—not even his feet most of the time.

PETER: Just for that I won't tell either of you where I hid it. Good grief, here come some customers and this place isn't even half cleaned up. Take off your apron, Jill, and Sally, try to look a little intelligent. (MRS. SLADE *and* MRS. THORPE *enter right.* PETER *hurries forward in his best business manner.*)

PETER: May I show you something, ladies, or do you just wish to—to prowl around?

MRS. SLADE (*Indignantly*): Prowl indeed! I'll have you know, young man—

MRS. THORPE (*Interrupting hastily*): Such a nice young man, too, Mildred. I'm sure he'll help us find what we want.

MRS. SLADE (*Sharply, peering at* PETER *over the top of her spectacles*): That's what he's paid to do, Carrie. Now, young man, we want something choice for a very dear friend. Price is no object, but let me warn you, we will not be taken in. We know fakes when we see them. We can smell them!

SALLY (*Brightly*): Why, you've both got the same secret method. Peter smells, too, don't you, Peter? (MRS. SLADE *stares at* SALLY *distastefully.* PETER *gives her a sharp nudge with his elbow.*)

PETER (*Hastily*): My *little* sister is just trying to be funny, ha, ha! Now, let me show you this table here. (*Points to small, antique table, up center*) It's a very old piece. It dates back to—to—let me see—yes, to 1602.

MRS. THORPE: Really—how delightful, Mildred. Just think, 1602!

MRS. SLADE: Young man, the Pilgrims didn't arrive in this country until 1620!

PETER (*Running his finger around the inside of his collar nervously*): Did I say 1602—ha, ha!

MRS. SLADE: You certainly did.

PETER: What I meant was 1702, of course. Just a slip of the tongue.

MRS. THORPE: I know how it is, young man. I was never good at dates myself. Why, I remember when I was in the eighth grade—

MRS. SLADE (*Sharply*): Nonsense, Carrie. If you can't remember dates, you certainly can't remember what happened when you were in the eighth grade. And as for you, young man, that slip of the tongue will cost you dearly. I wouldn't even consider making a purchase in this shop now. I told you we would not be taken in. Come, Carrie. (MRS. SLADE *exits with her nose in air.* MRS. THORPE *follows, waving her hand timidly in silent farewell as she goes out the door.*)

JILL: Well, I must say, that was a fine mistake to make. Even Sally would have known better than that. (*Bitterly*) And price was no object—oh, dear!

SALLY: What I can't understand is how you tell the difference between the smell of an antique and the smell of a fake. How can you tell, Peter?

PETER (*Bitterly*): You and your smart remarks. (*Mimicking her*) Peter smells, too, don't you, Peter? That's what threw me off.

JILL: When Sally opens her mouth, she always puts her foot in it.

PETER: Both feet. Now she's probably spoiled a good sale for Mother.

SALLY (*Crestfallen*): I want to help Mother just as much as you do, Peter Todd!

PETER: Well, then be still and keep your nose out of things that don't concern you. (*Turning to* JILL) Let's start moving the furniture around. I'm tired of seeing things in the same place all the time. Give your shop a new look and people will take a second look—that's my motto. (*He and* JILL *set to work to rearrange the antiques.*)

SALLY (*To herself*): But if I keep my nose out of things, how will I know how they smell?

JILL (*Glancing toward shop door*): Look who's coming— old Mr. Higgins. We'll never be able to get rid of him. He looks at everything and never buys anything. Mother says he's a dreadful nuisance besides being a little cracked.

PETER: Let Sally take care of him. She can't do any harm there. (*They continue to arrange antiques.*)

SALLY (*Aside*): Maybe I'll even sell him something. Then they'll change their tune. (MR. HIGGINS *enters. He walks with little, mincing steps.*)

MR. HIGGINS: My, how pretty the bells are. I never tire of listening to them. I even hear them in my dreams.

SALLY (*Hurrying forward*): Good morning, Mr. Higgins. I'd just love to show you everything we have.

MR. HIGGINS: Oh, I've come to buy today—not just to look. Genevieve—that's my dear wife, you know—gave me a whole purse full of money to spend. Wasn't that sweet of her? And because she was so sweet I'm going to spend it all on her. (PETER *and* JILL *finish arranging the furniture and exit left, carrying broom and dusters.*)

SALLY (*Softly*): Whoopee—let's go! (*To* MR. HIGGINS) How about this very old table? (*She leans forward and sniffs appreciatively.*) It dates back to—let me see—did Peter say 1602 or 1702? Well, anyway, what difference do a few years make, more or less. It's the smell that counts.

MR. HIGGINS (*Sniffing at table*): My, my, what a nice, musty odor. I do like a nice, musty odor now, don't you? I am sure dear Genevieve would like it, too. What is the price?

SALLY: How much do you have?

MR. HIGGINS: Fifty-seven dollars and seventeen cents— exactly. I counted it just before I came.

SALLY: Well, that's what this table costs, fifty-seven dollars and seventeen cents—exactly.

MR. HIGGINS (*Clapping his hands*): Goodie, goodie, goodie! How pleased Genevieve will be. Here's my purse. It's all in there. I must take this table right home to show my dear wife. (MR. HIGGINS *leaves with the table.* SALLY *is skipping about excitedly as* JILL *and* PETER *return.*)

PETER: My, this place certainly looks better. There's just that one bare spot to fill in. We can put that little, old table there. (*Looks around for it*) Where the dickens has it gone?

SALLY (*Giggling*): I sold it.

PETER *and* JILL: Sold it!

SALLY: Yes, to Mr. Higgins. Now, who's helping Mother?

PETER (*Accusingly*): Sally Todd, did he pay you for it?

SALLY: Of course—fifty-seven dollars and seventeen cents. He said his dear wife Genevieve had given it to him to spend.

PETER: Fifty-seven dollars and seventeen cents!

JILL: I don't believe it!

SALLY (*Holding out purse*): Here it is. He even gave me his purse. (PETER *snatches it hurriedly and dumps bills and loose change out on bottom shelf.*) You see. I'm a supersalesman!

PETER: You certainly are! It just so happens that these bills are play money—the kind they use on the stage. You sold that table for exactly seventeen cents!

SALLY (*Wailing*): Oh, no!

JILL: You can't even trust her with a crackpot. As if Mrs. Higgins would give her husband fifty-seven dollars. She's so stingy, I'm surprised she even let him get away with seventeen cents.

PETER (*Gloomily*): We'll never be able to get the table back from her, never in the world. (SALLY *bursts into tears and rushes out of the shop, right.* PETER *puts seventeen cents into cash box on bottom shelf.*) I guess I'll wander over to the auction and see if I can improve our situation with some really smart bidding.

JILL: And while you're gone, I think I'll improve this chair with a nice coat of bright blue paint. I never can understand why Mother likes chairs to look quite so— quite so sat in. I'll see if I can find the paint that was left over from the bathroom floor. (JILL *exits left into house.* PETER *looks around and then climbs up on a chair and takes down cracked teapot from top shelf.*)

PETER (*Smugly*): Nobody'd ever guess that this is where I'm keeping the cash while Mother's away. (*Pulls out roll of bills*) Let me see—I think twenty-five dollars ought to see me through. (*He peels off some bills, puts remainder back and replaces teapot as* JILL *returns with paint can and brush.*)

JILL: Whatever are you doing up there?

PETER: Uh—ah—just looking to see if you got all the dust off this top shelf. (*Runs his finger over the top shelf and examines it critically*)

JILL: Well, of all the nerve!

PETER: Can't let the help get careless, you know. As manager of Mother's business, I have to be on my toes all the time.

JILL: Humph—some manager you are!

PETER (*Airily*): Just wait until I come back from the auction. Then you'll see how good I am.

JILL: You'd better be careful how you spend Mother's money, that's all I have to say.

PETER: They can't outsmart me. Just you take care of the customers while I'm gone and keep Sally out of mischief. (PETER *exits right and* JILL *begins painting the chair with bright blue paint.* SALLY *tiptoes into shop, takes the seventeen cents from change box on shelf and departs without being heard.* JILL *stands back to admire her first few strokes.*)

JILL: I'm sure Mother will like this. (MR. SNIFTER *enters, carrying a magnifying glass. He leans over* JILL'S *shoulder to peer through his magnifying glass at chair she is painting.*) Oh, good morning, sir, may I help you?

MR. SNIFTER (*Peering at* JILL *through his glass*): When I find what I want I'll let you know, miss. (*He walks about the shop, giving everything a close inspection. Finally, he climbs up on a chair and takes down the cracked teapot carefully.*) Here's exactly what I want, young lady—it's a gem—a rare old bit of English pottery—a masterpiece!

JILL (*In amazement*): Not that horrible old teapot! Mother never expected to sell that.

MR. SNIFTER (*Ecstatically*): A real beauty. I see it is marked only two dollars. I will give you ten. When I see what

I want, I'm willing to pay for it. I don't believe in haggling.

JILL (*Faltering*): I—I'm not sure Mother would want me to sell something for more than she thinks it's worth.

MR. SNIFTER (*Solemnly*): Let me be the judge of that, my dear. Here is your ten dollars.

JILL: Well, let me wrap it up for you, anyway.

MR. SNIFTER: Hide such rare beauty beneath wrapping paper—never! I wouldn't think of letting it out of my hands for a moment. Goodbye, goodbye. (*He exits, clutching the teapot tightly to him.*)

JILL (*Weakly*): Goodbye. Do come again! (MRS. BOUNCE *enters. She is fanning herself with a newspaper.*) Good morning, madam.

MRS. BOUNCE: Good morning, my dear. What do you have in bargains for today? I always go bargain-hunting on Mondays.

JILL: What—what sort of bargain were you looking for?

MRS. BOUNCE: Oh, something marked down from ten dollars to ninety-eight cents. Some little thing like that, you know.

JILL: Well, there's a cup my sister broke this morning. I just finished mending it a short while ago. You could have that for a quarter.

MRS. BOUNCE (*Fanning herself rapidly*): The very idea! What do you take me for. A cheapskate? (*She sits down on freshly painted chair.*)

JILL (*Clapping her hand over her mouth in dismay*): Oh, my goodness gracious, get up out of that chair quickly!

MRS. BOUNCE: Well! I have never been so insulted in my life. I shall certainly take my trade elsewhere in the future. (*She starts to stand, but her dress sticks to the paint as she rises.*) Oh, my beautiful new dress—ruined! You will pay for this, young lady, or I'll call the police.

JILL (*Falteringly*): How much—how much did it cost?

MRS. BOUNCE: Ten dollars on the bargain counter. Worth a great deal more, I'm sure. I'm really letting you off cheaply considering my injured feelings.

JILL (*Hurriedly handing over money received from* MR. SNIFTER): Here is your ten dollars. I'm very sorry it happened. (MRS. BOUNCE *flounces out and* JILL *wipes her brow with a despairing hand.*) First Peter, then Sally, now me. Oh, dear, what will Mother think of us? I'm beginning to believe it would be a good idea if we learned something about the business instead of thinking we were such know-it-alls. No wonder Mother didn't want us to try to sell anything. I do hope that Peter turns up something good at the auction. (PETER *enters, lugging a huge metal kettle with him.*) For goodness' sake, Peter Todd, don't tell me that's what you bought!

PETER (*With a flourish*): You see before you, my fine woman, the very kettle in which the Pilgrims cooked their first Thanksgiving dinner! The auctioneer said so.

JILL: The auctioneer said that?

PETER: Well, he said they could have cooked their first Thanksgiving dinner in it—that it was certainly big enough.

JILL: Peter Todd, how much did you pay for that kettle?

PETER: Oh, I was smart. When the bid went up to five dollars, I said, very coolly, mind you, twenty-five—just like that. You could have heard a pin drop. Nobody made another bid. I had the kettle at my own price.

JILL: Well, I should think so. Peter, you're crazy. Why, Mother has kettles right here in the shop that sell for less than five dollars!

PETER (*Feebly*): Not ones that came over in the *Mayflower*.

JILL: Oh, so now it came over in the *Mayflower*. Of all the ridiculous things!

PETER: We—we could paint 1620 on the bottom of it.

JILL: Oh, we could, could we? Just wait till Mother hears about this.

PETER: Oh, all right then, I'll pay Mother back out of my allowance. I only took twenty-five dollars out of the teapot, and there's plenty more there.

JILL: Out of the teapot? What are you talking about?

PETER: Why, that's where I put the cash—in the old tea-pot on the top shelf. (*Turns to point towards it*) Why, where is it? What did you do with it?

JILL (*Dismayed*): Oh, dear—this is dreadful!

PETER: What do you mean?

JILL: I sold that teapot!

PETER: You didn't—you're fooling.

JILL (*Sobbing*): I wish I were. The man gave me ten dol-lars for it.

PETER: Ten dollars for that old, cracked teapot that's been hanging around here for the last couple of years!

JILL: He s-said it was a rare old bit of English p-pottery, a—a masterpiece!

PETER (*Darkly*): He must have looked inside.

JILL: Maybe he did. He had a magnifying glass. It's all your fault, Peter Todd, taking the money out of the cash box where Mother had it locked up.

PETER (*Sitting down and dropping his chin into his hands glumly*): Yeah, I guess it is. No wonder Mother was worried about leaving us alone. We sure have gummed up the works. You're the only one who hasn't done something really dumb.

JILL (*Dejectedly*): Oh, yes, I did, too. I had to give a woman the ten dollars I got for the teapot when she ruined her dress sitting on that freshly painted chair.

PETER (*Disgustedly*): You'd think we had money to burn the way we've been tossing it around. And that chair doesn't look so hot either. I guess if Mother wanted it painted she would have done it herself.

JILL: All we have to show for our efforts is seventeen cents in the cash box.

PETER: What are we going to do now?

JILL (*Pulling herself together determinedly*): Well, first off we're going to put things back in the shop the way Mother had them. Then you can go to the paint store and get some turpentine to clean the paint off that chair. And when Mother comes home, we're going to confess everything and tell her that we really want to learn how to run the shop like grown people so she can feel safe to go away and leave us in the future. It's fun to be smart about things but not smart-alecky.

PETER (*Groaning*): Smart-alecky—that's me all right. But just straightening things up again isn't going to put the money back in the cash box.

JILL: I've thought of that. I've decided to sell my coral necklace to Mrs. Jenkins. Every time she comes in the shop she asks if I will part with it. I know she's willing to pay quite a bit of money for it. Anything that's hard to get goes way up in value in Mrs. Jenkins' eyes.

PETER (*Excitedly*): And I could sell this old striking watch that Grandfather gave me. (*He takes large watch from his pocket and* JILL *takes off the coral necklace which she is wearing.*) Maybe we can make up everything that we lost.

JILL (*Doubtfully*): But you've always valued that watch so much, Peter.

PETER: I value Mother's good opinion more. (*As they talk, they slip watch and necklace into their pockets and start rearranging the furniture.*) By the way, where's Sally?

JILL: I don't know. I haven't seen her since she sold that table to Mr. Higgins. Maybe she's going around trying to smell out some good antiques!

PETER: Well, without any money, she can't do much harm.

(*Peering into cash box*) By the way, where is that seventeen cents?

JILL: It was right there in the change box a while ago.

PETER: It's gone now. Do you suppose that old teapot snatcher got his mitts on that too? (SALLY *enters right, holding something behind her.*)

JILL: Sally Todd, where have you been? A fine help you are.

PETER: And what have you got behind you?

SALLY: I have something for Mother—so there.

JILL: Show it to me this instant—this instant, do you hear. As if we aren't in enough trouble already!

SALLY: Oh, all right. Here. (PETER *and* JILL *stare in amazement at a glass object she holds out to them.*)

JILL: Sally, how did you get that valuable old paperweight? Mother's been dickering with Mrs. Higgins for that for years. She says it's worth a great deal of money!

SALLY (*Admiring paperweight*): Isn't it pretty. See the roses under the glass.

PETER (*In hushed tones*): You didn't steal it, did you?

SALLY (*In disgust*): Of course not. I bought it for seventeen cents!

PETER: A likely story!

JILL: Out with it, Sally—tell us everything. We might as well know the worst at once.

SALLY: I just took the seventeen cents Mr. Higgins paid me this morning and went to see Mrs. Higgins. She was having a garden party. And what do you think—she was serving tea from the little table her husband bought this morning! It had a lace cloth on it and a bowl of roses and her best china. You could see she was proud of it.

JILL: What happened then?

PETER: Yeah, what happened then?

SALLY: I just told her I had come to buy the rose paper-weight my mother liked. I told her I would pay her seventeen cents for it.

JILL: Good grief, what did she say?

SALLY: She just laughed in that nasty way she has and said, "Run along home now, dear. Can't you see I'm entertaining company?" And I said, "Oh yes, I can see that—on a table that isn't paid for yet!"

JILL: Oh, Sally, you didn't!

SALLY: Yes, I did. She almost ran into the living room and got me the paperweight. And then she positively thrust it at me. I said politely, "Here's your seventeen cents." Just like that.

JILL: Well, I never.

SALLY: There was just one thing that troubled me.

PETER: Really? Not your conscience by any chance?

SALLY (*Wide-eyed*): Certainly not. My conscience is as clear as—as the glass in that paperweight. I thought it was a good deal all round. Mrs. Higgins got something she wanted and now Mother will have something she wanted.

PETER: We certainly have the makings of one antique dealer in this family anyway. Maybe it pays to put your foot in your mouth every time you open it.

JILL: You didn't tell us what the one thing was that was troubling you.

SALLY: Well, it's just this—(MR. SNIFTER *bursts into the shop holding the cracked teapot in his hand.*)

MR. SNIFTER (*Shouting*): It's an outrage, that's what it is! Selling me a teapot with a crack in it! I demand my money back! Do you hear, I demand my money back! (PETER *seizes teapot excitedly, lifts off lid and dumps money onto a chair.*)

PETER (*Joyously, handing him money*): Here's your ten

dollars, sir, and welcome. Maybe you need a stronger magnifying glass!

MR. SNIFTER (*In bewilderment*): You mean to say that money was in the teapot all the time? (PETER *and* JILL *both nod.*) And I was asking for my ten dollars back. I should have my head examined. (*He grins weakly and backs out of the shop.*)

SALLY: What's all this about?

JILL (*Laughing*): Oh, just a little tempest in a teapot! Now maybe you'll tell us what it is that's still troubling you. It's the only thing that hasn't been cleared up.

SALLY: Well, it's just that this paperweight doesn't have that good, old, musty smell. I've sniffed and sniffed but it's just no use. Do you suppose Mother might have been mistaken about its value?

PETER: Ye gods! Just don't go by anything I say any more. From here on in, we're going to take lessons from you! (*Curtain*)

THE END

The King's Calendar

by Janice Auritt Oser

Characters

KING
PRIME MINISTER
KETTLEKIN, *Minister of Pots and Pans*
BANGLE, *Minister of Buttons and Bows*
TALLY, *Minister of the Piggy Bank*
CALENDAR-MAKER
BETTINA ⎱
WHEATINA ⎰ *Princesses*
QUEEN
TWO LADIES-IN-WAITING
ASTRONOMER

SETTING: *The throne room of the palace in the State of Confusion.*

AT RISE: KING *sits on throne reading a comic book. There is a knock on the door.*

KING (*Quickly sitting on comic book*): Enter! (PRIME MINISTER *enters.*)

PRIME MINISTER (*Bowing as low as possible*): Your Majesty. (*Straightens up with difficulty*)

KING: Good day, Prime Minister. You wanted to see me?

PRIME MINISTER: Yes, Your Majesty. If you recall, today

is the day for the Ministers of the State of Confusion to make their reports on affairs of state.

KING: Ah, yes. How are the affairs of state going?

PRIME MINISTER: They're in a terrible state of affairs, Your Majesty.

KING: What! Terrible, you say? What is happening to the State of Confusion?

PRIME MINISTER: The Ministers are here to give you their reports themselves, Your Majesty.

KING: Well, let them come in! (PRIME MINISTER *bows and goes to door to admit Ministers.*)

PRIME MINISTER (*Announcing*): Kettlekin, Minister of Pots and Pans. (KETTLEKIN *enters, approaches throne, bows low, and stands to one side.*) Bangle, Minister of Buttons and Bows! (BANGLE *approaches throne, bows, and steps aside.*) Tally, Minister of the Piggy Bank. (*Pause*) Minister of the Piggy Bank! (*After a brief pause, he cups hands to mouth and shouts.*) I say, Tally, Minister of the Piggy Bank! (TALLY *runs on breathlessly, carrying a large sheaf of papers. He quickly approaches throne, bows, steps to one side next to other Ministers, and shuffles papers with thumb and forefinger as others address* KING. KETTLEKIN *steps forward, bows again, and holds out his bright red hands as he speaks.*)

KETTLEKIN: The Pots and Pans Department is working day and night, Your Majesty. As you can see, even I have dishpan hands, but no sooner do we get the pots clean than the pans are dirty, and by the time we clean the pans, the pots are dirty. There just aren't enough hours in the day, Your Majesty. (*Steps back, wringing his hands*)

BANGLE (*Steps forward, bows*): The Buttons and Bows Department is working all the time, Your Majesty. But no sooner do we get one button sewed on than another button falls off. As you can see, I don't have a single button on my own coat. (*Shows coat*) There just aren't enough hours in the day, Your Majesty. (*Steps back*)

TALLY (*Steps forward, giving papers a last-minute shuffle*): The staff of the Piggy Bank has been working very hard, Your Majesty.

KING: Yes? That's fine. (*Rubs his hands*) And how much money do we have in the Piggy Bank?

TALLY (*Looks earnestly through papers, then at* KING): I don't know.

KING: You don't know? What do you mean, you don't know!

TALLY: By the time we get one year's finances straightened out, the next year is almost over. The years just aren't long enough, Your Majesty. (*Steps back*)

PRIME MINISTER: To sum it up, Your Majesty, there aren't enough hours in the day, and the years aren't long enough.

KING: Well, we'll fix that! Ministers, send me the Royal Calendar-Maker!

MINISTERS (*Bow, in unison*): Yes, Your Majesty. (*File out*)

KING: Not enough hours in the day and the years aren't long enough, huh? That's easy enough to fix. We'll put more hours in the day and we'll make the years longer! (CALENDAR-MAKER *enters.*)

CALENDAR-MAKER (*Bows*): You wanted to see me, Your Majesty?

KING: Yes, Calendar-Maker. How many hours are there in a day, and how long is a year?

CALENDAR-MAKER: There are twenty-four hours in a day, Your Majesty, and a year is about 365 days long.

KING: Well, change it.

CALENDAR-MAKER (*Surprised*): Change it, Your Majesty?

KING: Yes. I want . . . let's see, now . . . thirty hours in the day and, oh, about 400 days in the year.

CALENDAR-MAKER: But, Your Majesty—

KING: No "buts" about it. Change the Royal Calendar and see that every man, woman and child in the State of Confusion hears about it immediately.

CALENDAR-MAKER (*Shrugs*): Yes, Your Majesty. (*Bows and exits*)

KING: That ought to do it. There will be plenty of time for everybody.

PRIME MINISTER: Yes, indeed, Your Majesty. (*A knock on the door is heard.* PRIME MINISTER *opens it, admits visitors and announces them.*) The Princess Bettina! (BETTINA *walks toward throne.*) The Princess Wheatina! (WHEATINA *approaches throne, and both curtsy before* KING.)

BETTINA (*Excitedly*): Papa, is it true that you've made the days longer?

WHEATINA (*Breaking in*): And the years longer, too?

BETTINA: May we stay up later?

WHEATINA: Do we have more holidays?

KING (*Holding his ears*): Just a minute! Let me think! I can't . . . (QUEEN *enters with* TWO LADIES-IN-WAITING.)

QUEEN: Henry! What have you done?

KING: Who, me?

QUEEN: Yes, Henry, you! With your new calendar you've put the people in a state of confusion.

KING: But that's where they were in the first place!

QUEEN: Well, you've made it worse.

KING: How so? I was only trying to give the people more time.

QUEEN: But the trouble is, Henry, that if you add hours to the day, then . . . then . . . (*Scratches head, turns to* LADIES-IN-WAITING) What *was* the trouble?

1ST LADY: Why, Your Majesty, if you add hours to the day, then we'll all be staying up long past nightfall, and we'll be going to bed just when it's getting light.

2ND LADY: And then the next day, we'll be going to bed while it's still light and getting up in the dark.

1ST LADY: And, Your Majesty, if you add all those days to the year, then the weather will be getting warm while it's still wintertime.

2ND LADY: It wouldn't be long, Your Majesty, before we'd be warm in the winter and cold in the summer.

BETTINA: What fun! We'd go sledding on the Fourth of July.

WHEATINA: And swimming at Christmastime.

KING: Oh my, how confusing! What went wrong with my new calendar?

QUEEN: I don't know, Henry, but you'd better fix it!

KING (*To* PRIME MINISTER): Send the Royal Calendar-Maker to me, immediately.

PRIME MINISTER (*Bows*): Yes, Your Majesty. (*Exits*)

KING: I don't understand. All I did was throw in a few more hours and days, and all of a sudden, day is night and night is day and winter is summer and summer is winter. . . . (*Moans*) Oh, my! (CALENDAR-MAKER *and* ASTRONOMER *enter, carrying several books to which they refer often for information during remainder of play.*)

CALENDAR-MAKER: You sent for me, Your Majesty?

KING: Ah, the Calendar-Maker. Yes, I sent for you. The ladies here have been pointing out certain minor difficulties in my calendar.

CALENDAR-MAKER: I see, Your Majesty.

KING: If you see, then please explain it to me. I don't see what's wrong.

CALENDAR-MAKER: Perhaps the Royal Astronomer had better explain it, Your Majesty.

KING: The Royal Astronomer? What does he have to do with my calendar?

ASTRONOMER: A great deal, Your Majesty. You see, the calendar we use is in the sky, and the sky, as you know, is what I, the Royal Astronomer, study.

KING: The sky? The only calendars I've ever seen were hanging on walls.

ASTRONOMER: Yes, Your Majesty, but those calendars merely give you information that has been gathered by studying the sky. You see, a year is about 365¼ days long because that is about how long it takes the Earth to travel around the sun.

KING: But we have no such thing as a quarter of a day!

CALENDAR-MAKER: That's right, Your Majesty. It's more convenient to wait until the four left-over quarters add up to a whole, and then we add another day to the year.

BETTINA: That's Leap Year!

CALENDAR-MAKER: That's right, Princess. Every fourth year we add another day to the month of February to make the years marked on our calendars come out even with the time it takes the earth to travel around the sun.

ASTRONOMER: So you see, Your Majesty, deciding upon the number of days in the year is not a simple matter. Our present system was arrived at only after hundreds of years of study, and even now it is not perfect. Our calendar runs twenty-six seconds fast each year, just as a clock may run fast, and in about three thousand years we shall have to make one year one day longer.

KING: Well, that's something, anyhow.

CALENDAR-MAKER: Yes, Your Majesty, but you see the difficulty in making each year 400 days long. Our calendar would then run slow; it would run behind the movement of the earth around the sun and it would not keep up with the seasons. Thus the calendar would show it to be wintertime while we would know it to be spring outside.

KING: But why can't we simply make winter longer?

ASTRONOMER: Because, Your Majesty, the length of the seasons is determined by the position of the Earth in respect to the sun. (*Reading from his book*) "As the

Earth travels around the sun, it tilts (CALENDAR-MAKER *makes motion with his arm.*) on its axis, which means that sometimes the North Pole is closer to the sun than the South Pole. But twice a year, on March 21 and about September 23, the Earth is not tilted (CALENDAR-MAKER *straightens arm*), and the North Pole (CALENDAR-MAKER *indicates fingers.*) and the South Pole (CALENDAR-MAKER *indicates elbow.*) are exactly the same distance from the sun. On these days, the hours of daylight and of darkness are equal, and they mark the beginnings and endings of the seasons. After March 21, the days grow longer and the nights shorter—that is the beginning of spring and then summer. Then, on about September 23, the hours of night and day are equal, and then the days grow shorter and the nights longer—that is the beginning of fall and winter, until we are back at March 21 and spring again."

CALENDAR-MAKER: And so, Your Majesty, if we were suddenly to make a year 400 days long, we would soon find the seasons all mixed up. As things are now, the seasons divide into four quarters the time it takes the Earth to go around the sun.

KING: I see. That is, I think I see. But why does my new calendar make day night and night day?

ASTRONOMER: Ah, Your Majesty, that is because there can be neither more nor less than twenty-four hours in a day. You see, the Earth, besides tilting on its axis, turns around as it moves about the sun. Let me show you. (*To* CALENDAR-MAKER, *bowing*) Will you do me the honor, kind sir, of being the sun?

CALENDAR-MAKER (*Bowing*): Delighted.

ASTRONOMER: Thank you. And I shall be the Earth. As the Earth goes around the sun (*Walks slowly around* CALENDAR-MAKER) it turns on its axis (*Turns around while walking*) and a full turn takes twenty-four hours.

CALENDAR-MAKER: That means, Your Majesty, that different parts of the Earth face the sun at different times. The sun doesn't really rise and set, it's just that the people in any given place on Earth are moving towards or away from the sun. (ASTRONOMER *stops walking and staggers dizzily.*) When we come in sight of the sun, it's daylight for us, and when we move away from the sun so that we can no longer see it, it's nighttime. And it takes twenty-four hours for the Earth to make a full turn so that we can see the sun again.

ASTRONOMER: Therefore, Your Majesty, if you were to increase the length of a day to thirty hours, you would not be keeping up with the turning of the Earth. You would still be counting the hours of the evening of one day when the Earth had already made a full turn and the morning of another day had begun.

KING: But there must be something we can do with the calendar. How about the months? Can we make them longer?

CALENDAR-MAKER: Yes, Your Majesty, we could make the months longer. (KING *looks pleased.*) But then we'd have to have fewer months in the year.

ASTRONOMER: Perhaps I should explain. (*Reading*) "A month is roughly the length of time it takes the moon to travel around the Earth—for the moon does travel around the Earth, just as the Earth travels around the sun. In olden times, people arranged their calendar according to the moon."

CALENDAR-MAKER: There was a difficulty with this, however, Your Majesty. It takes the moon only a little more than twenty-nine days to travel around the Earth, and twelve of these months made only . . . let's see, twelve times twenty-nine is . . . (*Mumbles calculations*) Oh, about 348 days, and that is some days less than a year —which is measured, as we have said, by the sun. For this reason, we have changed the lengths of the months by a few days so that twelve months add up to a year. If you add more days to the months, then twelve months will add up to more than a year.

KING: Hmmm. And can there be no more than seven days in a week?

ASTRONOMER: As a matter of fact, Your Majesty, the fact that we count seven days to a week is based on what you might call a mistake.

KING: A mistake? All these years we've been making a mistake?

ASTRONOMER: Not exactly, Your Majesty. But the people of ancient times could see only five planets in the sky, and they thought of them as gods. They also considered the sun and the moon to be gods. That made seven gods, and when they set aside one day of the week for the worship of each of these gods, that made seven days in the week.

CALENDAR-MAKER: Of course, today we know that there are eight planets, besides the Earth. If the people of ancient times had had telescopes to look at the sky with, there might now be more than seven days in the week.

KING: Well, let's change that now, by all means.

CALENDAR-MAKER: But Your Majesty, fifty-two weeks of seven days each add up to almost exactly one year, and if you make the weeks longer, there will have to be fewer of them in a year.

KING: Oh dear, how can anything as simple-looking as a calendar be so complicated?

CALENDAR-MAKER: It isn't really so complicated, Your Majesty. It's just that a calendar is more than a piece of paper or cardboard; it's a way of keeping track of the time according to the sun.

KING: I certainly wouldn't want the Royal Calendar to go against the sun. Change it back, fix it, repair it, mend it!

CALENDAR-MAKER (*Bows*): Yes, Your Majesty. (*Exits with* ASTRONOMER.)

BETTINA: Papa, does that mean that we can't stay up later?

WHEATINA: Does that mean that we won't have any extra holidays?

KING: I'm afraid so, Princesses. But get back to work now —remember there are only twenty-four hours in a day.

PRINCESSES: Yes, Papa. (*Exit*)

KING: Oh my, *now* what can we do?

QUEEN: Do about what, Henry?

KING: The Ministers reported to me today that they don't have enough time to do their work, and I can't give them any more time.

QUEEN: Give them less work, then.

KING: How can I do that?

QUEEN: Tell Kettlekin, the Minister of Pots and Pans to throw away some of his pots and pans so he will not have so many of them to clean.

KING: Hm-m-m. Good! Very good! I'll tell him that.

QUEEN: And tell Bangle, the Minister of Buttons and Bows, to use snaps.

KING: Snaps! Very clever! And Tally, the Minister of the Piggy Bank?

QUEEN: Well, we'll have to speed things up in the Piggy Bank.

KING: Yes, but how?

QUEEN: Why, we'll spend the money faster!

KING: Good! Spend the money faster . . . (*Does a double take*) What! (QUEEN *smiles sweetly, takes* KING *by hand, as curtain falls.*)

THE END

Abe Buys A Barrel

by Mary Nygaard Peterson

Characters

ABE LINCOLN, *twenty-four*
BILL BERRY, *his partner*
JACK KELSO, *his friend*
MENTOR GRAHAM, *the schoolteacher*
MRS. HORNBUCKLE, *a customer*
RUSSEL GODBEY, *a farmer*
JIM JENSEN, *a traveler*
HANNAH JENSEN, *his wife*
PETER
REBECCA } *their children*

TIME: *A summer morning in 1833.*

SETTING: *The Lincoln-Berry general store in New Salem, Ill.*

AT RISE: ABE LINCOLN *is lying on the counter reading a book. There is a period of silence, broken after an interval by the sound of someone rattling the door. It gradually occurs to* ABE *that someone is trying to get in. He turns the book face down on the counter, goes to the door and opens it.*

ABE: Come in, Mrs. Hornbuckle.

MRS. HORNBUCKLE (*Entering*): Is the store open? I didn't really know whether you were here yet or not.

ABE: I'm here. I just hadn't gotten around to opening the door yet.

MRS. HORNBUCKLE: That's all right, Mr. Lincoln. I wouldn't want you to open it any earlier than usual just for me.

ABE: There's no one I'd rather open it for. What can I do for you this morning?

MRS. HORNBUCKLE: I'd like half a pound of tea. I didn't realize I was out of it, and I just don't enjoy my breakfast without it.

ABE: You shall have your tea, ma'am. (*He measures out tea, weighs it, puts it in paper packet, and hands it to* MRS. HORNBUCKLE.) Here you are. I hope you enjoy your breakfast.

MRS. HORNBUCKLE (*Taking tea*): I will now, thanks to you. And here is your money. (*She digs deep into a worn, old-fashioned purse and hands him coin.*)

ABE: Thank you. Come in again, won't you?

MRS. HORNBUCKLE: Oh, I will, thank you. (ABE *escorts her to door, and she goes out. He returns to counter, picks up book again, and sits on counter, his legs dangling over the edge.*)

ABE (*Muses*): "To thine own self be true. . . . Thou canst not then be false to any man." (*Pause*) "To thine own self be true"— Hm-m-m. (*Door opens and* BILL *enters wearily.*)

BILL (*Approaching counter*): Howdy, Abe. How's business? (*He pushes his straw hat back on his head and looks around.*)

ABE: Same as usual, Bill. Not rushing. All I've sold this morning is a half pound of tea. (ABE *gets down from counter and starts to straighten merchandise. He takes weight off scale and as he looks at it, stops suddenly, obviously upset.*) Jumping crickety!

BILL: What's the matter, Abe?

ABE: I charged Mrs. Hornbuckle for half a pound of tea and used only a four-ounce weight on the scale!

BILL: Oh, well, never mind—the old girl can afford it. And we need the money a lot worse'n she does.

ABE: Maybe so, but she's still got another fourth of a pound of tea coming to her. I'll measure it out right now before I forget. (*He measures out a small packet of tea, writes her name on it, and leaves it on the counter.*)

BILL: Suit yourself, Abe. (*He shrugs.*) But I just don't see how we're goin' to stay in business the way things are goin'. Have you any money, Abe?

ABE (*Jingling a few coins in his jeans*): Not more'n a few cents left from what Coleman Smoot paid me for pitchin' hay for him last week. But Russ Godbey promised to come in today to pay me for the work I did at his place. I have plenty of places to spend it, too. Need new pants, for one thing. I remember I had to split four hundred rails for each yard of cloth in these jeans. Nancy Miller sewed them up for me. They sure have been good pants, but you can't expect anythin' to last forever.

BILL (*He goes to the door, right, and looks out.*): I'll bet there are a *hundred* people in New Salem, an' not a soul stirring. Where do they keep themselves? (*He turns back into the room in disgust.*) No business. I might just as well have stayed in bed. (*He sits on a chair, tilts it back against the wall, then pulls his hat down over his eyes.*) Call me if you need me, Abe. I'm bone tired. (*It is quiet in the room.* ABE *picks up his book and paces up and down reading it.* JACK KELSO *enters, right, carrying a fishing pole.*)

JACK: Is this the firm of Lincoln and Berry—dealers in general merchandise?

ABE (*Laughing*): Depends on who's askin'. If it's bill collectors, we just moved out of town—forwardin' address unknown. (*Then, changing his tone.*) What's on your mind, Jack?

JACK: Fishin'. It's a perfect morning for fishin'. How about comin' with me? I'll fish an' you can read—an' if the fish won't bite, we can talk.

ABE (*Doubtfully*): I don't know, Jack. Maybe I'd better not—someone might want to buy something. We could sure use a few customers. Besides, Bill's sleepin' an' I kinda hate to wake him up just to tell him I'm goin' fishin'.

JACK: I'm in no hurry—the fish can wait. (*He takes a book out of his pocket, pushes a chair up against a wall, and settles himself down to read.* ABE *sits with his book.* RUSSEL GODBEY *enters.*)

GODBEY: Hello, Abe. I brought in your pay, just like I said I would.

ABE: That's good. My bank account's gettin' kinda low— an' my pants are gettin' kinda high—as you can see.

GODBEY (*Shifts about uncomfortably*): Well, now, Abe, I kinda hoped you wouldn't need to be paid in cash.

ABE (*Crestfallen*): Why, ah—are things runnin' kinda low for you, too, Russ?

GODBEY: Just seems like I can't make both ends meet, Abe —had to get me a new plow if I wanted to stay in farmin'. Then the Missus said she had to get clothes for the young'uns—seems they had nothin' to wear.

ABE: In that case, why don't we just forget the whole thing? I know it takes a heap of money where there's a family of young'uns to support.

GODBEY: Oh, I don't want to forget it, Abe. I always aim to pay my debts, somehow. I wondered if you might have any use for these two buckskins? (*Shows him skins*) They're real nice skins.

ABE (*Feeling skins*): Why, yes, Russ—I'd be glad to take the skins for pay. They *are* real nice skins.

GODBEY: Thanks, Abe, for bein' so accommodatin'. If there's ever anythin' we can do for you, all you have to do is name it.

ABE: I'll sure do that, Russ. (GODBEY *exits, right.* ABE *folds the skins up and puts them away.*)

JACK: I see you're gettin' rich fast, Abe—just like me.

ABE: I wouldn't worry about gettin' rich, if I could just break even. Well, I guess there go my new pants. (*He shrugs and grins.* JENSEN *enters, right. He stands uncertainly near the door until* ABE *looks up and sees him.*) Howdy, stranger. I didn't see you standin' there. Something I can do for you?

JENSEN (*Wringing his hands nervously*): Well, ah—I've got a barrel out in my wagon. I wondered if you might be interested in buyin' it?

ABE: What's in the barrel?

JENSEN (*Shifting his feet uneasily*): Oh—nothin', I guess —just junk. We're movin' West, an' I'd like to get the thing out of the way.

ABE: Well, I don't rightly need a barrel, but I can look at it, I guess. (ABE *and* JENSEN *exit.* BILL *shifts his position but continues sleeping.* JACK *reads.* MENTOR GRAHAM *enters and looks around.*)

MENTOR: Abe here?

JACK: Out buyin' a barrel.

MENTOR: A barrel of what? (JACK *shrugs.* ABE *enters with* MRS. JENSEN *and her two children.*)

ABE: Now you just sit here an' make yourself comfortable, Mrs. Jensen. (*He takes a chair and places it near the counter for her.*) An' you two young'uns sit here. (*He picks up children and sets them on counter.*) We'll see that you get some crackers an' milk to take away that hungry feelin'.

JACK: I'll get it for 'em, Abe. Where do you keep the milk?

ABE: There's a bucket of milk in the back room. Bowling Green brought it over—his wife told him I was gettin' too skinny, an' she wanted to fatten me up a little. (*He laughs and starts to leave, then notices that* MENTOR *has come in.* JACK *exits.*) Be with you in a minute, Mentor. (*He waves and exits, right.* JACK *comes in from the storeroom, left, with three tin cups on the lid of a box.*)

JACK: Here you are, kids. Do you like milk? (*He offers it to them and they accept it eagerly, but shyly, and nod their heads.* MRS. JENSEN *takes a cup, also.*)

MRS. JENSEN: Thankee, kindly. It's long since we ate, an' I'm sure I don't know where our next meal's comin' from. Peter, Rebecca—where's your manners? Did you say thanks for the milk?

JACK: That's all right. Let them enjoy themselves. (*He reaches into large bin, takes out two handfuls of crackers and puts them on box lid, which he holds out to children.*)

PETER *and* REBECCA (*Helping themselves*): Thankee. Thankee.

MRS. JENSEN (*Helping herself*): Thankee, mister.

JACK: Eat all you want—all you can hold. Abe wants you to. (*He puts the lid between the children and returns to his chair.*)

MENTOR (*Looking inside the covers of the book on the counter*): Looks like Abe borrowed this from you, Jack.

JACK: Yep. He reads everything he can get his hands on—makes no difference what it is.

MENTOR: I know. He'll *get* somewhere, some day—with that brain of his.

JACK: Yep. The place he'd like to get most right now is out of debt. He sure worries about those debts of his. (ABE *enters, rolling a barrel in on its rim.*)

ABE (*Speaking over his shoulder*): This'll come in real handy, one of these days. (MR. JENSEN *follows* ABE, *but says nothing.* ABE *digs into his pocket.*) Here's four bits. I know it's not much, but it's all I can pay.

MR. JENSEN: Thankee, mister. That's about all it's worth, I reckon. (*Then, to his wife*) You ready to start, Hannah? (MRS. JENSEN *rises and helps the children down.*)

MRS. JENSEN: Come on, Peter, Rebecca. Your Pappy's ready to start.

ABE: Wait a minute. (*He reaches into candy jar and gives each of the children a piece of candy.*) Here's a horehound drop for each of you. Suck on that an' the way won't seem so long.

MRS. JENSEN (*Almost tearfully*): Thankee kindly, sir. We all feel much better, now. (*Then, to the children*) What do you say to the man—Peter, Rebecca?

PETER *and* REBECCA (*Shyly*): Thankee, sir.

ABE: That's all right. (*He escorts them to the door.*) Good luck to you out West! (*They exit, and* ABE *walks back to counter.*)

JACK: What a store! Seems to me you're givin' out more'n you're takin' in.

ABE: Oh, I dunno. The barrel *might* come in handy some day. You never can tell. Why, I might even have to wear it if I don't earn enough money for some new clothes soon.

JACK (*Jeering*): Now, Abe, you won't need clothes for a long time. Didn't Godbey just pay you a couple of perfectly good buckskins?

ABE (*Looks thoughtful for a moment, and then suddenly*): You're dead right, Jack. I know just what I can do with those buckskins—I can take them over to Jack Armstrong's and have his wife fix my pants with them —you know, sew them on the bottom and the insides

of the legs! They'll wear like iron. Maybe I'll never
need to buy another pair of pants.

JACK: Well, now you have that settled, why don't we set
a match to this ol' barrel an' go fishin'?

MENTOR (*He peers into it*): Wonder what all that junk is.
It's almost full. (*He gingerly reaches inside barrel.*)

ABE: You've got me curious now. (*Reaches into barrel*) I
don't imagine it's anything very valuable. When poor
folks throw away somethin', it's generally not worth
much. Well, what do you know? (*He begins tugging on
something, and pulls out an old bonnet.*) Anyone need
a new bonnet? (*He plops it on* JACK's *head.*) Makes you
look real handsome, Jack.

JACK (*Flinging the hat away from him*): Hey! Have a
heart.

ABE (*Continuing to dig*): New shoes, anyone? (*He hauls
out a pair of high-heeled, pointed ladies' shoes, tied
together.*) Looks like they'd about fit you, Mentor. (*He
dangles them enticingly in front of* MENTOR *but* MEN-
TOR *refuses to touch them.* ABE *lets them fall to the
floor.* BILL *stirs, yawns, and wakes up to find* ABE
lifting some garments out of the barrel.)

BILL: What in the world have you there, Abe?

ABE: Just a barrel I bought from a hard-up stranger.

BILL (*Grumpily*): We're plenty hard-up ourselves, without you buyin' junk that other folks throw away.

ABE (*Comfortingly*): Don't worry, Bill. I paid for it out
of my own pocket—a whole fifty cents.

BILL (*Pacified*): Well, that's different. Though I can't see
how you have any extra money to spend. I know I
don't. Russ Godbey must have been in to pay you.

ABE (*Absently*): He was. (*He continues to take things
out of barrel*) Well, look what I found! (*He holds up
a big book.*)

JACK: A book! Say, you should like that, Abe.

ABE: Yep. Maybe this *isn't* all junk. (*He reads the title from the back of the book.*) *Blackstone's Commentaries on English Law.* Hip, hip, hooray! (*He flings his arms jubilantly into the air and dances a few awkward hops.*)

JACK: Sounds like kinda dull readin' to me. Too bad it isn't Shakespeare.

ABE (*Decidedly*): No, sir-ee. This is the book fellows have to read before they can become lawyers. John Stuart over in Springfield was tellin' me. He said I could even read this by myself, an' then if I could pass the bar examinations, I could be a lawyer. (*He looks thoughtful.*) There should be—I wonder if—(*He reaches into barrel again.*) There should be more—yes, sir, here's another! (*He takes out another huge volume. He puts it on top of the first one, on the floor, and pulls out another.*) An' here's the third one, and the fourth. (*He examines the last one.*) Yes, sir, they're all here! (*He hugs them all and cavorts about with them.*) Boy, oh, boy, oh, boy! This is my lucky day!

BILL (*Unbelieving*): You gonna *read* all those big books, Abe?

ABE: Not read 'em, Bill—*study* 'em. Why, these books must have cost almost a fortune. I could never own them, except by accident. An' to think we almost set a match to 'em!

JACK: You think you'll really be a lawyer some day, Abe?

ABE: Maybe. John Stuart said if I ever did pass those bar examinations, he'd be glad to take me into his law office with him, over in Springfield. (*Suddenly thoughtful, then, seeming to lose his confidence.*) Only one thing bothers me about bein' a lawyer, though.

JACK: What's that?

ABE: The way I talk. I know I don't talk right. A lawyer's

got to know how to talk—he's got to make speeches to the court an' jury, an' they'd just laugh at me the way I talk now. I could never win a case.

BILL: Shucks, Abe. What difference does it make how you talk—long as people understand what you're sayin'? You sound all right to me.

MENTOR: No, Abe's right. We all know how smart Abe is. He's going to amount to something some day—maybe even be a famous man. He ought to learn to talk right.

ABE: But what's a fellow to do when he has to earn a livin'? I can't take time out to go to school. Why, I don't reckon I've been to school a year all together in my life, so far.

BILL: I still say it doesn't matter. Look at President Andy Jackson—d'you s'pose he knows any more'n you do? I'll bet he doesn't know half as much—an' he got to be President. What more d'you want?

MENTOR (*Thoughtfully*): I was just thinking, Abe. Vanner has a grammar book over at his place—*Kirkham's Grammar*. I saw it over there, and I'm sure he'd let you borrow it. You could study it odd minutes here at the store, and I could help you at night if you needed any help.

ABE: You'd be willin' to do that?

MENTOR: Be glad to, Abe.

ABE: Then I'll sure go over to Vanner's an' borrow that book right now. (*He looks at* BILL.) You goin' to stay awake now, Bill?

BILL (*Grumpily*): Guess I can if I have to. No business anyhow.

ABE (*Stuffing letters into the band inside his hat*): I might as well move the United States Post Office into my hat an' deliver these letters at the same time . . . (*Looks around and sees* MRS. HORNBUCKLE'S *tea. He stuffs package into his pocket.*) an' take Mrs. Hornbuckle's tea to her. (*He heads for the door, looks back as he steps out, and calls.*) So long, I'll be seein' you.

JACK (*Howling*): Abe! Oh, Abe—aren't you goin' fishin' with me? (*When there is no answer, he shrugs in despair.*) That's Abe for you! Six miles out to Vanner's and six miles back—for a grammar!

MENTOR (*Smiling*): I guess he's gone off on a tack of his own, now.

BILL: An' when he does that, there's no turnin' him back or stoppin' him. You can bank on that. (*He goes behind the counter ready to wait on customers.*) He'll be a lawyer for sure, now.

MENTOR: And here's another thing you can bank on— when he *is* a lawyer, he'll be a mighty good one. Wait and see!

JACK (*Musing half to himself as the others watch him*): Abe will be a mighty good lawyer. And maybe he'll be even more than a lawyer. Why, maybe some day Abe will even get to go to Washington—as a Congressman or a Senator. Why, it wouldn't surprise me if Abe Lincoln even became President of the United States some day. President Abraham Lincoln! I'll bet Abe could do it. (*Curtain*)

THE END

The Magic Fishbone

by *Charles Dickens*

Adapted by *Mary Nygaard Peterson*

Characters

KING WATKINS THE FIRST
QUEEN
PRINCESS ALICIA, *their daughter*
FREDDIE, *their son*
CHILDREN, *their other sons and daughters*
MR. PICKLES, *the fishmonger*
GOOD FAIRY GRANDMARINA
PEGGY, *the maid*
PRINCE WONDERFUL

TIME: *Long, long ago.*
SETTING: *A street in the kingdom of King Watkins.*
BEFORE RISE: MR. PICKLES, *the fishmonger, enters right with his pushcart full of fish.*

MR. PICKLES: Fresh fish for sale! Fresh fish for sale! (KING WATKINS *enters left.*)
KING: Good morning, Mr. Pickles. (*He looks at fish.*) Do you have some good fish this morning?
MR. PICKLES: Good morning, King Watkins. Yes, Your Majesty, I have some lovely fresh fish—just off the boat. Would you be interested in some of this nice salmon?

(GOOD FAIRY GRANDMARINA *enters right quietly, unnoticed by the other characters.*)

KING (*Leaning forward and looking at it*): Yes, indeed. Just the thing for my dinner. I'll take that one.

MR. PICKLES: An excellent choice, Your Majesty. I'm sure the Queen will be pleased. (*He wraps the fish.*)

KING: I hope so. (*He takes package and starts toward right.*)

MR. PICKLES (*As he exits left*): Fresh fish! Fresh fish for sale! (GOOD FAIRY GRANDMARINA *stops* KING *as he comes near the exit.*)

KING (*Bowing slightly*): How do you do, madam?

FAIRY: You're King Watkins the First, aren't you?

KING: Yes, Watkins is my name.

FAIRY: Papa of the lovely princess, Alicia?

KING: Yes. But you must be a fairy to know all this about me.

FAIRY: Certainly, I'm a fairy. I'm called Good Fairy Grandmarina.

KING (*Inclining his head*): I'm very happy to have met you, Good Fairy. (*He turns to go.*)

FAIRY: Wait.

KING (*Returning to her*): Yes?

FAIRY: When you get home, I want you to invite Princess Alicia to have some of that fish with you. (*She points to the package.*)

KING (*Protesting*): Oh, it might not agree with her.

FAIRY (*Stamping her foot*): Agree with her! Agree with her! Stuff and nonsense! That's just an excuse. You're selfish and greedy. You want to keep all that fish for yourself.

KING (*Wearily*): Very well. To please you, I'll invite the Princess Alicia to share the fish with me. (*He turns to go again.*)

FAIRY: Wait.

KING (*Turning to her again*): Yes?

FAIRY: Don't be so impatient. (KING *bows slightly in apology.*) After the princess has eaten, you will notice that she has left a fishbone on her plate.

KING: A very unusual discovery, I am sure.

FAIRY: That remark was not necessary. However, I shall overlook it this time. (KING *makes a slight bow again.*) Tell the princess to dry the bone carefully, rub it, and polish it until it resembles mother-of-pearl. After that, she must take care of it, as a present from me.

KING (*Sarcastically*): She will be very grateful, I'm sure. Perhaps we should polish all the other bones as well.

FAIRY: I am quite losing patience with you. You have no right to jump to conclusions.

KING (*Sincerely*): I'm sorry. Forgive me.

FAIRY: This once. (*She stamps her foot in emphasis.*) Now! Tell the princess that the bone is a magic present. It can be used only once, but that once it will bring her whatever she wishes for—provided she wishes at the right time.

KING (*Gratefully*): Thank you, Good Fairy. I will certainly give Princess Alicia your message. (*Both exit.*)

* * *

TIME: *That evening.*

SETTING: *The palace dining room.*

AT RISE: KING, QUEEN, *and* PRINCESS ALICIA *are seated at the table. They have just finished eating.* PEGGY *is serving, and as the others talk she may remove some of the dishes, tidy up, etc.*

KING: Did you enjoy your fish, Alicia?

ALICIA: It was the best salmon I've ever tasted, Father. Did you buy it from Mr. Pickles?

KING: As a matter of fact, I did. Something rather odd happened while I was buying the fish this morning.

QUEEN: Odd?

ALICIA (*Leaning forward*): Odd, Father?

KING: Yes. I met a fairy there—Good Fairy Grandmarina, she said her name was.

ALICIA: How quaint!

KING: Yes. The strangest part of it was that she seemed to know so much about our family. As a matter of fact, she asked me to give you a message.

ALICIA: Me, Father?

KING: Yes, you. She said I should tell you to polish that bone on your plate.

ALICIA (*Holding up the bone and looking at it*): This fishbone, Father?

KING: Yes, my dear. It may sound odd, but that is what she said. She said you should dry it and polish it until it resembles mother-of-pearl, and then you are to keep it as a present from her.

QUEEN: Ridiculous!

ALICIA: Isn't that odd? (PEGGY *comes closer and bends over to look. Then she sniffs in disdain.*)

KING: The Good Fairy said to tell you that the bone contains magic, but the magic may be used only once. Just one time, it will grant you whatever you wish—if that wish is made at the proper time.

ALICIA (*Beginning to polish vigorously*): If that is the case, I'd better take care of it. (QUEEN *looks upset.* KING *goes to her and leans over her.*)

KING: Is something the matter, dear? You look so pale.

QUEEN (*Putting the back of her hand to her forehead*): Oh, I do feel faint.

KING: Alicia, come help your mother.

ALICIA (*Rising*): Mother, let me help you. (*Together, they help the* QUEEN *to the divan.*)

KING: We'll make you as comfortable as we can, my dear. (*He turns to* PEGGY.) Bring some cold wet cloths, Peggy. Then bathe Her Majesty's forehead.

PEGGY (*Haughtily*): Not me, sir. I'm no nurse. I quit.

KING: You quit? At a time like this?

PEGGY: I most certainly do. This place has turned into a madhouse lately. All those children to take care of, and the cooking to do—and the cleaning and everything. I don't blame the other servants for quitting. I'm quitting, too, right now. I've had enough of working my fingers to the bone. (*She takes off her apron and cap and hangs them over the back of a chair. Then she prepares to leave.*)

KING (*Following her*): Oh, please, don't leave now, Peggy. We need you so! We'll raise your wages.

PEGGY: If you'd only pay me the wages I have coming! But don't worry, you can keep my back wages. You probably need the money worse than I do. (*She exits.*)

KING (*Rubbing* QUEEN's *hands*): Oh, what shall we do, now?

ALICIA (*Bravely*): We'll be all right, Father. I'm a good nurse. Don't worry.

KING (*Pacing the floor*): If only we had some money, we could hire help and make things easier for everyone. But pay day isn't until next week, and I can't expect my people to pay me before then.

ALICIA (*Fanning* QUEEN): Don't worry, Father. A little extra work won't hurt us. We'll do our best.

KING: You're a good girl, my dear. I don't know what we'd do without you. (*He begins stacking up remaining dishes and carries out a load of them.*)

ALICIA: You're better now, aren't you, Mother?

QUEEN: Oh, I feel so weak. Yet I hate to be a burden upon you. (KING *reappears.*)

ALICIA: Don't worry about that, Mother. I'm strong. I won't mind doing Peggy's work.

KING (*Thoughtfully*): Alicia, I was wondering what became of that magic fishbone.

ALICIA (*Reaching into her pocket*): It's right here, Father, in my pocket.

KING: You haven't lost it?

ALICIA: No, Father. Why?

KING (*Uncomfortably*): Oh, nothing—I just wondered. (*Sound of* CHILDREN *shouting comes from offstage. They cry, "Alicia, Alicia."*) The children! Who is with them?

ALICIA: No one, Father. I fed them their dinner and sent them into the palace yard to play. (CHILDREN *burst into the room.*)

CHILDREN (*Ad lib*): Alicia, Alicia! Freddie hurt himself. Look at him! (*Etc.*)

ALICIA: Oh, no! (*She turns to* FREDDIE, *kneels before him and examines the hand tenderly.*) What happened to you, brother dear?

FREDDIE (*Sobbing*): It hurts, Alicia. Oh, it hurts. (*He wails.*)

CHILDREN (*Ad lib*): We were running—playing tag— Freddie tripped and fell on his hand and cut it. He really hurt himself! (*Etc.*)

ALICIA: (*Sympathetically*): Oh, dear! Well, we must bandage it up. Get the bandages, children, and towels and some water. You know what to do.

CHILDREN (*Rushing off*): All right! We will, Alicia. We will. (*Etc.*)

ALICIA: Now don't cry, Freddie. Alicia will soon have it fixed up good as new. (*She hugs him.*)

QUEEN (*Moaning*): Oh, my head. Will troubles never end? (KING *goes to the* QUEEN *to comfort her.*)

KING: Alicia—

ALICIA (*Looking up*): Yes, Father?

KING: I was just wondering, dear. Whatever became of that fishbone?

ALICIA: My magic bone?

KING: Yes.

ALICIA (*Feeling pocket*): Why, it's still right here in my pocket. Why, Father?

KING (*Shifting uncomfortably*): Oh, nothing, I was just wondering. (CHILDREN *dash back in with basin, towel, bandages, medicine.*)

CHILDREN (*Ad lib*): Here's a basin of water, Alicia—some towels— Here are some bandages, Alicia— I brought you some medicine. (*Etc.*)

ALICIA: Thank you, my dears. Thank you. We'll soon have Freddie fixed up good as new. (*She moves* FREDDIE *to a chair beside the table.*) Now, let's put the basin and the other things right here. (*She points to place on the table.* CHILDREN *do as she directs, then stand around to watch while she bandages the hand.*)

KING (*Walking the floor*): If only Peggy hadn't quit, she would have been here to help you. Oh, if only it were pay day!

QUEEN (*Dramatically*): If only I felt better!

ALICIA (*Completing her task*): There you are! Good as new! (FREDDIE *gets down off the chair, holds up his hand to be admired, and gives* ALICIA *a broad smile.*) Now! Who will help me with the dishes?

CHILDREN (*Ad lib shouting*): We will. We will, Alicia. (*Etc.*) (*They troop offstage.*)

ALICIA (*To* KING): Father—

KING: Yes?

ALICIA: Since all the servants have left, we will have to think about feeding the children.

KING (*Uncomfortably*): Yes?

ALICIA: There was only enough cereal left for their dinner. What shall we do about supper? Do you think you should go to the market and buy something—or shall I?

KING (*Uncomfortably*): My dear, we have no money.

ALICIA (*Shocked*): No money at all?

KING: None at all. (*He turns his pockets out for her to see.*) And we won't have any until pay day, next week.

ALICIA (*Walking the floor thoughtfully, as* KING *watches her*): Isn't there some way we could earn some?

KING: I don't see how. The people wouldn't want their King to be digging ditches, or mending fences. It would make them feel sad if they thought we were poor.

ALICIA: Perhaps if I got a job?

KING: You are needed right here, my dear. How would your eighteen little brothers and sisters get along without you? Who would wash their faces, and dress them, and feed them, and play with them, and tell them stories? Who would care for your mother?

ALICIA (*Thoughtfully*): Yes, I see that. (*With decision*) I suppose we'll just *have* to use our magic fishbone.

KING: You still have it? It isn't lost?

ALICIA (*Indignantly*): Of course, it isn't lost, Father. I just didn't want to ask for help as long as there was something we could do for ourselves. (*She thinks a while longer.*) But now, I just don't see how we can get along without help from someone. The children will soon be crying for food. (*She shakes her head.*) I just *can't* think of any other way to help them. So, (*She draws the bone from her pocket, holds it up to look at it and kisses it impulsively.*) I wish it were pay day! (*Immediately a shower of money descends upon them, thrown from offstage.*)

KING: Pay day! All this beautiful money! (*He begins to gather it up, kneeling on the floor.*) Now our servants will come back. (GOOD FAIRY GRANDMARINA *enters.*)

FAIRY: Yes, King Watkins, now your servants will come

back, and you will be able to spare the Princess Alicia.

KING (*From his knees on the floor*): Spare Alicia? What do you mean? We'll never be able to spare Alicia.

FAIRY (*Firmly*): Oh, yes, you will. Alicia is coming with me.

ALICIA (*Bewildered*): Going with you? Where? (*She glances about the room and gestures toward it with outspread hands.*) How can I leave? Father is right—the children and mother need me.

FAIRY (*Firmly*): They will be all right. You have used your magic fishbone wisely. Since it will be of no more use to you, I will take it back. (*She does so.*) But from now on, Your Majesty, (*Bows to* KING) you will have a pay day every week. You will be able to pay your servants often, and they will be glad to stay with you.

KING: That will be a big help, I must say. (*Turns to* QUEEN) Won't it, my dear?

QUEEN (*Sitting up*): I should say so. I feel better already. (*She gets up and stands beside* KING, *holding his arm.*)

FAIRY (*Putting her arm around* ALICIA): And this fine girl will be able to lead a life of her own.

KING: But where are you taking her? I think we have a right to know.

FAIRY: In the next kingdom lives a handsome and wealthy prince—Prince Wonderful. He asked me to find him a wife who will be unselfish, kind, loving, and true. Naturally, I thought of Alicia right away. But, just to be sure, I decided to put her to a test. So, I slipped that magic fishbone into her salmon when no one was looking.

KING: So that's why you made such a fuss over that bone! You knew it was there. You put it there.

FAIRY (*Haughtily*): Naturally. I wanted to see what Alicia would wish for. Did she wish for something selfish— for beauty, or riches, or a fine palace to live in? (KING *shakes his head firmly.* FAIRY *nods in agreement*) You're right. She did not. Did she wish for her work to become lighter—for her burdens to be removed? (KING *shakes head.* FAIRY *again nods in agreement.*) She did not. (*She points her finger several times in emphasis.*) Instead, she asked for help for her family—and then only when she could think of no other way to help them.

KING: She has been a wonderful daughter. We love her very much.

FAIRY: And she will make a wonderful Queen, one who will not shirk her duties. (*She looks at* QUEEN, *who seems embarrassed*)

KING: But how do you know Alicia wants to go? Perhaps she would rather spend her life here with us, looking after her ailing mother.

FAIRY: Ailing, my foot! But we can easily find out. (*Turns to* ALICIA) My dear, would you like to marry the charming Prince Wonderful and rule over his castle?

ALICIA (*Clasping her hands and speaking ecstatically*): Oh, yes! It will be the dream of my life come true! (*At her words,* PRINCE WONDERFUL *throws open the door and enters.*)

QUEEN (*Impressed*): Oh! Isn't he handsome!

KING (*With awe*): Prince Wonderful! (ALICIA *draws back modestly. The* CHILDREN *enter noisily.*)

CHILDREN: We did the dishes, Alicia. The dishes are done. (*When they see* PRINCE, *they become shy.*) A prince! Isn't he handsome? (*Etc.*)

PRINCE (*Holding out his hand to* ALICIA): Come. My palace is empty without you. (ALICIA *takes his hand, and they exit.*)

ALL (*With wonder*): They will live happily ever after! (*Quick curtain*)

THE END

Aesop, Man of Fables

by Ernestine Phillips

Characters

TANCRED, *a Greek merchant*
AESOP ⎫
CYRUS ⎬ *slaves*
SHEBA ⎭
IADMON, *a rich merchant of Samos*
CROESUS, *King of Lydia*
SOLON, *an Athenian legislator and philosopher*
XANTHUS, *the King's chamberlain*
SLAVES
PURCHASERS

SCENE 1

TIME: *The sixth century B.C.*
SETTING: *The slave market of Samos.*
AT RISE: *On a platform at one side stand several* SLAVES.
A group of PURCHASERS, *including* IADMON, *stands below.* TANCRED *enters from opposite side of stage, followed by* AESOP, CYRUS, *and* SHEBA, *who carry bundles.* AESOP'S *sack, although the largest, is practically empty.*

TANCRED: Wait here, Cyrus and Sheba. Aesop, come with me. (TANCRED *goes to talk with* IADMON *and* AESOP *follows him.*)

481

SHEBA: How weary I am of this journey. You know, Cyrus, when the master told me to choose my bundle, I did not dream that the smallest one would prove so heavy.

CYRUS: And we laughed at Aesop for choosing the largest one!

SHEBA: Who but Aesop would figure out that the bundle of food would grow lighter day by day, while blankets and cooking pots seem to grow heavier!

CYRUS: Do you know what Master Tancred said when I objected to Aesop's trick, Sheba? (SHEBA *shakes her head.*) He said, "Aesop is a smart fellow. His purchaser must pay well for him."

SHEBA: Aesop should bring a good price. (AESOP *joins them.*)

AESOP: Let us hope for Tancred's sake that I do, Sheba. Our master bids us rest while he arranges for our placement in this market. (*They set down their bundles.*)

SHEBA: I hope it will not take long, for it is so hot here.

AESOP: Tancred will leave us as comfortable as possible. I know he regrets that his loss of money requires him to sell us. I am sorry to lose a good master.

CYRUS: I for one shall be glad to have a new master.

SHEBA: So shall I. Life is so dull in the house of Tancred.

AESOP: The country mouse thought his life was dull.

SHEBA (*Tartly*): As no doubt it was!

AESOP: Let me tell you how it all came about. The city mouse came to visit the country mouse. The country mouse served his relative the best he had—oatmeal, bacon, beans, and bread crusts, but the town mouse sniffed, "How can you abide such poor fare? Come with me to the city and I'll show you the pleasures and plenty of a palace." The country mouse willingly accompanied his friend back to the city. After they arrived at the great palace that night, the city mouse proudly took his cousin on a tour of the pantry, kitchen, and storeroom. When they entered the grand dining room they found the remains of a banquet still on the table. While the two mice were feasting upon the food and resting upon a velvet couch, the country mouse said, "The country was never like this!" Suddenly, the door flew open to admit several people and two large cats. The two mice barely escaped with their skins. When the palace was again quiet, the country mouse whispered, "Goodbye, cousin." "What! Are you going so soon?" said the city mouse. The country mouse replied, "Yes. I'd rather nibble crusts and moldy beans in peace than eat cakes and cheese in fear."

SHEBA: You may be right, Aesop. I may wish myself back in the country, but I'd still take that life in the palace if I had the chance.

CYRUS: Any place is preferable to this dirty slave market!

AESOP: That is what the fish thought when he felt the heat of the frying pan. "There is no bearing this," he cried as he leaped into the fire. Instead of mending matters, he was worse off than before.

CYRUS: Must you forever moralize about our being content with our lots because they could be worse!

SHEBA: Aesop does have a point, Cyrus. A bad master would be worse than the fleas and dirt of this slave market. (*Shudders*) Oh, Aesop, have we no hope, then?

AESOP: There is a chance that Iadmon may buy us.

SHEBA: Who is Iadmon?

AESOP (*Pointing*): The man talking with Tancred.

SHEBA (*Impatiently*): But *who* is he?

CYRUS: Is he not the rich merchant of Samos?

AESOP: The same. Iadmon is reputed to be a kind master. (IADMON *and* TANCRED *approach*.)

SHEBA: Sh-h-h, here they come. Let's all try hard to please him. (CYRUS, SHEBA, *and* AESOP *drop to their knees*.)

IADMON: Ah, Tancred, your slaves appear well trained.

TANCRED: They are fine slaves, Iadmon, and I would not part with them willingly. I'll make you a fair price for them.

IADMON (*Walking around* CYRUS, SHEBA, *and* AESOP *and looking them over critically*): Stand up, slaves. (*They stand.*) Turn around. (*They turn. To* SHEBA) What is your name, girl?

SHEBA: Sheba, master.

IADMON: What are your skills?

SHEBA (*Boldly*): I'm a fine cook and I can manage any household—no matter how large or fine.

IADMON (*To* CYRUS): And you, my man, what are you called?

CYRUS: Cyrus, master. You'll find no better man with horses nor a handier man with tools than myself. And gardens bloom under my care.

IADMON: I'm afraid I haven't sufficient work to keep a man of your talents busy. (*To* AESOP) What about you, fellow? What can you do?

AESOP: Nothing, master.

IADMON (*In surprise*): Nothing! What do you mean?

AESOP: Since Cyrus and Sheba do everything, what is there left for me to do?

IADMON (*Laughing heartily*): I'll find something for you. Tancred, I'll buy this slave.

TANCRED: I'll make you a bargain price on the three.

IADMON: No. I need only one. Come to my house and we'll complete the business.

TANCRED: Very well. (*To* CYRUS *and* SHEBA) You two report to the master of the slave market. I'll return shortly. (AESOP *waves goodbye to* SHEBA *and* CYRUS *and follows* IADMON *and* TANCRED *offstage.*)

SHEBA (*Mimicking*): "Nothing!" Aesop says, "Nothing," and Iadmon chooses him!

CYRUS (*Striding about furiously*): Iadmon must be mad. (*Sighs*) At least we are rid of Aesop's eternal story-telling. (SHEBA *puts her face in her hands and weeps.*) What's the matter now?

SHEBA: I—I'll miss Aesop. He kept life from being totally dreary. I even liked his fables.

CYRUS: But you just said . . .

SHEBA: That was jealousy speaking. I'm truly glad for Aesop and wish him good fortune.

CYRUS: So, he has charmed even you! (*Curtain*)

*   *   *

SCENE 2

TIME: *A few years later.*

SETTING: *A room in Iadmon's home in Samos.*

AT RISE: IADMON *and* XANTHUS *are resting on a low couch. There is a basket of fruit on a low table. The men nibble on the fruit while they talk. Beside* IADMON *there is a gong.*

XANTHUS: How I envy you the peace of your island, Iadmon.

IADMON: It has been a hard struggle for us to reach our present state of democracy, Xanthus. Now that we have thrown off the twin yokes of monarchy and aristocracy, it is my hope that we can progress in painting, sculpture, and literature.

XANTHUS: That is a fine dream, Iadmon, a fine dream. I never expect to see its like in Lydia during my lifetime.

IADMON: How goes your life as the King's chamberlain?

XANTHUS: It is filled with problems. Even now, King Croesus is contemplating war with the King of Persia.

IADMON: Will King Croesus not be satisfied until he conquers every nation under the sun?

XANTHUS: Nay, if Croesus won the world he'd seek a way to imprison the stars.

IADMON: I must tell Aesop your words. He has a fable that is exactly to the point.

XANTHUS: Who is Aesop?

IADMON: One of my slaves.

XANTHUS: I would like to hear the fable of this slave.

IADMON (*Strikes gong*): Aesop will be pleased by your interest. He loves telling stories better than working.

XANTHUS: I would not tolerate a lazy slave.

IADMON: Aesop is physically lazy, but he works hard with his mind. As he is frail of body, he would not likely live long otherwise. (AESOP *enters.*)

AESOP (*Bowing*): You rang, master?

IADMON: I would have you tell Xanthus your story of Fortune and the beggar.

AESOP: Gladly, master. (*Bows again*) As you know the story so well, would your guest enjoy hearing it as a dialogue?

IADMON (*Rising eagerly*): An excellent suggestion, Aesop.

AESOP (*To* IADMON): May I use this basket? (IADMON *nods.* AESOP *picks up basket, empties out remaining fruit, and hangs it over his arm. He speaks to* XANTHUS) My master, good sir, is Sir Fortune. He meets a poor beggar—played by myself—wandering down a road. (*Hunching his back,* AESOP *slowly crosses the stage, whining.*) Will life ever deal with me justly? My clothes are rags, my body starved. Will none take pity on me? Why do other people who have so much give so little? They aren't even happy with their possessions. There (*Pointing at* XANTHUS) sits a man worth thousands of drachmas, yet he never stops working to earn more. How silly he is! Now, I would be content with only a very small sum. (*Shaking his head, he hobbles on in silence.* IADMON, *playing the role of Sir Fortune, strides to meet him.*)

IADMON: I will deal with you justly, old man. Hold out your basket and I'll fill it with gold.

AESOP (*Holding out basket with fawning eagerness*): Oh, happiness! Sir, pour me this gold.

IADMON: Be warned, beggar. If a single coin falls from your basket, all the gold will turn to dust. (*Pantomimes pouring of gold.* AESOP *pretends to stagger under the weight of the basket.* IADMON *pauses.*)

AESOP: Don't stop!

IADMON: Your basket is beginning to break.

AESOP (*Whining*): It will hold. Pray continue!

IADMON (*Pouring again*): Haven't you enough now?

AESOP: Just a few more, please!

IADMON (*Pours again, then stops*): It's quite full now. Take care.

AESOP (*Whining*): There is room for one more. Just one more coin, please, sir. (IADMON *pantomimes the dropping in of a single coin. The basket appears to tip sideways.* AESOP *clutches it desperately, but it drops upside down. He lunges after it to grovel on the ground, grasping after "coins" that aren't there.*) Oh, my basket! Oh, my coins! Dust! Dust! All is dust! (IADMON *turns away from* AESOP, *who shakes his fist after him.*) That was a mean trick! You could at least have left me the price of a new basket. But no! The rich have no sympathy for the poor. (*Returning to his own character,* AESOP *rises, straightens his back, and bows.* IADMON *sits near* XANTHUS.)

XANTHUS: If only Croesus were half as wise as your slave, he would realize that in grasping for too much, a man may lose all. It is my fear that, like the beggar, Croesus will overreach himself if he stretches out his hand to grasp Persia. Several of us in Lydia have been wondering if you islanders of Samos would care to— (*He stops, as he glances toward* AESOP) . . .

IADMON: You may speak freely before Aesop.

XANTHUS: Good. The question is—if Croesus persists in his foolishness, should not he and his threat be removed?

IADMON (*Thoughtfully*): As a friend, you have my sympathy, Xanthus, but as a citizen of Samos, I must remind you that we hope to remain at peace with Croesus. You can expect no help from us in furthering any plot against the King.

XANTHUS (*Shuddering*): There is no plot. We would not dare. It's too risky. We merely discuss the possibilities. Anything done would be in absolute secrecy.

IADMON (*Thoughtfully*): In secrecy! In that case, perhaps . . . (AESOP *moves and catches his eye.*) Why, Aesop, have you another fable for our guest?

AESOP (*Bowing*): Good sirs, many frogs once lived very happily in a marshy swamp where they could splash to their heart's content. Life was pleasant and careless, when one day a frog suggested that they needed a king and constitution. After much discussion, they referred the matter to Jove, the great god. "Jove," they cried, "send us a king to rule over us and keep us in order." Jove laughed and threw down a great log that landed with such a mighty splash that it frightened the frogs away. However, when they realized that the log never moved of itself, the boldest of the frogs ventured to touch it. He jumped upon it. Nothing happened. He danced a jig. Log-jigging soon became a popular sport among the frogs. But growing tired of their dumb king, they petitioned Jove again, "Send us a real king to rule over us." Jove grew very angry with the frogs and sent them for their king a great stork, who immediately began eating them. The frogs were sorry, but it was too late. (*Bows.* XANTHUS *and* IADMON *gaze at* AESOP *thoughtfully.*)

XANTHUS (*Nodding*): You are right, Aesop. In making a change, we could go from bad to worse. Perhaps King Croesus may see his error before it is too late. I wonder . . . (*Thoughtfully, staring at* AESOP) Croesus is a lover of wisdom. The great philosopher Solon is even now visiting in his court. (*To* IADMON) Your slave Aesop would please the King. You have but to name his price.

IADMON (*Hesitates*): Aesop is so valuable to me, I doubt that I could put a price on him. Still, the matter is grave. (*After a moment of silence he turns to* AESOP.) Aesop, what do you think about going to Lydia to King Croesus?

AESOP (*Bowing*): Your will is mine, master.

IADMON: Even so, I would know your feelings.

AESOP: I have heard of the wonders of the court of King Croesus—how it is filled with beautiful treasures and is the gathering place of the world's wisest men. Although I would gladly see this court and hear these men, I should not like to end up like the proud horse.

IADMON: Tell us about this proud horse.

AESOP: One day a horse in the fine trappings of nobility met a poor donkey creeping under a heavy load. "Behold, serf," the horse addressed the donkey. "Do you know that when I carry my master, the whole weight of the State rests upon my back? Out of my way, slave, lest I trample you in the dirt!" The poor donkey slunk out of the horse's way, thinking with envy, "If I could change places with that noble horse, how happy I should be!" The donkey was still brooding upon the inequality of their positions when a few weeks later he came upon the same horse, feeble and limping, pulling a common cart of bricks. "How did this come about?" the donkey asked in amazement. "It was the fortune of war," the horse replied. "My master was a soldier and he rode me into battle where I was shot, hacked, and maimed—and thus you see the catastrophe of my fortune." (AESOP *bows.*)

IADMON: Do I understand that you would rather remain with me than increase your fortune in the service of King Croesus?

AESOP: You have been a gentle master, sir, and I have never heard the same said of Croesus.

IADMON: And you a faithful servant, Aesop. Summon my secretary so that I may instruct him to draw up a writ that will make Aesop the slave into Aesop the freedman.

AESOP (*Dropping to his knees before* IADMON): Thank you, master, thank you.

IADMON: Rise, Aesop. (AESOP *rises.*)

XANTHUS: Well done, Iadmon, although I regret that you have cost us both a slave and the possible favor of King Croesus.

AESOP: But if my good master Iadmon gives me leave, I shall gladly accompany you to Lydia, Xanthus.

IADMON: Your life is now your own, Aesop. Make of it what you will.

AESOP: Then I shall go to Lydia. (*Curtain*)

*   *   *

SCENE 3

TIME: *A few weeks later.*

SETTING: *The throne room at the court of King Croesus in Lydia.*

AT RISE: SHEBA *is on her knees scrubbing the floor.* CYRUS *enters.*

CYRUS: How goes it, Sheba?

SHEBA: Slowly. It takes hard scrubbing to clean tile floors, Cyrus.

CYRUS: You should have told the King's chamberlain that you are a good cook.

SHEBA: Not I! Two bad masters have cured me of bragging.

CYRUS (*Wryly*): I'm so weary of grooming horses, I wish I had told Xanthus that I knew nothing about them.

SHEBA: You were sick of vegetable gardening under our last master. (*Thoughtfully*) Perhaps Aesop had the right idea. "Nothing." (*Laughs*) I often wonder what his "nothing" has brought him.

CYRUS: It has brought him just as far as our bragging has brought us.

SHEBA: What! Is Aesop here in the palace of King Croesus?

CYRUS: Yes, he arrived last night with Xanthus. I suppose Xanthus purchased him from Iadmon.

SHEBA: I'm so glad! Now we shall all be together again!

CYRUS: What do masters see in a scrawny slave like Aesop?

SHEBA: They see brains! (*Thoughtfully resumes scrubbing*) I wonder if Aesop could persuade Xanthus to give me some cloth for a new robe? (AESOP *enters unobserved and stands listening with a smile.*) Yes, Aesop could do it. He'd know just the right fable to persuade Xanthus that I need a new robe. It will be long, soft, and a lovely red. How jealous the cook will be when she sees it! (AESOP *bursts into laughter.* SHEBA *jumps to her feet.*) Aesop! How wonderful to see you!

AESOP (*Taking her hand*): How are you, Sheba?

CYRUS: Sheba is pretending to be glad to see you because she wants you to do something for you, Aesop.

AESOP: I'll see what I can do about that robe, Sheba. Meanwhile, I am reminded of a certain milkmaid . . .

SHEBA (*Grabbing up her scrubbing implements*): I've already met that milkmaid. (*Laughs*) I'd enjoy hearing it again, but if Xanthus catches his slaves gossiping in the royal reception room, he'll have us whipped! (*She exits.* XANTHUS *enters.*)

XANTHUS: Aesop, King Croesus will receive you here.

AESOP: Thank you, Xanthus. (XANTHUS *exits.*)

CYRUS (*In surprise*): "King Croesus will receive you!" Strange words to address to a slave.

AESOP: Iadmon gave me my freedom, Cyrus. (XANTHUS *re-enters.* CYRUS *exits hastily, staring back in amazement as he goes out.*)

XANTHUS: Aesop, King Croesus and Solon are coming. When there is occasion, I'll present you. Until then, stand you to one side. (AESOP *nods.* XANTHUS *hurries to the entrance to bow as* KING CROESUS *and* SOLON *enter.*)

CROESUS (*Sits on throne*): Sit you before me, Solon. (SOLON *takes the chair facing* CROESUS.) I've followed your political career in Athens with astonishment. Any man who can persuade his fellow citizens to adopt laws he suggests, and then to keep them during his absence is certainly the greatest of the seven sages.

SOLON: You flatter me, Your Majesty, for I am not the wisest of the wise.

CROESUS: Ah, you are modest! (*Beckons to* XANTHUS *with sceptre.* XANTHUS *advances, bowing.*) Welcome home, Xanthus. We have missed you. Solon, this is our chamberlain. He is a most valuable man to the court.

SOLON (*Nods to* XANTHUS): Happy is the valuable man.

XANTHUS: Our court is honored by your presence, Solon. If it please Your Majesty, I would present a freedman— Aesop, the man of fables.

CROESUS: Let him come forward. (AESOP *steps forward and bows.*) You arrive at an auspicious moment, Aesop. I am seeking the wisest of men. I believe that Solon is the man, but he denies it. Who do you think is the wisest of the wise?

AESOP: Choosing such a one, Your Majesty, is a task even more difficult than describing the chameleon.

CROESUS: How so?

AESOP: I can best explain by a fable. (CROESUS *nods*.) Once two gentlemen traveling across the plains of Africa had a violent disagreement about the color of the chameleon. They readily agreed that he had a fish-shaped head, a lizard body, a long tail, and four paws with three fingers, but when it came to his color one said, "Red," and the other said, "Green." "You never saw a green chameleon!" one cried. "Oh, but I did," cried the other. "I watched him basking in the sun for the better part of an hour." "The sun blinded your eyes," said the first man. "No," answered the second, "I saw him clearly in the shade, and he was green." The two men had almost come to blows when a third man interfered. "You are both mistaken," he said. "The chameleon is coal black. I saw one only last night." "Not so," said the others. "I can prove it," the man cried, "for here I have him in my handkerchief." To the astonishment of all three, the chameleon was neither red, green, nor black, but white—as white as the handkerchief upon which it lay. "Get about your business, gentlemen," said the chameleon. "You are all right, and all wrong. Believe henceforth that you cannot make every man's judgment submit to your own. Others as well as you have eyes."

CROESUS (*Laughs*): Very good, Aesop. Now tell me of yourself.

AESOP: I was born of merchant parents in Phrygia, Your Majesty.

CROESUS: Then you were born free? How lost you your freedom?

AESOP: During one of Your Majesty's raids on Phrygia, my parents were killed. I, a small child, was captured and sold into slavery. After belonging to several masters, it was my good fortune to be sold to Iadmon, the best of masters for any slave.

CROESUS (*Slyly, winking at* XANTHUS): What think you of Aesop's naming Iadmon as the best of masters, Xanthus?

XANTHUS: I can only applaud his choice, Your Majesty. Iadmon has proven his goodness by giving Aesop his freedom.

CROESUS: Tell me, has freedom brought you happiness, Aesop?

AESOP: Freedom has brought me to your court, Your Majesty.

CROESUS: And does my court equal happiness?

AESOP: For those who appreciate its beauty and wisdom, it does.

CROESUS (*Pleased*): I must remember to quote your words to complaining subjects. Solon, define for us the happy man.

SOLON: No man can judge truly of his happiness until he can look back on the whole of his life, Sire.

CROESUS: I disagree! I attained the absolute in happiness when I was engaged in battle. Ah, the dreams of power and conquest that came to me then. If reality could but compare!

AESOP: Truly, all men seek happiness in dreams, O King. May I present to you a fable that the slave Sheba brought to my mind today? In a humorous way, it portrays what Your Majesty has just expressed about dreams.

CROESUS: Certainly.

AESOP: I'll need the assistance of the girl Sheba for this fable.

CROESUS: Fetch her! (AESOP *exits.*)

SOLON: How rare to find a man who has been a slave and has so wise a mind.

XANTHUS: Sire, what think you of entrusting Aesop with the job of distributing the portions of money owed to the citizens of Delphi?

CROESUS: I like it well. Such a true diplomat as Aesop will surely make a wise distribution. (AESOP *returns with* SHEBA, *who carries an earthen jar containing pieces of paper.*)

AESOP (*Whispers to* SHEBA): Do you understand?

SHEBA: Of course. Will this get me the robe?

AESOP: I hope so. (*Bowing to* CROESUS) O King (*Turning and bowing again*) and good sirs, this maid is Sheba. She is taking a jar of milk to market.

SHEBA (*Placing jar on her head and passing in front of them*): When I've sold this fine milk, I will have some money. With the money I can buy a few chicks from Androcles, the farmer. They will lay eggs in a few months, and I'll sell them to the merchants. With my egg money I'll buy a bolt of material from the clothier and make myself a new robe . . . long, soft, and a lovely red color. Then, when I go to market, all the citizens will admire me. The other ladies will be jealous, but I'll just toss my head. (*She tosses her head; the jar falls from her head and breaks into pieces, scattering scraps of paper around the floor to resemble milk. The others roar with laughter.*)

CROESUS: Excellent! Excellent! Don't count your chickens before they hatch! Young woman, you shall have a boon. Name it. (SHEBA *stands in frightened silence*)

AESOP: Sheba would like a new robe, Your Majesty.

CROESUS: She shall have it. Xanthus, see to it.

SHEBA (*Curtsying*): Oh, thank you, Sire, but please give

Aesop the robe instead. Since he has no master to feed and clothe him, he needs the robe more than I.

CROESUS: Well said, girl. You shall each have a robe!

SHEBA: Oh, thank you, Your Majesty.

CROESUS: Aesop, we have a commission for you. Come with us into the garden and you shall hear the details. Solon, are you coming?

SOLON: I'll join you presently. (CROESUS, XANTHUS, *and* AESOP *exit.* SOLON *watches* SHEBA *pick up fragments of jar.* CYRUS *enters.*)

SHEBA: Oh, Cyrus, I'm to have a new robe! Aesop managed it for me.

CYRUS: Good for you!

SHEBA: It's like a dream, with Aesop being free, and King Croesus giving him a commission and giving me a red robe.

CYRUS (*Laughs*): How do you know it will be red?

SHEBA: Aesop will see that it is red!

CYRUS: He probably will. For a slave who started out doing nothing, Aesop has done very well indeed.

SHEBA: Some day he'll be as famous as King Croesus and Solon.

SOLON: You compliment me above my deserts, my child, for Aesop's simple tales will be remembered long after the gold of Croesus and the wisdom of Solon are forgotten. Centuries hence people will still be laughing at Aesop's fables and treasuring the lessons of life they teach. (AESOP *re-enters.*)

SHEBA (*Rushing to* AESOP): Aesop, Solon has been saying such wonderful things about you . . . how people will still be telling your fables thousands of years from now, and . . .

AESOP (*Interrupting with a smile*): Stop, Sheba, lest you persuade me to exaggerate my own importance as the fly did.

SHEBA: Oh, tell us about the fly!

AESOP: One day a fly that was sitting on a coach wheel said to himself, "My, what a dust I am raising." Again, he sat upon the horse's back and said, "How fast I am driving!" (*They all laugh heartily as the curtain falls.*)

THE END

Mrs. Gibbs Advertises

by Mary Thurman Pyle

Characters

MRS. GIBBS	BETTY
HANNAH, *her housekeeper*	BILLY
JACK	MARY JANE
TIM	CHARLIE
ELSIE	TWO BOYS
ERNEST	OTHER CHILDREN

SETTING: *The living room of Mrs. Gibbs' home.*

AT RISE: MRS. GIBBS *sits at desk facing audience. She is looking at the morning paper and smiling with satisfaction.* HANNAH *enters from left carrying a breakfast tray.*

HANNAH: You'll have your breakfast in here, won't you, Mrs. Gibbs?

MRS. GIBBS: Yes, thank you, Hannah. (HANNAH *puts tray on desk.*) Here's the advertisement we put in the paper, Hannah. It looks very nice, and we're almost sure to get some answers.

HANNAH (*Picking up paper and reading it out loud*): "Good homes wanted for four terrier puppies. Call at 410 Pine St. after 9:00 a.m. on Thursday." (*She looks at clock.*) It's just eight-thirty, so you will have plenty of time to eat your breakfast before anyone comes.

MRS. GIBBS (*Starts to nibble at her toast*): I'm sure I will. I *do* hope we are successful in finding good homes for all four of those puppies. You'll feel better about parting with them then.

HANNAH: They're right nice pups. You're sure you couldn't let me take them with us to the summer cottage?

MRS. GIBBS: We've been over all that, Hannah. I really can't let you take the dogs. They would bark and scratch up the garden and—and other things.

HANNAH: I guess they would.

MRS. GIBBS: You can give the puppies away and board the mother dog while we are in the country. That's best. Of course you brought them when you came to work this morning?

HANNAH: They're in a basket in the kitchen—all four of 'em, cute as can be. Maybe we won't get four answers to the ad. (*The doorbell rings.* HANNAH *opens the front door.* JACK *enters, cap in hand, eager.*)

JACK: Is this the place where I can get a dog for nothing?

HANNAH: Why, yes, but you're early. The ad said after nine o'clock.

JACK: I know—but I wanted to get here early so I could be sure to get one of them.

MRS. GIBBS: Let the boy come in, Hannah. Come in, little boy. (JACK *enters.*) I'm Mrs. Gibbs, and (*Gesturing*) this is Hannah, who has the dogs to give away.

JACK: My name's Jack. (*Looks around*) You got 'em in here?

MRS. GIBBS: Bring the basket with the puppies, Hannah. (HANNAH *goes out left.*) Can you give a good home to a pet?

JACK: I've been wantin' a dog like anything, ma'am, and my dad saw the ad in the paper this morning and at first my mom said nothin' doin', a puppy was too much trouble—but I said I'd take care of it, and then she said I could.

MRS. GIBBS: That's splendid.

JACK: I'm going to spend the money I made shovelin' snow to buy the license and a collar. I sure do want that pup. (*The doorbell rings just as* HANNAH *re-enters with a large basket, which she puts on a chair before she answers the door.* TIM, *a small, thin boy, enters.*)

TIM (*Excitedly*): Is this the place that wants dogs for homes—I mean homes for dogs?

HANNAH: Come in.

TIM: I heard about this ad in the paper—and *I* can give a good home to a pup. My name's Tim Andrews.

MRS. GIBBS: And I'm Mrs. Gibbs. So you would like to have a puppy?

TIM: I sure would! My mother wants it, too. We live by ourselves and she works out a lot and she said a dog would be company for me.

MRS. GIBBS: Splendid! You two boys have first choice. The puppies are in that basket. (*The boys go eagerly to the basket and look in, as* HANNAH *stands nearby.* JACK *immediately reaches for one of the puppies.*)

HANNAH: Don't take it out yet. Just look and see which you like best.

JACK: I get first go. (*Looks a minute*) I want that one with the white spot on its head.

TIM: Can I have that little fellow there? (*He points.*) I kinda think he'd like me.

HANNAH: And you would take good care of him?

TIM (*Awed by his good fortune*): Sure I will! He can even sleep in my bed. (*The doorbell rings.*)

MRS. GIBBS: Do you suppose that's another boy? So *soon?* (HANNAH *answers the bell.* ELSIE, *in sweater and skirt, stands there. She has a newspaper turned to the ad.*)

ELSIE: I saw this ad—or rather, my big brother did—and I came right over. (*Sees boys*) Am I too late?

HANNAH: Come in. You're not too late. A girl this time, Mrs. Gibbs. (ELSIE *enters and makes a beeline for the basket.*)

ELSIE (*Looking in*): Oh, aren't they *darling!*

JACK (*Pointing into basket*): That one's mine—with the white spot on its head.

TIM: And that one's mine—the little fellow.

ELSIE: I like the spotted one best. Isn't he *adorable?* I'm going to call him Domino. (JACK *and* TIM *are scornful of this chatter.*)

TIM (*To* ELSIE): You haven't even spoken to *her* yet. Her name's Mrs. Gibbs. She lives here.

ELSIE (*To* MRS. GIBBS): Please excuse me. I didn't even notice you, I just wanted to see the puppies so badly.

MRS. GIBBS: Certainly, my dear. (*To* HANNAH) Please take the breakfast tray away, Hannah. I don't think I'll have time to eat any more breakfast. (HANNAH *takes the tray.*)

HANNAH: I made some little blankets to wrap the puppies in. I'll bring them. (*She goes off with tray.*)

MRS. GIBBS (*To* ELSIE): So little girls like dogs, too?

ELSIE: Oh, yes! I'm absolutely *wild* about dogs. I had one once, but it was run over. (*Quickly*) But we've moved and we have a big yard now. And my brother is going to build a nice little doghouse for Domino—only of course I didn't know he was going to be called that until I saw him.

JACK: A doghouse? Say, that's a good idea!

MRS. GIBBS: And you would really take good care of one of the puppies? You see, they belong to Hannah, my housekeeper, but we are going to my summer cottage soon, and she has no one to leave them with. And I can't let her take them because I can't be annoyed by them.

ELSIE (*Outraged*): *Annoyed* by them! Oh, Mrs. Gibbs, how could such darling little things like these puppies annoy you? Why, they'd make *my* summer perfect!

MRS. GIBBS: I fancy we think differently about a good many things, child. What's your name?

ELSIE: Elsie Smith. (*The doorbell rings.*)

MRS. GIBBS: I'll answer this time myself. (*She goes to door to admit* ERNEST, *a serious, studious-looking boy.*)

ERNEST (*Entering*): Good morning. I saw this ad in the paper.

MRS. GIBBS: Come in. You're in the right place.

ERNEST: I would like to have one of the puppies mentioned in this ad. (*Seeing others*) Is there one left?

MRS. GIBBS (*Genially*): There is just one left. Over there in the basket. (ERNEST *goes quickly to the basket and looks in.*) You boys show our new caller the puppy that's left. (*To* ERNEST) These children have already selected theirs.

ERNEST: That's all right—just so it's a dog, that's all I care. I like them all.

JACK: That one's left—the white one with the black ears.

ERNEST (*Enthusiastically*): Well, say! I think he's best of all. (*To* MRS. GIBBS) Can I really have him? I'll take good care of him. I'm reading a book on the proper care of dogs. (*The doorbell rings.* MRS. GIBBS *goes to door.* BETTY *and* BILLY *enter. Both wear faded and patched clothing, but are very neat and clean.*)

MRS. GIBBS: Good morning. Why, there are two of you this time.

BETTY: Yes, but only Billy, my little brother, wants a dog. Only of course it would be my dog too, and I'd help take care of it.

BILLY (*Very definitely*): I came for a dog.

MRS. GIBBS: Come in, children—but I'm sorry to say you have a disappointment in store for you. There are only four puppies, and we've already had four applicants.

BILLY (*To* BETTY): Where's my dog? You said we were going to get a puppy for our very own.

BETTY: But, Billy, honey, you just heard the lady. We're too late. (HANNAH *enters, holding four little blankets. She also carries a pad and pencil.*)

HANNAH: My! Some more children. I thought I heard the doorbell, but I was stacking the dishes.

MRS. GIBBS: That's quite all right. I answered the doorbell. The trouble is, we haven't enough dogs to go around.

BETTY: We'd better be going. Come on, Billy.

BILLY (*Quiet but firm*): No! I want a puppy first. The paper said they were here.

MRS. GIBBS: I'm sorry. You're a nice little boy, and I like you. But there were only four puppies, and they're taken. (*She sits in chair at right.*)

BETTY: But I came early on purpose. It's not even nine yet. Daddy said we could have the puppy and Billy has his heart set on it.

HANNAH: Too bad Queenie didn't have more than four pups. I'm going to take the names and addresses of the children who take the pups so I can keep track of 'em. We could take this little boy's name, too, in case Queenie has any more.

MRS. GIBBS: Yes, we could. (*Doorbell rings.*) Could that be another answer to our advertisement? (HANNAH *answers.* MARY JANE, *an expensively dressed girl, enters.*)

MARY JANE: Good morning. I came in answer to an ad. Is your mistress at home?

HANNAH: Yes, miss, she is—but they're *my* pups, and they're all gone.

MARY JANE: All gone? But the paper said nine o'clock, and it's only ten minutes to.

HANNAH: Can't help that. The others got here before you.

MARY JANE (*Coming in*): I beg your pardon. (*To* MRS. GIBBS) I'm Mary Jane Armstrong. You probably know my parents.

MRS. GIBBS: The Henry Armstrongs? I know your mother quite well. We belong to the same club.

MARY JANE (*Smiling ingratiatingly; with assurance*): I'm so happy to meet you, Mrs. Gibbs. I just know you are going to let me have one of those puppies. Naturally, I can give it a very good home, and I do love pets so much.

JACK (*Fearing to lose his dog*): These dogs are all given away. I was here first, and I've chosen mine.

TIM (*Also sensing danger*): And I have, too—the little black and tan one.

ELSIE: I was third, and I've chosen one, too.

ERNEST: And the last is mine. She said so. (*To* MRS. GIBBS) You did, didn't you?

BILLY: I want a pup. My sister brought me here to get it.

BETTY: But we were too late, Billy.

MARY JANE: Well, our chauffeur brought me and is waiting outside in the car to take me and the puppy home. I'll be dreadfully disappointed if I don't get one. (*Doorbell rings.* HANNAH *gives* MRS. GIBBS *a quizzical look, then goes to door and opens it.* CHARLIE, *a somewhat pugnacious boy, is standing there.*)

CHARLIE (*Slightly out of breath*): Is this the place—

HANNAH (*Not waiting for him to finish*): Yes, it is, but the puppies are all gone.

CHARLIE (*Belligerently*): What d'you mean, all gone? (*He edges his way past* HANNAH, *but forgets to take off his cap.*) The paper said nine o'clock, and I'm here on time. What's it all about, anyway?

MRS. GIBBS: Take off your hat, young man. (CHARLIE *does so.*) I don't like your manner, but I'll explain the situation, nevertheless. We have only four puppies. Hannah, my housekeeper, owns them and the mother dog, Queenie. But when we go to the country for the summer, she has no one to leave the dogs with, and I can't let her take them with us.

ERNEST: Why? Dogs like the country.

MRS. GIBBS: But I don't like dogs—or rather, I've nothing against dogs except that they bark and tear things up.

CHARLIE: Well, I got here at the time the paper said. (*He recognizes* JACK.) Oh! So you're here already.

JACK: So what?

CHARLIE: You cheated, getting here ahead of the time the paper said.

JACK: I did not cheat. The ad didn't say you couldn't come early.

CHARLIE: I'll get even with you, Jack Henderson. You just wait!

JACK: You just try to do anything to me or my dog and see what happens!

MRS. GIBBS: Boys! Don't quarrel. (*She goes over to basket and looks at puppies.*) Which one do you want, Jack?

JACK: That one. (*Points*) And you've already said I could have it.

CHARLIE: I want a puppy! I'm not going home until I get one.

MRS. GIBBS (*To* JACK): Do you know this boy?

JACK: Sure. Charlie Doyle. He lives next door to me.

MRS. GIBBS: Well, then! Why not share a pet? (*Looks in basket again*) You know, they really are cute little animals.

ELSIE (*Vehemently*): They're perfectly adorable!

MARY JANE: I think we should draw straws or something. Otherwise, it just isn't fair. I intended to take my pet to our country place for the whole summer—and that certainly would be giving it a good home.

MRS. GIBBS (*Laughing*): And I have a country place but don't want to be bothered with a lot of little dogs there.

BILLY: My sister and I could go to the country with you and help take care of the puppies. Then you wouldn't have to give any of them away.

MRS. GIBBS: What an extraordinary idea.

BETTY: Billy, honey, be quiet. Come on, let's go. (*She tries to pull* BILLY *toward the door, but he pulls back. The doorbell rings again.*)

CHARLIE: That must be the rest of the kids.

HANNAH: The rest?

CHARLIE: Sure. There was a whole bunch of them coming up the street, but I was on my bike and I beat 'em. (*Disgusted*) And now I can't even get a dog. (*Doorbell rings again.*)

MRS. GIBBS: Whatever shall we do, Hannah? (HANNAH *replies by stalking to the door. A number of boys and girls are outside, and they all talk at once: "Is this where the puppies are?" "There's an ad in the paper."* HANNAH *tries to answer but cannot make herself heard.* TWO BOYS *slip past her into the room.* MRS. GIBBS *goes to the door and tries to speak over the noise, but she cannot be heard.*)

CHARLIE (*Loudly, to* MRS. GIBBS): You want these kids to be quiet?

MRS. GIBBS: Yes, of course.

CHARLIE (*Going to door and shouting*): Hey, you kids! Pipe down. You heard me—pipe down. You'd better do as I say or I'll make you wish you had.

1st Boy: You and who else? (CHARLIE *starts to chase the* Two Boys *who have pushed into the room.*)

CHARLIE: Scram!

2ND Boy: We want to talk to the lady.

1st Boy: I came to get a puppy for free. (*Under* CHARLIE's *bullying manner, other children gradually quiet down and come in.*)

CHARLIE (*To* MRS. GIBBS): You can explain it to them now.

MRS. GIBBS: Dear, dear! I hardly know whether I care to. They're so—so noisy!

HANNAH: I'll explain it. Boys and girls! The puppies we advertised about have all been given away. If Queenie had only known so many children would want her puppies, maybe she would have had more. (*Some of the children laugh at this.*) We're sorry—but you'll have to go away now.

CHARLIE (*Still masterful*): Go on! You heard her. (*The group turns away, ad-libbing remarks of disappointment.* HANNAH *stands at the door as they go out.*)

MRS. GIBBS: Well! I had no idea children liked dogs so much.

ELSIE: You'd like them yourself if you'd get to know them. I'm sure you would.

MRS. GIBBS (*Looking into basket*): Which is yours?

ELSIE: The spotted one—Domino.

MRS. GIBBS (*Chuckling*): Domino? A very original name. He is a cute fellow.

TIM: So's mine. I think I'll call him Runt.

ERNEST: Mine's going to be called Jasper.

MRS. GIBBS: Hannah, please give the children the puppies. (HANNAH, *back to audience, takes out puppies, which may be stuffed animals, one by one, wrapping each in a little blanket. The new owners receive them with eagerness and ad-lib thanks.*)

MARY JANE: I'm so disappointed I could cry.

CHARLIE: Why doesn't your father buy you a dog?

MARY JANE: I wanted one of these. I thought it would be so nice to give a homeless dog a good home.

BILLY: I want one, too. Maybe I could have the mother dog—although the puppies are nicer.

HANNAH: Have Queenie? I should say not! Put your names and addresses on this sheet of paper, and if there are ever any more pups, we'll let you know.

MARY JANE: I'll give you my address, although I'll probably buy a dog. (*She writes name on paper.*)

JACK (*To* CHARLIE): You could have Spot over at your house part of the time. (CHARLIE *does not respond.*)

MARY JANE: Goodbye, Mrs. Gibbs. My mother said she thought the address in the ad was where you live and that you were a very lonely woman. But you don't look lonely right now. I do hope you enjoy your summer in the country.

MRS. GIBBS: Thank you. (MARY JANE *goes out.* ELSIE, ERNEST *and* TIM *write down names.*)

JACK: Doing anything special this afternoon, Charlie?

CHARLIE: Nothin' special. Why?

JACK: Would you help me build a doghouse for Spot?

CHARLIE (*Trying not to appear too eager*): I guess so.

JACK: I have some boards left over from our new garage.

CHARLIE: And we have some paint. We can paint it white with red trim.

JACK: Come on! Oh, my name and address. (*He stops at desk and hastily scribbles, then goes to door.*) Thanks for the pup. (*He and* CHARLIE *dash off.*)

ERNEST: And for mine. (*He looks at* MRS. GIBBS *and then at* HANNAH.) I'll take good care of Jasper. I'm reading a book on the care of dogs.

TIM: I'll walk with you, Ernest. I want you to tell me

what that book says. Goodbye and thanks. (TIM *and* ERNEST *go out.*)

ELSIE: Really, Mrs. Gibbs, you would like dogs if you would just have them around a while. I know you would. (*Notices* BILLY *still standing there*) I'm so sorry you didn't get a puppy. (*With a struggle, then straightening up, with resolution*) You can have mine. (*Holds it out*) I'll get another one some time, maybe.

BETTY (*Restraining* BILLY): Oh, no. We couldn't take yours. You got here before we did. The puppy belongs to you.

ELSIE (*Relieved*): Well—all right. Goodbye.

MRS. GIBBS: Goodbye, my dear. (ELSIE *goes out.*) That was a wonderful thing for that child to do—offering to give her dog away.

HANNAH: It certainly was.

BETTY: Did you say I could leave our name and address? (HANNAH *indicates the paper and* BETTY *writes.*) In case Queenie has any more puppies.

BILLY: I hope she has some more very soon.

BETTY: Billy! (*Apologetically*) I try to teach him good manners.

MRS. GIBBS: He's a nice little boy and you're doing a good job. And now, goodbye, children. (*They ad-lib goodbyes and go out.*)

HANNAH: I'll say that's one ad that brought results.

MRS. GIBBS: Hannah, couldn't you do something to make it up to that little fellow?

HANNAH: I know what we could do. I thought of it a minute ago.

MRS. GIBBS: Well, what do you suggest? A little present, perhaps?

HANNAH: Take him and his sister with us to the country for a few weeks—or maybe a month.

MRS. GIBBS (*Gasps*): Take them with us—to my country place?

HANNAH: That's what country places are for—children and dogs. You won't have the dogs, but maybe you can give some children who can't afford it, a vacation in the country.

MRS. GIBBS: Whatever made you think of that?

HANNAH: When the little boy said he could come to the country with us and take care of the dogs.

MRS. GIBBS: That was quaint, wasn't it? (*Ponders a moment*) Hannah, do you understand children?

HANNAH: Yes, I understand them.

MRS. GIBBS: Billy and Betty are nice children.

HANNAH: Maybe the other little girl could come, too— The one who offered her dog.

MRS. GIBBS: Yes, Elsie. And one of the boys looked awfully pale and thin—the one who is going to call his dog Runt.

HANNAH: I kind of liked the one who's reading the book on the care of dogs.

MRS. GIBBS: It's a good thing we have their names and addresses. (*Thoughtful again*) It would be more work for you, Hannah.

HANNAH: I wouldn't mind. I get lonesome in the country.

MRS. GIBBS: Maybe I've been lonely and didn't know it. (*Suddenly*) We really ought to take Queenie, as company for the children. (*Begins to get enthusiastic over the new idea*) Leave the kitchen work for the time being, Hannah. Here, sit down. We've a great deal of planning to do. (*The two women are seated with the sheets of paper before them when the sound of a dog barking is heard off.*)

HANNAH: Oh, Mrs. Gibbs, I'm sorry. I forgot to tell you I brought Queenie with me this morning. But I put her outside and I didn't think you would hear her.

MRS. GIBBS: Go get Queenie and bring her in here. I'd like to get acquainted. (*They smile happily, as the curtain falls.*)

THE END

Pocahontas, the Tomboy Princess

by Helen M. Roberts

Characters

POWHATAN, *Chief of the Algonquins*
TWO SQUAWS, *about 16*
POCAHONTAS (MATOAKA), *11 or 12*
FOUR INDIAN GIRLS, *friends of Pocahontas*
MOTHER
INDIAN RUNNER
OPECHANCANOUGH, *brother of chief*
WARRIORS
JOHN SMITH, *28*
OPITCHAPAN, *second brother of chief*
QUEEN OF APPOMATTOX
TWO EXECUTIONERS

SETTING: *The council fire of Powhatan, in Virginia, January 5, 1608.*
AT RISE: CHIEF POWHATAN *is seated near the fire on a wooden throne. A young squaw is seated on each side of him.* POCAHONTAS *is playing around the fire with* FOUR INDIAN GIRLS, *who are about her age. They are playing their idea of a game such as "Follow the Leader."*

POCAHONTAS (*Preparing to jump over the fire*): What's the matter with you girls? You don't follow me very well.

1ST GIRL: Oh, Matoaka! Don't try to jump over the fire! It's bad luck! Besides, you'll burn your feet.

POCAHONTAS: Nonsense! Do you dare me to do it?

2ND GIRL: *I* dare you to do it! But surely you won't!

POCAHONTAS: Well, here I go! (*Runs and clears the fire*) It's really nothing! Let me see you do it now.

GIRLS: We couldn't! It's too dangerous! We don't want to burn our feet!

POCAHONTAS: But what's the use of playing "Follow the Leader" if you don't follow?

3RD GIRL: Don't choose the hardest things to do, then.

4TH GIRL: You do tricks more like a boy than a girl.

POCAHONTAS: I want to be as brave as any boy and do anything that a boy can do. There's nothing in the whole world I admire so much as skill and bravery.

1ST GIRL (*Sadly*): Don't you like to play with us any more, Matoaka?

POCAHONTAS (*Kindly*): Of course I do! The boys wouldn't play with me anyway, even if I am a princess.

2ND GIRL: Now if you would dance like a princess, we might be able to follow you.

POCAHONTAS: Oh, dancing is not much fun, unless it's a war dance. See if you can do this! (*She turns a somersault, and the others follow, clumsily.*)

4TH GIRL: We did that! It was fun!

MOTHER (*Approaching from left*): Matoaka! Matoaka!

POCAHONTAS: What is it, Mother?

MOTHER: That's what I want to know! What is all this tumbling around you are doing?

POCAHONTAS: We're playing "Follow the Leader," but the girls don't play it very well.

MOTHER: They could follow you well enough if you did what a girl of your age should be doing!

POCAHONTAS (*Rebelliously*): Ah! I'll have to do *those* things soon enough!

MOTHER: It's time for you to come home now to grind the corn and prepare the venison for the men's supper. You know how they grumble if everything is not ready when they want it.

POCAHONTAS (*Running around her mother playfully*): Look at Father sitting there on the council throne! He won't be ready to eat for hours! (*Stops and pleads*) Please let us play for a while longer.

1ST GIRL: *We'll* have to go soon to help our mothers too, Matoaka.

2ND GIRL: My father gets very angry if we keep him waiting.

POCAHONTAS (*Sighing loudly*): Well, if we all have chores to do, we'll all go—but not for a little while.

MOTHER: Then you want *me* to go home and do your work for you as well as my own, do you?

POCAHONTAS (*Gaily*): Would you do it, Mother?

MOTHER: I suppose so! I never saw such a child for getting her own way from her father and mother. None of the other children can do it.

POCAHONTAS (*Clapping her hands*): Oh, thank you, Mother! Thank you! I'll be home soon. Before you go, watch me do this!

MOTHER: What is it, now?

POCAHONTAS: It hasn't a name, but I call it a handspring! Come on and follow me, girls! If you liked turning somersaults, you will like this. It's a little harder, though. Watch me carefully, first! (*They all watch her turn a handspring, as an* INDIAN RUNNER *rushes in, and they collide and fall down.*)

RUNNER (*Getting up hastily*): Pardon me, Princess.

POCAHONTAS: Why don't you look where you're going?

POWHATAN (*Laughing, fondly*): Ah, my little Matoaka! You don't act much like a Princess. You are a regular tomboy. You are very playful and mischievous. You are *Pocahontas*.

GIRLS (*Ad lib*): She is Pocahontas! She is Pocahontas! Po-ca-hon-tas! (*Etc.*)

POCAHONTAS (*Standing up to brush herself off*): I'd rather be Pocahontas than—than some people I know!

POWHATAN: Hush, my child! The Chief must hear what news the runner brings. What is it, lad?

RUNNER (*Breathlessly*): Great news, O King! Your brother, Opechancanough, is approaching with a white prisoner.

POWHATAN: A white prisoner! Are you sure?

RUNNER: Yes, Chief. I saw him with my own eyes.

POCAHONTAS (*To* GIRLS): A white man! I've never seen one before!

3RD GIRL: Hush! The runner is speaking.

RUNNER: Your brother captured him after a long chase. He had found the way to your sacred land, even into the burial grounds of your ancesters.

POWHATAN: That is bad—very bad! We shall have to punish this man.

POCAHONTAS (*Running toward left and looking offstage*): Here they come, Father! Here they come!

GIRLS (*Dancing excitedly, as they follow* POCAHONTAS): Here they come! Here they come! Many warriors and their prisoner!

POWHATAN (*Shouting*): Bring the prisoner before me! (OPECHANCANOUGH *and* OPITCHAPAN *enter with* WARRIORS *carrying tomahawks or bows.*)

OPECHANCANOUGH: Greetings, my Brother Powhatan! We bring you a white prisoner. (CAPTAIN JOHN SMITH *is brought before them.*)

POWHATAN: What is your name, Paleface?

SMITH: I am Captain John Smith.

POWHATAN: What are you doing in my territory, Captain Smith?

SMITH: I didn't know it was your territory, Chief Powhatan. I traveled up this river to find a route to the great western waters.

POWHATAN: You should have stayed in your own land across the sea. This land belongs to Indians.

OPECHANCANOUGH: This man and his companions entered our sacred burial grounds, my brother. We killed his companions.

POWHATAN: Have you other charges against him, Opechancanough?

OPECHANCANOUGH: Many other charges, Powhatan. When we pursued him, he strapped his Indian guide to him as a shield against our arrows.

POCAHONTAS (*Excitedly, to* GIRLS): Why the Paleface is as brave as an Indian chief and as crafty, too.

GIRLS (*Ad lib*): Sh! Don't talk so loud, Pocahontas! (*Etc.*)

POWHATAN: How, then, did you capture such a wily man?

OPECHANCANOUGH: He almost escaped to his boat. Fortunately for us, he slipped into a bog and nearly drowned before we caught him.

POWHATAN: This story interests me, brother. Before we go further in the trial, I wish the hand-washing ceremony for the prisoner. (*Calls*) Queen of Appomattox! Bring out the water bowl to wash his hands! (*She obeys.*)

SMITH: Thank you, Chief Powhatan!

POWHATAN: You don't need to thank me, Captain Smith! (*Chuckling*) So you fell in a mud-hole and gave up, eh?

SMITH: I threw away my gun, hoping for mercy.

OPECHANCANOUGH: We granted him mercy, all right—but only that *you* might punish him the more, O Chief.

POWHATAN: You can depend on me.

QUEEN OF APPOMATTOX (*Bringing in bundle of feathers to dry* SMITH's *hands*): There, my Chief. The ceremony is performed. (*Exits*)

POWHATAN: What else has the prisoner done?

OPECHANCANOUGH: Our younger brother, Opitchapan, will tell you that.

OPITCHAPAN (*Approaching* POWHATAN): This paleface prisoner wounded many of our warriors in the chase. His gun crashed like the great thunder, and several men fell.

POWHATAN (*Rising in anger*): What? This prisoner has killed our men?

OPECHANCANOUGH: More swiftly than the arrow, more deadly than the lightning, more loudly than the mighty thunder, death struck our companions!

POCAHONTAS (*Whispering loudly*): The Paleface is a great and powerful man!

POWHATAN (*Sternly*): What have you to say for yourself, Captain Smith?

SMITH (*Bravely*): I shot only to save my life. I did not want to kill your warriors.

POWHATAN: Now it is *our* turn to repay you. (*To council*) What is your will, brothers?

WARRIORS (*Murmuring angrily, then shouting, ad lib*): Kill him! Death to the prisoner! (*Dancing wildly around fire, shouting and singing*) Kill him! Death to the prisoner! (*Etc.*)

POWHATAN (*After a few moments*): Captain Smith, we have three charges against you, any one of them serious enough for the death penalty. First, you and your paleface friends have taken much of our country, killing our game and taking our food. Second, you yourself have entered our sacred ground where no outsider dares tread.

Third, you have wounded and killed several of my men before you were caught. Have you anything to say?

WARRIORS (*Dancing wildly about, ad lib shouting*): Kill him! Death to Paleface! Kill him! (*Etc.*)

POWHATAN (*Raising his hand for silence*): Hush, my people. We shall act with justice. (*To* SMITH) Have you anything to say, Captain Smith?

SMITH (*Shaking his head*): Nothing—except to ask for mercy.

POWHATAN (*Smiling*): We will give you mercy—a quick death! Brothers, bring the white stones. (WARRIORS *go off and return with two white stones which they place before* CHIEF POWHATAN.)

OPECHANCANOUGH: Here are the death stones, O Mighty Chief!

POWHATAN: Good. Now, Executioners, bring your clubs and tomahawks here. (Two EXECUTIONERS *come forward, clubs and tomahawks poised.*)

1ST EXECUTIONER: Here are the powerful clubs and sharp tomahawks, O Chief!

POWHATAN: Throw the prisoner on the stones, and we shall show him how quickly our justice will follow his evil deeds. (SMITH *is shoved toward stones.*)

2ND EXECUTIONER: Place his head on the large rock, ready for our mighty blows.

POCAHONTAS (*Coming forward, frightened*): No, no! They must not do it.

GIRLS (*Pulling her back, ad lib*): Hush, Pocahontas! It is the will of the council! You must not interfere. (*Etc.*)

POCAHONTAS (*Rushing forward again*): No! They must not kill him. They *shall not* kill him!

POWHATAN: Are your clubs ready, my braves?

1ST EXECUTIONER: Ready, O Chief!

POWHATAN: When I drop my hand, let your blows fall!

(*He raises his hand,* and EXECUTIONERS *raise clubs and tomahawks.*)

POCAHONTAS (*Suddenly rushing to* SMITH's *side, then kneeling before* POWHATAN): You must not do it!

WARRIORS (*Angrily, ad lib*): Kill him! He is our enemy! He must die! (*Etc.*)

POCAHONTAS (*Lifting* SMITH's *head as if to protect him from blows of tomahawks*): He is brave! He must not be killed.

POWHATAN (*Holding up his hand for silence*): What is the meaning of this behavior, daughter?

POCAHONTAS (*Pleadingly*): The Paleface is not worthy of death. He is young and brave. He will make a good warrior for you, venerable Father.

POWHATAN (*Smiling fondly*): I can never refuse you anything, my child! He is your prisoner. (*To* EXECUTIONERS) Put down your clubs.

POCAHONTAS: And you will really spare his life? (CHIEF *nods.*) Then you are free, white man, free! (*Lifts his head.*)

SMITH (*Rising, with a smile, bows deeply to* POCAHONTAS): Thank you for my life, Indian maiden. It may not be worth much, but it's the best life I have!

POWHATAN (*Sternly*): You may spend it making arrows and beads for my daughter.

SMITH: And what is your name, I pray, young maiden?

POWHATAN (*Gruffly*): Indian maidens do not tell their names to strangers. You may call her Pocahontas.

SMITH: Pocahontas! Would you like this compass as a little gift of thanks from me? (*Takes it from his pocket, along with a string of beads.*) See how it points to the north, always! You could never get lost with such a fine instrument to guide you!

POWHATAN: Even a young Indian girl needs no such

trickery to guide her. She knows direction by the sun or the stars. Don't you, Pocahontas?

POCAHONTAS: Why, of course! But I *would* like those pretty beads, if I may have them.

SMITH: They are yours to keep. A present from Captain John Smith to Princess Pocahontas. (*Bows*)

POCAHONTAS (*Looking at beads, then putting them around her neck*): I will always be your friend, Captain Smith, just as I have been today.

SMITH: And I shall always treasure that friendship, Pocahontas! (*Curtain falls.*)

THE END

The Day the Moonmen Landed

by Rose Kacherian Rybak

Characters

MOON MAYOR MUGGINS
THREE LUNAR ASTRONAUTS
MR. MCGUIRE
MR. CASEY
MR. O'CONNOR
KATHLEEN, *a baton twirler*
IRISH CHILDREN
JOSE
CARMEN

ROSITA
ANNA
PABLO
MEXICAN CHILDREN
TWO BOYS (*Dragon*)
CHINESE PARADERS
MARIA
ITALIAN CHILDREN

TIME: *Present light year.*

SETTING: *The Moon Office of Moon Mayor Muggins is at left. At center and right is bare stage where Earth scenes are played. A backdrop of skyscrapers, factories, farms, etc., is upstage. Moon and Earth scenes, played at left and right stage, respectively, are indicated by spotlight.*

AT RISE: *Spot on Moon Office.* MOON MAYOR MUGGINS *is pacing up and down in front of the screen. He glances impatiently at his watch.*

MOON MAYOR MUGGINS: Where are those men? I called the Astronaut Training Center an hour ago, and they're still not here! (*Goes to desk and picks up telephone*)

Calling Cape Can-Have-It-All. . . . This is Moon Mayor Muggins. What happened to those astronauts I sent for? How are they going to explore the universe when they can't even find their way to my office? (*Pause*) What do you mean, they got tied up in traffic? Never mind—I think I hear them coming now. (THREE ASTRONAUTS, *one in green, enter and step forward in turn.*)

1ST ASTRONAUT (*Saluting*): Lunar Astronaut Number 1 reporting, sir.

2ND ASTRONAUT (*Saluting*): Lunar Astronaut Number 2 reporting, sir.

3RD ASTRONAUT (*Saluting*): Lunar Astronaut Number 3 reporting, sir.

MOON MAYOR MUGGINS: At ease, men. First, I want an account of why it took you one hour to float here from Cape Can-Have-It-All!

1ST ASTRONAUT (*Apologetically*): Well, sir, you know the bottlenecks on those moonbeams.

2ND ASTRONAUT: Especially since the Gravity Commissioner made them all one way.

MOON MAYOR MUGGINS: All right, all right. Traffic is only part of the problem around here lately.

3RD ASTRONAUT: Is that why you've called us here today, sir?

MOON MAYOR MUGGINS: Precisely. The Moon is becoming so overcrowded that immediate steps must be taken to provide more elbowroom. We've used up all the cities, suburbs and farms, so there's only one way to go . . .

1ST ASTRONAUT: Into outer space.

MOON MAYOR MUGGINS: Precisely. Now, on this universe chart there is a nearby planet called Earth, which should satisfy our needs very adequately. The ideal country on Earth is called America.

2ND ASTRONAUT: And we are going to annex it. Is that right, Chief?

MOON MAYOR MUGGINS: Not so fast! Before we do any large-scale invading, we must secure a typical American and study his habits and ways, so that we can make the proper adjustments for Earth life.

3RD ASTRONAUT: How will we go about this mission, sir?

MOON MAYOR MUGGINS: The plan is this. At the right atmospheric moment, one of you will be launched by rocket to a prearranged spot. When you are directly over the spot, you will parachute to ground safely. Find a typical American, radio back immediately, and I will arrange a return rocket to pick you both up. This must all be done within twenty-four hours.

1ST ASTRONAUT: What happens if we fail?

MOON MAYOR MUGGINS: Then you are fated to spend your life on this new planet, Earth. So you see how dangerous this assignment is. And you (*Putting his hand on* 1ST ASTRONAUT's *shoulder*) will be the first to try! Now, all the scientific data points to one good landing area this month. It is a street named Fifth Avenue in New York City. That is where you will find yourself.

1ST ASTRONAUT: Just one question, sir. When will the launching take place?

MOON MAYOR MUGGINS: The day for the Fifth Avenue launching will be (*Pause*) March 17th! (*Shakes hands with* 1ST ASTRONAUT) Good luck. (*The spotlight goes out, as they exit left. Spotlight shines on group of* IRISH CHILDREN *at right, with instruments, playing "Mac-Namara's Band" or similar song.* KATHLEEN *is twirling baton.* MR. CASEY, MR. McGUIRE, *and* MR. O'CONNOR *are watching them and looking offstage at parade. After one chorus,* 1ST ASTRONAUT *enters holding parachute.*)

MR. McGUIRE (*Pointing offstage*): What do you call this?

MR. CASEY: I haven't missed a St. Patty's Day parade in twenty years, but I never saw the likes of this float!

MR. O'CONNOR (*Angrily*): That Houligan clan can dream of more ways to steal the show each year.

1ST ASTRONAUT: Is this Fifth Avenue, New York City?

MR. CASEY (*Sarcastically*): Well it isn't County Cork!

1ST ASTRONAUT: Are you a typical American?

MR. CASEY (*Indignantly*): Castin' aspersions on my citizenship, are you now?

MR. O'CONNOR: Be polite, can't you, Casey? You can see he's an out-of-towner. Probably from Dublin.

KATHLEEN: And bless his heart, he's painted himself all green.

1ST ASTRONAUT: Oh, that's not paint, ma'am, that's my natural color.

KATHLEEN: Natural color? They must be making that old Irish tea a lot stronger than they used to.

MR. MCGUIRE: Sure, and they'll be puttin' the old Irish shillelagh to us if we don't get on with this parade. Will you be marching with us, friend?

KATHLEEN: You can stand next to me, sir. I find your manners quite charming.

1ST ASTRONAUT: How warm and friendly these typical Americans are. I confess it will be hard to leave them. (*Piano chord heard.*)

MR. MCGUIRE: There's our cue. Give it everything you've got, folks. (*All sing "When Irish Eyes Are Smiling."*)

MR. CASEY: There's the reviewing stand ahead. Let's step lively as we go by. (*They march down center aisle.*)

KATHLEEN (*Speaking from aisle*): Are you enjoying our parade, sir?

1ST ASTRONAUT (*Speaking from aisle*): Never have I enjoyed myself more, Kathleen, and never did I find a nicer companion.

KATHLEEN: Must you go back to your home now?

1ST ASTRONAUT: Go back to my home? Why, no, I don't

have to go back anywhere. In fact, I think I'll make New York City my home. Erin go bragh! Don't I sound like a typical American already? (*Spotlight goes out right as they exit. Spotlight shines left, on Moon Office.* MOON MAYOR MUGGINS *is pacing back and forth.*)

MOON MAYOR MUGGINS: Eight months—eight long months and still no word from my first astronaut. (2ND *and* 3RD ASTRONAUTS *enter.*)

2ND ASTRONAUT: You sent for us, Chief?

MOON MAYOR MUGGINS: Yes, I did. Here it is November, and we've had no word from our astronaut. I can't wait any longer. This mission to bring back a typical American from Earth has been delayed too long. Astronaut Landing Agency reports that conditions for a good landing exist in a place called Texas. You (*Putting his hand on* 2ND ASTRONAUT's *shoulder*) will be dropped by parachute in that vicinity. Remember to bring back a typical American immediately.

2ND ASTRONAUT: You can count on me, Chief. (*Spotlight goes out as they exit left. Spotlight shines on* CARMEN, ROSITA, ANNA *and* PABLO *at right. They are holding maracas and claves, and chattering.* JOSE *enters, carrying his guitar.*)

JOSE: Hello, amigos. I'm sorry I'm late.

CARMEN: Hurry, Jose! We finished gathering all the strawberries long ago, and we can't celebrate the harvesting of the crop without you!

ROSITA: It's not Jose we need, it's his guitar. Who ever heard of a Mexican celebration without music?

CARMEN: After working all day in the hot Texas sun, perhaps Jose doesn't have the energy to play for us.

JOSE: You underestimate the energy and spirit of Mexican farmhands, Carmen. (*All laugh.* 2ND ASTRONAUT *enters.*)

526 THE DAY THE MOONMEN LANDED

ANNA: Who is this coming from the north field?

PABLO: He must be new in the area. Never saw him before.

ROSITA: Let's be nice to him. You know how much we appreciated it when we first crossed the border from Mexico and people were kind. (*Turning to* 2ND ASTRONAUT) Hello, are you new here?

2ND ASTRONAUT: Well, you might say I'm passing through. Are you typical Americans?

PABLO: Oh, si, si. Why don't you join our celebration? Come, let us sing. (CHILDREN *sing Spanish song.*)

2ND ASTRONAUT: What wonderful rhythm. I could hardly keep my feet from tapping.

ANNA: Why should you stop yourself from dancing? We can remedy that in a minute. Musicians, are you ready? (CHILDREN *do Mexican Hat Dance to music.*)

2ND ASTRONAUT: Where I come from, there's nothing to compare with that. What are those instruments you are holding?

JOSE: These are maracas. They are dried-out gourds filled with pebbles. When you shake them in time to the music, they make a happy sound.

ROSITA: And these are claves—little sticks that beat the rhythm. (*Claps sticks together*)

2ND ASTRONAUT: Do you think if I stayed here with you that I could someday learn to make such happy music?

CHILDREN: Si, si—stay here with us, amigo.

2ND ASTRONAUT: That settles it. Muchos gracias, amigos. Now I am a typical American, too! (*Spotlight goes out, as they exit, right. Spotlight shines left on Moon Office.* MOON MAYOR MUGGINS *is pacing back and forth.*)

MOON MAYOR MUGGINS: This is terrible, this is awful! My second brightest astronaut is gone, lost forever. (3RD ASTRONAUT *enters.*)

3RD ASTRONAUT: Lunar Astronaut reporting, sir.

MOON MAYOR MUGGINS: Welcome! You know why I've called you. Two out of two attempts have been failures. Astronaut, I am counting on you.

3RD ASTRONAUT: I have a suggestion, sir. I have studied the reports and charts, and there seems to be a place called San Francisco, California, where I can surely corner one of those elusive Americans.

MOON MAYOR MUGGINS: Have you checked the landing space available?

3RD ASTRONAUT: Yes, sir, it looks like an ideal location.

MOON MAYOR MUGGINS: Very well, we will drop you in San Francisco, California. If you have trouble in your first target area, you will proceed to another part of town where you may have better luck. Any questions?

3RD ASTRONAUT: No, sir. I anticipate a quiet, peaceful mission.

MOON MAYOR MUGGINS (*Resting his hand on* 3RD ASTRONAUT'S *shoulder*): My boy, you're my last hope. The others have all failed to return.

3RD ASTRONAUT: I know, sir, and I promise to do the job.

MOON MAYOR MUGGINS (*Shaking his hand*): Goodbye and good luck. (*Spotlight goes off as they exit left. Spotlight shines right on* 3RD ASTRONAUT *in center, looking around curiously.*)

3RD ASTRONAUT: Here I am in San Francisco, California, and everything is just as quiet as I expected. (*Suddenly from rear of auditorium the Chinese parade begins. 2* BOYS *dressed as the Dragon lead, followed by* CHINESE PARADERS *throwing colored streamers and rattling their noisemakers. They march down the aisle to the accompaniment of a Chinese record, march onstage and pause before* 3RD ASTRONAUT.)

CHINESE PARADERS: Happy Chinese New Year, Western friend! (*They march around stage, then go down aisle and out of the auditorium as they entered.*)

3RD ASTRONAUT (*Staring after them, then suddenly running to edge of stage*): I have failed in my mission! I became so engrossed with those typical Americans that I forgot to capture one of them. Oh, well, their dragon leader would never have fit into our rocket ship anyway. Moon Mayor Muggins ordered me to another part of town if I had any difficulty, so I think I'll try going in that direction . . . (*Exits left.* ITALIAN CHILDREN *enter from right and do Italian dance. Towards the end of the dance,* 3RD ASTRONAUT *enters.*) These Americans look a little different from the last group but they're just as noisy. Imagine, people so happy that they dance in the streets. What amazing people these Americans are!

MARIA: Ciao, amico, welcome to La Festa, the feast. Have you tasted my pizza yet? You look half-starved. Come on Rosa, Tony, Gina. While I fatten up our visitor, you serenade him a little!

3RD ASTRONAUT: Oh, you are all too kind! (CHILDREN *sing Italian song.*)

MARIA: What do you think of our song, signor?

3RD ASTRONAUT: It's just out of this world, Maria, or should I say in my newly-found American way, Com'è bella! (*They exit right, as spotlight goes off, then shines left on Moon Office.* MOON MAYOR MUGGINS *is pacing back and forth.*)

MOON MAYOR MUGGINS: This is unbelievable, fantastic! Three of my best Moonmen have all deserted this beautiful place to stay in a place called America. It must be a very wonderful and special place. There's only one way to find out the truth! I shall go myself to this ideal place where everyone wants to live. Let's see the latest scientific report. (*Goes over to universe chart*) Best conditions for a landing exist in a place called Times Square subway in New York at 5 P.M. This should be good! Here I go! (*Exit. Lights dim, spot on bare stage right.*)

OFFSTAGE VOICE: Last stop, Times Square! All out! (*There is a mad stampede across stage from all directions, in which* MOON MAYOR MUGGINS *ends up on the floor, all disheveled.*)

MOON MAYOR MUGGINS: It's lunacy, that's what it is— lunacy. Calling Cape Can-Have-It-All! (*Begging*) Take me home, please!! (*They exit left, as spotlight goes out. Spotlight shines left on Moon Office.* MOON MAYOR MUGGINS *is sitting dejected, his head in his hands.*) There's nothing left for me now. All my friends have gone to that horrible place. And I was so sure that America would be a very wonderful place . . . (3 ASTRONAUTS, *and all* CHILDREN *enter*)

1ST ASTRONAUT: But it *is* a wonderful place, Moon Mayor. We came for a visit with our typical American friends to prove it to you!

MOON MAYOR MUGGINS: Typical? How can you say each one is typical when they all look so different?

2ND ASTRONAUT: But that is the wonderful thing about America. Regardless of how they look, they are all the same wonderful kind of Americans!

CHILDREN: Even you would make a wonderful American, Mayor Muggins!

MOON MAYOR MUGGINS (*His spirits lifted*): Do you really think so? Could I try?

ALL: Yes, yes. (*They eagerly take his hands and lead him to center of stage, where all join hands and sing "America the Beautiful," as curtain falls.*)

THE END

The Wizard of Oz

by L. Frank Baum
Adapted by Lynne Sharon Schwartz

Characters

NARRATOR
DOROTHY
WITCH OF THE NORTH
THREE MUNCHKINS
SCARECROW
TIN WOODMAN
COWARDLY LION
SOLDIER
WIZARD OF OZ
LOVELY LADY
WICKED WITCH OF THE WEST
KING OF THE WINGED MONKEYS
WINGED MONKEYS
GLINDA, *the Good Witch of the South*
AUNT EM

SCENE 1

BEFORE RISE: NARRATOR *enters and goes to a lectern at one side in front of curtain.*

NARRATOR: Once upon a time there was a little girl named
Dorothy, who lived in the great Kansas prairies with
her Uncle Henry, who was a farmer, and her Aunt Em,
and her dog, Toto.

One day they heard a low wail of the wind, and they
saw the long grass bowing in waves; they heard a sharp,
whistling sound in the air, and they knew that a great
storm, a cyclone, was coming. (*Howling sound of wind
is heard from offstage*) Uncle Henry ran out to take
care of the cattle, and Aunt Em ran to a trapdoor in
the floor, calling to Dorothy to follow her. But at that
moment Toto jumped out of Dorothy's arms and hid
under the bed. As Dorothy reached to get him, the
house shook so hard that she lost her footing and fell
down on the floor. Then the house whirled around two
or three times and rose slowly through the air, and
Dorothy felt as if she were going up in a balloon. The
house was in the exact center of the cyclone, and it was
carried miles and miles up into the air. The wind was
shrieking loudly, but soon the house felt very calm,
and Dorothy crawled into her bed and fell asleep. When
she awoke, she found herself in a strange place. (NAR-
RATOR *exits as curtain rises.*)

SETTING: *A field. A backdrop portrays the front of a cottage. Two silver shoes can be seen sticking out from
under the house.*
AT RISE: DOROTHY *is standing near the doorway holding
her dog, Toto.*

DOROTHY: I wonder where I am! All I can remember is
whirling around and around. (*Looks around.* WITCH
OF THE NORTH *and* THREE MUNCHKINS *enter.*)
WITCH OF THE NORTH (*Going to* DOROTHY *and bowing*):
You are welcome, most noble Sorceress, to the land of

the Munchkins. We are so grateful to you for having
killed the Wicked Witch of the East, and for setting
our people free from bondage.

DOROTHY: You are very kind, but there must be some
mistake. I have not killed anyone.

WITCH OF THE NORTH (*Laughing*): Your house did, anyway, and that is the same thing. See! (*She points to
the corner of the house.*) There are her two feet, sticking out from under the house.

DOROTHY (*Dismayed*): Oh, dear. The house must have
fallen on her. Whatever shall we do?

WITCH OF THE NORTH: There is nothing to be done. She
was the Wicked Witch of the East, and she made the
Munchkins her slaves. Now they are set free, and are
grateful to you.

DOROTHY: Who are the Munchkins?

WITCH OF THE NORTH: They are the people who live in
this land of the East. These are three of my Munchkin
friends. (THREE MUNCHKINS *bow to* DOROTHY.) I am the
Witch of the North.

DOROTHY: Oh, gracious! Are you a real witch?

WITCH OF THE NORTH: Yes, indeed. But I am a good witch,
and the people love me.

DOROTHY: I thought all witches were wicked.

WITCH OF THE NORTH: Oh, no, that is a great mistake.
There were four witches in all the Land of Oz, and two
of them, those who live in the North and the South,
are good witches. Those who lived in the East and the
West were wicked witches; but now that you have
killed the Wicked Witch of the East, there is but one
Wicked Witch left, the one who lives in the West.

1ST MUNCHKIN (*Who has been peering at the feet of the
Wicked Witch*): Look! Look! Her feet have disappeared. (*All run to look.*)

WITCH OF THE NORTH: She was so old that she dried up

quickly in the sun. That is the end of her. But the silver
shoes are yours, and you shall have them to wear. (*Gives
shoes to* DOROTHY)

2ND MUNCHKIN: There is some charm connected with
these silver shoes, but what it is, we never knew.

DOROTHY: Thank you. (*Puts shoes on*) Now, can you help
me find my way back to my aunt and uncle?

3RD MUNCHKIN: There is a great desert all around this
land, and no one can live to cross it.

WITCH OF THE NORTH: I am afraid, my dear, that you will
have to live with us.

DOROTHY (*Starting to cry*): But I want to go back to
Kansas.

WITCH OF THE NORTH (*Taking off her cap and looking
inside*): Perhaps we will get a magic message from the
cap to help us. (*Reading*) It says, "Let Dorothy go to the
City of Emeralds." Is your name Dorothy, my dear?

DOROTHY: Yes. Where is the City of Emeralds?

WITCH OF THE NORTH: It is in the center of the country,
and is ruled by Oz, the Great Wizard.

DOROTHY: Is he a good man?

WITCH OF THE NORTH: He is a good Wizard. Whether he
is a man or not I cannot tell, for I have never seen him.

DOROTHY: How can I get there?

WITCH OF THE NORTH: You must walk. It is a long journey,
through a country that is sometimes pleasant and sometimes dark and terrible. However, I will use all the
magic arts I know of to keep you from harm, and I will
give you my kiss. No one will dare injure a person who
has been kissed by the Witch of the North. (*Kisses*
DOROTHY *on the forehead*) The road to the City of
Emeralds is paved with yellow brick, so you cannot
miss it. When you get to Oz, do not be afraid of him,
but tell him your story and ask him to help you. Goodbye, my dear.

MUNCHKINS (*Bowing*): Goodbye, Dorothy.

DOROTHY: Goodbye, and thank you. I will start on my journey right away. (WITCH *and* MUNCHKINS *exit. Lights dim to indicate the passage of time. While the stage is dark, the* SCARECROW *enters and stands on a high stool at one side. There is a pole in back of the stool which he pretends to be attached to. When the lights come up,* DOROTHY *is walking across the stage, holding Toto. Suddenly she notices the* SCARECROW.) I'm sure I saw the Scarecrow wink at me, but it couldn't be. He's just made of straw.

SCARECROW: Good day.

DOROTHY (*Surprised*): Did you speak?

SCARECROW: Certainly. How do you do?

DOROTHY: I'm pretty well, thank you. How do you do?

SCARECROW: I'm not feeling well. It's very tedious being perched up here night and day to scare away crows.

DOROTHY: Can't you get down?

SCARECROW: No, because this pole is stuck up my back. If you will please take away the pole, I shall be greatly obliged to you. (DOROTHY *goes to* SCARECROW *and pretends to lift him off pole. He steps down and lowers his arms.*) Thank you very much. I feel like a new man. (*Stretches and yawns*) Who are you, and where are you going?

DOROTHY: My name is Dorothy, and I am going to the Emerald City to ask the great Oz to send me back to Kansas.

SCARECROW: Where is the Emerald City? And who is Oz?

DOROTHY: Why, don't you know?

SCARECROW (*Sadly*): No, indeed; I don't know anything. You see, I am stuffed, so I have no brains at all.

DOROTHY: Oh, I'm awfully sorry.

SCARECROW: Do you think if I go to the Emerald City with you, that Oz would give me some brains?

DOROTHY: I cannot tell, but you may come with me if you like.

SCARECROW: I think I shall. You see, I don't mind my legs and arms and body being stuffed, because I cannot get hurt. But I don't like to be thought a fool. (*As they talk,* TIN WOODMAN *enters, unseen by the others, and stands at one side of the stage with his ax raised; he groans, first softly, then louder.*)

DOROTHY (*Looking around*): I'm sure I heard someone groan. (*Sees* TIN WOODMAN *and goes to him*) Oh! Did you groan?

TIN WOODMAN: Yes, I did. I've been groaning for more than a year.

DOROTHY (*Sympathetically*): What can I do for you?

TIN WOODMAN: Get an oilcan and oil my joints. They are rusted so badly that I cannot move them at all. You will find an oilcan right in front of my cottage a few steps further in the woods.

DOROTHY: Very well. You wait here. (*Pause*) Of course, you must wait here, for you can't move. (*She runs off-stage and returns immediately carrying oilcan.*) Where are your joints?

TIN WOODMAN: Oil my neck, first. (DOROTHY *does so.* SCARECROW *helps by moving* TIN WOODMAN's *head from side to side gently.*) Now oil the joints in my arms. (DOROTHY *does so.* SCARECROW *bends* TIN WOODMAN's *arms.* TIN WOODMAN *sighs and lowers his ax.*) This is a great comfort. I have been holding that ax in the air ever since I rusted in a rainstorm, and I'm glad to be able to put it down at last. Now, if you will oil the joints of my legs, I shall be all right once more. (*They oil his legs.*) Thank you so much. I might have stood there always if you had not come along, so you have certainly saved my life. How did you happen to be here?

DOROTHY: We are on our way to the Emerald City to see the Great Oz. I want him to send me back to Kansas, and the Scarecrow wants him to put a few brains into his head.

TIN WOODMAN (*After thinking for a moment*): Do you suppose Oz could give me a heart?

DOROTHY: Why, I guess so. It would be as easy as giving the Scarecrow brains.

TIN WOODMAN: True. If you will allow me to join your party, I will also go to the Emerald City and ask Oz to help me.

SCARECROW: Come along. We'd be pleased to have you. But if I were you, I should ask for brains instead of a heart, for a fool with no brains would not know what to do with a heart if he had one.

TIN WOODMAN: I shall take the heart, for brains do not make one happy, and happiness is the best thing in the world. (*A great roar is heard, and the* COWARDLY LION *rushes in. He knocks the* SCARECROW *over, and strikes the* TIN WOODMAN, *who falls to the ground.* DOROTHY *drops Toto, in her surprise, and the* LION *rushes toward him.* DOROTHY *snatches him up, and then slaps the* LION *on the nose.*)

DOROTHY: Don't you dare to bite Toto! You ought to be ashamed of yourself, a big beast like you, biting a poor little dog!

LION (*Rubbing his nose*): I didn't bite him.

DOROTHY: No, but you tried to. You are nothing but a big coward.

LION (*Hanging his head in shame*): I know it. I've always known it. But how can I help it?

DOROTHY: I'm sure I don't know. To think of your striking a stuffed man like the poor Scarecrow!

LION: Is he stuffed?

DOROTHY (*Helping the* SCARECROW *up and patting his clothes into shape*): Of course he's stuffed.

LION: That's why he went over so easily. Is the other one stuffed also?

DOROTHY (*Helping* TIN WOODMAN *up*): No, he's made of tin.

LION: Then that's why he nearly blunted my claws.

SCARECROW: What makes you a coward?

LION: It's a mystery. I suppose I was born that way. All the other animals in the forest naturally expect me to be brave, for the Lion is everywhere thought to be the King of Beasts. I learned that if I roared very loudly every living thing was frightened and got out of my way. If the elephants and the tigers and the bears had ever tried to fight me, I should have run myself—I'm such a coward. But just as soon as they hear me roar they all try to get away from me, and of course I let them go.

SCARECROW: But that isn't right. The King of Beasts shouldn't be a coward.

LION: I know it. (*He wipes a tear from his eye with the tip of his tail.*) It is my great sorrow, and it makes my life very unhappy. But whenever there is danger my heart begins to beat fast.

TIN WOODMAN: You ought to be glad of that, for it proves you have a heart. I have no heart at all, so it cannot beat fast. But I am going to the great Oz to ask him for one.

SCARECROW: And I am going to ask him to give me brains, for my head is stuffed with straw.

DOROTHY: And I am going to ask him to send Toto and me back to Kansas.

LION: Do you think Oz could give me courage?

SCARECROW: Just as easily as he could give me brains.

TIN WOODMAN: Or give me a heart.

DOROTHY: Or send me back to Kansas.

LION: Then, if you don't mind, I'll go with you, for my life is simply unbearable without a bit of courage.

DOROTHY: You will be very welcome, for you will help to keep away the other wild beasts. I think it will be a long and difficult journey. (*They start to exit as curtain falls.*)

*   *   *

SCENE 2

TIME: *A few days later.*

SETTING: *Outside of Oz's throne room.*

BEFORE RISE: DOROTHY, SCARECROW, TIN WOODMAN, *and* LION *enter, all wearing green spectacles.*

DOROTHY: I am so glad to be here. I thought we would never arrive.

TIN WOODMAN: Let us hope that the great Oz will see us. The soldier said that no one has asked to see Oz in many, many years. (SOLDIER *enters.*)

DOROTHY (*To* SOLDIER): Have you seen Oz and asked him about us?

SOLDIER: Oh, no, I have never seen him, but I gave him your message. When I mentioned your silver shoes he was very much interested. He said he would grant you an audience, but if you come on an idle or foolish errand he may be angry and destroy you all in an instant.

SCARECROW: But it is not a foolish errand, nor an idle one. It is important.

SOLDIER: Very well, then. But each of you must enter his presence alone. And you must not remove the green spectacles.

DOROTHY: Why?

SOLDIER: Because that is the rule. Otherwise the bright-
ness and glory of the Emerald City would blind you.

DOROTHY: Thank you. That is very kind of Oz. (*Bell
rings.*)

SOLDIER: That is the signal. You must go into the throne
room by yourself. (SOLDIER *exits with* SCARECROW, TIN
WOODMAN, *and* LION, *as curtain rises.*)

SETTING: *The throne room. All the furnishings are green.
Suspended over the throne at center is a tremendous
papier-mâché head, with a mouth that moves.*

AT RISE: DOROTHY *walks hesitantly into room.*

OZ (*Speaking while hidden behind screen at one side*):
I am Oz, the Great and Terrible. Who are you, and why
do you seek me?

DOROTHY (*Speaking to the head*): I am Dorothy, the Small
and Meek. I have come to you for help.

OZ: Where did you get the silver shoes?

DOROTHY: I got them from the Wicked Witch of the East,
when my house fell on her and killed her.

OZ: What do you wish me to do?

DOROTHY: Send me back to Kansas, where my Aunt Em
and Uncle Henry are. I am sure Aunt Em will be
dreadfully worried over my being away so long.

OZ: Why should I do this for you?

DOROTHY: Because you are strong and I am weak; because
you are a Great Wizard and I am only a helpless little
girl.

OZ: But you were strong enough to kill the Wicked Witch
of the East.

DOROTHY: That just happened. I could not help it.

OZ: Well, I will give you my answer. You have no right
to expect me to send you back to Kansas unless you do

something for me in return. Kill the Wicked Witch of the West.

DOROTHY: But I cannot!

OZ: You killed the Wicked Witch of the East, and you wear the silver shoes, which have a powerful charm. There is now but one Wicked Witch left in all this land, and when you can tell me she is dead, I will send you back to Kansas—but not before.

DOROTHY (*Beginning to weep*): I never killed anything, willingly, and even if I wanted to, how could I kill the Wicked Witch? If you, who are Great and Terrible, cannot kill her yourself, how do you expect me to do it?

OZ: I do not know, but that is my answer, and until the Wicked Witch of the West dies, you will not see your uncle and aunt again. Remember that the Witch is wicked—tremendously wicked—and ought to be killed. Now go, and do not ask to see me again until you have done your task. (*Blackout, during which* DOROTHY *exits; head is removed, and the* LOVELY LADY *enters and sits on the throne. Lights come up.* SCARECROW *enters and bows.*)

LADY: I am Oz, the Great and Terrible. Who are you, and why do you seek me?

SCARECROW: I am only a Scarecrow, stuffed with straw, and I have no brains. I come to you praying that you will put brains in my head instead of straw, so that I may become as much a man as any other.

LADY: Why should I do this for you?

SCARECROW: Because you are wise and powerful, and no one else can help me.

LADY: I never grant favors without some return, but this much I will promise. If you will kill the Wicked Witch of the West for me, I will bestow upon you a great many brains, and such good brains that you will be the wisest man in all the Land of Oz.

SCARECROW (*Surprised*): I thought you asked Dorothy to kill the Witch.

LADY: So I did. I don't care who kills her. Until she is dead I will not grant your wish. Now go, and do not seek me again until you have earned the brains you so greatly desire. (*Blackout, during which* SCARECROW *and* LADY *exit;* OZ *appears and sits on the throne, as a horrible beast. Lights up.* TIN WOODMAN *enters.* OZ *roars.*)

OZ: I am Oz, the Great and Terrible. Who are you, and why do you seek me?

TIN WOODMAN: I am a Woodman, and made of tin. Therefore I have no heart, and cannot love. I pray you to give me a heart that I may be as other men are.

OZ: Why should I do this?

TIN WOODMAN: Because I ask it, and you alone can grant my request.

OZ: If you indeed desire a heart, you must earn it.

TIN WOODMAN: How?

OZ: Help Dorothy kill the Wicked Witch of the West. When the Witch is dead, come to me and I will then give you the biggest and kindest and most loving heart in all the Land of Oz. (*He roars again as the lights black out, and he goes behind the screen.* TIN WOODMAN *exits. When lights go on again, there is a great "Ball of Fire" hanging over the throne.* COWARDLY LION *enters, frightened.*)

OZ (*Behind screen*): I am Oz, the Great and Terrible. Who are you, and why do you seek me?

LION: I am a Cowardly Lion, though I am supposed to be King of the Beasts. I am frightened of everything I see, and so I have come to you to ask if you will give me courage.

OZ: Why should I do this for you?

LION: Because you are great and powerful, and you alone can help me.

OZ: I will grant you courage only if you will do something for me. Help Dorothy kill the Wicked Witch of the West.

LION: But how can I do that if I am a coward?

OZ: I do not know, but after you have killed her, you may come back to me and I will make you the most courageous beast in all the forest. Remember, I am Oz, the Great and Terrible. (*The Ball of Fire shakes in the air, and the* LION *cringes as the curtain falls.*)

*   *   *

SCENE 3

BEFORE RISE: NARRATOR *enters and goes to lectern.*

NARRATOR: The next morning the four friends met and marveled at the many forms the Great Wizard could take. Then they started for the castle of the Wicked Witch of the West. At night, Dorothy and Toto and the Lion lay down to sleep, while the Scarecrow and the Tin Woodman kept watch.

Now, the Wicked Witch of the West had an eye that was as powerful as a telescope and could see everywhere. As she stood in front of her castle she looked out and saw Dorothy lying asleep with her friends around her. She was furious to find them in her country, and tried many ways to capture them, but was unsuccessful. She was a powerful witch, though, and thought of one last idea. (*Curtain slowly opens.*)

SETTING: *Before the castle of the Wicked Witch of the West. A backdrop depicts the front of the castle.*

AT RISE: WICKED WITCH *is onstage, holding a broom and*

a bucket of water; she peers around, then takes cap from her head.

WICKED WITCH: The only way left to destroy these strangers is with the Golden Cap. This must be my last command to the Winged Monkeys, for I have commanded them twice already. (*Puts cap on her head and recites, first standing on left foot*) Ep-pe, pep-pe, kak-ke! (*Standing on right foot*) Hil-lo, hol-lo, hel-lo! (*Standing on both feet and crying out loudly*) Ziz-zy, zuz-zy, zik! (*A low, rumbling sound is heard and* WINGED MONKEYS *enter.*)

KING OF MONKEYS: You have called us for the third and last time. What do you command?

WICKED WITCH: Go to the strangers within my land and destroy them all except the Lion. Bring that beast to me, for I shall harness him like a horse, and make him work.

KING OF MONKEYS: Your commands shall be obeyed. (MONKEYS *run out.*)

NARRATOR: The Monkeys flew to Dorothy and her friends. First they seized the Tin Woodman and dropped him in a valley covered with sharp rocks, where he lay battered and dented. Then they caught the Scarecrow and pulled the straw out of his clothes. They made a small bundle of his hat and clothes and threw it into the branches of a tall tree. (NARRATOR *exits as* WINGED MONKEYS *enter with* DOROTHY, *who holds Toto.*)

KING OF MONKEYS (*To* WICKED WITCH): We have obeyed you as far as we are able. The Tin Woodman and the Scarecrow are destroyed, and the Lion is tied up in your yard. The little girl we dare not harm, nor the dog she carries with her, for the Witch of the North has kissed her forehead and left her mark. Your power over our band is now ended. (MONKEYS *exit.*)

WICKED WITCH (*To* DOROTHY): Aha! I have tried many ways to capture you, and at last I have you for my slave. See that you mind everything I tell you, for if you do not I will make an end of you. You will clean the pots and kettles and sweep the floor and tend the fire.

DOROTHY: You are a very wicked witch for destroying my friends and tying up the Lion, but your power cannot last long. I have a special charm in my silver shoes that I got from the Wicked Witch of the East, and it will help me to get rid of you.

WICKED WITCH (*Staring at shoes*): The silver shoes! Give them to me!

DOROTHY: No!

WICKED WITCH (*Pushing* DOROTHY *down and grabbing one shoe*): There, you silly little girl. You cannot struggle against a powerful witch like me. Now I have your shoe and your charm will be useless.

DOROTHY: You wicked creature! You have no right to take my shoe from me.

WICKED WITCH: I shall keep it, just the same, and someday I shall get the other one from you, too.

DOROTHY (*In a rage*): Oh! (*Seizes bucket of water and dashes it over* WICKED WITCH, *who begins to shrink. NOTE: She does this by curling up slowly under her wide cloak and sinking to the floor, so that soon she is completely hidden under the cloak.*)

WICKED WITCH: See what you have done? In a minute I shall melt away.

DOROTHY (*Frightened and astonished*): I'm very sorry, indeed.

WICKED WITCH: Didn't you know water would be the end of me?

DOROTHY: Of course not. How could I?

WICKED WITCH: Well, in a minute I shall be all melted, and you will have the castle to yourself. I have been wicked in my day, but I never thought a little girl like you would ever be able to melt me and end my wicked deeds. Look out—here I go! (*Hides under cloak*)

DOROTHY (*Taking broom*): I may as well get her out of here. And take my shoe, too. (*Puts shoe back on*) Perhaps I shall take her Golden Cap also. (*Puts cap on*) It fits perfectly! (*She "sweeps" the* WICKED WITCH *offstage.*) Now I must go back to the Emerald City for my reward. But how can I save the Scarecrow and the Tin Woodman and the Lion? (*She looks about.*) And I am afraid I am hopelessly lost. What can I do? (*She sits down wearily, takes off the cap, and idly looks inside it.*) Oh, look! There's a charm in the cap! It's a magic rhyme. Maybe it will help me. (*Puts cap on and recites, standing on left foot*) Ep-pe, pep-pe, kak-ke! (*Stands on right foot*) Hil-lo, hol-lo, hel-lo! (*Louder, standing on both feet*) Ziz-zy, zuz-zy, zik! (WINGED MONKEYS *enter.*)

KING OF MONKEYS: What is your command? We can take you anywhere within the Land of Oz in a moment's time.

DOROTHY: I wish to go to the Emerald City, but I must rescue my friends and take them with me.

KING OF MONKEYS: We will carry you there, and we will find your friends and take them with us, have no fear. (MONKEYS *take* DOROTHY *and run offstage as curtain falls.*)

*   *   *

SCENE 4

SETTING: *Oz's throne room.*

AT RISE: *The throne is empty;* Oz *is hidden behind screen.* DOROTHY, SCARECROW, TIN WOODMAN, *and* LION *are onstage.*

DOROTHY: That was a good ride.

LION: Yes, and a quick way out of our troubles. How lucky it was that you took that wonderful cap, Dorothy.

DOROTHY: I wonder where Oz is. I don't see anything.

OZ (*From behind screen*): I am Oz, the Great and Terrible. Why do you seek me?

DOROTHY (*Looking around*): Where are you?

OZ: I am everywhere, but to the eyes of common mortals I am invisible.

DOROTHY: We have come to claim our rewards, O Great Oz.

OZ: What rewards?

DOROTHY: You promised to grant us all our wishes when the Wicked Witch was destroyed.

OZ: Is she really destroyed?

DOROTHY: Yes, I melted her with a bucket of water.

OZ: Dear me, how sudden. Well, come to me tomorrow, for I must have time to think it over.

TIN WOODMAN: You've had plenty of time already.

SCARECROW: We won't wait a day longer.

DOROTHY: You must keep your promises to us. (LION *lets out a great roar so that* DOROTHY *jumps, drops Toto, and tips over the screen. There is a crash, and they see a little old man with a bald head.*)

TIN WOODMAN (*Raising his ax and rushing toward* OZ): Who are you?

OZ: I am Oz, the Great and Terrible (*Trembles*), but don't strike me—please don't—and I'll do anything you want me to.

DOROTHY (*Dismayed*): I thought Oz was a great head.

SCARECROW: And I thought Oz was a lovely lady.

TIN WOODMAN: And I thought Oz was a terrible beast.

LION: And I thought he was a Ball of Fire.

OZ: No, you are all wrong. I have been making believe.

I'm supposed to be a Great Wizard, but I'm just a common man.

SCARECROW: You're more than that. You're a humbug, a fake!

OZ: Exactly! (*Rubs his hands together in pleasure*) But don't speak so loudly or you will be overheard, and I shall be ruined.

TIN WOODMAN: But this is terrible. How shall I ever get my heart?

LION: Or I my courage?

SCARECROW: Or I my brains?

OZ: My dear friends, I pray you not to speak of these little things. Think of me, and the terrible trouble I'm in since you found me out.

DOROTHY: Doesn't anyone else know you're a humbug?

OZ: No one but the four of you.

DOROTHY (*Bewildered*): But I don't understand. How was it that you appeared to me as a great head?

OZ: That was one of my tricks. Everything has been a trick.

SCARECROW: Really, you ought to be ashamed of yourself for being such a humbug.

OZ: I am—I certainly am—but it was the only thing I could do. You see, I was born in Omaha—

DOROTHY: Why, that isn't very far from Kansas!

OZ: No, but it's farther from here. (*Shakes his head sadly*) I worked in a circus as a balloonist—that's a man who goes up in a balloon on circus day, to draw a crowd of people together. One day the ropes of my balloon got twisted, so that I couldn't come down again, and I floated miles through the air until I landed in this strange and beautiful country. The people here, who saw me come down gently from the clouds, thought I was a great wizard. They were afraid of me and promised to do anything I wished, so to amuse myself and to keep the good people busy I ordered them to build this city and my palace. Because the country was so green and beautiful I called it the Emerald City. I have been good to the people, and they like me. But one of my greatest fears was the Witches, who had magical powers, while I had none at all. That is why I was so pleased to hear that your house had fallen on the Wicked Witch of the East, and why I was so willing to promise anything if you would do away with the other Witch. But I am ashamed to say now that I cannot keep my promises.

DOROTHY: I think you are a very bad man.

Oz: Oh, no, my dear. I'm really a very good man, but I'm a very bad Wizard, I must admit.

SCARECROW: Can't you give me brains?

Oz: You don't need them. You are learning something every day. A baby has brains, but it doesn't know much. Experience is the only thing that brings knowledge, and the longer you are on earth the more experience you are sure to get.

SCARECROW: That may all be true, but I shall be very unhappy unless you give me brains.

Oz: Then I will try to give you brains. I cannot tell you how to use them, however; you must find that out for yourself. (Oz *goes to cabinet and fills a cup with powder, then goes to* SCARECROW *and pretends to pour the powder into his head.*) The main ingredient is bran. Hereafter you will be a great man, for I have given you a lot of bran-new brains!

SCARECROW: Oh, thank you, thank you. And I'll find a way to use them, never fear.

DOROTHY (*To* SCARECROW): How do you feel?

SCARECROW: I feel wise indeed.

LION: Now, how about my courage?

Oz: You have plenty of courage, I am sure. All you need is confidence in yourself. There is no living thing that

is not afraid when it faces danger. True courage is facing
danger when you are afraid, and you have plenty of
true courage.

LION: Perhaps I have, but I'm scared just the same. I shall
really be very unhappy unless you give me the sort of
courage that makes one forget he is afraid.

OZ: Very well, I will get some for you. (*Goes to cupboard,
takes down green bottle, and pours contents into a
green dish. He offers it to the* LION, *who sniffs at it
disdainfully.*) Drink.

LION: What is it?

OZ: Well, if it were inside of you, it would be courage.
You know, of course, that courage is always inside a
person; so that this really cannot be called courage until
you have swallowed it. Therefore I advise you to drink
it as soon as possible. (LION *drinks.*) How do you feel
now?

LION (*Happily*): Full of courage!

TIN WOODMAN: How about my heart?

OZ: Why, as for that, I think you are wrong to want a
heart. It makes most people unhappy. If you only
knew it, you are in luck not to have a heart.

TIN WOODMAN: That must be a matter of opinion. For
my part, I will bear all the unhappiness without a
murmur, if you will give me a heart.

OZ: Very well. (*Goes to cabinet, takes out paper heart and
pins it carefully on* TIN WOODMAN's chest) Isn't it a
beauty?

TIN WOODMAN (*Looking down at it*): It is, indeed. But
is it a kind heart?

OZ: Oh, very kind. It is a heart that any man might be
proud of.

TIN WOODMAN: I am very grateful to you, and shall never
forget your kindness.

DOROTHY: And now, how am I to get back to Kansas?

Oz (*Sighs*): We shall have to think about that for a while. (*Curtain*)

*   *   *

Scene 5

Before Rise: Narrator *enters and goes to lectern.*

Narrator: Oz thought for several days, and finally decided that he and Dorothy should leave in a balloon. Dorothy worked hard on making the balloon and it was soon ready, but at the moment they were to take off, she realized that she had lost Toto. She hurried through the crowd looking for him, but by the time she found him the balloon was already sailing overhead, and Oz could not bring it back. She was very sad, and cried because she thought she would never get back to Kansas. Finally a soldier who felt sorry for Dorothy came and told her that Glinda, the Good Witch of the South, might help her. Glinda was the most powerful of all the Witches, and ruled over the Quadlings. The road to her castle was full of dangers to travelers, but Dorothy decided to go nevertheless, because it was her last hope, and her faithful friends went along to protect her. (Narrator *exits as curtain rises.*)

Time: *A few days later.*
Setting: *A room in Glinda's castle.*
At Rise: Dorothy, Scarecrow, Tin Woodman, *and* Lion *enter.*

Dorothy: This must be Glinda's castle. Isn't it beautiful?
Tin Woodman: She must be an especially good witch, and I know she will help you, Dorothy. (Glinda *enters.*)
Glinda: I am Glinda, the Good Witch of the South. I

have heard of how you landed here on the cyclone, child. What can I do for you?

DOROTHY (*Curtsying*): My greatest wish is to get back to Kansas, for Aunt Em will certainly think something dreadful has happened to me.

GLINDA: I am sure I can help you. But if I do, you must give me the Golden Cap.

DOROTHY: Willingly, for it will be of no use to me now. (*Gives her cap*)

GLINDA: I think I will need it just three times. (*To* SCARECROW) What will you do when Dorothy has left us?

SCARECROW: I will return to the Emerald City, for Oz has made me its ruler, and the people like me. The only thing that worries me is how to cross the tremendous mountain bordering your land. On our journey here the Winged Monkeys carried us over.

GLINDA: By the Golden Cap I shall command the Winged Monkeys to carry you again to the gates of the Emerald City, for it would be a shame to deprive the people of so wonderful a ruler. (*To* TIN WOODMAN) What will become of you when Dorothy leaves?

TIN WOODMAN: The Winkies, in the land of the West, were very kind to me, and wanted me to rule over them after the Wicked Witch of the West was melted. If I could get back again I should like nothing better than to be their ruler forever.

GLINDA: My second command to the Winged Monkeys will be that they carry you safely to the land of the Winkies. Your brains may not be as large as those of the Scarecrow, but you are really much brighter than he is when you are well polished—and I am sure you will rule the Winkies wisely and well. (*To* LION) When Dorothy has returned to her home, what will become of you?

LION: The beasts in the forest on the outskirts of your land have made me their king, because during our journey here I saved them from a wicked monster. If only I could get back to them I should pass my life there very happily.

GLINDA: My third command to the Winged Monkeys shall be to carry you to your forest. Then, having used up the powers of the Golden Cap, I shall give it to the King of the Monkeys, so that he and his band may be free forever after.

SCARECROW, TIN WOODMAN, LION (*Ad lib*): Thank you. You are so kind to us. (*Etc.*)

DOROTHY: You are certainly as good as you are beautiful. But you have not yet told me how to get back to Kansas.

GLINDA: Your silver shoes have wonderful powers. They can carry you across the desert, anywhere in the world. In fact, if you had known their power you could have gone back to your Aunt Em the very first day you came to this country.

SCARECROW: But then I should not have had my wonderful brains. I might have passed my whole life in the farmer's cornfield.

TIN WOODMAN: And I should not have had my lovely heart. I might have stood and rusted in the forest till the end of the world.

LION: And I should have lived a coward forever, and no beast in all the forest would have had a good word to say to me.

DOROTHY: This is all true, and I am glad I was of use to these good friends. But now that each of them has what he most desired, and a kingdom to rule besides, I think I should like to go home.

GLINDA: All you have to do is knock your heels together three times and command the shoes to carry you wherever you wish. They will take you in only three steps, each step made in the wink of an eye.

DOROTHY (*Joyfully*): I shall command them at once. (*Hugs* LION, SCARECROW *and* TIN WOODMAN) Goodbye, goodbye, everyone. You have all been such good friends, and I will never forget you.

SCARECROW, TIN WOODMAN, LION (*Ad lib*): Goodbye, Dorothy. We shall always remember you, too. (*Etc.*)

DOROTHY (*Bows to* GLINDA): I am so grateful for your kindness. (*She stands solemnly and clicks heels together three times.*) Take me home to Aunt Em! (*Blackout, crash of thunder, and curtain quickly closes. Lights come up on apron of stage to reveal* DOROTHY *sitting on the floor, with no shoes on, holding Toto. She stands up, looking dazed.*) Good gracious, here I am in Kansas! (*Points offstage*) And there is Uncle Henry's new farmhouse, and there are the cows in the barnyard. Oh! I've lost the silver shoes. They must have fallen off in the air. (AUNT EM *rushes in and takes* DOROTHY *in her arms.*)

AUNT EM: My darling child! Where in the world have you been?

DOROTHY: In the Land of Oz. (*Gravely*) And here is Toto, too. And, oh, Aunt Em, I'm so glad to be at home again. (*They embrace as curtain falls.*)

THE END

The Baking Contest

by Shirley Simon

Characters

ESMERELDA GRIFFIN
GRISELDA GRIFFIN
PENNY GRIFFIN
OLD WOMAN
PRINCE RICHARD PRITCHARD GOOROMAY
TWO PAGES
TWO LADIES
COURTIERS

TIME: *Long ago.*
SETTING: *In front of palace courtyard of Prince Richard Pritchard Gooromay. There is a small pond downstage center, a tree at the left, and a large stone or rock in front of tree.*
AT RISE: ESMERELDA *and* GRISELDA *enter left, each carrying basket covered with a white napkin.*

ESMERELDA: Let's stop here by this pond, cousin. We could rest a moment.
GRISELDA: We could also admire our lovely selves. (ESMERELDA *and* GRISELDA *set baskets down and sit beside pond. They preen and stretch.*)

ESMERELDA (*Standing up*): How beautiful we are, Cousin Griselda.

GRISELDA (*Also standing*): How gorgeous we are, Cousin Esmerelda. (*Sings to tune of "Clementine"*)

> Esmerelda, Esmerelda.
> Gorgeous creatures that we are—
>   Just to find girls
>   Half so lovely
> One would have to travel far.

ESMERELDA (*Sings*):

> Oh, Griselda. Oh, Griselda.
> Stunning creatures that we be—
>   One would have to
>   Travel far to
> Find the likes of you and me.

GRISELDA: One of us will surely win the heart of the Prince. (*Fanfare is heard offstage.* 1ST PAGE *and* 2ND PAGE *enter from courtyard, followed by* COURTIERS *and* LADIES.)

1ST PAGE (*Shouting*): Last call! Last call! Today is the day of the Baking Ball. (*Clearly and slowly*) Prince Richard Pritchard Gooromay will choose a bride this very day.

2ND PAGE: He loves pies and tarts and cakes. He wants a *pretty* girl who *bakes*. (1ST PAGE *and* 2ND PAGE *exit right, repeating their verses as they go. They are followed by* COURTIERS *and* LADIES) Last call! Last call!

ESMERELDA: Griselda, we are lost. You are fair, and I am (*Smirks*) beautiful, but let's face it—

GRISELDA: We're both terrible cooks.

ESMERELDA: The pie I have in my basket (*Peeks in, makes face*) is all soggy and miserable.

GRISELDA: My cake (*Peeks into her basket*) is flat and ugly.

ESMERELDA: If only—if only—

GRISELDA: We had our looks—

ESMERELDA: And (*Nods head toward left*) *her* cooking ability.

GRISELDA: Cousin Penny is on her way here now with *her* entry for the baking contest. She was baking a mince pie and a chocolate cake. (*Sniffs*) Oh, yum! I smelled them. Now if *we* had that pie and cake—

ESMERELDA (*Giggling*): Griselda! (*Whispers to* GRISELDA. *They clap hands over mouths, nod heads and jump up and down.* ESMERELDA *runs to the left and looks down the road.*) She's coming! Penny's coming! (PENNY *enters left, carrying large basket.*)

PENNY (*Sweetly*): Good day to you, cousins.

ESMERELDA: Good day to you, cousin. (*Pokes* GRISELDA) You tell her, cousin.

GRISELDA: We thought—(*Covers mouth with hand to suppress laughter*) Is that your entry for the baking contest, cousin?

PENNY (*Patting basket*): Here I have my chocolate cake and my mince pie.

ESMERELDA: Give them to us, cousin. Whichever one of us is chosen by the Prince will reward you.

GRISELDA: You will be named palace cook.

PENNY (*Shocked*): Oh, no! That wouldn't be honest! Besides, I want to enter the contest.

ESMERELDA: You! The Prince wants a pretty bride. Look at her, Griselda! (*Snaps fingers*) Her nose turns up!

GRISELDA (*Pulling* PENNY'S *hair*): Straight hair!

ESMERELDA: Freckles. Ugh!

PENNY (*Backing away*): I know I'm no raving beauty.

ESMERELDA: That you're not indeed.

PENNY (*With spirit*): Pretty is as pretty does, and I do pretty well, thank you. Now if you will excuse me, cousins, I shall be on my way.

GRISELDA: Wait! There was someone to see you, cousin.

He was looking for you. He's waiting down the lane, past the willows.

ESMERELDA: He has a message from your papa out at sea.

GRISELDA: He has one from your dead mama, too.

PENNY: From my—(ESMERELDA *shoves* GRISELDA *so hard* GRISELDA *staggers and almost falls.*)

ESMERELDA: She means he once knew your mama—before we all came to live with our aunt. Here. (*Takes basket from* PENNY) We'll hold your basket, cousin.

PENNY (*Running to right*): Up the lane, did you say? Under the willows? (*Exits right*)

ESMERELDA: You fool! You would overdo it!

GRISELDA: Oh, come on. She went, didn't she? (*Opens the basket*)

ESMERELDA: Here, cousin. We'll put her pie in my basket and her cake in yours.

GRISELDA: We'll put our (*Makes a face*) stuff in *her* basket. (*They transfer pies and cakes, leave* PENNY'S *basket in front of tree, then pick up their own baskets and hide behind tree.* PENNY *enters right.*)

PENNY (*Disappointed*): No one was there, cousins. Cousins? (*Looks around*) They must have gone on without me. (*Picks up her basket*) My goodness, this basket is heavy. (*Looks into basket*) These aren't *my* cake and pie. Where are my chocolate cake and my mince pie? Oh, dear! What will I do? (*Exits left.* GRISELDA *and* ESMERELDA *come out from behind tree, giggling.*)

GRISELDA: Good work, cousin. Soon one of us will be chosen by the Prince. When I am chosen by the Prince, cousin, I will see that you have an important place at the palace and many beautiful gowns. You may be one of my ladies-in-waiting.

ESMERELDA (*Stamping her foot*): Oh, no, I won't be your lady-in-waiting, you fool! I will be the bride of the Prince. (OLD WOMAN *enters right, approaches as* Es-

MERELDA *speaks, and puts her hand on* GRISELDA'S *arm*.)

GRISELDA (*Tossing her head*): Don't be ridiculous. I will be his bride. (*Notices* OLD WOMAN) What is it, old woman? (*Impatiently*) What do you want? (*Shoves* OLD WOMAN)

OLD WOMAN (*Timidly*): A bite of food. (*Points to basket*)

GRISELDA: Oh, no, you don't! Not a bite! Not a sniff! This chocolate cake is to be entered in the Prince's baking contest. Prince Richard Pritchard Gooromay will choose *me* for his bride.

ESMERELDA: He will choose *me*! (OLD WOMAN *now goes to* ESMERELDA. *She puts hand on* ESMERELDA, *who shoves her so hard that* OLD WOMAN *staggers and falls*.) Away from me, you old nanny-granny! This mince pie will win the heart of the Prince.

OLD WOMAN (*From the ground*): Please, just a taste!

ESMERELDA: Not a sniff! Not a whiff! (ESMERELDA *and* GRISELDA *start to leave*.)

OLD WOMAN (*Stands up*): Wait! (ESMERELDA *and* GRISELDA *turn, startled*. OLD WOMAN *points finger at them*.) You are mean and selfish and miserable.

ESMERELDA (*Pulling* GRISELDA *with her*): Come along, cousin. She is mad! Baa, you old granny-nanny! (ESMERELDA *and* GRISELDA *exit into courtyard*.)

OLD WOMAN: Granny-nanny, am I? (Two LADIES *enter left, carrying baskets*.) A bite to eat, kind ladies? (LADIES *shake their heads*.)

1ST LADY: Oh, no. We're in a hurry. We must get to the palace.

OLD WOMAN: All of you? You're all entering the baking contest?

2ND LADY: Yes, of course. The Prince will be ready to choose his bride in a little while.

1ST LADY: Just as soon as he has tasted all the entries.

OLD WOMAN: Oh, dear. I hope he won't get indigestion.

2ND LADY: Not Prince Richard. He loves to eat.

OLD WOMAN: All the same, he is subject to indigestion from foods improperly cooked.

1ST LADY: How do you know?

OLD WOMAN (*Quickly*): I've heard tell. (*Mournfully*) A bite to eat, a bite to eat. (LADIES *exit right into courtyard, ignoring* OLD WOMAN. PENNY *enters left, carrying basket.*)

PENNY: Good day to you, old woman. (*Sits down on stone*) I'm *so* tired. I baked all morning. I made a chocolate cake and a mince pie. (*Sighs*) They disappeared right after my cousins—(*Thoughtfully*) I do believe— Well, never mind.

OLD WOMAN: A chocolate cake and a mince pie, you say. What have you here? (*Points to basket*)

PENNY: Currant buns. I had some all ready to bake for dinner, and I popped them into the oven. I couldn't give them the time and trouble I took with the chocolate cake and the mince pie, but they are good. Everything I bake is good. (*Puts hand into her pocket*) I have here the recipes from my dear dead mama.

OLD WOMAN (*Putting hand on* PENNY's *arm*): May I have a bite to eat, child? I'm so tired and hungry.

PENNY (*Full of concern*): You poor dear. (*Gets up*) Come sit on this stone. (*Offers basket*) Help yourself. Eat as much as you like.

OLD WOMAN: Thank you, child. (*Takes a bun*) Wouldn't you, too, want to be the bride of Prince Richard Pritchard Gooromay?

PENNY: I was hoping, although I know I'm no beauty.

OLD WOMAN: Pretty will be as pretty may do.

PENNY: That's what my mama used to say. It is better that you should not be hungry than that I should have buns for the contest.

OLD WOMAN (*Eats another bun*): Never lose hope, child.

(*Eating another bun,* PENNY *reaches hopefully for the basket.* OLD WOMAN *snatches it and runs into the courtyard.* PENNY *is left standing alone. She covers her face with her hands and sits down on stone. Fanfare is heard offstage.* 1ST PAGE *and* 2ND PAGE *march out through courtyard entrance, blowing trumpets. They are followed by* LADIES, COURTIERS, PRINCE RICHARD PRITCHARD GOOROMAY, GRISELDA, ESMERELDA, *and, finally,* OLD WOMAN.)

1ST PAGE: Hear ye! Hear ye! Harken! Prince Richard Pritchard Gooromay will choose a bride right away.

OLD WOMAN (*Running to* PRINCE RICHARD, *puts hand on his arm*): Wait! Wait, my child. Before you decide, taste these. (*Holds out* PENNY'S *basket*) They were baked by this lovely girl. (*Indicates* PENNY)

PRINCE RICHARD (*Tasting bun*): Yum! (*Tastes another*) Oh, dear.

OLD WOMAN: What is wrong? Are they not delicious?

PRINCE RICHARD: Granny! Darling Granny! They are indeed delicious. You have made things even more difficult for me. I was just about to choose between the chocolate cake of this lady (*Holds up basket, indicates* GRISELDA, *who simpers and bows low*) and the juicy mince pie of this lady. (*Indicates* ESMERELDA, *who does likewise.* PENNY *goes over to look into their baskets.*) Now that I've tasted these currant buns—I'm completely confused.

OLD WOMAN: No need to be confused, dear Richard.

PENNY: That's my chocolate cake, and that's my mince pie. (*Points to* ESMERELDA *and* GRISELDA) You took my basket, cousins. You entered *my* cake and *my* pie in the contest.

OLD WOMAN (*To* PRINCE RICHARD): See what I mean?

ESMERELDA *and* GRISELDA (*Together*): We did not!

ESMERELDA: Anyway, you can't prove it.

OLD WOMAN (*Slyly*): If they baked that cake and that pie, surely they can give you the (*Shouts*) *recipes!*

PRINCE RICHARD: Yes, that's it. The recipes will prove who baked the pie and cake. What are the recipes?

GRISELDA: The recipes! Er—er—I took three bags of flour (LADIES *gasp.*) and I added—er—I added *chocolate.* (*Pleased with herself*) Yes, that's it. I added chocolate— it is a chocolate cake—and I added—(*Quickly*) pumice and anise and granice.

PRINCE RICHARD: Granice? What's granice?

GRISELDA: It's like granite, but it's ground. (PRINCE RICHARD *makes a face.*)

ESMERELDA: My recipe for mince pie, Your Highness, is— Well, you buy a pound of minces at the market and you mince them. And you add—er—you add— (*Quickly*) spice twice and nice mice, and you mince them.

PRINCE RICHARD: Ugh! It is obvious that these ladies have never baked anything!

PENNY: Here are the recipes, Your Highness. (*Reaches into pocket and hands recipes to* PRINCE RICHARD)

PRINCE RICHARD (*Reading*): Yes. Yes. This is the girl. What is your name, girl?

PENNY: I am Penny, Your Highness.

PRINCE RICHARD: You are a fine cook, Penny, an accomplished girl.

OLD WOMAN: She is as sweet as she is accomplished, grandson.

PRINCE RICHARD: Granny, I almost made a terrible mistake. Why did you not use your magic to stop me?

OLD WOMAN: Didn't need to, grandson. The truth is better than the best magic. Better have these two (*Indicates* GRISELDA *and* ESMERELDA) sent to the palace kitchen until they at least learn to make buns for breakfast.

PRINCE RICHARD: Good idea.

OLD WOMAN: And learn not to be so bad-tempered and selfish.

GRISELDA (*Stamping her foot*): Who says we are bad-tempered, you old crone? (*Shakes her fist, screams*) We are ladies!

ESMERELDA (*As she shakes* GRISELDA): Quiet, you idiot! That's his granny! His real granny! (ESMERELDA *and* GRISELDA *begin to fight, shove each other, pull hair, tussle. They are stopped by* 1ST PAGE *and* 2ND PAGE *who hold them, arms behind back.* ESMERELDA *and* GRISELDA *continue to struggle and kick.*)

OLD WOMAN (*Sweetly*): Pretty will be as pretty may do. Congratulations, grandson. You will be happy with Penny.

PRINCE RICHARD: I know it. (*Eats a bun*) Yum! What a cook!

ESMERELDA (*Breaking away from* 1ST PAGE): She's *not* pretty, Your Highness.

GRISELDA: She has freckles.

ESMERELDA: And straight hair!

PRINCE RICHARD: Freckles are fetching, and I *like* straight hair. (*Eats a bun*) And I *love* to eat. Penny *will* be my wife. (*Sings to tune of "Au Clair de la Lune" as he holds* PENNY's *hand*)

> I think freckles fetching.
>   Penny is so sweet.
> She will be my bride and
>   Fix good things to eat.
> She will be my princess;
>   She will be my wife.
> She will fix me goodies
>   Each day of my life.

(PRINCE RICHARD, PENNY *and* OLD WOMAN *join hands and dance, circle to the right and then to the left.* 1ST PAGE *and* 2ND PAGE *drag off* ESMERELDA *and* GRISELDA.)
ALL (*Singing together*):

> He thinks freckles fetching.
>> Penny is so sweet.
> She will be his bride and
>> Fix good things to eat.
> She will be his princess;
>> She will be his wife.
> She will fix him goodies
>> Each day of his life. (*Curtain*)

THE END

The Queen's Mirror

by Margaret E. Slattery

Characters

QUEEN DANDELION	PATRICIA
JOCKO	RAG
LADY JANE	TAG
BAKER JOHN	PRINCE STEPHEN
MRS. BAKER JOHN	KING HENRY

TIME: *Once upon a time.*

SETTING: *The throne room in the palace of Queen Dandelion.*

AT RISE: QUEEN DANDELION *is seated on the throne.* LADY JANE *sits beside her, sewing.* JOCKO, *the Court Jester, is sprawled on the floor on the other side of the room, playing with jacks and a ball.*

QUEEN DANDELION (*Leans elbow on arm of chair, rests head on hand, sighs, leans other elbow on other arm of chair, moves head to that hand and sighs, taps foot on floor, sighs loudly, finally jumps up*): Oh, I'm so bored, bored, bored!

LADY JANE: Shall I play you a tune on my lute, Queen Dandelion?

QUEEN DANDELION: Lute, flute—you don't know one tune from another.

JOCKO: Perhaps if you would pay some attention to the people, you wouldn't be so bored.

QUEEN DANDELION: Never mind the people. If they don't bother me, I won't bother them. Fetch me my mirror, Lady Jane. I wish to admire myself. (LADY JANE *exits. The sound of pots and pans falling is heard.*) What was that?

JOCKO (*As he runs over and looks out*): Cook just left. I suppose it's because you haven't paid him any wages in two years. We're getting very poor.

QUEEN DANDELION: Nonsense. I refuse to be poor. Amuse me, Jocko.

JOCKO: Gladly. (*Turns a few somersaults or handsprings*) When is a ship not a ship?

QUEEN DANDELION: When?

JOCKO: When it's ashore. Ha! Ha!

QUEEN DANDELION: I must have been insane when I hired you. (LADY JANE *enters with mirror.*) Ah, here is my mirror. It always cheers me up to see my lovely face. (*Looks in mirror, then lets out a shriek*) What is the meaning of this? I asked for my mirror, and you have brought me this picture of a hideous grinning monster.

LADY JANE: But that is your mirror.

JOCKO (*Peering over* QUEEN DANDELION's *shoulder*): That's your hair all right.

QUEEN DANDELION: But those purple teeth. Those yellow eyes. (*She hands* JOCKO *the mirror, walks backwards away from it, covers her face with her hands, walks up to mirror, uncovers her eyes and shrieks.*) Oh, it's too awful. (*Door slams offstage.*)

JOCKO (*Looking out*): Oh, my, all the chambermaids just left.

QUEEN DANDELION (*Shaking her fist at* LADY JANE): You did something to this mirror when you washed it.

LADY JANE: No, no. I'm always very careful.

QUEEN DANDELION: I've always looked so radiantly beautiful in this mirror. You've ruined my favorite mirror. You're fired. Leave this palace and never come back.

LADY JANE: But it's raining.

QUEEN DANDELION: Leave at once. (QUEEN DANDELION *exits*.)

LADY JANE: Oh, Jocko, now we won't be able to get married and live in our own little cottage.

JOCKO: Don't worry. I'll find out what's the matter with that mirror. You wait just outside the palace grounds.

LADY JANE: Oh, please be quick, Jocko! (LADY JANE *exits. JOCKO picks up the mirror and examines it, peering closely at the frame and testing it with his finger. QUEEN DANDELION enters. JOCKO puts the mirror down quickly.*)

QUEEN DANDELION: I can't understand about that mirror. I usually look so beautiful. (*She goes up and sits on throne.*) Oh, well, I think I'll have my tea now. Lady Jane!

JOCKO: Gone!

QUEEN DANDELION: So she is, foolish girl. Cook! Cook! Cook!

JOCKO: Gone!

QUEEN DANDELION: But who is to fix my tea? This is outrageous! Prime Minister!

JOCKO: Gone! (*He does a somersault and gets up.*) In fact, Queen Dandelion, the palace is empty.

QUEEN DANDELION: How dare they?

JOCKO (*As he sits down on floor and starts playing jacks again*): I don't know how you're going to manage. You have no money.

QUEEN DANDELION: I'll think of something. (*She clasps her hands behind her back and strides about room.*) I'll collect more taxes and hire new servants.

JOCKO: Who will collect the taxes for you? You've turned

everybody against you, and nobody wants to work for you.

QUEEN DANDELION: Hm-m-m. (*Strides about again*) I have an idea. Get me a big piece of cardboard and a paintbrush. (JOCKO *exits.* QUEEN DANDELION *walks about, deep in thought.* LADY JANE *enters carrying an umbrella over her head.*)

LADY JANE: Queen Dandelion! Please, Queen Dandelion, may I come back?

QUEEN DANDELION: Get out, get out, get out! You're fired! (LADY JANE *exits.* QUEEN DANDELION *picks up mirror and looks in it.*) Ah, how awful! (*She calls after* LADY JANE.) And don't come back. (JOCKO *enters with cardboard and paintbrush.*) Ah, good. Wait till you see my wonderful idea. (QUEEN DANDELION *kneels on floor and paints with brush.*) There. See? (*She rises and holds up sign. It reads "Rooms for Rent."*)

JOCKO: "Rooms for Rent!" You're going to take in boarders?

QUEEN DANDELION: Certainly. Put this in the window. (JOCKO *puts sign in window.*) Now let's see. How much should we charge for the Gold Room? Is it bigger than the Silver Room?

JOCKO: But Queen Dandelion, you don't know anything about renting rooms.

QUEEN DANDELION: I can do anything I put my mind to. I'm noted for that. (LADY JANE *enters.*)

LADY JANE: It's stopped raining, but it's getting awfully cold. Can't I come back?

QUEEN DANDELION: Out of my sight, wretched girl! (LADY JANE *exits.*) I'll teach people to ruin mirrors belonging to me. (*Knocking is heard at door*) See who that is. (JOCKO *exits and comes back with* BAKER JOHN *and* MRS. BAKER JOHN. *They are carrying a tray with buns and some paper bags.*)

BAKER JOHN: We saw your sign. I'm Baker John.

MRS. BAKER JOHN: And I'm Mrs. Baker John. We wish to board here and sell our bakery goods. (*She points to her husband.*) He burned down our bakery shop. (*She puts tray on small table.*)

BAKER JOHN: Well, I only did it once.

MRS. BAKER JOHN: Once was enough. Imagine falling asleep while the buns were baking! Come along. Let's unpack. (*They exit.*)

QUEEN DANDELION: There you are. Two boarders already. We'll have tea now, and eat some of their buns. Push that table out while I get the teapot. (QUEEN DANDELION *exits.* JOCKO *pushes table to center of room and arranges chairs around it.*)

RAG (*Offstage*): Halloo!

TAG: Ship ahoy! (RAG *and* TAG *enter, dragging a large canvas bag.*)

RAG: Anybody aboard? (QUEEN DANDELION *enters, carrying a teapot.*)

QUEEN DANDELION: What's all this riff-raff doing in my throne room?

RAG: I'm Rag.

TAG: I'm Tag.

RAG: Have ye a room for a couple of weary sailors?

QUEEN DANDELION: Sailors! I should say not.

RAG: We can pay you in gold pieces.

QUEEN DANDELION: Gold, eh? All right. You can stay in the Gold Room. (RAG *and* TAG *exit.*)

JOCKO: When are you going to let Lady Jane come back?

QUEEN DANDELION: Never. She ruined my mirror. (PATRICIA *enters.*)

JOCKO: Good day, miss.

PATRICIA: Good day. I'd like to rent a room. I hope they don't cost much.

JOCKO: Have you come far?

PATRICIA: Yes, very far. I'm quite tired.

JOCKO: Well, sit down. We're just about to have tea. (JOCKO *and* PATRICIA *sit down.* QUEEN DANDELION *goes and gets tray of buns and dumps them on the table.*)

QUEEN DANDELION (*Sitting down*): Teatime! Tea is served. (BAKER JOHN *and* MRS. BAKER JOHN *enter and sit down.*)

MRS. BAKER JOHN: We'll send you a bill for these buns later, Queen Dandelion.

QUEEN DANDELION: Don't be impertinent. (RAG *and* TAG *enter dragging their large canvas bag.*)

RAG: I'm hungry.

TAG: I'm starving.

JOCKO: Why didn't you leave your bag in your room?

RAG: Yes, why didn't we, Tag?

TAG: Oh, we're just absent-minded, I guess. (*They sit down.*)

JOCKO (*To* PATRICIA): What did you say your name was, miss?

PATRICIA: It's ah—er—Patricia.

MRS. BAKER JOHN: That looks like a dairymaid's dress. Are you a dairymaid?

PATRICIA: Well, you could say that. (PRINCE STEPHEN *comes running in.*)

PRINCE STEPHEN: Quick! Quick! Hide me!

QUEEN DANDELION: Can you pay? This isn't a charity home, you know. It's a boarding-palace.

PRINCE STEPHEN (*As he throws some money on table*): There's some money. Quick! I must hide.

QUEEN DANDELION: Well, you can rent the Emerald Room.

JOCKO: It's the third door on your left. (PRINCE STEPHEN *exits.*)

QUEEN DANDELION: Ho, hum, I think I'll go take a nap. (QUEEN DANDELION *exits.*)

BAKER JOHN: I think I'll go bake some buns.

MRS. BAKER JOHN: I'll come with you. All we need now is for you to burn the palace down. (BAKER JOHN *and* MRS. BAKER JOHN *exit*.)

RAG: Let's look around, Tag. (RAG *and* TAG *exit*.)

JOCKO: I'd certainly like some nice butter with these buns. Could you churn some, miss?

PATRICIA: I don't know how to churn butter.

JOCKO: A dairymaid who doesn't know how to churn butter? What kind of a dairy do you come from?

PATRICIA: From a—oh, never mind. (PATRICIA *rushes out*.)

JOCKO: We certainly have some very strange boarders. (LADY JANE *enters*.)

LADY JANE: Hello, Jocko.

JOCKO: Oh, you'd better go. Queen Dandelion will be furious if she sees you.

LADY JANE: Jocko, I'm not going to stay out there and get pneumonia. If you don't find out what's wrong with that mirror soon, I'm going to get a job as lady-in-waiting at King Henry's palace, and marry somebody else.

JOCKO: But I have some good ideas about it. Wait! (LADY JANE *exits*.) Well, it's a good thing there is one person in this palace who can keep his head. Namely, me. (BAKER JOHN *enters and goes behind table*.)

BAKER JOHN: Well, I'd better go out and find some customers. (*Starts filling bags with buns.* PRINCE STEPHEN *comes tiptoeing in*.)

PRINCE STEPHEN: Sh-h-h. I'm hiding. Shhh.

JOCKO: Who are you hiding from?

PRINCE STEPHEN: Sh-h-h. How do you sell those buns, Baker?

BAKER JOHN: A dozen to the bag.

PRINCE STEPHEN: Quick! Here's some money. I'll have a bag. (BAKER JOHN *hands him a bag, and* PRINCE STE-

PHEN *tiptoes toward door*.) If anybody comes looking for me, I just left for China. (PRINCE STEPHEN *exits*.)

BAKER JOHN: Well, I'm off. I wonder if my hat is on straight. (*He picks up mirror from chair*) Eek!

JOCKO: What's the matter?

BAKER JOHN: Why, the mirror shows a big pig in a baker's cap and apron.

MRS. BAKER JOHN (*Offstage*): Baker John! Come here a minute.

BAKER JOHN: Coming! (*Shakes head*) I don't understand. What kind of a mirror is that? (*Exits*)

JOCKO (*Going over to table, he opens a bag of buns*): One, two, three, four, five, six, seven, eight, nine, ten, eleven. Hm-m-m. That's a funny kind of dozen. Baker John looked like a greedy pig. Hm-m-m. I have an idea. (PATRICIA *enters*.) You have a little bit of soot on your face, miss.

PATRICIA: Where? Where? (*She touches her face.*)

JOCKO: Here, see in the mirror. (*He stands behind her and hands her the mirror.*)

PATRICIA: Oh, my! (*She puts the mirror down quickly.*)

JOCKO (*Bows*): How do you do, Princess Patricia. I can't see the crown on your head, but the mirror can.

PATRICIA: Oh, don't tell. Please don't tell.

JOCKO: But why are you dressed as a dairymaid?

PATRICIA: I'm disguised. My father wants me to marry a prince he has chosen for me, and I know he'll turn out to be old and ugly.

JOCKO: Haven't you ever seen him?

PATRICIA: No. He was supposed to come to our palace today, but I ran away last night. (QUEEN DANDELION *enters*.)

QUEEN DANDELION: I'm going to give this mirror one more chance. (*She looks in it.*) Aah! Horrible! Well, goodbye to you, mirror. (*She holds it over her head and starts to throw it on the floor.*)

JOCKO: Oh, don't do that, Your Majesty. I think that mirror is bewitched.

QUEEN DANDELION: Bewitched! Such nonsense!

JOCKO: I'll show you. (*He hands mirror to* PATRICIA.) Your Highness, will you look in this mirror, please.

QUEEN DANDELION: Your Highness! (PATRICIA *looks in mirror.*) Good gracious, the mirror shows a beautiful princess with a crown on her head.

JOCKO: You see, Patricia is a princess, and this mirror shows her as she really is. Baker John looked in the mirror and saw a greedy pig, because that's what he is. He puts eleven buns in a bag and calls it a dozen. This mirror shows people as they really are.

QUEEN DANDELION: But I looked in and saw a hideous, ugly, miserable—how dare you!

JOCKO: I'm afraid it's true. The mirror is bewitched.

QUEEN DANDELION: But who could have bewitched it?

JOCKO: Have there been any witches or fairies around here lately?

QUEEN DANDELION: Well, my Fairy Godmother paid me her annual visit last week—she must have done it. What's the world coming to when a person's Fairy Godmother plays tricks on her?

JOCKO: She did it for your own good.

QUEEN DANDELION: Oh, how can anyone be so mean to me? Boohoo! (*Cries*)

JOCKO: All you have to do is reform. (LADY JANE *enters.*)

LADY JANE (*Sneezing*): Achoo!

JOCKO: Psst! (*Waves at her*) Go away!

QUEEN DANDELION (*Looks up*): What was that?

LADY JANE (*Sneezing*): Achoo! Achoo! It's so cold out.

QUEEN DANDELION: Why, you're shivering. You poor thing!

JOCKO: Oh, you said something nice. Let's look in the mirror. (*He holds up the mirror and looks over her shoulder.*)

QUEEN DANDELION: I think I look better.

JOCKO: You do. Those three green spots are gone from your nose.

QUEEN DANDELION: Oh, I must say something else nice. Here. (*She hands* JOCKO *the mirror, and runs over to* LADY JANE.) I hope you don't catch cold. (*She runs back to mirror.*) Oh, that's better. (*She runs back to* LADY JANE.) I'm sorry I sent you into exile. (*She runs back to mirror.*) Oh, better and better. (*She runs to* LADY JANE.) You'd better go and get warm. You can use my room. (*She leads* LADY JANE *to door and calls out as* LADY JANE *exits.*) You can wear all my clothes. (*She comes back to mirror.*) Oh, I'm getting nicer and nicer, and looking better and better.

RAG (*Offstage*): Oh, ho, for the rolling waves.

JOCKO: Let's hide, and find out what those sailors are really like. (QUEEN DANDELION, JOCKO *and* PATRICIA *hide.* RAG *and* TAG *enter.*)

RAG: Well, let's see how we are doing. (*He puts bag on floor and they sit on either side of it.* TAG *reaches in and pulls out gold crown.*)

TAG: I wonder if King Henry has missed his crown yet.

RAG: Ha, ha! Very few thieves could steal the crown right off a king's head.

TAG: Well, we can't leave here without taking something. How about this mirror? (*He picks up mirror and looks in.*) Oh! Look! It shows a man behind prison bars. Why, he looks like me.

RAG: Let's see. (*He runs over, grabs mirror and looks in.*) No, he doesn't. He looks like me.

TAG (*Grabbing mirror and holding it up*): Like me!

RAG: Like me! Look at that wicked face. (*Stamps foot*)

Me, me, me! (QUEEN DANDELION, PATRICIA, *and* JOCKO *come out.*)

PATRICIA: You're not sailors at all. You're thieves.

JOCKO: Send them to prison, Queen Dandelion.

QUEEN DANDELION: Rag and Tag, go to prison.

RAG: You have no guards.

TAG: You can't keep us here. (*He starts to gather up bag and crown.*)

JOCKO (*Grabs his arm*): Leave those alone.

RAG: Come on, Tag. Let's run!

QUEEN DANDELION: No, you don't. Help! Help! Baker John! (BAKER JOHN *comes running on stage.*)

BAKER JOHN: What is it? What is it?

QUEEN DANDELION: Arrest those thieves.

BAKER JOHN: Thieves! Help, thieves. (MRS. BAKER JOHN *comes running onstage, waving rolling pin.*)

MRS. BAKER JOHN: Thieves! Thieves! Is someone stealing our buns?

QUEEN DANDELION: Arrest these thieves! (BAKER JOHN *and* MRS. BAKER JOHN *grab* RAG *by his arms, and* JOCKO *and* QUEEN DANDELION *grab* TAG. *They all exit as* PATRICIA *enters.*)

PATRICIA: My goodness, this is a very strange palace! (PRINCE STEPHEN *enters, tiptoes around room.*)

PRINCE STEPHEN: He's not here, is he? (*Looks out window*)

PATRICIA: Oh, you missed all the excitement. They just arrested the thieves who stole King Henry's crown.

PRINCE STEPHEN: King Henry! King Henry! Is he here? Oh, I must hide!

PATRICIA: No, no, come back. He's not here. What's the matter?

PRINCE STEPHEN: Oh, nothing. I'm just nervous. I think I'll have another bun to calm my nerves. That baker owes me one anyway. There were only eleven in the bag.

(*He turns around and goes over to the table in the corner, with his back to the audience.* KING HENRY *enters.*)

KING HENRY: I'm King Henry. Where's my son, Prince Stephen?

PRINCE STEPHEN (*Whirling around*): Father!

KING HENRY: It's no use hiding. Come along. The marriage has already been arranged.

PRINCE STEPHEN: I won't marry Princess Patricia.

PATRICIA: Who?

PRINCE STEPHEN: They tell me she's ugly and stupid and mean.

PATRICIA: Wait—wait—

KING HENRY: Stuff and nonsense. Come along.

PRINCE STEPHEN: She hits people with a big stick if they so much as say "Good Morning."

PATRICIA (*Walking between them*): Wait—listen—

PRINCE STEPHEN (*Talking over her shoulder*): No, Father, I refuse to marry Princess Patricia.

PATRICIA: Oh, please marry me. You're so handsome.

PRINCE STEPHEN: Oh, I'd be glad to marry you. You're nice.

PATRICIA: But I am Princess Patricia. I ran away from my palace because they told me that *you* were stupid and ugly and mean. (QUEEN DANDELION, JOCKO, BAKER JOHN, *and* MRS. BAKER JOHN *enter.*)

QUEEN DANDELION (*As she dusts off hands*): Well, those rascals will stay in prison a long time.

PATRICIA: This is Prince Stephen.

PRINCE STEPHEN: And I'm going to marry Princess Patricia.

MRS. BAKER JOHN: Isn't that sweet?

KING HENRY (*As he picks up crown from floor*): Why, what's my crown doing here?

QUEEN DANDELION: Oh, it's a long story.

KING HENRY: Well, I'm a little tired. Perhaps, madam, if I might have the honor of calling on you tomorrow, we could talk. Now come along, Stephen and Patricia. We must make plans for the wedding. (KING HENRY *exits with* PRINCE STEPHEN *and* PATRICIA.)

QUEEN DANDELION: Oh, I think King Henry likes me. How nice.

BAKER JOHN: Your Majesty, as a reward for helping you arrest those thieves, could we become cooks here?

QUEEN DANDELION: Good. I haven't had a decent meal all day.

JOCKO: I'd be careful if I were you, Queen Dandelion. After all, you've reformed and you'll want an honest cook. Baker John sells eleven buns as a dozen, remember.

MRS. BAKER JOHN: I told you to stop doing that.

BAKER JOHN: Well, I never will again.

JOCKO: Why don't you take him on trial, Your Majesty? Then, in a week, the mirror will tell us if he really has changed.

QUEEN DANDELION: Good idea. Baker John, fix my supper at once!

JOCKO: Queen Dandelion!

QUEEN DANDELION: I mean—fix my supper (*Bows*), please. (BAKER JOHN *and* MRS. BAKER JOHN *exit.*)

JOCKO: I'm sorry, Your Majesty, but it's been such an exhausting day that I don't think I can do any tricks to amuse you. (*He gets down on floor and tries to do a somersault, but falls over.*)

QUEEN DANDELION: That's all right. (*She climbs up on throne.*) Now that I've reformed, I have a lot of work to do. (*She takes out paper and pencil.*) Let's see. There's Queen Eleanor—I insulted her at her last dinner party. There's Duchess Marie—I refused to go to her daughter's wedding. I made fun of Lady Agatha's hat. I put salt in the sugar bowl when General Battle was here last month. My goodness, I have been naughty. So don't worry about amusing me, Jocko. I'll be so busy being nice to people, I'll never be bored again! (*Curtain*)

THE END

Posies for the Potentate

by Martha Swintz

Characters

KING RUDOLPH OF HAPPIDAZIA
QUEEN LETITIA OF HAPPIDAZIA
PRINCESS ALICE
PRIME MINISTER
MESSENGER
WIZARD OF RATZENCATZIA
CUTHBERT CACKLEBAIT
COURTIERS

SETTING: *Throne room in the royal palace.*
AT RISE: KING RUDOLPH OF HAPPIDAZIA *is sitting on his throne, talking with the* PRIME MINISTER. *The* KING *holds a large book on his lap.*

PRIME MINISTER: Flower pots!
KING: Flower pots. All that you can get. It says right here on page 22, "to achieve the best results you must have adequate equipment." I want adequate flowerpots. (*Ordering*) Minister, attend to it.
PRIME MINISTER: Yes, King Rudolph, I'll order a dozen immediately.
KING: A dozen! My good man, we are planting a kingdom,

not a window box. The land of Happidazia shall be
bathed in fragrance.

PRIME MINISTER (*Aside*): This idea smells anyway. (*To
KING*) I'll see that it is taken care of. But, King Rudolph,
suppose Queen Letitia discovers you've been reading
those "Pamphlet of the Week Club" books again. I
don't think she will be very pleased about that. She
still remembers your early pamphlet projects.

KING: She will never find out until it's too late. She
thought she had me fooled when she canceled my subscription to the "Pamphlet of the Week Club" but I
fooled her. I took out a new subscription for Flopsy,
our royal dog.

PRIME MINISTER (*Patiently*): Do we need anything besides
flowerpots?

KING: Let's see here. (*Reads*) "Plant the seeds." Seeds? We
haven't any. Put them on the list. (*Sounds of movement
and talking offstage*)

BOTH: The Queen!

KING: Go, quickly, and send out these orders before my
wife finds out. (PRIME MINISTER *exits.*) She mustn't find
me with another book! (*Sits on book.* QUEEN *and* COUR-
TIERS *enter. The* QUEEN *carries a large mop and dustcloth.*)

QUEEN (*Walking toward* KING *and glancing around room*):
Good morning, Rudolph. (*To herself*) Now where shall
I start?

KING: Good morning, Letitia. Who's your friend? Looks
like she could use a permanent.

QUEEN: You know very well this is the week for the royal
housecleaning. Although it is difficult enough with the
litter of your various projects lying about. Some day I'm
going to throw out all the old wrecks around here.

KING: Don't give me any ideas, my dear.

QUEEN (*To* COURTIERS): We'll start with the thrones. I'm

going to clean this place thoroughly—top to bottom, over and under.

KING: Under? Under what?

QUEEN: The thrones, of course. Now get up and don't stand on ceremony.

KING: I'm not standing on ceremony. I want to sit on my throne.

QUEEN: Rudolph, get up!

KING: DON'T SHOUT! Why don't you wait until tomorrow?

QUEEN: I'm going to clean this room right now.

KING (*Begrudgingly*): Oh, all right. (KING *rises gingerly, clutching book behind him. Moves away from* QUEEN)

QUEEN: Rudolph, you're hiding something behind your back. What is it?

KING: Why—nothing, dear. (KING *and* QUEEN *circle each other.* QUEEN *points mop right at* KING, *who backs away.* COURTIER *who is dusting bumps into* KING, *causing him to drop book.* QUEEN *pounces on it.*)

QUEEN: A book!

KING: Why so it is. Now how do you suppose it got in here?

QUEEN: You know exactly how it got in here. You brought it. And you promised me you wouldn't read any more of that "Pamphlet of the Week Club" drivel. (*Looks at book*) "The Art of Growing Flowers," by Cuthbert Cacklebait. Is he the same one who started you collecting fishing tackle and building canoes?

KING: And what is wrong with collecting fishing tackle and building canoes?

QUEEN: Nothing, except that there aren't any fish or lakes within five hundred miles of Happidazia.

KING: The Water Commissioner is working on *that* now. Besides, there is enough water for flowers, and I'm going to grow them.

QUEEN: What are you going to plant them in, the millions

of old bottles we have in the basement left from the time you started building ship models to put inside bottles?

KING: Now that was an excellent idea. The trouble with you is that you get discouraged too quickly. (PRIME MINISTER *enters and bows before* KING.)

PRIME MINISTER: Sire, I've ordered twelve hundred.

QUEEN: Twelve hundred what?

PRIME MINISTER: Flowerpots, Your Highness. Flowerpots.

QUEEN: Oh, no. (*Falls in a faint, dropping book.*)

PRIME MINISTER: I do believe the Queen is laid up.

KING: No, just laid out. But never fear, I have my handy pocket edition of "First Aid for the Home" here in my robe. (*Takes book from inside of gown.* PRINCESS ALICE *enters and runs to* QUEEN.)

PRINCESS: Mother! (*Looking about*) What has happened here? Father, you've done something again. Quickly, help me. (PRINCESS ALICE *and* COURTIERS *work to revive the* QUEEN. KING *stands to one side and reads his book.*)

KING (*Reading*): "If the victim is in pain . . ." But she's not in anything. The least she could do is act like a victim. (QUEEN *sits up slowly.* KING *picks up dustcloth and fans* QUEEN *with it.*)

QUEEN: Oh, all I can see are flowerpots. They're waving around me. Oh, dear. I'm surrounded by flowerpots.

KING: I'm no flowerpot!

PRINCESS: What on earth is going on around here?

QUEEN: Earth! Oh, don't mention that word. Flowers grow in earth. They thrive in earth!

KING: You're learning, dear.

QUEEN: Alice, come to your poor mother. His Majesty has been reading again.

PRINCESS: Father, not again! You promised us you were through after the rabbit farm. We were up to our necks in little white bunnies.

KING: Why didn't somebody tell me about their love of family life? But flowers don't multiply—I don't think so anyway. (MESSENGER *enters*.) What do you want?

MESSENGER: Your Majesty, there is an odd creature at the gate who begs to speak to you on important business.

QUEEN: You seem to collect odd creatures.

KING: You should know. (*To* PRIME MINISTER) Well, we had better see him. He may be selling something, and I love free samples. Minister, go with this Messenger and show our guest to the throne room. (PRIME MINISTER *and* MESSENGER *exit*.) And now, let's get all of this claptrap out of the way. We are holding court. (*All scurry to hide cleaning implements.* KING *and* QUEEN *sit on thrones. In a few minutes* PRIME MINISTER *enters, glancing behind him at intervals. The* WIZARD OF RATZENCATZIA *follows at a distance.*)

PRIME MINISTER: Sire, this—uh—gentleman has come to us from very far away.

QUEEN: He looks as though he never arrived. Who is he?

WIZARD: Your Highness, I am known as the Wizard of Ratzencatzia. I have come a great distance to the land of Happidazia for I have heard tales of your fair daughter.

KING: We like her. Would you like to meet her? (PRINCESS *draws away*.) Come now, Alice, don't be shy.

PRINCESS (*To* KING): I don't like him, Father. He has a strange look about him.

WIZARD (*Aside*): So this is Princess Alice. When I marry her, I shall have this country and its resources in my power. (*To* QUEEN) Your Highness, she is lovelier than I had hoped. Although her beauty cannot compare with yours.

KING: This man's not strange; he's a liar.

QUEEN: Quiet, Rudolph! Mr. Wizard, you are too kind. What can we do for you?

WIZARD: I have come in the hope that I might win the hand of this lovely Princess.

KING (*To* MINISTER): Doesn't he want the rest of her?

WIZARD: I shall put all of my power at your disposal if I may have your greatest treasure.

KING (*To* MINISTER): What's he talking about? Is he going to rob the royal treasury?

PRIME MINISTER: What difference would it make? We haven't any money. Give the moths a change of scenery.

QUEEN: Rudolph, he wants to marry Alice.

KING: Well, why didn't you say so? What—marry Alice? He can't. Nobody can marry Alice until I say he can, and I don't want to—not yet. Do you want to marry him, Alice?

PRINCESS: Oh, no. There's something evil about him. Tell him to go away.

KING: Go away. The Princess doesn't want to get married today. Maybe tomorrow—

WIZARD: Don't be hasty, O King. Remember, I can grant any wishes you make. I can perform wonderful feats of sorcery at your command.

KING: Thanks, but we have a very spooky court magician right here. Besides, the local boys might complain if you cut in on their business.

WIZARD: Sire, I am *not* an ordinary magician. I've been working for years on my own never-fail spells. I have a terrific ten-minute thriller that I'll show you for half price.

KING: I told you that we are not giving away daughters today. That's final!

WIZARD: Do not anger me, Sire. I should hate to resort to witchcraft in such charming company.

KING: Just charm yourself right out of here, and we'll be satisfied. Pick up your broomstick and fly home.

WIZARD (*Starting to exit*): I shall leave now but I'll be

back. You will be more ready to hear me then. (*Exits*)

PRINCESS: Perhaps you shouldn't have spoken to him so strongly.

KING: Now don't you worry. Your daddy can take care of any old wizard or witch that comes along. Look at your mother—isn't she the soul of happiness?

QUEEN (*Angrily*): I've had enough. I'll speak to you later, Rudolph. (QUEEN *and* COURTIERS *exit.*)

KING: We're going to have quite a crowd in here later on. Now to business. Minister, how's the garden coming along?

PRIME MINISTER: Bloomingly, Sire—if I may make a pun. In fact, I think I'd better tend to the garden right now. (*Exits*)

PRINCESS: Father, must you continue with this foolish idea of yours?

KING: It's not foolish. My flowers will be beautiful. Cuthbert Cacklebait says that flowers are the source of life.

PRINCESS: They may end yours. Who is Cuthbert Cacklebait?

KING: He is an editor for the "Pamphlet of the Week Club." His books are very popular.

PRINCESS: Not around here. I hope Mother never meets him.

KING: Well, she will. I've had a letter from him and he's coming here to discuss subscriptions—with Flopsy. (*Laughs to himself*)

PRINCESS: They must really need subscribers. I had better warn Mother. (*Exits*)

KING: And now—(*Reaches around for book but finds it gone. Frantically searches under drapes, out window, etc. Finds book where* QUEEN *dropped it when she fainted.*) Back to Cuthbert. Nobody understands me around here. It will be wonderful when Cacklebait arrives. Somebody on my side for a change. (KING *is deep in reading, as* WIZARD *creeps back in. He carries a book.*)

WIZARD: King Rudolph, I would have a word with you.

KING: Are you back again?

WIZARD: I wish to repeat my offer.

KING: Once was enough. I'm busy. This is my one chance to read in peace. Can't you see I'm an unhappy man?

WIZARD: You are? Perhaps I can be of help. I have many powers at my command.

KING: No amount of black magic could help me. You see, I like to read books but nobody will ever let me. Even you must have a favorite volume of curses.

WIZARD: I certainly do. "Classic Curses for Crafty Conjurers." Keep it with me all the time. (*Pats book*)

KING: But there is more to it than just reading. I want to plant a garden. I want to plant the entire land of Happidazia with flowers.

WIZARD (*Aside*): This may be my chance to get the kingdom. (*To* KING) Don't despair. I can help you.

KING: Plant my flowers? And maybe even a few trees and shrubs?

WIZARD: That might take a little extra homework, but I think I could manage it.

KING: Hooray! (*Dances down from throne and hugs* WIZARD) When shall we start?

WIZARD: Not so fast, King Rudolph. Remember, a man of my talents doesn't come along every day. There is a certain talent fee involved. My manager would hate me if I didn't collect something.

KING: I'll have money printed at once.

WIZARD: I don't need money. No, Sire, if I plant this garden for you, you must give me Princess Alice as a reward.

KING: This is a pretty stiff bargain. I'll have to think about it. Turn your back, please. (WIZARD *turns away as* KING *searches furiously through book.*) Cuthbert, don't desert me now. (*Pause*) No, there isn't a single thing about exchanging princesses for gardens.

WIZARD: Are you ready?

KING: Not yet. I have to make up my mind. (*Itemizing on fingers*) First, Alice is as pretty as a flower and she smells as good, too. Second, flowers require much care and they get buggy in the summertime. Alice takes care of herself quite well and, at least, I've never heard her complain about bugs.

WIZARD: Your Majesty—

KING: WILL YOU KEEP QUIET! I must have absolute silence.

WIZARD: I'll breathe softly.

KING (*Continuing*): Flowers will make Alice happy too, though. I can't plant Alice but I can plant flowers. Wiz, (WIZARD *turns*) it's a deal.

WIZARD: You are wise, O King. (*Aside*) He's all mine along with this silly country of his. (*To* KING) Let us begin. Take those pillows from the thrones and place them on the floor.

KING: My wife won't like this.

WIZARD: She hasn't seen anything yet! I shall prepare myself for the spell. I usually have a fanfare before I perform but I suppose I'll have to put up with this. (WIZARD *reads book as* KING *peers over his shoulder.*)

KING: That looks good. Very wizardly.

WIZARD: I shall now assume the position. Move over. (*Lies down on floor*) I really should have a black cat. Can you purr?

KING: I'll try. (*Screws up his face and tries to purr*)

WIZARD: I suppose you'll have to do. Put my hat on my chest. (KING *does so.*) Now close your eyes. No peeking! (PRIME MINISTER *enters.*)

PRIME MINISTER: Excuse me, Sire, there's a gentleman in

the outer hall. (*Sees* WIZARD) What's this? Is he in-capacitated?

KING: No, entranced. The Wizard is growing my garden.

PRIME MINISTER: He needs a flower bed not a feather bed!

WIZARD: Quiet! Can't you see I'm working?

PRIME MINISTER: Looks like a pretty soft job to me.

WIZARD (*Chanting*):

> "Spirits of the world attend me,
> Answer to my magic powers,
> Let the land of Happidazia,
> Burst into a realm of flowers."

(*Raises arms up straight*)

PRIME MINISTER: Has rigor mortis set in?

WIZARD: This will take time. I knew I needed that cat.

KING (*Going to window*): Wait a moment. The land around the castle is turning green. There are little buds and blossoms springing up everywhere! You're wonder-ful.

WIZARD: It wasn't so much. Say, this feels good. Mind if I take a nap?

PRIME MINISTER: I don't understand any of this, but there is still a man in the outer hall. He wants to see you about the "Pamphlet of the Week Club."

KING: What's his name?

PRIME MINISTER: Cuthbert Cacklebait. He said he had an appointment.

KING: So he did. Send him in. Let him see what a real gardener can do. (PRIME MINISTER *exits.*)

WIZARD (*Getting up*): Don't forget our bargain, King Ru-dolph. Your garden is finished. Now I want the Princess.

KING: Oh, that. Well, you know, she might not like this.

WIZARD: Your promise was made. A king never breaks his word. (QUEEN, PRINCESS, *and* COURTIERS *enter hur-riedly.*)

KING: That's true. Here she is; ask her yourself.

QUEEN (*Greatly disturbed*): Rudolph, something is happening around here. There are buttercups on the balconies, daisies in the drawing-room and petunias in the pantry.

KING: Isn't that wonderful!

QUEEN: Wonderful? I can't turn around without seeing some big green thing.

KING: The Wizard has planted my garden for me. The land of Happidazia shall be a blooming paradise.

PRINCESS (*To* WIZARD): You did this for Father?

WIZARD: It was my pleasure.

PRINCESS: In return for what?

WIZARD: For you, Princess Alice.

PRINCESS: Father! Is this true?

KING: Well, now—

QUEEN: Rudolph?

KING: Yes. (CUTHBERT CACKLEBAIT *enters.*)

CACKLEBAIT: Am I interrupting?

QUEEN: Who are you?

CACKLEBAIT: I am Cuthbert Cacklebait, editor for the "Pamphlet of the Week Club."

QUEEN: Throw him out! He's responsible for all of this.

CACKLEBAIT: My dear madam—

QUEEN: Don't you "dear madam" me! If you don't leave you'll be editing a murder story—your own.

CACKLEBAIT: I merely came to find out if Mr. Flopsy wants his subscription renewed.

QUEEN: The only new thing we need around here is a new king with a new head! Alice, we're leaving.

WIZARD: I'll take care of Princess Alice from now on.

PRINCESS: You will not!

CACKLEBAIT: This sounds tremendous. May I have the publishing rights?

QUEEN: You'll have funeral rites in a few minutes. Alice! (QUEEN, PRINCESS *and* COURTIERS *exit.*)

KING: I'm awfully sorry, Wiz, but her mind is made up.

WIZARD: And so is mine. You have the garden; I want the Princess.

KING: Then I guess you'll have to take the garden back.

WIZARD: There's not much of a market for used gardens these days, King Rudolph.

CACKLEBAIT: I'm an expert on gardens. Can I help?

KING: Who are you?

CACKLEBAIT: That question has gotten me into more trouble lately.

KING: I remember. You're Cuthbert Cacklebait. You started all of this—stop it!

CACKLEBAIT: King Rudolph, I don't know what you're talking about. However, never let it be said that the "Pamphlet of the Week Club" deserted a sinking subscriber.

KING: Come with me. We'll have a very private conference out of the hearing of sinister sorcerers. (KING *and* CACKLEBAIT *exit.*)

WIZARD: So—he's trying to back out on me. I'll fix him. I'll take that garden and turn it into a nightmare. First, I'll get rid of all those flowers. Then I'll plant—I'll plant—*onions!* Big, juicy onions. The land of Happidazia will burst into tears all because of me. Ha-ha. Now to re-arrange the pillows. (*Busily pushes pillows together, gets out reference book and lies down.*) I do wish I had that cat! (*Chanting*)

> "Spirits of the world attend me,
> Since the King won't grant my dreams,
> Let onions grow instead of flowers,
> And make tears run out in streams."

(*Shoots both arms and legs into air*) That took a lot out of me. I guess I'm getting to that age. (*Sounds of weeping offstage*) Ah, I'm getting results. (KING *and* CACKLEBAIT *enter.*)

CACKLEBAIT: Yours is indeed a sad story, King Rudolph. (*Takes out large handkerchief and sniffs into it*) I can understand your unhappiness. (*Begins to cry*) Books are such a joy to me.

KING: There, there, my boy. (*Also begins to cry into handkerchief*) Don't take it so seriously. We'll think of something.

CACKLEBAIT (*Weeping harder*): If we could just get rid of this wizard.

WIZARD: I won't leave until I take the Princess with me. (QUEEN, PRINCESS *and* COURTIERS *enter, weeping into handkerchiefs.*)

QUEEN: Oh, Rudolph, we were sitting among the flowers eating bread and honey when all at once they wilted and—

KING: There, there, dear, don't worry. I'll plant some more flowers.

PRINCESS: Papa, we've made you cry, too. (PRIME MINISTER *enters, also weeping.*)

PRIME MINISTER: Sire, I was riding through the country when all at once I just began to cry and cry. Everyone else is crying, too. Gloom has descended on the kingdom. (CACKLEBAIT *exits quietly while* WIZARD *moves closer to the* PRINCESS.)

KING: I feel just fine. (*Sobbing*)

WIZARD (*Aside*): I may (*Gets out handkerchief*) have overdone this a bit. (*To* KING) Is this the land of Happidazia? Is this King Rudolph's joyous kingdom? Where's the Chamber of Commerce? Wait until I tell the folks at home about this! Will they laugh! (*Bursts into tears*)

KING: What will I say at the Kings' Convention next

month? They'll throw me out of the Lodge. (*To* WIZ-ARD) Do something. Do something! (CACKLEBAIT *enters carrying large onion. He has a book in a pocket of his coat.*)

CACKLEBAIT: Sire, I suspected foul play. Here is the answer to your weeping nation. Onions!

ALL: Onions!

CACKLEBAIT: Onions. This old goblin here turned your garden into a huge onion patch.

PRINCESS: Father, you don't know what he'll do next. I'd better give in and marry the old buzzard.

WIZARD: That's wizard. Watch your pronunciation.

CACKLEBAIT: Wait! I have here a copy of the new "Pamphlet of the Week Club" selection. It is "Cooking for Two." In it there is a graphically illustrated color section on onions. (*Takes book from coat and begins to read*)

WIZARD: Close that book!

QUEEN: Don't you dare.

CACKLEBAIT (*Reading*): "Onions should be peeled under water to avoid shedding tears."

ALL: Under water?

CACKLEBAIT: That's what it says.

WIZARD: King Rudolph, I demand your daughter. You can't flood the entire country.

CACKLEBAIT: Oh, yes he can. Issue a proclamation!

KING: Minister, issue a proclamation.

PRIME MINISTER (*Weeping*): I'd love to. (*Takes out pencil and paper and scribbles furiously*)

CACKLEBAIT: Tell the people to cry and cry. Tell them to collect their tears and throw them into the fields. We will create lakes, rivers and streams of tears. We will drown those onions in their own juice.

WIZARD: Curses!

KING: Issue that proclamation immediately! (PRIME MIN-

ISTER *exits*.) And now, Sir Ratzencatzia, we are through with you.

WIZARD: I'll not give up easily. You'll hear from me again.

CACKLEBAIT: Now, just a minute. I don't think you are a bad fellow. Would you be interested in a little business proposition?

WIZARD: I might be. This wizarding seems to be falling off a bit.

CACKLEBAIT: The "Pamphlet of the Week Club" has been looking for a new department. How would you like to become editor of a new series, "The Spell of the Week"? We'll start a campaign for bigger and darker magic.

WIZARD: Not *magic*, please—sorcery. Professional ethics, you know. Think how proud my dear mother would be of me—a real editor. It's a deal. I'm going to get my reference books. An honorable wizard! (WIZARD *exits as* PRIME MINISTER *enters*.)

PRIME MINISTER: It's working. We are well on the way to having a beautiful salt lake in the middle of Happidazia.

KING: Where are the plans for my canoes and fishing tackle? I knew I would want them some day.

QUEEN: Mr. Cacklebait, how can we ever thank you?

CACKLEBAIT: If I may be allowed to remain here and . . . cultivate, I shall consider myself amply rewarded.

KING: We will be proud to have you. And I have some dandy ideas for the Club.

QUEEN: Rudolph! That will do. Alice, why don't you go out and watch the moon rise over the new lake?

PRINCESS: An excellent idea. Mr. Cacklebait?

CACKLEBAIT: Simply delightful. Shall we? (PRINCESS *and* CACKLEBAIT *exit*.)

KING (*Relaxing on throne*): Now you see, I'm not such a bad fellow after all.

QUEEN: At least you're a very lucky fellow. Wouldn't it be

splendid if that Mr. Cacklebait turned out to be our son-in-law?

KING: I'll say. Just think, then I'd be certain of having a life subscription to the "Pamphlet of the Week Club." (QUEEN *collapses. Curtain.*)

THE END

The Saga of Davey Rocket

by Ruthe Massion Tausheck

Characters

COSMA DIMPLEWART, *the heroine*
ATOM DIMPLEWART, *her father*
RADIA DIMPLEWART, *her mother*
GREAT-GRANDFATHER DIMPLEWART, *a uranium prospector*
DAVEY ROCKET, *the hero*
SCORPIO, *the villain*
ROBERT THE ROBOT

TIME: *An evening in 1990.*

SETTING: *The dining room of the Dimplewart home, on planet Earth. At center is a table with four chairs around it. Upstage center is a cupboard lined with small bottles. On one side is an intercom speaker and on the other side is the space-a-phone, which looks like a television set, with a large picture into which a person can step. It has modernistic knobs, dials, etc.*

BEFORE RISE: ROBERT THE ROBOT *appears from behind the curtain, carrying cue cards, which he puts on an easel at one side of the apron of the stage. The top card reads,* CUE CARDS.

ROBERT (*Mechanically*): Greetings to you in the audience. Welcome to our gay nineties melodrama. The melodramas of old had a prompter to cue the audience. Since our melodrama takes place in the nineteen-nineties, the old-time prompter has become mechanized. Tonight you will get your cues from me, Robert the Robot. (*He holds up* APPLAUSE *cue card and bows.*) Let the curtain open!

*　　*　　*

AT RISE: RADIA DIMPLEWART *takes four pills from each of four bottles on the shelf. In front of each chair at the table she places four pills.*

ROBERT: As you can see, it is dinner time at the home of the Dimplewart family. Radia Dimplewart is hard at work preparing dinner. (*He holds up cue card,* TO-NIGHT'S MENU: ONE GROUND MEAT PILL. ONE MASHED PO-TATO PILL. TWO EGG PILLS.)

RADIA (*Calling into intercom*): Atom! Dinner is on the table. Our daughter, Cosma, will be home from work any minute. You'd better clean up for dinner.

ATOM (*Voice offstage, as over intercom*): I just finished feeding Robert his nightly quart of oil. I'll be right in.

RADIA (*Into intercom*): Bring Great-grandfather Dimple-wart with you. He's probably out on the patio tending that potted meteorite plant that cousin Abel Baker sent him from Saturn last summer. (*She arranges pills on table and looks impatiently toward left.*) Where is every-one tonight?

ATOM (*As he enters and sits at table*): What are you look-ing so worried about, Radia? I'm here.

RADIA: I slave around this place all day, wearing my finger-nails down pushing buttons. The rest of you could at least get to the table on time. Where is Great-grand-father Dimplewart?

ATOM: He'll be right in. He's out on the patio trying to

fix old Betsy, his Geiger counter. He hasn't been the same since old Betsy has been having those wild spells.

RADIA: He's been prospecting this place since the uranium rush of 1961. It's silly of him to think he would find anything after all these years.

ATOM: I know, but it keeps him happy.

GREAT-GRANDFATHER (*Enters, carrying Geiger counter*): Evening, folks. Where's Cosma?

RADIA (*Wringing hands*): She's always home from her job at the interplanetary phone exchange by this time. I can't understand what's keeping her. I'm really worried. (COSMA *flings open door, rushes in, closes the door and leans against it.* ROBERT *holds up cue card,* THE HEROINE. WHISTLES AND APPLAUSE.)

COSMA: Woe is me! Woe is me!

RADIA: What is the trouble, Cosma? You look as pale as the Milky Way.

COSMA: Mother dear, I am so truly frightened. When I got off the atomic bus, that horrible Mr. Scorpio was waiting for me. He followed me to the suburban monorail. I ran all the way home from there, trying to escape him. (*There is a loud pounding at the front door.*)

ATOM (*Booming voice*): Who is it?

SCORPIO (*Offstage*): It is I, Scorpio! (ROBERT *holds up sign,* THE VILLAIN. *He puts sign down.*)

ATOM: Enter if you dare. (SCORPIO *flings open door and enters. He strikes a villainous pose, while* ROBERT *holds up cue card,* BOO.)

SCORPIO: Aha! There you are, my lovely little golden star. Did you really think you could escape me? Not Scorpio, owner of the largest used helicopter business in town. (*Laughs*)

COSMA: How dare you force your way into my home?

SCORPIO (*With false sweetness*): My dear Miss Dimplewart,

you do me an injustice. Do you think I would be so crude as to enter another's home? (*Villainously*) This is no longer your home; it now belongs to me! (SCORPIO *produces an aged document and holds it for all to see.*)

ATOM: You know full well this house is all paid for. In the days when I was gainfully employed as a dishwasher repair man, I made good money.

SCORPIO: Aha, but the Dimplewart clan has only been leasing the lot that this house is on.

GREAT-GRANDFATHER: That's mighty true, but we are supposed to have ninety-nine years in which to purchase this lot.

SCORPIO: According to this document, today is the last day. (*Sneers*) Do you have the money?

ATOM: You know full well we don't have the money. You just admitted that this house is all paid up. It is legally ours. How dare you say it belongs to you?

SCORPIO: The fine print. You didn't read the fine print. (GREAT-GRANDFATHER *snatches the document from* SCORPIO, *then pulls spectacles from his pocket and places them on the end of his nose. He scans paper and shrugs.*)

GREAT-GRANDFATHER: Here, Radia, you read it. (RADIA *holds lorgnette up to her eyes, brings paper close to her face, then holds it farther away.*)

RADIA: I do see several little dots. That must be the fine print. (COSMA *takes a long telescope from top of cupboard and looks at paper.*)

COSMA: It says: "The Dimplewart family has the right to lease the lot for ninety-nine years. During that time no one else has any rights to the lot. At the end of the 99th year, the lessees must either purchase the lot or give up any and all rights to it. If the lessees have not done so by the stroke of nine o'clock on the final day, then any and all dwellings or possessions located upon the lot shall become the property of the holder of this document. Deadline, November 18, 1990." Then this is the last day!

SCORPIO: Just as I said. You know how hard land is to find on the planet Earth. I will have this house blown to atomic dust, and I will use the lot to expand my helicopter business.

COSMA (*On knees pleading*): Please, Scorpio, take pity. Have mercy. Isn't there anything that will prevent you from sending us poor Dimplewarts homeless into the crowded universe?

SCORPIO (*Twirling his mustache*): There is only one thing that I want more than land. That, my dear, is you. Come with me and be mine, and I will tear up the lease rental.

COSMA: No! No! A thousand times no! I'd rather die than say yes.

ATOM: Never fear, daughter. (*To* SCORPIO) This document says the deadline is nine o'clock. So leave and don't darken my door until nine o'clock.

SCORPIO: Curses! I go, but I will return. Soon! (*He takes document and exits.* ROBERT *holds up cue card,* HISS AND BOO.)

COSMA (*Weeping*): What will we do? Whatever in the universe will we do?

GREAT-GRANDFATHER: In my day there was always a brave young hero to save a lady in distress.

COSMA (*Dabbing tear from cheek*): That is the solution! There is only one person who could save us—my own true hero, Davey Rocket.

RADIA: True. He is the one to save us. But this week he is stationed on Satellite National Park.

ATOM: Everyone knows that the satellite only spins over our town once every two hours.

GREAT-GRANDFATHER: Great Jupiter! We need him right now. We can't do anything without a hero.

COSMA: We can't give up hope. I'm going to call Satellite National Park on the space-a-phone and find out if he can get here in time to save us. (COSMA *goes to the space-a-phone. She sits down, turns knobs and dials, and speaks into microphone.*) This is (*Insert name of town and state in which play is produced*), Planet Earth. I would like to put in a call to Davey Rocket, Satellite National Park. (DAVEY ROCKET *appears in the picture of the space-a-phone.*)

DAVEY ROCKET: Hello, Davey Rocket speaking. (ROBERT *holds up cue card,* HOORAY, CHEERS, AND APPLAUSE.)

COSMA: Davey, my hero! Save us from the clutches of Scorpio. If we don't pay him the money for our lot by nine o'clock tonight, he will burn our house and turn us out homeless.

DAVEY ROCKET: The villain! Never fear, my own true love. I, Davey Rocket, shall rocket to Earth and save you.

COSMA: He will be here in half an hour. Can you get here by then?

DAVEY ROCKET: It is humanly impossible! But then, *I* am Davey Rocket. For you, my fair earthling, I will try anything. Pray that the winds are not against me. Take hope, my sweet love. (DAVEY ROCKET *disappears from view.*)

RADIA: Will he be here in time to save us?

COSMA: It will depend on the prevailing winds over (*Insert name of town*).

RADIA: The winds over (*Insert name of town*)? He'll never make it!

ATOM: There is only one thing left to do. We must scrape together enough money to pay Scorpio. How much do we owe him, anyway? (COSMA, RADIA, *and* GREAT-GRANDFATHER *indicate they don't know by shaking their heads or shrugging.*)

ROBERT (*Holds up cue card,* $1,350): The price of the lot is $1,350.

ATOM: If we earth people still used dishes, I'd still be working as a dishwasher repair man. Then we wouldn't be in this financial mess.

RADIA: Take Halley's comet by the tail, Atom, and quit blaming yourself. In the thirty years you were fixing washers, you earned enough to pay for this house, didn't you?

ATOM: I'd still be earning money, if it hadn't been for the invention of capsule meals. It was a sad day for me when the government catapulted all our dishes into outer space.

GREAT-GRANDFATHER: I wonder if the people on Mars ever solved the mystery of all those flying saucers.

COSMA (*Taking envelope from pocket*): Here is my very first pay envelope from my new job at the interplanetary space-a-phone exchange. (*Puts each item on table*) A coupon for two free calls to Venus, a token for the jet express to the moon, and six dollars.

RADIA: That's a beginning. All we need now is one thousand three hundred and forty-four dollars. What about you, Gramps? I know you've been collecting dimes in that old sock of yours for three decades.

GREAT-GRANDFATHER: You wouldn't want me to give up my savings, would you? You know how I've had my heart set on a new Geiger counter.

ATOM: You'd better give your money to the cause, for the good of all of us. Besides, you still have old Betsy. (ATOM *points to Geiger counter.*)

GREAT-GRANDFATHER: I know, but Betsy's broken. Every time I try to take a snooze out on the patio, she gets to ticking so loud I can't get any sleep.

RADIA: You aren't even going to have a patio to try to sleep on if we don't collect enough money.

GREAT-GRANDFATHER: Well, if you put it that way. (*Reluctantly he takes an old stocking from his pocket. He counts out coins.*) There! It still doesn't do any good. I'm going out to have one last look at the old patio. (*Picks up Geiger counter*) Come on, Betsy.

RADIA: You'd better grab some dinner first. (GREAT-GRANDFATHER *picks up four pills and pops them into his mouth. He starts to exit, then goes to the cupboard and takes a pill from one of the bottles.*)

GREAT-GRANDFATHER: You forgot my bicarbonate pill! (*He exits.*)

ATOM: That leaves you, Radia. Do you have any money? (RADIA *shakes her head.*) I wish I had only part of what I put into Robert. (ROBERT *walks to table and deposits three bolts, two screws and a nut. He goes back to cue station.*) That makes $56, three bolts, two screws and a nut. It just isn't enough. I guess I'd better go pack my tool kit. (RADIA *scoops eight pills from table. She hands four to* ATOM.)

RADIA: Here's your dinner. You'll need it. We all will. (RADIA *and* ATOM *pop pills into their mouths.*) I might as well start packing my fingernail polish. Cosma, you sit down and eat while you are waiting for Davey. (RADIA *and* ATOM *exit.* COSMA *sits at the table and picks up a pill.*)

COSMA: I let them down, didn't I, Robert. All I had to do was say I would go with Scorpio, and all of their troubles would have been solved. (SCORPIO *peeks through the curtains.* ROBERT *holds up cue card,* THE VILLAIN APPROACHES. SCORPIO *enters through curtains.* ROBERT *holds up cue card,* "HERE HE IS.")

SCORPIO: Aha, my fair damsel! At last you are alone. (ROBERT *holds up cue card,* BOO.)

COSMA: How dare you enter and force your attentions on me?

SCORPIO: Come away with me to my space satellite, and you will save your family.

COSMA: You must be mad, mad, mad to think I would go anywhere with you. And to the hog farm satellite where you live! Ugh!

SCORPIO: (*Looks at wrist watch*). In five minutes it will be nine o'clock. You had better change your mind.

COSMA: (*Paces floor*). What will I do? What will I do? (*She goes to window*.) Look at poor Gramps out there—prospecting with old Betsy, right up to the last.

SCORPIO: Time does not stand still, my dear Cosma. Make your decision. Let me remind you that in the days of your great-grandfather's youth, the hog farms were here on the planet Earth.

COSMA: If my brave ancestors could survive the hog farm, I guess I could try to endure it. But could I endure you? No, never!

SCORPIO: Curses! Spurn my attentions, will you? (SCORPIO *chases* COSMA *around the room. He eventually catches her by the hand.* COSMA *is struggling to free herself when* DAVEY ROCKET *enters.* ROBERT *holds up cue card,* THE HERO. *It is followed by cue card,* LOUD APPLAUSE AND CHEERS. DAVEY ROCKET *bows to the audience, flexes muscles and expands chest.*)

COSMA (*Still struggling*): Davey, my hero, help! (DAVEY ROCKET *removes ray gun from his holster and takes calm, careful aim.* SCORPIO *is struck by its paralyzing rays and holds his pose.*)

DAVEY ROCKET: Cosma, my sweet one. Are you all right?

COSMA: (*Coming to* DAVEY ROCKET *and looking adoringly at him*): Everything will be all right now that you are here, Davey.

SCORPIO: What happened? I can't move.

DAVEY ROCKET: I have paralyzed you with my stun gun.

You will be unable to move until I release you with my un-stun gun. (ATOM *and* RADIA *enter.*)

ATOM: (*Carrying tool kit*): What's all the commotion?

RADIA (*Carrying cosmetics case*): Davey, you have come!

SCORPIO: Release me! You can't keep me here forever. When I do get free, I will have the law on you Dimple-warts. And you, Davey Rocket, I will see to it that you are dishonorably discharged from the Space Cadets. You can't hold me without charges. (GREAT-GRAND-FATHER *enters, carrying Geiger counter and waving a rock.*)

GREAT-GRANDFATHER: Old Betsy isn't broken after all. She's ticking like crazy because of this thing I found out on the patio. (DAVEY ROCKET *takes both the rock and the Geiger counter from* GREAT-GRANDFATHER, *and examines the ore with the counter.*)

DAVEY ROCKET: This is uranium ore. But as much as I hate to say it, this land does belong to Scorpio.

GREAT-GRANDFATHER: That may be true. But we still own all the possessions that are on this land. (*He takes old-fashioned pocket watch from vest pocket.*) For two and a half more minutes anyway.

SCORPIO: What difference does that make? This ore is from my land.

GREAT-GRANDFATHER (*Picking up ore*): Not this piece of ore. This came from the potted meteorite plant my cousin sent me from Saturn last summer.

SCORPIO: Curses! Well, you can't use that rock as payment on the lot. I refuse to accept it. (*He laughs villainously.*) In two more minutes, your time will be up.

RADIA: Cosma, tell Davey to do something clever to save us.

COSMA: Davey, do something clever to save us. After all, you are the hero.

DAVEY ROCKET: I am the hero and I should be able to think of something to save you. But my true sky-blue honesty forces me to un-stun Scorpio.

SCORPIO: At last! You had all better prepare to leave the premises. (*He laughs.* DAVEY ROCKET *takes his un-stun gun from the holster. He looks at the Geiger counter, which is in his other hand. As he approaches* SCORPIO, *he continues to look at the counter.*)

DAVEY ROCKET: Hold on here! You are radioactive, Scorpio. But why?

SCORPIO: Release me immediately, and stay out of my pockets. (DAVEY ROCKET *replaces gun in holster and puts Geiger counter on table. He frisks* SCORPIO.)

DAVEY ROCKET: Your pockets, eh? Aha! (DAVEY ROCKET *takes a rock from* SCORPIO's *pocket.*) This ore is just like Great-grandfather's rock!

SCORPIO: I forbid you to get anything out of my other pocket.

DAVEY ROCKET: And what do we have here? (*He takes a letter from* SCORPIO's *other pocket.*) A letter addressed to Mr. Scorpio. I quote: "We have assayed the ore you sent us from your property at (*Name of city and state*). It is highly radioactive. We are returning one of the less radioactive samples you sent us. Enclosed you will find the sum of $1,350 for the remaining ore." It is signed "Chief of the Uranium Commission."

SCORPIO: Curses!

DAVEY ROCKET: That settles that. The money you received for the ore was not rightfully yours. The authorities will see to it that you are banished from here to your hog farm satellite for eternity.

SCORPIO: Curses, curses, curses!

ATOM: Does that mean we get to keep our home, Davey?

DAVEY ROCKET: Yes, you do. The money Scorpio received for the ore really belongs to the Dimplewarts. That makes the lot paid for. So the house is yours, lot and all. (COSMA *rushes to* DAVEY ROCKET *and throws her arms around him.* RADIA, COSMA, *and* GREAT-GRANDFATHER *crowd around them.*)

COSMA: Davey, what about us?

DAVEY ROCKET: I shall never leave you again. We will be married immediately, and we will live happily ever after.

COSMA: Oh, Davey, my own true love. Where will we go on our honeymoon?

DAVEY ROCKET: Where else, honey? To the moon! (*They embrace, as the curtain falls.*)

THE END

Mr. Lazy Man's Family

by Muriel Ward

Characters

JANET FOREST
KITTY FOREST
MARGARET FOREST, *their mother*
DAVID FOREST, *their father*
G. L. HANSON, *president of the Masonville Machinery Co.*
BOB HOWE, *magazine writer*

TIME: *About seven o'clock in the evening.*
SETTING: *The Forests' living room.*
AT RISE: JANET FOREST *is sitting in an armchair, her legs dangling over the side. She is alone, writing in a notebook and thinking out loud.*

JANET (*Thoughtfully*): Let's see . . . "It happened in old Maracaibo; the moon was beginning to rise." (*Writing*) "The breeze dripped with perfume of orchids, when I saw that look in your eyes." (*Triumphantly*) There! That's the first verse done already.
KITTY (*Entering*): Oh, here you are, Janet. I've been looking for you. I want you to do me a favor.
JANET: You would! And it all depends. First I want *you* to give me your opinion of the new song I'm writing.

I'm calling it, "That Night in Venezuela." Here's how it starts: "It happened in old Maracaibo; the moon was beginning to rise. The breeze dripped with perfume of orchids, when I saw that look in your eyes." (*Pauses*) What do you think?

KITTY: I think that orchids don't smell, but your song makes up for that.

JANET: Kitty! That's a fine thing to say to your own sister. And just see if you get any favors from me!

KITTY: But you're the one who asked me for my opinion of it. (*Trying diplomacy*) It'll probably sound better when it's finished. I was comparing it with your song, "Spring in the Belgian Congo"—and nothing could compare with that, Janet. That beats them all!

JANET (*Pleased*): Do you really think so?

KITTY: Positively. Now about that favor. I just want you to lend me a dollar. That's all I need. With that and what I've got saved, I can buy the cutest little monkey at Donaldson's Pet Shop.

JANET: A monkey? Will he get along with my turtle and baby crocodile and your canary?

KITTY: Sure he will. They'll love each other. And the monkey can even be yours part time, if you lend me the dollar.

JANET: That means when I want to take him for a walk or show him to my friends, you won't make a fuss?

KITTY: Of course not. Only I get first call on him because I'm putting up all the money except for your dollar. And if Mom and Pop don't object, we can get another monkey later to keep this one company, and it'll be all yours if you save the money for it.

JANET: O.K. It's a deal.

KITTY (*Excited*): Swell! Thanks lots, Janet. I've got a wonderful name picked out for my little monkey already. I'm going to call him Darwin—in honor of that man who started the evolution theory. We've been learning about it in biology class.

JANET: Darwin—I like that idea. They say he was the first one to notice a family resemblance between monkeys and people, so I don't think he'd mind if we called *our* monkey Darwin.

KITTY: And Darwin has such a nice, distinguished sound too. I thought I'd get the monkey tonight. The store closes at nine, so I'll run down before then. The sooner the better. Only I wouldn't mention it to Mom or Pop first, would you?

JANET: No . . . it'll be nicer to surprise them, I think. The money's in my bureau drawer. I'll get it for you whenever you're ready to go. (MRS. FOREST *enters.*)

MRS. FOREST: I want to talk to you both. I've just had the most unnerving experience in the bathroom. (JANET *looks up expectantly.*) There's a slimy creature in the tub! This creature is about a foot long.

JANET (*Smiling*): Oh, no, Mom. It's 8½ inches. Not a millimeter more.

MRS. FOREST: Well! I was certain one of you would be responsible for it. Where did you get that—that giant lizard?

JANET: It's a baby crocodile, and I bought it in the same pet shop where Kitty gets her animals.

MRS. FOREST: Can't you girls ever go past that pet shop without buying something? The canary's all right, and I don't mind the turtle—except that you never know where he's going to crawl. Someone's going to sit on him or step on him some day. But that—that reptile in the bathtub. Janet, would it break your heart if I asked you to take it back where you got it?

JANET: Yes, it certainly would.

MRS. FOREST (*Coaxingly*): But I'd buy you some nice tropical fish to take its place.

JANET (*Stubbornly*): I don't want fish. I bought the crocodile because it has a real personality. Honest. So can I keep the croc, huh, Mom?

MRS. FOREST: But Janet, it's out of the question to keep it in the bathtub.

JANET: The bathtub's the best place for it. It can't climb out and get stepped on while it's in there. And when anyone wants to take a shower or a bath, he can just give it to me to hold.

MRS. FOREST: But, Janet—(*She is interrupted by a man's loud exclamation of annoyance offstage.*)

KITTY: What's happened to Pop?

MR. FOREST (*Offstage, indignantly*): Margaret!

MRS. FOREST (*Calling back*): Yes, dear?

MR. FOREST (*In the doorway*): Where in blazes did that repulsive animal in the bathtub come from?

MRS. FOREST: Oh, have you seen it too? I was just talking to the girls about it.

MR. FOREST: I've seen it, all right. At first I thought I was having a hallucination. A real live alligator in the house! Where did it come from?

JANET: It's not an alligator, Pop, it's a crocodile.

MR. FOREST (*Annoyed*): Oh, what's the difference!

JANET: Well, the alligator is a member of the crocodile family, but the alligator differs from the crocodile in having only slightly webbed feet, a shorter, more blunt snout, and a difference in arrangement of teeth. Now the crocodile—

MR. FOREST (*Interrupting*): All right! I humbly acknowledge my ignorance, but get that thing out of the tub, please, so I can take a bath.

JANET (*On her way out, sadly*): Sometimes I'm disappointed in this family.

MR. FOREST (*Feelingly*): Sometimes I'm positively frightened by it!

KITTY: I'll come with you, Janet. You and I still have some business to transact, you know. (KITTY *and* JANET *exit.*)

MR. FOREST (*To* MRS. FOREST): I'd like everything to look as nice as possible around here tonight because we're having company, Margaret. (*They sit down.*)

MRS. FOREST: Really, dear? Who?

MR. FOREST: The head of my company—Mr. G. L. Hanson, President of the Masonville Machinery Company!

MRS. FOREST: Well! What is he coming here for, David?

MR. FOREST: I think it's to offer me a promotion and the title of Production Manager at the plant!

MRS. FOREST: Oh, how wonderful. I'm very proud of you, dear. I know you can handle it.

MR. FOREST: Well, I haven't got it yet. I know they've been considering another man for the job, too. But Mr. Hanson's coming here to visit us is a pretty encouraging sign. He likes to see how his employees act when they're not on the job, and what kind of a home life they have. He's kind of old-fashioned and hasn't much of a sense of humor, from what I've seen of him. He's one of these really conservative businessmen, you know. Strictly for hard work and no nonsense. But I guess he's O.K. when you get to know him.

MRS. FOREST: Yes, I'm sure he is. And I'm sure you'll get the promotion, too, if it's given on the basis of hard work. Because I know how hard you do work, and how you even bring work home some nights. I really don't know what they'd do without you.

MR. FOREST: Well, thank you, Margaret. But don't say that to Mr. Hanson. He might decide to find out. I just want everything to look in good order tonight, as it always does when you're home—and most of all for Janet and Kitty to behave themselves and make a good impression.

MRS. FOREST: I'll speak to them about it, David. They're usually pretty well behaved anyway. It's just that they think of doing and saying the funniest things sometimes. But that's healthy imagination, I'm sure.

MR. FOREST: It's imagination all right, but it's not always healthy for the rest of us. Well, I have to go wash up and shave anyway.

MRS. FOREST (*Rising, starting to exit*): Yes, and I'd better go see what Janet has done about that crocodile. (*Pausing in doorway*) David, what kind of a personality do you suppose that crocodile has?

MR. FOREST: A man-eating personality, that's his kind. He looked at me a little while ago as though he were estimating my weight to the pound! (*They both exit. A moment later* JANET *and* KITTY *enter from another direction, still discussing the proposed secret purchase of a monkey. They drop casually into chairs.*)

JANET: I don't know if it's such a good idea to buy the monkey right now, Kitty. Mom and Pop weren't so happy over the crocodile.

KITTY: But they didn't *insist* you had to take it back. So it seems to me now is the *best* time to get Darwin. While they're in a good mood, you see. They didn't refuse you a new pet, so why should they object if I bring in the cutest monkey you ever saw?

JANET: I don't know why, but they might. (*As phone rings*) I'll get it. It's probably Marge. (*She picks up the phone and speaks into it*) This is the Forest Hand Laundry. Send your shirts to us today and they'll stop looking old and gray. (*Slight pause*) Oh, hello, Marge— I thought it would be you.

KITTY: You'd better stop answering the phone like that.

JANET (*To* KITTY): Quiet, I can't hear. (*Into phone*) No, not you, Marge. I was talking to Kitty. What's new? (*Listens for a minute while* KITTY *wanders over to a table and takes a piece of candy. Motions to* KITTY *to bring her one.*) I want some too. (*Takes a piece from the dish* KITTY *offers.*) Yeah, I'm listening, Marge. A writer for *Family Magazine* and he was at your house a little while ago. What did he want? . . . O.K., I'm listening. . . . Yeah. . . . Really? . . . That's exciting. Wait till I tell Kitty—just a second. (*Turning to* KITTY) A writer from *Family Magazine* was at Marge's house. The magazine is sending men around to interview families and find the most outstanding family in Masonville. The family they pick is going to have a story written about them and pictures in the magazine, and a prize of $100! This man was interviewing people on our block, so he'll probably come here tonight too! Kitty, wouldn't it be wonderful if *we* could win the prize for being outstanding?

KITTY: It certainly would.

JANET: I'm sure they want unusual people with lots of color to write about, not just the ordinary kind. When he comes here, you and I can show him how unusual we are, O.K.?

KITTY: Fine. But I'd better go now and buy my monkey before the store closes. You and Marge will probably be on the phone for hours.

JANET: O.K., see you later. And think up some unusual things about our family in the meantime.

KITTY: I'll think on the way. (*Exits*)

JANET (*Into phone again, getting comfortably settled for long chat*): Sorry, Marge. Kitty's gone now, so tell me more. . . . They're looking for people with unusual occupations or interesting hobbies? . . . It sounds as if they want something really different all right, something more than just a family with kids that go to school and a father that just works at a regular ordinary job, and a mother that's never done anything but keep house.

. . . Did he tell you what he wanted right away? . . . Oh no? Just said something about taking a little survey of the family? . . . When did you find out? When he was leaving? . . . Oh, that's how they do it.

MRS. FOREST (*Poking her head in the door*): Oh, you're busy on the phone, I see. Well, I'll come back later and talk to you. I have a dozen and one things to attend to.

JANET (*To her mother*): O.K., Mom. If the doorbell rings, I'll answer it. I have Marge on the phone, and we have dozens of things to tell each other.

MRS. FOREST: Yes, I guess you have. The last time you saw her was at least two hours ago. (*Exits*)

JANET (*Into phone*): You still there, Marge? . . . Good. Wouldn't it be something to have your picture all over town in that magazine, and to win the money too! He'll probably finish this block tonight. When do you suppose the magazine will decide? . . . Very shortly, he said? . . . This was his last evening on the assignment! Then the other interviewers must be finished or nearly finished too. (*Jumps as the doorbell rings*) Our bell, our doorbell's ringing, Marge. That must be *him!* Oh Marge, thanks for calling. Have to run. I won't let him know you told us about it. G'bye. (*Hangs up phone hurriedly and runs out to answer the door. Murmur of conversation is heard offstage, and* JANET *returns, ushering in* MR. G. L. HANSON, *her father's boss.*) Won't you sit right down in here, please? My parents are home, but they're both busy right now, so if there's anything at all I can do for you or *tell* you about them, I'll be very glad to.

HANSON: All right, young lady. How about sitting here with me and talking to me a little, while I wait for them?

JANET (*Highly pleased*): Fine!

HANSON: May I ask your name, please?

JANET: Oh, sure—I'm Janet. And I have a sister Kitty, who's a year younger than I am—she's thirteen, and there's Mom and Dad. (*Struck by inspiration*) Mom used to work in a circus.

HANSON (*Startled*): Really?

JANET (*Crossing her fingers behind her*): Yes—she was a bareback rider. Used to ride horses as if she were born on one. She almost was, I guess. She was brought up circus-minded. And I was born on a circus train when it was traveling through—ah, Texas. Somewhere between Dallas and Ft. Worth. Mom says she never can remember just where it was—she traveled around through so many towns.

HANSON: Very interesting. Was your father with her? (JANET *is interrupted by* KITTY, *who peeks cautiously into the room, then briefly holds up a large, oddly wrapped package.*)

KITTY: I have him, Janet. I have Darwin. Be back in a minute. (*Disappears down the hall*)

JANET (*To* HANSON): That's Kitty. She'll be back. Yes, Pop was with Mom in the circus. He was a roustabout—helping to move the tents and animals and everything.

HANSON: And how long did that go on?

JANET: Oh, only till I was about four, and ready to start school. We moved to Masonville then. Mom hasn't been in any circuses since and Pop's had a job here for ten years.

HANSON (*Thinking aloud*): Yes, ten years is correct.

JANET: Oh—do you know about Pop's job?

HANSON (*Dryly*): A little.

JANET: Well, it's not very exciting, but my father's a very unusual man, and anything's likely to happen. He invents things in his spare time and—(*Quickly and mean-*

ingfully addressing KITTY *as she enters the room*) Kitty, this gentleman is interested in learning about the *family*. (*To* HANSON) This is my sister, Kitty—we both go to the high school.

KITTY (*Sitting down*): How do you do?

HANSON: How do you do, Kitty? Now, what's this about your father inventing things?

JANET: He does, doesn't he, Kitty?

KITTY: Oh, yes. Lots of things.

HANSON: Like what, for instance?

KITTY: Well, he invented a kind of a stand that's on a bracket that sticks to the wall with suction so you can read in bed without holding the book. He calls that the "Lazy Man's Librarian." It's upstairs if you want to see it.

HANSON: Not now, thank you. But this is all *very* interesting.

JANET: Pop also invented a thing that's like a long pair of tongs—extra-long, for reaching things that are far away without having to get up from your chair. He calls that the "Lazy Man's Butler." It's out in the kitchen if you'd like to see it.

HANSON: No, no thanks. I can picture it very well! This is most enlightening. (MRS. FOREST *enters*)

MRS. FOREST: Oh—I didn't know we had company.

KITTY: Mom, this man is interested in Pop's inventions. We were telling him about the Lazy Man's Librarian and the Lazy Man's Butler. Pop thought them up all by himself, didn't he?

MRS. FOREST: That's right. Also the Lazy Man's Shoe-Shiner and the Lazy Man's Window-Washer.

KITTY (*Triumphantly, to* MR. HANSON): See!

HANSON (*Indignantly*): Yes, I see. It's pretty obvious I'm in the home of Mr. Lazy Man! Tell me, Mrs. Forest, is it true that you're "circus-minded," and that you used to travel around all over the country roustabouting and riding horses like you were born on one?

MRS. FOREST (*Surprised*): What? Circus-minded? (KITTY *and* JANET *groan.*) Well, yes, I guess I am. I never miss a circus that comes to town. Were the girls telling you about how Mr. Forest and I used to travel? That was a long time ago, but we always did love traveling. And I used to do quite a bit of riding when I was younger. I loved horses, and people did tell me I was quite a good rider. (*Sighs of relief from* KITTY *and* JANET.) But all that's not important. Haven't you come to see my husband? Kitty, go and tell your father— (MR. FOREST's *voice is heard offstage, shouting angrily.*)

MR. FOREST (*Offstage*): Kitty! Janet! Margaret! Get that monkey out of here! (*Appears in doorway and suddenly sees* MR. HANSON.) Oh—Mr.—Mr. Hanson! (*Flustered*) Good evening—I didn't know—

HANSON (*Coldly, interrupting*): Never mind. I was leaving anyway. As President of the Masonville Machinery Company, I have a good number of responsibilities. One is finding a new Production Manager for the plant— and I *don't* expect to find him here. Good night, Mr. Lazy Man. Good night, everyone! (*Stalks out firmly,* MR. FOREST *following him and protesting in a bewildered way.*)

MR. FOREST (*As he goes out*): But Mr. Hanson—I don't get it! What happened? What's the matter? (*Door slams offstage, then silence.*)

MRS. FOREST (*Sternly*): Girls, what on earth is this all about?

JANET (*Weakly*): Was that—Pop's *boss,* Mother? I thought it was a man from *Family Magazine,* looking for an unusual family.

KITTY: So did I!

MRS. FOREST: You see the damage you've done, don't you? You must have given him a terrible impression of us, and it looks as if you've cost your father an important promotion at the plant. You've really done it this time!

JANET (*Repentant*): I'm sorry, Mother, honest.

KITTY: Me too, Mom. (*Doorbell rings.*)

MRS. FOREST (*Jumping a little nervously*): I'll go this time. You stay here and behave yourselves. (*Exits*)

KITTY (*To* JANET): What if this is the man from *Family Magazine*?

JANET: Well, if we could just get picked as the most outstanding family in Masonville and have a story about us in the magazine—I'll bet Pop could get any job in town he wanted.

KITTY (*Pleased*): Yes—and think of the money too!

JANET: I *am* thinking! (MRS. FOREST *enters with a young man,* BOB HOWE, *and offers him a chair.*)

MRS. FOREST: Please come in and have a seat, Mr.—Mr.?

HOWE: Howe—Bob Howe. Thank you. (*He sits as* MRS. FOREST, JANET *and* KITTY *seat themselves again.*)

MRS. FOREST: My husband, Mr. Forest, has just—stepped out for awhile, but I expect him back soon. Is there anything we can do?

HOWE: Well, yes, I'm sure there is. The company I work for has asked me, and other representatives, to make a little survey in Masonville for special purposes. And we'd appreciate your answering a few questions about your family, all of you, and telling us a bit about your interests, your work, your hobbies—and so on.

MRS. FOREST: I see. Well, my husband is David Forest and he works for the Masonville Machinery Company. That is, I *think* he still works for them. I'm a housewife and these are my two daughters, (*Indicating*) Kitty and Janet. That's the whole family.

KITTY (*Eagerly*): How do you do!

JANET: Delighted to meet you, Mr. Howe.

HOWE: How do you do, girls. How old are you?

KITTY: I'm thirteen and Janet's fourteen.

HOWE (*Taking out a small notebook and beginning to jot down an occasional note*): Do you do anything else besides run this very attractive house?

KITTY: Well, Mom collects old—

MRS. FOREST (*Interrupting, warningly*): Kitty! No, Mr. Howe, I don't have time for much else—outside of working with the Parent-Teachers Association, some Red Cross work occasionally, and a few church activities, of course.

HOWE (*Busily taking notes*): I see. And the girls, what do they do? Besides go to school, I mean.

JANET: Why, I write real Irving Berlin type—

MRS. FOREST (*Interrupting*): Janet takes piano lessons. And Kitty—well, Kitty doesn't take lessons on anything because she can't hold still long enough. She's very fond of animals—Janet is, too.

KITTY: We have the cutest—

MRS. FOREST (*Interrupting*): They have a canary and a couple of other small pets. (*As phone rings and she sees* JANET *rising to answer it*) I'll answer the phone, dear. It may be your father. Or Mr. Hanson. (*Glancing at* HOWE) I'd better take it on the extension outside, if you'll excuse me for a minute, Mr. Howe.

HOWE (*Rising*): Certainly.

MRS. FOREST (*Warningly*): Girls, I'll be back right away.

KITTY: Yes, Mom.

HOWE (*Politely stands till* MRS. FOREST *has left the room. Sitting again, to* KITTY): What were you saying your mother collects?

KITTY: Old empty bottles—all shapes and sizes. She has lots in the cellar.

HOWE: Anything in them?

KITTY: Not any more there isn't.

HOWE (*Taking notes again*): And did you start to tell me you write songs?

JANET (*Excitedly*): Yes, I do. I've written dozens of them.

HOWE: Get any published?

JANET: Not yet—but it's just a matter of time. Would you like to hear some of them?

HOWE: Well, how about some of the titles?

JANET: Oh, there's "Rainy Day in Nova Scotia," "Panama Canal Blues," "One Way Ticket to Scranton," "Dreaming of My Sweet Egyptian Home," and lots of others.

HOWE (*Grinning*): Sounds like a travelogue.

JANET (*Seriously*): I like to write about far-off, mysterious places.

HOWE: I see. You could supply me with a copy of the words to some of these songs if necessary, couldn't you?

JANET: Oh yes. I have a notebook full of them.

HOWE: Good. About your pets—what other pets have you besides your canary?

KITTY: Janet has a baby crocodile and a turtle—not one of those tiny turtles you can hardly see, but a nice size. He just fits comfortably on a dinner plate. (*Importantly*) And I have a monkey named Darwin—just got him tonight, but I don't know if Mom and Pop will let me keep him.

HOWE (*Amazed*): And this is what your mother meant by "small pets"?

JANET: Well, you see, I don't think Mom likes everyone to know what an *unusual* family we are. She's a little shy about it. She might not want us to mention Pop's inventions to you, but it's true he has invented several things.

KITTY: That's right—they all work too, Mr. Howe, and they're all around the house. Working for a machinery company, Pop knows a lot about machines. And he likes

to rig up things that run electrically. He says everything he's invented saves lots of time.

JANET: Of course it doesn't always. Sometimes it takes
longer, but all his inventions are lots of fun. We like
to use them. We think Pop's really a genius.

KITTY: Yes—another Thomas Edison.

HOWE: That's wonderful. What *are* some of his inventions?

JANET: There's the "Lazy Man's Librarian," the "Lazy
Man's Butler," the "Lazy Man's Shoe-Shiner," the "Lazy
Man's Window-Washer" and oh—lots of others. The
shoe-shiner is one of the inventions that runs by a
motor, so you don't have to clean and polish your
shoes by hand and tire out your arm with a lot of
rubbing.

HOWE: Sounds terrific!

KITTY: Oh, it is! Once in a while something happens inside the works—"a bug gets into the machinery," Pop
says—and then it chews up your shoe, but the rest of the
time it works fine.

HOWE (*Intrigued by all this*): That's really amazing.
Could we take pictures of some of these inventions, do
you suppose?

KITTY: I don't think Pop would mind, do you, Janet?

JANET: No, I don't think so. We could talk to him about
it later and tell him if other people are interested in his
inventions—and they should be, too—then it's his duty
to publicize them, right?

KITTY: Right! Just let Janet and me handle it for you,
Mr. Howe.

JANET: Yes. There's a right time for everything, Pop always says, so my sister and I will take care of it for
you at the right time. When would you want to take
pictures?

HOWE: Well, I'll have to consult with some other people

first. You see, I work for *Family Magazine*. You've heard of it, haven't you?

JANET (*Thoughtfully*): Yes—I think so.

KITTY: Once or twice.

HOWE: Good. We've been conducting a search for an outstanding, really interesting family, and yours is the most interesting family I've met during my part in the search. If I can convince my two other associates on this project that your family is "it," so to speak, there'll be a story with pictures about you—and your pets— illustrating all the interesting things you've been telling me. Besides that, there's a cash prize of $100.

JANET: Oh, Kitty! Isn't this thrilling!

KITTY (*Dreamily*): Yeah.

HOWE: Mind you, now, I haven't said this is definite yet. I'll have to put the details before my associates and compare notes with them, and then let you know.

JANET: Could you phone us as soon as you decide? It would mean a lot to Kitty and me. (*Dejectedly*) We're not in such good favor with Pop at the moment. In fact, this could be a matter of life or death.

HOWE: Why?

JANET: Oh, it's a long story. We did something we shouldn't have, and it may cost Pop his job—but if it does, I'll quit school and go to work, that's what I'll do. Even though it would mean giving up the presidency of the Poetry Club at high school.

HOWE: Well, I hope it doesn't come to that.

KITTY: So do we!

HOWE: I'll phone you then, in any event. And I'd better be going if I'm to get my report in to the office. (HOWE *rises as* MRS. FOREST *re-enters the room.*)

MRS. FOREST: Please excuse me for keeping you waiting so long, Mr. Howe. (*To girls*) Your father is bringing Mr. Hanson back with him.

JANET: Mom—is everything going to be all right?

MRS. FOREST: I hope so. Your father said he's been explaining things to Mr. Hanson. Mr. Hanson listened to him, but your father wasn't making any headway until a fortunate thing happened just as Mr. Hanson was about to get into his car. One of the company inspectors came along and told him that he'd just turned in a report showing that production was 22 per cent higher in the department your father supervises than it was before your father took charge. Mr. Hanson seemed impressed with that, and when the inspector left them, he said he'd come back here to talk things over with your father.

HOWE: Is Mr. Forest a department head at the Masonville Machinery Company?

JANET: Yes—and he may be promoted to Production Manager very soon.

MRS. FOREST: Janet! (*To* HOWE) My daughters are always optimistic, Mr. Howe.

HOWE: I see. Well, in any case, I know that's a pretty important job your husband is being considered for, Mrs. Forest. I hope he gets the promotion. And now I really must leave in a hurry. As I was explaining to your daughters, I work for *Family Magazine,* and on a magazine we have deadlines to meet, you know.

MRS. FOREST: Oh, I see. Are you sure there's nothing I can do for you right now?

HOWE: No, thank you. Your daughters have been very helpful, and I've explained my business to them so they can tell you all about it when I leave. Goodnight, everyone. (*Turning to* KITTY *and* JANET) I'll try to phone you our decision this evening—perhaps in a little while.

JANET *and* KITTY: Thanks!

HOWE (*Exiting*): Good night, Mrs. Forest.

MRS. FOREST (*Mystified*): Good night, Mr. Howe. (*Follows him off*) I'll see you to the door.

KITTY: Janet, I think we did it, don't you?

JANET: I sure hope so. (*They both whirl around the room excitedly, pleased with themselves.* MRS. FOREST *returns, and eyes this exhibition of energy.*)

MRS. FOREST: Now, if your uninformed mother may ask, what is *this* all about?

KITTY: *Family Magazine* wants to write a story about an interesting family in Masonville, and Mr. Howe says ours is the most interesting one he's seen.

JANET: And he's practically promised us that our family will be written up in the magazine with lots of pictures of us and our animals and Pop's inventions and $100.

MRS. FOREST: What!

KITTY: Janet means we're going to get $100 in cash besides. If we win, that is.

MRS. FOREST: Well, of all things! It sounds rather nice at that.

JANET: Oh, it'll be wonderful, Mother!

MRS. FOREST: Well, it seems that way, but don't count on it till we hear from Mr. Howe again. Since he didn't make it definite, it may not even happen. You shouldn't — (*She is interrupted by* MR. FOREST'S *entry with* MR. HANSON.)

MR. FOREST (*Looking a little worn after his ordeal, but striving to be cheerful*): Well, we're back, folks. Mr. Hanson wants to get really acquainted with the family.

MRS. FOREST (*Smiling*): I'm so glad. Let me take your hat, Mr. Hanson, and let's all sit down and be comfortable. Why don't you try this chair? (*Indicates comfortable armchair*)

HANSON: Thank you, I will. (*Gives* MRS. FOREST *his hat and sits as she places the hat on a table*) Yes, I'm back again, Mrs. Forest, and girls, and I'd like to apologize for my hasty departure before. I realized later that it wasn't very polite of me.

MRS. FOREST: That's quite all right. We're very glad you came back so we can straighten out the misunderstanding.

JANET: Oh, yes! You see, Kitty and I didn't know you were Pop's boss. We thought you were someone else— a magazine writer looking for interesting people—so we made up some things, I'm afraid—just a few little things about our circus background and Pop being a roustabout.

KITTY: Those things were just—well, talk, you know. Except for the inventions. Pop has made lots of wonderful inventions!

HANSON (*Smiling*): I see. I wondered very much about those things you girls told me.

MRS. FOREST (*Quickly*): It's not that they're in the habit of telling stories, Mr. Hanson. They're always truthful with their father and me, but sometimes, well, sometimes their imaginations run away with them when they get enthusiastic about something.

HANSON: I can understand that. I have a daughter myself. And some of the things she dreams up—well, that's another story. But, as I was saying, I started wondering about those things your daughters told me, Mrs. Forest, especially after we met a company inspector who gave me some very impressive statistics on the job your husband's been doing. So while Mr. Forest was phoning you, I phoned our plant and got some more details on his background. That was when I found out the circus story was—well, misinformation, and that Mr. Forest actually has a very fine background in mechanical engineering and production. That confirmed—and increased—the original understanding I had before coming here tonight.

MR. FOREST: You can't imagine how pleased I am to hear you say that, Mr. Hanson.

HANSON: I should have realized I was making a snap decision before, and that's not a wise thing to do, not wise at all. You've impressed me very favorably, David. Your record at the plant is superior—very superior indeed, and I'm taking this opportunity to offer you the position of Production Manager of the Masonville Machinery Company. (*The family utters exclamations of delight.*) What do you say, David?

MR. FOREST: I say, it's wonderful—the opportunity I've been hoping and working for, Mr. Hanson. I'm very glad to accept the job.

HANSON: Fine! Then it's all settled. And call me G.L., won't you?

MR. FOREST (*Heartily*): Yes, sir—G.L.!

HANSON: Good. Now that that's all settled, we can sit back and have a nice, sociable talk, can't we?

MR. FOREST: By all means!

MRS. FOREST: It's very nice that we have this opportunity to get acquainted. You know, my husband's promotion makes me just as happy as it does him because I know— (*Phone rings.* JANET *rushes to answer.*)

JANET: I'll get it! (*Into phone*) Hello? . . . Yes, this is the Forest residence. . . . Mr. Howe? . . . Oh, yes, Mr. Howe. This is Janet Forest. Did you decide yet? . . . Yes? Our family has been picked! (*To the others in the room*) Did you hear that? *Family Magazine* thinks we're outstanding and unusual! (MR. *and* MRS. FOREST *and* HANSON *look surprised.*)

KITTY: Hooray for us!

JANET (*Into phone*): Thank you so much for calling Mr. Howe. And thanks for everything. . . . You'll bring a photographer over tomorrow? Wonderful! Goodbye! (*As she is hanging up phone, she suddenly notices something on the floor. Bends down and picks up some small objects which she rushes to show the others.*) Look—everybody! Baby turtles—five of them. My turtle Montgomery just became a mother!

HANSON: You know, you really are the most unusual family in Masonville! (*They laugh, as the curtain falls.*)

THE END

The Crimson Feather

by Frances B. Watts

Characters

FRITZ	HILDA
MARTA, *his wife*	HANS
AMELIA ⎫ *their children*	FRIEDA
KARLI ⎭	PEDDLER
WILHELM	GENIE

SETTING: *The kitchen of a peasant cottage.*

AT RISE: FRITZ *is sitting cross-legged on a bench, sewing a pair of trousers.* MARTA *is rolling dough on the kitchen table. She is humming happily.*

FRITZ (*Rises from bench and holds up the trousers*): There, Marta, Herr Kraut's trousers are finished. He will be the best dressed man in the village, if I do say so myself.

MARTA: What a fine tailor you are, Fritz! The clothes you make are truly perfect. (*Rolls dough vigorously*) And my pies will soon be ready for the oven.

FRITZ: Good. I am hungry. It has been a busy day, but also a happy one. (*Walks over to a chair by the table and sits down*)

MARTA (*Anxiously*): I wonder where Karli and Amelia are. They should be home from school by this time.

627

FRITZ: Perhaps they are playing with their friends. At any rate, we need not worry about them. They are good children.

MARTA: Indeed, yes. We are so fortunate. Our children are well behaved, and we have a warm cottage and good food to eat. I wish that everyone in the world could have a home as happy as ours. (KARLI *and* AMELIA *enter from door at left. They are excited.*)

FRITZ: Ah, here they are now. Hello, children.

KARLI *and* AMELIA: Hello, Papa. Hello, Mama.

AMELIA (*Dancing about the room*): Guess what! Karli and I are going to be in the school Festival next month!

MARTA: How wonderful! Papa and I will be so proud.

KARLI: We have been practicing the song and dance we are going to do. That is why we are home so late. Would you like to see us do it?

FRITZ: Yes! Right away! (MARTA *sits down in the other chair by the table.* KARLI *and* AMELIA *each remove one shoe, then step to front center.*)

KARLI *and* AMELIA (*Singing to the tune of "Oh, Where, Oh, Where, Has My Little Dog Gone" and making appropriate gestures*):
Oh, who, oh, who could have taken my shoe?
Oh, who, oh, who could it be?
I was wearing them both just an hour ago,
And now one is gone, as you see.
Oh, how, oh, how can we dance for you now?
Oh, how, oh, how dance in one?
    (*They hold up the foot with shoe on it.*)
Perhaps what we'll do since we can't dance in two,
Is try dancing for you in none.
(*They each remove other shoe, and dance a bouncy waltz. They hum as they dance. When dance is finished, they fall down laughing and put on their shoes.* FRITZ *and* MARTA *applaud.*)

FRITZ: Bravo! I see we are going to enjoy the Festival very much indeed. (*A knock is heard at the door.*)

MARTA: Hello! Someone is at the door! Karli, will you please see who is there?

KARLI (*Opens door at left*): It's a peddler. Shall I ask him to come in?

MARTA: Very well. I do not wish to buy any wares, but perhaps he would like to step in to rest for a moment. (PEDDLER *enters with a large pack on his back.* FRITZ *and* MARTA *stand up.*)

PEDDLER (*Lowers his pack*): Greetings, good frau. Greetings, Herr Tailor. What will you buy today? (*Changing to verse*)

I have bean pots to sell and fry pans as well;
I have sandals and candles and clocks,
Shiny pie tins, needles and pins,
And beautiful stockings and socks.
I have thread and wool yarn, should you have things to
    darn;
I've molasses and glasses and leather.
If you need none of these, I have, if you please,
This beautiful fine crimson feather.

(*Snatches a crimson feather from his pack and holds it up high*)

AMELIA: Oh, it is beautiful! Do you use it to decorate a bonnet?

PEDDLER (*Indignantly*):

Decorate a bonnet?
Why, child, you *wish* upon it!

MARTA: Wish upon a *feather?*

PEDDLER:

Yes, you wish upon this feather,
Just three wishes altogether.
And a genie will appear each time you do.
Yes, you wish upon this feather,

Just three wishes altogether.

And the wishes that you make will all come true.

KARLI: Why, the crimson feather must be magic! It must cost a great deal of money.

PEDDLER:

The feather may be sold

For one small piece of gold.

AMELIA (*Clapping her hands with joy*): Only one piece of gold! Oh, Papa, may we buy the crimson feather?

KARLI (*Tugging at* FRITZ's *arm*): Oh, please, Papa. Imagine! Three wishes for only one piece of gold!

FRITZ (*Strokes chin thoughtfully*): What do you say, Marta? Shall we buy this crimson feather?

MARTA: We are very happy as we are. However, there may come a time when we would like to wish for something more. Yes, Fritz, let us buy the crimson feather.

KARLI *and* AMELIA: Hooray! Hooray! (FRITZ *takes gold from his pocket and pays* PEDDLER, *who gives him the feather.*)

PEDDLER (*Puts pack on back*): Just say, "I wish," when you make a wish. You have three wishes; that is all. (*Exits quickly*)

AMELIA (*Jumping with excitement*): Oh, I can hardly wait to make our wishes! What shall they be? Gold? A castle? Beautiful clothing? How can we ever decide?

MARTA: We must not be hasty, child. We have only three wishes and we must be careful not to waste them.

FRITZ (*Puts the feather on the table*): Yes, we must think and act very cautiously.

KARLI: That is true. We must be careful or we may wish for the wrong things.

MARTA: I am not sure that we need rich clothes, or gold or a castle. Would these things make us any happier than we are now?

FRITZ: I do not know. Who can tell?

AMELIA (*Swings* KARLI *around by clasping his hands tightly*): Oh, I'm so excited. I can hardly wait to tell our friends about our good fortune. I wish that Hilda and Hans and Wilhelm and Frieda were here so we could tell them about our feather! (*Sound of clashing cymbals is heard.* GENIE *enters. He pulls in* HILDA, HANS, WILHELM, *and* FRIEDA. GENIE *bows with a sweep of his cape and exits.*)

FRITZ (*Clasps forehead in despair*): Ach, Amelia! You have wasted one of our three wishes. You wished that your friends were here, and here they are!

MARTA (*Scolding*): Amelia, how could you be so thoughtless!

KARLI (*Stamps his foot. To* AMELIA): You're a knucklehead! That's what you are!

WILHELM (*Bewildered*): What's going on? I was home reading a book. Suddenly, I felt a great gust of wind, and a genie appeared. Now I am here. What happened?

HILDA: The same thing happened to me, only I was helping Mama with the supper.

HANS: I was milking the cow when I was snatched away.

FRIEDA (*Rubbing her eyes*): And I was taking a nap. How did I get here?

FRITZ (*Leads* WILHELM, HILDA, HANS *and* FRIEDA *to the door*): You must leave now, boys and girls. We will explain some other time. (AMELIA *runs over and starts shoving them out.*)

WILHELM (*Crossly*): Don't push me! I am going! (*Exits*)

FRIEDA (*Crossly*): I am leaving! I never stay where I am not welcome! (*Exits*)

HANS (*Crossly*): All right. I'll go back to my cow. She is more polite than some people I know. (*Exits*)

HILDA (*Crossly*): Don't push me! I didn't ask to come here! (*Exits. All stare angrily at* AMELIA. AMELIA *hangs her head in shame.*)

MARTA: Oh, Amelia, why didn't you hold your tongue? Now we have only two wishes left.

FRITZ: You are careless, daughter. I cannot abide carelessness.

KARLI (*Runs up to* AMELIA): Knucklehead! Knucklehead!

AMELIA: Stop it! (*She slaps* KARLI. KARLI *slaps her back, and they start to tussle.* FRITZ *separates them and shakes* KARLI. AMELIA *runs over to a chair, puts her head down on the table and sobs loudly.*)

FRITZ (*Still shaking* KARLI): Is that the way for a gentleman to behave? Haven't I told you never to strike your sister? (KARLI *begins to howl.* AMELIA's *sobs grow louder.*)

MARTA (*Puts her hands over her ears*): Stop it! I can't endure all this noise! Oh, I wish you children would stop crying! (*The sound of cymbals is heard.* GENIE *enters. With a sweep of his cape he runs lightly about the room. The crying stops abruptly. He exits.*)

FRITZ (*Stalks angrily over to* MARTA): Now see what you have done! You have wasted our second wish by wishing for the children to stop crying. What a dumbbell you are!

MARTA (*Indignantly*): In all our married life you have never called me such a name! If you think I am a dumbbell, I will behave like one. I shall not speak for the rest of the evening. Nor will I cook the supper! (*She sits down and folds her arms stubbornly.* FRITZ *frowns at her and taps his foot in anger.*)

KARLI: Mama, you must speak to us! We are sad when you are angry.

AMELIA: Please cook supper, Mama. I'm hungry! (MARTA *ignores their pleas.*)

KARLI (*Picks up the crimson feather from the table*): Oh, I wish we had never bought this wicked crimson feather from the peddler. I wish it were out of the cottage, and we were happy again. (*Sound of cymbals is heard.* GENIE *enters. Whirling his cape, he runs up to* KARLI, *snatches away the feather, and exits.*)

MARTA (*Rushes to* FRITZ *and throws her arms about him*): Oh, my dear, will you forgive me? I do not know what possessed me. How could I ever have been so unkind and cross? I'm so sorry.

FRITZ: And I am sorry that I was rude to you and rough with my son. Will you forgive me, Karli?

KARLI: Certainly, Papa. I am sorry that I struck my sister. (*He puts his arm around* AMELIA.) Will you forgive me, Amelia?

AMELIA: Of course. I was impolite to my friends, and I hope they will forgive me. It was all my fault anyway, because I made the first careless wish.

MARTA (*Walks over to* AMELIA): No, my child. All of us were to blame. The moment we bought the crimson feather we became selfish and greedy.

FRITZ: We became so greedy that there was no room in our hearts for love.

KARLI: Then you are not angry with me for wishing the crimson feather out of the cottage? It was our last wish.

FRITZ: The last wish and the best wish. Now our minds will be free of greed, and our home will be happy again.

MARTA (*Goes to table and begins to roll dough*): I think we will all feel happier once I get these pies baked and on the table.

AMELIA: Good, Mama! I'm so hungry!

KARLI: And I, too!

FRITZ (*Sits down in chair and smiles at children*): Let us hear some happy sounds once more. Perhaps you children will perform that gay song and dance again, yes?

KARLI *and* AMELIA: Certainly, Papa. (*Smiling happily, they repeat their song and dance.*)
Oh, who, oh, who could have taken my shoe?

Oh, who, oh, who could it be?
I was wearing them both just an hour ago,
And now one is gone, as you see.
Oh, how, oh, how can we dance for you now?
Oh, how, oh, how dance in one?
Perhaps what we'll do, since we can't dance in two,
Is try dancing for you in none.
(*They fall to the floor laughing, as curtain falls.*)

THE END

Miss Louisa and the Outlaws

by Frances B. Watts

Characters

MISS LOUISA, *the schoolteacher*
THEODORE ⎤
WILLIAM ⎟
ANNABELLE ⎬ *pupils*
CLARA ⎟
REGINA ⎦
OTHER PUPILS
BENNY ⎤ *outlaws*
DEAD-EYE DAN ⎦
SHERIFF
SHERIFF'S ASSISTANT

TIME: *A day in October, at the turn of the century.*
SETTING: *A one-room schoolhouse.*
AT RISE: MISS LOUISA *is standing at her desk. The pupils sit at attention, with their hands folded.*

MISS LOUISA: For our history lesson this afternoon you all were to learn the first three stanzas of "Paul Revere's Ride." Theodore, would you come to the front of the room and recite, please?

THEODORE (*Rises uneasily from his desk and walks slowly*

to front. Recites haltingly): Uh—uh—"Listen, my—children, and you—shall hear." Uh—uh—

MISS LOUISA (*Sternly*): I see that you haven't studied your lesson, Theodore. You will stay after school and learn the lines before you leave this afternoon. Do you understand?

THEODORE (*Mumbles as he slinks back to his seat*): Yes.

MISS LOUISA: Remember your manners! Yes *what*, Theodore?

THEODORE (*Straightens up and speaks with respect*): Yes, *Miss Louisa.*

MISS LOUISA: William, let's see how well you have learned the stanzas.

WILLIAM (*Stumbles to front, stares up at ceiling and recites slowly*): Uh—uh. "Listen, my children, and you shall hear." Uh—uh. "Of the midnight ride of Paul Revere." Uh—uh— (*Fidgets*)

MISS LOUISA: Another shirker! William, you will join Theodore after school. Do you understand?

WILLIAM (*Mumbles as he returns to his seat*): Yes.

MISS LOUISA: Yes, *what*, William?

WILLIAM (*With respect*): Yes, *Miss Louisa.*

MISS LOUISA (*Sighs*): Boys and girls, I realize that this poem may seem a bit dull and uninteresting. But I'm asking you to memorize it in hopes that you will recognize the courage and strength some of our forefathers possessed when they founded our great country. Do you have any idea what courage is?

CLASS (*After a moment's hesitation*): No, Miss Louisa.

MISS LOUISA: Well, courage is behaving bravely when you are most afraid. All of us, at some time, have been afraid. Those who discipline themselves and control fear in times of stress are exhibiting courage. Is that clear?

CLASS: Yes, Miss Louisa.

WILLIAM (*In a whispered aside to* THEODORE): Ha, I'll bet

Miss Louisa has never been afraid in her life! All she ever does is scare *us* to death!

THEODORE (*Aside*): You said it. What does she know about fear? All she has in her veins is ice water!

MISS LOUISA: Annabelle, do you think that you can recite the lines for us?

ANNABELLE: Yes, Miss Louisa. (*She goes confidently to front and recites*):
"Listen, my children, and you shall hear
Of the midnight ride of Paul Revere."
(*She recites first two verses. Then outlaws enter down right. They draw their guns.*)

BENNY: Stay where you are!

THEODORE (*Fearfully*): Outlaws! It's Benny, the Kid, and Dead-Eye Dan! The ones who robbed Dodge City Bank last week!

WILLIAM: It is! It is! Their pictures are up in the Post Office. Wanted, dead or alive! A hundred dollars reward! (*The children scream with terror. Some of them run to the back of the room.*)

MISS LOUISA (*Rapping on desk with a ruler. Speaks sternly*): Back to your seats, everyone! How often have I told you never to leave your seats without permission! (*Timidly, but obediently, children return to seats.*)

DAN: Nobody's going to get hurt, kiddies, as long as you set there quiet.

MISS LOUISA (*With great dignity*): Watch your grammar in front of my pupils, sir. The proper expression is—*sit there quietly*—not—*set there quiet*.

DAN (*Baffled*): Huh? Oh. As long as you *sit there quietly*.

BENNY: Just in case somebody tipped off the Sheriff that we're in town, my pal Dan and me are going to hide out here till the two-thirty freight train comes through. Then we'll make our getaway. So don't anybody get any bright ideas like yelling out the window or running for help, see? (*Flourishes gun while the children cower in fear.*)

DAN (*Nodding at two vacant desks in row nearest to audience*): Let's take a load off our feet, Benny. May as well be comfortable till train time.

MISS LOUISA (*Firmly*): Just a moment, Daniel! I believe that is your name. You and Benjamin will kindly wipe your feet on this mat before you sit down. (*Points to mat in doorway*)

BENNY (*In confusion*): Say, what is this? Dan and me got guns. We don't have to take orders from you.

MISS LOUISA: It's Dan and *I* have guns, sir. And as long as you and Benjamin take refuge here, I shall insist that you obey the laws and rules of our schoolhouse. Kindly wipe your feet, gentlemen! (*She stares at the men.*)

DAN (*Grudgingly*): All right. All right. We'll wipe our feet.

MISS LOUISA: Mind your manners, sir. When I speak to you, you are to answer, "Yes, Miss Louisa." Do you understand?

BENNY and DAN (*Meekly*): Yes, Miss Louisa. (*They wipe their feet, then tiptoe to the vacant desks. They keep guns in hand.*)

BENNY (*Aside to DAN, seems puzzled*): I don't know why we let this schoolteacher lead us around by the nose. By all rights we ought to tie her up in the closet.

MISS LOUISA (*Brisk and efficient*): Well, boys and girls, we shall continue our history lesson tomorrow. It is now time for music. Let's have a song. A jolly one. How about "Old MacDonald Had a Farm"?

REGINA: We can't sing, Miss Louisa. We—we're too scared! (*Lays head on desk and sobs*)

MISS LOUISA: Afraid, Regina? Of what is there to be afraid? As far as we are concerned, we simply have two extra pupils in our room. We will follow our usual schedule. (*Coolly takes pitch pipe from her pocket and sounds the key. Class begins to sing "Old MacDonald." * MISS LOUISA *interrupts song by rapping with ruler. Speaks to outlaws*) Benjamin and Daniel, why aren't you singing?

DAN (*Bewildered*): Huh? Why should we sing?

CLARA (*Earnestly*): Because, when we have music in this school, everybody sings.

ANNABELLE (*Nods*): And that means *everybody*. It's a school rule.

MISS LOUISA (*To children*): Clara and Annabelle, this is not your affair. (*To outlaws, firmly*) When we start to sing again, you will sing. Do you understand?

BENNY (*Mumbles*): Yes.

MISS LOUISA: Yes *what*, Benjamin?

BENNY: Yes, Miss Louisa. (MISS LOUISA *blows pipe again and waves her arms as she leads the song. The children's spirits rise noticeably as they progress through the various animal sounds of the song. The faces of the outlaws are comically serious as they sing along with the children. When song ends,* MISS LOUISA *crosses over to window and gazes out with a worried frown.*)

BENNY (*Hops up and draws gun*): Stay away from that window, ma'am. We're not giving you the chance to signal for help.

DAN (*Draws gun*): You may be a schoolmarm, but you can't outsmart us. Nobody has ever outsmarted Benny, the Kid, and Dead-Eye Dan.

MISS LOUISA (*Stays at window. Speaks matter-of-factly*): It looks a bit like rain. William, will you and Theodore please go out and bring in the flag? (WILLIAM *and* THEODORE *rise to obey.*)

BENNY (*To* MISS LOUISA): Do you think we're stupid? Why, the minute those kids leave this room they'll run for the Sheriff.

WILLIAM (*Nervously*): Don't insist that we go, Miss Louisa! It really doesn't look like rain.

MISS LOUISA: There are cumulus clouds forming in the west. It is October; showers begin suddenly in fall. (*To outlaws*) It is a rule of our school that we never allow the American flag to become wet. One of you may accompany the boys, if you wish. But our flag must not be rained upon! Do you hear? (*The outlaws exchange exasperated looks, then finally nod agreement.*)

BENNY: Oh, all right then.

MISS LOUISA (*Sternly*): What did you say?

BENNY (*Meekly*): Yes, Miss Louisa. (*He heads toward the door and motions to* WILLIAM *and* THEODORE *to precede him. They exit.* DAN *keeps his gun drawn.*)

MISS LOUISA: Now, boys and girls, we will have a spelling bee. Regina and Clara may be captains. You may start choosing teams, girls. (*CLARA and* REGINA *proceed to choose sides, calling out various children's names. The teams line up on opposite sides of stage and face audience.* BENNY, THEODORE *and* WILLIAM *enter. They wipe their feet carefully.* WILLIAM *hands flag to* MISS LOUISA, *who folds it and puts it upon her desk.*)

REGINA (*Continuing with the choosing*): I choose Theodore for my team. (*THEODORE takes his place.*)

CLARA: I choose William. (*WILLIAM takes his place.*)

REGINA: I choose Daniel. (*DAN takes his place, and tucks gun in holster.*)

CLARA: I choose Benjamin.

BENNY: Say, what is this? What's going on?

DAN (*With enthusiasm*): A spelling bee, pal. Ain't you never been in a spelling bee before?

MISS LOUISA: *Haven't you ever,* Daniel. Watch that grammar!

DAN: Haven't you ever been in a spelling bee before?

BENNY: No, and I'm not going to now. Besides, it'll be train time soon. We have to stay on the alert.

MISS LOUISA (*Pauses, then nods sympathetically*): Very well, Benjamin. I will excuse you from participating in the spelling bee. Naturally, it would be most embarrassing for you to be spelled down by a group of young children.

BENNY (*Blustering*): Who's scared of being spelled down? Look, maybe I haven't had much schooling, but I'm not so dumb that a bunch of little kids can lick me at spelling.

MISS LOUISA: I admire your spirit, Benjamin. You won't mind joining Clara's team then. (*Waits patiently for* BENNY *to line up*)

BENNY (*Sighs in resignation*): Oh, all right.

MISS LOUISA (*Severely*): What's that, Benjamin?

BENNY: Yes, Miss Louisa. (*He takes his place at the end of* CLARA'*s line and puts gun in holster.* MISS LOUISA *stands with a spelling book at center stage and calls out words for the children to spell.* DAN *and* BENNY *are caught up in the spirit of competition. They cheer and applaud the spellers along with the others. All spell correctly until* BENNY'*s turn.*)

MISS LOUISA: Now, Benjamin, I would like you to spell the word, "thief."

BENNY (*Raises eyes to ceiling*): Uh—Uh. Lemme see. T—h. T-h-e-i-f.

MISS LOUISA: That is wrong, Benjamin. The correct spelling is t-h-i-e-f. You may take your seat.

WILLIAM (*Aside*): Gee whiz! He *is* a thief, and he can't even spell it!

BENNY (*Stomps sulkily to his desk*): Aw, so what if I'm not a good speller. I still make a good living. (*Sound of a train whistle is heard. It gradually increases in volume.*)

DAN (*Rushes to window*): Yeow! There goes the two-thirty freight train!

BENNY (*Running over to window, stamping angrily*): I told you it was time to get out of here! But you had to let that crazy schoolteacher talk us into a spelling bee!

DAN: All right. All right. So at least *I* didn't miss my spelling word. (*The children still stand in their lines, but they buzz with excitement.* SHERIFF *and* ASSISTANT *enter suddenly.*)

SHERIFF (*Draws gun, catching outlaws off guard*): Hands up! (*Outlaws raise hands.* SHERIFF *and* ASSISTANT *steer them toward the door, as children cheer.*)

THEODORE: Sheriff, how did you know the outlaws were here?

SHERIFF: I didn't know, son. But I gathered that something was wrong when I happened to look out of my office window and saw that the school flagpole was bare. Why, you know as well as I do that, unless it's raining, Miss Louisa never lowers the flag until sundown. It's a rule of the school. Remember, Miss Louisa was my teacher, too.

MISS LOUISA (*To* SHERIFF): I was hoping you'd notice that the flag was down, and would remember that rule, Rodney. Apparently my pupils remember *some* things that I teach them.

ANNABELLE (*Laughing*): Miss Louisa was just like Paul Revere's friend. She used a signal to tell about the enemy!

MISS LOUISA: That's right, Annabelle. (*To outlaws*) And if you gentlemen were the slightest bit educated about the ways of the weather, you would have known that cumulus clouds in the west rarely mean immediate rain.

BENNY (*To* DAN): I had a hunch that we should have tied that teacher up in the closet the minute we came in!

DAN: Could *you* have tied her up?

BENNY (*Scratches his head in bewilderment*): No, I guess I couldn't have at that. There's something about Miss Louisa. Well, you just can't imagine tying her up in a closet. (*Pauses*) She doesn't scare easy, and before you know it, you're half-scared of *her*.

MISS LOUISA: The proper grammar, Benjamin, is—She doesn't scare easily.

BENNY: Yes, Miss Louisa.

SHERIFF: Well, we'll take these scoundrels down to jail where they belong. You'll receive the hundred dollars' reward in a few days, Miss Louisa.

MISS LOUISA: Thank you, Rodney. I believe it will be just enough money to take the children on an outing to the Dodge City music festival. (*The children shout with delight.* SHERIFF *and* ASSISTANT *exit with outlaws.*)

MISS LOUISA: And now, children, I believe that I will dismiss you for the rest of the afternoon.

CLASS: Hooray! Hooray for Miss Louisa! (*They exit noisily.* WILLIAM *and* THEODORE *remain in their seats.*)

MISS LOUISA (*Sitting down limply at her desk. She holds her head in her hands. In a few minutes she looks up and sees the boys*): Well, boys, why are you still here?

THEODORE: You asked us to stay and learn the first three stanzas of "Paul Revere's Ride," Miss Louisa.

MISS LOUISA: Oh, so I did. Well, I will excuse you just this once. You see, I'm feeling a bit shaky. (*Rubs forehead*)

WILLIAM (*Thoughtfully*): Miss Louisa, you were afraid when the outlaws were here, weren't you?

MISS LOUISA: Oh, yes. Very much afraid. I did everything in my power to delay them, so that they might miss the train and be captured. Yet, I longed for them to leave before they decided to use those wicked guns on some of us.

THEODORE: Well, you didn't act scared. Not one bit!

WILLIAM (*Stoutly*): Naturally, she didn't! She behaved

bravely when she was most afraid. That's *courage*. Remember?

MISS LOUISA (*Smiling*): Perhaps I taught you something today after all. (*She takes flag from desk and hands it to* WILLIAM.) Before you leave, boys, please hoist the flag again. It's several hours yet until sundown. We must abide by the rules of the school, you know.

WILLIAM (*With admiration*): Yes, Miss Louisa.

THEODORE (*With a quick bow of respect*): Yes, indeed. Goodbye, Miss Louisa. (*Boys exit, as curtain falls.*)

THE END

School for Jesters

by Constance Whitman

Characters

KING WILLIAM THE WISE
PRINCESS LILAC
LADY CRACKWHIP, *headmistress of the Royal School of Jesters*
DRUVO, *the King's court jester*
BOODLES ⎫
SCRIMSCRAM ⎬ *pupils at the Royal School*
MELISSA ⎪
OTHER JESTERS ⎭
COURTIERS
THREE HERALDS

SETTING: *The main classroom of the Royal School for Jesters.*

AT RISE: *The* JESTERS *are practicing their lessons—doing somersaults, jumping jacks, and making funny faces.* MELISSA *is trying to stand on her head, down left, and* BOODLES *and* SCRIMSCRAM *are helping her, as* LADY CRACKWHIP *watches.* DRUVO *enters hurriedly from right, pauses, and knocks on door frame.* BOODLES *and* SCRIMSCRAM *help* MELISSA *to her feet; other* JESTERS *stop to listen; and* LADY CRACKWHIP *runs to door.*

LADY CRACKWHIP: Who is it?

DRUVO: If it is not I, surely it is someone else; but since I am me, then it is I, the King's court jester.

LADY CRACKWHIP: Druvo, is that you?

DRUVO (*Striding in*): Lackaday and a hey, nonny, nonny, it *is* I, Lady Crackwhip—once your star pupil and now court fool to King William the Wise. (DRUVO *bows with a flourish. Then he jumps up and kicks his heels together.*) Tell me, what is a jester who falls in love with a simpleton?

BOODLES: What, Druvo?

DRUVO: A jester who falls in love with a simpleton is a court fool who courts a fool! (*He laughs and does jig step.* MELISSA *steps forward.*)

MELISSA: And what is a jester who pretends to be wise and really isn't?

SCRIMSCRAM: What *is* a jester who pretends to be wise, Melissa?

MELISSA: He is a court fool who fools the court! (*All laugh.*)

DRUVO (*Aside*): There's a foolish fool. (*Holds head with hands*) But I'm forgetting myself. Lady Crackwhip, the King is on his way here this very minute, and he has sent me ahead to see that all is in order for the Court Jester Competition. Are the three contestants ready?

LADY CRACKWHIP: Oh, chalices and palaces, whatever shall we do? I didn't expect the King until at least ten minutes from now.

DRUVO: If you didn't expect the King, perhaps, then, you are ready for the Princess. (*He slaps his side, does jig step, and laughs.*) Anyway, she's coming, too.

MELISSA: How can she be coming "too," Druvo, if she's celebrating her twelfth birthday today? She must be coming "twelve," if she's coming at all.

BOODLES: She must be coming "fourteen," then—because

she's twelve, and she's coming too! (*All do jig steps and laugh.*)

LADY CRACKWHIP: *Please,* jesters, we've no time for merriment right now. We must organize ourselves for the Competition. Flagons and dragons, we'll never be ready in time! (LADY CRACKWHIP *directs other* JESTERS, *as they place two thrones on upstage platform for the* KING *and the* PRINCESS. *They place cushions on platform for the* COURTIERS. MELISSA *stands down right and clasps her hands.*)

MELISSA: Oh, if only I can win today! All my life I've dreamed of being a jester in King William's court. (LADY CRACKWHIP *comes up to* MELISSA.)

LADY CRACKWHIP: Lieges and sieges, Melissa, stop daydreaming! (*Gesturing*) Come, help us with the cushions. (MELISSA *and* LADY CRACKWHIP *help* JESTERS *arrange cushions on platform upstage.* DRUVO *crosses left and gestures to* BOODLES *and* SCRIMSCRAM, *who join him. They bow their heads and huddle together.*)

BOODLES: Is everything set for the Competition, Druvo?

DRUVO: Of course, everything's set. Being the wisest jester in this or any other kingdom, I shall, of course, be able to answer every riddle that the King and the Princess ask you.

SCRIMSCRAM: But what if *we* don't know the answers?

DRUVO: That's just the point. I shall stand behind the King and the Princess and signal the answer to you.

BOODLES: You're a genius, Druvo. (DRUVO *blows on his fingernails and polishes them against his chest.*)

DRUVO: It's nothing. (*Suddenly*) Now, what do I get in return? (BOODLES *and* SCRIMSCRAM *reach into their pockets and take out bags of gold. Each gives bag to* DRUVO, *who weighs it in his hand, and then puts it in pocket.*)

SCRIMSCRAM: If we don't win, do we get our gold back?

DRUVO: Don't be ridiculous. One of you is bound to win, and I'll give the gold back to the other one. But, with me helping you, I think it will be a tie, and the King will have to make you both the winners.

BOODLES (*Jumping up and down*): Oh, just think, all those delicious (*He pats his stomach.*) banquets!

SCRIMSCRAM (*Jumping up and down*): And we'll see the tournaments from the Royal Box!

DRUVO: Quiet, you two! There's one thing more I must know. Who is the third contestant?

BOODLES *and* SCRIMSCRAM (*Pointing*): Melissa.

DRUVO: That one? (*Disdainfully*) *She* won't give you any trouble. A girl jester. Bah! (*Trumpet fanfare is heard.* DRUVO *turns and looks off right, then, excitedly*) The King is coming! Remember, a good fool never acts like one. (*Aside, to audience*) This may be one court fool who *will* fool the court! (*Fanfare is heard again, and* KING, PRINCESS, COURTIERS, *and* HERALDS, *who carry slates and chalk, enter right.* LADY CRACKWHIP *runs to meet them.*)

LADY CRACKWHIP (*Curtsying*): Welcome, Your Majesties. Welcome to the Royal School for Jesters. (*JESTERS bow.* LADY CRACKWHIP *escorts* KING *and* PRINCESS *to thrones.* DRUVO *and* COURTIERS *sit or stand nearby, and* HERALDS *stand at right and* JESTERS *at left.*)

KING (*As he walks to throne*): Thank you, Lady Crackwhip.

PRINCESS LILAC (*Pulling at* KING's *robes*): Daddy, Daddy, it's almost time, isn't it?

KING: Yes, dear. The Competition will begin in a few moments. (*He sits on throne.*) Heralds, announce the Court Jester Competition. (*PRINCESS settles herself on throne.* 1ST HERALD *steps forward.*)

1ST HERALD: Hear ye, hear ye! Today is the Princess Lilac's twelfth birthday. (*PRINCESS smiles.*)

JESTERS *and* COURTIERS (*Ad lib*): Hurray! Happy Birthday! Hurray for the Princess! (*Etc.*)

2ND HERALD (*Stepping forward*): And in honor of the occasion, the King is giving her a very special present—a court jester of her very own.

3RD HERALD (*Stepping forward*): Let the three contestants for the Court Jester Competition step forward and announce themselves. (BOODLES *steps forward and bows to* KING *and to* PRINCESS.)

BOODLES: I am called Boodles, Your Majesties. (*As he steps back into place,* SCRIMSCRAM *bumps into him.*)

SCRIMSCRAM: Excuse me.

BOODLES: You idiot! (*To* KING) Excuse us, Sire. (SCRIMSCRAM *bows to* KING *and to* PRINCESS.)

SCRIMCRAM: My name is Scrimscram, Your Majesties. (SCRIMSCRAM *resumes place, and* MELISSA *comes forward and curtsies to* KING *and to* PRINCESS.)

MELISSA: And I am Melissa, Your Highnesses. (*She curtsies again and goes to stand with* BOODLES *and* SCRIMSCRAM.)

KING: Now, the Princess and I shall ask the contestants riddles. And the Heralds shall keep score. (HERALDS *step forward and display slates.*)

PRINCESS: And the one who gives the most correct answers will be my very own court jester! (*To* KING) You begin, Daddy.

KING: All right, Lilac. (*Strokes his chin as he thinks*) Boodles, I shall ask you the first riddle. (BOODLES *steps forward;* DRUVO *steps up behind* KING'S *throne.*) How many coins can you put in an empty bag?

BOODLES (*Wrinkling his forehead as he thinks*): Could you say that again, Your Majesty?

KING: Certainly, Boodles. How many coins can you put in an empty bag? (BOODLES *looks at* DRUVO, *who holds up one finger.*)

BOODLES: Oh, of course, Your Majesty—one!

PRINCESS: Why, Boodles, why? (*She claps her hands with excitement.*)

BOODLES: Why, Princess Lilac? Because . . . because . . . because after there's one coin in it, I guess the bag won't be empty any more! (*He laughs, and* COURTIERS *laugh. As* BOODLES *steps back into place, he pats his stomach and says, aside*) Oh, those banquets, yum!

KING: Very good, Boodles. Now, let's try Scrimscram. (SCRIMSCRAM *steps forward and fidgets with his hands.*) Scrimscram, what does a hippopotamus have that no other animal has?

SCRIMSCRAM (*Putting hand to head in bewilderment*): What *does* a hippopotamus have that no other animal has? (*He looks at* DRUVO, *who holds up his thumb and index finger to indicate something small, and then makes a rocking motion with his arms.* SCRIMSCRAM *squints, as he watches and thinks.*) Oh, yes, of course—the one thing that hippopotamuses have that no other animal has is baby hippopotamuses! (*He laughs, and* COURTIERS *laugh. As* SCRIMSCRAM *returns to place, he says, aside*) The tournaments! I'm so excited!

KING: Very, very good. I can see this contest is going to be close. Now, a riddle for Melissa. (MELISSA *starts to step forward, then turns to* LADY CRACKWHIP.)

MELISSA: Wish me luck, Lady Crackwhip.

LADY CRACKWHIP: Good luck, my child. Thrones and scones, my child, good luck! (MELISSA *steps forward.*)

KING: Now, Melissa, what is it that you cannot see, yet is always before you? (MELISSA *purses her lips.*) Can you tell me the answer, Melissa?

MELISSA: May I have a little more time, Your Majesty? (DRUVO *looks at* BOODLES *and* SCRIMSCRAM *as he points to* MELISSA *and sneers.*)

KING: Of course, my dear. (MELISSA *paces up and down in front of* KING. *Suddenly she looks up, smiling.*)

MELISSA: I know, Your Majesty. What is always before you and yet can't be seen is—the future! (COURTIERS *nod in agreement; and* BOODLES *and* SCRIMSCRAM *look at each other in surprise.* DRUVO *scowls.*)

KING: Very good, all of you. Heralds, what is the score so far?

1ST HERALD (*Consulting slate*): One point for Boodles.

2ND HERALD (*Consulting slate*): One point for Scrimscram.

3RD HERALD (*Consulting slate*): And one point for Melissa.

PRINCESS: It's a tie! It's a tie!

BOODLES *and* SCRIMSCRAM: A tie! A tie!

DRUVO (*Crossing his arms on his chest*): Humph!

KING: What was that, Druvo?

DRUVO: I just said, I suppose the next round will decide things.

PRINCESS: Now it's my turn, Daddy. (DRUVO *carefully steps behind* PRINCESS's *throne.*) Boodles, there were three princesses walking in the garden under one umbrella. Why didn't they get wet? (BOODLES *steps forward and looks at* DRUVO, *who points up to sky and then shakes his head.*)

BOODLES: Because they were shaking their heads?

KING: What was that, Boodles?

PRINCESS: Don't be silly, Boodles. Think hard. (DRUVO *stamps his foot angrily and pantomimes answer again.*)

BOODLES: Oh, now I get it. The three princesses didn't get wet because it wasn't raining! (COURTIERS *laugh.*)

PRINCESS (*Clapping her hands*): Right, Boodles. (BOODLES *steps back into place.*)

BOODLES (*To* SCRIMSCRAM): Almost lost out on the banquets that time.

PRINCESS: Now, Scrimscram, tell me, (SCRIMSCRAM *steps*

forward.) what has one eye but cannot see? (DRUVO *pantomimes sewing motions*.)

SCRIMSCRAM: Um—um—a tournament—er, I mean, a *needle* has one eye but cannot see. (COURTIERS *nod in agreement*.)

PRINCESS: Right, Scrimscram. (SCRIMSCRAM *steps back into place*.) And, Melissa, (MELISSA *steps forward*.) why do the birds fly south?

MELISSA (*Curtsying*): Because they can't walk that far, Your Highness. (*All laugh, and* DRUVO *stamps his foot, angrily*.)

KING: Very good, Melissa. Now, Heralds, the score! (HER-ALDS *huddle together, whispering and comparing slates*.)

HERALDS (*Together*): It's a tie.

COURTIERS: It's a tie?

PRINCESS: What will we do, Daddy? I don't know any more riddles.

KING: And neither do I.

MELISSA: Your Majesty . . .

KING: Yes, Melissa.

MELISSA: You've seen that we can answer riddles. Why don't you see if we can make them up, too?

PRINCESS (*Clapping her hands*): Good, good! (BOODLES *and* SCRIMSCRAM *look at each other fearfully*.)

KING: An excellent suggestion. (*Gestures with his fore-finger, as he suddenly thinks of idea*) And you may ask the riddles of Druvo!

DRUVO: Ah—ah, Your Majesty, I don't really see the need for that.

KING: But, of course, Druvo, for I'm sure none of us will be able to answer the riddles. It will be good practice for you anyway.

DRUVO (*Reluctantly*): Yes, Sire. (*He steps down from be-hind throne and stands before* JESTERS.)

KING: Boodles, you may start.

BOODLES: Y-Yes, Your Majesty. Um—um—Druvo, what is the best way to catch a squirrel in the palace garden?

DRUVO (*Snapping his fingers*): That's easy. Climb up a tree and act like a nut! (*All laugh.* BOODLES *nudges* SCRIMSCRAM, *who finally steps up.*)

SCRIMSCRAM: Druvo, what has keys but can't open locks?

DRUVO (*Laughing*): Mon*keys*, tur*keys*, and don*keys*! (COURTIERS *applaud.* DRUVO *waves hand and scoffs.*) Child's play.

PRINCESS: Melissa, it's your turn. Ask him a hard one.

MELISSA: Let me see. . . . Druvo, what can pass before the sun without making a shadow?

DRUVO (*Thoughtfully*): Hm-m. What can pass before the sun without making a shadow? (*Rubs his chin.*) If a man passes before the sun, he casts a shadow. (*He scratches his head.*) And if the moon passes before the sun, its shadow makes an eclipse. . . .

KING: What's the matter, Druvo?

PRINCESS: Don't you know the answer, Druvo? (DRUVO *stamps his foot.*)

DRUVO: Your Majesties are being beguiled. There *is* no answer to this riddle.

KING: Are you sure of this? Boodles, Scrimscram, do you know the answer to Melissa's riddle?

BOODLES: I don't know the answer, Your Majesty.

SCRIMSCRAM: Nor I, Your Majesty.

DRUVO: There can't be any answer, Sire. I'll wager my reputation as the wisest fool in this or any other kingdom.

MELISSA: But there *is* an answer, Your Majesty.

KING: If there *is* an answer, Melissa, and you can tell it to us, you will be the official winner of the Court Jester Competition.

PRINCESS: Tell us, Melissa, what can pass before the sun without making a shadow?

MELISSA (*Curtsying*): The wind, Princess Lilac.

COURTIERS: The wind!

3RD HERALD (*Holding up slate with* MELISSA's *score*): Melissa is the winner! (COURTIERS, JESTERS, *and* LADY CRACKWHIP *crowd around* MELISSA.)

ALL: Hurray! Hurray for Melissa! (PRINCESS *rises and walks over to* MELISSA. *Meanwhile,* DRUVO *runs out, unnoticed by others.*)

PRINCESS: Daddy, is Melissa to be my very own court jester?

KING (*Smiling*): Yes, indeed, my dear. She is your very own court jester, just as Druvo is *my*—(*Looks around and stops suddenly*) Druvo, where *is* Druvo?

BOODLES: Where *is* he? I want my gold back.

PRINCESS: Come, Melissa, you must help us find Druvo. (*All look about the stage for* DRUVO.) Druvo? Druvo? (MELISSA *runs off.*)

SCRIMSCRAM: I hope we find him soon. He didn't earn the gold I gave him, and I want it back. (MELISSA *returns, leading* DRUVO *by the hand. He wears a dunce's cap.*)

MELISSA: Here he is.

PRINCESS (*Pointing*): And he's wearing a dunce's cap!

LADY CRACKWHIP: Wizards and vizards, whatever are you doing with that, Druvo? My star pupil, wearing a dunce's cap? Why only the bad jesters in my school ever have to wear that!

DRUVO (*Sadly*): Well, I've been bad. (BOODLES *and* SCRIMSCRAM *run up to him.*)

BOODLES: You certainly *have*.

SCRIMSCRAM: We want our gold back. (DRUVO *takes out bags of gold and gives one bag to* BOODLES *and another to* SCRIMSCRAM.)

KING: What's that? Bags of gold? What have you done, Druvo?

DRUVO: It's a long story, Your Majesty. (DRUVO *ap-*

proaches throne.) I tried to help Boodles and Scrimscram win the contest.

KING: And they each gave you a bag of gold in return?

PRINCESS: You mean, Boodles and Scrimscram didn't get the answers on their own?

DRUVO (*Hanging his head*). No, Princess Lilac. And then, and then (*He starts to cry*.), and then I couldn't even answer Melissa's riddle.

KING (*Sternly*): I am very angry, Druvo. Most angry, in fact. At least you have not spoiled everything, though, since even *with* your help, Boodles and Scrimscram could not beat Melissa.

PRINCESS: Then Melissa is still my jester?

KING: Yes, my dear. She, at least, has won the contest fair and square. (*Turning to* DRUVO) But because you tried to spoil the Competition, Druvo, I shall not let you attend the Tournament of the Knights of the Nobility next week.

DRUVO (*Meekly*): Yes, Your Majesty.

KING: And because you were unable to answer Melissa's riddle, I shall send you back to the Royal School for Jesters for a refresher course. Your jokes have been getting stale recently, anyway.

DRUVO: Yes, Your Majesty.

LADY CRACKWHIP: Oh, moats and groats, my own Druvo, back again!

KING: And now, let us have some entertainment. Melissa. . . .

MELISSA (*Curtsying*): Gladly, Your Majesty. But, before I begin, may I beg one favor of you?

KING: Certainly, child.

MELISSA: Well, then, if Druvo proves his skills right now, will you lighten his punishment?

KING: What do you mean, Melissa?

MELISSA: Watch. (*She gestures for* DRUVO *to join her*.)

Come on, Druvo. Let's show King William. (DRUVO *looks bewildered, but joins her. She takes dunce's cap off his head and tosses it aside. Then she curtsies to court and walks from* COURTIER *to* COURTIER *as she makes up poem.*)

A jester ought to be happy;
A jester ought to be gay;
A jester ought to spread merriment
All along his way.

(*She gestures to* DRUVO *to say something.*)

DRUVO (*To court*): Who can tell me the definition of a fat jester?

COURTIERS (*Ad lib*): A fat jester? What is a fat jester? Tell us, Druvo. (*Etc.*)

DRUVO: A fat jester is a round clown who clowns around! (*All laugh.*)

MELISSA:

A jester's the wisest teacher,
Though he's called the royal fool;
His jokes will teach you lessons,
For laughter is his school.

DRUVO:

He can tease a princess or scold a king;
He should show them right from wrong.
But he always teaches with a joke
Or corrects them with a song.

(MELISSA *walks over to* KING.)

MELISSA: Your Majesty, why is a king like an owl and a lion but not like an elephant?

KING: Why *is* a king like an owl and a lion but not like an elephant?

MELISSA:

A king is as wise as an owl;
He rules like the lion, and yet
He hasn't an elephant's memory—

A king *can* forgive and forget!

KING: "Forgive and forget". . . . I understand, Melissa. (DRUVO *approaches throne.*)

DRUVO:
I've learned my lesson, Your Majesty;
I'll be good forever after.
My only wish is to dance and sing
And fill the palace with laughter.

KING: And so you shall, Druvo. And perhaps you shall see the Tournament as well. (*Rising, turns to* PRINCESS) Come, Lilac, your birthday banquet is waiting. Let us return to the castle with our *two* new jesters.

DRUVO *and* MELISSA: Bravo! Hooray!

COURTIERS: Bravo! (*Fanfare is heard as* KING *and* PRINCESS *lead* COURTIERS *offstage.* DRUVO *and* MELISSA *start to exit, then run back to center stage.*)

DRUVO: Melissa, what letter in the alphabet never gets lost?

MELISSA: I don't know, Druvo. Tell me.

DRUVO: "D" never gets lost, because you always find it in THE END! (*They laugh. Then they stop, run over to side of stage, and pick up sign reading,* THE END, *which they show to audience.*)

DRUVO *and* MELISSA (*Reading sign*): THE END. (*They run offstage as curtain falls.*)

THE END

Production Notes

TREASURE IN THE SMITH HOUSE

Characters: 2 male; 3 female.
Playing Time: 20 minutes.
Costumes: Modern dress. Mrs. Smith has a scarf around her head when she enters for the first time. Darlene and Diane wear aprons.
Properties: Slips of paper, broom, dustpan, carved box, yardstick, newspaper, sack of groceries, book, letter.
Setting: The living room of the Smith house. The furnishings are old-fashioned but attractive and comfortable. Upstage center is a brick fireplace, and near it bookcases filled with books. Armchairs with tables are placed around the room. On the tables are china ornaments and bric-a-brac. There are exits right and left.
Lighting: No special effects.

ON THE FENCE

Characters: 4 male; 3 female.
Playing Time: 20 minutes.
Costumes: Modern dress. Tom wears jeans. Horace wears a suit and has glasses.
Properties: Washing, pail of whitewash, two brushes, ball, harmonica, bicycle, large red handkerchief, two pitchers of lemonade, glasses, plate of cookies, baseball.

Setting: A backyard. Along the back of the stage runs a wooden fence with posts. At right is a bench. At left is a clothesline. Bushes and flowers may be added to give a realistic effect.
Lighting: No special effects.

THE KEY TO UNDERSTANDING

Characters: 7 male; 3 female; 18 male or female.
Playing Time: 15 minutes.
Costumes: Children of the Nations wear traditional costumes of the countries they represent. Children representing the United Nations wear suits or dresses. Innkeeper and Innkeeper's Wife wear aprons over their clothes. Other characters wear everyday clothing.
Properties: Food, glasses, plates, paper money, board with keys on it, twelve large cardboard keys and one enormous cardboard key, large caldron, signs reading "Door of Understanding," "General Assembly," "Security Council," "International Court of Justice," "Secretariat," "Trusteeship Council." and "Economic and Social Council."
Setting: Scene One represents an inn, with a counter and several small tables with chairs. Scene

Two takes place before the curtain. Scene Three represents the United Nations, and is the same as Scene One except that the counter has been removed and the tables placed end to end to make one long conference table.
Lighting: No special effects.

THE ROSY-CHEEKED GHOST

Characters: 7 male; 5 female. Male or female extras as desired.
Playing Time: 15 minutes.
Costumes: Ghosts wear sheets. Scary Larry has rosy cheeks at first, but when he returns he has white cheeks. Witches wear traditional black witches' dresses and peaked hats. Professor Gruesome wears a monster costume. The children wear Halloween costumes.
Properties: Trick or treat bags for children; diplomas for Professor Gruesome.
Setting: An old deserted barn, the classroom of Spookane Ghoul School. Cornstalks, straw, and old boxes and crates are strewn around the room. The stage should look as mysterious as possible, and should be rather cluttered.
Lighting: No special effects necessary. Lights may be dimmed before the children enter.

CINDER-RILEY

Characters: 2 male; 5 female; at least 3 male for prop boys; as many male and female as desired to be dancers.
Playing Time: 20 minutes.
Costumes: The Leprechaun wears a brown tunic, tights, a cap and a kerchief. The Stepmother and Stepsisters wear long gowns, crowns, and comical putty noses. The Stepmother wears a cloak.

Cinder-Riley wears a long gown, a crown, and silver slippers (the gown should be expendable, since it must be cut). The Fairy Godmother wears a housedress, two aprons, two mop caps, and two pairs of shoes. Jack wears a crown of potatoes, a tattered shirt, and breeches decorated with green patches. The Dancers may wear green and white costumes; the boys may wear gold ties and the girls, gold kerchiefs.
Properties: Stick and red hanky for Leprechaun; large portable screen decorated with a coat of arms or other royal device; light card table covered with long tablecloth; papers, quill pen and inkstand (on top of table); broom; reticule containing huge shears for Fairy Godmother.
Setting: The stage is bare, and all necessary furnishings are brought on and removed as indicated in the text. The backdrop may be hung with drawings of large knives, forks, spoons and skillets.
Lighting: No special effects.

THE DREADFUL DRAGON

Characters: 7 male; 8 female; as many male and female extras as desired.
Playing Time: 25 minutes.
Costumes: Colorful Chinese costumes; those of the Empress, the Prince, and the Goddesses should be more elaborate. As the dragon, all the Prince needs is a ferocious head which he sticks out of the cave when he speaks.
Properties: Sewing, trays of food, thunder sheet, drumstick, sweetmeats.
Setting: At rise the stage is bare except for a screen on which has been painted a Chinese god; on the other screen is a sign saying

"Street of the Locusts." For Chang's home the Property Man brings in two stools, a small box, a kettle and a basket. For the cave scene, the Property Man sets up a stream (made of rippled blue paper tacked to wood), mountains (heavy paper painted various shades of purple, brown and green and pasted to large cartons), and a cave (beaver board cut in an arch and nailed between two wooden standards). Across the top is painted, "Cave of the Dreadful Dragon."

Lighting: If possible, flashes of lightning to accompany the rolls of thunder should be used. Color spots for the cave scenes are also effective.

THE MYSTERY OF THE GUMDROP DRAGON

Characters: 9 male; 4 female; 6 male or female.

Playing Time: 25 minutes.

Costumes: Court costume. The Prince and Princess should be dressed mainly in white (with touches of red for the Prince), and Sir Licorice in black. The clowns are dressed in clown costume. The town crier wears a black cape and hat; the court writer wears tights, a short jacket, and a cap with a quill in it. The wizard wears a long cloak and a hat covered with astrological symbols. The dragon should be dressed in a fanciful green costume.

Properties: Handkerchief and piece of paper, for court writer; inkwell; toy white rabbit and wand, for wizard; chains, for Sir Licorice.

Setting: The stage represents the throne room of the kingdom of Candyland throughout. There is a throne at center stage for the Princess, and a table to the right on which an inkwell is placed. The stage may be decorated in keeping with the Candyland theme. There are chairs for the ladies-in-waiting.

Lighting: The lights dim and brighten to simulate moonlight, as indicated in Scene 2.

THE BOOKWORM

Characters: 4 female; 5 male; 7 male or female.

Playing Time: 20 minutes.

Costumes: Betty and Librarian wear modern dress. Librarian wears eyeglasses. Bookworm wears a tubular-shaped garment of dark material encircled with bright stripes; he has antennae on his head and large, dark-rimmed eyeglasses. Reference Books wear large posters representing books. Each poster has a letter on it, so that together they spell out the word "library." Storybook characters wear clothing appropriate to the parts played.

Properties: Books and cards.

Setting: A public library. There are bookcases full of books across the back of the stage. (A painted backdrop may be used if desired.) Upstage right are the librarian's desk and chair. A tall stool is at center. Upstage left there may be one or two reading tables.

Lighting: No special effects.

Sound: Bell ringing.

THE COURT OF KING ARITHMETIC

Characters: 8 male; 4 female; 10 male or female.

Playing Time: 25 minutes.

Costumes: Timothy wears school clothes. The others wear suitable court dress with the appropriate arithmetic symbols on the fronts of their costumes. Lord Calculation has a pair of eyeglasses hanging on a cord around his neck.

Properties: Fans, mirrors or flowers for Princesses, sceptre, huge book, tiny pocket-sized book, large magnifying glass, magician's wand, arithmetic book, arithmetic assignment papers.

Setting: The throne room of King Arithmetic's palace. The King's throne stands on a raised platform, and steps leading to throne hold cushions which form seats for the four Princesses. There are doors at left and right.

Lighting: No special effects.

A PRINCE IS WHERE YOU FIND HIM

Characters: 7 male; 6 female.
Playing Time: 20 minutes.
Costumes: Court costumes. Guards wear uniforms. Cook wears white apron, hat. Beggar wears rags.
Properties: Tennis racket, apple, wristwatch, tennis net, and satchel.
Setting: The throne room in the palace of the kingdom of Pneumonia. Two thrones stand upstage center, with a sundial slightly to their left. There are exits at left and right.
Lighting: No special effects.

THE MAGIC BOOKSHELF

Characters: 5 male; 5 female.
Playing Time: 20 minutes.
Costumes: Sally is dressed in school clothes; Tim, in pajamas, bathrobe, and slippers. The Fairy Godfather wears a long robe and a tall, pointed hat. Peter Pan is dressed in green tights and jacket, and a green cap with a feather. Cinderella wears a ball gown and carries a glass slipper. Alice in Wonderland wears a starched dress and pinafore, with a black velvet ribbon around her hair. Jack the Giant Killer wears tights and a jacket, with a knife in his belt. Dorothy wears a simple dress; Red Riding Hood, a red cape. Christopher Robin is dressed in short pants with suspenders and a striped jersey.

Properties: Several books, a blanket, lightweight baseball bat, teddy bear, basket with cookies in it.

Setting: The living room in Sally's and Tim's house. A door, a window, some bookshelves and two large easy chairs pulled close together are the important furnishings. Other furniture may be added as desired.

Lighting: No special effects.

A MESSAGE FROM ROBIN HOOD

Characters: 11 male; male extras to be soldiers and outlaws.
Playing Time: 20 minutes.
Costumes: The outlaws wear tunics and tights of Lincoln green. The necks of the tunics may be plain or finished with wide scalloped collars of brown or red. Some of the outlaws may wear triangular hats with feathers and narrow brims. The soldiers wear bright uniforms, the Sheriff, an especially ornate uniform. Duffy is dressed as an outlaw.
Properties: Bows, arrows, quarterstaves (long poles tipped with metal), swords, goose feathers and knife for Duffy, scroll, horn.
Setting: The backdrop depicts a forest. At right center is a log. A large oak tree stands at upstage center with a smaller tree on either side. There are several trees along the right and left walls.
Lighting: No special effects.

A Turtle, A Flute, and the General's Birthday

Characters: 15 male; 1 female. As many male extras as desired for officers or band members.

Playing Time: 20 minutes.

Costumes: Revolutionary period costumes. Soldiers' uniforms should be quite ragged and officers' uniforms newer.

Properties: Flute tied to string, other flutes or recorders, knife, buckets of water, cleaning rags, broom, bellows, bundles of grain, food, pots, stuffed turtle; table setting, including white tablecloth, silver candlesticks, dishes and cutlery.

Setting: The kitchen and dining room of the farmhouse which served as General Washington's headquarters at Valley Forge. The kitchen end of the room is divided from the dining end by a screen. The kitchen has an open fireplace, cranes with heavy pots, a plain table and stools, cooking utensils, and a sideboard with china and pewter on it. The dining room has a large table with plain chairs. In Scene 3, the table is set for a banquet. Scene 2 may take place before curtain. If desired, an old wagon wheel, leafless branches, etc., may suggest a lonely road outside of the camp.

Sound: Band music. If possible, a real band with Revolutionary period instruments should be used.

Lighting: No special effects.

Valentine's Day

Characters: 6 male; 3 female; any number of male or female extras to be elves, King's followers and offstage voices.

Playing Time: 15 minutes.

Costumes: The fairies and elves wear the traditional costumes; the elves may wear an assortment of bright-colored hats, tops, etc. Little Valentine wears modern dress. Jack the Knave should wear a cloak; a large heart is pinned to the front of his costume. Teardrop Dan may wear a blue and silver costume. The King and Queen and their followers wear royal robes. The Queen has a large arrow pin on her dress.

Properties: Tray of tarts, sleigh bells (offstage), arms for elves, handkerchief for gag, rope, bugle (offstage), lace handkerchief, rose, tart for Tompkins, bells (offstage).

Setting: A forest glen. There is a fallen log at center. Tree trunks, rocks, and giant toadstools furnish seats, and later are used as hiding places for the elves. There is a large tree upstage right.

Lighting: If possible, the stage should be dimly lighted to suggest night.

Saving the Old Homestead

Characters: 7 male; 3 female.

Playing Time: 20 minutes.

Costumes: Clothing appropriate to the period. Pansy should have an apron. Murdock should have a top hat and cloak. All the men might wear mustaches.

Properties: Bills, embroidery, envelope containing blank paper, vase of flowers, stocks, gun, gag, handkerchief, rope, pipe, ring.

Setting: The living room set consists of a table covered with an ornate, fringed cloth, a rocker and a straight chair. An old-fashioned kerosene lamp is on the table, and a sampler with "Home Sweet Home" is hanging on the wall. The woods scene should have at least three trees. On one tree should be a sign pointing to the saw mill. The trees do not have to be taken down for the saw mill scene. The saw mill scene can be as simple or as elaborate as desired. The saw itself can be made of a piece of heavy cardboard. Cut a circular saw with a two-foot diameter; cut saw-teeth around the edge. Paint the saw a light color and fasten it to a hand grindstone. The grindstone should be fastened to a sturdy frame and arranged so that someone in back of the scene can turn it and push it slightly so that the saw seems to be getting closer to the girl lying in its path. Caroline can be lying on a rough table that serves as the saw table. William is tied to a chair nearby.

Lighting: No special effects.

Oleo Numbers: An oleo number consists of songs, dances and recitations. Between the scenes the audience might be entertained by oleo numbers, including songs like "Bicycle Built for Two," "Tavern in a Town," "Put on Your Old Gray Bonnet," etc. The Master of Ceremonies may heckle the piano player, stop the singing and start it over again, etc.—all in good humor, of course.

THE EMPEROR'S NEW ROBES

Characters: 5 male; 4 female; 1 Fan Bearer and 2 Storytellers may be male or female; male and female extras to be Courtiers and voices from audience.

Playing Time: 30 minutes.

Costumes: Traditional Japanese kimonos for entire cast except Taro

and Danzo, who wear dark tunics with large pockets; they wear single pigtails. Emperor has mustache and wears long underwear under his robe.

Properties: Hand mirror, fan, tape measure, writing pad, ink and brush, table, fan on long pole, loom, boxes of jewels and silks, food, candles—one burnt low in a candlestick, goblet or cup, canopy, lanterns, blanket.

Setting: The Audience Chamber in the Palace of the Emperor of Japan, and the Flower Path before the Palace. A divan on a raised platform is at center, rear. A full-length mirror is on wall at right. A cushion for each Storyteller is placed at downstage right and left. Steps lead down to the Flower Path which may be the aisle of the auditorium. The aisle seat in each row may be decorated with artificial flowers to represent the Flower Path.

Lighting: If possible, lights should dim at the end of Scene 1 to indicate the approach of night and come up slowly at the beginning of Scene 2 to indicate daybreak.

FATHER HITS THE JACKPOT

Characters: 4 male; 6 female.

Playing Time: 30 minutes.

Costumes: Mr. and Mrs. Evans, Sheila, Cindy, Patrice and Tommy wear modern everyday clothes on first appearance. In Scene 2, Patrice wears several sweaters on top of each other, and Cindy wears an exaggerated "movie" costume: spike heels, long black satin dress, feather in hair, fan, etc. The Cook wears chef's hat and apron. The TV commentator wears a high hat; the Reporter wears an old felt hat pushed far back on his head. Aunt Marion wears old-fashioned clothes, hat, large handbag and umbrella; around her neck is the key to the handbag.

Properties: Pen, checkbook, stack of bills, and newspaper for Mr. Evans; sewing or knitting for Mrs. Evans; nail polish for Sheila; movie magazine for Cindy; magazine and coupon to tear out, pencil, for Patrice; envelope containing check; large bunch of grapes for Tommy; check for TV Commentator; stage money, pad and pencil, for Reporter; checkbook for Aunt Marion; old doorbell or bicycle bell for sounds of doorbell and telephone.

Setting: The Evans living room. There are two doors: an exit at left which leads outdoors, and a door at backstage center which connects with the other rooms of the house. There is a couch upstage left, with a low coffee table in front of it. A desk stands near downstage right, with telephone, stack of bills, etc., on it. There is a chair for the desk, and several other chairs and small tables, etc. are placed around the stage.

Lighting: No special effects.

THE MYSTERY RING

Characters: 8 female.
Playing Time: 15 minutes.
Costumes: Everyday, modern dress.
Properties: Two slips of paper, wrapped ring box, ring with red stone, two newspapers.
Setting: The front lawn of the Foster home. The only furnishings required are a table and two chairs. Bushes and flowers may stand about the stage. There may also be a croquet set, if desired. Exits are at right and left.
Lighting: No special effects.
Sound: Offstage telephone bell.

THE GYPSY LOOK

Characters: 3 male; 3 female.
Playing Time: 20 minutes.
Costumes: Modern dress. Nora later puts on a head scarf and hoop earrings. When Sue re-enters, she wears slacks, a bright shirt, a sash, a head scarf, earrings, and a small black mustache.
Properties: Suit, books, purse, hoop earrings, small suitcase.
Setting: A comfortably furnished living room. There are entrances at upstage left and right. At center is a table, and on the table are papers, books, a basket of apples and a dish of candy. Downstage right is a large easy chair. Several smaller chairs and other furniture are placed around the room.
Lighting: No special effects.

POET'S NIGHTMARE

Characters: 4 male; 4 female.
Playing Time: 25 minutes.
Costumes: Modern dress.
Properties: Knitting, papers, pad, pencils, books, ice skates.
Setting: The living room of the Martin home. Downstage right is a couch, downstage left, a large armchair. Near the chair is a small table, and on the table is a telephone. Upstage right is a desk. Bookcases and other chairs and tables may be placed around room.
Lighting: No special effects.

THE FEAST OF THE THOUSAND LANTERNS

Characters: 9 male; 3 female; male or female extras for guards and people in the crowd.
Playing Time: 15 minutes.
Costumes: All characters wear typi-

cal Chinese robes with big sleeves. The Emperor has on a plain robe for the first part of the play; he later appears in royal robes. The sellers may carry merchandise on poles, or on yokes hung across their shoulders.

Properties: Lanterns for people and for the Seller of Lanterns (one should be plain and broken); drawstring bag with coins for Chang; covered cage for Seller of Birds; feathers; parasols for Seller of Parasols; four golden tassels for Old Woman; several colorfully wrapped packages of food for Seller of Refreshments; token, parchment and purse for Emperor; light-weight table holding a decorated lantern covered by a dark cloth.

Setting: An open space.

Lighting: If desired, the lantern on the table can cover a flashlight or table lamp. Seng can then switch the lamp on. The other lanterns may also have flashlights concealed in them and these may be turned on at the same time.

Sound: Offstage gong, as indicated.

THE COURAGE PIECE

Characters: 6 male; 3 female.

Playing Time: 25 minutes.

Costumes: The girls and Mother are dressed in peasant costumes. Johnny wears short trousers, and has a coat on when he first appears. The other boys also wear short trousers and jackets. Neighbor Dunn is dressed in a dark suit and has a long coat. The Leprechaun should wear a green costume, with long tight-fitting trousers and a pointed hat.

Properties: Pots and pans, rug, pillow, broken pitcher, bread, knife, bowl, basket, bottles, jug of water, turf, large coin, wallet, shamrock,

sheet of metal to simulate thunder.

Setting: The old-fashioned kitchen of an Irish cottage. Upstage center is a large fireplace with a mantel above it. On the mantel are an oil lamp, some pots and pans, and a large can. On one side of the fireplace is a large casement window, and near it a little stand. There is also a large table in the room, with some crude chairs placed near it.

Lighting: The lights should be dimmed when the storm begins, and they may be turned up for a moment to indicate lightning. The lamp on the mantel should be turned off as indicated in the text, and turned up again when the Leprechaun touches it.

THE HONORED ONE

Characters: 8 male; 4 female. Page may be male or female.

Playing Time: 15 minutes.

Costumes: King wears traditional royal robes and crown. Prime Minister wears long dark costume. Jester wears colorful tights and cap, and carries a baton with bells attached. Farmer wears workman's clothes; Ballerina wears dance costume; Rich Man wears elaborate clothing and jewelry. Doctor and Scientist wear short white coats over their clothes; Nurse wears a white uniform. Singer may wear fancy dress. Artist wears a smock over his clothes. Old Woman wears simple, old-fashioned clothes.

Properties: Basket or tray of fruit, large money box, painting, rolling cart with microscope, test tubes and other scientific instruments on it, wreath of flowers.

Setting: A room in a palace. There is a throne at center.

Lighting: No special effects.

Sound: Music for Ballerina and Singer as indicated.

ANGEL OF MERCY

Characters: 5 male; 4 female; boy's voice (offstage).

Playing Time: 20 minutes.

Costumes: Scene 1: the girls are dressed in clothes of the period. Scene 2: Florence wears a long, dark dress with a white apron over it. Mary is dressed in the same fashion. Dr. Goodale wears a white uniform. Dr. Hall is dressed in military uniform of the period. Scene 3: Florence wears a plain, long black dress and hat with a veil that covers her face. The other characters are dressed in elaborate clothes of the period. The servant wears a butler's uniform.

Properties: Embroidery work, basin, bandages, stationery, scrubbing brush, pail, kerchief, shawl, kerosene lamp, pencil, candy, fruit, piece of notepaper.

Setting: Scene 1: The living room of the period. At the center rear is a large globe with a footstool beside it. At left stage is an elaborate divan. Other chairs and tables are placed about the room. Scene 2: At the right is a rough, unpainted table with a bench behind it and another to the side. An unlighted lamp stands on the table. On the opposite side of the stage are shelves stacked with shirts, socks, slippers, flannels, etc. A bench stands beside the shelves. Scene 3: Living room of the period. A large divan is on one side of the stage with a chaise longue on the other, with an elaborate footstool beside it. A serving table laden with fruit and sweets is between the divan and the chaise longue.

Lighting: No special effects in first and third scenes; Scene 2: the stage should be quite dark.

FIESTA THE FIRST

Characters: 9 male; 7 female; as many as desired for crowd.

Playing Time: 20 minutes.

Costumes: Girls wear bright cotton skirts with white blouses and may have flowers in their hair. Maria's skirt is shorter than those of the women. Jane wears a school dress. Boys are dressed in jeans and white cotton shirts with bright-colored sashes around their waists. The Mayor wears a large sombrero. Father wears a business suit.

Properties: Two large baskets full of vegetables; green beads, for Maria; rubber ball, for Carlos; coins, for Pedro; cooking utensils and pancakes for Cook's stall; assorted dolls for Dollmaker.

Setting: The stage represents a market place. There are several stalls (desks decorated with crepe paper), one with dolls, one with cooking utensils, and one empty.

Lighting: No special effects.

THE CROSS PRINCESS

Characters: 4 male; 6 female.

Playing Time: 15 minutes.

Costumes: Any costumes suitable for royalty.

Properties: Tray of food, paper, pencils, books, small black books, ball and bat, large book, two small bags of gold.

Setting: The bedroom of the Princess. It is crowded with toys of all kinds—dolls, skates, sleds, balls, etc., and has a big bookcase full of books. There is a bed that should be high enough for Edward and Catherine to crawl

under. A table and some chairs complete the furnishings.
Lighting: No special effects.

THE SECRET OF THE WINDMILL

Characters: 4 male; 5 female.
Playing Time: 15 minutes.
Costumes: Modern everyday dress. Grandmother may wear more traditional Dutch clothing.
Properties: Books, papers, pencils, lamp, lamp shade, vase, Edam cheese, large packing case filled with old clothes, dishes, etc., silverware, glasses, plates, trays, earrings, ring, 3 shiny stones.
Setting: The Van Dyke living room in Amsterdam. A table covered with books and papers is upstage center; there are chairs around it. A small sofa is at front left, and right front is a comfortable chair beside an end table which holds an old lamp and a vase.
Lighting: No special effects.

A DOCTOR FOR LUCINDA

Characters: 4 male; 2 female.
Playing Time: 15 minutes.
Costumes: Old-fashioned dress. Jacqueline and Lucinda wear long, bright-colored dresses. Jacqueline wears an apron and her clothes are not as attractive as those of her mistress. The male characters all wear knee breeches. The Squire wears a white shirt and a bright-colored vest. Luke is dressed in brown, and Jeremy in black. Jeremy wears a black cape. Robin has a large hat which he can pull down to cover most of his face. He wears a long brown cape to cover his clothes which are similar to those of the Squire.
Properties: Pillow, two purses full of money.
Setting: A room in Squire Geronde's home. The furnishings may be as simple or as elaborate as desired. All that is essential is a comfortable-looking chair for Lucinda. Other tables, chairs, couches, etc., may be added to complete the furnishings. There are exits at right and at left. A window, upstage center, revealing the garden, is not necessary but it would enhance the action of the play.
Lighting: No special effects.

THIRTEEN

Characters: 13 female.
Playing Time: 25 minutes.
Costumes: Everyday modern dress.
Properties: Pencil, books, papers and pinking shears for Susan; handbag containing envelope for Carol; covered cake plate containing cake for Roberta; purse (containing penny), sweater and umbrella for Bonnie; shoes for Joan; purse with mirror for Patty.
Setting: A comfortable living room. A little right of center is a couch with a coffee table in front of it. Several gay cushions are on the couch. An easy chair is at center. There is a desk near the left wall, with a straight chair behind it and a wastebasket near it. A telephone is on the desk. Lamps, end tables, other chairs and hassocks may be added as desired. A door at upper right leads to the other rooms of the house, a door at left to the front porch.
Lighting: No special effects.

VISIT TO THE PLANETS

Characters: 9 male; 7 female; 3 male or female.
Playing Time: 25 minutes.
Costumes: Space suits for Leif and Mark. School dresses for the girls.

Sun wears a bright yellow dress. Mercury wears summer clothing —shorts and a light, bright-colored shirt. Venus wears a filmy dress and veils. Earth may wear a dress with the outline of North and South America on it. Mars carries sword and shield, and may wear armor. Jupiter wears a suit. Saturn's robe has rings. Uranus has a white beard and leans on a stick. Neptune carries a trident. Pluto wears a heavy coat and scarf. Comet Head and Tail wear a cardboard costume painted to resemble a comet. Meteor wears a cardboard costume.

Properties: Monkey wrench, hammer, bowl-shaped helmets, Make-it-Snow gadget, and another complicated gadget, for the boys. Mirror for Venus.

Setting: Scene 1 is in the playground of the school. At right center is a space ship. The space ship is a flat cardboard cut-out, about 12 feet tall, painted silver. It is placed in front of a small platform, about 4 feet high, which has three steps attached to it. The steps are used to enter the space ship. On the upstage side, not visible to the audience, is a small fire extinguisher of the carbon dioxide type. When the ship "blasts off," an adult behind the ship sets off the fire extinguisher and starts to lift the space ship.

For Scenes 2 and 3 the stage is bare, except for a black backdrop, on which constellations are painted in phosphorescent paint.

For Scene 3, the boys have a jet-propelled space scooter, a lightweight cardboard cut-out, which they wear as a harness. The boy in the rear uses an aerosol spray for the jet effect when they move.

Scene 4 is the same as Scene 1, except that instead of the rocket ship, a pile of debris is in the middle of the stage.

Lighting: Scenes 2 and 3 should be played with dim light. The Sun may be lighted with a spotlight. There are flashes of light when the space ship blasts off, and also just before the Comet enters.

THE INVISIBLE DRAGON
OF WINN SINN TU

Characters: 3 male; 1 female; 1 male or female.

Playing Time: 25 minutes.

Costumes: Peach Blossom wears a Chinese robe, with or without sleeves. She wears flowers in her hair. The Baron, Wun Sun Tu and the peasant wear a basic costume of Chinese pajamas—silk for the Baron and cotton for the others. Wide colored sashes, slippers or sandals, and long queues complete their attire. The dragon wears green tights or pajamas. An outer garment, mask, long tail, and pipe-cleaner antennae may be added, if desired.

Properties: Long string attached to inside of Wun Sun Tu's sleeve; bent safety pin; worm made of cloth; mat with long string attached; "peach tree" (rod, decorated with crepe paper, placed in flower pot); flat slab of wood with door and door frame construction braced onto one end, and on which are a low table and two small stools; potted plant and trowel; large gong or brass tray hung on upstage center screen; clapper made of stick and padded cloth; long mustaches on adhesive tape, lightly stuck to inside of Wun Sun Tu's sleeve; scarf for Wun Sun Tu; three trays of bright plastic dishes; medicine bottle and spoon;

feather, "rock" made of sponge or foam material, attached to clapper with string.

Setting: Three large folding screens are placed at stage left, stage right, and upstage center. These may be painted to represent a landscape with mountains, sky, and cherry blossoms. On the center screen hang the gong and clapper with the "rock" set on top of the screen, and attached to the clapper with a string.

Lighting: No special effects.

THE REBELLIOUS ROBOTS

Characters: 5 male; 5 female; 6 male or female for Robots.

Playing Time: 20 minutes.

Costumes: Agatha wears a dress and apron. Henry wears slacks and a sport jacket. Mayor Portly wears a formal suit and has a pillow stuffed in his clothes. Children wear everyday school clothes. Robots are dressed identically, except that each has a wide belt of a different color; on the back of each one is a large box with dials, knobs, buttons, etc.

Properties: Large box marked "candy," tied with string, with smaller boxes inside it; scissors, coiled tubing, boxes with colored buttons on them, wastebaskets filled with paper, paper play money, flowers, wrapping paper, paper bag, handkerchief, shopping bag, small slips of paper, and jewelry.

Setting: A gift shop. At one side is a display of flowers. At the other side is a display of jewelry, candy, and other gifts. Various signs are placed around the store, giving gift suggestions, price information, etc.

Lighting: No special effects.

THE MYSTERIOUS STRANGER

Characters: 4 male; 3 female.

Playing Time: 25 minutes.

Costumes: Modern dress. Bernice wears an apron. Mr. and Mrs. Lister wear hats and coats when they leave. The officers wear uniforms.

Properties: Magnifying glass, paper, plaid cap, false beard, briefcase, stalk of celery, tray of sandwiches covered with napkin, magazine, box of chocolates, paper knife, books, small valise containing gold slippers, blue sock, toothbrush with blue handle, rags, and papers.

Setting: A comfortably furnished living room. A sofa, chairs, a table or two and a desk furnish the room. On the desk are the telephone, and some books and papers. Lamps are placed around the room, and there are some magazines on the table. Door at upstage center leads to reception hall and upper stairway. The door at upstage right leads to the rest of the house.

Lighting: No special effects.

TEAPOT TROUBLE

Characters: 3 male; 5 female.

Playing Time: 25 minutes.

Costumes: Modern dress. Jill wears an apron over her dress and a coral necklace around her neck. Peter has a large pocket watch. Mrs. Slade wears spectacles.

Properties: Broom, dusters, purse with coins and play bills, cup, cracked teapot with bills inside, can of blue paint and brush, magnifying glass, newspaper, ten-dollar bill, large kettle, glass paperweight.

Setting: The interior of an antique shop. Shelves upstage hold old dishes, copper bowl, clocks, glassware, etc. On one of the bottom shelves is a cash box. On the top shelf is an old teapot. Upstage center is a small antique table. Up right is door to shop with bells that tinkle as customers enter. At left is a door leading to house. Other furnishings—chests, spinning wheels, old chairs, etc.—can be added to give the set an authentic appearance.

Lighting: No special effects.

THE KING'S CALENDAR

Characters: 7 male; 5 female; if desired there may be more than two Ladies-in-Waiting.
Playing Time: 25 minutes.
Costumes: King, Queen, and Princesses wear royal garb. The Ministers and Ladies-in-Waiting are dressed as court attendants. The Calendar-Maker and Astronomer wear dark clothing and look very learned with spectacles on the ends of their noses and pencils behind their ears.
Properties: Comic book, stacks of papers, several books.
Setting: Throne room of the palace.
Lighting: No special effects.

ABE BUYS A BARREL

Characters: 7 male; 3 female.
Playing Time: 25 minutes.
Costumes: Abe wears a calico shirt and a pair of jeans several inches too short for him. The jeans are held up by one suspender. The other men also wear shirts and jeans; Mentor Graham is more neatly dressed than the others. Bill Berry wears a straw hat. The women wear long skirts and long-sleeved tops of plain gray or brown. The children may be barefoot.
Properties: Books for Abe and Jack,

purse for Mrs. Hornbuckle, tea, scales, small bags, coins, fishing pole for Jack, two buckskins for Godbey, three tin cups of milk, box lid, crackers, letters, hat for Abe, barrel containing the following items: old bonnet, lady's shoes, garments, and four large volumes.
Setting: A small general store. A counter runs along the upstage wall. Behind the counter are some shelves containing bolts of material, groceries, etc. Near the counter is a large barrel of crackers. Brooms, shovels, hoes, etc., lean against the walls. There are boxes and jars on the counter containing thread, needles, candy, etc. On the counter also is a scale which requires weights for balancing. There are several straight-backed chairs in the store. A door at right leads outside, a door at left to the rear of the store.

THE MAGIC FISHBONE

Characters: 4 male; 4 female; as many other male or female as desired for royal children. (Dickens specified eighteen.)
Playing Time: 15 minutes.
Costumes: Court costumes, if desired, for royal family and Prince Wonderful. King's clothing should be rather shabby, and Princess Alicia should be dressed neatly, not showily. Children may be dressed as commoners. King and Queen wear crowns, and Princess Alicia and Prince Wonderful may wear small coronets. Good Fairy is dressed as an old-fashioned, elderly lady. Mr. Pickles wears street clothes, with white dish towel as an apron, and a white cap. Peggy wears a black dress and apron and cap.
Properties: Pushcart, wrapping pa-

per, and fish, for Mr. Pickles; fishbone (real or imaginary) and fan,
for Alicia; bandaging material,
basin, towels, and a small bottle
for children; dishes, coins.
Setting: The dining room of the
palace of King Watkins. It is a
simple room with a dining table
and chairs for three people.
There is a divan or couch with
pillows on one side of the stage.
Lighting: No special effects.

AESOP, MAN OF FABLES

Characters: 7 male; 1 female; male
and female extras as desired for
slaves and purchasers.
Playing Time: 25 minutes.
Costumes: Short tunics of coarse
cloth for the male slaves; long
tunic for Sheba. Classical long
Greek robes for Tancred, Solon
and Iadmon. Croesus wears a
sleeveless robe and a wreath of
laurel on his head. Solon, Xanthus, and Croesus have beards.
Properties: Three bundles, gong,
basket of fruit, pail and scrub
brush, sceptre, earthen jar containing small pieces of white paper.
Setting: A simple backdrop and
movable columns will give the
necessary changes of setting. For
furnishings, Scene 1 requires a
platform; Scene 2, a low couch
and a low table; Scene 3, a throne
on a platform and a chair.
Lighting: No special effects.

MRS. GIBBS ADVERTISES

Characters: 7 male; 5 female; male
and female extras.
Playing Time: 20 minutes.
Costumes: Modern dress.
Properties: Newspaper, tray with
breakfast dishes, large basket with
four toy dogs or bundles in it,
four little blankets, pad, pencil.
Setting: The living room of Mrs.
Gibbs' home. It is richly and
tastefully furnished. A desk is
upstage center, a sofa, right.
Other chairs and tables with
lamps are placed around room,
pictures are on the walls, and
expensive-looking bric-a-brac is
placed around on the tables.
Lighting: No special effects.

POCAHONTAS, THE TOMBOY PRINCESS

Characters: 7 male; 9 female; extras.
Playing Time: 20 minutes.
Costumes: Powhatan wears raccoon
skins and there is a coronet of
feathers on his head. The Indian men may wear feather coronets, and shorts; the Indian
women wear coronets of feathers,
full gowns with ropes around
waists, and hair hanging down.
John Smith is dressed in a shabby,
dirty colonial costume.
Properties: Tomahawks, bows,
clubs, two large rocks, string of
bright beads, compass.
Setting: There may be a large pile
of crumpled red crepe paper to
represent fire in the center of the
stage. Nearby is a wooden throne.
There may be a few camp stools
about, and one on each side of
the throne.
Lighting: No special effects.

THE DAY THE MOONMEN LANDED

Characters: 11 male; 5 female; as
many extras as desired.
Playing Time: 20 minutes.
Costumes: Moonmen wear "space-
suits," one all green. They
wear beanies with wires for
antennae. Irish children wear
street dress with green capes and
green ties for boys; Kathleen

wears majorette outfit. Mexican children wear colorful peasant outfits, with shawls and straw hats for the girls. Italian children wear bright, frilly costumes. The dragon should have a crepe paper costume with grotesque face painted on front; paraders wear Chinese costumes.

Properties: Telephone, umbrellas decorated with strings for parachutes, baton, musical instruments, guitar, maracas, claves, paper streamers, noisemakers.

Setting: The Moon scenes are played at left in the office of Moon Mayor Muggins. There is a screen upstage decorated with pictures and models of planets, satellites, and universe charts, and a desk downstage with a telephone. The Earth scenes are played at right and center. The stage is bare, and a backdrop of skyscraper, factories, farms and other typical American scenes, is upstage. The scenes are indicated by a spotlight.

Sound: Music as indicated.

Lighting: Spotlight left for Moon scenes and right for Earth scenes, as indicated.

The Wizard of Oz

Characters: 6 male; 6 female. Narrator and Munchkins may be male or female. Male and female extras. The Wizard of Oz in his various disguises may be played by different actors if desired.

Playing Time: 30 minutes.

Costumes: Dorothy wears everyday dress and carries a basket. The Witch of the North and the Wicked Witch of the West wear traditional witches' costumes, with pointed hats and long black cloaks. The Wicked Witch has a golden cap. Glinda wears a long, flowing white dress. The Munchkins wear odd, old-fashioned blue costumes. The Scarecrow wears a baggy shirt and overalls, and a straw hat; wisps of straw stick out of his costume. The Tin Woodman wears a silvery costume and helmet, and carries an ax. The Cowardly Lion wears a lion costume with a long tail. The Soldier wears a green uniform. The Winged Monkeys wear monkey costumes with wings attached; the King of the Monkeys has a crown. The Wizard of Oz wears a beast costume, and then an old-fashioned suit. Lovely Lady wears a long, colorful gown. Aunt Em wears an old-fashioned long dress with an apron.

Properties: Toy dog, silver shoes, oilcan, four pairs of green spectacles, papier-mâché head attached to a string, broom, bucket of water, cup, powder, green bottle of liquid, green dish, small red paper heart, yellow rug. Ball of fire may be constructed from a circular piece of oak tag painted red and orange, with pointed flames drawn at the edges. This may be suspended by a string from the ceiling, or supported on a stand from below.

Setting: Scene 1 takes place in a cornfield. There is a backdrop depicting the front of Dorothy's house. Later a stool with a pole on it is brought on for the Scarecrow. Scenes 2 and 4 take place in Oz's throne room. There is a large throne at center and a folding screen is at one side. The furnishings may be lavish and should all be green. Scene 3 takes place before the castle of the Wicked Witch of the West; a backdrop depicts the front of the castle. Scene 5 takes place in Glinda's castle. Simple but attractive furnishings may be used. Some of the furnishings used for Oz's throne room may be used for Glinda's castle as well.

Lighting: Lights dim and black out as indicated. Spotlight is used for Narrator.

Sound: Rumbling of cyclone; crash of thunder; bell.

THE BAKING CONTEST

Characters: 3 male; 6 female; male and female extras.

Playing Time: 20 minutes.

Costumes: The people of the court and Esmerelda and Griselda are dressed in finery. Penny and Old Woman are in poor clothes.

Properties: Three baskets, pie, cakes, buns, trumpets, and recipes.

Setting: The entrance to the courtyard of the palace. There is a small pond downstage center. A brick wall goes across the stage, about two-thirds of the way back. There is an opening at center, through which characters enter and leave the palace courtyard. There is one tree at the left and a large stone or rock in front of tree.

Lighting: No special effects.

THE QUEEN'S MIRROR

Characters: 6 male; 4 female.

Playing Time: 20 minutes.

Costumes: Court costumes for Queen Dandelion, King Henry, Prince Stephen, and Lady Jane. Queen Dandelion wears a crown and Prince Stephen wears a coronet. King Henry wears a royal cape. Baker John and Mrs. Baker John wear white aprons, and Baker John wears a cook's cap. Patricia wears a peasant's costume. Rag and Tag wear sailors' costumes.

Properties: Jacks and ball, mirror, large piece of cardboard, paint and brush, tray of buns and paper bags for buns, teapot, large canvas duffel bag, coins, crown, umbrella, rolling pin, paper and pencil.

Setting: The throne room of a palace. The throne, a chair, and a small table are needed. The rest of the room may be furnished as simply or as elaborately as desired.

Sound: Pots and pans falling.

POSIES FOR THE POTENTATE

Characters: 5 male; 2 female; as many boys and girls as desired for Courtiers.

Playing Time: 25 minutes.

Costumes: King and Queen wear royal robes and crowns; Princess may wear a gown and a small crown; Prime Minister, Messenger and Courtiers wear court dress. Cuthbert Cacklebait may wear a business suit. The Wizard has on a weird costume with a high pointed hat. He carries a large book. The King carries a First Aid booklet under his robe.

Properties: Large book for King; pencil and paper for Prime Minister; large mop and dustcloth for Queen; handkerchiefs for Cacklebait, Wizard and members of the Court; large onion; book for Cacklebait.

Setting: Two thrones with removable cushions stand in the rear of the stage at the center. The room should have a window and some rich-looking draperies.

Lighting: No special effects.

THE SAGA OF DAVEY ROCKET

Characters: 5 male; 2 female.

Playing Time: 25 minutes.

Costumes: All characters wear clothes with a futuristic look. (Sequins will help to give this effect.) Radia has long fingernails which extend two inches beyond her fingers. Atom wears overalls. Great-Grandfather has a long, white beard and wears a battered hat, a vest, and a gaudy long-sleeved plaid shirt. Scorpio wears black clothes, with top hat and tails, and has a mustache and goatee. Davey Rocket wears a space suit or a superman costume and has a two-holster gun belt.

Properties: Easel with cue cards as indicated in text, five or more bottles with candy "pills" in them, document, spectacles, lorgnette, telescope, envelope, coupon, token, paper money, three bolts, two screws, a nut, stocking stuffed with play coins, two toy ray guns, a tool kit, a cosmetics case, two rocks, a pocket watch, a letter, and a "Geiger counter" with a fancy dial.

Setting: The dining room of a futuristic home. In the center is a table with four chairs around it. Upstage center is a cupboard lined with small bottles. Beside the cupboard is a window. On one side of the room there is a large speaker, which represents the intercom. On the other side is the space-a-phone, which looks like a television set, with a large picture into which a person can step, and with modernistic knobs, dials, lights, etc. It may have two microphones, one for the person phoning and one for the person being phoned. Doors at left and right lead outside and to the rest of the house.

Lighting: A spotlight may be used, if desired, to call attention to Robert the Robot when he shows a cue card.

Sound: Ticking of Geiger counter.

MR. LAZY MAN'S FAMILY

Characters: 3 male; 3 female.
Playing Time: 25 minutes.
Costumes: Everyday dress.
Properties: Notebooks and pencils for Janet and Bob Howe, candy, large oddly wrapped package, five small objects representing baby turtles.
Setting: An attractive and comfortable living room. There are several armchairs, a sofa, and several small tables with lamps. On one of the tables is a telephone, on another, a candy dish. Entrances are at left and right.
Lighting: No special effects.

THE CRIMSON FEATHER

Characters: 6 male; 4 female.
Playing Time: 15 minutes.
Costumes: Genie wears a cape, turban, and heavy Oriental make-up. Other characters wear peasant costumes—full skirts and kerchiefs for the girls; bright shirts, short trousers, and Tyrolean hats for the boys.
Properties: Pair of trousers, needle, thread, rolling pin and dough, red feather, peddler's pack, various items for pack.
Setting: A small cottage kitchen. At center of stage are a table and two kitchen chairs. There is a bench down right. Other furniture, fireplace, etc., may be added as desired.
Lighting: No special effects.
Sound: Offstage cymbals when Genie appears.

MISS LOUISA AND THE OUTLAWS

Characters: 6 male; 4 female. Any number of girls and boys may take part as pupils.

Playing Time: 20 minutes.

Costumes: Miss Louisa wears a dark old-fashioned gown and spectacles. The outlaws, sheriff and assistant wear the typical costumes associated with these characters; they have guns and holsters. The children should wear old-fashioned clothing.

Properties: Ruler, pitch pipe and spelling book for Miss Louisa; flag for William.

Setting: A one-room schoolhouse. Miss Louisa's desk is up right. Rows of children's desks (or tables and chairs) should be placed at an angle so that the audience will be able to see the children. At least one window should be in the rear wall. The door is down right. There is a mat in doorway. Slates, books, globes, maps, a stove, a blackboard, etc., may be added.

Lighting: No special effects.

Sound: Offstage train whistle.

SCHOOL FOR JESTERS

Characters: 7 male; 3 female; male and female extras for Jesters and Courtiers.

Playing Time: 20 minutes.

Costumes: Jesters wear traditional caps with bells, colorful patchwork costumes and, if possible, shoes with turned-up toes. Others wear appropriate court dress.

Properties: Slates and chalk for Heralds, bags of gold, dunce's cap.

Setting: The main classroom of the Royal School for Jesters. There is a raised platform upstage for thrones, and above it is a sign reading, "Royal School for Jesters." Two thrones and several cushions are at side of stage at beginning of play. At one side of stage, facing away from audience, is sign reading "The End," for use as indicated in text. There is a door at right.

Lighting: No special effects.

Sound: Knock on door, trumpet fanfare.